Marketing Management

Second Edition

CONNECT FEATURES

Interactive Applications

Interactive Applications offer a variety of automatically graded exercises that require students to **apply** key concepts. Whether the assignment includes a *click and drag*, *video case*, or *decision generator*, these applications provide instant feedback and progress tracking for students and detailed results for the instructor.

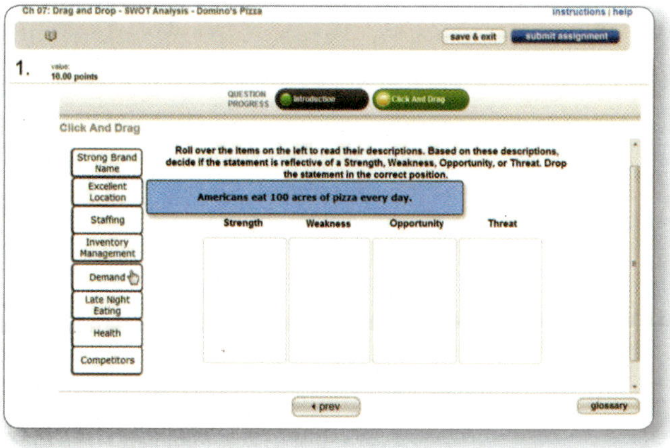

eBook

McGraw-Hill Connect Plus® includes a media-rich eBook that allows you to share your notes with your students. Your students can insert and review their own notes, highlight the text, search for specific information, and interact with media resources. Using an eBook with Connect Plus gives your students a complete digital solution that allows them to access their materials from any computer.

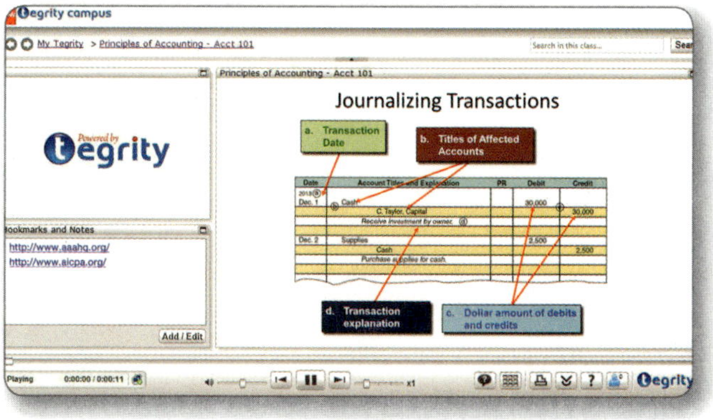

McGraw-Hill Tegrity®

Make your classes available anytime, anywhere. With simple, one-click recording, students can search for a word or phrase and be taken to the exact place in your lecture that they need to review.

EASY TO USE

Learning Management System Integration

MH Campus® is a one-stop teaching and learning experience available to use with any learning management system. MH Campus provides single sign-on to faculty and students for all McGraw-Hill material and technology from within the school website. MH Campus also allows instructors instant access to all supplements and teaching materials for all McGraw-Hill products.

Blackboard® users also benefit from McGraw-Hill's industry-leading integration, providing single sign-on to access all McGraw-Hill Connect® assignments and automatic feeding of assignment results to the Blackboard grade book.

POWERFUL REPORTING

Connect generates comprehensive reports and graphs that provide instructors with an instant view of the performance of individual students, a specific section, or multiple sections. Since all content is mapped to learning objectives, Connect reporting is ideal for accreditation or other administrative documentation.

Marketing Management

Second Edition

Greg W. Marshall
ROLLINS COLLEGE

Mark W. Johnston
ROLLINS COLLEGE

Mc
Graw
Hill
Education

MARKETING MANAGEMENT, SECOND EDITION

Published by McGraw-Hill Education, 2 Penn Plaza, New York, NY 10121.

This book is printed on acid-free paper.

1 2 3 4 5 6 7 8 9 0 DOW/DOW 1 0 9 8 7 6 5 4

ISBN 978-0-07-802886-1
MHID 0-07-802886-8

Senior Vice President, Products & Markets: *Kurt L. Strand*
Vice President, Content Production & Technology Services: *Kimberly Meriwether David*
Managing Director: *Paul Ducham*
Executive Brand Manager: *Sankha Basu*
Executive Director of Development: *Ann Torbert*
Development Editors: *Sean M. Pankuch and Jane Beck*
Digital Product Analyst: *Kerry Shanahan*
Marketing Manager: *Donielle Xu*
Director, Content Production: *Terri Schiesl*
Content Project Manager: *Dana M. Pauley*
Content Project Manager: *Susan Lombardi*
Senior Buyer: *Sandy Ludovissy*
Design: *Margarite Reynolds*
Cover Image: © *Bernard Jaubert/imagebroker/Corbis*
Senior Content Licensing Specialist: *Jeremy Cheshareck*
Typeface: *10/12 Palatino LT Std*
Compositor: *Laserwords Private Limited*
Printer: *R. R. Donnelley*

Library of Congress Cataloging-in-Publication Data

Marshall, Greg W.
Marketing management / Greg W. Marshall, Rollins College, Mark W. Johnston, Rollins College.—Second edition.
pages cm
Includes bibliographical references and index.
ISBN 978-0-07-802886-1 (alk. paper)—ISBN 0-07-802886-8 (alk. paper)
1. Marketing—Management. I. Johnston, Mark W. II. Title.
HF5415.13.M3699 2015
658.8—dc23 2013049003

www.mhhe.com

To Patti and Justin

-Greg

To Susan, my love, and Grace, my joy, thank you

-Mark

ABOUT THE AUTHORS

Greg W. Marshall

Greg W. Marshall is the Charles Harwood Professor of Marketing and Strategy in the Roy E. Crummer Graduate School of Business at Rollins College in Winter Park, Florida, and is also the academic director of the Executive DBA program there. For three years he served as vice president for Strategic Marketing for Rollins. He earned his PhD in Business Administration from Oklahoma State University, taking a marketing major and management minor, and holds a BSBA in marketing and an MBA from the University of Tulsa. Before joining Rollins, Greg was on the faculty at the University of South Florida, Texas Christian University, and Oklahoma State University. He currently also holds an appointment as professor of Marketing and Strategy at Aston Business School in Birmingham, United Kingdom.

Prior to returning to school for his doctorate, Greg's managerial industry experience included 13 years in consumer packaged goods and retailing with companies such as Warner Lambert, Mennen, and Target Corporation. He also has considerable experience as a consultant and trainer for a variety of organizations and has been heavily involved in teaching Marketing Management at multiple universities to both MBA and undergraduate students.

Greg is editor of the *Journal of Marketing Theory and Practice* and from 2002–2005 was editor of the *Journal of Personal Selling & Sales Management*. His published research focuses on the areas of decision making by marketing managers, intraorganizational relationships, and sales force performance. He is past president of the American Marketing Association Academic Division and also was a founder and served for five years on its Strategic Planning Group. He is a Distinguished Fellow and past president of the Academy of Marketing Science and is a Fellow and past president of the Society for Marketing Advances.

Mark W. Johnston

Mark W. Johnston is the Alan and Sandra Gerry Professor of Marketing and Ethics in the Roy E. Crummer Graduate School of Business at Rollins College in Winter Park, Florida. He earned his PhD from Texas A&M University and holds a BBA and an MB from Western Illinois University. Before joining Rollins, Mark was on the faculty at Louisiana State University. Prior to his academic career, he worked in industry as a sales representative for a leading distributor of photographic equipment. His research has been published in a number of professional journals including *Journal of Marketing Research, Journal of Applied Psychology, Journal of Business Ethics, Journal of Marketing Education, Journal of Personal Selling & Sales Management,* and many others.

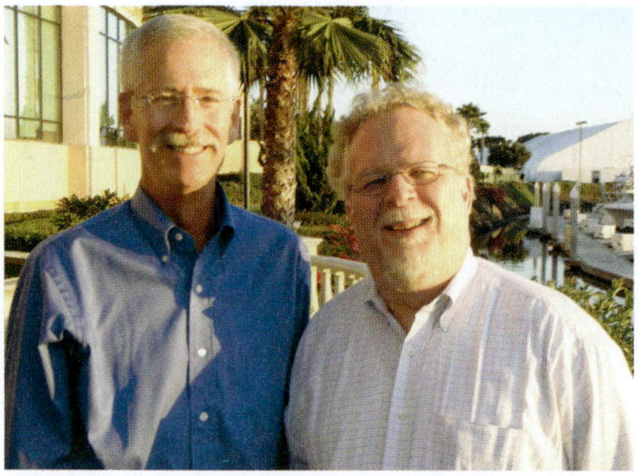

Mark has been retained as a consultant for firms in a number of industries including personal health care, chemical, transportation, hospitality, and telecommunications. He has consulted on a wide range of issues involving strategic business development, sales force structure and performance, international market opportunities, and ethical decision making. Mark also works with MBA students on consulting projects around the world for companies such as Tupperware, Disney, and Johnson & Johnson. He has conducted seminars globally on a range of topics including the strategic role of selling in the organization, developing an ethical framework for decision making, improving business unit performance, and structuring an effective international marketing department.

For more than two decades Mark has taught Marketing Management, working with thousands of students. His hands-on, real-world approach has earned him a number of teaching awards.

PREFACE

INTRODUCTION

No doubt about it, the field of marketing is *really changing*. The changes in the practice of marketing management are dramatic and important, and call attention to a number of organizational issues in today's business milieu that differ from the past. In general, marketing management today is:

- Very strategic—customer centricity is now a core *organizational* value.
- Heavily enabled by technology and data.
- Focused on facilitating *value* for the customer.
- Concerned with internal alignment of people, processes, systems, and strategies to effectively compete through a customer focus.
- Accountable to top management through diligent attention to metrics and measurement.
- Oriented toward service as the driver of product.
- Focused on a long-term customer relationship–centered understanding of the need to develop deep commitments from current profitable customers while also cultivating new ones.
- "Owned" by everybody in the firm, to one degree or another.
- Critically committed to exhibiting the utmost ethical behavior in all dealings.

In contrast, marketing management in the past has been:

- Much less strategic in nature.
- Very 4Ps oriented—more tactical.
- Less relationship-centered, thus focused on shorter time horizon decision making.
- Less focused on the ability to consistently deliver value for the customer.
- Oriented toward product as the core deliverable.
- Done by marketing *departments.*
- Much less accountable to upper management in terms of measurement of marketing success.

WHY WE WROTE THIS BOOK

Given the dramatic changes in the field of marketing, it is a sure bet that the job of leading and managing marketing's contributions to the organization and its customers, clients, partners, and society at large has changed at a concurrent level. Yet, the typical marketing management book on the market today does not effectively capture and communicate to students how marketing management is really practiced in the 21st century world of business. Clearly, it is time for an updated approach to teaching and learning within the field. This book is designed to fulfill that need.

We hear it from colleagues all the time—the complaint that the book they are using in their marketing management course "doesn't say what I believe the students need to hear" or that it "is too simplistic—like a marketing principles book" or that it "doesn't match what my MBAs actually do on the job" or that it "reads like an encyclopedia of marketing" or that it "has too much about everything and not enough focus on anything." During the development process for this book, we heard comments like these and others from hundreds of colleagues in focus groups, in written reviewer comments, and in numerous conversations around the world about the course. As a result, we became convinced that such comments truly are pervasive among instructors who teach marketing management, whether as the introductory MBA course, capstone undergraduate course, or first focal course after the undergraduate marketing principles course. Many marketing management instructors are looking for a book that is:

- Written for today's students in an up-to-date, user-friendly, yet professional and thorough style.
- Able to strike an effective balance between presenting the new world order of marketing at the strategic, operational, and tactical levels.
- A step up from the previous norm in terms of support materials for the classroom.

Marshall/Johnston's *Marketing Management, 2e* has taken great effort to represent marketing management the way it is actually practiced in successful organizations today. In our view, leading and managing the aspects of marketing to improve individual, unit, and organizational performance—**marketing management**—is a *core business activity.* Its relevance is not limited to just marketing departments or marketing majors. And business students of all backgrounds should appreciate the impact of effective marketing management on their own professional careers as well on as the overall success of their organizations. Bottom line, the ability to do great marketing management is relevant to *everyone in a firm.*

The content of the book reflects the major trends in the managerial practice of marketing, and the pedagogy is crafted around *learning and teaching preferences in today's classroom.* Above all, it is written in a style that is appealing for both students and instructors so that students will actually enjoy reading the material and instructors will be proud to teach from it and confident about presenting its up-to-date, professional, and thorough approach to their courses.

STRUCTURE OF THE BOOK

Marshall/Johnston's *Marketing Management, 2e* has six major parts, reflective of the logical sequence of building blocks for the course.

- **Part One: Discover Marketing Management.** In this part, students gain an understanding of the dynamics of the field. Significant attention is paid to framing the importance of studying marketing to future success as a manager. To kick off the marketing planning theme early in the course, Part One includes comprehensive coverage of this aspect along with an example marketing plan.
- **Part Two: Use Information to Drive Marketing Decisions.** It has often been said that information is the fuel that fires the engine of marketing management decision making. With this in mind, Part Two focuses on effective management of information to better understand customers, both in the consumer and business marketplaces. Effective segmentation, target marketing, and positioning are at the core of successful marketing and this part provides a modern managerial treatment of these critical topics, including connecting CRM capabilities with other relevant competencies and capabilities of successful marketers.
- **Part Three: Develop the Value Offering—The Product Experience.** This "product suite" of chapters presents a coherent and comprehensive drill-down into today's world of product strategy, branding, and new-product development. Reflective of the notion that service is a key driver of product success, we devote a separate chapter to making important links between service and the overall offering.

- **Part Four: Price and Deliver the Value Offering.** Part Four begins with a fresh, managerially relevant treatment of pricing decision making followed by an integrative approach to the multitude of modes at a manager's disposal today by which an offering can be made available to customers through channels and points of interface.
- **Part Five: Communicate the Value Offering through the Elements of Integrated Marketing Communications.** With the rise of social media and the dramatic changes in the deployment of marketing communications, this new "marketing communications suite" of chapters has been created for *Marketing Management, 2e* to best feature the array of new-age and traditional marketing communication vehicles available to managers.
- **Part Six: Bring It All Together—Global and Performance Dimensions.** Global marketplace issues are presented based on the idea that today, truly *all marketing is global.* The final chapter in the book is unique in marketing management books, in that it is the first of its kind to focus on comprehensive approaches to selecting and executing marketing metrics for decision making. As such, it is useful as a resource chapter for numerous other topics in the course including the development of a marketing plan.

KEY FEATURES OF THE BOOK

ETHICAL DIMENSION 3

The Source of the Click

Internet ad spending is currently $100 billion and is projected to reach more than $160 billion by 2016. The pay structure has evolved along two distinct lines. About half of all Internet ads are priced based on the number of people viewing the ad, similar to traditional television advertising. The other model for Internet advertising charges by the click. If someone views an ad and then chooses to click on the ad through to the advertiser, the advertiser pays a fee ranging from a few pennies to $20. A critical assumption is the click's legitimacy; it is supposed to represent someone actively seeking information from the advertiser's site.

Two companies control the vast majority of Internet ad placements—Yahoo and Google. While Google and Yahoo generate most of their revenue on legitimate websites, they also send ads to affiliated sites, known as "domain parking websites," which are basically advertising sites with very little content. Publicly they state these sites provide a useful service by directing Internet surfers to relevant information. However, companies are starting to express concern that some of these sites may actually be generating illegitimate clicks, clicks by individuals (or other computers) who are not legitimate potential customers.

Click fraud, estimated at more than $1 billion, has become a big issue for many Internet advertisers. Websites with names such as "insurance1472.com" are dummy sites located primarily in Asia and Eastern Europe that generate false clicks. The process works like this. First, ABC Company contracts with Google or Yahoo to advertise on the Internet and negotiates the fee ABC will pay for each click from an ABC ad to the company website. Second, Google or Yahoo displays the ad on legitimate websites but also sends the ad to domain parking websites. Third, these sites distribute the ads to parked websites that are often just lists of ads. Fourth, the owner of the parked website sends out a list of sites to individuals known collectively as "paid-to-read groups." These individuals' role is to click on ads for which they receive a small payment. Finally, Google or Yahoo charges ABC Company for the click, then shares part of the revenue with the domain parking website, which shares it with the other participants in the fraud.

72 PART TWO Use Information to Drives Marketing Decision

At the broadest conceptual level, members of society at large can be viewed as a stakeholder for marketing, a concept called **societal marketing.** As one example, the concept of environmentally friendly marketing, or *green marketing*, has been a growing trend in socially responsible companies. Today the movement has evolved into a part of the philosophical and strategic core of many firms under the label **sustainability,** which refers to business practices that meet humanity's needs without harming future generations.[11] Sustainability practices have helped socially responsible organizations incorporate *doing well by doing good* into their overarching business models so that both the success of the firm and the success of society at large are sustained over the long term. Ethical Dimension 1 takes a look at environmentally friendly marketing at several firms.

"Purpose Marketing, or "Pro-Social Marketing," is growing as a marketing strategy. This growing popularity can be attributed to an increasing number of consumers who say what a company stands for influences their purchasing decisions. Companies, such as Panera Bread, must communicate their core values through their use of the marketing mix. Panera is known for its quick serve restaurants, but it's also charitable, actively working with other organizations including Feeding America. In order to create awareness of its social consciousness, Panera launched its "Live consciously. Eat deliciously" campaign. The initiative will have a significant presence on social media sites, including Facebook and Twitter, exposing this new positioning to millions of fans. Purpose marketing with this type of sincerity has the potential to appeal to consumers on an emotional level and further drive customer loyalty. This trend moves marketing beyond push brand messaging and instead engages consumers in a much more meaningful way.[12]

Value and Exchange Are Core Marketing Concepts

Throughout the various topics encompassed within this book, the idea of value as a core concept in marketing will be a central theme. From a customer's perspective, we define **value** as a ratio of the bundle of benefits a customer receives from an offering compared to the costs incurred by the customer in acquiring that bundle of benefits.[14] Another central tenet of marketing is the concept of **exchange,** in which a person gives up something of value to them for something else they desire to have.[15] Usually an exchange is facilitated by money, but not always. Sometimes people trade or barter nonmonetary resources such as time, skill, expertise, intellectual capital, and other things of value for something else they want. For any

ETHICAL DIMENSION

Reflective of the centrality of ethical practices to marketing management, each chapter includes a real-world example of business ethics related to chapter material. These lively boxed features highlight how ethical issues permeate every marketing decision.

POP-OUT EXAMPLES

Each chapter contains numerous pop-out examples so that students can immediately connect chapter content to real-world application.

MANAGEMENT DECISION CASE

At the end of each chapter is a case drawn from the business headlines. Students are engaged by the currency of the problem and asked to develop solutions using chapter material. The cases are just the right size for today's classroom use—not too short but not too long!

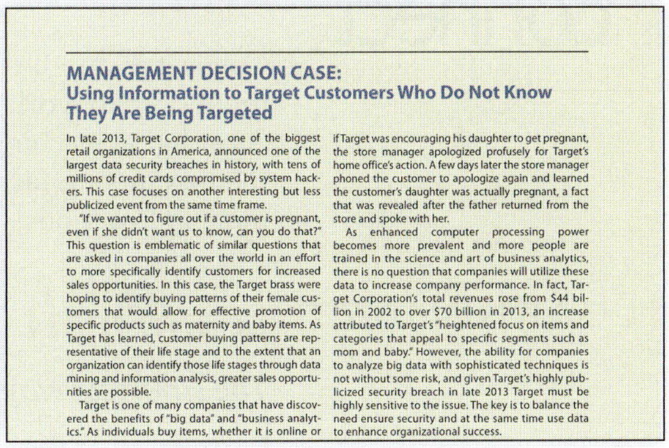

MANAGEMENT DECISION CASE:
Using Information to Target Customers Who Do Not Know They Are Being Targeted

In late 2013, Target Corporation, one of the biggest retail organizations in America, announced one of the largest data security breaches in history, with tens of millions of credit cards compromised by system hackers. This case focuses on another interesting but less publicized event from the same time frame.

"If we wanted to figure out if a customer is pregnant, even if she didn't want us to know, can you do that?" This question is emblematic of similar questions that are asked in companies all over the world in an effort to more specifically identify customers for increased sales opportunities. In this case, the Target brass were hoping to identify buying patterns of their female customers that would allow for effective promotion of specific products such as maternity and baby items. As Target has learned, customer buying patterns are representative of their life stage and to the extent that an organization can identify those life stages through data mining and information analysis, greater sales opportunities are possible.

Target is one of many companies that have discovered the benefits of "big data" and "business analytics." As individuals buy items, whether it is online or if Target was encouraging his daughter to get pregnant, the store manager apologized profusely for Target's home office's action. A few days later the store manager phoned the customer to apologize again and learned the customer's daughter was actually pregnant, a fact that was revealed after the father returned from the store and spoke with her.

As enhanced computer processing power becomes more prevalent and more people are trained in the science and art of business analytics, there is no question that companies will utilize these data to increase company performance. In fact, Target Corporation's total revenues rose from $44 billion in 2002 to over $70 billion in 2013, an increase attributed to Target's "heightened focus on items and categories that appeal to specific segments such as mom and baby." However, the ability for companies to analyze big data with sophisticated techniques is not without some risk, and given Target's highly publicized security breach in late 2013 Target must be highly sensitive to the issue. The key is to balance the need ensure security and at the same time use data to enhance organizational success.

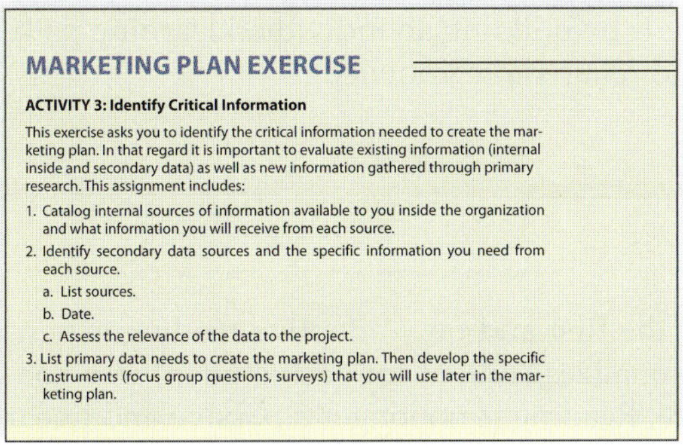

MARKETING PLAN EXERCISE

ACTIVITY 3: Identify Critical Information

This exercise asks you to identify the critical information needed to create the marketing plan. In that regard it is important to evaluate existing information (internal inside and secondary data) as well as new information gathered through primary research. This assignment includes:

1. Catalog internal sources of information available to you inside the organization and what information you will receive from each source.
2. Identify secondary data sources and the specific information you need from each source.
   a. List sources.
   b. Date.
   c. Assess the relevance of the data to the project.
3. List primary data needs to create the marketing plan. Then develop the specific instruments (focus group questions, surveys) that you will use later in the marketing plan.

MARKETING PLAN EXERCISE

Each chapter connects that chapter's key content to a semester-long marketing plan project activity. Marshall/Johnston's *Marketing Management, 2e* is the only marketing management book to effectively thread a marketing planning focus throughout the textbook itself. Whether or not a semester marketing plan project is used by the instructor, the marketing plan exercise feature does a great job of tying together important planning concepts for students in a methodical, stepwise manner.

GLOSSARY OF TERMS

A complete glossary of key terms and definitions is provided at the end of the book. The glossary serves as an important reference as well as a handy study aid for students preparing for exams.

OTHER FEATURES IN EACH CHAPTER

- *Learning objectives:* These set the stage at the beginning of the chapter for what students will achieve by reading and studying the chapter. Each objective reappears in the margin at the relevant point in the chapter so students can track their progress.
- *Summary:* At the end of each chapter, a summary reminds students of the highlighted topics.
- *Key terms:* Terms are bolded throughout the chapter and connected with definitions in the Glossary.
- *Application questions:* These engaging questions at the end of each chapter are designed to direct students' thinking about the topics to the next level of application. Throughout the book all of these questions have been specially designed to simulate managerial decision making.

SUPPLEMENT PACKAGE

Marshall/Johnston's *Marketing Management, 2e* is committed to having the best supplement package in the marketing management textbook arena.

Mc Graw Hill Education connect® MARKETING

Connect

Connect is an all-digital teaching and learning environment designed from the ground up to work with the way instructors and students think, teach, and learn. As a digital teaching, assignment, and assessment platform, Connect strengthens the link among faculty, students, and coursework, helping everyone accomplish more in less time.

LEARNSMART®

LearnSmart

The smartest way to get from B to A

LearnSmart is the most widely used and intelligent adaptive learning resource. It is proven to strengthen memory recall, improve course retention, and boost grades by distinguishing between what students know and what they don't know, and honing in on the concepts that they are most likely to forget. LearnSmart continuously adapts to each student's needs by building an individual learning path. As a result, students study smarter and retain more knowledge.

SMARTBOOK™

SmartBook

A revolution in learning

Fueled by LearnSmart, SmartBook is the first and only adaptive reading experience available today. SmartBook personalizes content for each student in a continuously adapting reading experience. Reading is no longer a passive and linear experience, but an engaging and dynamic one where students are more likely to master and retain important concepts, coming to class better prepared.

Practice Marketing

McGraw-Hill's Practice Marketing is a 3D, online, multiplayer game that enables students to gain practical experience by applying the skills they learn in a highly interactive and engaging environment. Using the knowledge built on their course, students become the marketing manager for a company entering the backpack market. By making decisions and seeing the results, players get feedback on their actions and learn by doing. Practice Marketing is the first in this series of new digital products from McGraw-Hill. Contact your local rep for more details.

Create

Instructors can now tailor their teaching resources to match the way they teach! With McGraw-Hill Create, www.mcgrawhillcreate.com, instructors can easily rearrange chapters, combine material from other content sources, and quickly upload and integrate their own content-like course syllabi or teaching notes. Find the right content in Create by searching through thousands of leading McGraw-Hill textbooks. Arrange the material to fit your teaching style. Order a Create book and receive a complimentary print review copy in 3–5 business days or a complimentary electronic review copy (echo) via e-mail within one hour. Go to www.mcgrawhillcreate.com today and register.

Tegrity Campus

Tegrity makes class time available 24/7 by automatically capturing every lecture in a searchable format for students to review when they study and complete assignments. With a simple one-click start-and-stop process, you capture all computer screens and corresponding audio. Students can replay any part of any class with easy-to-use browser-based viewing on a PC or Mac. Educators know that the more students can see, hear, and experience class resources, the better they learn. In fact, studies prove it. With patented Tegrity "search anything" technology, students instantly recall key class moments for replay online or on iPods and mobile devices. Instructors can help turn all their students' study time into learning moments immediately supported by their lecture. To learn more about Tegrity, watch a two-minute Flash demo at http://tegritycampus.mhhe.com.

Blackboard® Partnership

McGraw-Hill Education and Blackboard have teamed up to simplify your life. Now you and your students can access Connect and Create right from within your Blackboard course—all with one single sign-on. The grade books are seamless, so when a student completes an integrated Connect assignment, the grade for that assignment automatically (and instantly) feeds your Blackboard grade center. Learn more at www.domorenow.com.

McGraw-Hill Campus™

McGraw-Hill Campus is a new one-stop teaching and learning experience available to users of any learning management system. This institutional service allows faculty and students to enjoy single sign-on (SSO) access to all McGraw-Hill Higher Education materials, including the award-winning McGraw-Hill Connect platform, from directly within the institution's website. With McGraw-Hill Campus, faculty receive instant access to teaching materials (e.g., ebooks, test banks, PowerPoint slides, animations, learning objects, etc.), allowing them to browse, search, and use any instructor ancillary content in our vast library at no additional cost to instructor or students. In addition, students enjoy SSO access to a variety of free content (e.g., quizzes, flash cards, narrated presentations, etc.)

and subscription-based products (e.g., McGraw-Hill Connect). With McGraw-Hill Campus enabled, faculty and students will never need to create another account to access McGraw-Hill products and services. Learn more at www.mhcampus.com.

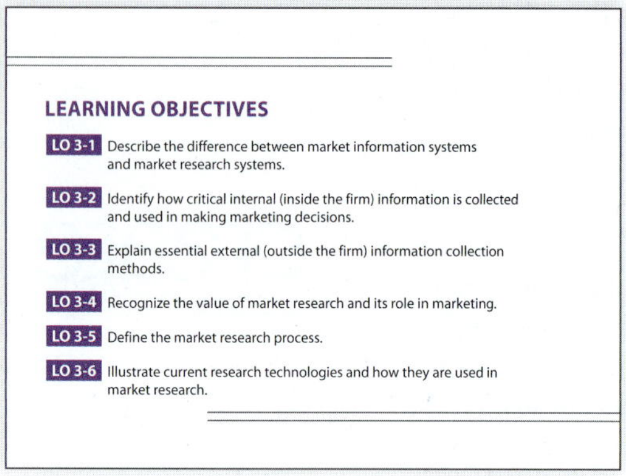
LEARNING OBJECTIVES

LO 3-1 Describe the difference between market information systems and market research systems.

LO 3-2 Identify how critical internal (inside the firm) information is collected and used in making marketing decisions.

LO 3-3 Explain essential external (outside the firm) information collection methods.

LO 3-4 Recognize the value of market research and its role in marketing.

LO 3-5 Define the market research process.

LO 3-6 Illustrate current research technologies and how they are used in market research.

Assurance of Learning Ready

Assurance of learning is an important element of many accreditation standards. Marshall/Johnston's *Marketing Management, 2e* is designed specifically to support your assurance of learning initiatives. As mentioned earlier, each chapter in the book begins with a list of learning objectives, which are then addressed throughout the chapter as well as in the end-of-chapter problems and exercises. Every test bank question is also linked to one of these objectives and indicates level of difficulty, topic area, Bloom's Taxonomy level, and AACSB skill area. EZ Test, McGraw-Hill's easy-to-use test bank software, can search the test bank by these and other categories, providing an engine for targeted Assurance of Learning analysis and assessment.

AACSB Statement

The McGraw-Hill Companies is a proud corporate member of AACSB International. Understanding the importance and value of AACSB accreditation, Marshall/Johnston's *Marketing Management, 2e* has recognized the curricula guidelines detailed in the AACSB standards for business accreditation by connecting selected questions in the test bank to the general knowledge and skill guidelines found in the AACSB standards.

The statements contained in Marshall/Johnston's *Marketing Management, 2e* are provided only as a guide for the users of this text. The AACSB leaves content coverage and assessment within the purview of individual schools, the mission of the school, and the faculty. While Marshall/Johnston's *Marketing Management, 2e* and the teaching package make no claim of any specific AACSB qualification or evaluation, we have labeled selected questions according to the six general knowledge and skills areas.

McGraw-Hill Customer Experience Group Contact Information

At McGraw-Hill, we understand that getting the most from new technology can be challenging. That's why our services don't stop after you purchase our products. You can e-mail our Product Specialists 24 hours a day to get product training online. Or you can search our knowledge bank of Frequently Asked Questions on our support website. For Customer Support, call 800-331-5094, e-mail mhsupport@mcgraw-hill.com, or visit www.mhhe.com/support. One of our Technical Support Analysts will be able to assist you in a timely fashion.

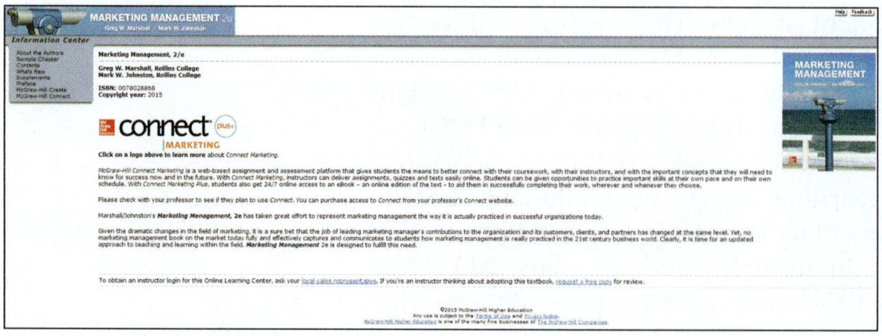

ONLINE LEARNING CENTER

Students using Marshall/Johnston's *Marketing Management, 2e* will have access to resources located on the Online Learning Center, including Chapter Quizzes.

CONCLUSION

Our overarching goal is to provide a marketing management book that truly captures the managerial practice of marketing in a way that is fully relevant to today's business students, professors, and managers. As stated earlier, we strongly believe that leading and managing the aspects of marketing to improve individual, unit, and organizational performance—**marketing management**—is a core business activity that is relevant to any MBA or undergraduate business student, regardless of his or her functional area of focus. At the end of the course, we want this book to allow marketing management instructors to have accomplished these key objectives:

- Clearly bring knowledge leadership in managerial aspects of marketing into the classroom, especially focusing on marketing management decision making in this new era of marketing.
- At the same time, cover the core areas of day-to-day management of marketing functions, but with a focus always on application and managerial decision making—not just basic "principles."
- Integrate the following themes as systematic focal areas of the course experience: marketing planning, leadership, metrics, value, customer centricity, globalization, ethics, technology and data-driven marketing, and marketing's interface with other business functions.
- Speak to today's students in an up-to-date, user-friendly, yet professional and thorough writing style with vivid examples of actual marketing managers and leaders doing their jobs and making decisions about marketing problems and opportunities.
- Offer a state-of-the-art supplement package that enhances instructional effectiveness and the student's learning experience.
- Ultimately, provide a book today's instructors will be proud to teach from, secure in the knowledge that students *will want to read it* and that it represents the field of marketing management the way it is practiced in today's business milieu.

Acknowledgments

The task of writing a textbook requires the talents of many dedicated people. First and foremost, we want to thank the McGraw-Hill team for sharing the vision of this project with us from the very beginning. Particularly given the dynamic nature of marketing management both as a professional field and as a course of study, it was critically important that throughout the development process the authors and the editorial, production, and marketing team remain steadfast in believing in the vision of the project. The high level of mutual enthusiasm never waned, and we commend McGraw-Hill for this.

In particular, we want to recognize and thank the following individuals at McGraw-Hill who played a significant part in the successful development of Marshall/Johnston's *Marketing Management, 2e.* Sankha Basu, Executive Brand Manager for Marketing, has worked with us for many years and is an outstanding editorial leader. His vision for the book is very consistent with ours and we appreciate his steadfast advocacy for the project. For this edition, we shifted Development Editors midstream from Sean Pankuch to Jane Beck. Both contributed greatly to the end result and we thank them for their contributions. As always, it was delightful to work with Dana Pauley, Content Project Manager, throughout the process of turning the second edition over to production. Prior to Dana's entry onto the project, Sue Lombardi did a great job in kicking off the turnover process for us. And our marketing manager Donielle Xu always practices the advice contained in *Marketing Management, 2e* with utmost professional skill. All of these great professionals made our job as authors much more enjoyable, and we are indebted to them for their significant contributions to the project. We have been McGraw-Hill authors for over 15 years and consider their team to be family.

Dan Goebel at Illinois State University did a masterful job in creating the new set of Management Decision Cases that add so much value to this new edition. Likewise, Jill Solomon at the University of South Florida developed an outstanding set of testing materials and PowerPoints to accompany the book—she truly is an outstanding instructor of marketing management herself and that talent comes through in the materials she has created for this second edition. Leroy Robinson at the University of Houston–Clear Lake worked tirelessly to create an outstanding Instructor's Manual to accompany this edition and to develop the interactive Connect exercises and the adaptive LearnSmart materials. His significant contributions ensure that *Marketing Management, 2e* contains relevant and engaging resources for instructors and students. Thanks to all three of you for a job well done!

In addition, we appreciate the contributions by several members of the Rollins College Crummer Graduate School of Business team. Morgan Filteau managed the art program for the book with creativity and skill. Each of the following folks contributed to the plethora of great current business examples featured in this edition: Jessica Dunn, Taylor Estes, Susanna Miller, and Larissa Raines. We deeply appreciate your exceptional contributions.

And finally, we want to offer a very special and heartfelt note of appreciation to our families, colleagues, and friends. Their encouragement and good humor throughout this process were integral to the end result.

Greg W. Marshall, ROLLINS COLLEGE

Mark W. Johnston, ROLLINS COLLEGE

February 2014

REVIEWERS

Many colleagues have participated in the developmental process of Marshall/Johnston's *Marketing Management, 2e* from the very beginning through focus groups, chapter reviews, and other means. Out thanks go to each of the following people for their guidance and suggestions throughout this process:

Kalthom Abdullah, *INTERNATIONAL ISLAMIC UNIVERSITY OF MALAYSIA*

Denise Ammirato, *WESTFIELD STATE COLLEGE*

David Amponsah, *TROY UNIVERSITY MONTGOMERY*

David Andrus, *KANSAS STATE UNIVERSITY*

Paul Arsenault, *WEST CHESTER UNIVERSITY OF PENNSYLVANIA*

Semih Arslanoglu, *BOSTON UNIVERSITY*

Chad Autry, *UNIVERSITY OF TENNESSEE–KNOXVILLE*

Parimal Baghat, *INDIANA UNIVERSITY OF PENNSYLVANIA*

William Baker, *SAN DIEGO STATE UNIVERSITY*

Roger Baran, *DEPAUL UNIVERSITY*

Danny Bellenger, *GEORGIA STATE UNIVERSITY*

John Bellenoit, *WESTFIELD STATE COLLEGE*

Parimal Bhagat, *INDIANA UNIVERSITY OF PENNSYLVANIA*

Subodh Bhat, *SAN FRANCISCO STATE UNIVERSITY*

Carol Bienstock, *RADFORD UNIVERSITY*

Diedre Bird, *PROVIDENCE COLLEGE*

Douglas Boyd, *JAMES MADISON UNIVERSITY*

Steve Brokaw, *UNIVERSITY OF WISCONSIN–LACROSSE*

Laura Buckner, *MIDDLE TENNESSEE STATE UNIVERSITY*

Tim Calkins, *NORTHWESTERN UNIVERSITY*

Barb Casey, *DOWLING COLLEGE*

Bob Cline, *UNIVERSITY OF IOWA*

Cathy Cole, *UNIVERSITY OF IOWA*

Mark Collins, *UNIVERSITY OF TENNESSEE–KNOXVILLE*

David Conrad, *AUGSBURG COLLEGE*

Bob Cutler, *CLEVELAND STATE UNIVERSITY*

Geoffrey Da Silva, *TEMASEK POLYTECHNIC*

Lorie Darche, *SOUTHWEST FLORIDA COLLEGE*

Patricia Daugherty, *MICHIGAN STATE UNIVERSITY*

F. Robert Dwyer, *UNIVERSITY OF CINCINNATI*

Michael Edwards, *UNIVERSITY OF ST. THOMAS*

Adel El-Ansary, *UNIVERSITY OF NORTH FLORIDA*

Alexander Ellinger, *UNIVERSITY OF ALABAMA–TUSCALOOSA*

Ken Fairweather, *LETOURNEAU UNIVERSITY*

Bagher Fardanesh, *JOHNS HOPKINS UNIVERSITY*

Andrew Forman, *HOFSTRA UNIVERSITY*

Fred Fusting, *LOYOLA COLLEGE OF MARYLAND*

Jule B. Gassenheimer, *ROLLINS COLLEGE*

Mahesh Gopinath, *OLD DOMINION UNIVERSITY*

Shiv Gupta, *UNIVERSITY OF FINDLAY*

Liz Hafer, *UNIVERSITY OF COLORADO–BOULDER*

Angela Hausman, *UNIVERSITY OF NORTH CAROLINA AT PEMBROKE*

Chuck Hermans, *MISSOURI STATE UNIVERSITY*

Asep Hermawan, *UNIVERSITAS TRISAKTI*

Mahmood Hussain, *SAN FRANCISCO STATE UNIVERSITY*

Donna Rue Jenkins, *WARREN NATIONAL UNIVERSITY*

Johny Johansson, *GEORGETOWN UNIVERSITY*

Amit Joshi, *UNIVERSITY OF CENTRAL FLORIDA*

Fred Katz, *JOHNS HOPKINS UNIVERSITY*

Craig Kelley, *CALIFORNIA STATE UNIVERSITY–SACRAMENTO*

Elias Konwufine, *KEISER UNIVERSITY*

Robert Kopp, *BABSON COLLEGE*

Michael Levens, *WALSH COLLEGE*

Cesar Maloles, *CALIFORNIA STATE UNIVERSITY–EAST BAY*

Avinash Malshe, *UNIVERSITY OF ST. THOMAS*

Susan Mantel, *INDIANA UNIVERSITY–PURDUE UNIVERSITY–INDIANAPOLIS*

Norton Marks, *CALIFORNIA STATE UNIVERSITY–SAN BERNARDINO*

Thomas Maronick, *TOWSON UNIVERSITY*

H. Lee Mathews, *OHIO STATE UNIVERSITY*

Melvin Mattson, *RADFORD UNIVERSITY*

Denny McCorkle, *UNIVERSITY OF NORTHERN COLORADO*

Michael Menasco, *CALIFORNIA STATE UNIVERSITY–SAN BERNADINO*

Morgan Miles, *UNIVERSITY OF TASMANIA*

Chad Milewicz, *UNIVERSITY OF CENTRAL FLORIDA*

Herb Miller, *UNIVERSITY OF TEXAS*

Mark Mitchell, *COASTAL CAROLINA UNIVERSITY*

Thomas Noordewier, *UNIVERSITY OF VERMONT*

Nicholas Nugent, *SOUTHERN NEW HAMPSHIRE UNIVERSITY*

Carl Obermiller, *SEATTLE UNIVERSITY*

Azizah Omar, *UNIVERSITI SAINS MALAYSIA*

Barnett Parker, *PFEIFFER UNIVERSITY*

Vanessa Patrick, *UNIVERSITY OF GEORGIA*

Dennis Pitta, *UNIVERSITY OF BALTIMORE*

Salim Qureshi, *BLOOMSBURG UNIVERSITY*

Pushkala Raman, *TEXAS WOMAN'S UNIVERSITY*

K. Ramakrishna Rao, *MULTIMEDIA UNIVERSITY*

Molly Rapert, *UNIVERSITY OF ARKANSAS–FAYETTEVILLE*

Richard Rexeisen, *UNIVERSITY OF ST. THOMAS*

Subom Rhee, *SANTA CLARA UNIVERSITY*

Robert Richey, *UNIVERSITY OF ALABAMA–TUSCALOOSA*

Torsten Ringberg, *UNIVERSITY OF WISCONSIN–MILWAUKEE*

Ann Root, *FLORIDA ATLANTIC UNIVERSITY–BOCA RATON*

David Rylander, *TEXAS WOMAN'S UNIVERSITY*

Mahmod Sabri Haron, *UNIVERSITI SAINS MALAYSIA*

Dennis Sandler, *PACE UNIVERSITY*

Matt Sarkees, *PENNSYLVANIA STATE UNIVERSITY*

Linda Saytes, *UNIVERSITY OF SAN FRANCISCO*

Shahid Sheikh, *AMERICAN INTERCONTINENTAL UNIVERSITY*

Susan Sieloff, *NORTHEASTERN UNIVERSITY*

Karen Smith, *COLUMBIA SOUTHERN UNIVERSITY*

Sharon Smith, *DEPAUL UNIVERSITY*

Jill Solomon, *UNIVERSITY OF SOUTH FLORIDA*

Ashish Sood, *EMORY UNIVERSITY*

Robert Spekman, *UNIVERSITY OF VIRGINIA, DARDEN SCHOOL*

James Spiers, *ARIZONA STATE UNIVERSITY*

Thomas Steenburgh, *UNIVERSITY OF VIRGINIA, DARDEN SCHOOL*

Geoffrey Stewart, *UNIVERSITY OF LOUISIANA–LAFAYETTE*

John Stovall, *GEORGIA SOUTHWESTERN STATE UNIVERSITY*

Ziad Swaidan, *UNIVERSITY OF HOUSTON AT VICTORIA*

Michael Swenson, *BRIGHAM YOUNG UNIVERSITY*

Leona Tam, *OLD DOMINION UNIVERSITY*

Niwet Thamma, *RAMKHAMHEANG UNIVERSITY*

Meg Thams, *REGIS UNIVERSITY*

Rungting Tu, *PEKING UNIVERSITY*

Bronislaw Verhage, *GEORGIA STATE UNIVERSITY*

Guangping Wang, *PENNSYLVANIA STATE UNIVERSITY*

Cathy Waters, *BOSTON COLLEGE*

Art Weinstein, *NOVA SOUTHEASTERN UNIVERSITY*

Darin White, *UNION UNIVERSITY–JACKSON*

Ken Williamson, *JAMES MADISON UNIVERSITY*

Dale Wilson, *MICHIGAN STATE UNIVERSITY*

Walter Wochos, *CARDINAL STRITCH UNIVERSITY*

Khanchitpol Yousapronpaiboon, *KHONKHEN UNIVERSITY*

Zach Zacharia, *LEHIGH UNIVERSITY*

Yong Zhang, *HOFSTRA UNIVERSITY*

Shaoming Zou, *UNIVERSITY OF MISSOURI–COLUMBIA*

BRIEF TABLE OF CONTENTS

part ONE
Discover Marketing Management 1

CHAPTER 1
Marketing in Today's Business Milieu 2

CHAPTER 2
Elements of Marketing Strategy, Planning, and Competition 26

part TWO
Use Information to Drive Marketing Decisions 61

CHAPTER 3
Manage Marketing Information 62

CHAPTER 4
Understand Business-to-Consumer Markets 94

CHAPTER 5
Understand Business-to-Business Markets 130

CHAPTER 6
Segmentation, Target Marketing, Positioning, and CRM 158

part THREE
Develop the Value Offering—The Product Experience 197

CHAPTER 7
Product Strategy and New-Product Development 198

CHAPTER 8
Build the Brand 238

CHAPTER 9
Service as the Core Offering 264

part FOUR
Price and Deliver the Value Offering 293

CHAPTER 10
Manage Pricing Decisions 294

CHAPTER 11
Manage Marketing Channels and Points of Customer Interface 322

part FIVE
Communicate the Value Offering through the Elements of Integrated Marketing Communications 359

CHAPTER 12
Promotional Strategy and New Media 360

CHAPTER 13
Advertising, Sales Promotion, and Public Relations 396

CHAPTER 14
Personal Selling and Direct Marketing 414

part SIX
Bring It all Together—Global and Performance Dimensions 441

CHAPTER 15
Understand the Global Marketplace: Marketing without Borders 442

CHAPTER 16
The Marketing Dashboard: Metrics for Measuring Marketing Performance 474

GLOSSARY G-1

PHOTO CREDITS PC-1

INDEX I-1

TABLE OF CONTENTS

part ONE

Discover Marketing Management 1

CHAPTER 01

Marketing in Today's Business Milieu 2

WELCOME TO MARKETING MANAGEMENT 3

MARKETING MISCONCEPTIONS 3

Behind the Misconceptions 3
Beyond the Misconceptions and Toward the *Reality* of Modern Marketing 6

DEFINING MARKETING 6

Value and Exchange Are Core Marketing Concepts 8

MARKETING'S ROOTS AND EVOLUTION 10

Pre-Industrial Revolution 10
Focus on Production and Products 10
Focus on Selling 11
Advent of the Marketing Concept 11
Post-Marketing Concept Approaches 12

CHANGE DRIVERS IMPACTING THE FUTURE OF MARKETING 14

Shift to Product Glut and Customer Shortage 15
Shift in Information Power from Marketer to Customer 15
Shift in Generational Values and Preferences 16
Shift to Distinguishing Marketing (Big M) from marketing (little m) 17
Shift to Justifying the Relevance and Payback of the Marketing Investment 19

YOUR MARKETING MANAGEMENT JOURNEY BEGINS 20

SUMMARY 21

KEY TERMS 21

APPLICATION QUESTIONS 21

MANAGEMENT DECISION CASE: GAINING A FOOTHOLD AMONG GIANTS WHILE BEING KIND 22

NOTES 23

CHAPTER 02

Elements of Marketing Strategy, Planning, and Competition 26

VALUE IS AT THE CORE OF MARKETING 27

The Value Chain 28
Planning for the Value Offering 30

MARKETING PLANNING IS BOTH STRATEGIC AND TACTICAL 30

ELEMENTS OF MARKETING PLANNING 32

Connecting the Marketing Plan to the Firm's Business Plan 32
Organizational Mission, Vision, Goals, and Objectives 35
Organizational Strategies 36
Situation Analysis 39
Additional Aspects of Marketing Planning 43

TIPS FOR SUCCESSFUL MARKETING PLANNING 46

VISIT THE APPENDIX FOR A MARKETING PLAN EXAMPLE 47

SUMMARY 48

KEY TERMS 48

APPLICATION QUESTIONS 48

MANAGEMENT DECISION CASE: HEWLETT-PACKARD AND THE CASE FOR STRATEGIC CHANGE 49

MARKETING PLAN EXERCISES 50

NOTES 50

APPENDIX Cloudcab Small Jet Taxi Service Abbreviated Example Marketing Plan 53

part TWO

Use Information to Drive Marketing Decisions 61

CHAPTER 03

Manage Marketing Information 62

MAKING GOOD MARKETING DECISIONS—THE NEED TO KNOW 63

MARKET INFORMATION SYSTEM 64

The Nature of a Market Information System 64
Internal Sources—Collecting Information Inside the Company 66
External Sources—Collecting Information Outside the Company 68

MARKET RESEARCH SYSTEMS 73

The Importance of Market Research to Managers 73
The Market Research Process 74
Market Research Technology 82
Market Research Challenges in Global Markets 84

SUMMARY 88

KEY TERMS 88

APPLICATION QUESTIONS 88

MANAGEMENT DECISION CASE: USING INFORMATION TO TARGET CUSTOMERS WHO DO NOT KNOW THEY ARE BEING TARGETED 89

MARKETING PLAN EXERCISE 90

NOTES 90

CHAPTER 04
Understand Business-to-Consumer Markets 94

THE POWER OF THE CONSUMER 95

INTERNAL FORCES AFFECT CONSUMER CHOICES 95

Personal Characteristics 95
Psychological Attributes 99

EXTERNAL FACTORS SHAPE CONSUMER CHOICES 106

Cultural Factors 106
Situational Factors 108
Social Factors 109

THE LEVEL OF INVOLVEMENT INFLUENCES THE PROCESS 114

Decision Making with High Involvement 114
Decision Making with Limited Involvement 115

THE CONSUMER DECISION-MAKING PROCESS 115

Problem Recognition 116
Search for Information 116
Evaluation of Alternatives 119
Product Choice Decision 120
Post-Purchase Assessment 121

SUMMARY 124

KEY TERMS 124

APPLICATION QUESTIONS 124

MANAGEMENT DECISION CASE: SMARTPHONES, SENIORS, AND PURCHASE DECISIONS 125

MARKETING PLAN EXERCISE 126

NOTES 126

CHAPTER 05
Understand Business-to-Business Markets 130

ORGANIZATIONAL BUYING: MARKETING TO A BUSINESS 131

DIFFERENCES BETWEEN BUSINESS AND CONSUMER MARKETS 132

Relationships with Customers 132
Number and Size of Customers 133
Geographic Concentration 133
Complexity of the Buying Process 133
Complexity of the Supply Chain 134
Demand for Products and Services Is Different in a Business Market 135

BUYING SITUATIONS 136

Straight Rebuy 136
Modified Rebuy 137
New Purchase 137

BUYING CENTERS 138

Members of the Buying Center 138
Pursuing the Buying Center 139

THE PLAYERS IN BUSINESS-TO-BUSINESS MARKETS 140

The North American Industrial Classification System (NAICS) 140
Manufacturers 141
Resellers 142
Government 143
Institutions 143

THE BUSINESS MARKET PURCHASE DECISION PROCESS 143

Problem Recognition 144
Define the Need and Product Specifications 144
Search for Suppliers 145
Seek Sales Proposals in Response to RFP 147
Make the Purchase Decision 147
Post-Purchase Evaluation of Product and Supplier 150

THE ROLE OF TECHNOLOGY IN BUSINESS MARKETS 151

E-Procurement 151

SUMMARY 152

KEY TERMS 152

APPLICATION QUESTIONS 152

MANAGEMENT DECISION CASE: ORGANIZATIONAL BUYING ON A GRAND SCALE 153

MARKETING PLAN EXERCISE 154

NOTES 154

CHAPTER 06
Segmentation, Target Marketing, Positioning, and CRM 158

FULFILLING CONSUMER NEEDS AND WANTS 159

WHAT IS SEGMENTATION? 160

Effective Segmentation 160

SEGMENTING CONSUMER MARKETS 161

Geographic Segmentation 161
Demographic Segmentation 163
Psychographic Segmentation 172
Behavioral Segmentation 174

Firms Use Multiple Segmentation Approaches Simultaneously 176
Segmenting Business Markets 176

TARGET MARKETING 177

Analyze Market Segments 177
Develop Profiles of Each Potential Target Market 178
Select a Target Marketing Approach 179

POSITIONING 180

Perceptual Maps 182
Sources of Differentiation 183
Positioning Errors 183

OBJECTIVES AND CAPABILITIES OF CRM 184

THE CRM PROCESS CYCLE 186

Knowledge Discovery 186
Marketing Planning 187
Customer Interaction 187
Analysis and Refinement 187

MORE ON CUSTOMER TOUCHPOINTS 188

CRM Facilitates a Customer-Centric Culture 188

SUMMARY 190

KEY TERMS 190

APPLICATION QUESTIONS 190

MANAGEMENT DECISION CASE: HOTEL CHOICES AND THEIR APPEAL TO DIFFERENT MARKETS 192

MARKETING PLAN EXERCISE 193

NOTES 193

part THREE

Develop the Value Offering—The Product Experience 197

CHAPTER 07

Product Strategy and New-Product Development 198

PRODUCT: THE HEART OF MARKETING 199

Product Characteristics 199
Product Classifications 202
Product Discrimination: Create a Point of Differentiation 205
Product Plan: Moving from One Product to Many Products 210
Product Decisions Affect Other Marketing Mix Elements 211

THE LIFE OF THE PRODUCT: BUILDING THE PRODUCT EXPERIENCE 213

Product Life Cycle Sales Revenue and Profitability 215
Product Life Cycle Timeline 215
Product Life Cycle Caveats 215

NEW PRODUCTS—CREATING LONG-TERM SUCCESS 218

"New" Defined 218
Reasons for New-Product Success or Failure 219

NEW-PRODUCT DEVELOPMENT PROCESS 220

Identify Product Opportunities 220
Define the Product Opportunity 223
Develop the Product Opportunity 225

CONSUMER ADOPTION AND DIFFUSION PROCESS 228

Consumer Product Adoption Process 228
The Diffusion of Innovations 229

SUMMARY 231

KEY TERMS 231

APPLICATION QUESTIONS 231

MANAGEMENT DECISION CASE: PRODUCT DEVELOPMENT AND RENEWAL IN THE TOY MARKET 232

MARKETING PLAN EXERCISE 233

NOTES 234

CHAPTER 08

Build the Brand 238

BRAND: THE FUNDAMENTAL CHARACTER OF A PRODUCT 239

Brands Play Many Roles 239
The Boundaries of Branding 242

BRAND EQUITY—OWNING A BRAND 243

Defining Brand Equity 243
Benefits of Brand Equity 245

BRANDING DECISIONS 247

Stand-Alone or Family Branding 248
National or Store Branding 250
Licensing 250
Co-Branding 250

PACKAGING AND LABELING: ESSENTIAL BRAND ELEMENTS 251

Package Objectives 251
Effective Packaging 255
Labeling 255

WARRANTIES AND SERVICE AGREEMENTS: BUILDING CUSTOMER CONFIDENCE 257

Warranties Help Define the Brand 257

SUMMARY 259

KEY TERMS 259

APPLICATION QUESTIONS 259

MANAGEMENT DECISION CASE: DEVELOPING AND GROWING BRAND EQUITY IN AN ICONIC BRAND 259

MARKETING PLAN EXERCISE 260

NOTES 261

CHAPTER 09

Service as the Core Offering 264

WHY SERVICE IS IMPORTANT 265

Service as a Differentiator 265
A New Dominant Logic for Marketing 265

CHARACTERISTICS OF SERVICES 266

Intangibility 266
Inseparability 267
Variability 268
Perishability 269

THE SERVICE-PROFIT CHAIN 269

Internal Service Quality 269
Satisfied, Productive, and Loyal Employees 271
Greater Service Value for External Customers 272
Customer Satisfaction and Loyalty 272
Revenue and Profit Growth 272

SERVICE ATTRIBUTES 274

Search Attributes 274
Experience Attributes 275
Credence Attributes 275
Importance of Understanding Service Attributes 276

SERVICE QUALITY 278

Gap Analysis 278
SERVQUAL: A Multiple-Item Scale to Measure Service Quality 283
The SERVQUAL Instrument 284

SERVICE BLUEPRINTS 287

SUMMARY 288

KEY TERMS 288

APPLICATION QUESTIONS 288

MANAGEMENT DECISION CASE: SERVICE AND THE STORY OF NETFLIX 289

MARKETING PLAN EXERCISE 290

NOTES 290

part FOUR

Price and Deliver the Value Offering 293

CHAPTER 10

Manage Pricing Decisions 294

PRICE IS A CORE COMPONENT OF VALUE 295

ESTABLISH PRICING OBJECTIVES AND RELATED STRATEGIES 297

Penetration Pricing 298
Price Skimming 298
Profit Maximization and Target ROI 299
Competitor-Based Pricing 300
Value Pricing 301

SELECT PRICING TACTICS 303

Product Line Pricing 303
Captive Pricing 305
Price Bundling 305
Reference Pricing 306
Prestige Pricing 306
Odd/Even Pricing 307
One-Price Strategy and Variable Pricing 307
Everyday Low Pricing (EDLP) and High/Low Pricing 308
Auction Pricing 309

SET THE EXACT PRICE 309

Cost-Plus Pricing/Markup on Cost 309
Markup on Sales Price 310
Average-Cost Pricing 310
Target Return Pricing 311

DETERMINE CHANNEL DISCOUNTS AND ALLOWANCES 311

Cash Discounts 311
Trade Discounts 311
Quantity Discounts 312
Seasonal Discounts 312
Promotional Allowances 312
Geographic Aspects of Pricing 312

EXECUTE PRICE CHANGES 313

UNDERSTAND LEGAL CONSIDERATIONS IN PRICING 314

Price-Fixing 314
Price Discrimination 314
Deceptive Pricing 315
Predatory Pricing 315
Fair Trade and Minimum Markup Laws 315

SUMMARY 316

KEY TERMS 316

APPLICATION QUESTIONS 316

MANAGEMENT DECISION CASE: PRICE UNBUNDLING: AN UNCOMMON WORD LEADING TO VERY NICE FINANCIAL RETURNS 317

MARKETING PLAN EXERCISE 318

NOTES 318

CHAPTER 11

Manage Marketing Channels and Points of Customer Interface 322

THE VALUE CHAIN AND VALUE NETWORKS 323

CHANNELS AND INTERMEDIARIES 326

FUNCTIONS OF CHANNEL INTERMEDIARIES 328

Physical Distribution Functions 328
Transaction and Communication Functions 329
Facilitating Functions 330

DISINTERMEDIATION AND E-CHANNELS 331

VERTICAL MARKETING SYSTEMS 332

Corporate Systems 332
Contractual Systems 332
Administered Systems 332

CHANNEL BEHAVIOR: CONFLICT AND POWER 333

SELECTING CHANNEL APPROACHES 334

Distribution Intensity 334
Channel Control and Adaptability 336
Prioritization of Channel Functions—Push versus Pull Strategy 336

LOGISTICS ASPECTS OF SUPPLY CHAIN MANAGEMENT 336

Order Processing 337
Warehousing and Materials Handling 338
Inventory Management 338
Transportation 338

LEGAL ISSUES IN SUPPLY CHAIN MANAGEMENT 339

Exclusive Dealing 339
Exclusive Territories 340
Tying Contracts 340

RETAILING 340

Offer Variety for Consumers 341
Separate Large Product Volume into Consumer Purchase Quantities 341
Maintain Inventory Levels 342
Make Additional Services Available to Consumers 342
Characteristics of Store Retailers 343
Types of Store Retailers 344
Non-Store Retailing 346

ELECTRONIC COMMERCE 348

Business-to-Consumer Electronic Commerce 348
Business-to-Business Electronic Commerce 350

SUMMARY 352

KEY TERMS 352

APPLICATION QUESTIONS 353

MANAGEMENT DECISION CASE: PUSHING SUPPLY CHAIN EFFICIENCIES TO THE MAXIMUM IN RETAILING 353

MARKETING PLAN EXERCISE 354

NOTES 355

part FIVE

Communicate the Value Offering through the Elements of Integrated Marketing Communications 359

CHAPTER 12

Promotional Strategy and New Media 360

ESSENTIALS OF PROMOTION AND INTEGRATED MARKETING COMMUNICATIONS (IMC) 361

The Rise of IMC 362
IMC Decision Making 363
IMC and the Promotion Mix 364
Push and Pull Strategies 364
Internal Marketing and IMC 366
Looking Ahead 366

COMMUNICATION PROCESS MODEL 366

Sender 367
Encoding Process 367
Message Transmission 368
Decoding Process 368
Receiver 368
Feedback Loop 368
Noise 369

HIERARCHY OF EFFECTS MODEL 370

Attention 370
Interest 371
Desire 371
Action 372

THE MARKETING MANAGER'S ROLE IN PROMOTIONAL STRATEGY 372

Identify Targets for Promotion 373
Establish Goals for Promotion 373
Select the Promotion Mix 375
Develop the Message 377
Select Media for Use in Promotion 378
Prepare Promotion Budget 378
Establish Measures of Results 380

NEW MEDIA 381

Online Communication Decisions 381
Mobile Growth Opportunities 384
Social Media Change the Conversation 386

SUMMARY 391

KEY TERMS 391

APPLICATION QUESTIONS 392

MANAGEMENT DECISION CASE: WATER IS LIFE: ATTRACTING ATTENTION TO A CAUSE THROUGH GUERILLA TACTICS 393

MARKETING PLAN EXERCISE 394

NOTES 394

CHAPTER 13

Advertising, Sales Promotion, and Public Relations 396

ADVERTISING 397

Types of Advertising 398
Advertising Execution and Media Types 401
The Role of the Creative Agency 404

SALES PROMOTION 404

Sales Promotion to Consumers 405
Sales Promotion to Channel Members 405

PUBLIC RELATIONS (PR) 407

Gaining Product Publicity and Buzz 407
Securing Event Sponsorships 408
Crisis Management 409

SUMMARY 410

KEY TERMS 410

APPLICATION QUESTIONS 410

MANAGEMENT DECISION CASE: ADVERTISING TO GAIN OR KEEP MARKET SHARE IN THE HYPERCOMPETITIVE INSURANCE SPACE 411

MARKETING PLAN EXERCISE 412

NOTES 413

CHAPTER 14

Personal Selling and Direct Marketing 414

TOWARD A MORE PERSONAL COMMUNICATION WITH THE CUSTOMER 415

PERSONAL SELLING—THE MOST PERSONAL FORM OF COMMUNICATION 415

Activities in Personal Selling 416
Sales in B2C versus B2B Markets 418
Classifying Sales Positions 418
The Personal Selling Process 419
Organizing the Sales Force 423
Managing the Sales Force 426

DIRECT MARKETING 431

Creating a Direct Marketing Campaign 432
Direct Marketing Channels 433

SUMMARY 435

KEY TERMS 435

APPLICATION QUESTIONS 435

MANAGEMENT DECISION CASE: PHARMACEUTICAL SALES: PRESSURE IS ON TO CHANGE THE SELLING PROCESS 436

MARKETING PLAN EXERCISE 437

NOTES 437

part SIX

Bring It all Together—Global and Performance Dimensions 441

CHAPTER 15

Understand the Global Marketplace: Marketing without Borders 442

MARKETING IS NOT LIMITED BY BORDERS 443

THE GLOBAL EXPERIENCE LEARNING CURVE 444

Companies with No Foreign Marketing 444
Companies with Foreign Marketing 445
International Marketing 445
Global Marketing 446
Essential Information 446
Emerging Markets 448
Marketing in Emerging Markets 449
Multinational Regional Market Zones 449
Marketing in Regional Market Zones 453

SELECT THE GLOBAL MARKET 453

Identify Selection Criteria 454
Company Review 454

DEVELOP GLOBAL MARKET STRATEGIES 455

Market Entry Strategies 455
Organizational Structure 459
Product 460
Consumers 460
Market Channels 462
Marketing Communications 464
Pricing 465

SUMMARY 468

KEY TERMS 468

APPLICATION QUESTIONS 468

MANAGEMENT DECISION CASE: A NEW GLOBAL COMPETITOR: COMMERCIAL JETLINER PRODUCTION BEGINS IN CHINA 469

MARKETING PLAN EXERCISE 470

NOTES 470

CHAPTER 16

The Marketing Dashboard: Metrics for Measuring Marketing Performance 474

THE MARKETING DASHBOARD 475

Goals and Elements of a Marketing Dashboard 475
Potential Pitfalls in Marketing Dashboards 477
Toward Your Own Marketing Dashboard 478

RETURN ON MARKETING INVESTMENT (ROMI) 478

Cautions about Overreliance on ROMI 479
Proceed with Caution 480

A SAMPLING OF OTHER MARKETING METRICS 481

Market Share 481
Penetration 481

Margin on Sales 482
Cannibalization Rate 483
Customer Lifetime Value (CLV) 483
Sales Force Effectiveness 483
Supply Chain Metrics 484
Promotions and Pass-Through 484
Cost per Thousand Impressions (CPM) Rates 484
Share of Voice 484
Click-Through Rates 485

DEVELOPING EFFECTIVE ACTION PLANS 485

Responsibility for the Action Plan 485
Timing of the Action Plan 486
Budget for the Action Plan 486
Measurement and Control of the Action Plan 487

FORECASTING FOR MARKETING PLANNING 487

Subjective Methods of Forecasting 487
Objective Methods of Forecasting 489
Selecting the Appropriate Forecasting Method(s) 493

THE MARKETING BUDGET 494

CONTROLS AND CONTINGENCY PLANNING 495

THE MARKETING AUDIT 497

SUMMARY 500

KEY TERMS 500

APPLICATION QUESTIONS 500

MANAGEMENT DECISION CASE: FORECASTING AND WANNABE BLOCKBUSTER FILMS 501

MARKETING PLAN EXERCISE 502

NOTES 502

GLOSSARY G-1

PHOTO CREDITS PC-1

INDEX I-1

PART 1

Discover Marketing Management

chapter 01

MARKETING IN TODAY'S BUSINESS MILIEU

chapter 02

ELEMENTS OF MARKETING STRATEGY, PLANNING, AND COMPETITION

CHAPTER 01

Marketing in Today's Business Milieu

LEARNING OBJECTIVES

LO 1-1 Identify typical misconceptions about marketing, why they persist, and the resulting challenges for marketing management.

LO 1-2 Define what marketing and marketing management really are and how they contribute to a firm's success.

LO 1-3 Appreciate how marketing has evolved from its early roots to be practiced as it is today.

LO 1-4 Recognize the impact of key change drivers on the future of marketing.

WELCOME TO MARKETING MANAGEMENT

Welcome to the world of marketing management! Now is a great time to be studying about marketing. In fact, marketing as a field of study has much to offer everyone, regardless of whether or not the word "marketing" appears in their job title. Whether your interest and training are in engineering, accounting, finance, information technology, or fields outside business, marketing is relevant to you. You can be confident that, when finished with this course about marketing management, you will emerge with a set of knowledge and skills that will not only enhance your personal effectiveness as a leader and manager regardless of area of responsibility or job title, but will also positively impact the performance of your work group and firm. Mastering great marketing is useful for anyone!

Despite the strong case for the value of learning about marketing, marketing is often misunderstood for a variety of reasons. So before we go any further, let's start by clearing the air. Before you learn about great marketing and how to successfully manage it, it is important to address some misconceptions and stereotypes about marketing. Getting these out in the open will give you the opportunity to challenge your own perceptions of the field. After this section, attention will quickly turn from marketing misconceptions to *marketing realities* in today's business milieu.

MARKETING MISCONCEPTIONS

LO 1-1

Identify typical misconceptions about marketing, why they persist, and the resulting challenges for marketing management.

When you think of *marketing,* what sorts of ideas and images initially come to mind? Close your eyes and think about the essence of the word. What images flow in? The images will vary depending on your age, your professional background, and whether you have worked in some aspect of the marketing field. Here is a short list of perceptions commonly conjured up about marketing:

- Catchy and entertaining advertisements—or perhaps the opposite, incessant and boring advertisements.
- Pushy salespeople trying to persuade someone to *buy it right now.*
- Incessant SPAM in your e-mail inbox and unwelcome solicitations on your smartphone.
- Famous brands and their celebrity spokespeople, such as Nike's athlete endorsers.
- Product claims that turn out to be overstated or just plain false, causing doubt about the trustworthiness of a company.
- Marketing departments "own" an organization's marketing initiative.

Exhibit 1.1 expands on the common stereotypes and misconceptions about marketing.

Behind the Misconceptions

Several important factors have contributed to the development of these misconceptions: marketing's inherent visibility and its tendency toward buzzwords and "spin."

Marketing Is Highly Visible by Nature Unlike most other key areas of business, marketing as a field is highly public and readily visible outside the confines of the internal business operation. Think of it this way: Most aspects of financial management, accounting, information technology, production, operations management, and human resource management take place behind the curtain of an organization, out of the general public's sight. But marketing is very different. A good portion of marketing is very public. Marketing is seen through the web page

EXHIBIT 1.1 | Marketing Misconceptions: What Marketing Is *Not*

MISCONCEPTION NO. 1: Marketing is all about advertising.

THE REALITY: Advertising is just one way that marketing is communicated to potential customers. Advertising is highly visible to the general public, so many people naturally think of advertising when they think of marketing. A famous axiom: *Good advertising makes a bad product fail faster.*

MISCONCEPTION NO. 2: Marketing is all about selling.

THE REALITY: The general public also experiences a lot of selling. Much of this day-to-day selling is in retail store environments. Selling, or more correctly "personal selling," is simply another method of marketing communication. Marketers have to decide on a mix of marketing communication approaches that (in addition to advertising and personal selling) might also include public relations/publicity, sales promotion, and direct marketing. Later chapters discuss how and when each might be most effective in communicating the message.

MISCONCEPTION NO. 3: Marketing is all about the *sizzle.*

THE REALITY: Yes, some aspects of marketing are inherently fun and glitzy. Hiring Tiger Woods as a celebrity spokesperson had to be a real thrill for everybody at Nike, not to mention the pleasure and fun it gave Nike fans. But marketing also has aspects that involve sophisticated research, detailed analysis, careful decision making, and thoughtful development of strategies and plans. For many organizations, marketing represents a major investment and firms are naturally reluctant to invest major resources without a reasonable level of assurance of a satisfactory payback.

MISCONCEPTION NO. 4: Marketing is inherently unethical and harmful to society.

THE REALITY: Marketing is no more inherently unethical than other business areas. The accounting scandals at Enron, WorldCom, and other firms in the early 2000s show that to be true. However, when some element of marketing proves to be unethical (or even illegal), it tends to be visible to the general public. Untrue advertising claims, arm-twisting sales tactics, and nonenvironmentally friendly product packaging are a few very visible examples of marketing not behaving at its best.

MISCONCEPTION NO. 5: Only marketers market.

THE REALITY: Everybody does marketing. Everybody has a stake in the success of marketing. Regardless of your position in a firm or job title, learning how to do great marketing is a key professional asset. People with strong marketing skills achieve greater success—both on the job and off. If you've never thought of yourself in the context of being a "personal brand" that needs to be effectively communicated, just consider how useful such an approach could be in job seeking or positioning yourself for a promotion.

MISCONCEPTION NO. 6: Marketing is just another cost center in a firm.

THE REALITY: The mind-set that marketing is a cost, rather than an investment, is deadly in a firm because costs are inherently to be reduced or avoided. When management doesn't view marketing as earning its keep—that is, marketing being able to pay back its investment over the long term—it becomes very easy for firms to suboptimize their success in the long run by avoiding investment in brand and product development in favor of cutting costs. This is the classic argument that successful firms must simultaneously monitor costs to ensure short-term financial performance while also investing in marketing to ensure long-term competitive strength.

that stimulates interest in seeking more product information, the (hopefully) good service received from the salesperson representing a firm's products, the enjoyment and interest generated from a clever advertisement on Super Bowl Sunday, or the well-stocked shelves at the neighborhood Target Store.

Of all the business fields, marketing is almost certainly the most visible to people outside the organization. While other fields also have negative stereotypical images (think accountants with green eyeshades or IT computer geeks), you'd be hard pressed to identify another business field about which nearly everyone has formed a deeply held set of images and opinions or about which nearly everybody thinks they know enough to confidently offer advice! Think about how many times casual conversation in a social setting turns to something marketing related. Have you ever had similar social exchanges about the ins and outs of financial management or the complexities of computerized production systems? Of course not, but it seems almost anybody is comfortable talking (and tweeting!) about elements of marketing—from the week's advertised specials at the supermarket to this year's fashion for kids heading back to school to the service received at a favorite vacation hotel—marketing is a topic everyone can discuss!

Marketing strategies, including pricing strategies, are not easily changed once established with the consumer. Penney (JCP) has faced difficulties since February 2012 when CEO Ron Johnson steered the retailer away from deep discounts, coupons, and super sale advertisements, instead offering everyday low pricing (EDLP). Johnson's ultimate goal was to transition the department store into a specialty store featuring in-store boutiques. However, customers did not respond favorably. The company reported four consecutive quarters of net losses. By February 2013, JCP announced it would be adding sales to select merchandise again and by late spring the same year Johnson was out as CEO, quickly followed by other top-management changes. JCP has since shifted to displaying manufacturer suggested retail pricing alongside its EDLP on select merchandise in order to educate the customer on the value of its EDLP approach. JCP may have recognized that its core customers were not ready for such a big change, and as a result it had to evolve (or devolve) its strategy. The company's challenge going forward is to regain those customers lost to competitors.[1]

Why is the notion that marketing is visible and accessible to nearly everyone so important to students of marketing management? The truth is, despite the fact that much of marketing is easily observable to just about anyone, marketing as a professional field worthy of serious study doesn't always get the respect it deserves, maybe in part because of its overexposure. The business functions of financial management, operations, IT, and the rest seem to be viewed by many MBA and undergraduate students (and also, unfortunately, by managers in many firms) as the more "serious" parts of an enterprise—topics that are perceived as more concrete, more scientific, and more analytical than marketing, thus implying they are topics worthy of more substantial investment in time, money, and other resources.[2] In the past, marketing has had few useful metrics or measures to gauge the performance impact of a firm's marketing investment, while other areas of the firm have historically been much more driven by measurement of results. The old adage "if it can't be measured, it can't be managed" has plagued marketing for years. This is changing, and today measurement of marketing's performance and contribution is a focal point in many firms.[3] In fact, so many great marketing metrics are available that we've included a whole chapter on the topic at the end of the book.

Marketing Is More Than Buzzwords Given the inherently transparent nature of marketing and the prior lack of ways to effectively measure its impact on a firm's success, it should be no surprise that some managers consider marketing to be little more than a necessary evil—a *cost* they reluctantly have to incur.[4] They're not sure *how* marketing works, or even *if* marketing really does work, but for competitive reasons—or maybe just because it's always been done—they continue to invest large sums of money in its many facets including market research, brand development, advertising, salespeople, public relations, and so forth. With so much ambiguity historically surrounding the management and control of marketing, a "flavor of the month" club mentality has developed around the field of marketing, often promoted by consultants and authors looking to make a quick buck by selling their latest and greatest ideas complete with their own catchy buzzwords for the program.

Anyone who doubts the pervasiveness of quick-fix approaches to marketing should visit a bookstore or online bookseller. Go to the business section and look at the marketing titles. Among the buzzwords right in the book titles are such gems as *guerilla marketing, permission marketing, holistic marketing, marketing warfare, marketing rainmaking, buzz marketing, integrated marketing* . . . the list goes on and on. Although each of these approaches may provide a germ of usefulness, the circus-like atmosphere surrounding the field has detracted from its position as a respectable business function.

Beyond the Misconceptions and Toward the *Reality* of Modern Marketing

Of course, buzzwords are just window dressing, and most popular press prescription approaches to marketing don't do much to improve the *long-term* performance of an organization. Effective marketing management isn't about buzzwords or quick fixes. Nor is the essence of marketing really about the kinds of stereotypical viewpoints identified earlier in this section. In today's business milieu, marketing is a central function and set of processes essential to any enterprise.[5] Moreover, leading and managing the facets of marketing to improve individual, unit, and organizational performance—**marketing management**—is a *core business activity*, worthy of any student's study and mastery.

Netflix was a leader in subscription streaming video content. New rivals have been establishing themselves in this market, providing similar service, pricing, and content. Netflix decided to use its favorable perception among families to differentiate itself. In 2012, the company made an exclusive deal to be the home for Disney's new releases along with offering older content beginning in 2016. In addition to licensing agreements, Netflix felt the pressure to create original content like rival streaming video producers, Amazon Prime and Hulu Plus. However, in its transition to original content, Netflix aimed to own the under-12 viewer segment. Early in 2013 it announced plans to create a children's series, *Turbo: F.A.S.T.*, which would be a spin-off of the Dreamworks film *Turbo*. Netflix recognized its appeal to parents as a service that provides endless hours of children's entertainment for an affordable monthly fee. Through its agreements with Disney and Dreamworks, as well as its new original content, Netflix has the potential to position itself as the go-to entertainment service for families with children.[6]

The chapters that follow lay the groundwork for developing the knowledge and skills around marketing that will allow you to build a more successful career as a leader and manager, regardless of department, area of specialization, level in the organization, or job title. Is marketing relevant to *you?* You bet it is because *everyone* in an organization does marketing in some way and must share ownership of its success or failure.

Learning about marketing management is not just about reading a book or taking a course, although dedication to these activities is a great starting point. Instead, great marketing is a lifelong journey that requires dedication to continuous learning and improvement of your knowledge and skills as a leader and manager. It is in this spirit that we enthusiastically invite you to begin your journey into the field of marketing management!

DEFINING MARKETING

LO 1-2

Define what marketing and marketing management really are and how they contribute to a firm's success.

Over 50 years ago, the late management guru Peter Drucker, often referred to as the father of modern management, set the stage for defining contemporary marketing and conceiving of its potential power. Consider this quote from Drucker, circa 1954 (emphasis added):

> If we want to know what a business is we have to start with its *purpose*. There is only one valid definition of business purpose: *to create a customer*. It is the customer who

determines what a business is. For it is the customer, and he alone, who through being willing to pay for a good or service, converts economic resources into wealth, things into goods. What the business thinks it produces is not of first importance—especially not to the future of the business and its success. What the customer thinks he is buying, what he considers "value" is decisive. . . . Because it is the [purpose of a business] to create a customer, [the] business enterprise has two—and only two—business functions: *marketing* and *innovation*.[7]

Consider the power of these ideas: a business built around the customer with resources and processes aligned to maximize customer value. Within this context, Drucker is not talking just about "marketing departments," but rather marketing in much broader terms. More on that distinction later. For now, consider this subsequent quote from Drucker circa 1973:

Marketing is so basic that it cannot be considered a separate function (i.e., a separate skill or work) within the business . . . it is, first, a central dimension of the entire business. It is the *whole business* . . . seen from the *customer's* point of view. Concern and responsibility for marketing must, therefore, permeate all areas of the enterprise.[8]

Clearly, Peter Drucker was a man whose business philosophy was way ahead of his time. Now fast forward to this decade. The American Marketing Association offers the following as its official definition of marketing:

Marketing is the activity, set of institutions, and processes for creating, communicating, delivering, and exchanging offerings that have value for customers, clients, partners, and society at large.

This definition is quite good because it

- Focuses on the more *strategic* aspects of marketing, which positions marketing as a core contributor to overall firm success.
- Recognizes marketing as an activity, set of institutions, and processes—that is, marketing is not just a "department" in an organization.
- Shifts the areas of central focus of marketing to *value*—creating, communicating, delivering, and exchanging offerings of value to various stakeholders.

Just who are the relevant stakeholders of marketing? **Marketing's stakeholders** include any person or entity inside or outside a firm with whom marketing interacts, impacts, and is impacted by. For example, internal stakeholders—those inside a firm—include other organizational units that marketing interacts with in the course of business. Strong, productive relationships between marketing and finance, accounting, production, quality control, engineering, human resources, and many other areas in a firm are necessary in order for a firm to do business successfully.[9] The range of external stakeholders—those outside a firm—is even broader and includes customers, vendors, governmental bodies, labor unions, and many others. One important challenge in marketing management is deciding how to prioritize these internal and external stakeholders in terms of their relevance and importance to the firm.[10] Most firms place the customer first, but a key question is: how do you decide which of the others deserve the most attention?

Green marketing isn't a theme one might expect to see Waste Management, Inc., conveying, yet they have a powerful environmental message.

At the broadest conceptual level, members of society at large can be viewed as a stakeholder for marketing, a concept called **societal marketing.** As one example, the concept of environmentally friendly marketing, or *green marketing,* has been a growing trend in socially responsible companies. Today the movement has evolved into a part of the philosophical and strategic core of many firms under the label **sustainability,** which refers to business practices that meet humanity's needs without harming future generations.[11] Sustainability practices have helped socially responsible organizations incorporate *doing well by doing good* into their overarching business models so that both the success of the firm and the success of society at large are sustained over the long term. Ethical Dimension 1 takes a look at environmentally friendly marketing at several firms.

"Purpose marketing," or "pro-social marketing," is growing as a marketing strategy. This growing popularity can be attributed to an increasing number of consumers who say what a company stands for influences their purchasing decisions. Companies such as Panera Bread must communicate their core values through their use of the marketing mix. Panera is known for its quick-serve restaurants, but it's also charitable, actively working with other organizations including Feeding America. In order to create awareness of its social consciousness, Panera launched its "Live consciously. Eat deliciously" campaign. The initiative will have a significant presence on social media sites, including Facebook and Twitter, exposing this new positioning to millions of fans. Purpose marketing with this type of sincerity has the potential to appeal to consumers on an emotional level and further drive customer loyalty. This trend moves marketing beyond push brand messaging and instead engages consumers in a much more meaningful way.[12]

Value and Exchange Are Core Marketing Concepts

Throughout the various topics encompassed within this book, the idea of value as a core concept in marketing will be a central theme. From a customer's perspective, we define **value** as a ratio of the bundle of benefits a customer receives from an offering compared to the costs incurred by the customer in acquiring that bundle of benefits.[13] Another central tenet of marketing is the concept of **exchange,** in which a person gives up something of value to them for something else they desire to have.[14] Usually an exchange is facilitated by money, but not always. Sometimes people trade or barter nonmonetary resources such as time, skill, expertise, intellectual capital, and other things of value for something else they want. For any exchange to take place, the following five conditions must be present:

1. There must be at least two parties.
2. Each party has something that might be of value to the other party.
3. Each party is capable of communication and delivery.
4. Each party is free to accept or reject the exchange offer.
5. Each party believes it is appropriate or desirable to deal with the other party.

Just because these conditions exist does not guarantee that an exchange will take place. The parties must come to an agreement that results in both being better off, hence the phrase in the AMA definition of marketing ". . . exchanging offerings that *have value* . . . (emphasis added)." Value implies that both parties win from the exchange.

Coca-Cola made new investments in its Simply Orange product line in order to provide a premium product for consumers. There has been an increasing trend in consumer behavior toward healthier eating (and drinking). In fact, the market for "still" beverages, including juices, has been outpacing the growth of sparkling

ETHICAL DIMENSION 1

The Green Product Challenge

Environmental awareness coupled with a sense of social responsibility is leading many companies to assess their environmental policies and business practices. Some companies such as General Electric are developing environmentally sensitive products while others such as Starbucks have adopted tough recycling programs that minimize environmental waste. Companies worldwide acknowledge a concern for the environment, seek to minimize environmental damage, and commit resources to their environmental programs.

One challenge for manufacturers around the world is to transform environmentally harmful products into environmentally friendly products. In some industries, making products more environmentally safe has been relatively straightforward. For instance, air conditioner manufacturers moved from the refrigerant known by the brand name Freon to a more environmental friendly product, Puron, that reduced chlorine emissions and depletion of the ozone layer.

In other situations, it is more difficult to create environmentally sensitive products. Consider Nike, a company that built its running shoe business through outstanding products and creative marketing communications. A key product feature for Nike has been a small pocket of air in its Nike Air shoes. The extra cushion was a significant product innovation when it was introduced and proved to be a major market differentiator for the company. However, the pocket of "air" was not just air; it also contained a small amount of sulfur hexafluoride, or SF6, a gas that damages the ozone layer.

In the early 1990s, questions about Nike's use of SF6 gas became public. While the Nike air cushion was a key factor in the company's success, Nike realized that continued use of SF6 posed an environmental problem. Unfortunately, replacing SF6 with a solution that minimized environmental damage while providing the same product benefits (long-lasting cushion and support) proved challenging.

After millions of dollars and almost two decades, a team of 60 Nike engineers replaced the old product with a new, greener solution using sophisticated manufacturing techniques to replace the SR6 with nitrogen. The Air-Max was the first shoe to incorporate the new technology. Interestingly, the new shoe actually increases comfort and weighs less than older models, making the environmentally sensitive solution the best business solution as well. Nike's focus on product performance and technical innovation created a better, environmentally friendly product that is successful in the marketplace.

As part of the product development process, Nike kept environmental groups informed of the progress. Although there were tensions as the process took longer than anyone planned, the communication between Nike and stakeholders helped minimize long-term negative publicity. The challenge for marketers is finding the right balance between consumer demand and environmental stewardship.[15]

Ethical Perspective

1. **Nike:** How would you prioritize what are often two conflicting demands: consumer product performance expectations and the demand for eco-friendly products?
2. **Consumers:** Would you choose a Nike shoe that provided less comfort but was more environmentally friendly? Would you pay a premium for an environmentally friendly Nike shoe?
3. **Environmental groups:** Nike took almost two decades to create a new sole for its air cushion; would you allow a company that much time to deal with an environmentally damaging product?

drinks in recent years. In order to develop its production in a growing beverage market, Coca-Cola is tackling the external variables that affect making juice. By using very sophisticated satellite and statistical models applied to securing a constant high-quality inflow of raw materials, Coke is able to provide its customers a standardized, 100% not-from-concentrate orange juice year-round. Bob Cross, the architect of Coke's juice algorithm (called the Black Book), said the program "... requires analyzing up to 1 quintillion decision variables to consistently deliver the optimal blend, despite the whims of Mother Nature." In addition, it includes information about the 600 flavors that are contained in an orange, as well as consumer preferences. As the juice is being bottled, "blend technicians" follow the recipe from the Black Book, even adding the natural flavors and fragrances that were lost in processing.[16]

EXHIBIT 1.2 | Marketing Yesterday and Today

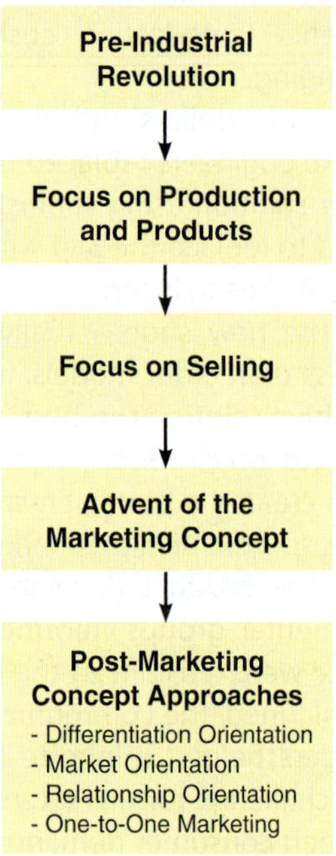

The AMA definition of marketing highlights marketing's central role in creating (or developing), communicating, delivering, and exchanging offerings that have value. But marketing's central focus hasn't always been on value and customer relationships, and the truth is that even today some firms lag in these areas. The next section offers perspectives on marketing's roots and evolution, and explains why some firms today are frozen in past approaches to marketing.

MARKETING'S ROOTS AND EVOLUTION

In the spirit of the old adage that he who ignores history is doomed to repeat its mistakes, here's a short marketing history lesson. Exhibit 1.2 illustrates the flow of marketing's evolution as a field. It is important to note that there are still firms that are "stuck in the past" in the way they approach marketing. That is, not all organizations have "fully evolved!" But hopefully the majority of firms seek to approach marketing from a 21st century perspective as we present throughout this book.

Pre-Industrial Revolution

LO 1-3

Appreciate how marketing has evolved from its early roots to be practiced as it is today.

Before Henry Ford and his contemporaries created assembly lines and mass production, marketing was done very much on a one-to-one basis between firms and customers, although the word *marketing* wasn't really used. Consider what happened when a person needed a new pair of shoes, pre-industrial revolution. One would likely go visit the village cobbler, who would take precise measurements and then send the customer away with instructions to return in a week or so to pick up the new shoes. Materials, styles, and colors would be limited, but customers likely would get a great fit since the cobbler created a customized pair of shoes for each person. And if they didn't fit just right, the cobbler would adjust the shoes to a customer's liking—right on the spot.

Focus on Production and Products

The industrial revolution changed nearly everything in business by shifting the focus from meeting demand one item at a time to mass production via assembly line. Maximizing production capacity utilization became a predominant concern. For the early part of the 20th century, the focus was on this **production orientation** of improving products and production efficiency without much regard for what was going on in the marketplace. In fact, consumers snapped up this new pipeline of reasonably priced goods, even if the products didn't give much choice in style or function. Having a Ford Model T was great, but as Henry Ford himself said, "People can have the Model T in any color—so long that it's black."[17]

A production orientation assumes that customers will beat a path to your door just because you have a great product that functions nicely; build a better mousetrap and they will come. You will learn throughout your study of marketing management that great products alone do not assure success. Unfortunately, firms that are stuck in a production orientation mentality likely will have great difficulty competing successfully for customers.

Focus on Selling

Around the end of World War I, production capacity utilization began to decline for several reasons. First, capacity had been increased greatly for the war. Second, a number of firms that had dominated their respective industries before the war now found themselves with stiff competition for sales because many new competitors had flooded into the marketplace. And third, financial markets were becoming more sophisticated and were placing more pressure on firms to continually increase sales volume and profits.

These factors resulted in the rise of many of the great sales organizations of today. A **sales orientation** suggests that, to increase sales and consequently production capacity utilization, professional salespeople need to "push" product into the hands of customers, both businesses and end users. For years, the most vivid image of a salesperson in the public eye was that of the peddler, the classic outside salesperson pushing product on customers with a smile, promise, and handshake. Gradually, customers of all kinds grew wary of high-pressure selling, sparking laws at all levels to protect consumers from unscrupulous salespeople. For many customers, the image of marketing became permanently frozen as that of the pushy salesperson. And just as with the production orientation, to this day some firms still practice mainly a sales-oriented approach to their business.

Advent of the Marketing Concept

After World War II, business began to change in many long-lasting ways. Business historians point to a number of reasons for this shift, including:

- Pent-up demand for consumer goods and services after the war.
- Euphoric focus on family and a desperate need to regain a normalcy of day-to-day life after years of war (which produced the baby boomer generation).
- Opening up of production capacity dominated for years by war production.
- Advent of readily available mainframe computing capability, and especially the associated statistical analytic techniques that allowed for more sophisticated market research.

In the 1950s, these forces, combined with growing frustration with high-pressure selling, sparked a shift in the focus of American business. The resulting business philosophy has been labeled the **marketing concept,** which is an organization-wide customer orientation with the objective of achieving long-run profits.[18] General Electric's *1952 Annual Report* is often cited as the first time the marketing concept was articulated in writing by a major corporation. Clearly delighted to herald its new-age management philosophy, GE wrote the following to stockholders in that report (in this historical period, the assumption was that business professionals would be male):

> [The marketing concept] . . . introduces the marketing man at the beginning rather than at the end of the production cycle and integrates marketing into each phase of the business. Thus, marketing, through its studies and research, will establish for the engineer, the design and manufacturing man, what the customer wants in a given product, what price he is willing to

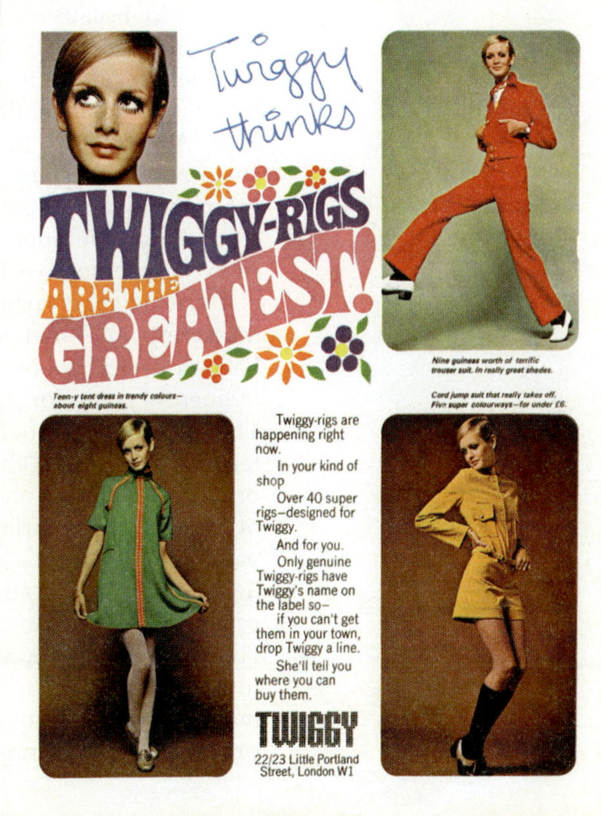

In the 1960s, Twiggy was an immensely popular model and is often regarded as one of the first supermodels. Her name and image were strong enough to promote a line of clothing, beginning a trend of celebrity connections to fashion that continues today.

pay, and where and when it will be wanted. Marketing will have authority in product planning, production scheduling, and inventory control, as well as in sales distribution and servicing of the product.[19]

The articulation of the marketing concept was a major breakthrough in business, and in the 1960s and '70s it spread like wildfire throughout companies of all kinds. Soon firms everywhere were adopting the practice of letting the market decide what products to offer. Such an approach required substantial investment in ongoing market and consumer research and also necessitated an organization-wide commitment to marketing planning. As a result, the idea of the marketing plan became codified in most organizations' business processes. We'll come back to the idea of marketing planning in Chapter 2.

The Marketing Mix The articulation of the marketing concept and its quick adoption across a gamut of industries quickly led to a major focus on teaching marketing courses in colleges and universities. In the mid-1960s, a convenient way of teaching the key components was developed with the advent of the **marketing mix,** or **4Ps of marketing,** originally for *p*roduct, *p*rice, *p*lace, and *p*romotion.[20] The idea was that these fundamental elements comprise the marketer's "tool kit" to be applied in carrying out the job. It is referred to as a "mix" because, by developing unique combinations of these elements, marketers set their product or brand apart from the competition. Also, an important rubric in marketing is the following: making a change in any one of the marketing mix elements tends to result in a domino effect on the others.

Today, the basic concept of the marketing mix still persists but with considerably greater sophistication than in the 1960s. The product is now regarded broadly in the context of an overall *offering,* which could include a bundle of goods, services, ideas (for example, intellectual property), and other components, often represented by strong overarching branding. Many marketers today are more focused on *solutions* than products—the characterization of an offering as a solution is nice because of the implication that a solution has been developed in conjunction with specific, well-understood customer wants and needs.[21] *P*rice today is largely regarded in relationship to the concept of value. *P*lace has undergone tremendous change. Rather than just connoting the process of getting goods from Point A to Point B, firms now understand that sophisticated, integrated supply chain approaches are a crucial component of business success.[22] And finally, to grasp the magnitude of changes in *p*romotion since the 1960s one need only consider the proliferation of high-tech media options available to marketers today, from the Internet to cell phones and beyond.

Over the years some authors have proposed various additions to the original marketing mix—that is, adding "more Ps." Especially outside the setting of marketing physical goods, as in the context of marketing services or ideas, the case is frequently made for the need to add more elements to the marketer's tool kit.[23] This issue has been hotly debated for years. You will find as you progress in your reading of this book that later on we follow the basic topical flow of developing, pricing, delivering, and communicating offerings that have value. Put in terms of the 4Ps of the marketing mix, Part Three of the book focuses on *developing* the value offering through product strategy and new product development, building the brand, and attention to service (the product "P"). Part Four focuses on pricing and delivering the value offering (the "price and place Ps"). Finally, Part Five provides a comprehensive look at how firms communicate the value offering to customers (the "promotion P"). Thus, the core elements of the original 4Ps of marketing are there but presented within the context of the terminology and work processes used by *today's* marketing managers.

Post-Marketing Concept Approaches

Close perusal of the definition of the marketing concept reveals several issues that still resonate widely in today's business milieu. The decisions to place the customer at the core of the enterprise (often referred to as a **customer-centric** approach to business), focus on investment in customers over the *long term*, and focus on marketing as an *organization-wide* issue (that is, not just relegated to a "marketing department") are all relevant and important topics in business classes and boardrooms today, and each will be discussed further in later chapters.[24] Referring again to Exhibit 1.2, the four evolutionary steps beyond the original marketing concept warrant further discussion now: differentiation orientation, market orientation, relationship orientation, and one-to-one marketing.

Differentiation Orientation More sophisticated research and analytical approaches have made it possible to do increasingly precise refinement of market segmentation, target marketing, and positioning of products to serve very specific customer groups, processes you will learn more about in Chapter 6. The idea is to create and communicate **differentiation**, or what clearly distinguishes your products from those of competitors in the minds of customers.[25] The ability for marketers to tailor and deliver different product messages to different groups also has been greatly enhanced by the proliferation of multiple types of media that can be used with great precision to communicate to very specifically defined customer groups.

Gap, a group of several major retail store brands for men's, women's, and children's clothing, began noticing that its clothing styles were not meeting customer expectations. They were creating clothing that was not clearly differentiated from that of competitors and Gap's brands were quickly losing market share. CEO Glenn Murphy decided to revamp their strategy and develop trendier styles. One result was the introduction of the sleek, "Mad Men" collection in Banana Republic, which proved to be extremely successful. Mad Men apparel began to appear on eBay selling for more than the store's retail price! As customers appreciated the more "fashionable" styles, the company's numbers also improved. Revenue per product has increased nicely since 2012, but it remains to be seen if these increased sales can be sustained. Nonetheless, the latest sales are promising for the struggling retailer.[26]

Market Orientation A great deal of research has been devoted to learning how a firm can successfully put the marketing concept into practice. Think of **market orientation** as the implementation of the marketing concept. The notion of market orientation, one component of which is **customer orientation**—placing the customer at the core of all aspects of the enterprise—takes the guiding business philosophy of the marketing concept and works to more usefully define just how to implement it within a firm.[27]

Relationship Orientation Marketing managers today recognize the power of securing, building, and maintaining long-term relationships with profitable customers.[28] The original marketing concept clearly recognized the need for an orientation toward the longer term in marketing—that is, not just making the next quarter's financial projections but rather cultivating customers for the long haul. The move toward a **relationship orientation** by firms has been driven by the realization that it is far more efficient and effective to invest in keeping and cultivating profitable current customers instead of constantly having to invest in gaining new customers that come with unknown return on investment.[29] Certainly most firms simultaneously focus on both current and new customers, but no company wants to be in a position of losing great customers and having to scramble to replace the associated lost revenue.

Customers drive the marketplace today, and it is critical that every organization pays close attention to customer wants and needs. Each year, global executive surveys indicate that leaders will push in the coming year to better understand their customers. Yet, some companies are reluctant to admit customers hold so much power in the marketplace. Rather than making the effort to effectively analyze offerings by customer preferences, companies conclude that marketing may be at fault. If there had been larger and better marketing campaigns, then sales would have been higher. For instance, after HTC's profits plummeted 79 percent year over year in the third quarter of 2012, the CEO focused squarely on marketing, overtly acknowledging that ". . . the most important thing is to have unique products that appeal to customers." However, he noted a lack of resources kept the company from performing in that manner. In actuality, a limitless marketing budget will not sustain a product that does not have value in the eyes of the consumer. Without an emphasis on the consumer, it will be nearly impossible for a business to survive long term.[30]

A relationship orientation draws its power from the firm's capability to effectively collect and use ongoing, real-time information on customers in marketing management decision making. Implementation of a relationship orientation is discussed in Chapter 6 in the context of customer relationship management (CRM). Much of CRM is designed to facilitate higher levels of customer satisfaction and loyalty, as well as to provide a means for identifying the most profitable customers—those worthy of the most marketing investment.[31]

One-to-One Marketing Remember the earlier example of the pre-industrial revolution cobbler who would customize a pair of shoes for each customer? In many ways marketing's evolution has come full circle back to a focus on creating capabilities for such customization. In their books and articles, Don Peppers and Martha Rogers popularized the term **one-to-one marketing,** which advocates that firms should direct energy and resources into establishing a learning relationship with each customer and then connect that knowledge with the firm's production and service capabilities to fulfill that customer's needs in as custom a manner as possible.[32]

Some firms come close to one-to-one marketing by employing **mass customization,** in which they combine flexible manufacturing with flexible marketing to greatly enhance customer choices.[33] Retailers have even entered into mass customization. The luxury brand Burberry allows customers to build their own trench coats. They are able to select from silhouettes of varying length, leather or fabric type, and several colors. Options also include sleeve length, lining, collar, buttons, and belts. Buyers are able to customize their perfect coat with the click of a few buttons.[34]

So far in this chapter we have explored common misconceptions about marketing and then moved well past the stereotypes to begin to gain a solid foundation for understanding what marketing management really is about today. Given the increasingly rapid pace of changes in today's business environment, it's highly likely that marketing's role will evolve even more rapidly than in the past. Let's look to the future to identify important change drivers that are sure to impact marketing over the next decade and beyond.

LO 1-4

Recognize the impact of key change drivers on the future of marketing.

CHANGE DRIVERS IMPACTING THE FUTURE OF MARKETING

A great way to systematically explore the future of marketing is by considering several well-documented broad trends that are likely to impact the future of the field. These trends are well under way, but their ultimate impact on marketing and on business in general is not yet fully known. Five key areas of shift, or change drivers, are

- Shift to product glut and customer shortage.
- Shift in information power from marketer to customer.
- Shift in generational values and preferences.
- Shift to distinguishing Marketing ("Big M") from marketing ("little m").
- Shift to demanding return on marketing investment.

Shift to Product Glut and Customer Shortage

Fred Wiersema, in his book *The New Market Leaders,* builds a powerful case that the balance of power is shifting between marketers and their customers, both in business-to-consumer (B2C/end user) markets and business-to-business (B2B) markets. He identifies "six new market realities" in support of this trend: Competitors proliferate, all secrets are open secrets, innovation is universal, information overwhelms and depreciates, easy growth makes hard times, and customers have less time than ever.[35]

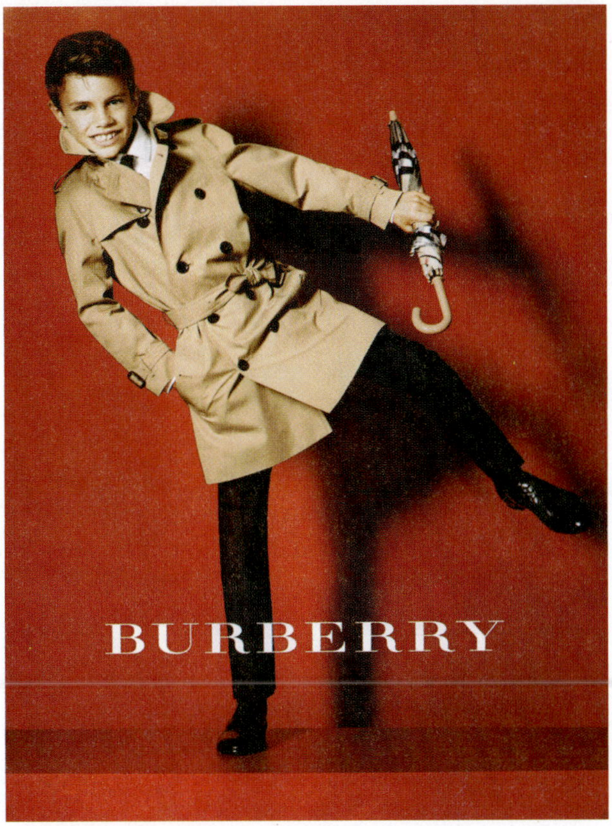

The highly customizable brand Burberry has extended its product line to children.

How do companies get the word out about new products? Some offer free samples to gain new customers. Many food chains have used this tactic. In early 2013, Pizza Hut leveraged itself with the buzz surrounding the Super Bowl. The company said it would give away free samples of its next "big pizza innovation" if the word "hut" was said at least once during the game. Not only did Pizza Hut have the potential to reach the millions of people tuning into the game, but they also recognized that game day is the busiest of the year for the pizza chain. As expected, "hut" was said and Pizza Hut followed through on their promise. Their restaurants across the nation gave away thousands of free "Big Pizza Sliders" in hopes that customers would talk about the product to their friends. And besides the game-day attention, the chain certainly also created a buzz in anticipation of their product innovation during the week prior to the giveaway.[36]

Wiersema's central point is that not only is a customer orientation desirable, but also in today's market it is a *necessity for survival.* Coming to grips with the impact of his six market realities greatly heightens the role of marketing in the firm as the nexus of an organization's customer-focused strategies.

Shift in Information Power from Marketer to Customer

Nowadays, customers of all kinds have nearly limitless access to information about companies, products, competitors, other customers, and even detailed elements of marketing plans and strategies. This is analogous to Wiersema's "All Secrets Are Open Secrets," but here we're talking about the customer's perspective. For decades, marketers held a degree of information power over their customers because firms had access to detailed and sophisticated information about their products and services that customers couldn't get without the help of somebody in the firm (usually

Like us on Facebook, and we will vaccinate zero children against polio.
Likes don't save lives. Money does. Buy polio vaccine for €4, and we will vaccinate 12 children against the deadly disease. Shop today at unicef.se.
unicef

Many companies encourage Facebook "likes," but this ad from Europe makes the point that UNICEF can't accomplish its mission with "likes" alone.

a salesperson). Now, customers are empowered to access boundless information about all kinds of products and services on the Internet.[37]

For competitive reasons, firms have no choice but to be more open about their businesses and products. Even if they wanted to, firms can't stop chat rooms, independent websites, web logs or blogs, and other customer-generated modes of communication from filling web page after web page with information, disinformation, and opinions about a company's products, services, and even company dirty laundry. Consider Walmart, one of the world's most successful companies. In recent years Walmart has been caught off guard by the number and voracity of uncontrollable information sources about it and its activities. Another example of this shift in information power is the physician/patient relationship. Between open direct-to-consumer advertising by pharmaceutical companies and innumerable websites devoted to every medical malady, more and more patients arrive at the doctor's office self-diagnosed and ready to self-prescribe![38]

The trend toward more information in the hands of the customer is not going to diminish. Marketing approaches must be altered to reflect and respond to this important change.

Shift in Generational Values and Preferences

Aspects of generational marketing will be discussed in more detail in Chapter 6. For now, the inexorable shift in values and preferences from generation to generation deserves mention as one of the key trends affecting the future of marketing. One clear impact is on the firm's message and the method by which that message is communicated. For example, GenY consumers tend to be much more receptive to electronic commerce as a primary mode of receiving marketing communication and ultimately purchasing than are prior generations.[39] As an example, in 2013 Girl Scouts of the USA introduced the Girl Scout Cookie Finder app. The app provides users with GPS coordinates for the nearest cookie sales location. For many, gone are the days of strictly relying on face-to-face selling.[40] This preference has clear implications for how marketing carries out its management of customer relationships across generations and also calls into question how much *value* younger customers derive from the different approaches to relationships. That is, do members of the younger generation appreciate, or even need, the kinds of close personal relationships companies like State Farm provide through their agents, or are they perfectly happy to interact with firms like GEICO, primarily through electronic means?

Generational shifts also impact marketing in terms of human resources. Consider how generational differences in attitudes toward work life versus family life, expectations about job satisfaction and rewards, and preferred modes of learning and working (e.g., electronic versus face-to-face) affect the ability of firms to hire people into various marketing-related positions. For example, firms often wish to differentiate themselves by offering great service to their customers. Yet, nearly all organizations are severely challenged today in hiring and keeping high-quality customer service personnel because of a severe shortage of capable, qualified customer care personnel.[41]

Generational changes are nothing new. In the context of both customers and organization members, understanding the generational differences and how to work to appeal to different generations' values and preferences is a critical part of marketing management. Today, the importance of this issue is accentuated and accelerated in marketing due to propensities among generational groups to differentially use technology and the impact of generational differences on workplace design and management practice.

> Generational changes have even been noticed in the competitive candy industry. Bazooka brand candy rebranded its product line to remain relevant, including its flagship Bazooka Joe that was revamped after 66 years to better position itself with younger, tech-savvy generations. Scott Utke, Bazooka's marketing director for its non-gum brands, said, "What we are trying to do is define what kids love about each of our brands at a more emotional level than just product benefit, which is what we've been doing in the past." In line with this strategy, the company began replacing the traditional miniature comic strips on its candy with quizzes and brainteasers that direct kids to digital content. Additionally, well-known product lines expanded into other product categories to provide more variety. For instance, a gummy version of Ring-Pop was released in order to have a presence outside the lollipop segment. The executive team has made an effort to reinvent its customers' experiences with the products for a new generation. Understanding generational preferences is critical to successful marketing strategies.[42]

Shift to Distinguishing Marketing (Big M) from marketing (little m)

Earlier it was established that the marketing concept is intended to be an overarching business philosophy in which firms place the customer at the core of the enterprise. Also, you have learned through reading some of the stereotypical impressions of what marketing is (and is not) that marketing—at least the *image* of marketing—can be fairly fragmented and often quite tactical in nature. How can marketing as a discipline that is both strategic and tactical be rectified?

Begin by thinking of marketing as occurring on two dimensions within an organization. These dimensions exist in tandem, and even intersect on occasion, but harbor fundamental differences in goals and properties. For convenience, we can distinguish these dimensions by capitalizing the word for one ("Marketing"—"Big M") and leaving the word in lowercase for the other ("marketing"—"little m"). Exhibit 1.3 portrays this relationship. Let's investigate these concepts further.

EXHIBIT 1.3 | Strategic and Tactical Marketing

Marketing (Big M) **Marketing (Big M)** serves as a core driver of business strategy. That is, an understanding of markets, competitors, and other external forces, coupled with attention to internal capabilities, allows a firm to successfully develop strategies for the future. This approach is often referred to as **strategic marketing,** which means a long-term, firm-level commitment to investing in marketing—supported at the highest organization level—for the purpose of enhancing organizational performance.

Going back to the AMA definition, marketing's focus as ". . . the activity, set of institutions, and processes for creating, communicating, delivering, and exchanging offerings that have value for customers, clients, partners, and society at large" contains substantial elements of Marketing (Big M): The core concepts of customer value, exchange, customer relationships, and benefit to the organization and its stakeholders are all very strategic in nature and help form the core business philosophy of a firm. Earlier we saw that the marketing concept includes a strong Marketing (Big M) thrust: ". . . an organization-wide customer orientation with the objective of achieving long-run profits." Certainly the core marketing concept characteristics of an organization-wide customer orientation and long-run profits are very strategic. Both the AMA definition of marketing and the long-standing marketing concept provide evidence of the centrality of Marketing (Big M) to the firm as a core business philosophy.

The concept of Marketing (Big M) necessitates several important actions on the part of the organization to maximize marketing's impact. Consider these action elements required for successful Marketing (Big M):

- Make sure *everyone* in an organization, regardless of their position or title, understands the concept of customer orientation, which places the customer at the core of all aspects of the enterprise. It doesn't matter whether or not the organization member directly interfaces with customers outside the firm. The point is that everybody has customers within the organization, and through the process of effectively serving those internal customers, the firm can better serve its external customers. In this way, everyone in the firm has a stake in the success of Marketing (Big M).
- Align all internal organizational processes and systems around the customer. Don't let the IT system, telecommunications system, billing system, or any other internal process or system become an impediment to a customer orientation. If the people inside a firm understand the power of a customer-centric business approach, but the internal systems don't support it, Marketing (Big M) won't be successful.
- Find somebody at the top of the firm to consistently champion this Marketing (Big M) business philosophy. The CEO is the most appropriate person for this role, perhaps manifest through the CMO (chief marketing officer). Like anything else of importance in a business organization, Marketing (Big M) takes resources, patience, and time to acculturate and implement, and it won't happen unless someone at the top is consistently supportive, with both resources and leadership.
- Forget the concept that the marketing department is where Marketing (Big M) takes place. Marketing (Big M) is not about what one department does or does not do. Marketing (Big M) is the basis on which an organization approaches its whole enterprise—remember Peter Drucker's words: "[Marketing] is the *whole business* . . . seen from the *customer's* point of view. Concern and responsibility for marketing must, therefore, permeate all areas of the enterprise." Drucker was right!
- Create *market-driving,* not just *market-driven,* strategies. It is imperative to study the market and competition as part of the marketing planning process. Firms today must break out of linear thinking when developing new products and markets. Certainly research on markets and customers can uncover unmet needs and offer guidance on designing products to fulfill those needs. But the process contributes little toward **market creation**—approaches that drive the market toward fulfilling a whole new set of needs that customers did not realize was possible or feasible before. Classic examples of market creation include Microsoft's revolution of the information field, Disney's creation of the modern theme park industry, and Apple's innovations in integrated communications with the iPhone and iPad. These were all market-driving strategies that created really new markets.

marketing (little m) In contrast, **marketing (little m)** serves the firm and its stakeholders at a functional or operational level; hence, marketing (little m) is often thought of as **tactical marketing**. In fact, marketing (little m) almost always takes place at the functional or operational level of a firm. Specific programs and tactics aimed at customers and other stakeholder groups tend to emanate from marketing (little m).[43] But marketing (little m) always needs to be couched within the philosophy, culture, and strategies of the firm's Marketing (Big M). In this way, Marketing (Big M) and marketing (little m) should be quite naturally connected within a firm, as the latter tends to represent the day-to-day operationalization and implementation of the former. Everything from brand image, to the message salespeople and advertisements deliver, to customer service, to packaging and product features, to the chosen distribution channel—in fact, all elements of the marketing mix and beyond—exemplify marketing (little m).

Understanding these two dimensions of marketing helps clarify much of the confusion surrounding the field today. It certainly helps explain much of the confusion surrounding what marketing management is supposed to be, and how and why the field tends to have a bit of an identity crisis both inside firms and with the public at large. Occasionally throughout this book, the Marketing (Big M), marketing (little m) notion will be brought up to add explanatory power to important points. But for the most part, we'll just use one version of the word, assuming we all understand it contains both levels.

Shift to Justifying the Relevance and Payback of the Marketing Investment

The final change driver affecting the future of marketing is a topic on the minds of many CEOs and CMOs today. The issue is how management can effectively measure and assess the level of success a firm's investment in various aspects of marketing has had. Appropriate and effective **marketing metrics** must be designed to identify, track, evaluate, and provide key benchmarks for improvement just as various financial metrics guide the financial management of the firm.[44] For many years, the Marketing Science Institute (MSI) has commissioned research for the marketing field funded by a number of large companies. Every two years, MSI publishes a list of research priorities that top organizations are willing to fund with large sums of money to further the practice of marketing management. In recent years, the topic of marketing metrics has been one of the highest priorities for most MSI member companies, especially connecting appropriate metrics to marketing management decision making.[45]

Metrics has become such an important issue that we devote much of Chapter 16 to the topic. Why the intense focus on metrics? Here are several important reasons:

- *Marketing is a fuzzy field.* Marketing has often historically viewed itself as working within gray area comfort zones of a business. That is, if what marketing contributed was mostly creative in nature, how can the impact of such activities effectively be measured? For the marketer, this can be a somewhat attractive position to be in, and historically many marketers probably took advantage of the idea that their activities were above measurement. Those days are over.
- *If it can't be measured, it can't be managed.* As with all aspects of business, effective management of the various aspects of marketing requires quantification of objectives and results. The marketing plan is one of the most important elements of a business plan. Effective planning requires metrics.

Although, marketing carries a stigma as a cost center, metrics such as ROI can indicate marketing success. A trend is marketing the use of Big Data—that is, collecting and using large amounts of data from consumers in order to make data-based consumer insights. A Nucleus Research Study indicated that 241 percent ROI can be achieved by applying data to business decisions. Caesars Entertainment heavily focuses its efforts on consumer data. The Total Rewards program was created to track about 80 percent of customer spending and led to the creation of the "luck ambassador" program. If a customer reaches a certain loss level at the casino, a luck ambassador delivers a special reward—such as show tickets or dinner—based on the customer's known preferences. Even though customers are not winners in the casino, they leave feeling happy and pleased with their experiences. This program also provided Caesars with valuable insight about its customers—0.15 percent of guests generated 12 percent of revenue. This dynamic use of consumer data will give the company a competitive edge in its marketing strategy.[46]

This AT&T sponsored display in a local YMCA calls out the dark side of smartphone communication—texting while driving. Technology has increased the channels of marketing communications, but at the same time created important new responsibilities for marketers to promote proper use.

- *Is marketing an expense or an investment?* Practicing marketers tend to pitch marketing internally as an investment in the future success of the organization. As an investment, it is not unreasonable that expected returns be identified and measured.[47]
- *CEOs and stockholders expect marketing accountability.* A few years ago, MSI published a report with the provocative title "Can Marketing Regain Its Seat at the Table?" The report centered on the fragmentation of marketing and ways marketing can recover its relevance in firms where it has become underutilized and undervalued, and has therefore lost its seat on the executive committee. One of the major conclusions of the report is that marketers need to create tools for ongoing, meaningful measurement of marketing productivity. More and more, CMOs are being held accountable for marketing performance in the same manner as are CFOs and leaders of other functional aspects of the business.[48]

This section has identified and examined several key change drivers that are sure to impact the future of marketing. Clearly, many other trends in the macro-level environment of business also affect marketing, including the obvious examples of globalization, ethnic diversification, and the growth and proliferation of technology.

YOUR MARKETING MANAGEMENT JOURNEY BEGINS

Some students take the marketing management course because they "have to" take it in order to fulfill a degree requirement, not necessarily because they see inherent value in marketing for their career as a leader and manager. It is our hope that if you initially fell into this category, you can now see that gaining the knowledge and skills required for marketing management will increase your worth as an asset to any firm, regardless of your position or job title.

As you progress through this course, keep in mind that marketing management is not so much a position or a job title as it is a process and a way of approaching decision making about important business opportunities and challenges. Our presumption throughout this book is that you are seeking knowledge and skills that will enable you to use marketing to its fullest potential to positively impact organizational performance. Be assured from the outset that a high level of personal and career value can be derived by investing time and energy now in mastering the leadership and management of marketing.

SUMMARY

Marketing as an activity, set of institutions, and processes adds value to a firm and its internal and external stakeholders in many ways. For a marketing manager to be successful, he or she must approach the job with a strong understanding of what it takes to do great marketing *today,* which, because of a variety of change drivers, is very different from doing marketing in the past. Leading and managing the facets of marketing in order to improve individual, unit, and organizational performance—marketing management—is a core business activity in today's business milieu, worthy of study and mastery by any student of business regardless of job title or professional or educational background.

KEY TERMS

marketing management 6
marketing's stakeholders 7
societal marketing 8
sustainability 8
value 8
exchange 8
production orientation 10
sales orientation 11
marketing concept 11
marketing mix (4Ps of marketing) 12
customer-centric 13
differentiation 13
market orientation 13
customer orientation 13
relationship orientation 13
one-to-one marketing 14
mass customization 14
Marketing (Big M) 17
strategic marketing 17
market creation 18
marketing (little m) 18
tactical marketing 18
marketing metrics 19

APPLICATION QUESTIONS

1. Consider the various marketing misconceptions introduced in this chapter.
   a. Pick any two of the misconceptions and develop a specific example of each from your own experience with firms and brands.
   b. How will it be beneficial for a new marketing manager to understand the misconceptions that exist about marketing?
   c. Can you come up with some other marketing misconceptions of your own—ones that are not addressed in the chapter?
2. In the chapter we make a strong case for the relevance of Peter Drucker's key themes today, even though much of his writing was done decades ago. Do you agree that his message was ahead of its time and is still relevant? Why or why not? Assume you are the CEO of a firm that wants to practice a market orientation. How will Drucker's advice help you to accomplish this goal?
3. Put yourself in the role of a marketing manager. From this perspective, do you agree with the concepts of societal marketing and sustainability? Why or why not? How does a focus on sustainability affect the marketing manager's role and activities? Identify two organizations that you believe do a great job of paying attention to sustainability and present the evidence that leads you to this conclusion.
4. Review the section on change drivers and select any two within the set that you want to focus on. Pick an organization of your choice and answer the following questions:
   a. In what ways does each of the change drivers impact the firm's ability to successfully do marketing?
   b. How is the firm responding to the change drivers in the way it approaches its business? What should it be doing that it is not doing at present?
   c. What role do you believe the marketing manager has in proactively preparing for these and future change drivers?

5. In the chapter you learned that harmonious performance of Marketing (big M) and marketing (little m) within a firm can lead to greater levels of success. Why is this true? What does it mean that these two need to be "harmonious"? What would be some likely negative consequences if they were out of sync?

MANAGEMENT DECISION CASE: Gaining a Foothold among Giants While Being KIND

Think of the snack foods you eat most often. What type of snacks does that include? For many of us, those we frequently eat are salty snacks, which include chips of various ingredients and flavors, pretzels, cheese curls, crackers, and nuts (hint: nuts are the most healthy of this bunch). Another option might be sweet snacks such as cookies, candy bars, other chocolate-based snacks, and cereal bars. Behind these various snack options are some of the largest companies in the food industry including behemoths such as Frito Lay, Kellogg, Hershey, Mars, General Mills, and Nabisco among others. All of these companies utilize immense resources to implement their marketing strategies in an effort to not only gain market share from competitors but also prevent others from entering the market.

So, if the competitive environment for the market is as described above, what in the world would make a firm think it could start a totally new snack food company and be successful? Apparently Daniel Lubetzky, founder of KIND Healthy Snacks, had a different idea of what it took to be competitive in the snack food market when he decided to enter it way back in 2003. Lubetzky looked at the playing field and decided that the competition was, in fact, not impenetrable. He found an opportunity to develop a product with all natural, healthy ingredients. In fact, a mantra of his organization is to put "nothing in the product that the typical consumer cannot pronounce." As a result, the ingredient list is an exercise in simplicity with easy-to-understand components that promote healthfulness in everyone who eats them.

Lubetzky also found opportunity in the *packaging* of his products. Instead of the typical opaque packaging for snack or candy bars that prevents one from viewing the actual physical product, KIND Healthy Snacks uses proprietary technology to produce clear wrappers for its snack items. Using this type of package distinguishes KIND from its competitors because it allows consumers to see what they will eat and not just assume the bar inside will look like the picture on the wrapper.

Another opportunity area for Lubetzky was the trend toward consumers supporting products that have the betterment of society as part of their mission. Visit the KIND website and you will find a quote by Henry James that reads, "Three things in human life are important: the first is to be kind; the second is to be kind; and the third is to be kind." Lubetzky's company operationalizes this quote by allowing users to post on their website their individual acts of kindness and the number of people impacted by those acts. In addition to giving exposure to individual acts of kindness (get it—KIND-ness), KIND itself supports one project each month with $10,000. Whether it's rebuilding a New Jersey firefighter's house after Hurricane Sandy, supporting Big Brothers and Big Sisters, or working with a nonprofit agency to fly soldiers home from overseas for the holidays, KIND is working to have a social impact on the communities it serves.

Clearly, KIND has embraced the concept of "Marketing" with all of its activities, institutions, and processes for creating, communicating, delivering, and exchanging offerings that have value for customers, clients, partners, and society at large. Evidence of this buy-in is the result the company has achieved. From the end of 2008 to the end of 2012, KIND's sales went from $15 million to $120 million, an 800 percent increase in just four years. This growth occurred despite losing Starbucks as a distributor of its snack items in all of its U.S.-based cafes. By continuing to connect with its customers through its high-quality, all-natural-ingredient products; its innovative packaging; and its commitment to the betterment of society, KIND hopes to continue to dynamically grow its business well into the future.

Questions for Consideration

1. What other aspects of the AMA definition of marketing might KIND exploit in the future to continue to grow its business?
2. Do you think consumers supporting brands and companies that strive to benefit society are a trend that will continue? Why or why not?
3. What other industries might be especially prone to entry by a smaller, more nimble, and more socially conscious competition? What are the prospects for a competitor being successful in those industries?

Sources: Clark, Patrick. "Why a Snack Bar Maker Turned Down a Deal with Starbucks." *Bloomberg Businessweek*, September 18, 2013, www.businessweek.com/articles/2013-09-18/why-a-snack-bar-maker-turned-down-a-deal-with-starbucks. Cuttler, Andrea. "Kind Bar: Taking It to the Next Level." *Vanity Fair*, June 7, 2012, www.vanityfair.com/online/beauty/2013/09/kind-bar-taking-it-to-the-next-level?utm_medium=App.net&utm_source=PourOver. Fast Company Staff. "The World's Top 10 Most Innovative Companies in Food." *Fast Company*, February 11, 2013, www.fastcompany.com/most-innovative-companies/2013/industry/food. KIND, www.kindsnacks.com/.

NOTES

1. Anne d'Innocenzio, "They're Back: J. C. Penney Adds Sales," *Yahoo News*, January 28, 2013, http://news.yahoo.com/theyre-back-j-c-penney-183215451.html.
2. Pola B. Gupta, Paula M. Saunders, and Jeremy Smith, "Traditional Master of Business Administration (MBA) versus the MBA with Specialization: A Disconnection between What Business Schools Offer and What Employers Seek," *Journal of Education for Business* 82, no. 8 (2007), pp. 307–12.
3. David W. Stewart, "How Marketing Contributes to the Bottom Line," *Journal of Advertising Research* 48, no. 1 (2008), p. 94.
4. Malcolm A. McNiven, "Plan for More Productive Advertising," *Harvard Business Review* 58, no. 2 (1980), p. 130.
5. Mitchell J. Lovett and Jason B. MacDonald, "How Does Financial Performance Affect Marketing? Studying the Marketing-Finance Relationship from a Dynamic Perspective," *Journal of the Academy of Marketing Science* 33, no. 4 (2005), pp. 476–85; and Ramesh K.S. Rao and Neeraj Bharadwaj, "Marketing Initiatives, Expected Cash Flows, and Shareholders' Wealth," *Journal of Marketing* 72, no. 1 (2008), pp. 16–26.
6. Justin Bachman, "With an Animated Series, Netflix Aims for Kids," *Bloomberg Businessweek*, February 13, 2013, www.businessweek.com/articles/2013-02-13/with-a-3d-animated-series-netflix-aims-for-kids#r=lr-fst.
7. Peter F. Drucker, *The Practice of Management* (New York: Harper and Row, 1954), pp. 37–38.
8. Peter F. Drucker, *Management: Tasks, Responsibilities, Practices* (New York: Harper and Row, 1973), p. 63.
9. Shaun Powell, "The Management and Consumption of Organisational Creativity," *Journal of Consumer Marketing* 25, no. 3 (2008), pp. 158–66.
10. Rosa Chun and Gary Davies, "The Influence of Corporate Character on Customers and Employees: Exploring Similarities and Differences," *Journal of the Academy of Marketing Science* 34, no. 2 (2006), pp. 138–47.
11. John Grant, "Green Marketing," *Strategic Direction* 24, no. 6 (2008), pp. 25–27.
12. Stuart Elliot, "Selling Products by Selling Shared Values," *New York Times*, www.nytimes.com/2013/02/14/business/media/panera-to-advertise-its-social-consciousness-advertising.html?pagewanted=all&_r=0.
13. Michael J. Barone, Kenneth C. Manning, and Paul W. Miniard, "Consumer Response to Retailers' Use of Partially Comparative Pricing," *Journal of Marketing* 68, no. 3 (2004), pp. 37–47; and Dhruv Grewal and Joan Lindsey-Mullikin, "The Moderating Role of the Price Frame on the Effects of Price Range and the Number of Competitors on Consumers' Search Intentions," *Journal of the Academy of Marketing Science* 34, no. 1 (2006), pp. 55–63.
14. Jyh-shen Chiou and Cornelia Droge, "Service Quality, Trust, Specific Asset Investment, and Expertise: Direct and Indirect Effects in a Satisfaction-Loyalty Framework," *Journal of the Academy of Marketing Science* 34, no. 4 (2006), pp. 613–28.
15. Stanley Holmes, "Nike Goes Green," *BusinessWeek*, September 25, 2006, pp. 106–08.
16. Duane Stanford, "Coke Engineers Its Orange Juice—with an Algorithm," *Bloomberg Businessweek*, January 31, 2013, www.businessweek.com/articles/2013-01-31/coke-engineers-its-orange-juice-with-an-algorithm#p1.
17. "Henry Ford Quotes," UBR Inc., www.people.ubr.com/historical-figures/by-first-name/h/henry-ford/henry-ford-quotes.aspx.
18. Louis E. Boone and David L. Kurtz, *Contemporary Marketing* (Hinsdale, IL: Dryden Press, 1974), p. 14.
19. General Electric Company, *1952 Annual Report* (New York: General Electric Company, 1952), p. 21.
20. Neil H. Borden, "The Concept of the Marketing Mix," *Journal of Advertising Research* 4 (June 1964), pp. 2–7; and E. Jerome McCarthy, *Basic Marketing: A Managerial Approach* (Homewood, IL: Irwin, 1960).
21. Bernard Cova and Robert Salle, "Marketing Solutions in Accordance with the S-D Logic: Co-creating Value with Customer Network Actors," *Industrial Marketing Management* 37, no. 3 (2008), pp. 270–77.
22. Evangelia D. Fassoula, "Transforming the Supply Chain," *Journal of Manufacturing Technology Management* 17, no. 6 (2006), pp. 848–60.
23. Mary Jo Bitner and Bernard H. Booms, "Marketing Strategies and Organizational Structures for Service Firms," in *Marketing of Services*, J. Donnelly and W. George, eds. (Chicago: American Marketing Association, 1981), pp. 47–51.
24. V. Kumar and J. Andrew Petersen, "Using a Customer-Level Marketing Strategy to Enhance Firm Performance: A Review of Theoretical and Empirical Evidence," *Journal of the Academy of Marketing Science* 33, no. 4 (2005), pp. 504–20; and Stephen L. Vargo and Robert F. Lusch, "Evolving to a New Dominant Logic for Marketing," *Journal of Marketing* 68, no. 1 (2004), pp. 1–17.
25. Sundar Bharadwaj, Terry Clark, and Songpol Kulviwat, "Marketing, Market Growth, and Endogenous Growth Theory: An Inquiry into the Causes of

Market Growth," *Journal of the Academy of Marketing Science* 33, no. 3 (2005), pp. 347–60.

26. K. Talley and D. Mattioli, "At Gap, Sales Gains Are Back in Style," WSJ.com, February 11, 2013, http://online.wsj.com/article/SB10001424127887323511 80457829573.
27. Vargo and Lusch, "Evolving to a New Dominant Logic for Marketing."
28. Mark W. Johnston and Greg W. Marshall, *Relationship Selling,* 2nd ed. (New York: McGraw-Hill/Irwin, 2008), p. 5.
29. George S. Day, "Managing Market Relationships," *Journal of the Academy of Marketing Science* 28, no. 1 (2000), pp. 24–31.
30. Chuck Wall, "The 31 Excuses Leaders Use to Avoid Understanding Their Customers (and How to Get Rid of Them)," *Forbes,* www.forbes.com/sites/onmarketing/2013/02/07/the-31-excuses-leaders-use-to-avoid-understanding-their-customers-and-how-to-get-rid-ofthem/.
31. Simon J. Bell, Seigyoung Auh, and Karen Smalley, "Customer Relationship Dynamics: Service Quality and Customer Loyalty in the Context of Varying Levels of Customer Expertise and Switching Costs," *Journal of the Academy of Marketing Science* 33, no. 2 (2005), pp. 169–84; and Girish Ramani and V. Kumar, "Interaction Orientation and Firm Performance," *Journal of Marketing* 72, no. 1 (2008), pp. 27–45.
32. Don Peppers and Martha Rogers, *The One-to-One Manager: Real World Lessons in Customer Relationship Management* (New York: Doubleday Business, 2002).
33. Jagdish N. Sheth, Rajendra S. Sisodia, and Arun Sharma, "The Antecedents and Consequences of Customer-Centric Marketing," *Journal of the Academy of Marketing Science* 28, no. 1 (2000), pp. 55–67.
34. Cotton Timberlake, "Retailers Cater to Customization Craze," *San Francisco Chronicle,* January 18, 2013, www.sfgate.com/business/article/Retailers-cater-to-customization-craze-4207186.php.
35. Fred Wiersema, *The New Market Leaders: Who's Winning and How in the Battle for Customers* (New York: Free Press, 2001), pp. 48–58.
36. "Big Game, Big Offer: Pizza Hut Expands Hut. Hut. Hut! Campaign with 'BIG' and 'EASY' Fan Offer on Next Big Innovation," *PR Newswire,* January 28, 2013, www.prnewswire.com/news-releases/big-game-big-offer-pizza-hut-expands-hut-hut-hut-campaign-with-big-and-easy-fan-offer-on-next-big-innovation-188667981.html.
37. Efhymios Constantinides and Stefan J. Fountain, "Web 2.0: Conceptual Foundations and Marketing Issues," *Journal of Direct, Data and Digital Marketing Practice* 9, no. 3 (2008), pp. 231–45.
38. Anonymous, "Search and Seizure," *Marketing Health Services* 28, no. 1 (2008), p. 6.
39. Barton Goldenberg, "Conquering Your 2 Biggest CRM Challenges," *Sales & Marketing Management* 159, no. 3 (2007), p. 35.
40. Natalia Angulo, "Girl Scout Cookie Finder App Helps You Find Your Thin Mints," *Fox News,* February 7, 2013, www.foxnews.com/tech/2013/02/07/girl-scout-cookie-finder-app-helps-buyers-find-their-thin-mints/.
41. Ruth Maria Stock and Wayne D. Hoyer, "An Attitude-Behavior Model of Salespeople's Customer Orientation," *Journal of the Academy of Marketing Science* 33, no. 4 (2005), pp. 536–53.
42. E. J. Schultz, "How Bazooka Candy Is Rebranding for a New Generation," *Advertising Age,* January 30, 2013, http://adage.com/article/cmo-strategy/bazooka-candy-reaching-a-generation/239475/.
43. Marco Vriens, "Strategic Research Design," *Marketing Research* 15, no. 4 (2003), p. 20.
44. Lovett and MacDonald, "How Does Financial Performance Affect Marketing?"; and Steven H. Seggie, "Assessing Marketing Strategy Performance," *Journal of the Academy of Marketing Science* 34, no. 2 (2006), pp. 267–69.
45. Marketing Science Institute, www.msi.org.
46. Sandra Zoratti, "Unleash the Brawn of Big Data with Small Steps," *Forbes,* February 12, 2013, www.forbes.com/sites/onmarketing/2013/02/12/unleash-the-brawn-of-big-data-with-small-steps/.
47. Thomas S. Gruca and Lopo L. Rego, "Customer Satisfaction, Cash Flow, and Shareholder Value," *Journal of Marketing* 69, no. 3 (2005), pp. 115–30.
48. Frederick E. Webster, Jr., Alan J. Malter, and Shankar Ganesan, "Can Marketing Regain Its Seat at the Table?" *Marketing Science Institute Working Paper Series,* Report No. 03-113 (2004).

CHAPTER 02

Elements of Marketing Strategy, Planning, and Competition

LEARNING OBJECTIVES

LO 2-1 Examine the concept of value and the elements and role of the value chain.

LO 2-2 Understand the conditions required for successful marketing planning, that marketing planning is focused on the value proposition, and that marketing planning is a dynamic process.

LO 2-3 Identify various types of organizational strategies.

LO 2-4 Conduct a situation analysis.

LO 2-5 Use the framework provided for marketing planning, along with the content in future chapters, to build a marketing plan.

VALUE IS AT THE CORE OF MARKETING

In Chapter 1, the concept of value was introduced as a core element of marketing. Value was defined from a customer's perspective as a ratio of the bundle of benefits a customer receives from an offering compared to the costs incurred by the customer in acquiring that bundle of benefits. From the late management guru Peter Drucker's early writings in the 1950s through to today's American Marketing Association official definition of marketing, it is clear that marketing plays a central role in creating, communicating, delivering, and exchanging offerings that have value.

Let's examine the idea of value a bit more carefully now. One can think of value as a ratio of benefits to costs, as viewed from the eyes of the beholder (the customer). That is, customers incur a variety of costs in doing business with any firm, be those costs financial, time, opportunity costs, or otherwise. For the investment of these costs, the customer has a right to expect a certain bundle of benefits in return. A **benefit** is some type of utility that a company and its products (and services) provide its customers. **Utility** is the want-satisfying power of a good or service.[1] Four major kinds of utility exist: form, time, place, and ownership. *Form utility* is created when the firm converts raw materials into finished products that are desired by the market. The other three utilities—*time, place,* and *ownership*—are created by marketing. They are created when products are available to customers at a convenient location when they want to purchase them, and facilities of *exchange* are available that allow for transfer of the product ownership from seller to buyer. Chapter 1 mentioned that facilitating exchange between buyers and sellers is another core element of marketing.

America's Milk Producers continue to market their product through strong personal appeals.

LO 2-1

Examine the concept of value and the elements and role of the value chain.

Since value is a ratio of benefits to costs, a firm can impact the customer's perceptions of value by altering the benefits, the costs, or both. Assume that a person is faced with the decision of buying one of two automobiles. One should expect that a purchase decision will be greatly influenced by the ratio of costs (not just monetary) versus benefits for each model. That is, it is not just pure price that drives the decision. It is price compared with all the various benefits (or utilities)

What is the value proposition of a Jimmy Dean food product? It is not just a quick meal. Jimmy Dean marketers learned that consumers want more than convenience. They also want homemade and healthy meals, even though they do not have a lot of time to prepare them. To address these desires, the company introduced Delights by Jimmy Dean breakfast sandwiches, which can be cooked in less than three minutes in the microwave. Options include turkey sausage, egg, and cheese; bacon, egg, and cheese; and egg white with spinach and mozzarella-style cheese options. All sandwiches are served on honey wheat flatbread and are 250 calories or less. The company also added turkey maple sausage patties to its line of refrigerated, fully cooked items. "Knowing that our consumers are rushed during the mornings and shouldn't have to forego [sic] a hearty breakfast at home, we've expanded our line of frozen and refrigerated convenience breakfast offerings to make it easier for them to enjoy their favorite Jimmy Dean breakfast in minutes," said Amy Grabow, VP, Marketing, Jimmy Dean brand.[3]

that Car 1 brings versus Car 2.[2] These benefits could relate to availability, style, prestige, features—all sorts of factors beyond mere price.

Recall that marketing is charged not just with *creating* offerings that have value, but also with *communicating, delivering,* and *exchanging* those offerings. When a firm communicates the **value proposition** of its products to customers, the value message may include the whole bundle of benefits the company promises to deliver, not just the benefits of the product itself.[4] For example, when South Korean–based Samsung first brought its brand to the United States, it communicated a message centered primarily on functionality at a moderate price—a strategy designed to provide an advantage over pricier Japanese brands. But over time, Samsung's value proposition has expanded to include innovativeness, style, and dependability—the latter of which was helped significantly by high ratings of many of the company's products by sources such as *Consumer Reports*.[5]

For years, firms have been preoccupied with measuring **customer satisfaction**, which at its most fundamental level means how much the customer likes the product. However, for firms interested in building long-term customer relationships, having satisfied customers is not enough to ensure the relationship is going to last. A firm's value proposition must be strong enough to move customers past mere satisfaction and into a commitment to a company and its products and brands for the long run. Such a commitment reflects a high level of **customer loyalty**, which increases **customer retention** and reduces **customer switching**.[6]

Social media have dramatically changed the way companies approach customer loyalty. Consumers are now able to "like" their favorite store on Facebook and "follow" their favorite restaurant on Twitter. Studies have shown that customers who connect with businesses via social media will go to the businesses more often and contribute more to their bottom lines. Understanding the importance of these platforms, Whole Foods has cemented itself as a social media giant. "We talk about shared interests with customers," said Natanya Anderson, Whole Foods' social media and community team leader. "We have lifestyle conversations at the brand level, and on a local level we showcase the folks behind the store, highlight local partners and in-season produce." By engaging with Whole Foods via social media, customers are able to receive special discounts and that keeps loyalists coming back again and again.[7]

Customer loyalty almost always is directly related to the various sources of value the customer is presently deriving from the relationship with the company and its brands. Except in situations of monopoly (which creates forced loyalty), loyal customers by definition tend to also experience a high level of satisfaction.[8] However, not all satisfied customers are loyal. If a competitor comes along with a better value proposition, or if a value proposition begins to slip or is not effectively communicated, customers who are presently satisfied become good candidates for switching to another company's products.[9]

The Value Chain

A highly useful approach to bringing together and understanding the concepts of customer value, satisfaction, and loyalty is the **value chain**. Created by Michael Porter in his classic book *Competitive Advantage,* the value chain serves as a means for firms to identify ways to create, communicate, and deliver more customer value within a firm.[10] Exhibit 2.1 portrays Porter's value chain concept.

Basically, the value chain concept holds that every organization represents a synthesis of activities involved in designing, producing, marketing, delivering, and supporting its products. The value chain identifies nine relevant strategic activities the organization can engage in that create/impact both sides of the value equation: benefits and costs. Porter's nine **value-creating activities** include five primary activities and four support activities.[11]

EXHIBIT 2.1 | Porter's Value Chain

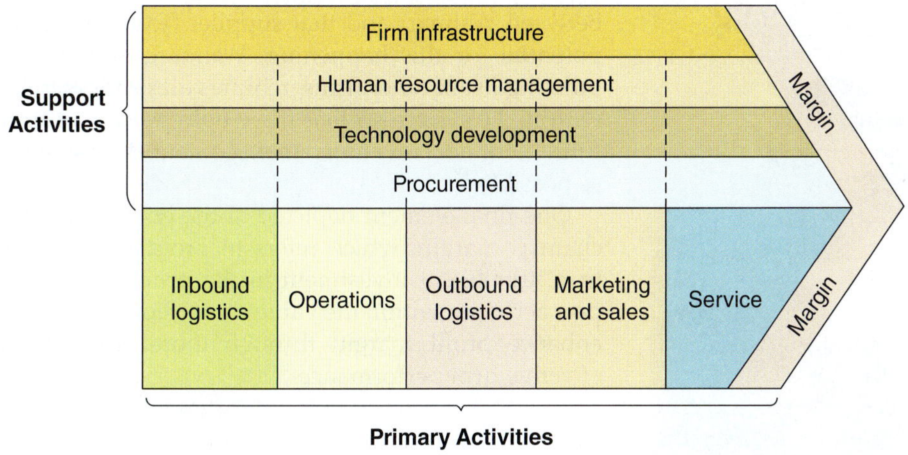

Source: Reprinted with the permission of The Free Press, a Division of Simon & Schuster Adult Publishing Group, from *Competitive Advantage: Creating and Sustaining Superior Performance*, by Michael E. Porler. Copyright © 1985, 1988 by Michael E. Porter. All rights reserved.

The five *primary activities* in the value chain are:

1. *Inbound logistics*—how the firm goes about sourcing raw materials for production.
2. *Operations*—how the firm converts the raw materials into final products.
3. *Outbound logistics*—how the firm transports and distributes the final products to the marketplace.
4. *Marketing and sales*—how the firm communicates the value proposition to the marketplace.
5. *Service*—how the firm supports customers during and after the sale.

The four *support activities* in the value chain are:

1. *Firm infrastructure*—how the firm is set up for doing business; are the internal processes aligned and efficient.
2. *Human resource management*—how the firm ensures it has the right people in place, trains them, and keeps them.
3. *Technology development*—how the firm embraces technology usage for the benefit of customers.
4. *Procurement*—how the firm deals with vendors and quality issues.

The value chain concept is highly useful in understanding the major activities through which a firm creates, communicates, and delivers value for its customers. CEOs in recent years have been concentrating on *aligning* the various elements of the value chain, meaning that all facets of the company are working together to ensure that no snags will negatively impact the firm's value proposition.[12] From a customer's perspective, when the supplier's value chain is working well, all the customer tends to see are the *results* of a well-aligned value chain: quality products, good salespeople, on-time delivery, prompt service after the sale, and so on. However, it takes only one weak link in the value chain and the whole process of cultivating satisfied and loyal customers can be circumvented.

Consider, for example, what happens if a glitch in the value chain of one of Walmart's vendors delays delivery of products at the peak selling season, resulting

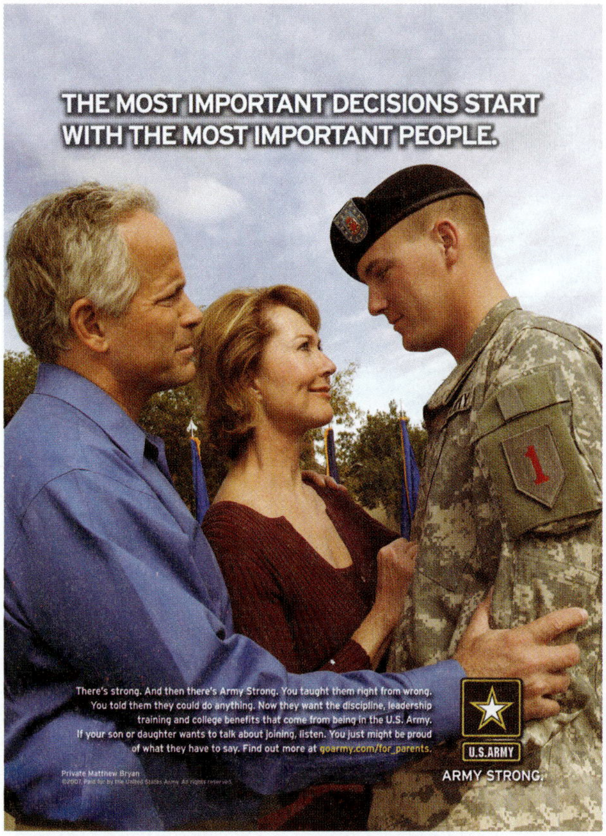

THE MOST IMPORTANT DECISIONS START
WITH THE MOST IMPORTANT PEOPLE.
There's strong. And then there's Army Strong. You taught them right from wrong.
You told them they could do anything. Now they want the discipline, leadership
training and college benefits that come from being in the U.S. Army.
If your son or daughter wants to talk about joining, listen. You just might be proud
of what they have to say. Find out more at goarmy.com/for_parents.
U.S.ARMY
ARMY STRONG.
Private Matthew Bryan

The U.S. Army does sophisticated marketing that leads to its ability to effectively appeal to recruits.

in stock-outs in Walmart stores. If this happens repeatedly, it can damage the overall relationship Walmart enjoys with its customers as well as the relationship between Walmart and that supplier. To minimize the potential for this happening, Walmart, as well as a growing list of other firms, requires all vendors to link with its IT system so that the whole process of order fulfillment and inventory management is as seamless as possible.[13]

One final element depicted at the end of the value chain is margin, which refers to profit made by the firm. Intelligent investment in the primary and support activities within the value chain should positively enhance profit margin through more efficient and effective firm performance.[14]

Planning for the Value Offering

The remainder of this chapter presents the approach that marketing managers use to plan for creating, communicating, and delivering the value offering. This is often referred to as **marketing planning**—the ongoing process of developing and implementing market-driven strategies for an organization—and the resulting document that records the marketing planning process in a useful framework is the **marketing plan**.[15]

MARKETING PLANNING IS BOTH STRATEGIC AND TACTICAL

LO 2-2

Understand the conditions required for successful marketing planning, that marketing planning is focused on the value proposition, and that marketing planning is a dynamic process.

Recall that one key trend identified in Chapter 1 was the practice of marketing on two dimensions or levels within an organization. Although these dimensions exist in tandem and even intersect on occasion, each holds fundamental differences in goals and properties. At the strategic level, Marketing (Big M) serves as a core driver of business strategy. That is, an understanding of markets, competitors, and other external forces, coupled with attention to internal capabilities, allows a firm to successfully develop strategies for the future. At the functional or operational level, marketing (little m) represents the specific programs and tactics aimed at customers and other stakeholder groups and includes everything from brand image, to the message salespeople and advertisements deliver, to customer service, to packaging and product features—in fact, all elements of operationalizing the marketing mix and beyond.[16]

The message of a marketing campaign is critical to its success. When Bud Light Platinum made a bold choice and selected Justin Timberlake as the new face of the brand, executives understood the message they were communicating to their customers. The brand's target consumer was identified as the nighttime party drinker and Anheuser-Busch believed that Justin best connected with their customers. The millennial generation has had an extreme influence on the Platinum brand. The marketing of the product has also had a particular musical focus. In the past, ads featured songs from Kanye West and Ludacris. "Justin Timberlake is one of the greatest creative minds in the entertainment industry, and his insights will help us further define Bud Light Platinum's identity in the lifestyle space. Since launching Bud Light Platinum last year, we've worked to align the brand closely with music. Partnering with Justin as he makes his return to music brings a new level of relevance and credibility to the brand," said Paul Chibe, VP-U.S. Marketing, Anheuser-Busch.[17]

Although these two levels of marketing are distinctly different in scope and activities, the common link is in the process of marketing planning. Marketing managers must be able to grasp both the big picture of strategy formulation and the details of tactical implementation. In fact, many a marketing plan has failed because either the formulation of the strategies was flawed or their implementation was poorly executed. A well-written marketing plan must fully address both Marketing (Big M) and marketing (little m) elements. Ultimately, the following must be in place for effective marketing planning to occur:

- *Everyone* in an organization, regardless of his or her position or title, must understand and support the concept of customer orientation, which, as you learned in Chapter 1, places the customer at the core of all aspects of the enterprise. Firms that promote and practice a high level of customer focus are often referred to as *customer-centric* organizations.[18]
- To operationalize a customer-centric approach, all internal organizational processes and systems must be aligned around the customer. A firm's internal structure and systems cannot be allowed to become an impediment to a customer orientation.[19] Anyone who has ever placed a phone call for service and been driven through a maze of phone transfers with a string of people (or machines) unable to help knows how poor structure and systems can impact customer satisfaction and loyalty!

Rite Aid is a customer-centric company. The company is the third largest pharmacy in the United States and is expanding its "NowClinic Online Care" services in stores. This program allows customers to go online and chat or have a video consultation with a doctor or nurse about an illness or injury and then retain a record of the consultation so they are able to share it with their primary care physician. A 10-minute consultation with a doctor costs $45. Chats with nurses are free. And after the consult, doctors can order prescriptions or refer patients to a specialist for more extensive care. Understanding and analyzing consumer trends and motivations led Rite Aid to pursue this strategy. Gone are the days when the customer has to wait to see a doctor. With the trend for technology also increasing, this concept addresses the desire for convenience as well.[20]

- The CEO and others at the top of the organization must consistently set the tone for market-driven strategic planning through the customer-centric business philosophy. As with a firm's internal structure and systems, its culture must be supportive of such an approach in order for a marketing plan to be successful. Upper management must also support the process through consistent investment of resources necessary to make it work. Marketing planning is not a "sometimes" process; rather, it should be a driving force in the firm day in and day out.[21]

At this point in the learning process about marketing management, you may begin to feel concerned that you are getting a lot of structure for marketing planning but not enough specific content to fill in the elements of the marketing plan template. That reaction is quite natural, as by design the depth of content for most of the various sections of a marketing plan is covered later in the book. Your next task is to familiarize yourself with the overall process and framework for marketing planning so that as the content pieces unfold chapter by chapter, it will be very clear how those pieces fit together into a complete marketing plan. Beginning with this one, each chapter ends with a "Marketing Plan Exercise." These are designed to help you make the connections between the content in each chapter and the requirements of your marketing plan template.

ELEMENTS OF MARKETING PLANNING

To get you started, we'll first walk through the process and content involved in marketing planning. A condensed framework for this process is presented in Exhibit 2.2. Then at the end of this chapter you'll find an abbreviated marketing plan example for the fictitious company CloudCab Small Jet Taxi Service. You'll want to look at that appendix for an example of what the key elements of a marketing plan look like in practice.

Connecting the Marketing Plan to the Firm's Business Plan

How does a marketing plan fit into a firm's overall business planning process? As we have learned, marketing is somewhat unique among the functional areas of business in that it has the properties of being both a core business philosophy (Marketing, Big M) and a functional/operational part of the business (marketing, little m). As such, all business-level strategy must be market-driven in order to be successful. Hence, the term **market-driven strategic planning** is often used to describe the process at the corporate or strategic business unit (SBU) level of marshaling the various resource and functional areas of the firm toward a central purpose around the customer.[22]

A great example of how these levels of planning fit together is General Electric. GE contains numerous SBUs that compete in very different markets, from lighting to jet engines to financial services. CEO Jeff Immelt oversees a **corporate-level strategic plan** to serve as an umbrella plan for the overall direction of the corporation, but the real action in marketing planning at GE is at the individual SBU level. Each GE business has its own **SBU-level strategic plan**, and part of GE's historical leadership culture has been to turn SBU management loose to run their

EXHIBIT 2.2 | Condensed Framework for Marketing Planning

- Ensure the marketing plan is connected to the firm's business plan including organizational-level mission, vision, goals, objectives, and strategies.
- Conduct a situation analysis.
  - Macro-level external environment
  - Competitive environment
  - Internal environment
- Perform any needed market research.
- Establish marketing goals and objectives.
- Develop marketing strategies.
  - Product-market combinations
  - Market segmentation, target marketing, positioning
  - Marketing mix strategies:
    - Product/branding strategies
    - Service strategies
    - Pricing strategies
    - Supply chain strategies
    - Integrated marketing communications strategies
- Develop implementation plans.
  - Programs/action plans for each strategy including timetable, assignment of responsibilities, and resources required
  - Forecasts and budgets
  - Metrics for marketing control
- Provide for contingency planning.

own businesses under their own plans, so long as they meet their performance requirements and contribute satisfactorily to the overall corporate plan.

Portfolio Analysis **Portfolio analysis**, which views SBUs and sometimes even product lines as a series of investments from which it expects maximization of returns, is one tool that can contribute to strategic planning in a multi-business corporation. Two of the most popular approaches are the **Boston Consulting Group (BCG) Growth-Share Matrix** and the **GE Business Screen**. These are portrayed in Exhibits 2.3 and 2.4.

The concept of the BCG approach to portfolio analysis is to position each SBU within a firm on the two-dimensional matrix shown in Exhibit 2.3. The competitive market-share dimension is the ratio of share to that of the largest competitor. The growth dimension is intended as a strong indicator of overall market

EXHIBIT 2.3 | Boston Consulting Group Growth-Share Matrix

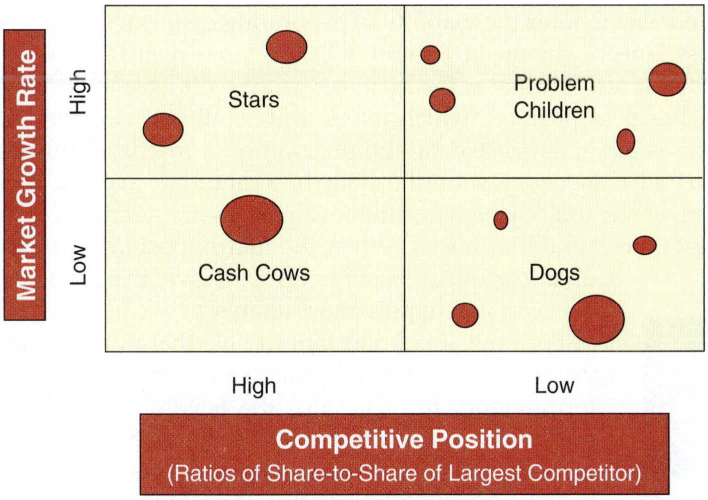

EXHIBIT 2.4 | GE Business Screen

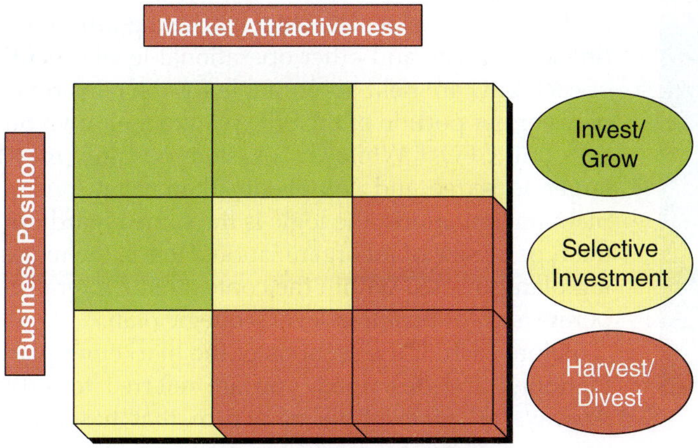

Business Position (high, medium, and low): Assess the firm's ability to compete. Factors include organization, growth, market share by segment, customer loyalty, margins, distribution, technology skills, patents, marketing, and flexibility, among others.

Market Attractiveness (high, medium, and low): For the market, assess size, growth, customer satisfaction levels, competition (quantity, types, effectiveness, commitment), price levels, profitability, technology, governmental regulations, sensitivity to economic trends, among others.[23]

"GE Business Screen," *Business Resource Software Online,* www.brs-inc.com/pwxcharts.asp?32, accessed January 4, 2014.

attractiveness. Within the BCG matrix you find four cells, each representing strategy recommendations:

- *Stars* (high share, high growth): important to building the future of the business and deserving any needed investment.
- *Cash Cows* (high share, low growth): key sources of internal cash generation for the firm.
- *Dogs* (low share, low growth): potential high cash users and prime candidates for liquidation.
- *Problem Children*, or Question Marks (low share, high growth): high cash needs that, if properly nurtured, can convert into stars.[24]

For purposes of strategy development, the BCG matrix approach is seductively simple and has contributed to decision making about internal cash generation and usage across SBUs. It has also morphed in application downward to often be applied to product lines and product groups, which is nominally possible so long as costs and returns can be properly isolated for investment decisions. But by nature of simplicity, BCG ignores other important factors that should go into this decision making and also ignores the viability of generating cash externally.

The GE Business Screen, shown in Exhibit 2.4, is a more realistic and complex portfolio model. It also evaluates the business on two dimensions—market attractiveness and business position, which refers to its ability to compete. The investment decision is again suggested by the position on a matrix. A business that is favorable on both dimensions should usually be a candidate to grow. When both market attractiveness and business position evaluations are unfavorable, the harvest or divest options should be raised. When the matrix position is neither unambiguously positive nor negative, the investment decision will require more analysis.

For now, it is important to note that portfolio analysis does not offer a panacea for corporate strategy formulation. In fact, since the heyday of the use of portfolio analysis in the 1970s and 1980s, firms are more cautious in its application and recognize that it is but one approach to strategy decision making.[25]

Marketing planning and strategy, while analytical in nature, often yield very funny marketing communications.

FRESH STEP® is a registered trademark of the Clorox Pet Products Company. Used with permission. FRESH STEP® advertisement. © 2013 The Pet Products Clorox Company. Reprinted with permission. Photographer: Jill Greenberg.

Functional Level Plans A firm's SBU plans all incorporate **functional-level plans** from operations, marketing, finance, and the other operational areas. Just as the individual SBU CEOs are held accountable for their unit's performance to Jeff Immelt within the context of GE's plan, the chief marketing officer, chief financial officer, and other operational-level executive of each SBU are held accountable for the performance of his or her portion of the SBU plan to their own business unit CEO.[26] While GE's system certainly may be larger in scope and complexity than many business planning situations, the logic is the same regardless of the type or size of an organization. Hence, the marketing plan is nested within the context of an overall corporate and/or business-level strategic plan.

Before each of the sections of the marketing plan is identified and described, you are referred to JetBlue Airways as an example of a firm that has become noted for successful marketing planning. Why JetBlue as an example? Clearly, JetBlue's not perfect, and in the turbulent airline industry it's really tough to do great marketing planning. During his tenure as chairman and CEO, JetBlue founder David Neeleman was quite transparent about his strategies and plans for the company, not only discussing them openly with the business press but also placing a substantial amount of organizational information on the company website. This approach has continued in the post-Neeleman era of the firm. And when JetBlue has made missteps, the company has been forthright in recognizing and addressing the errors. As each of the elements of the marketing planning process is described below, JetBlue will be used as a thematic example of each piece in practice.

Organizational Mission, Vision, Goals, and Objectives

Marketing planning does not occur in a vacuum; it must connect with the firm's overall mission and vision. A **mission statement** articulates an organization's purpose, or reason for existence. A well-conceived mission statement defines the fundamental, unique purpose that sets a company apart from other firms of its type and identifies the scope of a company's operations, products, and markets.[27]

Most mission statements also include a discussion of what the company would like to become in the future—its **strategic vision**. According to ex-GE CEO Jack Welch, "Good business leaders create a vision, articulate the vision, passionately own the vision, and relentlessly drive it to completion."[28] The vision of what the firm is capable of in the future and where it *wants* to go, as championed by its top leadership, sets the tone for everything that follows in the planning process. **Goals**, general statements of what the firm wishes to accomplish in support of the mission and vision, eventually become refined into specific, measurable, and (hopefully) attainable **objectives** for the firm.[29] Objectives at the corporate and SBU level provide the benchmarks by which organizational performance is assessed. Unfortunately, despite a formal mission, vision, goals, and objectives, it is all too easy for senior management and even the board of directors to become distracted and stray off course. Such action can create major problems both inside and outside the company, as demonstrated by the HP scandal featured in Ethical Dimension 2.

JetBlue Airways took to the air February 11, 2000, flying from John F. Kennedy International Airport in New York to Fort Lauderdale in Florida. Today, the upstart airline is rapidly becoming a major player, serving more than 50 cities (including several Caribbean locations) with nearly 100 aircraft, and it has ambitious plans for continued growth. The company's vision is to offer great service with low fares—and make a profit—even when other air carriers are struggling to survive. Several important goals back up this vision:

- Start and remain well-capitalized.
- Fly new planes.
- Hire the best people.
- Focus on service.
- Practice responsible financial management.

To date, JetBlue has mostly stayed true to course. While most of the major carriers continuously bleed red ink, JetBlue, though not perfect in bringing in every quarter's sales and profit goals, appears to be much more stable financially than the majority of other airlines. Much of the airline's success can be attributed to great market-driven strategic planning.

In terms of specific and measurable objectives, Neeleman established high performance expectations for financial results, operational processes, and customer satisfaction and loyalty. As mentioned earlier, JetBlue's website is very transparent in laying out company leaders' plans for the firm—Neeleman was always quite confident that the company had created a unique value offering that few (if any) competitors could readily duplicate. In the winter of 2007, JetBlue suffered

ETHICAL DIMENSION 2

HP's Ethical Scandal Impacts Marketing Strategy

Developing a strategic marketing focus in an organization requires a commitment from senior management. As you just read, according to Jack Welch, good managers create, articulate, become passionate about, and focus the company on a vision. That requires a clear focus on what *is* and, critically, what *is not* important to the firm.

Many issues confront senior managers and it is easy to lose focus. For example, senior management is rightfully concerned about competitors or even the general public gaining access to sensitive company information (for example, financial data, cost figures, future marketing strategies, product plans, and pricing programs). To help protect sensitive data from getting into the wrong hands, companies implement sophisticated security measures. At the same time, the Sarbanes-Oxley Act of 2002 (commonly referred to as SOX) established specific procedures and processes to ensure ethical conduct at the highest levels of a company including the board of directors and senior management.

Hewlett-Packard (HP), one of the world's leading technology companies, has experienced a series of ethical and legal failures over the last several years. Beginning with the leaking of sensitive documents, illegal wiretapping of Board members (and the subsequent dismissal of several Board members as well as firing of employees), firing of the CEO over submitting false expense reports, and other lapses, the company's reputation has been severely damaged, sales have dropped, and the stock price is down. As the company tried to deal with these ethical and legal issues, bad strategic decisions were made such as the acquisition of software company Autonomy for $11 billion and the subsequent write-down of nearly $9 billion as well as the decision to move out of manufacturing computers then reversing that decision. While not directly related to these strategy faux pas, the ethical lapses certainly created a challenging and difficult environment inside HP.

Were the people involved simply unethical by nature? Evidence suggests just the opposite. Indeed, one of the fired HP officers was the ethics chief for the company and also a well-respected attorney. While stopping the leak of sensitive information was a valid goal, poor—and even illegal—decisions were made about how to accomplish that goal. At the same time, the fired CEO, Mike Hurd, had done a good job at HP but made bad ethical decisions about an inappropriate relationship with an employee and subsequently submitting false expense reports. At critical decision moments, no one stepped back to reflect and ask important questions like: Does this make sense? Is this activity appropriate or ethical?

Employees report considerable conflict as the company has dealt with changes to ethical procedures and policies. Current CEO Meg Whitman has acknowledged that the scandals and subsequent poor management decisions have been a distraction and damaged HP's customer confidence in its brands. When management gets distracted by ethical scandals, the company loses strategic focus and the company's brands could lose market share to competitors who take advantage of the scandalized firm's weakness in the marketplace.[30]

Ethical Perspective

1. **Senior Management:** How should senior management incorporate ethical standards at all stages of the marketing planning process?
2. **Marketing Managers:** A company's brands can be quickly impacted by negative publicity surrounding ethical scandals. How might they be impacted and what might a marketing manager do to reestablish a brand damaged in this way?
3. **The Public:** Company image and trust can be regained by top leadership's quick public acknowledgment of an ethics problem accompanied by plans for changes in practice. What could HP's leaders have done better?

a highly publicized operational meltdown at its JFK airport home base due to a massive snow and ice storm, and Neeleman was right there on the website and in the public media. In addition to offering an apology, he also provided full refunds, free replacement tickets, and travel vouchers to stranded passengers and established the first passengers' bill of rights in the industry.

In developing a marketing plan, the marketing manager must proceed in the process with a strong understanding of and commitment to the firm's mission, vision, goals, and objectives. JetBlue's well-conceived and executed marketing plan is an integral element in its success.

LO 2-3

Identify various types of organizational strategies.

Organizational Strategies

At the firm level, a **strategy** is a comprehensive plan stating how the organization will achieve its mission and objectives. Put another way, strategy is like a road map to get the organization where it wants to go, based on good information gathered in advance. The choice of which direction a firm should go ultimately boils down to a *decision* by a firm and its managers. Strategy has two key phases: formulation (or development) and execution. And it occurs at multiple levels in the firm: corporate level, SBU (or business) level, and functional level (marketing, finance, operations, etc.). As we have discussed, the strategies developed and executed at each of these levels must be aligned and directed toward the overall organizational mission and goals.

A firm's **generic strategy** is its overall directional strategy at the business level.[31] Fundamentally, all firms must decide whether they wish to (or are able to) *grow,* and if not, how they can survive through *stability* or *retrenchment.* Exhibit 2.5 provides options for generic strategies for each of these three directions. The choice of generic strategy is usually driven by resource capabilities of the firm, as well as the competitive landscape. In the growth-oriented business culture in the United States, stockholders and financial analysts are constantly interested in knowing a firm's next growth strategy and can become quickly disenchanted, even with firms that are growing but at a slower than predicted rate. Yet, sometimes for reasons related to the competitive landscape or resource constraints, the best generic strategy for a firm may not actually be growth but stability or retrenchment instead. Interestingly, the pressure to constantly achieve accelerated growth is much less intense in many business cultures outside the United States.

Michael Porter identifies three primary categories of **competitive strategy**: low cost, differentiation, and focus (or niche). Exhibit 2.6 describes each of these, and Exhibit 2.7 illustrates them further within a matrix format. Porter's overarching premise is that firms must first identify their **core competencies**, or the activities the firm can do exceedingly

JetBlue communicates a strong value proposition for taller fliers who are frustrated with other airlines.

EXHIBIT 2.5 | Generic Business Strategies

Growth

- Organizations that do business in dynamic competitive environments generally experience pressure to grow in order to survive. Growth may be in the form of sales, market share, assets, profits, or some combination of these and other factors. Categories of growth strategies include:
  Concentration—via vertical or horizontal integration.
  Diversification—via concentric or conglomerate means.

Stability

- The strategy to continue current activities with little significant change in direction may be appropriate for a successful organization operating in a reasonably predictable environment. It can be useful in the short term but potentially dangerous in the long term, especially if the competitive landscape changes.

Retrenchment

- An organization in a weak competitive position in some or all of its product lines, resulting in poor performance and pressure on management to quickly improve, may pursue retrenchment.
- Essentially, retrenchment involves pulling assets out of underperforming parts of the business and reinvesting in aspects of the business with greater future performance potential.

Source: J. David Hunger and Thomas H. Wheelen, *Essentials of Strategic Management*, 4th ed. (Upper Saddle River, NJ: Prentice Hall, 2007).

EXHIBIT 2.6 | Competitive Strategy Options

Cost Leadership

- The organization strives to have the lowest costs in its industry and produces goods or services for a broad customer base. Note the emphasis on *costs*, not *prices*.

Differentiation

- The organization competes on the basis of providing unique goods or services with features that customers value, that they perceive as different, and for which they are willing to pay a premium.

Focus (or Niche)

- The organization pursues either a cost or differentiation advantage, but in a limited (narrow) customer group. A focus strategy concentrates on serving a specific market niche.

EXHIBIT 2.7 | Competitive Strategy Matrix

Competitive Scope \ Competitive Advantage	Lower Cost	Differentiation
Broad Target	Cost Leadership	Differentiation
Narrow Target	Cost Focus	Focused Differentiation

well. When these core competencies are superior to those of competitors, they are called **distinctive competencies**. Firms should invest in distinctive competencies, as they offer opportunity for **sustainable competitive advantage** in the marketplace, especially if the competencies cannot be easily duplicated or usurped by competitors. Sources of differential advantage will be developed further in Chapter 6.

As illustrated in Exhibit 2.8, Miles and Snow propose several categories of firms within any given industry based on **strategic type**. Firms of a particular strategic type have a common strategic orientation and a similar combination of structure, culture, and processes consistent with that strategy. Four strategic types are prospectors, analyzers, defenders, and reactors—depending on a firm's approach to the competitive marketplace.

JetBlue has historically followed an internal growth strategy. As some of its rivals continue to falter, it will be interesting to see how aggressive JetBlue might become in terms of growth through concentration via acquisitions. Like its much larger competitor Southwest Airlines, JetBlue executes a low-cost strategy in the

EXHIBIT 2.8 | Miles and Snow's Strategy Types

- **Prospector:** Firm exhibits continual innovation by finding and exploiting new product and market opportunities.
- **Analyzer:** Firm heavily relies on analysis and imitation of the successes of other organizations, especially prospectors.
- **Defender:** Firm searches for market stability and production of only a limited product line directed at a narrow market segment, focusing on protecting established turf.
- **Reactor:** Firm lacks any coherent strategic plan or apparent means of effectively competing; reactors do well to merely survive in the competitive marketplace.

Source: Adapted from Raymond E. Miles and Charles C. Snow, *Organizational Strategy, Structure, and Process*, McGraw-Hill, 1978.

competitive marketplace. Because it has no unions, hedges on fuel prices, and standardizes the types of planes flown, JetBlue enjoys numerous cost advantages over the competition. However, JetBlue differs from Southwest in that its strategy (in the context of Exhibit 2.8) is cost focus, while Southwest's is cost leadership. The difference is that Southwest—especially with its acquisition of AirTran Airways—has defined the scope of its competitive marketplace much more broadly than has JetBlue; for instance, Southwest is basically a nationwide carrier, while JetBlue focuses on some specific geographic markets. In terms of strategic type, JetBlue can be labeled a prospector. It has enjoyed strong **first-mover advantages** by providing television, movies, and games in every seat along with comfy leather accoutrements and plenty of legroom—all at bargain prices! Exhibit 2.8 provides typical characteristics of firms that fall into each of the strategy types.

To summarize, for purposes of marketing planning, it is necessary to be mindful of the organizational strategies in play when developing marketing strategies. One could reasonably argue that a fine line exists between organization-level strategies and marketing strategies, and, in many firms, the market-driven strategies developed within the context of the marketing plan ultimately rise to the organizational level.[32] Fortunately, the distinction is moot so long as the strategies developed and implemented are fully supportive of the organization's mission, vision, and goals.

Situation Analysis

LO 2-4

Conduct a situation analysis.

The marketing manager must perform a complete **situation analysis** of the environment within which the marketing plan is being developed. The situation includes elements of the macro-level external environment within which the firm operates, its industry or competitive environment, and its internal environment.[33] Think of external environmental factors as those a firm must be mindful of and plan for, yet has little or no direct ability to impact or change. On the other hand, internal environmental factors include the firm's structure and systems, culture, leadership, and various resources, all of which are under the firm's control. Ironically, when undertaking a situation analysis, managers often have more difficulty assessing the internal environmental components than the external, perhaps because it is much more difficult to self-assess and potentially criticize that for which the managers are responsible.[34]

Macro-Level External Environmental Factors Major categories for analysis within the external environment include:

- *Political, legal, and ethical.* All firms operate within certain rules, laws, and norms of operating behavior. For example, JetBlue has myriad regulations administered by the Federal Aviation Administration, the National Transportation Safety Board, and the Transportation Security Administration. In the airline industry, the regulatory environment is a particularly strong external influence on firms' marketing planning.

- *Sociocultural/demographic.* Trends among consumers and in society as a whole impact marketing planning greatly. Many such trends are demographic in nature, including changing generational preferences and the rising buying power of minority groups domestically and consumers in developing nations in the global marketplace.[35] Speaking of generational preferences, JetBlue jumped on the video game trend among children and teens by providing in-seat games, much to the delight of parents who no longer have to entertain the kids for the duration of the flight.

Demographic factors influence a company's marketing strategy. For example, Kmart's approach to attracting the 18 to 34 age group is completely different versus other age brackets. To capture more of the younger demographic, the retailer has introduced clothing collections from Selena Gomez, Sofia Vergara, Adam Levine, and Nicki Minaj. It has also increased its online fashion presence. They now maintain a fashion blog and have developed an interactive feature on their website that allows users to put together entire outfits. Kmart is heavily involved with New York Fashion Week, creating the "Kmart Concierge" service, which delivers on request small essentials to fashion designers, editors, and bloggers. This was done in hopes of swaying the younger generation to view the brand as a fashionable store. While this transition will not occur overnight, the company anticipates a positive trend for purchases within this demographic in the near future.[36]

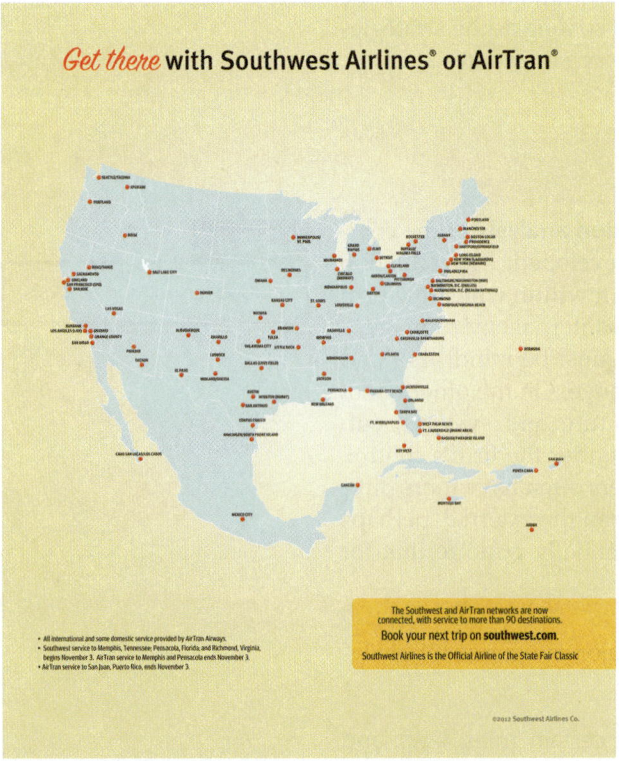

Southwest and AirTran merged and together they compete by offering more destinations at lower prices. Annually they carry more passengers inside the U.S. by far than any other airline.

- *Technological.* Constantly emerging and evolving technologies impact business in many ways. The goal is to try to understand the future impact of technological change so a firm's products will continue to be fresh and viable. JetBlue ordered a number of new downsized "regional jets," planes that carry about 50 passengers and allow for entry into smaller, underserved markets. The airline is banking on these attractive, comfortable new aircraft to provide a market edge over the competition.
- *Economic.* The economy plays a role in all marketing planning. Part of a marketing plan is a forecast and accompanying budget, and forecasts are impacted by the degree to which predicted economic conditions actually materialize.[37] Fuel prices are a major economic cost element for any airline. JetBlue was a pioneer in hedging against rising fuel prices—that is, making speculative long-term purchase commitments betting on fuel prices going up.
- *Natural.* The natural environment also frequently affects marketing planning.[38] JetBlue's highly publicized winter weather fiasco at JFK airport in 2007 prompted immediate changes in the way the company communicates with its customers. And on a broader scope, the concept of environmentally friendly marketing, or *green marketing,* has been a growing trend in socially responsible companies.

Sustainability, which refers to business practices that meet humanity's needs without harming future generations, has evolved into a part of the philosophical and strategic core of many firms.

Competitive Environmental Factors The competitive environment is a particularly complex aspect of the external environment. Let's identify several factors, or forces, that comprise a basis for assessing the level and strength of competition within an industry. The forces are portrayed in Exhibit 2.9 and summarized below:

- *Threat of new entrants.* How strong are entry barriers based on capital requirements or other factors? A cornerstone of JetBlue's initial market entry success was the fact that it was exceptionally well-capitalized. Not many new airlines are.
- *Rivalry among existing firms.* How much direct competition is there? How much indirect competition? How strong are the firms in both categories? JetBlue's industry contains a number of firms that are much larger, but based on JetBlue's unique value proposition, few of them can deliver the same customer experience that JetBlue can.
- *Threat of substitute products.* Substitutes appear to be different but actually can satisfy much or all of the same customer need as another product. Will teleconferencing PC-to-PC (using products such as Skype) reach a point in the near future such that business travel is seriously threatened, thus impacting JetBlue and other airlines?
- *Bargaining power of buyers.* To what degree can customers affect prices or product offerings? So far, JetBlue has not been in much head-to-head competition

EXHIBIT 2.9 | Forces Driving Industry Competition

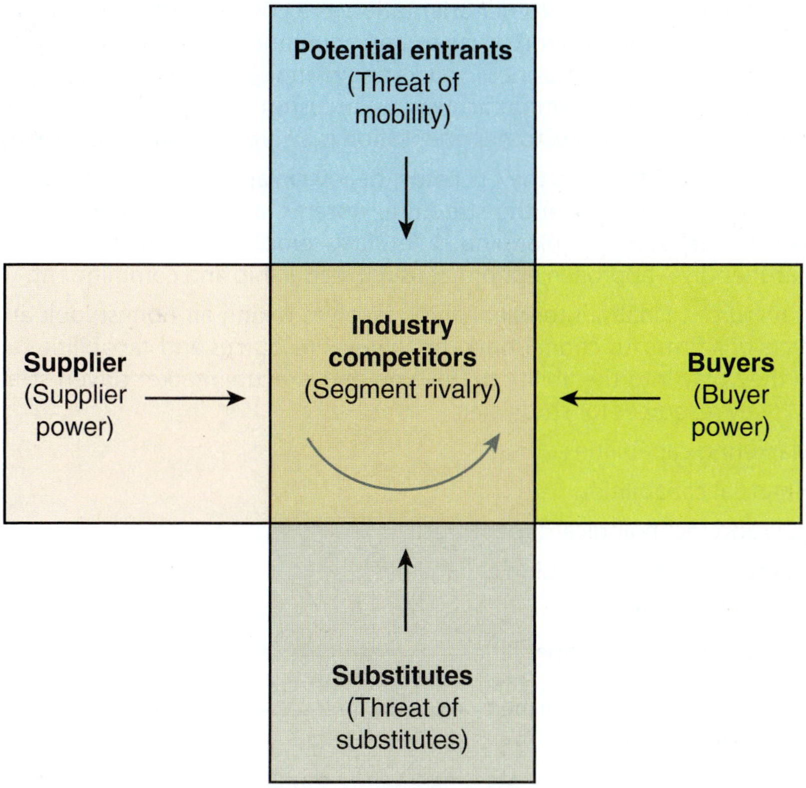

Source: Reprinted with the permission of The Free Press, a Division of Simon & Schuster Adult Publishing Group, from *Competitive Strategy: Techniques for Analyzing Industries and Competitors* by Michael E. Porter. Copyright © 1980, 1988 by The Free Press. All rights reserved.

with Southwest/AirTran, Spirit, Allegiant, Frontier, or other low-fare carriers in its primary markets. Should this change, passengers will have more power to demand even lower fares and/or additional services from JetBlue.

- *Bargaining power of suppliers.* Suppliers impact the competitive nature of an industry through their ability to raise prices or affect the quality of inbound goods and services. Jet fuel literally fires the airline industry's economic engine. Also, few manufacturers of commercial aircraft still exist. Both of these factors point to a competitive environment with strong supplier power.

One other competitive force not directly addressed by Porter is the *relative power of other stakeholders.* This force is becoming more and more relevant in assessing industry competitiveness. The level of activity by unions, trade associations, local communities, citizen's groups, and all sorts of other special-interest groups can strongly impact industry attractiveness.[39] Founder David Neeleman established JetBlue as a non-union shop with the goal of keeping it that way by hiring the very best people and treating the people right. The union environment in the airline industry adds multiple complexities to the ability to stay competitive.[40]

Internal Environmental Factors Major categories for analysis in the internal environment include:

- *Firm structure and systems.* To what degree does the present organizational structure facilitate or impede successful market-driven strategic planning? Are the firm's internal systems set up and properly aligned to effectively serve customers? David Neeleman had his organizational chart right on the company website and talked openly about being a lean and mean operation. It's hard to find much evidence that JetBlue's structure and systems offer impediments to its marketing planning.
- *Firm culture.* As discussed previously, successful marketing planning requires a culture that includes customer orientation as a core value. If a firm's culture does not value and support a customer orientation and customer-centric approach to the overall business, marketing planning will likely disappoint.[41] A close review of the communication with customers on JetBlue's website provides evidence that customer orientation is a core value at the company.
- *Firm leadership.* Of course, the CEO must believe in and continuously support (financially and otherwise) the structure, systems, and culture necessary for market-driven strategic planning.[42] JetBlue's employee-friendly—and customer-friendly—approach epitomizes such leadership and commitment.
- *Firm resources.* Finally, internal analysis involves taking an honest look at all aspects of a firm's functional/operational-level resources and capabilities and how they play into the ability to develop and execute market-driven strategies.[43] Key resources for study are:
  - Marketing capabilities.
  - Financial capabilities.
  - R&D and technological capabilities.
  - Operations and production capabilities.
  - Human capabilities.
  - Information system capabilities.

JetBlue historically has performed better than almost all the competition on all these resource dimensions.

Summarize the Situation Analysis into a SWOT Upon completion of the situation analysis, a convenient way to summarize key findings is into a matrix of strengths, weaknesses, opportunities, and threats—a **SWOT analysis**. Exhibit 2.10 provides a template for a SWOT analysis. Internal analysis reveals strengths and

EXHIBIT 2.10 | SWOT Analysis Template

INTERNAL FACTORS / EXTERNAL FACTORS	**Strengths (S)** List 5–10 *internal* strengths here	**Weaknesses (W)** List 5–10 *internal* weaknesses here
Opportunities (O) List 5–10 *external* opportunities here	**S/O Based Strategies** Generate strategies here that use **strengths** to take **advantage** of **opportunities**	**W/O Based Strategies** Generate strategies here that take **advantage** of **opportunities** by **overcoming weaknesses**
Threats (T) List 5–10 *external* threats here	**S/T Based Strategies** Generate strategies here that use **strengths** to **avoid threats**	**W/T Based Strategies** Generate strategies here that **minimize weaknesses** and **avoid threats**

Source: J. David Hunger and Thomas H. Wheelen, *Essentials of Strategic Management*, 5th ed. (Upper Saddle River, NJ: Prentice Hall, 2011). Reprinted from *Long Range Planning* 15, no. 2 (1982), Hans Weihrich, "The TOWS Matrix—A Tool for Situational Analysis," p. 60. Copyright 1982 with permission of Elsevier and Hans Weihrich.

weaknesses, while external analysis points to potential opportunities and threats. Based on the situation analysis and SWOT, it is now possible to begin making decisions about the remainder of the marketing plan.

Besides helping a marketing manager organize the results of a situation analysis, the SWOT analysis template is also useful in beginning to brainstorm marketing strategies that might be appropriate depending on which of four possible combination scenarios predominate in a firm's situation: internal strengths/external opportunities, internal strengths/external threats, internal weaknesses/external opportunities, or internal weaknesses/external threats. During the situation analysis it is essential to begin to critically and realistically examine the degree to which a firm's external and internal environments will impact its ability to develop a marketing strategy. The more honest and accurate the portrayal provided by the SWOT analysis, the more useful the remainder of the marketing planning process will be.

Additional Aspects of Marketing Planning

Additional elements of marketing planning are identified below. As they derive their content primarily from future chapter topics, reference is made where relevant to the chapters from which the content can be derived.

Perform Any Needed Market Research Part Two of the book focuses on using information to drive marketing decisions. In particular, Chapter 3 discusses collecting and analyzing market information. Chapters 4 and 5 outline key aspects of understanding customers in consumer and business markets, respectively. Chapter 6 includes ideas on how customer relationship management (CRM) enhances marketing planning and decision making. JetBlue has an effective CRM system that is supported through its TrueBlue loyalty program and other means. It also engages in ongoing market and consumer research to pinpoint trends and opportunities.

The Mall of America in Minneapolis, Minnesota, is the largest mall in the United States. Managing and measuring customer satisfaction can be a challenging process, given the mall welcomes 40 million shoppers annually. Mall administration sensed that some additional analytical power was needed and found a revolutionary product called Kipsu. This sophisticated CRM system allows the users to text a specified phone number and anonymously report about their experiences. The Mall of America began using the product in November of 2010. To give an example of the impact, custodians at the mall now have an informal competition to determine which bathrooms receive the fewest complaints!. Mall management staff members receive real-time metrics and updates from both the customers and the employees. Joseph Reuter, cofounder of Kipsu, said, "We are revolutionizing the service cultures of our clients. By scientifically dissecting the nuances of communication in service environments, we provide discipline over data and accountability." The success of the Mall of America is proving his statement is correct.[44]

Establish Marketing Goals and Objectives What is expected to be accomplished by the marketing plan? Based on what is learned from the situation analysis, competitor analysis, and market research, goals and objectives can now be developed related to what the marketing manager intends to accomplish with the marketing plan. JetBlue's marketing goals focus on enhancing the safety, comfort, and fun of customers' travel experience, building high satisfaction and loyalty among JetBlue users, and attracting new users to the brand.

Develop Marketing Strategies As we mentioned earlier, marketing strategies provide the road map for creating, communicating, and delivering value to customers. An overarching decision that must be made is which combinations of products and markets to invest in. A product-market combination may fall into one of four primary categories, as illustrated by Exhibit 2.11, Igor Ansoff's Product-Market Matrix:

EXHIBIT 2.11 | Product-Market Combinations

		Product Emphasis: Existing Products	Product Emphasis: New Products
Market Emphasis	Existing Markets	**Strategy = Market penetration** Seek to increase sales of existing products to existing markets	**Strategy = Product development** Create growth by selling new products in existing markets
	New Markets	**Strategy = Market development** Introduce existing products to new markets	**Strategy = Diversification** Emphasize both new products and new markets to achieve growth

Source: From H. Igor Ansoff, *The New Corporate Strategy*, John Wiley & Sons, 1988. Reprinted with permission of John Wiley & Sons, Inc.

- **Market penetration strategies** involve investing in existing customers to gain additional usage of existing products.
- **Product development strategies** recognize the opportunity to invest in new products that will increase usage from the current customer base.
- **Market development strategies** allow for expansion of the firm's product line into heretofore untapped markets, often internationally.
- **Diversification strategies** seize on opportunities to serve new markets with new products.

JetBlue began business with a primary focus on product development. The clean new planes, comfy leather seats, full spectrum entertainment console, and friendly staff were all welcomed by fliers as a long overdue change from other airlines' cattle-call mentality. However, more recently the company has focused on taking its winning formula into a number of new geographic markets. This market development strategy dramatically increased the number of cities on JetBlue's route system and especially increased opportunities for customers from underserved smaller cities such as Sarasota, Florida; Westchester County, New York; and Tucson, Arizona, to experience the airline. JetBlue has also added numerous international destinations into the travel mix such as Cancun, Aruba, and Nassau.

Krispy Kreme was once one of the most popular doughnut shops in the United States. In fact, in 2003, the brand earned the title "America's hottest brand" from *Fortune* magazine. When one of your authors lived in Tampa, the store on Kennedy Boulevard burned down and it was a banner headline the next day in the *Tampa Tribune!* The company was forced to reevaluate its strategy, however, when Dunkin' Donuts emerged and began offering specialty coffee drinks. The Atkins diet also became a fad around the same time period and swayed consumers away from carbohydrates. Krispy Kreme reevaluated its strategy and then began focusing on its coffee offerings. Through careful planning and implementation, the brand saw stock prices increase by 60 percent in one year. Beverages now account for 12 percent of the company's revenue and are targeted to increase to 20 percent of total revenue within a year. Krispy Kreme has even developed an app and a desktop widget to alert users when the doughnuts are fresh out of the oven. Bottom line: its marketing plan propelled it to financial success many industry analysts thought they would never see again.[45]

Create an Implementation Plan Including Forecast, Budget, and Appropriate Marketing Metrics As pointed out earlier, strategy *development* is only part of marketing planning. The other part is strategy *implementation,* including measuring results. The process of measuring marketing results and adjusting the marketing plan as needed is called **marketing control**.

In a marketing plan, every strategy must include an implementation element. Sometimes these are called action plans or programs. Each must discuss timing, assign persons responsible for various aspects of implementation, and assign resources necessary to make the strategy happen.[46] Forecasts and their accompanying budgets must be provided. Then, appropriate metrics must be identified to assess along the way to what degree the plan is on track and the strategies are contributing to achievement of the stated marketing objectives. Chapter 16 provides the background necessary for selecting marketing metrics appropriate for various marketing objectives and strategies, as well as instruction on preparing action plans for implementation, developing forecasts and budgets, establishing controls and contingency plans, and conducting a marketing audit.

On the JetBlue website, the Investor Relations and Press Room sections provide compelling evidence that the company is highly oriented toward measurement of marketing results. And although the airline industry as a whole has suffered in

Lego has executed a highly successful strategy by expanding into Legoland theme parks with locations in California, Florida, Denmark, Germany, Malaysia, and the UK.

recent years due to increased costs, JetBlue has generally received better reviews than most other airlines from Wall Street analysts in part because of the clarity of JetBlue's goals, metrics, and controls.

Develop Contingency Plans A final step marketing managers should take is to develop contingency plans that can be implemented should something happen that negates the viability of the marketing plan.[47] As you've learned, in marketing planning, flexibility and adaptability by managers are critical because unexpected events and drastic changes in various aspects of the external environment are the norm rather than an exception. To address this eventuality, a firm should incorporate contingency plans into the process.

Contingency plans are often described in terms of a separate plan for a worst-case, best-case, and expected-case performance against the forecast. That is, the implementation of the marketing strategies would be different depending on how performance against the forecast actually materializes. If better, the firm could quickly shift to a best-case implementation scenario. If worse, then the shift would be to a worst-case scenario. Having these contingency plans in place avoids scrambling to decide how to adjust marketing strategies when performance against a forecast is higher or lower than expected.

When developing contingency plans, the firm should be realistic about the possibilities and creative in developing options for minimizing any disruption to the firm's operations should it become necessary to implement them. Some firms use contingency planning to reduce the chances they would make a public relations blunder when confronted with an unexpected challenge that generates negative publicity in the media such as product tampering or failure, ethical or legal misconduct of an officer, or some other aspect of their operation that garners bad press.[48]

Recently, JetBlue has had to invoke a contingency plan for growth due to higher jet fuel costs (the entire industry has felt the impact). For all airlines, fuel costs have raised ticket prices and squeezed profit margins, drastically affecting achievement of forecasts. In reaction to a worst-case scenario, JetBlue has cut orders for new planes and postponed entry into some new market areas that it would like to develop. At best, in this environment JetBlue hopes to achieve stability in the short run at its current size and would also obviously benefit if other competitive carriers decide to stop operating.

TIPS FOR SUCCESSFUL MARKETING PLANNING

LO 2-5

Use the framework provided for marketing planning, along with the content in future chapters, to build a marketing plan.

Developing a marketing plan is an essential process for firm success. In addition to its direct impact on a firm's ability to compete, ongoing marketing planning also has a strong internal organizational benefit of providing a rallying point for developing creative ideas and for gaining input from important stakeholders throughout the various areas within an organization.[49] Who should be involved in marketing planning? The answer is: anyone from any unit at any level whose contribution and participation in the process will enhance the likelihood of a successful outcome. Marketing planning provides a unique opportunity for organization members to contribute to the success of a firm in a very concrete and visible way.

Here are a few final tips for having a successful marketing planning experience.

1. *Stay flexible.* Don't forget that marketing plans are not set in stone. Markets and customers change, competitors do unexpected things, and the external

environment has a nasty habit of creating unexpected surprises. Great marketing managers understand when to adjust a plan. Nimble organizations tend to be much more successful in their marketing strategies.

In his provocative book *The Rise and Fall of Strategic Planning,* strategy expert Henry Mintzberg builds the case that organizations sometimes spend so much time focused on planning for the long term that they miss the opportunities presented by the next customer who walks through the door.[50] Mintzberg's concern is valid and points to the need for viewing planning as an ongoing, organic process in which managers exhibit flexibility and adaptability to changing market conditions. Marketing plans are not written in stone—that is, after a plan is prepared, myriad changes in the firm's external and internal environments, may create a need for marketing managers to quickly alter their strategies in the marketplace.[51] The more nimble a company is in changing course to address new conditions as they arise, the more successful its marketing strategies will be.

2. *Utilize input, but don't become paralyzed by information and analysis.* Great marketing managers value research and analytics, but also know when to move forward with action.
3. *Don't underestimate the implementation part of the plan.* This is such a common mistake it is nearly synonymous with poor marketing planning. The quality of the action plans and metrics often make or break the success of the plan. Put another way, a good plan on paper is useless without effective implementation.
4. *Stay strategic, but also stay on top of the tactical.* Remember that marketing has these two levels of interrelated issues, and both the strategic and tactical elements have to be right for the plan to be successful.
5. *Give yourself and your people room to fail and try again.* Marketing planning is by no means a predictable science. It is more realistic to think of it as both science and art, and creativity and risk-taking are to be rewarded. All great marketing managers have experienced both success and failures in marketing planning. As in baseball, it's not one or two times at bat but rather the long-term batting average that separates the great from the average performer.

VISIT THE APPENDIX FOR A MARKETING PLAN EXAMPLE

Often the best way to learn is through example, so in the appendix to this chapter we have provided an abbreviated example marketing plan for the fictitious company CloudCab Small Jet Taxi Service. Take this opportunity early in the course to familiarize yourself with the flow and content, albeit abbreviated, of a typical marketing plan.

In addition, at the end of each chapter you will find a Marketing Plan Exercise that is designed to highlight aspects of that chapter as they pertain to a manager's ability to build an effective marketing plan. Use these activities to build your own knowledge and skill in the marketing planning process.

SUMMARY

Marketing planning is an ongoing process of developing and implementing market-driven strategies for an organization. Great marketing planning is essential for success in the marketplace. Once established, marketing plans are not set in stone. Instead, marketing managers must be flexible enough to constantly assess changes in the external and internal environments and adjust strategies and tactics accordingly. The chapter introduces the essential elements of marketing planning. The content elements for completing the various aspects of the template are covered in the chapters throughout the remaining three parts of the book.

KEY TERMS

benefit 27
utility 27
value proposition 28
customer satisfaction 28
customer loyalty 28
customer retention 28
customer switching 28
value chain 28
value-creating activities 28
marketing planning 30
marketing plan 30
market-driven strategic planning 32
corporate-level strategic plan 32
SBU-level strategic plan 32
portfolio analysis 33
Boston Consulting Group (BCG) Growth-Share Matrix 33
GE Business Screen 33
functional-level plans 34
mission statement 35
strategic vision 35
goals 35
objectives 35
strategy 36
generic strategy 37
competitive strategy 37
core competencies 37
distinctive competencies 38
sustainable competitive advantage 38
strategic type 38
first-mover advantages 39
situation analysis 39
SWOT analysis 42
market penetration strategies 45
product development strategies 45
market development strategies 45
diversification strategies 45
marketing control 45

APPLICATION QUESTIONS

1. What is a value proposition? For each of these brands, articulate your perception of their key value proposition:
   a. Caterpillar earth mover
   b. Apple iPad
   c. Facebook
   d. McDonald's hamburgers
   e. FedEx overnight delivery service
2. Consider the concept of the value chain. Identify a firm that you believe does an especially good job of investing in elements in the value chain to gain higher profit margins versus competition. Which two or three elements in the value chain does that firm handle especially well? For each of those elements, what does it do that is better than its competition?
3. Why is it so important for marketing managers, when engaged in marketing planning, to successfully deal with both Marketing (Big M) and marketing (little m) elements? What would be the likely negative outcome if a marketing plan paid a lot of attention to strategies and little attention to tactics? What would be the likely negative outcome of the reverse?
4. Consider firms in any area of the retail business. Using Miles and Snow's strategy types, identify the following: (1) a firm that you believe is a prospector; (2) a firm that you believe is an analyzer; (3) a firm that you believe is a defender; and

(4) a firm that you believe is a reactor. What characteristics of each led you to conclude they belong in their respective strategy type?

5. Historically, the theme park industry in Orlando is heavily affected by a large number of macro-level external environmental factors. From each of the five major categories of macro-level external factors, identify a specific example of how some element within that category might impact a theme park's marketing planning for the next couple of years. Be sure to explain *why* you believe each of your examples will be important for marketing managers to consider as they develop their marketing plans.

MANAGEMENT DECISION CASE: Hewlett-Packard and the Case for Strategic Change

How can a company that generates $111 billion in annual sales be considered a laggard in its industry? Well, if that company is Hewlett-Packard (HP for short), the answer is when that company loses roughly half its market value since 2010, when that $111 billion sales figure represents a 7.4 percent decline from the previous year, and when many of that company's main products are considered old and unappealing by a vast majority of customers. Needless to say, HP has many strategic challenges ahead as it strives to regain customers, market share, and profits.

Actually, HP has a proud history of being one of the top technology firms in the world. The company literally was founded in a California garage in 1939 on $538 of investment capital by Bill Hewlett and Dave Packard. Over the years, HP has introduced some of the most innovative products in several different industries. The company's very first product was purchased by Walt Disney Studios to produce the film *Fantasia*. Other product innovations by HP include a cesium-beam standard clock in 1964 that helped maintain international time standards, the first desktop calculator in 1968, the first scientific hand-held calculator in 1972, the first desktop mainframe computer in 1982, and the amazingly successful line of HP laser jet printers.

Despite this prior product innovation history, the company found itself in deep trouble in the late 2000s. A situation analysis at that time would have revealed an economy that was not very conducive to new investments in technology. The recession that began in 2008 was one of the steepest in U.S. history, with fallout effects for years with sluggish economic growth and relatively high unemployment. The sociocultural environment was one in which consumers began heavy use of smartphones and tablets as the primary access to social media and other electronic resources. Furthermore, today's consumers were becoming more interested in maintaining and sustaining the natural environment. Finally, the technology and competitive situation had changed as companies like Google, Apple, IBM, and Microsoft shifted to software and cloud computing. For a company like HP that earns much of its revenue from hardware like computers and printers, those trends collectively were not a welcome development. Their competitive responses over the past several years seem confusing, for example, their flip-flops on whether to be in or out of the PC business.

Clearly, HP has much work ahead of itself to right the ship. In an effort to change its fortunes, a few years ago the company hired former eBay CEO Meg Whitman. Determining how the company will reach its growth targets in the future is of paramount importance for Ms. Whitman and her leadership team. Regardless of the strategy they ultimately implement, how HP is able to adjust its strengths and weaknesses to take advantage of opportunities and minimize threats in the external environment will heavily impact the trajectory of their success in returning the venerable firm to its former position as a technology leader with innovative products and services that are preferred by customers.

Questions for Consideration

1. As HP continues to make changes to its overall strategy, what other aspects of the situation analysis beyond those elements mentioned above should Meg Whitman and other leaders pay special attention to?
2. What strengths does HP have that they can use to take advantage of various opportunities or minimize threats in the external environment?
3. Given what you know about HP and its situation, what product-market strategy or strategies would you recommend the company adopt to improve its performance and return on investment?

Sources: Sam Gustin, "Why Hewlett-Packard Suddenly Doesn't Look So Bad," *Time Magazine*, October 10, 2013, http://business.time.com/2013/10/10/why-hewlett-packard-suddenly-doesnt-look-so-bad/; "William Hewlett and David Packard: 1995 Lemelson-MIT Lifetime Achievement Award Winners," Lemelson MIT, http://web.mit.edu/invent/a-winners/a-hewlettpackard.html.

MARKETING PLAN EXERCISES

ACTIVITY 1: Elements of a Marketing Plan

In the chapter, you learned that marketing planning drives the activities of the marketing manager and you were provided a framework for marketing planning. Before you move further through this course, it is important to be sure that you understand the flow and content of a typical marketing plan.

1. Read the annotated marketing plan example presented in the appendix to this chapter.
2. Make notes about any questions you may have about the example plan, and be prepared to bring those questions to class for clarification.
3. An electronic template for your marketing plan that is essentially based on Exhibit 2.2 in the chapter (which is the same format used in the CloudCab Small Jet Taxi Service example in the appendix) can be accessed at www.mhhe.com/marshall2e.

ACTIVITY 2: Situation Analysis

In the chapter you also learned about the key situation analysis areas of external macro-level environmental factors, competitive forces, and internal environmental factors that marketing managers must consider in marketing planning. You also saw how this information can be conveniently summarized and portrayed in a SWOT analysis.

1. Using the chapter discussion on situation analysis along with Exhibit 2.10 as a guide, develop a short list of internal strengths and weaknesses and external opportunities and threats. Focus on issues that you believe will be most important to your marketing planning over the next year or so.
2. Exhibit 2.10 suggests that you consider the four different scenario combinations of the SWOT to begin to brainstorm possible strategies. Based on what you know at present, develop one idea for a marketing strategy that might be appropriate for each of the four situational scenario combinations represented in the exhibit—that is, one strategy that uses internal strengths to take advantage of external opportunities you have identified; one strategy that uses internal strengths to avoid external threats you have identified; one strategy that takes advantage of opportunities by overcoming internal weaknesses you have identified; and one strategy that minimizes internal weaknesses and avoids external threats.

NOTES

1. Peter C. Verhoef, "Understanding the Effect of Customer Relationship Management Efforts on Customer Retention and Customer Share Development," *Journal of Marketing* 67, no. 4 (October 2003), pp. 30–45.
2. Stephanie Coyles and Timothy C. Gokey, "Customer Retention Is Not Enough," *Journal of Consumer Marketing* 22, no. 2/3 (2005), pp. 101–06.
3. Business Wire (press release), "Jimmy Dean® Brand Warms up Mornings with the Launch of Several New Tasty Breakfast Offerings," *MarketWatch,* WSJ.com, February 5, 2013, www.marketwatch.com/story/jimmy-dean®-brand-warms-up-mornings-with-the-launch-of-several-new-tasty-breakfast-offerings-2013-02-05.
4. Anders Gustafsson, Michael D. Johnson, and Inger Roos, "The Effects of Customer Satisfaction, Relationship Commitment Dimensions, and Triggers on Customer Retention," *Journal of Marketing* 69, no. 4 (October 2005), pp. 210–18.
5. Seongjae Yu, "The Growth Pattern of Samsung Electronics: A Strategy Perspective," *International Studies of Management & Organization* 28, no. 4 (Winter 1998/1999), pp. 57–73.
6. Michael D. Johnson, Andreas Herrman, and Frank Huber, "The Evolution of Loyalty Intentions," *Journal of Marketing* 70, no. 2 (April 2006), pp. 122–32.
7. M. F. Emerson, "Learning Social Media Tricks from the Big Boys," *New York Times,* February 22, 2013, http://boss.blogs.nytimes.com/2013/02/22/learning-social-media-tricks-from-the-big-boys/.
8. Kusum L. Ailawadi and Bari Harlam, "An Empirical Analysis of the Determinants of Retail Margins: The

Role of Store-Brand Share," *Journal of Marketing* 68, no. 1 (January 2004), pp. 147–65.

9. Frederick F. Reichheld, *Loyalty Rules! How Leaders Build Lasting Relationships in the Digital Age* (Cambridge, MA: Harvard Business School Press, 2001).
10. Michael E. Porter, *Competitive Advantage* (New York: Simon & Schuster, 1985).
11. J. David Hunger and Thomas H. Wheelen, *Essentials of Strategic Management,* 4th ed. (Upper Saddle River, NJ: Prentice Hall, 2007).
12. Eric M. Olson, Stanley F. Slater, and G. Tomas M. Hult, "The Performance Implications of Fit among Business Strategy, Marketing Organization Structure, and Strategic Behavior," *Journal of Marketing* 69, no. 3 (July 2005), pp. 49–65.
13. Thomas L. Friedman, *The World Is Flat: A Brief History of the Twenty-First Century* (New York: Farrar, Straus and Giroux, 2005).
14. Wayne McPhee and David Wheeler, "Making the Case for the Added-Value Chain," *Strategy and Leadership* 34, no. 4 (2006), pp. 39–48.
15. Roland T. Rust, Katherine N. Lemon, and Valarie A. Zeithaml, "Return on Marketing: Using Customer Equity to Focus Marketing Strategy," *Journal of Marketing* 68, no. 1 (January 2004), pp. 109–27.
16. Richard W. Mosley, "Customer Experience, Organisational Culture, and the Employer Brand," *Journal of Brand Management* 15, no. 2 (November 2007), pp. 123–35.
17. E. J. Schultz and Rupal Parekh, "Justin Timberlake Is the New Face of Bud Light Platinum," *Advertising Age,* February 7, 2013, http://adage.com/article/news/justin-timberlake-face-bud-light-platinum/239672/.
18. P. Rajan Varadarajan, Satish Jayachandran, and J. Chris White, "Strategic Interdependence in Organizations: Deconglomeration and Marketing Strategy," *Journal of Marketing* 65, no. 1 (January 2001), pp. 15–29.
19. Karen Norman Kennedy, Jerry R. Goolsby, and Eric J. Arnold, "Implementing a Customer Orientation: Extension of Theory and Application," *Journal of Marketing* 67, no. 4 (October 2003), pp. 67–81.
20. Ron Southwick, "$45 for 10 Minutes: Rite Aid Expands Online Doctor's Appointments to Four More Cities," *MedCity News,* March 3, 2013, http://medcitynews.com/2013/03/45-for-10-minutes-rite-aid-expands-online-doctors-appointments-to-four-more-cities/.
21. Rust, Lemon, and Zeithaml, "Return on Marketing."
22. Karen Dubinsky, "Brand Is Dead," *Journal of Business Strategy* 24, no. 2 (March/April 2003), pp. 42–43.
23. "GE Business Screen," *Business Resource Software,* www.brs-inc.com/pwxcharts.asp?32.
24. "The Experience Curve—Reviewed: IV. The Growth Share Matrix or The Product Portfolio," *Boston Consulting Group,* www.bcg.com/documents/file13904.pdf.
25. Andrew E. Polcha, "A Complex Global Business' Dilemma: Long Range Planning vs. Flexibility," *Planning Review* 18, no. 2 (March/April 1990), pp. 34–40.
26. Robert Slater, *Jack Welch and the GE Way: Management Insights and Leadership Secrets of the Legendary CEO* (Boston: McGraw-Hill, 1998).
27. Hunger and Wheelen, *Essentials of Strategic Management.*
28. Noel Tichy and Ram Charan, "Speed, Simplicity, Self-Confidence: An Interview with Jack Welch," *Harvard Business Review,* September–October 1989, p. 113.
29. Mohanbir Sawhney and Jeff Zabin, "Managing and Measuring Relational Equity in the Network Economy," *Journal of the Academy of Marketing Science* 30, no. 4 (Fall 2002), pp. 313–33.
30. Lorraine Woellert, "HP's Hunsaker Papers," *BusinessWeek* Online, October 4, 2006, www.businessweek.com/technology/content/oct2006/tc20061003_396787.htm.
31. Bishnu Sharma, "Marketing Strategy, Contextual Factors, and Performance: An Investigation of Their Relationship," *Marketing Intelligence & Planning* 22, no. 2/3 (2004), pp. 128–44.
32. Mark B. Houston, Beth A. Walker, Michael D. Hutt, and Peter H. Reingen, "Cross-Unit Competition for Market Charter: The Enduring Influence of Structure," *Journal of Marketing* 65, no. 2 (April 2001), pp. 19–35.
33. David Mercer, *Marketing Strategy: The Challenge of the External Environment* (Thousand Oaks, CA: Sage, 1998).
34. Robert L. Cardy, "Employees as Customers?," *Marketing Management* 10, no. 3 (September/October 2001), pp. 12–14.
35. Regina D. Woodall, Charles L. Colby, and A. Parasuraman, "Evolution to Revolution," *Marketing Management* 16, no. 2 (March/April 2007), p. 29.
36. Ted Marzili, "K-Mart Not Cool with the 18–34 Demo Just Quite Yet," *Forbes,* February 13, 2013, www.forbes.com/sites/brandindex/2013/02/13/k-mart-not-cool-with-the-18-34-demo-just-quite-yet/.
37. Chaman L. Jain, "Benchmarking the Forecasting Process," *Journal of Business Forecasting Methods & Systems* 21, no. 3 (Fall 2002), pp. 12–16.
38. Rajdeep Grewal and Patriya Tansuhaj, "Building Organizational Capabilities for Managing Economic Crisis: The Role of Market Orientation and Strategic Flexibility," *Journal of Marketing* 65, no. 2 (April 2001), pp. 67–81.
39. Hunger and Wheelen, *Essentials of Strategic Management.*

40. Gary Chaison, "Airline Negotiations and the New Concessionary Bargaining," *Journal of Labor Research* 28, no. 4 (September 2007), pp. 642–57.

41. Kennedy et al., "Implementing a Customer Orientation."

42. Ross Goodwin and Brad Ball, "What Marketing Wants the CEO to Know," *Marketing Management* 12, no. 5 (September/October 2003), pp. 18–23.

43. Robert Inglis and Robert Clift, "Market-Oriented Accounting: Information for Product-Level Decisions," *Managerial Auditing Journal* 23, no. 3 (2008), pp. 225–39.

44. Patrick Hanlon, "Google Pushes Marketing Talk-Back Button," *Forbes,* February 8, 2013, www.forbes.com/sites/patrickhanlon/2013/02/08/google-pushes-marketing-talk-back-button/.

45. Robert Farzad, "Krispy Kreme's Unlikely Comeback," *Bloomberg Businessweek,* February 22, 2013, www.businessweek.com/articles/2013-02-22/krispy-kremes-unlikely-comeback.

46. Robert L. Cardy, "Employees as Customers?," *Marketing Management,* Vol. 10, Iss. 3, September/October 2001, pp. 12–14.

47. Denis Smith, "Business (not) as Usual: Crisis Management, Service Recovery, and the Vulnerability of Organisations," *Journal of Services Marketing* 19, no. 5 (2005), pp. 309–21.

48. Tobin Hensgen, Kevin C. Desouza, and Maryann Durland, "Initial Crisis Agent-Response Impact Syndrome (ICARIS)," *Journal of Contingencies and Crisis Management* 14, no. 4 (December 2006), pp. 190–98.

49. William B. Locander, "Staying within the Flock," *Marketing Management* 14, no. 2 (March/April 2005), pp. 52–55.

50. Henry Mintzberg, *The Rise and Fall of Strategic Planning* (New York: Financial Times Prentice Hall, 2000).

51. Polcha, "A Complex Global Business' Dilemma."

APPENDIX

CLOUDCAB SMALL JET TAXI SERVICE Abbreviated Example Marketing Plan

NOTE TO READER

This is an *abbreviated version* of a marketing plan for a fictitious firm, CloudCab Small Jet Taxi Service. This appendix is designed to walk you through the main steps of marketing planning. The idea is to provide you with an example early in the course so you will have a better understanding throughout the chapters of how the pieces of a marketing plan come together. Chapter 2 is devoted to the topic of marketing planning, providing a marketing plan framework and explaining the parts. That framework is used to develop this abbreviated example. Note that in practice most marketing plans contain more depth of detail than is provided here. Also, remember that each chapter ends with a Marketing Plan Exercise designed to guide you in applying the concepts from that chapter to a marketing plan.

SITUATION ANALYSIS

CloudCab seeks to provide solutions for the time-conscious traveler using quick, luxurious jet transportation. The small company was founded by former pilot Travis Camp and is now poised to be a first-mover into the California/Nevada/Arizona market. CloudCab will provide an alternative to frustrating waits at the airport and long car rides at a fair price for its customers.

CloudCab will use small, underutilized airports and a new class of Very Light Jet (VLJ) to quickly and comfortably transport customers from one city to another. Its customers will come primarily from businesses needing quick, on-demand transportation. Initially, CloudCab will not face much direct competition, so its biggest challenge will be to convince customers of its benefits over more traditional products.

Macro-Level External Environment

Political and Legal

Like all companies using the skies, CloudCab is subject to the rules set forth by the Federal Aviation Administration and other regulatory bodies. Fortunately, smaller jets have many of the same air privileges as their larger counterparts. This ensures access to needed airspace and air traffic control services.

The political and legal environment has the potential to become an even more positive factor for CloudCab as business expands. CloudCab uses smaller, underutilized airports, thereby drawing traffic away from congested major hubs and increasing the efficiency of the entire system. If CloudCab is successful, this may actually induce lawmakers to provide incentives for companies like CloudCab.

Furthermore, larger airports are already facing capacity strain. If CloudCab ties up the governmental resources needed by larger planes carrying more passengers, there may be pressure to limit the use of small jets at large airports.

Sociocultural

The macro-trend of consumers leading time-poor lives continues as both individuals and companies strive to be more efficient in their day-to-day operations. Coupled with an increase in waiting times at major airports due to heightened security procedures, this has led today's consumers to be even more conscious of the time spent in transit. Many are willing to spend extra money on faster, more convenient travel options.

Technological

Until recently, small jet service on a large scale was prohibitively expensive. The limited number of people willing to pay for such service could not compensate for the high cost of the jet itself. Due to changes in technology and the advent of the VLJ, this has begun to change. Several companies have been able to produce VLJs for the relatively low price range of $1 million to $3 million each. Using these efficient three-to-six-passenger jets, a taxi-like air service is now economically feasible.

Economic

The overall state of the economy will have a large impact on CloudCab's success, since business travel declines precipitously during economic downturns. Since some industries inherently require more travel than others (e.g., consulting, sales) and thus have a larger impact on demand for CloudCab services, CloudCab should particularly watch the health of these industries as predictors of demand for its own services.

CloudCab is also heavily dependent on the availability and price of oil. Higher oil prices will erode CloudCab's margins, while shortages may effectively stall the business. The risk involved in relying on a potentially price-volatile resource must be effectively managed to ensure success.

Competitive Environment

Threat of New Entrants

If CloudCab is successful it may entice others to enter the market. CloudCab's business is very capital intensive, though not as much so as a traditional airline due to smaller, lower-cost jets and a limited operating area. Still, the capital needs are sufficient to deter entry by many.

The biggest hurdle facing new entrants is the lead time necessary to procure the VLJs. This requires planning years in advance of actual operation due to backlogs in manufacturing and high demand. Thus, if a company is not in the business now, it would likely be at least a few years until it was able to enter. In the meantime, CloudCab would have some warning that a new competitor was coming.

Rivalry among Existing Firms

Fortunately, CloudCab will be one of the first to market, so initially there will not be many direct competitors. For a while, companies currently pursuing similar strategies should have ample market share to coexist peacefully, especially since most are geographically concentrated. However, it is just a matter of time before a few establish themselves as the dominant brands and expand nationally, increasing the rivalry and pushing some weaker players out of business.

CloudCab will face some indirect competition from the start from other private jet options. These include partial ownership plans and pay-by-the-hour membership cards. Until now, these have been the solutions of choice for speedy, luxurious travel.

Threat of Substitute Products

CloudCab's greatest threat will likely come from substitute products. Consumers have a variety of options when it comes to transportation. For regional travel, they can choose to fly on a traditional airline, drive their car, or in some cases take a bus or train. These options do not provide nearly the same level of comfort and speed as air taxis, but they do accomplish the task of getting a person from Point A to Point B at a significantly lower cost. Also, for business travelers, technology solutions such as videoconferencing and even PC-driven solutions such as Skype Internet phone service make physical travel to some types of meetings nonessential. If national security travel limitations develop or an economic downturn forces firms to cut business travel, these substitutes will predominate.

Bargaining Power of Buyers

CloudCab primarily competes in the business-to-business (B2B) market space, and it will be catering to only a few customers per flight on a limited number of flights. This means that any one customer's decision to use CloudCab has a large proportional impact, especially during CloudCab's early years. CloudCab will have to treat each customer well because it cannot afford to lose any. Still, a single traveler will not be able to demand, or bargain for, changes from CloudCab because the cost of making those changes will likely be larger than the revenue collected from that one buyer. On the other hand, a major corporate client—supplying many passengers over time—would wield considerable power.

Bargaining Power of Suppliers

CloudCab uses a single manufacturer for its jets; thus the level of dependency is high. If the jets are not ready in time or do not meet specifications, CloudCab could be put out of business. If CloudCab's manufacturer is not able to fulfill its contract, CloudCab might have to wait years to have an order filled with another supplier. Consequently, CloudCab's supplier is in a strong position to bargain for better terms.

At present, the supplier has relatively few buyers, one of them being CloudCab. So as a buyer, CloudCab also has some bargaining power. This makes the two interdependent and reduces the incentive for the supplier to treat CloudCab unfairly.

Internal Environment

Firm Structure

CloudCab, being relatively new, is far smaller than most businesses in the airline industry. Having few employees makes communication easy and response to change quick to occur. Realizing that the company's success depends heavily on customer adoption of the new offering, CloudCab executives' actions are driven primarily by the needs of the market.

CloudCab is led by founder and CEO Travis Camp. Robert Fray, chief operating officer and close friend of Camp, has been crucial in developing cost-saving measures to ensure CloudCab's prices are as competitive as can be. Other officers include Thomas Puck, chief financial officer; Elizabeth Vars, chief marketing officer; and Jeffery Brown, chief technology officer. All have airline industry experience, and Camp and Fray are former commercial pilots. The firm is in the entrepreneurial stage of its corporate development.

CloudCab is privately held and funded primarily through the investments of Travis Camp and Robert Fray, who combined have a controlling interest in the company. The rest of the funding has been obtained mostly from venture capital firms seeking returns based on a five-year time horizon.

Firm Culture

CloudCab is built on seizing opportunities to better serve the customer. It epitomizes a "lean and mean" culture. New ideas for improvements in efficiency and service quality are encouraged in this customer-centric culture. CloudCab has formalized reward systems for outstanding performance and attitude to promote high morale and productivity among its employees.

Firm Resources

Marketing capabilities: CloudCab has a strong, close-knit marketing team with a combination of experienced hands and recent college graduates. Several employees have ties with local media in major cities that can be used upon product launch.

Financial capabilities: CloudCab is well-financed through equity investments. It has purchased outright the 15 VLJs it plans to use in its operations. Current cash reserves should easily cover initial marketing and ongoing operating expenses, though investors have pledged further funds if needed.

R&D and technological capabilities: Lacking R&D capabilities in-house, CloudCab has chosen to purchase all aircraft and related systems from qualified vendors and outsource needed maintenance on those aircraft and systems. CloudCab values keeping its systems current and ensuring the firm is in a position to take advantage of any oncoming industry breakthroughs in jet technology.

Operations capabilities: CloudCab presently has the capacity to serve four city locations in California and Nevada (see the Market Research section of this document). Following success in these markets, CloudCab will be able to expand using its fully scalable communications and logistics tracking systems.

Human capabilities: CloudCab's employees are capable and committed. Many employees have received stock and stock options as part of their compensation, tying the interests of company and employee together. CloudCab is presently staffed with 45 people and has plans to employ a total of 80 people when fully operational. Many functions such as maintenance, security, and janitorial work will be outsourced.

Information systems capabilities: CEO Camp is a strong believer in customer relationship management (CRM). Every time a customer flies, he or she will be given the option to fill out a comment card, the contents of which will be entered into CloudCab's central database. Employees of CloudCab with customer contact will also be able to make notes on customer observations. Both of these data sources will be coded categorically and used to assist in customer development and planning. Popular flight times and routes will also be tracked to better assist in modification of product offerings.

SWOT SUMMARY/ANALYSIS

External / Internal	Key Strengths (S)	Key Weaknesses (W)
	Customer focus Speed to market Industry knowledge	Untested product Unknown brand Limited geographic reach
Key Opportunities (O)	**S/O Based Strategies**	**W/O Based Strategies**
Time-conscious travelers VLJ availability Small airports underutilized	Use VLJs to provide quick transportation between small airports	Focus on and invest in building the brand and offering in a small market first
Key Threats (T)	**S/T Based Strategies**	**W/T Based Strategies**
Traditional flights and cars Larger airports overcrowded Possibility of new, better jets	Demonstrate benefits over alternatives, avoid large airports, and stay tech aware	Don't try to compete against bigger airlines for mainstream customers

MARKET RESEARCH

To determine which locations to serve, CloudCab first gathered secondary data on air traffic patterns, popular destinations among private jet owners, and travel frequency for business and leisure. This allowed CloudCab to see where similar services were already being used for comparison.

CloudCab then gathered primary data on travelers' aspirations for where they would like to see CloudCab operate and what features they would want the service to have. This was done through a combination of focus groups and surveys. Focus groups were comprised of travel purchasers within businesses, business travelers themselves, and upper-income leisure travelers. Surveys were distributed via e-mail with a goal of gaining responses from both business and leisure travelers.

All of the data were analyzed to form a complete picture of what travel patterns are like now, what they may be in the future, and what factors (translated into customer benefits) would create demand for CloudCab services. CloudCab used the data to select its first four cities for operation: San Francisco, Los Angeles, Reno, and Las Vegas.

Research also revealed the following findings:

- In general, there seems to be a greater demand for sky taxis from business than from leisure travelers.
- Leisure travelers plan further ahead and have less need of on-demand service.
- Both leisure and business travelers want luxurious accommodations.
- Business travelers have more need of one-way flights than do leisure travelers.
- Time is the biggest priority for business travelers, while comfort is the biggest for leisure travelers.
- Some businesses, such as consulting and sales, have a greater need for on-demand travel than others.
- There is a "sweet spot" in income level among leisure travelers where they are wealthy enough to afford CloudCab services but not wealthy enough to own their own jet.

MARKETING GOALS AND OBJECTIVES

Goal

The goal of CloudCab is to be the preferred provider of on-demand short flight service.

Objectives

Within the first 12 months of operation, CloudCab will:

1. Sell 5,500 flight itineraries.
2. Attain a rating of "highly satisfied" customer satisfaction scored by 90 percent of customers.
3. Achieve repeat purchase by 50 percent of customers.

MARKETING STRATEGIES

Product-Market Combinations

CloudCab will use a product development strategy to introduce its new on-demand jet service into the California/Nevada/Arizona market. Based on CloudCab's market research, the product will first be made available in San Francisco, Los Angeles, Reno, and Las Vegas. If the product is successful there, then CloudCab will gradually add more service locations. Once a firm foothold in the region is established, CloudCab will expand into new markets in other regions.

Initially, CloudCab will depart only from the four selected cities. However, customers will be able to use the service to fly round-trip to *any airport* they choose within the region of operation. For one-way flights,

CloudCab will provide service only between selected cities, making the plane instantly available at that location for the next flight.

Market Segmentation, Target Marketing, Positioning

Segmentation

The market for on-demand small jet service can be easily divided between business travelers and leisure travelers. Leisure travelers can be further divided based on income levels, and business travelers can be further divided based on industry and other variables such as firm size. Of all possible segments, CloudCab has identified three that have especially high potential to be CloudCab customers:

- Leisure travelers with annual incomes between $300,000 and $1 million.
- Business travelers making B2B sales calls.
- Business travelers on assignment for mid-to-large-size consulting firms.

Target Marketing

CloudCab evaluated each of these segments to determine its focus for initial investment. The first segment, leisure travelers, has the means to afford CloudCab's service and could be a highly profitable market if effectively reached. However, its preference for round-trips over one-way and its tendency to book travel arrangements in advance does not fit well with CloudCab's on-demand service. Leisure travelers are also far less concentrated and thus harder to reach with marketing communications.

The second segment, business travelers in sales, would be easier to reach and would need CloudCab's one-way flights between select cities. Sales calls are a combination of previously scheduled appointments and client requests, making the demand for on-demand service in this group mixed. Sales professionals are often under pressure to keep traveling costs down though, making the profitability of serving this segment questionable.

The third segment, business travelers in consulting, shares sales professionals' need for one-way flights and on-demand service. Yet compared to sales professionals, there is less pressure to keep travel costs down since time and level of service to the client take precedence, and travel and other expenses are often billable to the client. Additionally, these travelers are largely concentrated in fewer firms, making it easier for marketing communications to reach this segment. Also, there is a substantial submarket of independent consultants from which to draw. For these reasons, CloudCab has decided to concentrate on the business consulting traveler segment as its primary target market. CloudCab will make its services available to other segments if they desire to use CloudCab, but CloudCab will not make any concentrated efforts to invest marketing dollars toward them in the beginning. Thus, high-income leisure travelers and sales professionals may be viewed as secondary target markets at present. No tertiary target markets have been identified as of yet.

Positioning

On one end of the travel spectrum, there exists the low-price, low-benefits group. This includes such offerings as traditional airfare and car transportation. Both involve a great deal of hassle, wasted time, and discomfort. The one advantage of this group is that it is affordable to the masses.

On the opposite end of the spectrum, there exists the high-price, high-benefits group. This group consists of private sole jet ownership, partial jet ownership similar to a time-share, and, on the lower side, pay-by-the-hour jet service. These options afford their customers a high degree of luxury and many time-saving features, but at a price well outside the range of most travelers, business or leisure.

In the middle of these two groups of travel options is a wide chasm. Until now, no company has been able to strike a happy medium between the two. Utilizing new technology and a unique business model, CloudCab seeks to position itself in this void with a focus on the B2B consulting market. Using its on-demand small-jet service, customers flying from select cities will be able to access many of the same benefits private jet owners enjoy, but without the exorbitant cost associated with it. CloudCab's service will be faster and more enjoyable than traditional airline flights or ground transportation, yet cost far less than private jet ownership. This appears to be a strong positioning with high upside potential for messaging to the primary target market.

Marketing Mix Strategies

Product/Branding Strategies

CloudCab's product benefits center on convenience, dependable service, and a quality image. CloudCab will primarily focus on service to small "executive airports" near the four start-up cities, with the exception of Las Vegas, for which travelers will have direct access to McCharren (the main Las Vegas airport) due to its proximity to the "strip."

To use CloudCab, customers will have two options. They will be able to either call a qualified customer service representative to book their flight or go online and enter their flight and payment information themselves.

Branding of CloudCab will evoke in customers the imagery of being quickly and comfortably transported "by a cloud" from one location to another. This will be communicated through the product name CloudCab as well as its logo, an airplane seat lightly resting in a fast-moving cloud.

Service Strategies

Customer service representatives and airport attendants will be noticeably a cut above the ordinary—polite and professional at all times, both on the phone and in person. Because of the firm's CRM capabilities to provide personalized service to its most valued customers, CloudCab employees will be able to easily enter information into an internal database under individual customer profiles. This will allow CloudCab to consistently meet the expectations of its customers without the customer having to express preferences every time CloudCab is used.

Pricing Strategies

The pricing decision for CloudCab is made more difficult due to the newness of its product offering and lack (so far) of strong competitors in its markets. In the early stages, penetration pricing can be effective to gain customer trial, expose customers to the excellent service quality, and build customer loyalty for the brand. Such an approach can also serve to keep planes in full service, making the most of a small fleet.

However, the penetration pricing strategy has to be tempered by attention to CloudCab's financial objectives for revenue, margins, and ROI. Chances are that, once a loyal customer base is developed, some incremental price increases can be taken without major disruption in the customer base.

CloudCab can communicate its positioning through price. Being first to market, CloudCab has the opportunity to set the value of its product in the mind of the customer. In setting a price, CloudCab must be careful to realistically assess the actual time savings and comfort customers can expect to receive, and what those benefits are worth to them. In this way, the price will work together with CloudCab's integrated marketing communications (IMC) strategies to effectively position the product and communicate value.

Supply Chain Strategies

CloudCab has purchased the needed operational systems to properly track its planes and ensure they are always where they need to be. Customer service representatives will use these systems to give customers information on flight availability and schedule new flights. CloudCab's outsource firms and supply chain partners will also have access to the system to ensure needed materials arrive where and when they are needed for everything from pillows to jet fuel.

Integrated Marketing Communications (IMC) Strategies

CloudCab will first use IMC to *create awareness* of CloudCab and *build interest* in the benefits of its service. All efforts will be focused on conveying a clear and consistent message. CloudCab's unique selling proposition will be that it is akin to a taxi service in the air, much quicker and more comfortable than other travel modes.

To convey this message, CloudCab will use targeted advertising, direct marketing, personal selling, and buzz marketing. Advertising will be limited to publications with high readership among the target market. Direct and interactive marketing—primarily via mail, e-mail, and the web—will be used to provide sales promotion incentives to customers to try CloudCab's service. Personal selling efforts will be made at consulting firms to attempt to gain contracts to make CloudCab one of the firm's transportation methods of choice. Finally, to generate buzz through public relations (PR), CloudCab will pitch stories to the media about its official launch date and first flight as a revolutionary way to travel.

Although these strategies should get CloudCab off the ground, over the long run the company will rely heavily on buzz generated by positive customer experiences to grow the business. The more people CloudCab effectively serves, the more potential brand ambassadors there will be. This should translate into an exponential sales growth for CloudCab.

IMPLEMENTATION

CloudCab possesses the needed resources for a successful launch early next year. The action plan below details the marketing communication initiatives CloudCab will undertake to increase market share and reach its goal of 5,500 flights in its first year of operation.

Marketing Action Plan for Initial Launch

Action	Date	Duration	Cost	Responsibility
Targeted print ads	December 1	4 months	$265,000	CMO Vars
CloudCab direct marketing to identified targets	February 1	3 months	$170,000	CMO Vars
Personal sales calls on key target firms	March 1	2 months	$210,000	CEO Camp and others
First CloudCab flight	May 1			COO Fray
Media coverage of first CloudCab flight	May 1	1 week	$ 3,000	CMO Vars

Monthly Sales Forecast to End of First Year

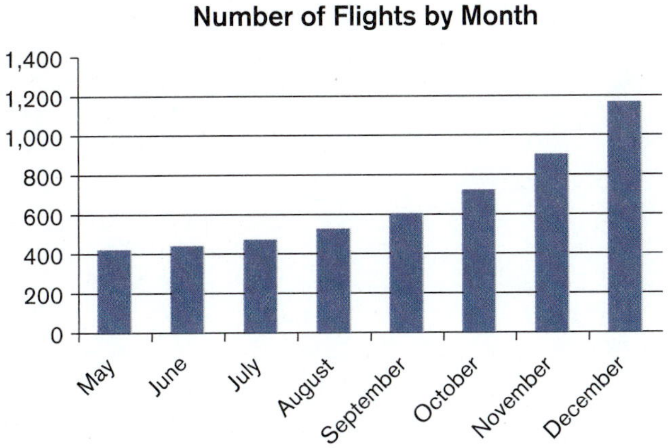

First-Year Budget

Using its forecasted sales volume, CloudCab can begin to establish a budget for its first year of operation. For now, CloudCab will use an estimated price of $1,200 per flight.

Revenue	5,287 × $1,200	$ 6,600,000
Fuel Costs		2,600,000
Promotional Activities		648,000
Salaries		1,200,000
Outsourced Systems		700,000
Operating Income		1,452,000
VLJ purchases		9,500,000
Net Income		$(8,048,000)

Marketing Control and Metrics

CloudCab must continually evaluate its marketing efforts to ensure its performance is on track against stated first-year objectives. The following metrics are associated with each objective.

Objective 1: Sell 5,500 Flight Itineraries

CloudCab will track sales to monitor if monthly targets are being met. If they are not, the market will have to be surveyed to determine awareness levels, and direct-mail response rates and personal selling closing ratios will be examined. In doing this, problem areas should be identified and resolved. If the problem cannot be addressed via CloudCab's current IMC mix, other elements may be added to the mix to find better ways of reaching the target audience.

Objective 2: Attain a Rating of "Highly Satisfied" Customer Satisfaction Scored by 90 Percent of Customers

Progress will be monitored by ongoing customer satisfaction measurement.

Objective 3: Achieve Repeat Purchase by 50 Percent of Customers

The CRM system will be utilized to track frequency of usage by customers.

CONTINGENCY PLANNING

CloudCab's product requires significant capital investment to bring to market and cannot be easily modified. Consequently, if CloudCab's target market does not respond to the product as planned, it would likely be easier to change the market to fit the product than to change the product to fit the market. If consultants do not find sufficient value in CloudCab and purchase at the anticipated level, then investment will be made against the secondary target market of salespeople.

In addition, CloudCab needs to closely track usage by leisure travelers. If it happens that, despite CloudCab's intentions, a larger than anticipated number of customers are leisure travelers or represent some business segment besides consulting, then CloudCab would consider refocusing its marketing efforts on both of these targets. It will have a contingency IMC plan in place that anticipates this eventuality.

PART 2

Use Information to Drive Marketing Decisions

chapter 03

MANAGE MARKETING INFORMATION

chapter 04

UNDERSTAND BUSINESS-TO-CONSUMER MARKETS

chapter 05

UNDERSTAND BUSINESS-TO-BUSINESS MARKETS

chapter 06

SEGMENTATION, TARGET MARKETING, POSITIONING, AND CRM

CHAPTER 03

Manage Marketing Information

LEARNING OBJECTIVES

LO 3-1 Describe the difference between market information systems and market research systems.

LO 3-2 Identify how critical internal (inside the firm) information is collected and used in making marketing decisions.

LO 3-3 Explain essential external (outside the firm) information collection methods.

LO 3-4 Recognize the value of market research and its role in marketing.

LO 3-5 Define the market research process.

LO 3-6 Illustrate current research technologies and how they are used in market research.

MAKING GOOD MARKETING DECISIONS—THE NEED TO KNOW

Information is power speaks to the importance of good information in decision making. Companies realize the right information at the right time and in the right format (a critical but often neglected part of the process) is essential for decision makers. Marketers are usually the ones entrusted with scanning the environment for changes that might affect the organization. As a result, creating procedures that collect, analyze, and access relevant information is a critical part of marketing management.[1]

A significant problem for most managers today is not having too little information but having too much. They frequently see interesting information that has no relevance to the immediate problem. As a result, companies need information systems that can collect and analyze huge amounts of information and then keep it for the right time and circumstance. Pulte Homes is one of the largest home builders in the United States. The company conducts research to learn how people move around in a home (the design flow), what features consumers want (for example, large master bedrooms and bathrooms), and what extras they want (upgraded countertops and wood trim). Also, Pulte studies demographic changes. For example, a large segment of the population, baby boomers (ages 50–68), is moving toward retirement; this may lead the company to design and build smaller homes with more special features. Also, volatility in the real estate market has led the federal government to adopt changes in real estate financing, and many states have followed suit with additional legislation. Finally, Pulte also needs to study changes in federal and state laws that affect home construction, such as the modifications to home building codes in New Jersey after Hurricane Sandy. These changes affect the homes people buy and, as a result, Pulte needs to be knowledgeable in all these areas.[2]

In addition to storing large amounts of data, marketing managers need a system to design and execute research that generates precise information. Consider the Apple iPhone. Before introducing a new model, Apple conducts tests with actual users to be sure the product fits their needs and performs as promised. The company also studies a wide range of other issues including competitors such as Samsung and long-term technology trends to identify key technologies for the iPhone now and in the future. Marketing managers need this information to make critical decisions as the iPhone is improved and the marketing plan put together. The success of the iPhone led competitors to incorporate similar features in their phones.

Apple Improved each iteration of the iPhone based on user experiences.

Post Cereal, newly independent from Ralcorp, its former parent company, faced declining sales of Honey Bunches of Oats. The third highest selling cereal brand in the United States, its sales fell 8.7 percent in 2012. After studying market trends, Post decided to capitalize on the surge in popularity of Greek yogurt and presented a new product—Honey Bunches of Oats Greek Honey Crunch—to Walmart and Target. Both retailers requested that it be on shelves within six months, leading Post to its fastest rollout in history with good success.[5]

These examples highlight the two fundamental types of market information decision makers need today. The first is data related to broad areas of interest such as demographic and economic trends, or the customer order fulfillment process inside the company. These data are used in strategic planning to help forecast potential new opportunities for company investment or deal with possible problems before they become a major issue for the company.[3] The second type of information needed addresses a specific question, for example, what is the best kitchen design for a retired baby boomer couple? Or what features would a young urban professional want in an iPhone? Questions like these require unique research designed to answer specific questions.[4] This chapter will examine both types of information needs. We'll start by discussing the market information system that is designed to bring together many different kinds information useful to the marketing decision maker. Then we'll look at market research, which is the process marketers use to conduct research on specific market questions.

MARKET INFORMATION SYSTEM

The Nature of a Market Information System

As noted earlier, marketing decision makers need limited amounts of the right data at any given time. Put simply, managers need what they need when they need it. When there is too much information, managers tend to either spend an excessive amount of time analyzing or get overwhelmed and ignore all the data. If they have too little information, managers are more likely to make poor decisions because they don't have all the facts. In either case, incorrect decisions are often the result. Exhibit 3.1 summarizes the various ways market research is used in making marketing decisions. As you can tell from Exhibit 3.1, market research takes many forms both inside and outside an organization.

LO 3-1

Describe the difference between market information systems and market research systems.

A **market information system (MIS)** is not a software package but a continuing process of identifying, collecting, analyzing, accumulating, and dispensing critical information to marketing decision makers. The MIS is really an "information bank" where data relevant to the company's marketing efforts are collected and stored until such time as management needs to "withdraw" them. Generally, this information is not specific to a particular problem or question; rather, it is important information that the marketing decision maker will need at the appropriate time.[6] A company needs to consider three factors in creating an MIS.

First, what information should the system collect? In evaluating internal and external information sources, companies need to consider not only what information is important but also the source of the data. Think about all the ways a company gets competitor data—salespeople and customers in the field, competitor materials and websites, business-related websites such as Hoover's, and many others. Because there are so many sources of information, decisions must be made about what information will be collected and where it will come from.

Second, what are the information needs of each decision maker? Not all managers need the same information. The CEO probably doesn't want or need daily sales figures across individual product lines, but the local sales manager does.

EXHIBIT 3.1 | Market Research Is Critical to Marketing Decisions

STAGES OR PROCESSES WITHIN MARKETING PLANNING	APPROPRIATE MARKET RESEARCH
Situation Analysis	
• Identification of competitive strengths and weaknesses • Identification of trends (opportunities and threats)	• Competitive barrier analysis • Analysis of sources of competitive advantage • Trend analysis • Positioning analysis • Identification of public and key issues concerns • Measure of market share
Selection of a Target Market	
• Analysis of the market • Selection of a target market	• Identification of segmentation bases • Market segmentation study • Needs assessment • Determination of purchase criteria • Buyer behavior analysis • Market demand estimation
Plan of the Marketing Mix	
• Product	• Product design assessment • Competitive product analysis • Competitive packaging assessment • Packaging trends assessment • Definition of brand image descriptors • Identification of brand name/symbol • New product ideation (concept development) • Package development or redesign
• Price	• Measure of price elasticity • Industry pricing patterns • Price-value perception analysis • Analysis of the effects of various price incentives
• Distribution	• Merchandising display assessment • Inventory management assessment • Location analysis (site analysis) • Market exposure assessment
• Promotion	• Message assessment • Content analysis • Copy testing • Media assessment • Media buy assessment
Marketing Control	
• Marketing audit	• Promotion effectiveness study • Assessment of effectiveness of marketing mix

Source: Reprinted from Donald R. Cooper and Pamela S. Schindler, *Marketing Research*, 2006. Copyright © 2006 The McGraw-Hill Companies, Inc.

A good MIS is flexible enough for managers to customize the information they receive and, in some cases, the format they receive it in.

Third, how does the system maintain the privacy and confidentiality of sensitive information? Company databases hold a great deal of confidential data on customers, suppliers, and employees. By limiting access to the data to those with a need to know, companies protect relationships and build trust.

Internal Sources—Collecting Information Inside the Company

LO 3-2

Identify how critical internal (inside the firm) information is collected and used in making marketing decisions.

At the heart of marketing is the relationship among the company, its products, and its customers. Critical to that relationship is a clear understanding of what is, and is not, working in the customer interface. Think about the senior manager at Microsoft who is concerned about rising dissatisfaction with customer support among its Office suite users. While there could be a number of reasons for this increase, the manager will first want to look at internal customer service metrics that include call wait times, ability of customer service representatives to handle the problems efficiently and effectively, number of customers who call back to address a problem, and a host of other metrics. These are all internal sources of data. By looking at such critical internal metrics collected as part of the market information system, management is able to do two things. First, in our example, management might see that an increase in call wait times has led to higher customer dissatisfaction. Here information is used to identify the problem. A second and more effective use of market information systems is to proactively address issues before they become a problem.[7] For example, management can set a benchmark stating that call wait times will not exceed two minutes. In this way, management can deal with a problem before it becomes a significant concern for the company. Of course, the investment in time and money needed to create and monitor such a system is significant.

A market information system can be as complicated as the company wants or can afford. It is expensive to collect and analyze data, and most companies don't maximize their existing information. Often, simply checking secondary sources such as legitimate websites will provide sufficient information for the marketing manager to make a decision in a particular situation. More formal information systems, however, provide a great deal more information that can help guide strategic decisions (changes in demographics can lead to new market opportunities) or address critical tactical issues (shorten call wait times for customer service).[8] Exhibit 3.2 identifies five common internal sources of data collected as a regular

EXHIBIT 3.2 | Internal Information Sources

part of doing business. Unfortunately, managers are often not aware of all the information in their own company.

From the Customer's Order to Order Fulfillment Tracking a customer's initial inquiry through to order placement, delivery, payment, and follow-up after the purchase offers insight about the customer as well as insight about how well the company is working. CRM systems use customer data collected through market information systems to help drive customer-centric strategies as discussed in Chapter 6. More specifically, the data collected and analyzed in a CRM system enable companies to:

- **Identify the frequency and size of customer orders.** By charting the frequency, size, and specific items included in an order, it's possible to assess customer satisfaction
- **Determine the actual cost of a customer order.** Tools such as activity-based cost accounting can allocate time and overhead costs to specific customers. By combining that with information from each customer order, it is possible to get accurate cost and profitability measures of individual customers.
- **Rank customers based on established criteria like profitability.** Not all customers are equal, and the customer mix changes over time. Companies need to understand how each customer rates on a defined set of criteria to better allocate current resources and develop strategies for future growth.
- **Calculate the efficiency of the company's production and distribution system.** Tracking customer orders makes it possible to assess many of the company's critical functions.

Heard on the Street—Sales Information System One of the best internal information sources is the sales force. Salespeople are on the front lines of the company-customer interface and have unique access to the customer. As a result, they are an excellent information source not only about the customer but also about market trends and even the competition.[9] This is particularly true in a business-to-business environment where salespeople are often the primary method for communicating with customers. Salespeople are usually the first to hear about changes with the customer, such as new personnel or the need for new products. What's more, as they interact with customers, salespeople frequently learn a great deal about competitor tactics and plans.

Regrettably, companies time and again fail to maximize this information source. While salespeople may share what they learn with local management or other salespeople, companies have traditionally not had formal systems of collecting and analyzing data from the sales force.[10] This is changing, however, as management creates formal sales information systems to collect, analyze, store, and distribute information from the field to appropriate decision makers in the company.[11] A sales information system includes:

- **Formal systems for collecting data (getting the data).** Many salespeople write call reports summarizing each sales call. Much of the information on a call report is relevant in a sales information system.

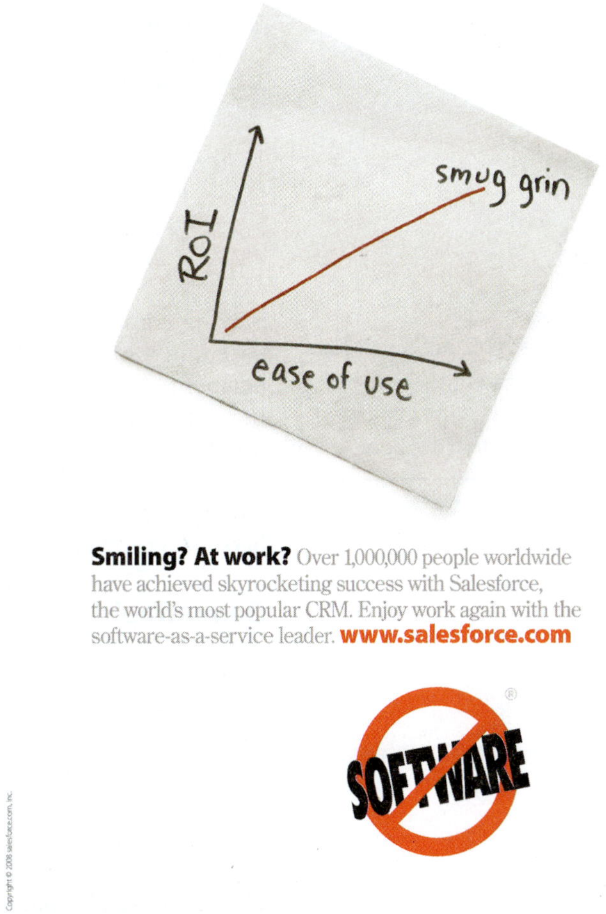

Salesforce.com has been successful providing online CRM applications that allow salespeople to access customer data easily. Moreover, its customizable applications encourage salespeople to input customer data into the company sales information system.

This includes products discussed with the customer, customer concerns, and changes in personnel.

- **Interpretation of data (analysis).** This may be done at the local level by sales managers who add additional insight to the "raw" data from the salesperson. In more sophisticated sales information systems, people at regional or national offices will analyze data from many salespeople looking for broad trends.
- **Distribution of data (getting the analysis to decision makers and back into the field).** A sales information system needs to distribute the information to management as part of a larger market information system. At the same time, it is important to get the information back out to the sales force. When trends, problems or solutions to problems, and opportunities are identified, salespeople benefit from learning quickly so they can respond in the field. Much of this information has a time value. If salespeople do not get the analysis in a timely manner, much of the benefit will be lost. For example, suppose a company learns from several salespeople that a major competitor is contacting customers about a new product. Getting this information to the entire sales force quickly will enable them to develop responses for their own customers.

Balancing research with management insight is a challenge. Nielsen, one of the world's leading media research organizations, is now able to track what you buy in addition to what you watch. By collecting purchase data from banks, the company, in theory, can match what people watch with what they buy. Marketers will soon be able to make "purchase based" media targeting decisions instead of "viewer based"; however, many companies are still not convinced the new approach works as well as the traditional methodology. Knowing when to make changes to marketing strategy requires management insight as well as reliable data.[12]

External Sources—Collecting Information Outside the Company

LO 3-3

Explain essential external (outside the firm) information collection methods.

Staying connected to the business environment is no longer optional. Success is based, in part, on both the quality and quantity of information available to management. As a result, most companies engage in collecting, analyzing, and storing data from the macro environment on a continuous basis known as **marketing intelligence**. The ability to do this well is a competitive advantage; successful companies accurately analyze and interpret environmental information, then develop strategies to take advantage of opportunities and deal with threats before they become a problem (see Exhibit 3.3).

Demographics Populations change over time, and companies must be aware of those changes. Not tracking and responding to demographic changes is a management failure because the data are easy to obtain and major changes occur slowly. Surprisingly, many companies do not do a good job of either learning about demographic trends or responding to them.

Demographics can be defined as the statistical characteristics of human populations, such as age or income, used to identify markets. They provide a statistical description of a group of people and are extremely useful in marketing for two reasons. First, *demographics help define a market.* How old is a typical customer? How educated? What is the typical customer's income? These are all demographic characteristics that help describe a market. For example, a typical Mercedes-Benz automobile owner in the United States is a male, successful, and over 50 years old. By analyzing demographics, a company can define not only the "typical"

EXHIBIT 3.3 | External Forces Affect Marketing Decisions

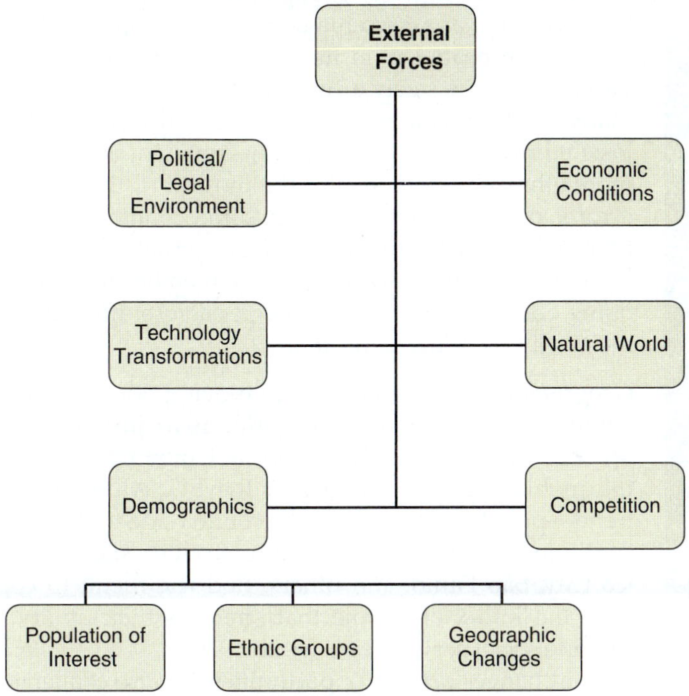

customer but also its market at large. Second, *studying demographics helps identify new opportunities.* As baby boomers age, they will need, among other things, retirement communities. This represents an opportunity for companies to build unique retirement properties specifically for baby boomers.

Companies that deal directly with consumers develop customer profiles based on demographic information and compare their profiles against those of competitors. For example, the typical Mercedes-Benz owner tends to be older than a BMW owner. Companies even create pictures of their "average" customer, highlighting key demographic data (age, gender, and ethnicity).

Populations of Interest Marketers are not interested in all groups, only populations of interest. The difficult part for many marketers is separating relevant demographic data from irrelevant. For example, does cell phone maker Samsung need to know that world population growth is faster in less developed countries (among less developed countries the population is growing at 2 percent per year while developed countries are growing at less than 1 percent)? Your first response might be no as Samsung is likely interested in more developed countries with established cellular networks and people who can afford the technology. However, while less developed countries do not need the more expensive Samsung Galaxy phones, they could use older, less expensive technology to encourage economic development and build a communication network. Targeting less developed countries may offer Samsung an opportunity to establish a market presence in these countries even as they develop economically.

Ethnic Groups Many countries are becoming more ethnically diverse as individuals increase their mobility. While some countries, such as the United Arab Emirates in the Middle East, have populations composed of a single ethnic group, others like the United States are much more ethnically diverse. Nearly three-quarters of the U.S. population is white, but trends project that whites will be less than 50 percent of the population in less than 30 years. Hispanics have shown the

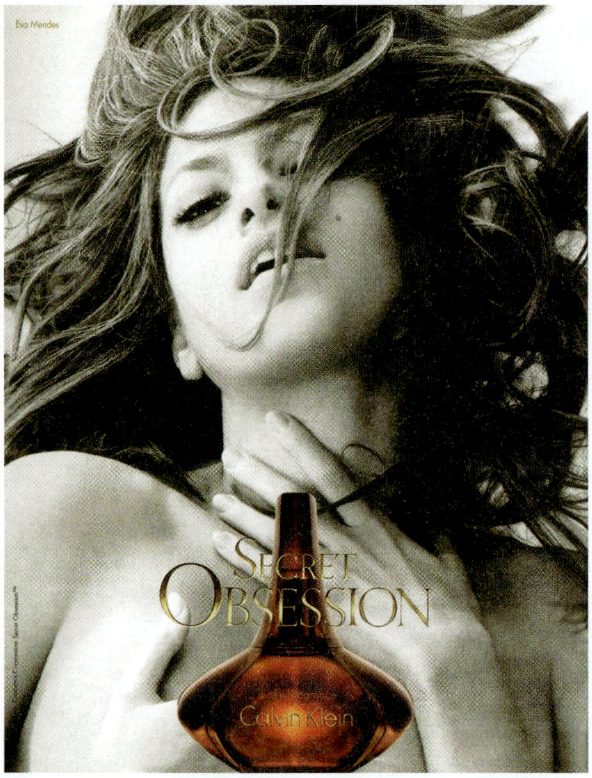

As the Hispanic population grows, advertisers continue to seek endorsements from Hispanic celebrities like Eve Mendes.

greatest increase among ethnic groups in the United States over the past 10 years. They are currently the second-largest minority group and are expected to continue growing as a percentage of the U.S. population.

The European Union has made it possible for individuals to move freely around member countries. While many of the member countries are still dominated by local ethnic groups, the European continent is becoming more ethnically diverse. For the most part, this leads to greater opportunities; however, some countries such as France find it difficult to assimilate certain groups into their culture. The market challenge then becomes developing effective marketing strategies across different ethnicities living in the same area.

Geographic Changes People are moving not only in the United States but around the world. As we just noted, the opening of borders in the European Union has increased the mobility of those living in the EU. A decades-old trend—people moving from the countryside to the city—continues around the globe and some cities, such as Mexico City, São Paulo, and others, find it difficult to cope with the influx of people that stretches their ability to provide social services (see Exhibit 3.4).

The changes present opportunities but also challenges. The growth of Asian cultures means many companies must adjust their marketing strategies to fit the unique needs of Asian consumers. Appliance companies such as Whirlpool have redesigned their products to fit in smaller Asian kitchens. Coincidentally, downsizing products is a strategy consistent with the migration of people to urban centers. Mr. Coffee, Braun, and others have created coffeemakers designed for single households in the smaller living environments often found in large cities.

Economic Conditions Companies are keenly interested in the ability of their customers to purchase products and services. It is not surprising then that a good

EXHIBIT 3.4 | Top 10 Cities in Population with Projected Growth Rates

Rank	Urban Area	Population (millions)			Rank		
		1990	2011	2025	1990	2011	2025
1	Tokyo, Japan	32.5	37.2	38.7	1	1	1
2	Delhi, India	8.3	22.7	32.9		2	2
3	Mexico City, Mexico	15.3	20.4	24.6	3	3	5
4	New York–Newark	16.1	20.4	23.6	2	4	6
5	Shanghai, China	13.3	20.2	28.4		5	3
6	São Paulo, Brazil	14.8	19.9	23.2	4	6	7
7	Mumbai (Bombay), India	12.4	19.7	26.6	5	7	4
8	Beijing, China	10.8	15.6	22.6		8	9
9	Dhaka, Bangladesh	6.7	15.4	22.9		9	8
10	Kolkata (Calcutta), India	10.9	14.4	18.7	7	10	

Source: UN-Habitat, *The State of the World's Cities 2012/2013: Prosperity of Cities* (2012).

understanding of current and future economic trends is important in an effective market information system. There are two principal types of economic knowledge. The study of individual economic activity (firm, household, or prices) is known as **microeconomics**. At the other end of the spectrum, **macroeconomics** refers to the study of economic activity in terms of broad measures of output (gross national product or GNP) and input as well as the interaction among various sectors of an entire economy. Both are important for marketing managers. Microeconomics helps marketing managers understand how individuals set priorities and make buying decisions. Macroeconomics, on the other hand, gives a "big picture" perspective for an economy and can be helpful at looking for broad economic trends.

Indicators such as the GNP measure the health of an economy and are helpful in spotting trends. For example, if the GNP goes up, it is generally viewed as a sign the economy is doing well. As an economy slows, the GNP will slow.

Technology Transformations Few areas in business have been more affected by technology than marketing. Technology has been one of the major catalysts for change in the marketplace. Faster, smaller, and easier-to-use computers and powerful software facilitate sophisticated analyses right on the desks of front-line managers from anywhere in the world. Complex supply chain and manufacturing processes coupled with Internet connectivity allow customers real-time access to the entire manufacturing process. Consider the online order process for HP. A consumer places the order online, gets a final price and expected delivery date, then follows it from the assembly plant literally to their front door with a tracking number from the shipping company.

Changing technology has radically altered the face of television by moving it onto computers. Formerly providers of DVDs, companies like Netflix and Amazon have become digital streaming services, allowing consumers to watch what they want, when they want in real time. Today these companies have taken the next step by creating original content, rather than serving as a vehicle for transmitting third-party-produced content.[13]

Marketing managers need to know the role of technology in their business today and also, perhaps even more importantly, its role in the future. Successfully assimilating technology into a business takes time and money. Almost every organization has had at least one negative experience with technology. Hershey Foods, for example, tried to bring a new CRM system online at the busiest selling season of the year for candy, Halloween, only to find problems implementing the system. The company estimated it was unable to fill $100 million worth of candy orders as a result of issues related to integrating the new software.[14] Read Ethical Dimension 3 to see a growing concern in collecting accurate information over the Internet.

Natural World Everyone lives on planet Earth, and business operates within the constraints of available natural resources. Two key issues drive marketers' need to know about the natural world. First, individuals, governments, and business all recognize the need to manage the available resources well. It took the world roughly 150 years to use 1 trillion barrels of oil; however, it is predicted the world will use the next trillion barrels by 2030 and, while there may be a lot of oil left, it will be harder to get and more expensive. Governments and businesses are concerned about the effect of increasing energy costs on economic growth. Other resources such as water are also becoming increasingly scarce in parts of the world. In the Western United States, for example, growth in communities such as Phoenix is considered in the context of water access, which limits future development as water becomes scarcer.

A second concern regarding the natural world is pollution. In some parts of the world, pollution takes a significant toll on the quality of life and economic

ETHICAL DIMENSION 3

The Source of the Click

Internet ad spending is currently $100 billion and is projected to reach more than $160 billion by 2016. The pay structure has evolved along two distinct lines. About half of all Internet ads are priced based on the number of people viewing the ad, similar to traditional television advertising. The other model for Internet advertising charges by the click. If someone views an ad and then chooses to click on the ad through to the advertiser, the advertiser pays a fee ranging from a few pennies to $20. A critical assumption is the click's legitimacy; it is supposed to represent someone actively seeking information from the advertiser's site.

Two companies control the vast majority of Internet ad placements—Yahoo and Google. While Google and Yahoo generate most of their revenue on legitimate websites, they also send ads to affiliated sites, known as "domain parking websites," which are basically advertising sites with very little content. Publicly they state these sites provide a useful service by directing Internet surfers to relevant information. However, companies are starting to express concern that some of these sites may actually be generating illegitimate clicks, clicks by individuals (or other computers) who are not legitimate potential customers.

Click fraud, estimated at more than $1 billion, has become a big issue for many Internet advertisers. Websites with names such as "insurance1472.com" are dummy sites located primarily in Asia and Eastern Europe that generate false clicks. The process works like this. First, ABC Company contracts with Google or Yahoo to advertise on the Internet and negotiates the fee ABC will pay for each click from an ABC ad to the company website. Second, Google or Yahoo displays the ad on legitimate websites but also sends the ad to domain parking websites. Third, these sites distribute the ads to parked websites that are often just lists of ads. Fourth, the owner of the parked website sends out a list of sites to individuals known collectively as "paid-to-read groups." These individuals' role is to click on ads, for which they receive a small payment. Finally, Google or Yahoo charges ABC Company for the click, then shares part of the revenue with the domain parking website, which shares it with the other participants in the fraud.

Adding to the challenge for advertisers is the difficult position of Google and Yahoo, who make more money when click fraud occurs. Both companies strongly deny any wrongdoing and actively police their ad placements. However, both have settled click fraud class action suits with advertisers and instituted a number of changes to their business model to curb the problem.[15]

Ethical Perspective

1. **Advertisers:** How would your view of Internet advertising change if the statistics related to the number of people who "click through" an ad were not accurate?
2. **Google and Yahoo:** While you are concerned with click fraud, the process actually generates significant revenue. What do you do?

growth in a community. In Mexico City, driving is limited for everyone to certain days during the week as congestion and smog create huge clouds of pollution that hang over the city. In China, government statistics show that of the lakes and rivers monitored for pollution levels, nearly 20 percent contained water considered unusable even for agricultural irrigation, causing losses in the billions of dollars.[16] These concerns influence marketers as they make decisions about how and where products are manufactured. For example, energy companies such as Chevron are investing billions to identify and develop more environmentally safe energy.

Political/Legal Environment Political judgments and, more broadly, the legal environment significantly affect company decisions and sometimes an entire industry. In 2003, the National Do Not Call Registry was created to minimize intrusive telemarketing calls. By registering, individuals protect themselves from telemarketing calls. Telemarketing companies are subject to significant fines if they call someone listed on the register. Millions of people signed up, and many companies were forced to reconfigure their marketing communications strategy.[17]

Local, state, and federal legislatures pass more business-related legislation than ever before. In addition, government agencies are more active in monitoring business activity. During the 1990s the Securities and Exchange Commission actively pursued several antitrust actions, the largest against Microsoft for illegal monopoly activity. As a result, Microsoft made changes to Windows 8 that opened it up to outside software vendors. More recently, the Dodd–Frank Wall Street Reform and Consumer Protection Act, passed in 2010, required banks and other financial institutions to dramatically change many aspects of their businesses including lending practices.

Competition One of the most important external environmental factors to consider is the competition. Companies want to know as much as possible about competitors' products and strategies. In highly competitive markets, companies are constantly adjusting their strategies to the competition. Airlines, for example, track competitor pricing and adjust their pricing almost immediately to changes in the marketplace. When one airline offers a sale in a specific market, competitors will soon follow with sales in the same market. Identifying, analyzing, and effectively dealing with competitors is the focus in Chapter 2.

MARKET RESEARCH SYSTEMS

Marketing managers are confronted with an unlimited number of problems, opportunities, and issues that require specific answers. Sometimes the information needed is not available from other sources or even from the company's own market information system. To get specific answers to important management questions, market research is necessary.

The Importance of Market Research to Managers

Consider the following:

- You are a marketing manager for Harley-Davidson Motorcycles, and 90 percent of your bikes are sold to men. You believe women are a great potential target market but have had little success selling Harleys to them. What do you do?
- You are the director of advertising for McDonald's, and the company is getting ready to roll out a new advertising campaign designed to increase sales of a new sandwich. However, senior management wants to know if it will work. What do you do?

The answers to situations like these lies in market research. **Market research** is the methodical identification, collection, analysis, and distribution of data related to discovering then solving marketing problems or opportunities and enhancing good decision making. Several things come out of this definition. Good market research:

LO 3-4

Recognize the value of market research and its role in marketing.

- **Follows a well-defined set of activities and does not happen by accident.** Rather, it comes as a result of the methodical identification, collection, analysis, and distribution of data.
- **Enhances the validity of the information.** Anyone can "Google" a topic and come up with a lot of information. However, following the market research process enhances the confidence that the research will discover then solve marketing problems and opportunities.
- **Is impartial and objective.** It does not prejudge the information or develop answers to fit an already decided outcome; rather, it enhances good decision making.

Market research is also big business. In 2012 nearly $19 billion was spent on market research worldwide with Europe ($8 billion) and the United States ($6.7 billion) conducting the most research.[18] Some of these departments, such as McDonald's internal research group, are larger than many research companies and spend hundreds of millions of dollars a year conducting market research for their own organizations. Exhibit 3.5 lists the top market research companies in the world.

EXHIBIT 3.5 | Top Five Market Research Companies in the World

Organization	Headquarters	Total Revenue
The Nielsen Company	New York	$5.43 billion
Kantar	London/Fairfield, CT	$3.33 billion
Ipsos	New York	$2.30 billion
Gfk SE	Nuremberg, Germany	$1.95 billion
IMS Health Inc.	Parsippany, NJ	$775 million

Source: 2013 Honomichl Report, June 30, 2013, *Marketing News,* p. 25.

The Market Research Process

LO 3-5

Define the market research process.

At the heart of the market research process is a search for understanding. Sometimes management seeks answers to a particular problem. In other situations, an opportunity needs to be evaluated before committing resources. By following the market research process, marketing managers can have greater confidence in the information they are receiving and, hopefully, make better informed decisions. As shown in Exhibit 3.6, the process consists of six steps.

EXHIBIT 3.6 | The Market Research Process

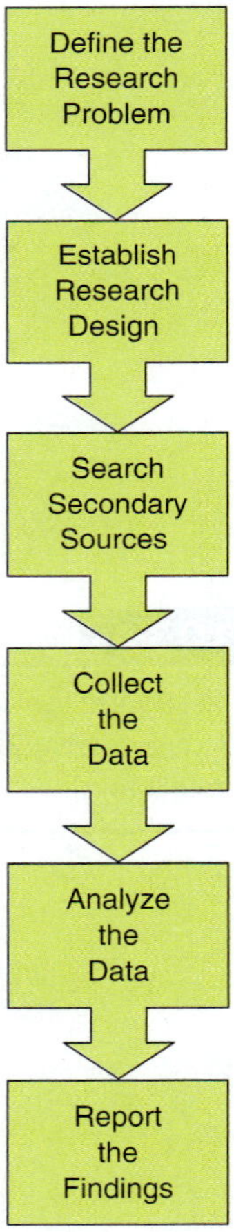

Define the Research Problem One of the biggest challenges facing a market researcher is accurately defining the problem. What exactly is the issue/opportunity/problem? Often managers are not clear about the problem and need help defining it. It is not uncommon for a market research professional to get a call that starts something like this, "I have a problem. Sales have been falling for six months and I am losing business to my competitors." The researcher knows that the real problem is not the company's declining sales; falling sales are the result, a symptom, of the real issue. Market research can be a useful tool helping senior managers identify and deal with the real issue.[19]

Given that management often does not have a clear understanding of the problem, defining the research problem involves two distinct steps. First, management, working with researchers and marketing decision makers, defines the **management research deliverable**. Exactly what does management want to do with this research? Keep in mind that decision makers are looking for information to help them make better, more informed decisions. For example, if you are the director of advertising for McDonald's, you want to increase sales of a new sandwich, and a new advertising campaign can help accomplish that goal. However, before you decide to spend a lot of money on the campaign, you want to know if it is going to be successful.

Once the management research deliverable has been identified, the next step is to define the **research problem**. Exactly what information is needed to help management in this situation? In our example that means assessing the target market's response to the new advertising campaign.

In the McDonald's example, the research problem is fairly straightforward. However, there are often multiple research problems and researchers will have to prioritize which problems to study first. Consider the example of Harley-Davidson motorcycles and targeting more female riders. Management may want to know:

EXHIBIT 3.7 | Research Design Activities

Activity	Question to Be Answered
Type of research	What kind of research needs to be done?
Nature of data	What kind of data do we need?
Nature of data collection	How should we collect the data?
Information content	What do we need to know?
Sampling plan	Who should be included in the research?

(1) How many women would be in the market for a motorcycle and, more specifically, how many women would be in the market for a large bike like a Harley? (2) What kind of motorcycle would they want to buy? (3) If Harley-Davidson were to create a new bike, how would loyal, dedicated Harley-Davidson owners react to it? You can begin to see why it is necessary for management and researchers to prioritize the problems and identify which research issues to address first.[20]

Establish the Research Design Following problem definition, companies must establish a research design, or a plan of action for attacking the research problem. Research designs consist of five activities, each of which is designed to address a specific question about the research process, as shown in Exhibit 3.7. It is critical that researchers develop and execute a research design so that decision makers can have confidence in the research findings. Effective market research is dependent on creating a research design and then executing it.[21] Conversely, and this is a problem for decision makers, bad market research cannot yield good information. When this happens, it severely limits management's confidence in the results.

While multiple designs often could work in any research situation, it is important to specify one design and follow it throughout the research. Decisions made at the research design stage affect the rest of the project, and it is not appropriate to start over once a project has begun. Let's examine each of these activities.

> Ten years of planning, design, and building culminated in the installation of Martha Jefferson Hospital in its new location. In creating the new space, designers relied on evidence-based design, which uses meticulous and cutting-edge research as the foundation for all decisions. This produces highly functional, effective, and relevant designs. It paid off for Martha Jefferson, which won eight prestigious patient satisfaction awards from Professional Research Consultants, and now performs "in the top 10 percent of hospitals nationwide."[22]

Type of Research: What Kind of Research Needs to Be Done? Not all market research involves complex, costly studies. People do market research all the time and don't think of it that way. For example, a salesperson who visits a website to learn more about a customer before a sales call is engaged in market research. The key is to fit the research to the unique requirements of the situation.

There are three basic types of research: exploratory, descriptive, and causal. While the complexity and methodology change for each type of research, it is not necessarily true that causal research is better than exploratory. Let's look at each research type more closely.

As the name implies, **exploratory research** is really about discovery. Reasons for conducting exploratory research include:

- Clarifying the research problem.
- Developing hypotheses for testing in descriptive or causal research.
- Gaining additional insight to help in survey development or to identify other research variables for study.
- Answering the research question.

Many times conducting exploratory research will provide sufficient information to answer the research question. Even if more sophisticated research is needed, exploratory research is usually the first step.

Descriptive research seeks to describe or explain some phenomenon. Often this involves something going on in the marketplace and can include issues such as:

- Identifying the characteristics of our target market.
- Assessing competitor actions in the marketplace.
- Determining how customers use our product.
- Discovering differences across demographic characteristics (age, education, income) with respect to the use of our product or that of our competitors.

Descriptive research uses many different methods including secondary data, surveys, and observation. Some of these methods are also used in exploratory research. The difference is how you use the information. Descriptive research uses a different, more restrictive and rigorous methodology than exploratory research.

Descriptive research identifies associations between variables; for example, the customers for Harley-Davidson motorcycles tend to be middle-aged, successful men. **Causal research** tries to discover the cause and effect between variables.

For example, in our Harley-Davidson example, does an increase in Harley-Davidson advertising directed toward men lead to increased sales of Harley-Davidson motorcycles? This can be particularly useful in making important marketing decisions. Consider a critical decision faced by all marketing managers: What effect will a price increase have on sales? Causal research can determine the change in the number of sales for different price levels. The types of research vary a great deal, so the question becomes what kind of research is appropriate in a given circumstance? The following factors help make that determination.

Benefit versus cost: Before making any other decisions about the type of marketing research to use, it is essential to assess the benefits versus the costs. Put simply, if the benefits of doing the research do not exceed the cost, don't do the research.

Time until decision: Decision makers sometimes have very little time between realizing a need for additional information and making the decision. When time is very short (a matter of days), it is simply not possible to conduct in-depth market research. The Internet can cut the time needed for a study from months to weeks, but when time is short researchers may have to rely on more exploratory research and the use of secondary data.

Nature of the decision: The more strategic the decision, the more important the information and the greater the need for primary data. Conversely, if the decision is primarily tactical (for example, decisions about where to place advertising), secondary data, like reviewing a medium's demographics and rate card, will likely be sufficient to make the decision.

Availability of data: Companies already have a lot of data as a result of CRM and other internal information systems. Consequently, it may not always be necessary to collect primary data when existing or secondary data will provide the necessary answers to the research problems.

Nature of Data: What Kind of Data Do We Need? Once the type of research has been determined, the next step is to evaluate what kind of data is needed for the research. The nature of the data will determine how the data are collected and is driven by the kind of research the company is undertaking.[23] The basic question is, does the research require **primary data**—data collected specifically for this research question—or will **secondary data**—data collected for some other purpose than the problem currently being considered—be sufficient? Even if primary data are collected, almost all research involves some secondary data collection, which we will talk about in the next section.

Primary data are collected using one of two approaches: qualitative and quantitative. **Qualitative research** is less structured and can employ methods such as surveys and interviews to collect the data; qualitative research employs small samples and is not meant to be used for statistical analyses. **Quantitative research** is used to develop a more measured understanding using statistical analysis to assess and quantify the results.[24] Now let's look at the nature of data collection.

Nature of Data Collection: How Should the Data Be Collected? No one technique is better than another, but it is important to use the right technique based on an assessment of the research problem and research type. Let's evaluate the various approaches to collecting primary data. Exploratory research techniques include focus groups and in-depth interviews.

Without question, the most widely used qualitative research technique is focus groups. Perhaps for this reason, it is also one of the most misused.[25] A **focus group** is a meeting (either in person or increasingly online) of 6 to 10 people that is moderated by a professional who carefully moves the conversation through a defined agenda in an unstructured, open format. Generally, the participants are selected on the basis of some criteria.[26] For example, they may be current customers or possess certain demographic characteristics (age, income, education), but they will all have at least one shared attribute.

The value of focus groups lies in the richness of the discussion. A good moderator can draw out a lot of information from the participants. For example, the marketing manager for Harley-Davidson might use focus groups to learn how women relate to motorcycles. The trade-off is a deeper understanding of each participant versus a more superficial knowledge of additional people. Herein lies the mistake many people make with focus groups. They assume that the results of a focus group are generalizable to a population of interest. This is not the case. Focus groups are not a representative sample and care should be taken to interpret the results properly. However, focus groups do provide insights on an issue that are useful to researchers as they develop quantitative research techniques. Focus group data provide a good starting point from which researchers can develop specific questions used in survey instruments.[27]

Another common qualitative technique is the in-depth interview. An **in-depth interview** is an unstructured (or loosely structured) interview with an individual who has been chosen based on some characteristic of interest, often a demographic attribute. This technique differs from focus groups in that the interview is done one on one rather than in a small group. The same advantages and disadvantages are present here as with focus groups so researchers most often use this technique to help formulate other types of research (surveys, observational research).

Descriptive research techniques include surveys, behavioral data, and observational data. Of the quantitative research techniques used to collect primary data, surveys, in their various forms, are the most prevalent. While they can be used informally in exploratory research, their most common purpose is in descriptive research. **Surveys** are structured questionnaires given to a sample group of individuals representing the population of interest and are intended to solicit specific responses to explicit questions.[28]

Harley-Davidson does market research to learn more about developing products that appeal to women.

There are a number of survey methods. Historically, mail and telephone surveys were most common. Today, electronic surveys have become widely adopted for their speed, ease of use, and relatively low cost. E-surveys can easily be done over the Internet using services such as Zoomerang or Survey Monkey.[29]

Behavioral data include information about when, what, and how often customers purchase products and services as well as other customer "touches" (for example, when they contact the organization with a complaint or question). When companies match this kind of information with demographic and psychographic information, they can see differences in purchase patterns. Behavior is usually more reliable than surveys because it is based on what the respondents actually do rather than what they say they are going to do.

In 2013 Raytheon developed a data mining software program called RIOT, Rapid Information Overlay Technology. This software tracks consumers via their social media accounts and predicts their future destinations using social media posts. Using the coordinates created by those social media posts, RIOT develops a list of tendencies for that individual and eventually predicts where they will be next. Among the many companies and organizations interested in the software is the federal government, which has expressed interest for use in law enforcement and national security.[30]

It is possible to get a lot of insight about people by simply watching what they do in various situations. **Observational data** are the behavioral patterns among the population of interest. One of the most common uses of this type of research is in retailing. Retailers watch how people move through a store, noting what aisles they go down and where they spend their time. In recent years a more intrusive approach to observational data has been used to actually examine people in a personal setting (for example, their homes). In this approach, the observer enters into the world of the individual rather than standing back and simply watching activities. Researchers see people in a very personal environment to better understand how people use and interact with products.

A variation of observational data is mechanical observation. **Mechanical observation** uses a device to chronicle activity. Some forms of mechanical observation are benign and not intrusive on the individual. Turnstiles, for example, record people coming into or going out of an area. Traffic counters record the number of cars on a given street for a set time period.

There are, however, mechanical devices that are more invasive. *Mechanical devices* can be very useful for researchers but are often used sparingly because of the cost and also the bias associated with the respondent's awareness of the device. Eye cameras can track the movement of an eye as the individual watches an ad. From this researchers can determine what the person sees first, what he is focusing on in the ad, and how his eyes move around the ad. Another device, the galvanometer, is attached to the skin and measures subtle changes in skin temperature. Researchers can then determine if the respondent found the ad interesting.

Information Content: What Do We Need to Know? A critical part of research design involves determining exactly what information is needed and how to frame the questions to get that information. From the questions used in focus groups to long questionnaires, it is important to consider the structure and wording as well as the response choices. Most often this issue comes up in designing questionnaires. As the most commonly used primary research technique, the survey questionnaire allows a lot of variability in its design and structure. Some surveys, such as the comment cards, are short and ask only a few questions. Others, such as new car satisfaction surveys, can be much longer and ask dozens of questions. No matter what the situation, careful attention must be paid to the design, structure, and format of each question. For years marketers have been interested in building and measuring customer loyalty.

Developed by Satmetrix, Bain & Company, and Frederick Reichfield, the Net Promoter Score (NPS) provides a simple measure of loyalty by asking one question: Would the customer recommend a brand to a friend or colleague? Many companies have measured a customer's willingness to recommend a product for many years, but the current approach suggests one question will measure loyalty accurately. Not everyone agrees, and critics point out the measure is not appropriate in all situations. For example, senior management, irrespective of current user preferences, often directs important capital expenditures, such as large IT purchases.[31]

Today, researchers must also consider the method of survey delivery. For example, mail surveys differ significantly from telephone surveys because respondents interact with the questions differently. Electronic surveys present a different challenge, although their structure is more easily adapted from a mail questionnaire.

Researchers must consider which of the many types of question formats is most appropriate for the situation. One of the most basic decisions is whether to use open-ended or closed-ended questions. **Open-ended questions** encourage respondents to be expressive and offer the opportunity to provide more detailed, qualitative responses. As a result, these kinds of questions are often used in exploratory research. **Closed-ended questions**, on the other hand, are more precise and provide specific responses. As a result, they allow for more quantitative analysis and are most often used in descriptive research. Frequently, questionnaires will contain a mix of open-ended and closed-ended questions to get both qualitative and quantitative information in a single survey.

Sampling Plan: Who Should Be Included in the Research? Once the other elements of the research design have been developed, it is time to consider who will be selected for the research. The most basic decision is whether to conduct a census or to sample a group of individuals from the population. A **census** is a comprehensive record of each individual in the population of interest, while a **sample** is a subgroup of the population selected for participation in the research. A census may seem like the better approach because everyone in the population is included in the study. Unfortunately, most of the time the number and diversity of the population are so large that it is simply not physically or financially possible to communicate with everyone. As a result, sampling is by far the preferred method of selecting people for market research.[32]

There are two basic approaches to sampling: probability and nonprobability sampling. It is important to keep in mind that one is not necessarily better than the other; rather, the key to making the right choice is to match the sampling approach with the research. Budgetary constraints will also likely influence the decision. **Probability sampling** uses a specific set of procedures to identify individuals from the population to be included in the research. From here, a specific protocol is identified to select a number of individuals for the research. As an example, suppose Bank of America is interested in finding out more about a group of its customers holding a certain kind of credit card. Let's assume there are 10 million customers holding this particular card. The bank wants to randomly choose 5,000 individuals for the survey. That means that everyone has a $5{,}000/10{,}000{,}000 = .0005$ chance of being selected. Next, Bank of America will create an algorithm to randomly identify 5,000 individuals from the list of 10 million. The algorithm ensures that, while everyone has a .0005 chance of being selected, only 5,000 will be sampled from the entire group.

A second approach is called **nonprobability sampling** and, as the name implies, the probability of everyone in the population being included in the sample is not identified. The chance of selection may be zero or not known. This type of sampling is often done when time and/or financial constraints limit the opportunity to conduct probability sampling. The most significant problem with nonprobability sampling is that it significantly limits the ability to perform statistical analyses and generalize conclusions beyond the sample itself.

Search Secondary Sources Secondary data are almost always part of market research. Searching a wide variety of sources and compiling additional information provide greater insight to the research problem and supplement the primary data collected for a specific study. We have already discussed the availability of information inside the company, so let's turn our attention to external sources of secondary data.

Government Sources Federal, state, and local governments are an important resource in collecting information on a variety of topics. For example, the U.S. Census Bureau publishes a library full of reports on business and consumer demographic trends. In 2012, the Census Bureau released the most recent Economic Census providing an in-depth analysis of business activity in the United States. Often, data are available by zip code, which can be useful for marketers in targeting specific groups of people. States also publish additional data on economic activity. Finally, local governments publish records such as business licenses as well as general economic activity in that area. Governments provide a great deal of information on a variety of activities. From here marketers can identify areas, even down to specific streets, and get detailed demographic information, which is very useful in a number of ways including targeted marketing communications campaigns.

Market Research Organizations A number of market research organizations publish data helpful to marketers. One resource many people are familiar with is Nielsen Media Research's TV ratings. The ratings are the basis for establishing national, cable, and local advertising rates. Another service well known to automobile enthusiasts is the J. D. Power automobile quality and customer satisfaction rankings. While automobile manufacturers pay a fee for more detailed information, the public has access to the overall rankings.

Other organizations publish data that can be useful to marketers in particular industries. For example, MMGY Global publishes several reports on both the leisure and business travel markets every year. These reports profile travel patterns and market segments in the travel industry. They are very useful for any business connected to the travel industry such as airlines, hotels, and cruise lines.

There are also information data services such as Information Resources, InfoScan, and Nielsen's ScanTrack that track scanner data from thousands of retailers. These organizations match sales data with demographic records to give a detailed picture of how well a product is doing in a particular area or within a certain target market. This information is useful for consumer products companies that want to assess the success of specific marketing activities (for example, how well is an advertising campaign working with a target market).

The Internet It is now possible to access a huge amount of information using search engines to identify hundreds, even thousands, of information sources. Care should be taken, however, to evaluate the validity of the data and the reliability of the source. Generally two kinds of data sources can be found on the Internet. The first is market research organizations (such as the ones we just discussed) willing to share or sell market data. A second source is "general knowledge" sites such as business publications, academic research sites, or other independent sources that have data applicable to the research problem.[33]

Advantages and Disadvantages of Secondary Data Sources As we discussed earlier, secondary data are almost always the first place to go in conducting a market research project. Even if primary data are collected, it is a good idea to see what has been done already that may be applicable now. Secondary data come with two primary advantages. First, it's a fast way to get information. Just a few minutes on a search engine can yield a lot of information. Of course, it takes much longer than that to look through it all. A second, and related advantage, is cost. Secondary data are relatively less expensive. Even if a company chooses to subscribe to organizations such as J. D. Power and Associates, thereby getting access to more detailed data, it is still more cost-effective than conducting a primary research study.

Of course, there are very distinct disadvantages. First and most important, secondary data will, almost by definition, not fit the research problem exactly. As a result, a specific answer to the research problem will not be possible using secondary data alone. Second, secondary data are not current. Sometimes the information may be only a few weeks or months old or it may be dated to the point where it is no longer useful for the current project. Third, without a clear understanding of the methodology used to collect and interpret the secondary data, one should be a little skeptical about its validity.[34]

More and more companies such as Nordstrom are moving to digital loyalty programs as opposed to physical. These programs not only create repeat business, but also capture data on their consumers. Eventually, this collection of data can be utilized by Nordstrom to better interact with its customers, create more appealing offers and incentives, and eventually help drive these consumers to the brick-and-mortar locations, or interact with the company online. Many large retailers are seeing opportunity in digital loyalty programs, in that they will provide differentiation from other retail applications and help influence consumer choices to return to a particular location rather than seeing them as a commodity.[35]

Collect the Data Now, it is time to find and engage the respondent to collect the data. **Data collection** involves access and distribution of the survey to the respondent, then recording the respondent's responses and making the data available for analysis. A company can choose to collect the data using its own resources or hire a market research firm to administer the data collection. The choice often depends on the company's internal expertise in market research as well as the resources required to complete the job.

This stage in the market research process presents several unique challenges. First, data collection is often the most costly element in the market research process. Second, the greatest potential for error exists as data are collected.[36] For example, respondents may not respond to certain questions or may fill out the survey incorrectly. Finally, the people collecting the survey may be biased or make mistakes.

Technology, in the form of online surveys, can help to mitigate some of the issues with data collection. For example, electronic survey methods are often more cost-effective than other survey methodologies. In addition, there is less chance of transcription error as no one has to input the data into a computer. Unfortunately, not everyone has access to a computer. As a result, certain target markets may be underrepresented if a survey requires completion of an online survey. Additionally, people may still input inaccurate responses.[37] We will talk about online research tools in the next section.

Photodex ProShow Gold is one of many software packages designed to enhance presentations. The presentation of a research report often includes sophisticated software designed to clearly present research findings and recommendations.

Analyze the Data Once the data are collected, coded, and verified, the next step is to analyze the information. The appropriate analysis is performed based on the research questions developed at the beginning of the research. A common mistake is using unsuitable analyses that are not supported by the data.

Analysis of the data will lead to findings that address the research questions. These findings are, in a sense, the "product" of the research. In most cases, researchers will also interpret the findings for decision makers.

Report the Findings The best research projects are only as good as the final report and presentation. If the research is done well but the report is poorly written and presented, managers will not benefit from the research. Exhibit 3.8 provides a basic framework for a research report. Note that, for managers, the key section of the report is the Executive Summary as it presents a summation of the analysis and essential findings. Keep in mind that managers are not really interested in the number of secondary data sources, the questionnaire design, or the sampling plan; rather, they want to see the findings.

EXHIBIT 3.8 | Outline of a Research Report

	Short Report		Long Report	
Report Modules	**Memo or Letter**	**Short Technical**	**Management**	**Technical**
Prefatory Information		**1**	**1**	**1**
Letter of transmittal		√	√	√
Title page		√	√	√
Authorization statement		√	√	√
Executive summary		√	√	√
Table of contents			√	√
Introduction	**1**	**2**	**2**	**2**
Problem statement	√	√	√	√
Research objectives	√	√	√	√
Background	√	√	√	√
Methodology		√ (briefly)	√ (briefly)	**3**
Sampling design				√
Research design				√
Data collection				√
Data analysis				√
Limitations		√	√	√
Findings		**3**	**4**	**4**
Conclusions	**2**	**4**	**3**	**5**
Summary and conclusions	√	√	√	√
Recommendations	√	√	√	√
Appendices		**5**	**5**	**6**
Bibliography				**7**

Source: Reprinted from Donald R. Cooper and Pamela S. Schindler, *Business Research Methods*, 12e (New York: The McGraw-Hill Companies, 2014), p. 502.

Market Research Technology

Market research has benefited from better, more cost-effective technology. The use of powerful software tools and online technologies brings research to any level in the organization. Sales managers can survey customers, analyze the results, and make decisions without costly, time-consuming external studies. Sophisticated software incorporating CRM and marketing decision support systems can do in-depth analyses that offer unique insights about customers or market trends not possible just a few years ago. In most respects, making market research tools available throughout the company has been a big success. Unfortunately, as the access to market research technology has increased, so has the misapplication of the technology. Without implementing the market research process presented earlier, no amount of technology can create worthwhile results.

LO 3-6

Illustrate current research technologies and how they are used in market research.

Online Research Tools Online research tools fall into three categories: databases, focus groups, and sampling. Each of these three categories offers unique opportunities to expand the reach and usefulness of market research. Let's examine each more closely.

Online (Cloud) Databases An **online database** is data stored on a server that is accessed remotely over the Internet or some other telecommunications network. Many, if not most, companies now have databases available to employees, suppliers, even customers. Information on orders, shipments, pricing, and other relevant information is available to salespeople and customer service personnel who need to access it.[38]

Independent online databases available from government and other sources are extremely useful tools in market research. Organizations such as the National Archives and Records Administration offer a wide range of databases with topic-specific data, all of which can be accessed for free. Fee-based services, while expensive, offer access to a wide range of information. Lexis/Nexis, for example, enables market researchers to access thousands of business and trade publications and market studies. Another company, IBISWorld, allows members to access hundreds, of industry overviews and analyses that have been conducted through research. These services make it possible to review market research reports, industry and company analyses, even market share information.[39]

Online Focus Groups The virtual focus group is becoming a viable alternative to the traditional focus group format (6 to 10 people in a room). Offering distinct advantages in terms of convenience and cost-efficiency, online focus groups provide data quickly and in a format that is usually easier to read and analyze. Traditional focus groups require someone to transcribe the spoken words into a transcript. With online focus groups, everything is already recorded by computer.

The primary disadvantage of online focus groups is that participants are limited to those with access to a computer or workstation. In addition, as people often participate remotely, it is not possible to verify who is actually responding to the questions. Measures can be employed to verify participation (for example, passwords), but the reality is that, in most cases, you must rely on the individual to be honest. One final problem is the lack of control over the environment. Traditional focus groups create an environment where participants are required to focus on the questions. Online focus groups enable participants to be at home, work, or even a remote location with wireless access. As a result, participants can become distracted and environmental factors can affect their concentration and responses.

Online Sampling If someone has access to a computer with an Internet connection, that person can complete a questionnaire. Online sampling has become increasingly

Gophers burrow through life without seeing the havoc they create.
They can't help having tunnel vision.
But you can. With proven business intelligence and analytic software from SAS.
www.sas.com/gophers
sas
THE POWER TO KNOW.

SAS offers powerful analysis tools to help managers more clearly understand market data.

popular as a data collection methodology. As with online focus groups, the primary advantages are convenience and cost-efficiency. Respondents are free to complete the survey when it is best for them, and sending a survey online is essentially free. Online survey companies such as QuestionPro offer a complete service from survey design and a variety of delivery methods (traditional e-mail, popup surveys, company newsletter integration, and others) to data analysis and presentation of findings.[40]

Statistical Software One of the real benefits of market research technology today is the ability to put powerful statistical software in the hands of front-line managers. With the proper training and data, it is now possible for managers to conduct analyses that were not possible even five years ago. Two software packages dominate desktop statistical analysis—SPSS and SAS. SPSS offers a range of marketing analytical tools. Its statistical software combines an easy-to-use interface with powerful statistical tools in a format that managers at all levels can use. The other widely used package is called SAS and it offers many of the same features. One of the real advantages of these packages is their ability to take the findings of the data analysis and create tables and reports.[41]

> Efficient Frontier, now owned by Adobe Acrobat, employs complex mathematics to optimize online advertising campaigns. The company's proprietary algorithms calculate a return on investment and rate of response for every ad placed by an advertiser. The goal is to eliminate guessing from ad placement and base it solely on statistical analysis based on data provided from the Internet.[42]

Interestingly, while dedicated statistical packages offer powerful analytical tools and outstanding reporting capabilities, probably the most widely used tool for analyzing business data is one almost everyone already has on his or her computer—Excel spreadsheets. Part of the Microsoft Office suite of products, Excel offers the ability to analyze data using formulas created by the user or statistical functions already embedded in the software. While not a dedicated statistical package, it is certainly a useful tool in basic data analysis.

Market Research Challenges in Global Markets

The primary difference between domestic and international research is that international market data are more difficult to get and understand than domestic data. In most Western European countries and the United States, it is much easier to access quality data than in the rest of the world. Let's examine some of the challenges market researchers face in finding, collecting, and then analyzing market data in foreign markets.

> Coping with the diversity of "global consumers" with strong regional subcultures is regarded as a challenge by 75 percent of senior marketers. A recent Millward Brown study found that only one in ten ads that tested exceptionally well in one country also tested well in another country—raising real questions about the cost efficiencies of cross-border campaigns. Add to this the growing tensions between local versus global control issues within the organization—which was identified as a significant challenge for more than 80 percent of senior marketers—and it becomes clear that there is a need for organizational design and digital platforms that create a multichannel, multidisciplinary approach to global marketing across all organizations.[43]

Secondary Data Exhibit 3.9 identifies the ten most expensive countries for marketing research. Note that while the United States and, to a lesser extent, Japan and the European Union are data-rich market environments, they are also among the most expensive countries in which to conduct marketing research. Unfortunately, that level of information is not found anywhere else in world. In certain areas, such as Central Europe, this is because they have only recently moved to open market economies. In other parts of the world, such as China and India, the culture does not encourage the free flow of information. This makes it difficult for any organization, even governments, to collect good information. Let's consider three major challenges researchers face as they collect data around the world.

Data Accessibility In the United States, businesspeople are accustomed to easily accessing information that simply does not exist in much of the world. The U.S. Census Bureau provides detailed information across a wide range of business sectors, including retailing and distribution, as well as specific data on many different economic and personal criteria such as income per capita, population by county, and zip code (broken down by gender, age, ethnic mix, and many other characteristics). From government sources (U.S. Census Bureau, Department of Commerce, EU Business Development Center), nongovernment business organizations (U.S. Chamber of Commerce, OECD), and private research organizations, a great deal of information is available to managers. The quantity and quality of data found in the United States are not available in most of the world.

Data Dependability A second major issue is the reliability of the data. Can the information be considered accurate? Regrettably, in many cases it cannot. Government agencies, particularly in developing countries, will distort data to present a more favorable analysis. The data are often reported incorrectly because people do not want the government to know the true figures, usually because of higher tax concerns. In other cases, governments want to present optimistic results that enforce government policies so they alter the data to reflect government accomplishments.

Data Comparability Comparing secondary data from foreign markets risks three other problems. First, developing countries often lack historical data, making it

EXHIBIT 3.9 | The Ten Most Expensive Countries for Research

Country	Global Index Scale
United States of America	241
Switzerland	239
Canada	229
Japan	222
United Kingdom	187
Sweden	168
Germany	165
Denmark	162
France	161
The Netherlands	156

Source: MarketingCharts Staff, "US the Most Expensive Country for Market Research," *Marketing Charts*, October 17, 2012.

much harder to assess long-term economic or business trends. Second, the available data are outdated so they are ineffective for making decisions in the current economic environment. Finally, terms used in reporting information are not consistent. Standardized business terminology used in industrialized countries has not been adopted by many developing regions, making it difficult for researchers to interpret data.

Primary Data Essential information about economic and general business trends can be gathered from secondary sources, but to get specific market data such as customer preferences, primary data are necessary. Collecting primary data presents many challenges for marketers that are almost always compounded in global markets. Some of the specific problems of international primary data collection include the following issues.

Unwillingness to Respond Cultural, gender, and individual differences create wide disparities in the willingness to provide personal information. The United States has an open information culture and people are much more willing to respond, but this openness is not shared around the world. In addition, government agencies such as the Securities and Exchange Commission require publicly traded companies to provide accurate business information including valid financial results. Nongovernment agencies such as trade associations report studies widely used in business. The National Realtors Association, for example, publishes quarterly data on the housing industry that is considered an accurate assessment of the real estate market in the United States.

As we discussed earlier, many people don't respond because they are concerned about government interference or additional taxes. However, concerns about privacy and how personal data are used generate a broad distrust of surveys among consumers and businesses. It is not difficult to understand these concerns. In countries formerly under the control of the Soviet Union (Czech Republic, Poland, Hungary, and others), for example, people were concerned that personal information provided to authorities could be used against them. After the fall of the Soviet Union, the historical problems created by decades of living in a closed society made it very difficult for companies such as A. C. Nielsen to collect valid consumer opinions and business data.

Unreliable Sampling Procedures Related to the quality of data noted earlier is the problem of unreliable or inadequate demographic information to conduct primary research. In many countries, there is no way to locate or identify who lives where or even how many people live in a given location, something businesspeople in the United States take for granted. In the United States, sophisticated global positioning system (GPS) devices can direct people to specific locations based on maps and other data stored on a hard drive. Consider the problem, then, if you are in a medium or small South American or Asian city where maps do not exist and street names are not even posted. The lack of reliable census information coupled with an inadequate infrastructure leaves market researchers in many countries with no accurate sampling frame from which to draw respondents.

Inaccurate Language Translation and Insufficient Comprehension Getting people in global markets to actually complete a survey presents three challenges. First, simply translating surveys can be a challenge. For example, Chinese

Mobile Internet usage is expected to continue growing at a phenomenal 66 percent a year over the next five years, greatly expanding the number of people using the Internet. By 2017 the average mobile user will watch 10 hours of video, listen to 15 hours of music, and download 15 apps each month. With the continuous digital movement, companies must be wise in choosing the medium by which they conduct research or attempt to create value for the consumer.[44]

is written with characters known as hànzi with each character representing a syllable of spoken Chinese with its own meaning. To read fluently in Chinese requires knowledge of more than 3,000 symbols. Second, word usage changes dramatically around the world. In the United States and Western Europe, "family" generally refers to the immediate family unit, including a father, mother, and their children, while in many Latin and Asian cultures "family" almost always includes the extended family, including all aunts, uncles, cousins, and grandparents. When a survey asks about family members, then, the responses could vary dramatically.

A final problem is insufficient language comprehension. In many parts of the world illiteracy rates are high, which rules out most survey methodologies (see Exhibit 3.10). In addition, some countries use multiple languages, making translation costly and increasing the likelihood of mistranslation. India, for example, recognizes 14 official languages with many additional nonofficial languages. Imagine writing a survey that would translate well into over a dozen languages.

EXHIBIT 3.10 | Global Literacy Rates

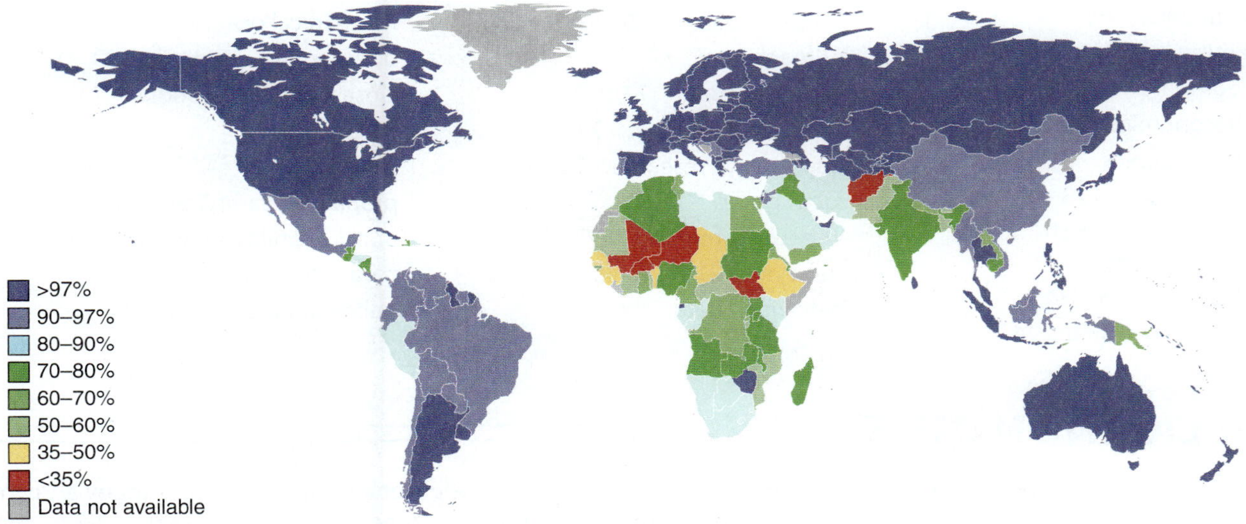

SUMMARY

Marketers know that accurate, relevant, and timely information is an essential element in marketing management. There are two sources of information: that which comes from outside the company and that which can be found internally. Being aware of environmental forces such as demographic profiles and changes, economic conditions, emerging technologies, changes in the natural world, and the political and legal environment enables marketers to create more effective short- and long-term marketing strategies.

Critical to assessing marketing information is a thorough understanding of the market research process. The process involves six specific steps: define the problem, establish the research design, search secondary sources, collect the data, analyze the data, and present the research findings. Researchers must follow the market research process to ensure the data are valid and useful for decision makers.

KEY TERMS

market information system (MIS) 64
marketing intelligence 68
demographics 68
microeconomics 71
macroeconomics 71
market research 73
management research deliverable 74
research problem 74
exploratory research 76
descriptive research 76
causal research 76
primary data 77
secondary data 77
qualitative research 77
quantitative research 77
focus group 77
in-depth interview 77
surveys 77
behavioral data 78
observational data 78
mechanical observation 78
open-ended questions 79
closed-ended questions 79
census 79
sample 79
probability sampling 79
nonprobability sampling 80
data collection 81
online database 83

APPLICATION QUESTIONS

1. Imagine you are the vice president of sales for a large security company and you have been asked to put together a sales information system that collects, analyzes, interprets, and distributes information from the sales force. How would you do it? What information would you ask salespeople to collect?
2. As a market manager at Lenovo, what key information from outside the company would be important to help in the design of a new laptop for small and medium-sized businesses?
3. The marketing manager for Disney Cruise Line wants to know what demographic trends will affect the cruise line business over the next five years. What kind of research is needed to address this question? Conduct some secondary research and try to identify two or three important demographic trends that might affect the cruise line business.
4. The market research director for John Deere has just received a call from the marketing manager in the company's lawn tractor division. The manager wants to know how the new advertising campaign is being received by current customers. Design a research study for this research. Be sure to include a problem definition and research design.
5. The alumni director at your institution wants to know how to serve the alumni better. Design a survey of no more than 10 questions that the alumni director can use to ask alumni about their interest in getting more involved with their school.

MANAGEMENT DECISION CASE:
Using Information to Target Customers Who Do Not Know They Are Being Targeted

In late 2013, Target Corporation, one of the biggest retail organizations in America, announced one of the largest data security breaches in history, with tens of millions of credit cards compromised by system hackers. This case focuses on another interesting but less publicized event from the same time frame.

"If we wanted to figure out if a customer is pregnant, even if she didn't want us to know, can you do that?" This question is emblematic of similar questions that are asked in companies all over the world in an effort to more specifically identify customers for increased sales opportunities. In this case, the Target brass were hoping to identify buying patterns of their female customers that would allow for effective promotion of specific products such as maternity and baby items. As Target has learned, customer buying patterns are representative of their life stage and to the extent that an organization can identify those life stages through data mining and information analysis, greater sales opportunities are possible.

Target is one of many companies that have discovered the benefits of "big data" and "business analytics." As individuals buy items, whether it is online or in a physical store location, they leave a data trail that can be collected, analyzed, and acted on by marketers in ways that were unheard of in the recent past. In Target's case, when a customer pays for purchases with a debit or credit card, that customer is assigned a unique internal customer identification number. Monitoring those purchases over time allows company personnel to collect information and make inferences about the shopper's lifestyle and family situation. For example, buying a small baseball glove, some animal crackers, and a DVD of the latest Pixar movie provides clues that a young boy may live in that household. With such information Target can provide coupons for age-appropriate clothing items, electronics, sporting goods, toys, and school supplies, thus increasing their chances to make more sales to that customer.

So, to answer the question posed in the opening of the case, it turns out that Target can identify its pregnant customers before those customers may want anyone to know they are pregnant! This point is illustrated best by a man who walked into a Target store clutching a coupon booklet demanding to see the store manager. That coupon booklet was addressed to the man's daughter, who was in high school at the time, and it contained coupons for things like cribs and baby clothes. Upon being asked by the upset customer if Target was encouraging his daughter to get pregnant, the store manager apologized profusely for Target's home office's action. A few days later the store manager phoned the customer to apologize again and learned the customer's daughter was actually pregnant, a fact that was revealed after the father returned from the store and spoke with her.

As enhanced computer processing power becomes more prevalent and more people are trained in the science and art of business analytics, there is no question that companies will utilize these data to increase company performance. In fact, Target Corporation's total revenues rose from $44 billion in 2002 to over $70 billion in 2013, an increase attributed to Target's "heightened focus on items and categories that appeal to specific segments such as mom and baby." However, the ability for companies to analyze big data with sophisticated techniques is not without some risk, and given Target's highly publicized security breach in late 2013 Target must be highly sensitive to the issue. The key is to balance the need ensure security and at the same time use data to enhance organizational success.

Questions for Consideration

1. A good portion of Target's success appears to be attributable to its internal market information system. What types of information from external sources might Target gather to augment its customer information and enhance analytical capability?
2. Aside from the downsides to using big data discussed in the case, what other possible issues exist for companies implementing market research/ customer insight technology in this manner? As younger consumers in general continue to share more of their life online, how might companies of different types utilize that information to their advantage?
3. What "dark sides" of big data and business analytics should Target be paying attention to? What might happen to Target if they are insensitive to the potential for such processes to offend some customers?

Sources: Charles, Duhigg "How Companies Learn Your Secrets," *New York Times*, February 16, 2012, www.nytimes.com/2012/02/19/magazine/shopping-habits.html?pagewanted=all; John, Jordan "The Risks of Big Data for Companies," *The Wall Street Journal Online*, October 20, 2013, http://search.proquest.com.proxy.lib.ilstu.edu/abiglobal/docview/1443270073/1416EA732968A4A12B/1?accountid=11578.

MARKETING PLAN EXERCISE

ACTIVITY 3: Identify Critical Information

This exercise asks you to identify the critical information needed to create the marketing plan. In that regard it is important to evaluate existing information (internal inside and secondary data) as well as new information gathered through primary research. This assignment includes:

1. Catalog internal sources of information available to you inside the organization and what information you will receive from each source.
2. Identify secondary data sources and the specific information you need from each source.
   a. List sources.
   b. Date.
   c. Assess the relevance of the data to the project.
3. List primary data needs to create the marketing plan. Then develop the specific instruments (focus group questions, surveys) that you will use later in the marketing plan.

NOTES

1. Anne L. Souchon, John W. Cagogan, David B. Procter, and Belinda Dewsnap, "Marketing Information Use and Organizational Performance: The Mediating role of Responsiveness," *Journal of Strategic Marketing* 12, no. 4 (2004), pp. 231–42.
2. "J.D. Power and Associates Reports: Del Webb Ranks Highest in Satisfying Buyers of Homes in Active Adult Communities," *PR Newswire,* September 13, 2006.
3. Roger Bennett, "Sources and Use of Marketing Information by Marketing Managers," *Journal of Documentation* 63, no. 5 (2007), p. 702; and Hean Tat Keh, Thi Mai Nguyen, and Hwei Ping Ng, "The Effects of Entrepreneurial Orientation and Marketing Information on the Performance of SME's," *Journal of Business Venturing* 22, no. 4 (2007), pp. 592–611.
4. Paul Ingenbleek, "Value-Informed Pricing in Its Organizational Context: Literature Review, Conceptual Framework, and Directions for Future Research," *Journal of Product and Brand Management* 16, no. 7 (2007), pp. 441–58.
5. E. J. Schultz, "How Post Pulled Off a Six-Month Cereal Launch," *Advertising Age,* February 11, 2013, http://adage.com/article/news/post-pulled-a-month-cereal-launch/239691/.
6. Gerrit H. Van Bruggen, Ale Smidts, and Berend Wierenga, "The Powerful Triangle of Marketing Data, Managerial Judgment, and Marketing Management Support Systems," *European Journal of Marketing* 35, no. 7 (2001), pp. 796–816.
7. Stephen F. King and Thomas F. Burgess, "Understanding Success and Failure in Customer Relationship Management," *Industrial Marketing Management* 37, no. 4 (2008), pp. 421–39.
8. Joao F. Proenca, Teresa M. Fernandez, and P. K. Kannan, "The Relationship in Marketing: Contribution of a Historical Perspective," *Journal of Macromarketing* 28, no. 1 (2008), pp. 90–106.
9. Sandra S. Liu and Lucette B. Comer, "Salespeople as Information Gatherers: Associated Success Factors," *Industrial Marketing Management* 36, no. 5 (2007), pp. 565–79.
10. Joel Le Bon and Dwight Merunka, "The Impact of Individual and Managerial Factors on Salespeople's Contribution to Marketing Intelligence Activities," *International Journal of Research in Marketing* 23, no. 4 (2006), pp. 395–412.
11. Jean Michel Moutot and Ganael Bascoul, "Effects of Sales Force Automation Use on Sales Force Activities and Customer Relationship Management Process," *Journal of Personal Selling and Sales Management* 28, no. 2 (2008), pp. 167–82.
12. Jack Neff, "Nielsen Now Tracks (Almost) Everything You Buy," *Advertising Age,* March 20, 2013, http://adage.com/article/media/nielsen-tracks-bank-statements-credit-card-transactions/240439/.
13. Brian Stelter, "A CBS Deal Bolsters Amazon's Challenge to NetFlix," *New York Times,* February 11, 2013, http://mediadecoder.blogs.nytimes.com/2013/02/11/amazon-and-cbs-announce-deal-on-rights-to-under-the-dome/.
14. Craig Stedman, "Failed ERP Gamble Haunts Hershey," *Computerworld* 33, no. 44 (1999), pp. 1–2.
15. Sajjad Matin, "Clicks Ahoy! Navigating Online Advertising in a Sea of Fraudulent Clicks," *Berkeley*

Technology Law Journal 22, no. 1 (2007), pp. 533–55; and Brian Grow and Ben Elgin, "Click Fraud," *BusinessWeek*, October 2, 2006, pp. 46–57.

16. Brad Plumer, "Will China Ever Get Its Pollution Problem under Control?" *Washington Post*, March 11, 2013, www.washingtonpost.com/blogs/wonkblog/wp/2013/03/11/will-china-ever-get-its-pollution-problem-under-control/.
17. Connie R. Bateman and JoAnn Schmidt, "Do Not Call Lists: A Cause for Telemarketing Extinction or Evolution," *Academy of Marketing Studies Journal* 11, no. 1 (2007), pp. 83–107; and Herbert Jack Rotfeld, "Misplace Marketing: Do-Not-Call as the U.S. Government's Improvement to Telemarketing Efficiency," *Journal of Consumer Marketing* 21, no. 4/5 (2004), pp. 242–59.
18. Thomas W. Miller, "At the Junction," *Marketing Research* 19, no. 4 (2007), pp. 8–14.
19. Alan Tapp, "A Call to Arms for Applied Marketing Academics," *Marketing Intelligence and Planning* 22, no. 5 (2004), pp. 579–96.
20. Dianne Altman Weaver, "The Right Questions," *Marketing Research* 18, no. 1 (2006), pp. 17–18.
21. Janice Denegri-Knott, Detiev Zwick, and Jonathan E. Schroeder, "Mapping Consumer Power: An Integrative Framework for Marketing and Consumer Research," *European Journal of Marketing* 40, no. 9/10 (2006), pp. 950–71.
22. Barbara Armstrong and Jennifer Schlimgen, "Smart Design: America's Most Beautiful Hospital Is More Than a Pretty Face (and Has the Results to Prove It)," *Forbes*, September 20, 2012, www.forbes.com/sites/barbaraarmstrong/2012/09/20/smart-design-americas-most-beautiful-hospital-is-more-than-a-pretty-face-and-has-the-reults-to-prove-it/.
23. Gordon A. Wyner, "Redefining Data," *Marketing Research* 16, no. 4 (2004), pp. 6–7.
24. Naomi R. Henderson, "Twelve Steps to Better Research," *Marketing Research* 17, no. 2 (2005), pp. 36–37.
25. David Stokes and Richard Bergin, "Methodology or 'Methodolatry'? An Evaluation of Focus Groups and Depth Interviews?" *Qualitative Market Research* 9, no. 1 (2006), pp. 26–38.
26. Clive Boddy, "A Rose by Any Other Name May Smell as Sweet but Group 'Group Discussion' Is Not Another Name for a 'Focus Group' Nor Should It Be," *Qualitative Market Research* 8, no. 3 (2005), pp. 248–56.
27. Jennifer Comiteau, "Why the Traditional Focus Group Is Dying," *Adweek*, October 31, 2005, pp. 24–27.
28. Gordon Wyner, "Survey Errors," *Marketing Research* 19, no. 1 (2007), pp. 6–7.
29. Catherine A. Roter, Robert A. Rogers, George C. Hozier Jr., Kenneth G. Baker, and Gerald Albaum, "Management of Marketing Research Projects: Does Delivery Method Matter Anymore in Survey Research," *Journal of Marketing Theory and Practice* 15, no. 2 (2007), pp. 127–45; and Sharon Loane, Jim Bell, and Rob McNaughton, "Employing Information Communication Technologies to Enhance Qualitative International Marketing Enquiry," *International Marketing Review* 23, no. 4 (2006), pp. 438–53.
30. Steve Henn and Melissa Block, "Data-Mining App Tracks People and Predicts Their Locations," NPR website, February 11, 2013, www.npr.org/2013/02/11/171737574/data-mining-app-tracks-people-and-predicts-their-location.
31. David Tiltman, "The Only Question You Need to Ask," *Marketing*, February 21, 2007, pp. 30–33; and Damon Darlin, "The Only Question That Matters, Surveys Are Tedious, Focus Groups Are Fickle. That's Why Intuit and GE Use a Radical New Research Technique to Keep Customers Happy and Revenue Growing," *Business 2.0* 6, no. 8 (2005), pp. 50–53.
32. Edward Blair and George M. Zinkhan, "Nonresponse and Generalizability in Academic Research," *Academy of Marketing Science Journal* 34, no. 1 (2006), pp. 4–8.
33. Peter Keliner, "Can Online Polls Produce Accurate Findings?," *International Journal of Market Research* 46 (2004), pp. 3–15; and Olivier Furrer and D. Sudharshan, "Internet Marketing Research: Opportunities and Problems," *Qualitative Market Research* 4, no. 3 (2001), pp 123–30.
34. N. L. Reynolds, A. C. Simintiras, and A. Diamantopoulos, "Theoretical Justification of Sampling Choices in International Marketing Research: Key Issues and Guidelines for Researchers," *Journal of International Business Studies* 34, no. 1 (2003), pp. 80–90.
35. Jane Intrieri, "Incentives for Customer Loyalty and Luxury Membership Programs," B2C Community website, March 28, 2013, www.business2community.com/loyalty-marketing/incentives-for-customer-loyalty-and-luxury-membership-programs-0449312; and Maggie Starvish, "Customer Loyalty Programs That Work," Harvard Business School website, July 27, 2011, http://hbswk.hbs.edu/item/6733.html.
36. Bill Blyth, "Mixed Mode: The Only 'Fitness' Regime?," *International Journal of Marketing Research* 50, no. 2 (2008), pp. 241–56.
37. Nick Sparrow, "Quality Issues in Online Research," *Journal of Advertising Research* 47, no. 2 (2007), pp. 179–91; and Elisabeth Deutskens, Ad de Jong, Ko de Ruyter, and Martin Wetzels, "Comparing the Generalizability of Online and Mail Surveys in Cross

National Service Quality Research," *Marketing Letters* 17, no. 2 (2006), pp. 119–32.

38. Kai Wehmeyer, "Aligning IT and Marketing—The Impact of Database Marketing and CRM," *Journal of Database Marketing & Customer Strategy Management* 12, no. 3 (2005), pp. 243–57; Joshua Weinberger, "Database Marketers Mine for Perfect Customer Segmentation," *Customer Relationship Management* 8, no. 10 (2004), p. 19; and Hoda McClymont and Graham Jocumsen, "How to Implement Marketing Strategies Using Database Approaches, "*Journal of Database Marketing & Customer Strategy Management* 11, no. 2 (2003), pp. 135–49.
39. R. Dale Wilson, "Developing New Business Strategies in B2B Markets by Combining CRM Concepts and Online Databases," *Competitiveness Review* 16, no. 1 (2006), pp. 38–44.
40. David Ward, "Master of All You Survey," *PRweek* 9, no. 38 (2006), p. 22.
41. Steve Ranger, "How Firms Use Business Intelligence," *BusinessWeek,* May 24, 2007, www.businessweek.com/globalbiz/content/may2007/gb20070524_006085.htm?chan=search; and Colin Beasty, "Minimizing Customer Guesswork," *Customer Relationship Management* 10, no. 6 (2006), p. 45.
42. "Efficient Frontier Releases Q! Search Engine Performance Report," *Business Wire,* April 17, 2008; and Robert D. Hof, "Efficient Frontier: Hacking Madison Avenue," *BusinessWeek,* July 24, 2006, p. 52.
43. Freddie Laker and Hilding Anderson, "Five Challenges for Tomorrow's Global Marketing Leaders: Study," *Forbes,* August 21, 2012, www.forbes.com/sites/onmarketing/2012/08/21/five-challenges-for-tomorrows-global-marketing-leaders-study/.
44. Cecilia Kang, "Mobile Internet Use Expected to Surge," *Washington Post,* February 6, 2013, http://articles.washingtonpost.com/2013-02-06/business/36937190_1_mobile-internet-mobile-devices-data-traffic.

CHAPTER 04

Understand Business-to-Consumer Markets

LEARNING OBJECTIVES

LO 4-1 Understand the value of knowing the consumer.

LO 4-2 Consider the role of personal and psychological factors in consumer decision making.

LO 4-3 Appreciate the critical and complex role of cultural, situational, and social factors in a consumer purchase decision.

LO 4-4 Understand the consumer decision-making process.

THE POWER OF THE CONSUMER

Teenage couple watching 3D movie.

It's a Friday night and a group of people are considering how to spend the evening. A consensus forms around watching a movie. The discussion focuses on two choices: visit the local multiplex theater to see a first-run showing of the latest hit movie or go to a friend's house and watch a classic on the 50-inch plasma television with surround sound. Ultimately, they decide to watch *The Avengers* at the friend's house. This interaction is repeated thousands of times each weekend and represents just one example of consumer decision making.

Marketers are fundamentally interested in learning about the process people use to make purchase decisions. In our example, the implications of the seemingly innocuous decision to watch a movie at home are very significant. Movie theaters are concerned because attendance has been falling for a decade while sales of DVDs and video on demand have been growing at double-digit rates. Theater owners are investing millions of dollars to get people to choose a night out at the movies instead of going home. At the same time, movie studios such as Paramount, Sony, Time Warner, and Disney are paying attention. Because they want to maximize revenue, they have shortened the time between theatrical release and DVD sales, in addition to making first-run movies available via video on demand.[1] Finally, theme parks such as Universal Orlando Resort are interested because they invest millions to combine successful movies with live-action shows and rides to extend the movie's experience.

LO 4-1

Understand the value of knowing the consumer.

Delivering value to the customer is the core of marketing, and a company can only do that with a thorough, accurate, and timely understanding of the customer. Complex forces influence consumer choices, and these forces change over time, which adds to the challenges marketers face. Exhibit 4.1 displays a model of the consumer decision process, which is a complex interaction of internal (personal and psychological characteristics) and external (cultural, situational, and social stimuli) forces that, joined with a company's marketing activities and environmental forces, affect the purchase decision process. This chapter will identify the internal and external forces affecting the process, then focus on the consumer decision process itself.

INTERNAL FORCES AFFECT CONSUMER CHOICES

Among the most difficult factors to understand are those internal to the consumer. Often, consumers themselves are not fully aware of the role these important traits play in their decision making. Compounding the challenge is the fact that these characteristics vary by individual, change over time, and affect decisions in complex ways that are difficult to know. Exhibit 4.2 identifies examples of internal forces.

Personal Characteristics

LO 4-2

Consider the role of personal and psychological factors in consumer decision making.

Personal attributes are frequently used to define an individual. Age, education, occupation, income, lifestyle, and gender are all ways to identify and classify someone. The *American Heritage Online Dictionary* defines **demographics** as "[t]he characteristics of human populations and population segments, especially when used to identify consumer markets." It is helpful to understand the demographics of a target market for two reasons. First, knowing the personal characteristics of a target market enables marketers to evaluate relevant statistics against competitors and the overall population using broad demographic studies like the U.S. Census reports. Comparing demographic data such as age and income to competitor data enables you to assess how your target markets match up with those of competitors. Second, personal characteristics like age, income, and education play

EXHIBIT 4.1 | Model of the Consumer Decision Process

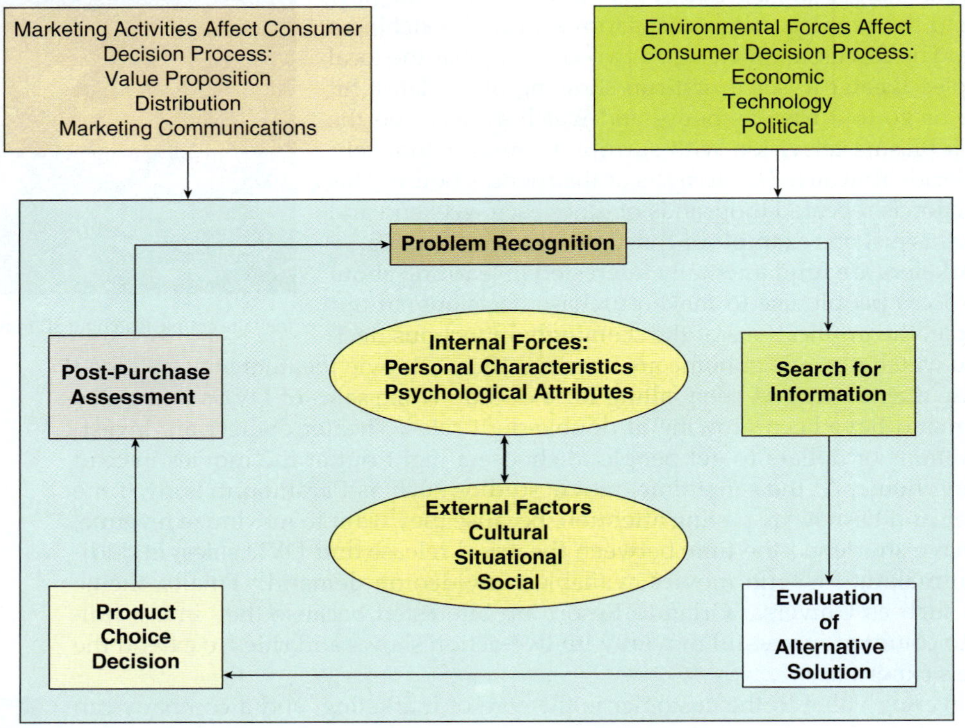

a critical role in consumer decision making, affecting information search, possible product choices, and the product decision itself.[2] Demographics are also an important tool in market segmentation, and Chapter 6 will explore how demographics are used to make decisions about targeting customer groups.

> The U.S. population is aging, with the first of the baby boomers (people born between 1946 and 1964) considering retirement options, health care planning, and lifestyle changes that offer companies in a number of industries growth opportunities.
> **Marketing opportunity:** Develop web portals to help retirees manage finances, health care, and other lifestyle issues for baby boomers.
> **Implementation strategy:** Increase the portability of services, enabling users to conduct transactions with their cell phones, and enhance international cell phone coverage.

EXHIBIT 4.2 | Internal Forces Affecting Consumer Choices

Personal Characteristics	**Psychological Attributes**
Age	Motivation
Education	Attitude
Occupation	Perception
Income	Learning
Lifestyle	Personality
Gender	

EXHIBIT 4.4 | Lifestyle Trends in the United States

	Trend	Marketing Example
Health-conscious eating	Americans are turning to healthier eating styles, which can be seen in most restaurants with new low-calorie and low-carbohydrate menus.	Olive Garden has created a new healthier menu to appeal to health-conscious lovers of Italian food.
Single-parent homes	Although the majority of families in the United States consist of two-parent homes, single-parent homes are increasing steadily.	Target, Walmart, and other retailers offer a wide range of books, DVDs, and other products targeted at single parents.
Online era	There has been a steady increase in online shopping and information gathering. This is only expected to increase as technology increases.	Amazon—One of the first and largest online shopping websites, Amazon continues to experience good growth, although not as fast as in the past.
Women in the workforce	In 2012, 46 percent of the workforce was made up of women and is continuously growing. As more and more women begin their careers, we have seen more and more men help in raising the kids.	Day care centers—Companies are including on-premise day care centers as part of their benefits packages; in addition, private centers continue to see significant growth.

to work and derives personal satisfaction from her employment. Other segments include trapped housewives who are married but prefer to work and trapped working women who would prefer to be at home but must work because of financial necessity or family pressure.

Marketing managers understand that men and women vary not only in the products they require but also in the marketing communications they are receptive to. For example, a significant majority of men and women use the Internet. The sites they visit differ a great deal.[6] In addition, women and men both read magazines, but the kinds of magazines they read vary greatly so marketers place ads in different magazines to reach both groups. Men prefer automotive and sports magazines while women choose health and epicurean magazines. In addition, the message itself varies by gender, with men preferring a "self-help" message and women responding to a "help others" communication. All this suggests that gender roles are a critical personal characteristic affecting consumer choices.[7]

Psychological Attributes

The consumer decision process involves a number of psychological forces that profoundly affect the consumer choice process. These forces drive the need, shape the content and format of information stored in memory, and have an effect on point of view about products and brands.

Motivation At any given time people experience many different needs. Most are not acted upon; however, when need reaches a particular strength or intensity, it becomes a motive that drives behavior. People prioritize needs, making sure that stronger, more urgent needs get met first. **Motivation** is the stimulating power that induces and then directs behavior. It is the force by which powerful unmet needs, or motives, prompt someone to action.

Many theories have been developed over the years to explain human motivation. Exhibit 4.5 provides a summary of four popular theories of motivation and how they are used in marketing. The best known and most popular of these theories is the Hierarchy of Needs, which was developed by psychologist Abraham

ETHICAL DIMENSION 4

Hello, Who Are You?

You probably thought your cell phone was just for phone conversations, right? Well, not anymore. Meet the new "sell phone," which combines Internet tracking data with your location to target very personal, specific ads right to your cell phone. Marketers are now testing technology tools that will deliver a message right to you about a store or promotion just as you pass that store. You will be able to see a Starbucks coupon pop up on your cell phone with a note that tells you the nearest Starbucks is one block away on your right.

Presently, the limiting factor is not the technology but the cellular service providers, who are not sure how best to move forward. Many advertisers are also taking a wait-and-see approach as everyone works through Federal Communications Commission (FCC) rules regarding use of private customer data such as location information. At this point, the FCC is requiring mobile advertisers to get an individual's permission to release sensitive customer data before the cellular service can release the information to the advertiser. Similar rules apply to e-mail, but spammers do not get the necessary permission before filling your mailbox.

Medio Systems and other companies are moving ahead and delivering targeted advertising to phones serviced by Verizon, T-Mobile, and others. Sprint Nextel is also implementing location-based targeted advertising. Advertisers see the potential to bypass much of the communications clutter that people disregard every day. By some estimates, people are exposed to as many as 3,000 ads each day, with the vast majority of the messages being ignored.

Cellular companies can locate a user within 50 to 300 meters and offer advertisers a captive audience. The marketing company collects Internet tracking data, then matches where the consumer has been on the Internet with his or her actual location. If someone has visited the Barnes & Noble website recently and her location shows her close to a Barnes & Noble, a specific message that could include a coupon or other promotion can be sent directly to the cell phone. In 2012 mobile ad spending was $8.5 billion, a miniscule amount compared to traditional advertising channels, but that number is expected to dramatically rise over the next few years to $37 billion in 2016.

A number of individuals and advocacy groups, however, are concerned about the potential invasion of consumer privacy. At minimum, advertisers will learn customer cell numbers, and many cell phone users are not happy about that prospect[8]

Ethical Perspective

1. **Advertisers:** The ability to reach targeted customers at the right moment has been the goal of advertising for decades. This new technology enables "just-in-time" advertising. As an advertiser, would you consider mobile advertising? How would you address customer concerns about privacy?
2. **Cellular service providers:** A potential source of revenue, the ability to target cell phone users, is available today and represents very little incremental cost to the service provider. Just because it is possible, should marketing companies be allowed to send mobile ads? How do you safeguard the privacy of your customer?
3. **Consumers:** Ensuring customer confidentiality is an essential element of the contract between cell service provider and consumers. Would you want to receive mobile ads?

Maslow. Maslow's theory proposes a series of needs that flow from lower order (physiological) to higher order (self-actualization). The theory suggests that people meet physiological needs such as hunger and sleep before they satisfy other needs. Once those needs are satiated, other needs become more important. At the highest level in the hierarchy, people seek human ideals related to justice, wisdom, and the meaning of life.[9] Maslow asserts that people never fully meet this need, and higher-order needs continue through an individual's life.

As is the case with any theory on motivation, the Maslow's Hierarchy of Needs theory is a good summary of human needs but should not be considered a comprehensive model. The model does not explain the level of intensity needed to move people from one need to the next. For example, how much financial security (a safety need) does someone need before social needs become a priority. In addition, research suggests that Maslow's hierarchy works better in Western cultures than in Eastern ones, where social needs take on a higher value than personal needs.

Marketing managers find Maslow's theory beneficial in identifying where products fit into an individual's overall needs. Products are often targeted at more than one set of needs. For example, dining at an upscale restaurant is certainly designed to satisfy the basic physiological need for food. However, the atmosphere and interior design encourage conversation with friends and a sense of belonging, thus meeting customers' social needs. Finally, if the restaurant is popular, it may address an individual's need for status, respect, and prestige, thus fulfilling a self-esteem need.

Demographics are key to illuminating target markets. A study by the Centers for Disease Control indicated that on an average day a U.S. adult got 11 percent of his or her calories from fast food. That changes when age groups are looked at in particular. People aged 20 to 39 eat more fast food (15 percent of daily calories) than people aged 60 and older (6 percent of daily calories). Obese individuals had higher fast food calorie intakes than skinny or normal-weight people. Additionally there was a difference between household incomes of young adults, in which those with low incomes ate more fast food than the affluent.

The overall fast food calorie intake has decreased since 2006. The cause of this change is not apparent, although the health-consciousness trend may be a factor. Only time will tell if the trend has staying power and how it may affect the likes of fast food giants including McDonald's and Yum! Brands.[10]

EXHIBIT 4.5 | Contemporary Theories of Motivation

	Theory	Key Elements	Marketing Implications
Maslow's Hierarchy of Needs Theory	Humans have wants and needs that influence their behavior. People advance only to the next level if the lower needs are meet.	**1. Physiological** **2. Safety** **3. Love/Social** **4. Self-Esteem** **5. Self-Actualization**	Individuals are not interested in luxuries until they have had basic needs (food, shelter) met.
Herzberg's Two-Factor Theory	Certain factors in the workplace result in job satisfaction.	**1. Motivators:** challenging work, recognition, and responsibility **2. Hygiene factors:** status, job security, salary, and benefits	Satisfying hygiene factors does not create a loyal employee or customer. For a company to really create satisfied employees it is important to focus on motivators.
Aldelfer's ERG Theory	Expansion on Maslow's hierarchy, placing needs in three categories.	**1. Existence** **2. Relatedness** **3. Growth**	People need a sense of belonging and social interaction. Creating a relationship with the customers extends the customers' satisfaction with the product.
McClelland's Achievement Motivation Theory	There are three categories of needs and people differ in the degree to which the various needs influence their behavior.	**1. Need for Achievement** **2. Need for Power** **3. Need for Affiliation**	Companies can be successful targeting one of three basic needs.

Attitude From religion to politics, sports to tomorrow's weather, people have an attitude about everything. An **attitude** is defined as a "learned predisposition to respond to an object or class of objects in a consistently favorable or unfavorable way."[11] Several key points come from this definition. First, attitudes are learned or at least influenced by new information. This is important for marketers because they seek to affect a person's attitude about a product. Second, attitudes are favorable or unfavorable, positive or negative. In other words, attitudes are seldom, if ever, neutral. As a result, marketers play close attention to people's attitudes about their products because they play an important role in shaping a person's purchase decision.

Initially, a person's attitudes are formed by their values and beliefs. There are two categories of values. The first refers to cultural values based on national conscience. Americans, for example, value hard work and freedom, among other things. In Japan, national values include reciprocity, loyalty, and obedience. The second category is personal values held by the individual. Products possessing characteristics consistent with a person's value system are viewed more favorably.

While values may be based, in part, on fact, beliefs are a subjective opinion about something. Since they are subjective (emotional and not necessarily based on fact) marketers become concerned that a negative product belief will create a negative attitude about that product, making the attitude more difficult to overcome.[12] It is also important to note that beliefs, once formed, are resistant to change. Personal experiences, marketing communication, and information from trusted sources, such as family members or friends, all shape a person's belief system.

Values and beliefs come together to shape attitudes about an object whether it is Coke, the environment, or your favorite sports team. This overall predisposition is the result, generally, of an individual's assessment of that object on several attributes. For example, an attitude about Coke could be based on attributes such as health, which could be a positive belief—Coke's caffeine give you energy—or a negative belief—Coke has a lot of sugar and calories. Coke is presented as a fun, youthful drink and youth is an American value.[13]

Because people's beliefs/values impact their purchase decisions, marketing managers try to learn about those beliefs/values. They do that by having customers check off rating scales that evaluate a product's performance on a list of attributes. This is important information because most attitudes result from an individual's assessment of an object using a **multiattribute model** that evaluates the object on several important attributes. Learning which attributes are used and how individuals rank those attributes is particularly helpful to marketers in creating specific marketing messages as well as the overall value proposition.[14] For instance, individuals who value the environment and ecology will place a higher priority on fuel economy and other environmentally friendly characteristics in the purchase of a car.

Coke promotes its fun brand image with bright and exciting graphic designs.

Perception People are inundated with information. Indeed, there is so much information that it is not possible to make sense of everything so people use a process called perception to help manage the flow of environmental stimuli. **Perception** is a system to select, organize, and interpret information to create a useful, informed picture of the world.

In marketing, perception of a product is even more important than the reality of that product because, in a very real sense, an individual's perception is his or her reality. Perception drives attitudes, beliefs, motivation, and, eventually, behavior. Since each individual's perception is unique, everyone's perceptual response to the same reality will vary. Two people will see an ad for a new Samsung LCD flat-panel television, but their perception of the ad will be very different. One may see a high-quality television worth the money, while the other sees an overpriced television that does not warrant a premium price. Their attitudes toward the ad and the product are affected by their perceptions.

Perception is shaped by three psychological tools: selective awareness, selective distortion, and selective retention.

Selective Awareness An individual is exposed, on average, to between 2,000 and 3,000 messages daily.[15] People cannot process, let alone retain, all those messages, so they employ a psychological tool known as **selective awareness** to help them focus on what is relevant and eliminate what is not. The challenge for marketers is breaking through people's decision rules, which are designed to reject the vast majority of stimuli they see every day.

Research provides several insights about these decision rules. First, not surprisingly, people are more likely to be aware of information that relates to a current unmet need. Someone looking to change cellular providers will pay more attention to ads from cellular companies than someone who is happy with her current service. Second, people are more receptive to marketing stimuli when they expect them. Customers entering an AT&T or Verizon Wireless store anticipate seeing mobile telephones and tablet computers and, as a result, pay more attention to them. Finally, people are also more likely to become aware of marketing stimuli when they deviate widely from what are expected. For several years, Allstate Insurance has run a series of ads called "Mayhem" in which a man in a business suit points out the problems someone might have without Allstate. In addition to the creativity behind this approach, one of the reasons the campaign did well was because it deviated from normal insurance ads. People didn't expect to see "Mayhem" talking about insurance.[16]

Selective Distortion Breaking through the customer's selective awareness is an important first step. However, even if a stimulus is noticed, there is no guarantee it will be interpreted accurately. Information can be misunderstood or made to fit existing beliefs, a process known as **selective distortion.**

The issue for marketers is that selective distortion can work for or against a product. If an individual has a positive belief about a powerful brand or product, information that is ambiguous or neutral will likely be interpreted positively. Even negative data can be adjusted to align with an individual's existing beliefs. For example, despite the negative implications of the information, a recall of Toyota Prius cars did not slow sales, in part, because people's perception of Toyota's overall quality offset the negatives associated with a product recall. On the other hand, a negative belief can lead to negative interpretation. In the 1990s General Motors worked hard to improve the quality of its cars. This came after several decades of being rated below Japanese cars from Toyota and Honda in terms of quality. Despite significant quality improvements validated by independent researchers like J.D. Power and Associates, people continue to believe GM car quality is inferior to that of Japanese cars. Sometimes a positive belief can work against a marketer, particularly when the belief leads to an incorrect interpretation.[17] When Eveready introduced the Energizer Bunny advertising campaign, it found people liked the commercials, but also found people believed the commercials were referencing Duracell batteries (Eveready's primary competitor). Part of the reason was that people strongly identified with Duracell (the brand had high brand recognition and market share) and distorted the information in the ads to fit their perception of Duracell.

Selective Retention Even if a stimulus is noticed and interpreted correctly, there is no guarantee it will be remembered. While selective awareness significantly controls the amount of information available to the individual's consciousness, selective retention acts as an additional filter. **Selective retention** is the process of placing in one's memory only those stimuli that support existing beliefs and attitudes about a product or brand. This is significant because **memory** is where people store all past learning events; in essence it is the "bank" where people keep their knowledge, attitudes, feelings, and beliefs.[18] There are two types of memory—short and long term. **Short-term memory** is what is being recalled at the present time and is sometimes referred to as working memory, while **long-term**

memory is enduring storage, which can remain with the individual for years and years. Marketing managers are particularly interested in understanding an individual's long-term memory recall about their brand.

Selective retention tends to reinforce existing attitudes and creates a real challenge for marketers trying to overcome negative beliefs and attitudes since people are less likely to be aware of or retain information to the contrary. Audi, despite strong products and sales, still suffers from negative perceptions because of product problems related to the Audi 5000. Some people still remember a problem with sudden acceleration in the car that led to several accidents. While later research suggested the problem was not as severe as originally reported, Audi has had trouble overcoming persistent consumer attitudes over the past 20 years.

As consumer trends push toward green and sustainability, some companies have pursued campaigns that address those issues. In late 2012, Swedish clothing retailer H&M announced that it planned to begin a clothing recycling initiative. The company noted that tons of clothing are thrown away each year, 95 percent of which could be reworn, reused, or recycled. At the start of the campaign, H&M encouraged its customers to bring in clothing of any brand to recycle. In return, the customers receive a voucher for future purchase at H&M. The recycling program began in February 2013. This comes at a time when "fast retailers," including H&M and Forever 21, were being criticized for encouraging younger consumers to treat clothing as disposable. H&M partnered with German company I:CO, which stands for "I collect," for this initiative. The collected clothing will be sent to I:CO facilities, where it will be sorted for reuse or recycle. This campaign was part of H&M's long-term goal to reduce the environmental impact of garments throughout their life cycle.[19]

One last point about perception regards a controversial issue—the effect of subliminal stimuli on perception. While people are aware of most stimuli around them, a number of other stimuli go unnoticed. In most cases, either the stimuli are presented so fast they are not recognized or they overload the individual and are "lost" in the person's consciousness. These stimuli are termed subliminal, and many critics of advertising suggest the stimuli can affect consumer behavior. Despite many claims to the contrary, however, research has uncovered no evidence that a subliminal message, whether sent deliberately or accidentally, has any effect on product attitudes or choice behavior.

Given the psychological processes people use to limit their awareness of marketing stimuli and control retention of any remaining information, it is easy to see why marketers must deliver a message over and over. Without repetition, the message is not likely to break through selective awareness and even less likely to be retained by the individual.[20]

Learning How does an individual become a consumer of a particular product? Most consumer behavior is learned through a person's life experiences, personal characteristics, and relationships.

Learning is any change in the content or organization of long-term memory or behavior. Learning occurs when information is processed and added to long-term memory. Marketers can therefore affect learning by providing information using a message, format, and delivery that will encourage customers to retain the information in memory.

There are two fundamental approaches to learning. The first, **conditioning**, involves creating an association between two stimuli. There are two types of conditioning: classical and operant. Classical conditioning seeks to have people learn by associating a stimulus (marketing information, brand experience) and response (attitude, feeling, behavior).[21] Recently, many companies have started using popular songs from the 1960s and 1970s in their advertising. When individuals, particularly baby boomers, hear that music, it connects them with positive memories and, not coincidentally, the product and brand being advertised. This is conditioned learning, by connecting the stimulus such as music with a response such as a positive association with a particular brand.

The other type of conditioning, operant conditioning, entails rewarding a desirable behavior, for example, a product trial or purchase, with a positive outcome that reinforces that behavior.[22] For example, many different types of food retailers offer product samples in their stores. Frito-Lay, for instance, offers free in-store samples of Doritos for the express purpose of getting people to try the product, enjoy the product, and finally purchase a bag of Doritos. Enjoying the Doritos reinforces the positive attributes of the product and increases the probability of a purchase. Since the consumer must choose to try the product for operant conditioning to occur, Frito-Lay wants to make the trial as easy as possible.

While conditioning requires very little effort on the part of the learner, **cognitive learning** is more active and involves mental processes that acquire information to work through problems and manage life situations.[23] Someone suffering from the flu and seeking information from their friends, doctors, or medical websites about the best over-the-counter remedy for their specific symptoms is engaged in cognitive learning. They are looking for information to help solve a problem. Marketers must understand consumers sometimes engage in this type of activity and be proactive in providing the information sought by the consumer. Consider a box of Theraflu caplets; Theraflu Daytime cold lists six symptoms right on the front of the box that the product will help relieve. This kind of information is critical at the point of purchase as an individual considers which product will help him feel better faster.

Personality When people are asked to describe someone, most of us do not talk about the person's age or education. Rather, our response generally reflects the individual's personality and is based on our interactions with that person in different situations. Our descriptions usually include various personality dimensions such as kind, outgoing, or gentle. **Personality** is a set of unique personal qualities that produce distinctive responses across similar situations.

Many theories of personality have been developed, but marketers tend to focus on personality trait theories because they offer the greatest insights on consumers. Personality trait theories all have two basic assumptions: (1) each person has a set of consistent, enduring personal characteristics and (2) those characteristics can be measured to identify differences between individuals. Most believe personality characteristics are formed at a relatively early age and can be defined in terms of traits such as extroversion, instability, agreeableness, openness to new experiences, and conscientiousness. These core traits then lead to outward characteristics, which are what people notice. For example, an extrovert would favor the company of others and be comfortable meeting new people. A conscientious person would exhibit behaviors that are considered careful, precise, and organized. Knowing the personality tendencies of a target audience can help marketers in developing product features such as mobile devices with Wi-Fi for extroverts so they can communicate easily with others or marketing communications that incorporate images consistent with the individual's personality.

GoPro initially targeted extreme athletes and other people who identified with excitement and ruggedness.

While it is certainly beneficial for marketers to know the personality characteristics of their target audience, another application is the association between a brand

and specific personality characteristics. This association is known as a **brand personality**. Research suggests that consumers purchase brands that have a personality consistent with their own.[24] Research on brand personality identified five traits:

- Sincerity (down-to-earth, honest, wholesome, cheerful).
- Excitement (daring, spirited, imaginative, and current).
- Competence (reliable, intelligent, and successful).
- Sophistication (upper class and charming).
- Ruggedness (outdoorsy and tough).

Knowing a brand's personality helps marketers connect their brand to a customer. For example, MetLife insurance has carefully considered its brand personality and arrived at the following characteristics: sincere and competent. Not coincidentally, these are characteristics that people in the market for insurance might find beneficial in an insurance company.

Nicholas Woodman launched GoPro in the mid-2000s. The company started by Woodman, family, and friends marketing their camera through surf, bike, and ski shops around the United States. The purpose of the camera was for sports enthusiasts to capture their adventures. The GoPro YouTube page neared 170 million views by fall 2012, which sparked a craze for user-generated videos posted online. However, the brand is not merely a niche business for thrill seekers. GoPro has gained a share of mainstream customers. Nearly 1 million HERO2 cameras were sold in 2011. With the rise of social media, there has been an increasing trend for people to document more of their lives to share with others. Now GoPro cameras are being used in ways that never would have been imagined when the company began. For instance, couples are leaving the cameras on tables at weddings rather than disposable cameras, fire departments are using them for training, and marine biologists use them for underwater research. As interest in the product rises, GoPro must continue to cater to its growing consumer segments' needs.[25]

EXTERNAL FACTORS SHAPE CONSUMER CHOICES

LO 4-3

Appreciate the critical and complex role of cultural, situational, and social factors in a consumer purchase decision.

While internal factors are fundamental in consumer decision making, forces external to the consumer also have a direct and profound effect on the consumer decision process. These factors shape individual wants and behavior, define the products under consideration, target the selection of information sources, and shape the purchase decision. Three wide-ranging external factors that have the most significant impact on consumer choices are cultural, situational, and social.

Cultural Factors

Culture is a primary driver of consumer behavior because it teaches values and product preferences and, in turn, affects perceptions and attitudes. Beginning in childhood and continuing on throughout life, people respond to the culture in which they live. In recent years, despite the globalization of communications and the universal nature of the Internet, people have developed a heightened awareness of their own culture and subculture.

Marketers need to be aware of culture for two reasons. First, learning a target market's culture is essential to an effective marketing strategy. Creating a value proposition that incorporates cultural cues is a prerequisite to success. Second, failing to understand cultural norms has a significant negative effect on product acceptance.

Culture **Culture** assimilates shared artifacts such as values, morals, beliefs, art, law, and customs into an organized system that enables people to function as members of society. In school, children learn basic cultural values through interaction with classmates and formal classroom learning. At a very early age, young people learn values and concepts about their culture. Among the values shared by Americans, for example, are achievement, hard work, and freedom, while Japanese value social harmony, hierarchy, and devotion.

While culture affects people in many ways, three factors are particularly relevant in consumer behavior: language, values, and nonverbal communications. **Language** is an essential cultural building block and the primary communication tool in society. At the most basic level it is important to understand the language, making sure that words are understood correctly.[26] However, language conveys much more about a society and its values. Scandinavian cultures, for example, place a high value on spending time together. They have more words to express "being together" than English does, and their meaning implies a more intimate sharing of thoughts and ideas. These concepts do not translate into the Anglo-American language and are not easily understood. In addition, language is such an important cultural element that frequently a culture will seek to protect its language. France, for example, has passed a number of laws to prohibit English words from being used in advertising, banning terms such as *crossover* and *showroom*.[27]

Cultural values are principles shared by a society that assert positive ideals. These principles are often viewed on a continuum. Consider the value of limited versus extended family. In the United States, the obligation and commitment to family are often limited to an individual's immediate family, including his or her parents, children, and siblings. Most Latin American cultures, on the other hand, have a more wide-ranging definition of family that includes extended family members such as cousins and grandparents and is also more inclusive with extended family members living together.

The last cultural factor is **nonverbal communication**. While a number of factors fall into this category (refer to Exhibit 4.6 for a more complete discussion), let's focus on two: time and personal space. The perception of time varies across cultures. Americans and Western Europeans place a high value on time and view it in discrete blocks of hours, days, and weeks. As a result, they focus on scheduling and getting as much done in a given period as possible. Latin Americans and Asians, on the other hand, view time as much more flexible and less discrete. They are not as concerned with the amount of work that gets done in a given time block. How does this affect marketing? Salespeople who have been trained in an American sales environment are often frustrated to find their Asian and Latin

EXHIBIT 4.6 | Nonverbal Communication

Nonverbal Communication: the means of communicating through facial expressions, eye behavior, gestures, posture, and any other body language

Positive nonverbal communication during a presentation	• Eye contact • Smiling • Steady breathing • Tone of voice • Moving closer to the person
Negative nonverbal communication during a presentation	• Swaying • Stuttering • Hands in pockets • Fidgeting • Looking at watch or clock

Caution: Nonverbal communication can contradict what is spoken if not used correctly.

American customers less concerned about specific meeting times and more concerned about spending time building a personal relationship.

Personal space is another example of nonverbal communication that varies across cultures. In the United States, for example, most business conversations occur between three and five feet, which is a greater distance than in Latin American cultures. Salespeople used to a three-to-five-foot distance can find it a little disconcerting when the space shrinks to 18 inches to three feet. Not understanding these differences can lead to confusion and embarrassment and even create a problem in the business relationship.[28]

Subculture As consumer behavior research has discovered more about the role of culture in consumer choices, it has become evident that beyond culture, people are influenced even more significantly by membership in various subcultures. A **subculture** is a group within the culture that shares similar cultural artifacts created by differences in ethnicity, religion, race, or geography. While part of the larger culture, subcultures are also different from each other. The United States is perhaps the best example of a country with a strong national culture that also has a number of distinct subcultures (see Exhibit 4.7).

Several subcultures in the United States have become such powerful forces that companies now develop specific marketing strategies targeted at those groups. Large companies such as Procter & Gamble and General Motors have begun targeting the Hispanic and African-American markets with specific products, distribution channels, and marketing communications. For example, Procter & Gamble created a line of beauty care products called Textures and Tones that includes new products, packaging, and promotional campaigns targeted specifically for African-American women in the United States and Latin America. L'Oreal, the cosmetics company, has a research center outside Chicago that focuses exclusively on the African-American market and has resulted in a number of products in its Soft-Sheen Carson and Mizani brands.[29]

Situational Factors

At various points in the consumer decision process, situational factors play a significant part. Situational factors are time-sensitive and interact with both internal and external factors to affect change in the consumer. Because they are situational, they are difficult, if not impossible, for the marketer to control. However, it is possible to mitigate their effects with a good marketing strategy.

Physical Surroundings People are profoundly affected by their physical surroundings. An individual viewing an ad on *CSI* will react differently whether watching the show alone or at a party with friends. Same show, same ad, but a

EXHIBIT 4.7 | Subculture Groups in the United States

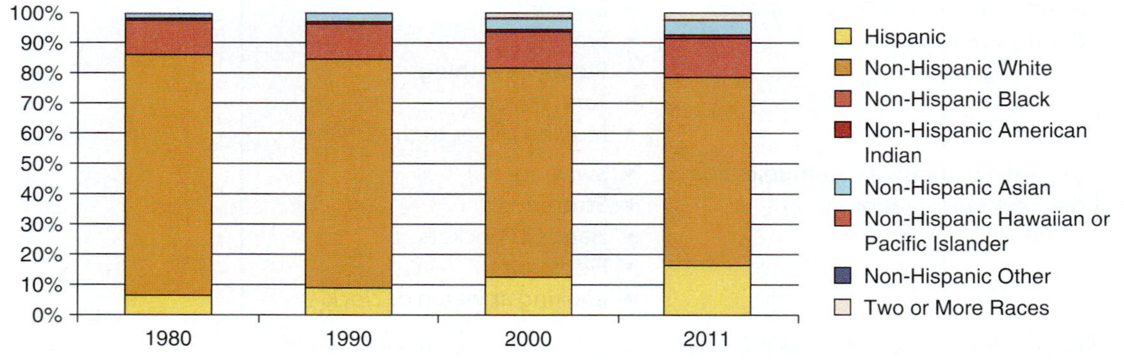

Source: *U.S. Census Bureau*, www.census.gov, accessed June 20, 2013.

different reaction as a result of the physical surroundings at the time the marketing message is being delivered. As we will see in Chapter 11, retailers devote a lot of time and resources to creating the right physical surrounding to maximize the customer's shopping experience. They know people respond differently to changes in color, lighting, or location of the product within the store; indeed, almost every element of the customer's experience is considered important in the consumer choice process.

> Children's hospitals are changing their interiors, promoting the healing properties of nature. Nemours Children's Hospital's 60-acre campus located outside of Orlando, Florida, is one such newcomer. The hospital acknowledges evidence that the presence of nature and natural lighting helps the healing process. Studies have shown, not only do views of nature help with healing, but also patients required less medication and experienced fewer complications. Aside from two outdoor terraces, the hospital has revamped its décor to suit the needs of patients and families as well. The ceilings in Nemours are a matte finish rather than metallic or glossy finishes present in other facilities. This is not for aesthetics but children's preference because they do not want to see themselves attached to machines while in bed. Nemours features fun amenities including colored lights in rooms and a saltwater aquarium maintained by Sea World. With research showing the benefits of new hospital configurations as well as considering the needs of patients and families, Nemours is establishing itself as a new breed of children's hospital.[30]

Personal Circumstances An individual's behavior is always filtered through his or her immediate personal circumstances. Parents with crying children shop differently than parents with small kids enjoying the experience, and parents without the kids along shop differently than parents with their children present. At the point of consumer choice, many things can influence the final purchase. If the line at the checkout is too long, people may eliminate certain discretionary items or forgo the entire purchase.

While it is not possible for marketers to control personal circumstances, it is important to understand how personal situations influence the choice process. Consider cold medicines such as Tylenol Cold Relief. Johnson & Johnson, maker of Tylenol Cold medicine, knows that people frequently purchase the product when they are not feeling well. As a result, the company makes the product readily available using a wide distribution channel.

Time Time is a critical situational factor that affects individuals throughout the consumer choice process. An emerging consumer trend in many industrialized countries is the willingness to trade time for money. This is evidenced in a study that reported a majority of Americans would like to have more time for family and are seeking ways to simplify their lives.[31] For many people, time is a resource to be used, spent, or wasted and, for these people, the issue is not always the best price but, rather, the best service. Increasingly, customers are asking if the purchase of this product will give them more time or be less of a hassle than another product. Automobile manufacturers and dealers have responded by creating more "hassle-free" shopping experiences. Instead of going through a difficult negotiation process to get the lowest price, dealers are offering low, fixed prices that reduce some of the hassle.

Social Factors

Humans are social beings. Everyone seeks social interaction and acceptance on some level. As people move through life, they affect and, in turn, are affected by various social factors. These factors include groups like their family, social class, and reference groups, as well as individual opinion leaders.

Family The first group any individual belongs to is the family. Families are the single most important buying group and they influence the consumer choice process in two ways. First, the family unit is the most influential teacher of cultural values. Children are socialized into a community and its values primarily through the family unit as they interact with parents, siblings, and extended family members. Second, children learn consumer behavior from their parents. As adults and later parents, they model the behavior first learned as a child.

The most basic definition of a **family** is a group of two or more people living together and related by birth, marriage, or adoption. Historically, in the United States and much of the world, the traditional family included a married couple with children of their own or adopted children. However, the last 40 years have witnessed changes in the family structure. In the 1970s the traditional family comprised 70 percent of all households. Today that number has dropped to a little under half of all households (48 percent).

New family structures are now much more prevalent. These emerging family structures create a number of challenges for marketers.[32] Single-parent households, for example, often report discretionary time is in short supply. Grocery stores have seized on this opportunity by creating deli bars that cater to working fathers and mothers who pick up dinner on their way home from work. Exhibit 4.8 provides a summary of the U.S. population by age.

The **household life cycle (HLC)** is fundamental to understanding the role of family in the consumer choice process (see Exhibit 4.9). The traditional family life cycle consists of a fairly structured set of activities that begins when single people get married (20s), start a family (30s), raise kids (40s to 50s), watch as the kids grow up and leave home (50s to 60s), and finally enter into retirement (60s and beyond). However, while this model is still relevant in many cases, several new models have emerged to reflect changes in the HLC. People are marrying later and putting off the start of a family. Women are having children later in life for a variety of reasons (marry later, focus on career). Couples raise kids then divorce and remarry, creating blended families, or they start new families of their own.

Each group in Exhibit 4.9 offers opportunities and challenges for marketing managers. From basic needs that motivate individuals to engage in the process through information search and then on to final purchase decision, each group thinks and behaves differently. It is essential to identify and understand the HLC group for each target market. Each group makes completely different choices based on its stage in the life cycle.[33] For example, two couples (35 years old, married, professionals)—one with two children, the other without—have very different lifestyles, values, and purchase priorities.

Individual responsibility in family decision making references the way individuals inside the family make decisions. There has been a great deal of research

EXHIBIT 4.8 | Population by Age

	1980	1990	2000	2010
<15	51,290,000	53,874,000	60,254,000	61,227,000
15–24	42,487,000	37,036,000	39,182,000	43,626,000
25–44	62,716,000	80,618,000	85,043,000	63,135,000
45–64	44,503,000	46,178,000	61,954,000	81,489,000
65+	25,550,000	31,084,000	34,992,000	40,268,000

Source: U.S. Census Bureau, "Families and Living Arrangements," www.census.gov/population/www/socdemo/hh-fam.html.

EXHIBIT 4.9 | Stages in the Household Life Cycle

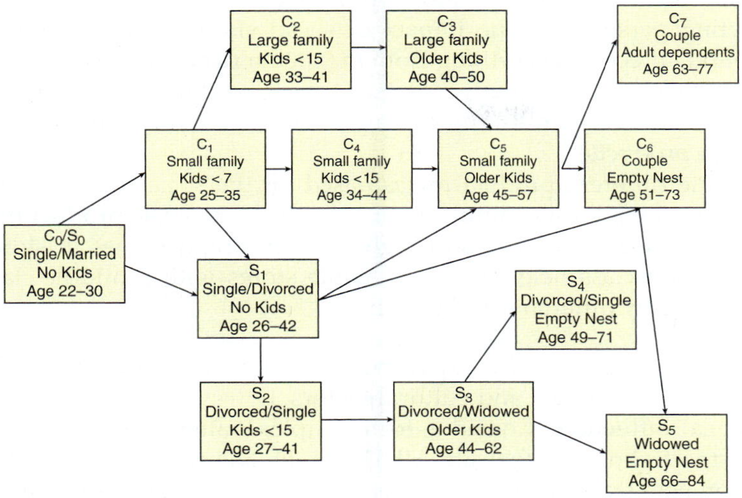

Source: Reprinted from *Journal of Marketing Research*, published by the American Marketing Association, Rex Y. Du and Wagner A. Kamakura in issue 43 (February 2006), pg. 126.

on the roles of various family members in the decision-making process. Across all the purchases in a household, research suggests, not surprisingly, that husbands and wives each dominates decision making in certain categories and jointly participate in others. For example, husbands tend to dominate insurance purchase decisions while wives are primary decision makers in grocery shopping.[34] Children, even at an early age, exert influence and dominate decisions for products such as cereal and indirectly influence decisions on things like vacations. However, traditional family responsibilities are changing as family units change. Single-parent households have shifted traditional purchase decisions. For example, single fathers must take on the responsibility for selecting their child's school.

Social Class In every society, people are aware of their social status; however, explaining the social class system to someone from outside the culture is often a challenge. People learn about social class and their social status at a very early age from their parents, school, friends, and the media. **Social class** is a ranking of individuals into harmonized groups based on demographic characteristics such as age, education, income, and occupation.

Most Western cultures have no formal social class system; however, there is an informal social ranking. These informal systems exert influence over an individual's attitudes and behavior. Two factors drive social status. Success-driven factors have the greatest effect on social status and include education, income, and occupation. Innate factors, the second category, do not result from anything the individual has done but, rather, are characteristics the individual has inherited from birth. Gender, race, and parents are the primary innate factors determining social status.

Social class is not the result of a single factor, such as income, but rather a complex interaction among many characteristics. While some social class drivers are not in the individual's control, people do make choices about their education and occupation. Therefore, it is possible for people, particularly in societies providing educational opportunities, to move into new social classes based on their achievements. In addition, the availability of easy credit, creative pricing, and new financing arrangements enable and even encourage people to engage in aspirational purchases. **Aspirational purchases** are products bought outside the individual's social standing. Over 50 percent of the luxury cars sold in the United States are leased. By offering special financing terms, individuals with lower income levels now drive a BMW, Mercedes-Benz, or Lexus. This enables people to drive a car they normally could not afford, an aspirational purchase.

From a marketing perspective, the impact of social status on consumption behavior is profound, affecting everything from the media people choose to view (lower classes watch more TV while upper classes tend to read more) to the products they buy (lower classes tend to buy more generics while the upper classes select more branded products).

Retail stores create different product mixes based on the social status of the shoppers at that store. Target, for example, maintains the same basic product mix across all its stores. However, it does add higher-priced brand names in stores serving primarily upper-class neighborhoods, while stores with a middle-class demographic get a slightly different product mix.

Opinion Leaders The previous discussion on external factors focused primarily on group influences such as social and cultural factors; however, external factors also include personal influences. Consider, for example, Walter Mossberg, technology writer for the technology website All Things D. His columns reviewing and commenting on new technologies are widely read and highly regarded. Jerry Yang, co-founder of Yahoo, says Mossberg is "one of the most trusted and influential voices in technology."[35] People listen and then respond to his columns. Wired Magazine notes that he is one of the most important technology writers and refers to him as "The Kingmaker." Mossberg is an example of an influential opinion leader. His expertise in technology products and services makes him an information source for many people and an opinion leader.

Opinion leaders fulfill an important role by classifying, explaining, and then bestowing information, most often to family and friends but occasionally to a broader audience, as is the case with Walter Mossberg. People seek out opinion leaders for a variety of reasons, including unfamiliarity with a product, reassurance about a product selection before purchasing, and anxiety resulting from high involvement with the purchase of a particular product. Anyone whose opinions are valued by the individual can be an opinion leader. For instance, the friend who enjoys cars could be an opinion leader about automobiles; the relative with a background in information technology might be the expert on technology.

While opinion leaders are often defined by product class, such as Mossberg's expertise in technology, another influential group has emerged. This new group, whose members are called **market mavens**, has information about many kinds of products, places to shop, and other facets of markets, and the members initiate discussions with consumers and respond to requests from consumers for market information.[36] The key difference between opinion leaders and market mavens is the focus on their market knowledge. Market mavens have a broader understanding and expertise that goes beyond product to include other elements of the purchase decision such as shopping experience and price.

In their role as information gatekeepers, opinion leaders and market mavens exert influence over an individual's product and brand choice. As a result, marketers seek to understand the roles of these two groups so they can identify the members and, in turn, encourage them to try a particular product. Marketers encourage these individuals using these activities:

- Market research. As a primary source of information for interested individuals, it is critical that opinion leaders and market mavens are familiar with a product and understand its advertising so they can convey the information accurately. Many market researchers focus on the way these individuals interpret messages to ensure the marketing mix is working correctly.
- Product sampling. Testing a product is an essential part of any gatekeeper's acceptance. As a result, the leaders are prime targets for product sampling.
- Advertising. Companies use opinion leaders and market mavens to influence decision makers whether it is a business leader or an individual consumer.

Barclay's (a global financial services company) hired Phil Mickelson as its spokesperson because he is an opinion leader. The company hopes Mickelson's qualities—successful, focused, and a winner—influence business leaders looking for financial services.

Reference Groups Everyone identifies with and is influenced by groups. In most cases, the individual may belong to the group or seek membership, while in other situations the group is perceived negatively and the individual works to disassociate himself. A **reference group** is a group of individuals whose beliefs, attitudes, and behavior influence (positively or negatively) the beliefs, attitudes, and behavior of an individual.[37] Three characteristics are used to categorize reference groups: association, desirability, and degree of affiliation.

The association with reference groups can be formal or informal. Students, for example, have a formal relationship with their college or university and, as a result, respond to and connect with other students at the school. At the same time, a student has a number of informal relationships with other groups. Circles of friends and classmates, while not a formal group, can exert a lot of influence over an individual.

A key characteristic impacting the degree a group affects the individual is the extent to which an individual desires to be associated with the group. **Desirability** is the extent and direction of the emotional connection an individual wishes to have with a particular group. Individuals can really want to belong to a group or not, and the linkage can be either positive or negative. Sports teams encourage participation at many levels. Like many cities, Boston has a number of established sports teams, including the Red Sox, Patriots, Celtics, and Bruins, each with thousands of supporters, though the level of support varies widely. Dedicated fans with the available resources become season-ticket holders, spending thousands of dollars to attend every game. Many Boston residents are not actively involved with any team or are ardent fans of one team but show less interest in the others. Some Boston residents may even support teams from other cities, perhaps the New York Yankees, and hold negative perceptions of the local team. As a result, the desirability of belonging to the reference group known as a "Boston sports fan" is person- and even team-specific.

The **degree of affiliation** indicates the amount of interpersonal contact an individual has with the reference group. **Primary groups** are marked by frequent contact, while less frequent or limited dealings are known as **secondary groups**. Individuals come in frequent contact with co-workers, close friends, and other groups such as religious, special-interest, or hobby groups that may be primary or secondary depending on the level of contact. Over time, the degree of affiliation will likely change; for example, when someone changes jobs, the primary group of co-workers will also change.

Over the last few years, Zumba has gained a large cult following. In 2011, the company surpassed its own goal of 10 million participants and continues to grow. In its beginnings with infomercial advertising, the brand attempted to sell fitness. However, in 2006, Zumba changed its messaging. It created an emotional appeal to its users in which customers would associate it with free and electrifying joy. CMO Jeffery Perlman was inspired by brands such as Harley-Davidson that had devoted customers. He wanted to understand what Zumba customers saw in the brand and looked to create a brand that could span other media and still maintain its personality. The company moved into apparel, shoes, accessories, and video games. Mr. Perlman concluded, "We want to craft an archetype of a Zumba enthusiast. If a yoga enthusiast is a tofu-eating, patchouli-smelling person, then Zumba enthusiast might have the baggy cargo pants, drive a Jeep Wrangler, and rip up her clothing. We're in the business of building a community."[38]

THE LEVEL OF INVOLVEMENT INFLUENCES THE PROCESS

One significant outcome of motivation, discussed earlier, is **involvement** with the product because it mediates the product choice decision. Involvement is activated by three elements: the individual's background and psychological profile, the aspirational focus, and the environment at the time of the purchase decision. As we noted, motivation is unique to each individual and drives purchase decisions. Aspirational focus is anything of interest to the buyer and is not limited to the product itself. It is possible to be involved with a brand, advertising, or activities that occur with product use.

Many people ride motorcycles, but far fewer ride Harley-Davidson motorcycles and, among Harley riders, some get tattoos of the Harley-Davidson logo. Clearly these people are highly involved beyond the product and associate strongly with the Harley lifestyle. Finally, the environment changes the level of involvement. Time, for example, can limit involvement if there is pressure to make a decision quickly but can enhance involvement if there is sufficient time to fully engage in the decision process. Involvement influences every step in the choice decision process, and, as a result, marketers create strategies based on high and low levels of involvement. For example, high-involvement purchases drive buyers to more cognitive learning such as the new car buyer who visits car dealers, checks out automotive websites, and seeks out the advice of automotive experts for information on cars in an effort to make an informed purchase decision. On the other hand, conditioning works well with low-involvement purchases such as the purchase of gasoline where people frequently purchase from the same station because of various factors such as price and location.[39]

Decision Making with High Involvement

Greater motivation that leads to greater involvement results in a more active and committed choice decision process. When someone is concerned with the outcome of the process, they will spend more time learning about product options and become more emotionally connected to the process and the decision. Someone stimulated to acquire new information is engaged in **high-involvement learning**. For example, someone interested in purchasing a new high-end digital camera will seek out product reviews on CNET.com or other online sources to discover information that will assist in the choice decision. Some, despite a brand preference, may be willing to experiment with other brands and seek out additional information looking for a new alternative. A high level of involvement usually means the entire process takes longer. High-involvement consumers report high levels of satisfaction in their purchase decision. This is not surprising since these consumers spend more time engaged in the decision process and, therefore, are more comfortable in their decision.

Even small-scale products can be time-consuming to buy. For women, discovering and investing in new beauty products can be an involved process. Birchbox, a New York City–based subscription service, delivers samples to its customers in the United States, Spain, France, and the United Kingdom. For a yearlong subscription of $120, Birchbox will deliver a box of samples monthly. It even bolsters an online shop in which it sells the full-sized versions of the sample products. The brand continues to expand its operations to also include sample subscriptions for men's products. As a leader in "discovery retail," Birchbox is allowing its product-conscious customers to discover new brands in a noncommittal way, allowing them to try new products without fear of waste. With operations only starting in September of 2010, the company already boasts over 400 brand partnerships. As its growth continues to boom, Birchbox is leading the way for high-involvement customers to find and potentially purchase a myriad of products.[40]

Decision Making with Limited Involvement

While high-involvement purchases are more significant to the consumer, the vast majority of purchases involve limited or low involvement. From the purchase of gasoline to the choice of restaurants, decisions are often made almost automatically, often out of habit, with little involvement in the purchase decision. The reality is that consumers tend to focus their time and energy on high-involvement purchases while making many purchases with little or no thought at all.

Low-involvement learning happens when people are not prompted to value new information. This is more prevalent than high-involvement learning because the vast majority of marketing stimuli occur when there is little or no interest in the information. People do not watch TV for the commercials; they watch for the programming, and advertising is just part of the viewing experience. Likewise, print advertising exists alongside articles and is often ignored. While people are not actively seeking the information, they are exposed to advertising and this, in turn, affects their attitudes about a brand. Research suggests that people shown ads in a low-involvement setting are more likely to include those brands in the choice decision process. Low-involvement consumers spend little time comparing product attributes and frequently identify very few differences across brands. Because the decision is relatively unimportant, they will often purchase the product with the best shelf position or lowest price with no evaluation of salient product characteristics.[41]

Marketers consider several strategies in targeting low-involvement consumers. The objective of these strategies is to raise consumer involvement with the product. Generally, time is the defining characteristic for these strategies. Short-term strategies involve using sales promotions such as coupons, rebates, or discounts to encourage trying the product and then hoping the consumers will raise their product involvement. Long-term strategies are more difficult to implement. Marketers seek to focus on the product's value proposition, creating products with additional product features, better reliability, or more responsive service to increase customer satisfaction. Additionally, strong marketing communications campaigns that speak to consumer issues or concerns can raise involvement with the product. A classic example of this tactic is Michelin's highly effective and long-running advertising campaign that links a relatively low-involvement product, tires, with a significant consumer concern, family safety. Tires are not typically a high-involvement product; however, when the voiceover on the commercial says, "Because so much is riding on your tires" while showing a baby riding in the car, consumer involvement in the product—and more specifically the brand—increases.

While a low-involvement consumer demonstrates little or no brand loyalty, he or she is also, by definition, open to brand switching. As a result, brands can experience significant gains in consumer acceptance with an effective, comprehensive marketing strategy.

THE CONSUMER DECISION-MAKING PROCESS

LO 4-4

Understand the consumer decision-making process.

Every day, people make a number of consumer decisions. From breakfast through the last television show watched before going to bed, people are choosing products as a result of a decision-making process. Learning about that process is a vital step for marketers trying to create an effective marketing strategy.

Years of consumer research have resulted in a five-stage model of consumer decision making. While not everyone passes through all five stages for every purchase, all consumers apply the same fundamental sequence beginning with problem recognition, followed by search for information, evaluation of alternatives, product choice decision, and finally post-purchase evaluation. Each time a purchase decision is made, the individual begins to evaluate the product in preparation for the next decision (see Exhibit 4.10)

EXHIBIT 4.10 | Consumer Decision-Making Process

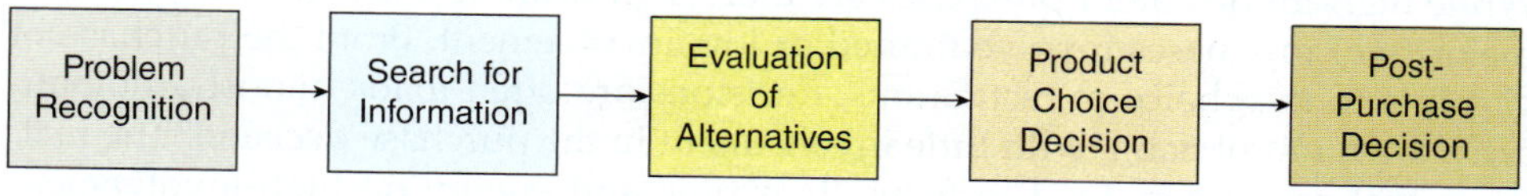

However, as noted earlier, someone driving home from work does not go through an extensive search for information or evaluate a number of alternatives in purchasing gasoline for the car. In all likelihood, the consumer buys from a station he or she knows well and shops at regularly. Nevertheless, this model is helpful because it illustrates what can be called the "complete decision-making process," which occurs when people are fully involved in the purchase.

Problem Recognition

Every purchase decision made by an individual is initiated by a problem or need that drives the consumer decision-making process. Problems or needs are the result of differences between a person's real and preferred states.

People live in the perceived reality of present time or **real state**. At the same time, people also have desires that reflect how they would like to feel or live in the present time and this is known as a **preferred state**. When the two states are in balance, the individual does not require anything and no purchase occurs. However, where there is a discrepancy in the two states, a problem is created and the consumer decision-making process begins.

The discrepancy, or gap, can be created by internal or external drivers. Internal drivers are basic human needs such as hunger and security. Someone is hungry (real state) and wants to eat (preferred state). This will lead to a number of choices: eat at home, dine out, or go to the grocery store. It may even trigger other options such as calling a friend, which addresses a need for social interaction. External drivers happen as people interact with the world. Some of these triggers result from a company's marketing efforts, but most arise when an individual experiences something that creates a desire, like seeing a friend driving a new car or hearing about a good new restaurant.

Despite internal or external stimuli, people do not respond to every gap between a real and preferred state. Sometimes the disparity is not sufficient to drive the person to action. A person may want a new car but does not act on that feeling because he or she lacks the financial resources or simply cannot justify the purchase. When the conflict between real and preferred states reaches a certain level, the decision-making process begins.

Marketers need to understand problem recognition for several reasons. First, it is essential to learn about the problems and needs of the target market to create value-added products. Second, key elements of an effective marketing strategy, particularly communication, are predicated on a good knowledge of problem recognition triggers. For example, the classic advertising campaign by the California Milk Processor Board, "Got Milk," spoke directly to the recognition of the problem—do you have milk in your refrigerator. The success of the campaign has been credited with reinvigorating the sale of cow's milk since the ads started running in the early 1990s.

Search for Information

Once a problem is recognized and action is required, people seek information to facilitate the best decision. The search for information is not categorical; rather, it operates on a continuum from limited to extensive. Consider the following examples. A couple notices the low-fuel light comes on as they are driving home from a party. The driver recalls their "local" station is on the way home and, without any additional information, stops at the station and fills up the car. This is an example of **minimal information search**. The same couple now finds out they are going to have a baby and realizes their Infiniti G coupe has to be replaced with a more practical vehicle. They engage in a thorough information search reviewing car magazines, soliciting opinions from friends and family, conducting online research on sites like Edmunds or KBB, and test-driving a number of new cars and SUVs before making a final purchase decision. This is an example of **extensive information search**. Between these two extremes is **limited information search**, which, as the name implies, involves some, albeit restricted, search for information. Suppose the wife from the couple in our previous examples has a cold. The husband stops at the drugstore to get her some medicine. At the cold medicine aisle he scans the boxes looking for the one that will provide "maximum relief" for his wife's symptoms. He may even ask the pharmacist for help in selecting the best choice. At this point he is engaged in a limited search for information. Generally, people do only the amount of information search they believe is necessary to make the best decision.

The Internet plays a significant role in consumers' purchasing decisions. According to a PricewaterhouseCoopers report, 83 percent of U.S. consumers (80 percent of global consumers) go online to research products before they buy those items in brick-and-mortar stores. The products Americans are researching include more than just large-ticket items. Seventy-three percent of U.S. consumers, and 60 percent of global consumers, research about clothing, shoes, toys, and health and beauty products before purchasing them. Even more, consumers are becoming more likely to multichannel shop. Globally, consumers are more comfortable shopping online. Consumers note the convenience of online shopping as the main reason for using that channel, with low prices being the second. Online shopping and research itself may take place over a variety of channels, whether it be computer, tablet, or cellular phone. With growing use of the Internet in retailing, companies are faced with integrating their channels of contact, including website, mobile, catalog, and call centers, to provide seamless service to their customers.[42]

Information Sources There are two basic sources of information: internal and external. **Internal information sources**, as the name implies, are all information stored in memory and accessed by the individual. This is always the first place people consider for information. Past experiences, conversations, research, preexisting beliefs, and attitudes create an extensive internal database that is tapped by the individual once the problem is recognized. In our example of the car low on gas, the driver searched internal information and found past experiences provided sufficient information to make a decision.

Even when additional information is needed, internal information is used to frame the external search. Price limits and key performance metrics, criteria often used in the evaluation of alternatives, are frequently derived from information stored in memory. People gather and process information even if they are not actively involved in the purchase decision process. Consequently, an individual's internal information is changing all the time. As people get older, gain more experience with a product or brand, and gather more information, they often rely more on internal information and conduct a less external information search.

The second fundamental source of information is external. Once people have determined internal information is not sufficient to make the purchase decision, they seek information from outside sources. **External information sources** include independent groups (sources), personal associations (friends and family), marketer-created information (sales brochures, advertising), and experiences (product trial and demonstrations).

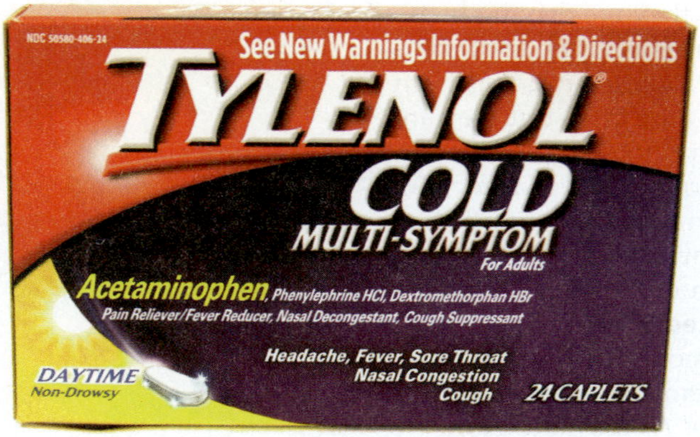

Tylenol Cold provides a great deal of information on the package to help consumers make a decision in the store at the point of purchase.

An organization's marketing communications represent only one source, albeit an important one, among several external information source options. However, company marketing communications can play an important role in influencing other sources of information such as personal contacts. For example, when Johnson & Johnson introduces new baby care products, it spends a lot of money providing product samples and information to pediatricians and nurses in an effort to support the company's direct marketing communications to young mothers. So even though consumers indicate company-sponsored marketing information is of limited value in making purchase decisions, the company's marketing efforts can play a more significant role when considered in light of their effect on other external information sources. Exhibit 4.11 is a summary of external information sources and highlights the diversity of available information resources.

Defining the Set of Alternatives At some point in the search for information, often during the internal information search, people begin to limit the number of alternatives under consideration. From a practical perspective, it is simply not possible to gather and process information on many different options. This is known as bounded rationality and defines people's limited capacity to process information.

People begin with a very large set of possible alternatives known as the **complete set**. This set includes a variety of options across different brands and perhaps even products. Consider a person looking for mobile, wireless Internet access. The complete set could include different product options (cell phone, laptop,

EXHIBIT 4.11 | Sources of External Information

External Information Sources	Example	Marketing Implications
Independent groups	*Consumer Reports* Consumer's Union	Favorable reviews from independent sources are an important source of external information. Marketers need a strategy to reach independent sources with relevant information.
Personal associations	Family/Friends	These associations can be an important external source of information in certain decisions. Marketers seek to influence reference groups and opinion leaders through favorable product reviews and effective marketing communications.
Marketer information	Advertising	Effective marketing communications reinforce messages to other external information sources such as independent groups.
Experiential	Product trials	Product samples for certain categories such as food are easy to provide. Encourage people to seek out product trials and demonstrations when a sample is not appropriate (electronics, automobiles).

or tablet computer) and brands (Apple, Dell, Sony, Samsung, Hewlett-Packard, Nokia, and Motorola). Based on the individual's choice criteria, however, this large set of possible options will be reduced. Keep in mind that the complete set is not *all* options available to the buyer; rather, the set is the options that the buyer is aware of when the search process begins. The extent of the buyer's knowledge about the problem and available options determines the set of possible alternatives in the complete set.

As consumers move through the search for information, certain products (laptop computer) may be eliminated in favor of others (tablet computer) and brands will be evaluated and discarded. The **awareness set** reduces the number of options. At a minimum, the number of different product categories, if considered, will be reduced and some brands discarded. Interestingly, the awareness set can include choices across product categories. In our example, it is still possible for a particular brand of cell phone to remain in the awareness set despite the fact they are different product categories. From the awareness set, individuals conduct an additional information search. Based on additional information and evaluation, a **consideration (evoked) set** is created, which encompasses the strongest options. It is from the consideration set that the product decision is made.

Marketers are vitally interested in learning about the information search process for two reasons. First, marketers must identify important external information sources so they can direct their resources to the most effective external sources. Second, they must learn how consumers choose products for inclusion in their awareness and consideration sets to create marketing strategies that increase the probability of being in the consideration set.

Evaluation of Alternatives

Concurrent with the search for information are the analysis and evaluation of possible product choices. As we discussed previously, consumers move, sometimes quickly, from many options to a more restricted awareness set and from there to a final consideration set from which a decision is made. During this process, the individual is constantly evaluating the alternatives based on internal and external information.

The consumer choice process is complex and ever changing. Environmental and personal factors at the moment of decision dramatically affect the purchase decision. As a result, it is impossible to develop a consumer choice model for every purchase. However, years of research suggest consumers make product choices primarily from three perspectives: emotional, attitude based, and attribute based.

Emotional Choice Not all purchases are made strictly for rational reasons. Indeed, product choices can be **emotional choices**, based on attitudes about a product, or based on attributes of the product depending on the situation. Frequently, the product choice encompasses a mix of all three. An individual goes to Starbucks for the personal pleasure of enjoying a cappuccino (emotional). That same person also considers Starbucks the best choice for getting together with friends after evaluating other choices (attitude based). Finally, the individual finds Starbucks' cappuccinos simply taste better than those of other competitors (attribute based).

While emotions have been considered an important factor in decision making for many years, it is only recently that marketers began to develop specific marketing strategies targeting emotion-based decisions. Product design and execution even focus on creating an emotional response to the product. From there, marketing communications connect the product to the target audience using images and words that convey an emotional connection. Exhibit 4.12 shows an ad that communicates emotion to the reader.

EXHIBIT 4.12 Ketel One Offers an Emotional Choice

Ketel One is connecting to their customers on an emotional level, reinforcing the old adage—"One picture is worth a thousand words."

Attitude-Based Choice Early in the evaluation of alternatives, people regularly use beliefs and values to direct their assessment. As consumers create the awareness set, they discard or include products and brands using existing attitudes. **Attitude-based choices** tend to be more holistic, using summary impressions rather than specific attributes to evaluate the options, and affect even important purchases such as a car or house. It is not uncommon for beliefs to affect the actual product decision. For example, "it is important to buy cars made in America" or the opposite, "foreign cars are better than American products." When two brands are judged to be relatively the same, people frequently look to existing attitudes to guide their decision. When someone responds to a question about why he bought a particular product with, "I always buy . . ." or "this is the only brand I use . . .," they are likely making an attitude-based choice decision.

Attribute-Based Choice By far the most prevalent approach to product decisions is **attribute-based choice** based on the premise that product choices are made by comparing brands across a defined set of attributes. These evaluative attributes are the product features or benefits considered relevant to the specific problem addressed in the purchase decision. Antilock brakes are a product feature that translates into a consumer benefit—better control in a hazardous situation. Most consumers could not describe how antilock brakes actually work but are quite aware of the benefits and would eliminate a car from the choice process if it failed to have that product feature. Not all evaluative attributes are tangible. Brand image, prestige, and attitudes about a brand or product can also be used as evaluative criteria.

Kohl's Department Stores has been successful targeting family-oriented "middle-class soccer moms." Recently, the company has targeted younger, professional women by bringing in designer labels such as Candies (shoes) and Elle. With a focus on value and convenience, Kohl's connects with customers on two key attributes critical to their purchase decisions.[43]

Product Choice Decision

The end result of evaluating product alternatives is an intended purchase option. Until the actual purchase, it is still only an "intended" option because any number of events or interactions can happen to dissuade or alter the final purchase decision. Four purchase event characteristics affect the actual choice decision:

Physical surroundings—the environment for the purchase. From store colors to the employees, consumers respond to their physical environment. For example, while the color red creates awareness and interest, it also creates feelings of anxiety and negativity. Blue is calmer and considered the most conducive in creating positive feeling with the customer. Crowding can have a negative effect on purchase decisions because, if the store becomes too crowded, people will forgo the purchase, perhaps going somewhere else.

Social circumstances—the social interaction at the time of purchase. Shopping is a social activity and people are influenced by the social interaction at the time of purchase. Trying on an outfit alone may lead to the purchase; however, when putting on the outfit while shopping with a friend, it is unlikely the clothing will be purchased if the friend does not like it.

Time—the amount of time an individual has to make the purchase. The product choice decision can be affected by time pressure. The consumer will be less willing to wait for the best solution and more likely to purchase an acceptable alternative.

State of mind—individual's state of mind at time of purchase. An individual's mood influences the purchase decision. People in a positive state of mind are more likely to browse. Negative mood states are less tolerant and lead to increased impulse and compulsive purchases.

As a result of these purchase event characteristics, the intended purchase can be altered despite the information search and evaluation process. Some of these characteristics are at least nominally in the marketer's control. Other characteristics, such as an individual's state of mind, are uncontrollable and must be dealt with at the moment of purchase by employees who, it is hoped, have the skills and training needed to handle difficult situations.[44]

The final purchase decision is not a single decision; rather, the consumer confronts five important decisions:

What: select the product and, more specifically, the brand. Included as part of the product choice are decisions about product features, service options, and other characteristics of the product experience

Where: select the point of purchase. Select the retailer and, increasingly, the channel—retail store (bricks) or online (clicks)—through which the product is to be purchased.

How much: choose the specific quantity to be purchased. For example, warehouse clubs, such as Sam's Club and Costco, offer consumer options on purchase quantity. If you have the ability to store products, it is possible to save money by purchasing in larger quantities.

When: select the timing of the purchase. The timing of the purchase can make a difference in the final purchase price. Car dealers traditionally offer better deals at the end of the month as they try to meet monthly sales quotas. Through sales and other marketing communications, marketers encourage consumers to purchase sooner rather than later.

Payment: choose the method of payment. The selection of a payment method makes a big difference to the consumer and marketer. Marketers want to make it easy for the consumer to purchase; however, not all payment methods are equal. Credit cards charge the retailer a fee that, in turn, is passed back to the consumer. One payment method, the debit card, is becoming popular with younger adults and combines the convenience of a credit card with the fiscal responsibility of using cash. Indeed, the consumer can often choose to not purchase the product at all, as other choices are available besides purchase. They can rent or lease products such as automobiles, making it possible to use products they could not normally afford.

Consumers make a number of decisions at the point of purchase. Often, the selection of where the product will be purchased is done in conjunction with the product evaluation.

Post-Purchase Assessment

Once the purchase is complete, consumers begin to evaluate their decision. Attitudes change as they experience and interact with the product. These attitudinal changes include the way the consumer looks at competitors as well as the product itself. At the same time, marketers want to foster and encourage the relationship and, as we will discuss in Chapter 6, increasingly focus resources to build the customer relationship. Most of a CRM program is built around the customer's experience after the purchase. The four critical characteristics of post-purchase assessment are dissonance, use/nonuse, disposition, and satisfaction/dissatisfaction.

Dissonance High-involvement, large purchases often lead to a level of doubt or anxiety known as **post-purchase dissonance**. Most purchases occur with little or no dissonance.[45] The likelihood of dissonance increases if one or more of the following purchase decision attributes are present: (1) a high degree of commitment that is not easily revoked; (2) a high degree of importance for the customer; (3) alternatives that are rated equally and a purchase decision that is not clear. Also, the individual's own predisposition for anxiety can create additional dissonance. Big-ticket purchases frequently include several of those characteristics. For example, buying a house, the single biggest purchase most people will ever make, is a big commitment that can be complicated when two or three homes are evaluated as more or less equal by the consumer.

How do consumers reduce dissonance? The single most effective method is a thorough information search and evaluation of alternatives. When consumers are confident that due diligence has been done, they have less anxiety after the purchase. If dissonance remains a problem, additional information can be sought to reduce anxiety and reinforce the decision. Marketers can direct marketing communications to reduce dissonance, particularly with large purchases such as automobiles. As part of a CRM program, many companies follow up with customers after the purchase to assess their satisfaction.

Use/Nonuse Consumers buy a product to use. Marketers are acutely interested in learning how customers use the product for several reasons. First, it is important the customer knows how to use the product correctly. Buying a new television can quickly become a negative experience if it is not set up properly. As a result, marketers want to be sure the customer understands how the product is to be used and any setup procedures that may be needed to ensure proper function. Second, a satisfied customer means a greater likelihood of additional purchases. Buying and riding a bicycle means the consumer is more likely to buy a helmet, light, bike rack, and other accessories.

Many products are purchased but not used or at least not consumed immediately. Some products are returned because the consumer has a negative experience such as a defective product. Marketers, of course, work to avoid a negative experience. Building customer relationships and making sure the customer understands the product and how it is to be used reduce the probability of consumers returning the product. Another potential post-purchase problem can be that the product is purchased and not used. In these situations, marketers seek to stimulate product usage. Campbell Soup Co. found customers frequently had several cans of soup on their shelf for long periods of time. The company developed a marketing communications program to encourage faster consumption of the product. Many packaged foods include expiration dates encouraging consumers to use the product quickly and repurchase.

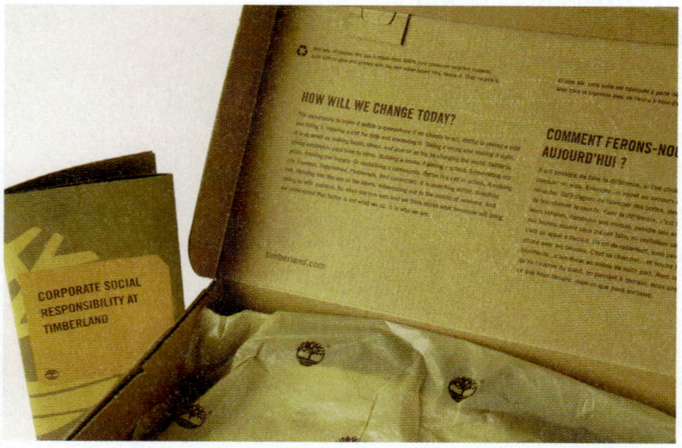

Timberland is one of many companies that uses recycled materials in its packaging.

Disposal Increasingly, marketers are concerned about how products are disposed of once they are no longer in use. Environmental concerns consistently rank as a major issue for consumers in many parts of the world. People living in the United States, for example, produce nearly 2,000 pounds (1 ton) of garbage per person every year. Once a product is consumed, in most cases, a physical object remains and needs to be disposed of. New technologies such as computer CPUs and monitors are particularly difficult to discard because they contain dangerous chemicals.

Environmentally friendly products encourage proper use and disposal. Companies including Coca-Cola use recycled materials in their manufacturing and packaging. At the same time, companies are encouraging consumers to recycle on their own. Dell and other computer companies have a program that encourages consumers to recycle their old computers.[46]

Satisfaction/Dissatisfaction Consumers evaluate every aspect of the product. As previously noted, this includes any dissonance present at the time of purchase, use or nonuse of the product, the product disposition, the purchase experience, and even the value equation. This results in the consumer's satisfaction or dissatisfaction with the product and purchase decision. In addition, various dimensions of the overall experience will be satisfactory or unsatisfactory. A customer may love the product but dislike the dealer or retailer.

Most products are evaluated on two dimensions—instrumental performance and symbolic performance. **Instrumental performance** relates to the actual performance features of the product and answers the question: Did the product do what is what supposed to do? **Symbolic performance** refers to the image-building aspects of the product and answers the question: Did the product make me feel better about myself? A product that performs poorly on instrumental dimensions will ultimately lead to dissatisfaction. However, for a consumer to be fully satisfied with the product, it must perform well both instrumentally and symbolically. A new Hyundai automobile may have scored high on instrumental performance but low on symbolic performance. Is the customer dissatisfied? No, but it is not certain that person will purchase another Hyundai.

There are two primary outcomes of consumer dissatisfaction with a product: a customer will either change his or her behavior or do nothing. When a customer has an unfavorable experience at the bank, she may not leave, but her opinion of the bank diminishes. Over time, this will erode the consumer's evaluation of the bank. The second result of consumer dissatisfaction is a change in behavior. The consumer may simply choose to stop shopping at that store or purchasing a particular product. Another option is to complain to management. Marketers are aware that for every complaint, there are eight "quiet" but dissatisfied consumers who chose to walk away. An even greater concern is consumers telling friends about a bad experience or complaining to government agencies. Finally, dissatisfied consumers who believe their legal rights have been violated may take legal action for damages related to the purchase experience.

SUMMARY

A thorough knowledge and understanding of customers is an essential element in developing an effective value proposition. For business-to-consumer companies this means learning about how and why consumers buy products and services. This chapter talks about the consumer buying decision process. We discuss the two complex, critical forces (internal and external) that shape the consumer decision-making process. We offer an in-depth analysis of the process a consumer uses in making a purchase decision. The distinction is made between high- and low-involvement decisions, which dramatically affects the degree to which the consumer engages in the entire buying decision process.

KEY TERMS

demographics 95
family life cycle 97
lifestyle 97
gender roles 98
motivation 99
attitude 102
multiattribute model 102
perception 102
selective awareness 103
selective distortion 103
selective retention 103
memory 103
short-term memory 103
long-term memory 103
learning 104
conditioning 104
cognitive learning 105
personality 105
brand personality 106
culture 106
language 107
cultural values 107
nonverbal communication 107
subculture 108
family 110
household life cycle (HLC) 110
social class 111
aspirational purchases 111
opinion leaders 112
market mavens 112
reference group 113
desirability 113
degree of affiliation 113
primary group 113
secondary group 113
involvement 114
high-involvement learning 114
low-involvement learning 115
real state 116
preferred state 116
minimal information search 117
extensive information search 117
limited information search 117
internal information sources 117
external information sources 117
complete set 118
awareness set 119
consideration (evoked) set 119
emotional choice 119
attitude-based choice 120
attribute-based choice 120
post-purchase dissonance 122
instrumental performance 123
symbolic performance 123

APPLICATION QUESTIONS

1. As we have discussed, understanding the consumers in a target market is critical to creating an effective value proposition. Assume you are the vice president of marketing for Regal Cinemas. What do you think is the demographic profile (including the age, income, and life cycle stage) of your largest target market? As part of a mini-market research project, visit a movie theater on a weekend and track the people entering. How old are they? Are they families or people meeting friends?
2. You are the marketing manager for the Bowflex Revolution Home Gym. You believe the product appeals to both men and women. As you develop the marketing strategy, what differences might you consider in the product based on whether a man or woman is buying? What about the marketing communications (message, choice of media)?
3. Disneyland has traditionally marketed to families; recently, however, new household life cycle patterns have led to changes in the marketing strategy. Identify three household life cycle stages that Disney may want to consider in the future.
4. The consumer decision process varies by purchase for each individual. Compare and contrast the consumer decision-making process you go through in buying gas for your car with the purchase of a new home entertainment system. How are the processes similar and how are the two purchase decisions different? Why do you think they are different?

MANAGEMENT DECISION CASE: Smartphones, Seniors, and Purchase Decisions

Picture this rather complex consumer purchase decision. An 82-year-old man (let's call him Jack) walks into to a Verizon Wireless store looking for a smartphone. However, Jack already is having serious reservations about his purchase because (a) he currently does not own even a basic cell phone let alone a smartphone, (b) up to now he's not been sure why he would need a smartphone, (c) he's really not interested in investing the time it will require to learn how to use the phone, which means (d) he's not convinced he will *ever* use it, and (e) if he doesn't think he will ever use it, then he's definitely not interested in being locked into the typical *two-year contract* required by most U.S. cellular providers.

The only reason Jack is in the market for a smartphone is because he is of the age where his children want him to be easily accessible so they can make sure he is "okay" at a moment's notice. Jack's mindset is that he knows the status of his own health at all times and figures that if his children want to know how he is, they can simply call his land line. The logic is that if he answers the land line, he's okay; if he doesn't answer the land line, he's well enough to be out of the house doing something else. So why all of the bother and fuss about buying a smartphone?

Like many seniors, Jack ultimately relents to the wishes of his children and makes the trek (driving by himself, of course) to the Verizon Wireless store. Once inside, he immediately comes in contact with a very enthusiastic 20-something salesperson (let's call her April) who is wielding a tablet-like device and talking nonstop about the latest gadgets and 4G service. After getting some basic information from Jack such as what kind of smartphone and data plan he has now (he doesn't have either), why he wants a smartphone (he doesn't want one, but his kids want him to have it), how he sees himself using the smartphone (he's not convinced he will use it), and what kind of options he's looking for in a phone and data plan (he's clueless), April shows Jack several different phones with various options while explaining that some phones require a data plan (which necessitates even more explanation) and others do not. Eventually Jack remembers that his children have talked a lot about the Apple iPhone and wonders if that would be appropriate for him. After considerably more explanation from the sales representative, Jack wears down and commits to the iPhone 4 because it is only 99 cents with a two-year contract. Feigning horror at Jack's choice, the sales representative immediately asks, "but what will your family and friends think if you are not using the newest phone (iPhone 5S at the time) and technology on the market?" After Jack finally stopped laughing at this seemingly ridiculous question, he simply said, "I think they will understand."

The interactions described between the consumer (Jack), his children (influencers), and the Verizon Wireless salesperson, April, illustrate many aspects of the consumer decision-making process. Although Jack does not personally recognize a problem with not having a smartphone, his children have been successful in convincing him that a problem does exist and influencing him to remedy the problem soon. Upon being convinced of the need for a smartphone, Jack (reluctantly) finds himself in information search mode when he enters the store and encounters the salesperson. There, he attempts to get his questions answered, but this is all so new to him that it is difficult to grasp many aspects of the information being provided. Nonetheless, he eventually is persuaded to make a decision about the type of phone and data plan he wants to purchase and a few minutes later he is walking out the door with his spiffy new phone activated for him to start using right away.

Fast-forward to a couple of months later—despite offers to help and extreme urging to do so, Jack's kids find that since he is not used to having a smartphone, he is still not in the routine of carrying it with him when he leaves the house. He also still has not set up his voicemail function, nor is he checking text messages. Frustrating as it is, this results in everyone reverting back to the old system of simply relying on the land line with Jack left holding the bag of paying for a two-year plan for a product that he uses minimally.

Customer needs and wants? They've obviously been overlooked so far in this scenario. Whether his children are able to educate him about the phone's features and, more importantly, convince him to ever carry and use the phone remains to be seen.

Questions for Consideration

1. After Jack purchases his phone and data plan, is it likely that he experienced cognitive dissonance with his purchase? What evidence makes you answer the way you did?
2. What social and/or cultural factors played a role in this consumer purchasing the smartphone and data plan? Which ones do you think were most important and why?
3. The scenario described in the case is an illustration that not only do companies have to overcome the hurdle of getting someone to buy their product but also have to educate consumers on the proper use of the product after purchase. Otherwise, the consumer has a product he/she may not properly use and thus achieves no value or satisfaction from the purchase! What steps could Verizon Wireless take in the post-purchase time frame to ensure that consumers get the maximum value and satisfaction out of their purchase and avoid outcomes such as Jack's?

MARKETING PLAN EXERCISE

ACTIVITY 4: Define Consumer Markets

For those marketing products to consumers (or through a channel that sells directly to consumers), understanding the purchase decision process of the target market is an essential element of the marketing plan. This exercise includes the following activities:

1. Develop a demographic profile of the customer to include
   a. Age
   b. Income
   c. Occupation
   d. Education
   e. Lifestyle (activities, interests, opinions)
2. Describe the motivation of the target consumer. Why is the consumer buying the product?
3. What external forces will influence the target consumer as he or she considers the purchase? For example, will the consumer's culture or subculture affect the purchase decision? How?
4. Describe the consumer's typical consumer purchase decision process? What is the likely process a consumer will go through in making the decision to purchase the product?

NOTES

1. S. Mark Young, James J. Gong, and Wim A. Van der Stede, "The Business of Selling Movies," *Strategic Finance,* 2008 89, no. 9 (2009), pp. 35–42; and Jon Silver and John McDonnell, "Are Movie Theaters Doomed? Do Exhibitors See the Big Picture as Theaters Lose Their Competitive Advantage?," *Business Horizons* 50, no. 6 (2007), pp. 491–501.
2. P. Sullivan and J. Heitmeyer, "Looking at Gen Y Shopping Preferences and Intentions: Exploring the Role of Experience and Apparel Involvement," *International Journal of Consumer Studies* 32, no. 3 (2008), pp. 285–99.
3. Tiffany Hsu, "Wineries Pour Efforts into Targeting Younger Drinkers," *Los Angeles Times,* March 1, 2013, http://articles.latimes.com/2013/mar/01/business/la-fi-young-wine-drinkers-20130228.
4. Paul G. Patterson, "Demographic Correlates of Loyalty in a Service Context," *Journal of Services Marketing* 21, no. 2 (2007), pp. 112–21.
5. Lisa E. Bolton, Americus Reed II, Kevin G. Volpp, and Katrina Armstrong, "How Does Drug and Supplement Marketing Affect a Healthy Lifestyle?" *Journal of Consumer Research* 34, no. 5 (2008), pp. 713–26.
6. Maureen E. Hupfer and Brian Detior, "Beyond Gender Differences: Self-Concept Orientation and Relationship-Building Orientation on the Internet," *Journal of Business Research* 60, no. 6 (2007), pp. 613–28; and J. Michael Pearson, Ann Pearson, and David Green, "Determining the Importance of Key Criteria in Web Usability," *Management Research News* 30, no. 11 (2007), pp. 816–29.
7. Parimal S. Bhagat and Jerome D. Williams, "Understanding Gender Differences in Professional Service Relationships," *Journal of Consumer Marketing* 25, no. 1 (2008), pp. 16–29.
8. Cara Peters, Christie H. Amato, and Candice R. Hollenbeck, "An Exploratory Investigation of Consumers' Perceptions of Wireless Advertising," *Journal of Advertising* 36, no. 4 (2007), pp. 129–46; "A Pocketful of Marketing," *Inc.,* 2008, p. 79; and Catherine Holahan, "The 'Sell' Phone Revolution," *BusinessWeek,* April 23, 2007, pp. 94–97.
9. Oliver M. Freestone and Patrick J. McGoldrick, "Motivations of the Ethical Consumer," *Journal of Business Ethics* 79, no. 4 (2008), pp. 445–68.
10. Mike Stobbe, "Adults Get 11 Percent of Calories from Fast Food," *Yahoo Health,* February 21, 2013, http://health.yahoo.net/news/s/ap/adults-get-11-percent-of-calories-from-fast-food.
11. M. Fishbein and I. Ajzen, *Belief, Attitude, Intention, and Behavior: An Introduction to Theory and Research* (Reading, MA: Addison-Wesley, 1975).
12. Maxwell Winchester and Jenni Romaniuk, "Positive and Negative Brand Beliefs and Brand Defection/Update," *European Journal of Marketing* 42, no. 5/6 (2008), pp. 553–68.

13. John Davis, "Did Seth Go to the Dark Side," *Inc.*, May 2008, pp. 21–24.
14. Pamela Miles Horner, "Perceived Quality and Image: When All Is Not 'Rosy,'" *Journal of Business Research* 61, no. 7 (2008), pp. 715–31.
15. Louise Story, "Anywhere the Eye Can See, It's Likely to See an Ad," *New York Times,* January 15, 2007, p. B1.
16. E.J. Schultz, "Inside Allstate's Strategy to Start Mayhem on Twitter," *Ad Age,* October 15, 2013, http://adage.com/article/digital/inside-allstate-s-strategy-start-mayhem-twitter/244690/
17. Joseph B. White, "Eyes on the Road: Good News, Bad News at Buick; Models Get Safer, Says J.D. Power, Then Get Dumped," *The Wall Street Journal,* August 14, 2007, p. D5.
18. Elizabeth Cowley, "How Enjoyable Was It? Remembering an Affective Reaction to a Previous Consumption Experience," *Journal of Consumer Research* 34, no. 4 (2007), pp. 494–510; and Moonhee Yang and David R. Roskos-Ewoldsen, "The Effectiveness of Brand Placements in the Movies: Levels of Placements, Explicit and Implicit Memory, and Brand Choice Behavior," *Journal of Communication* 57, no. 3 (2007), pp. 469–82.
19. Shan Li, "Calling All Stained T-Shirts: H&M Offers to Recycle Your Clothes," *Los Angeles Times,* December 6, 2012, http://articles.latimes.com/2012/dec/06/home/la-fi-mo-hm-recycle-clothes-20121206.
20. Ming-tiem Tsai, Wen-ko Liang, and Mei-Ling Liu, "The Effects of Subliminal Advertising on Consumer Attitudes and Buying Intentions," *International Journal of Management* 24, no. 1 (2007), pp. 3–15; and Sheri J. Broyles, "Subliminal Advertising and the Perpetual Popularity of Playing to People's Paranoia," *Journal of Consumer Affairs* 40, no. 2 (2006), pp. 392–407.
21. Brian D. Till and Sarah M. Stanley, "Classical Conditioning and Celebrity Endorsers: An Examination of Belongingness and Resistance to Extinction," *Psychology and Marketing* 25, no. 2 (2008), pp. 179–94.
22. Gordon R. Foxall, M. Mirella, and Yani de Soriano, "Situational Influences on Consumers' Attitudes and Behaviors," *Journal of Business Research* 58, no. 4 (2005), pp. 518–33.
23. Marcus Cunha Jr., Chris Janiszewski, and Juliano Laran, "Protection of Prior Learning in Complex Consumer Learning Environments," *Journal of Consumer Research* 34, no. 6 (2008), pp. 850–68.
24. Jennifer L. Aaker, "Dimensions of Brand Personality," *Journal of Marketing Research* 34, no. 3 (1997), pp. 347–63; Jennifer Aaker, Susan Fournier, and S. Adam Brasel, "When Good Brands Do Bad," *Journal of Consumer Research* 31, no. 10 (2004), pp. 1–17; and Robert Madrigal and David M. Boush, "Social Responsibility as a Unique Dimension of Brand Personality and Consumers' Willingness to Reward," *Psychology and Marketing* 25, no. 6 (2008), pp. 538–52.
25. Peter Burrows, "GoPro Widens the View of Its Customer Base," *Bloomberg Businessweek,* October 19, 2012, www.businessweek.com/articles/2012-10-17/gopro-widens-the-view-of-its-customer-base.
26. Katja Magion-Muller and Malcolm Evans, "Culture, Communications, and Business: The Power of Advanced Semiotics," *International Journal of Marketing Research* 50, no. 2 (2008), pp. 169–82.
27. David Pearson, "French Language Purists Put Brakes on Car Makers," *The Wall Street Journal,* April 4, 2007, p. B5b.
28. Mark W. Johnston and Greg W. Marshall, 2013, *Contemporary Selling*, 4e, Routledge Publishing, p. 180.
29. Lauren Foster, "Ethnic Shopper Sets Tone for Beauty Contest: Cosmetics Giants Need to Woo Consumers across Color Spectrum," *Financial Times,* April 12, 2005, p. 27.
30. Shawn Bean, "A New Kind of Children's Hospital," Parenting.com, December 20, 2012, www.parenting.com/artcle/childrens-hospital?page=0,2.
31. Alexandra Montgomery, "U.S. Families 2025: In Search of Future Families," *Futures* 40, no. 4 (2008), pp. 377–89.
32. Julie Tinson, Clive Nancarrow, and Ian Brace, "Purchase Decision Making and the Increasing Significance of Family Types," *Journal of Consumer Marketing* 25, no. 1 (2008), pp. 45–56.
33. Rex Y. Du and Wagner A. Kamakura, "Household Life Cycles and Lifestyles in the United States," *Journal of Marketing Research* 43, no. 1 (2006), pp. 121–32.
34. Palaniappan Thiagarajan, Jason E. Lueg, Nicole Ponder, Sheri Lokken Worthy, and Ronald D. Taylor, "The Effect of Role Strain on the Consumer Decision Process of Single Parent Households," *American Marketing Association, Conference Proceedings 17* (Summer 2006), p. 124.
35. Alan Deutschman, "The Kingmaker," *Wired,* May 2004, www.wired.com/wired/archive/12.05/mossberg.html.
36. Caroline Goode and Robert East, "Testing the Marketing Maven Concept," *Journal of Marketing Management* 24, no. 3/4 (2008), pp. 265–81; and Lawrence F. Feick and Linda L. Price, "The Market Maven: A Diffuser of Marketplace Information," *Journal of Marketing* 51, no. 1 (1987), pp. 83–98.
37. Katherine White and Darren W. Dahl, "Are All Out-Groups Created Equal? Consumer Identity and Dissociative Influence," *Journal of Consumer Research* 34, no. 4 (2007), pp. 525–40; Jennifer Edson Escalas

and James R. Bettman, "Self-Construal, Reference Groups, and Brand Meaning," *Journal of Consumer Research* 32, no. 3 (2005), pp. 378–90; and Terry L. Childers and Akshay R. Rao, "The Influence of Familiar and Peer-Based Reference Groups on Consumer Decisions," *Journal of Consumer Research* 19, no. 2 (1992), pp. 198–212.

38. Alexandra Bruell, "How Zumba Built a Brand with a Cult Following in Just a Few Years," *Advertising Age*, August 20, 2012, http://adage.com/article/cmo-interviews/zumba-built-a-cult-a-years/236737/.

39. Hans H. Baurer, Nicola E. Sauer, and Christine Becker, "Investigating the Relationship between Product Involvement and Consumer Decision Making Styles," *Journal of Consumer Behavior* 5, no. 4 (2006), pp. 342–55; Salvador Miquel, Eva M. Capillure, and Joaquin Aldas-Maznazo, "The Effect of Personal Involvement on the Decision to Buy Store Brands," *Journal of Product and Brand Management* 11, no. 1 (2002), pp. 6–19; and Laurent Gilles and Jean-Noel Kapferer, "Measuring Consumer Involvement Profiles," *Journal of Marketing Research* 22, no. 1 (1985), pp. 41–54.

40. Meghan Casserly, "Birchbox Goes Global, Acquires Paris-Based CopyCat 'JolieBox,'" *Forbes*, September 13, 2012, www.forbes.com/sites/meghancasserly/2012/09/13/birchbox-goes-global-acquires-paris-based-copycat-joliebox/.

41. Zafar U. Ahmed, James P. Johnson, Xiz Yang, and Chen Kehng Fatt, "Does Country of Origin Matter for Low Involvement Products? *International Marketing Review* 21, no. 1 (2004), pp. 102–15; and Wayne D. Hoyer, "An Examination of Consumer Decision Making for Common Repeat Purchase Product," *Journal of Consumer Research* 11, no. 3 (1984), pp. 822–30.

42. Sue McPartlin and Lisa Feigen Dugal, "Understanding How US Online Shoppers Are Reshaping the Retail Experience," PricewaterhouseCoopers (2012), www.pwc.com/en_US/us/retail-consumer/publications/assets/pwc-us-multichannel-shopping-survey.pdf.

43. Carrie Coolidge, "Discount Chic," *Forbes*, April 7, 2008, p. 108.

44. On Amir and Jonathan Levav, "Choice Construction versus Preference Construction: The Instability of Preferences Learned in Context," *Journal of Marketing Research* 45, no. 2 (2008), pp. 145–61.

45. Mohammed M. Nadeem, "Post Purchase Dissonance: The Wisdom of 'Repeat' Purchase," *Journal of Global Business Issues* 1, no. 2 (2007), pp. 183–94.

46. Mark Borden, Jeff Chu, Charles Fishman, Michael A. Prospero, and Daniell Sacks, "50 Ways to Green Your Business," *Fast Company*, no. 120 (November 2007), pp. 90–99; and "Coca-Cola Enterprises Forms Recycling Unit for Package Recycling," *Automatic Merchandiser* 49, no. 10 (October 2007), p. 12.

CHAPTER 05

Understand Business-to-Business Markets

LEARNING OBJECTIVES

LO 5-1 Recognize the importance of B2B marketing.

LO 5-2 Understand the differences between B2C and B2B markets.

LO 5-3 Understand the critical role of the buying center and each participant in the B2B process.

LO 5-4 Learn the B2B purchase decision process and different buying situations.

LO 5-5 Comprehend the role of technology in business markets.

ORGANIZATIONAL BUYING: MARKETING TO A BUSINESS

LO 5-1

Recognize the importance of B2B marketing.

Many people believe marketing is focused primarily on consumers—the ultimate users of the product. This is due at least in part to the fact that most people experience marketing as a consumer. The reality, however, is that large consumer products companies purchase hundreds of billions of dollars of products and services every year. General Motors, for example, spends over $60 billion a year on products and services. Everyone knows Hewlett-Packard (HP) and General Electric (GE) because of the products they sell to consumers, but these companies derive most of their revenue from selling to other businesses. Many companies that are primarily consumer oriented, such as Oracle, sell in the business-to-business (B2B) market as well.

Oracle made a strategic minority investment in Proteus Digital Health. Proteus is a leading digital health company. It developed ingestible and wearable sensors that are FDA approved and marketed in the United States and Europe. Proteus Digital Health is developing a new product category called Digital Medicines. These devices would include pharmaceuticals with the FDA-approved sensor inside. Upon ingestion, the sensor communicates with the wearable sensor to capture physiological responses and behaviors. Along with its investment, Oracle will also work alongside Proteus in conducting clinical trials exclusively to provide clinical investigators worldwide the ability to measure information about medication ingestion, dose timing, and other physiological responses for patients enrolled in clinical trials. The companies are anticipated to integrate Proteus's ingestible sensor with Oracle's leading clinical trial products including Oracle Health Sciences InForm, Oracle Life Sciences, Data Hub, and Oracle Health Sciences Cloud. Clinical trial sponsors, service providers, investigators, and patients are expected to benefit from the new technology and continuous real-time information about when a dose of medicine is actually ingested by a patient.[1]

In many cases, companies are selling products that end up as components in a finished product. GE is a world manufacturing leader in commercial jet engines that power half of the jets flying today. Also, companies must purchase products to help them maintain their business. Lenovo is a global company providing IT solutions to companies worldwide. Its products are not a component of another product but, rather, help a business run better. While many companies serve business-to-consumer markets, all companies operate in a business-to-business market, as we will see in this chapter. From GE to Walmart, companies must understand and work with other companies as part of their business operations.[2]

In this chapter, we explore **B2B markets**. The first part of the chapter defines business-to-business markets and delineates the differences between B2B markets and consumer markets. Next, we discuss the business market purchase decision process, which is different from the process consumers use in making a purchase decision. Finally, the significant role of technology in business-to-business market relationships will be presented.

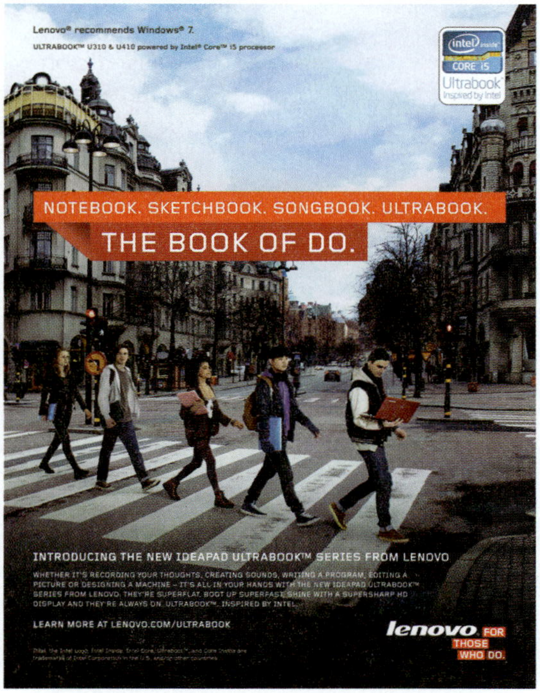

Lenovo markets its products to both consumers and businesses.

DIFFERENCES BETWEEN BUSINESS AND CONSUMER MARKETS

LO 5-2

Understand the differences between B2C and B2B markets.

Business markets and consumer markets are not the same. Six distinct differences dramatically affect marketing strategy and tactics (see Exhibit 5.1). These differences create unique opportunities and challenges for marketing managers because success in consumer marketing does not translate directly to business markets and vice versa.

Relationship with Customers

As we discussed in Chapter 4, many consumer product companies now focus on building strong relationships with their customers. However, even when a relationship is cultivated with the customer, it is impersonal and exists primarily through electronic communication or direct mail.

The opposite is true in business markets. The nature of business markets requires a more personal relationship between buyer and seller. Every relationship takes on additional significance as the sales potential of each customer increases. A strong personal relationship is critical because business customers demand fast answers and good service and, in general, want a close relationship with suppliers.[3] As a result, companies selling in a B2B market invest more resources to foster and maintain personal contact with their customers than in a consumer market. In some cases, companies even invest in their suppliers to strengthen the relationship.

Rival auto manufacturers Ford and General Motors began collaborating with each other to develop 9- and 10-speed transmissions jointly for use in cars, crossovers, pickups, and SUVs. The transmissions will be for both automatic front-and rear-wheel-drive gearboxes. The collaboration is being done in order to get the new technology to market faster. This new agreement builds on an 11-year partnership that resulted in more than 8 million front-wheel-drive 6-speed transmissions that were sold in each company's portfolio of vehicles. Based on GM and Ford's production forecasts, the volume for each type of new transmission will reach approximately 1 million by the year 2018. These manufacturers trail others in the use of higher geared transmissions. The new technology will improve the fuel economy, lower emissions, and improve performance in vehicles. The collaboration will result in identical hardware in the Ford and GM transmissions, while each company will develop its own software to integrate it into the vehicle.[4]

A more personal relationship most often connotes a greater emphasis on personal selling and, increasingly, technology. Customers want direct communication with company representatives and prefer someone they know and trust. The individual most responsible for maintaining a relationship is the salesperson. Personal selling also offers companies the most effective method for direct communication with the customer. Technology has greatly improved the quality and quantity of communications between buyer and seller. However, one-on-one personal communication is still the most important tool in developing and maintaining a strong customer relationship in business markets.

At the same time, technology plays a critical role in connecting buyer and seller. Integrating IT systems that enhance sales response times, provide better customer service, and increase information flow is now an accepted element in a successful B2B customer relationship. Customers demand not only a personal relationship with their vendors but also an efficient one. Most companies now require vendor Internet connectivity to increase efficiency.

EXHIBIT 5.1 | Differences between Business and Consumer Markets

	B2B Market (Business)	B2C Market (Consumer)
Relationship with customers	Invest more in maintaining personal relationships	Impersonal; exist through electronic communication
Number and size of customers	Fewer but larger customers	More customers but buy in smaller, less frequent quantities
Geographic concentration	Suppliers located strategically by the buyers	Could be anywhere in the world
Complexity of buying process	Complex process that can take a long time (years in some cases) and involve more people	Fewer people, often just one, directly involved in the purchase decision and the purchase decision is often based on personal and psychological benefits
Complexity of supply chain	Direct from supplier to manufacturer	Complex with products moving through the channel to reach the consumer
Demand for products	Derived from consumer demand, fluctuates with changes to consumer demand, and more inelastic (less price sensitive)	Consumer perceptions about their own needs mitigated by environmental factors and marketing stimuli

Number and Size of Customers

Business markets are characterized by fewer but larger customers. Goodyear, for example, may sell one set of tires to a consumer over the course of three years, but every year the company sells millions of tires to Ford Motor Company. Add up all the major automobile companies, and there are fewer than 25 business customers for Goodyear. Not surprisingly, the company maintains a dedicated sales force just for the automobile manufacturers.

The large size and small number of customers place a higher value on each customer. Although consumer products companies value customer relationships, it is not possible to satisfy every customer every time nor is it economically feasible. However, in a business market setting, losing even one large customer has striking implications for a company.[5] Walmart is Procter & Gamble's single biggest customer accounting for 17 percent of company sales (roughly equivalent to $9 billion). At its Arkansas office, P&G has a 300-member staff dedicated to one customer—Walmart.

Geographic Concentration

Business markets tend to concentrate in certain locations.[6] Historically, the automobile industry concentrated in the Midwest, particularly Detroit, and technology firms dominated Silicon Valley in California. As a result, their suppliers congregated nearby. A software developer, for example, that wants to be close to its primary customers should set up an office in San Jose, California. While the Internet allows people to live anywhere, the nature of business relationships means companies want to have a strong presence near their best customers.

Complexity of the Buying Process

The B2B customer buying process, discussed later in the chapter, is more complex than the consumer purchase decision process. It takes longer and involves more people, making the seller's job more challenging. In addition, as companies connect with customers, the number of relationships increases and it is difficult for one individual, the salesperson, to keep up with the complexity of the relationships.[7] Companies also face competing forces in critical decisions about their products (see Ethical Dimension 5).

Complexity of the Supply Chain

The movement of goods through a channel to the ultimate consumer requires a high level of coordination among the participants. A **supply chain** is the synchronized movement of goods through the channel. It is far more integrated than ever before as companies seek to keep production costs low, provide maximum customer input and flexibility in the design of products, and create competitive advantage. At the same time, the supply chain in B2B markets is generally more direct with suppliers and manufacturers working closely together to ensure efficient movement of products and services.

ETHICAL DIMENSION 5

Implications of Biofuels

As the United States and many other industrialized countries wrestle with the high cost of energy, few energy options offer a dual win for consumers—environmentally sensitive and fuel efficient. Coal, for example, is prevalent in some parts of the world, including the United States, but is harmful to the environment. Solar and wind power generation are clean energy sources but are difficult to harness in sufficient quantities to make a significant impact on the use of fossil fuel. One source of energy that both reduces the dependence on oil and offers cleaner burning is ethanol. Produced from corn, ethanol lowers the use of fossil fuel and has been a critical piece of the federal government's plan to lessen U.S. dependence on foreign oil. Current plans call for renewable fuels such as ethanol to account for 15 percent of gasoline burned in the United States by 2017. The move to biofuels is also happening in other parts of the world. Europe requires that over 6 percent of its diesel fuel come from plants.

The benefits of biofuels do not come without a cost. Livestock farmers have experienced a dramatic increase in the price of corn, doubling from $2 a bushel to over $4 a bushel. This price increase is due primarily to huge increases in demand for corn to make ethanol. Nearly 40 percent of all corn production in the United States goes toward the making of ethanol.

This focus on greater energy independence and more environmentally friendly fuel is creating difficult choices for companies, government officials, and farmers. Ethanol is becoming more readily available, but higher feed corn prices have led to higher prices for meat and poultry at the grocery store. Chicken feed costs, for example, are increasing an estimated $1.5 billion per year. Ultimately, some predict competition for bio products as producers choose between using corn and other plants for fuel or food.

Around the world, difficult choices are being made. In Germany, increased demand for rapeseed, used as a biofuel in Europe, has led to steep price increases for other uses of the product, such as cooking oil and protein meal. Indonesia and Malaysia suffered significant air pollution recently as millions of acres of forests were cleared to plant oil palms used in biofuels in Asia.

The use of corn as a biofuel is not particularly efficient as it takes 7 gallons of fossil fuel to produce 10 gallons of ethanol. Additionally, while it does produce lower greenhouse gases, the comparison with fossil fuels is not dramatic. Researchers are looking for more efficient biofuels. Pine groves, prairie grass, and other plants have even greater potential than corn, producing cleaner fuel with less energy.

From consumers to energy companies and farmers, the increased use of biofuels means choosing, at least in some cases, between greater energy dependence and higher food prices as limited quantities of critical plants raise prices for a variety of products.[8]

Ethical Perspective

1. **Oil companies:** Should they invest in alternative fuel technologies such as ethanol to reduce fossil fuel consumption?
2. **Consumers:** Should they be willing to pay higher food prices to achieve greater energy independence and cleaner-burning fuel?
3. **Farmers:** Should they be required to invest in greater production of critical biofuel plants such as corn?

Demand for Products and Services Is Different in a Business Market

Product demand in business markets is different from consumer demand on three critical dimensions: derived demand, fluctuating demand, and inelastic demand. All three offer unique challenges and opportunities for marketers. For example, two of the three differences (derived and fluctuating demand) deal with the relationship between B2B and B2C demand and suggest B2B marketing managers must first understand their customer's markets before they can sell to the customer. The final dimension (inelastic demand) is an opportunity for a seller but must be managed carefully to maintain a successful relationship.

Derived Demand Demand for B2B products originates from the demand for consumer products, or, put another way, demand for B2B products is **derived demand**. If consumers are not buying Ford cars and trucks, then there is no need for Ford to purchase Goodyear tires. Therefore, it is important for Goodyear to understand the consumer market for automobiles for two reasons. First, knowing what consumers are looking for in a car is critical to designing tires for those cars. Second, knowing the consumer automobile market is essential to create a value proposition that speaks to Ford's need to sell more cars and trucks to consumers.

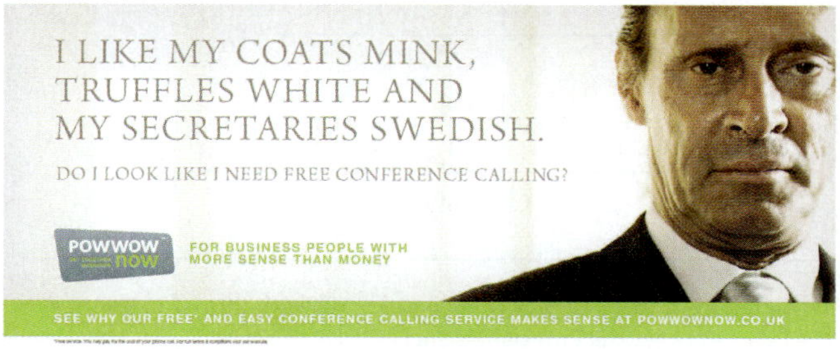

Powwownow appeals to business customers with this humorous ad. "For business people with more sense than money." Courtesy powwownow. co.uk

In addition to the demand for specific Ford products, such as the Flex or Mustang, Goodyear scans the environment for anything that might affect consumer demand. Environmental factors have long-term and short-term effects on consumer product choices. For example, long-term economic factors such as the rapid rise in the price of gasoline have had a significant negative effect on the sales of SUVs, and short-term factors like a hurricane in Florida or the Southeast can limit distribution and sale of products in those areas for a while. B2B sellers understand that business customer success frequently means finding ways to assist them in their consumer markets. This is a challenge for business marketers because, despite having a great product and providing great service at a competitive price, they may still not get the business because consumer demand for their business customer's product is weak.

In order to make its services more efficient for its customers, OfficeMax announced a new search engine, with content and navigation improvements, on its OfficeMax Workplace business-to-business e-commerce site. This will deliver faster and more streamlined online shopping for its customers. The changes to the site began in early 2013, during which time the company experienced increases in conversion rates, average revenue per visit, and positive customer feedback around site navigation and functionality. In order to make these changes, OfficeMax gathered input from business customers on what site changes would be the most helpful. Executive Vice President and President of OfficeMax Workplace John Kenning stated, "Listening to our customers helped us shape these search and navigation upgrades and further supports our commitment to being a strategic partner, delivering solutions that help address the needs of their businesses. Our customers are telling us how much they enjoy shopping on our improved site and how quick and convenient the shopping experience is."[9]

Fluctuating Demand The relationship between consumer demand and demand for business products presents a real challenge for business-to-business marketers. Small changes in consumer demand can lead to considerable shifts in business product demand and is referred to as the **acceleration effect**. This makes

EXHIBIT 5.2 **Examples of Elastic and Inelastic Demand**

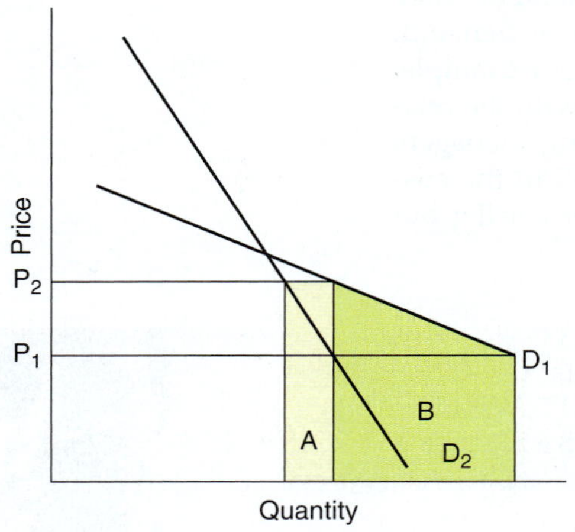

Reprinted from Stephen Slavin, *Economics*, 10th ed., 2011. Copyright © 2011 The McGraw-Hill Companies, Inc.

forecasting the sale of consumer products important because making even a small mistake in estimating consumer demand can lead to significant errors in product production.

Inelastic Demand Business products experience fairly **inelastic demand**, meaning changes in demand are not significantly affected by changes in price. Apple, for example, will not buy more processors from Intel if Intel lowers the price nor will it buy fewer chips if Intel raises the price until the price increase becomes so high that Apple considers alternative vendors. Apple designs some of its computers around Intel processors and to change vendors creates disruption and costs in other areas of the manufacturing process. Price increases, particularly incremental changes, are often accepted because manufacturers are hesitant to disrupt manufacturing processes, which, in turn, creates inelastic demand in the short run. Exhibit 5.2 has two demand curves, D_1 and D_2. As price rises from P_1 to P_2 the demand changes. The more elastic demand curve is the one with the largest shaded area—B. Demand in business-to-business markets is generally more inelastic than in consumer markets, which means changes in price have less effect on demand—the smaller shaded area A. This makes D_2 an example of inelastic demand.

BUYING SITUATIONS

People involved in making business **buying decisions** face many choices as they move through the purchase decision process. Business buying decisions vary widely based on the

- Nature of the purchase (large capital outlay like that needed for a new manufacturing plant versus simply ordering office supplies).
- Number of people involved in the decision (one or many).
- Understanding of the product being purchased (new to the firm or a familiar product purchased many times before).
- Time frame for the decision (short time requiring an immediate purchase decision or a longer lead time).

Some decisions require little or no analysis before the purchase decision. Others require updating information or changing existing purchase orders before the purchase decision can be made. Finally, some decisions require an in-depth analysis of the product. These three scenarios are referred to as straight rebuys, modified rebuys, and new purchases (see Exhibit 5.3).

Straight Rebuy

Many products are purchased so often that it is not necessary to evaluate every purchase decision. Companies use a wide range of products on a consistent basis (office supplies, raw materials) and simply reorder when needed. This type of purchase is called a **straight rebuy**. Increasingly, this is done automatically via secure Internet connections with approved or preferred suppliers. Far fewer people are involved with the purchase decision; often it is handled by one person in the purchasing department.

EXHIBIT 5.3 | Types of Buying Situations

Straight rebuy	Reorder products that are used on a consistent basis
Modified rebuy	Familiar with product and supplier but still seek additional information
New purchase	First-time purchase of product or service

The goal of business sellers in straight rebuy situations is to become the preferred supplier. A company given approved status must be diligent and mindful of competitors seeking to displace it. Companies not on the approved list are called **out suppliers**. Their primary task is to obtain a small order, an opening, then leverage that opportunity to gain additional business. This is a challenge, however, if the approved supplier is doing a good job of meeting the customer's needs. From time to time, many companies order small quantities from nonapproved suppliers just to keep the approved supplier from becoming too complacent or to evaluate a potential new vendor.[10]

Modified Rebuy

A **modified rebuy** occurs when the customer is familiar with the product and supplier but is looking for additional information. Most often this need for change has resulted from one or more of three circumstances. First, the approved supplier has performed poorly or has not lived up to the customer's expectations. Second, new products have come into the market triggering a reappraisal of the current purchase protocols. Third, the customer believes it is time for a change and wants to consider other suppliers.

All three situations create opportunities for out suppliers to gain new business. When a purchase contract is opened up for a modified rebuy, it represents the best opportunity for a new supplier. At the same time, however, the current approved supplier seeks to maintain the relationship. The approved supplier almost always has the advantage, particularly if it has a close relationship with the customer, because it knows the people involved and usually gets access to critical information first.

New Purchase

The most complex and difficult buying situation is the new purchase. A **new purchase** is the purchase of a product or service by a customer for the first time. The more expensive, higher the risk, and greater the resource commitment, the more likely the company will engage in a full purchase decision process (outlined later in the chapter).

This process almost certainly involves a group throughout the entire decision process, even though the final decision may rest with a single individual. Because the company's purchasing personnel have had very little experience with the product, they seek information from a variety of sources. First and foremost, vendor salespeople are a key source of information about the product's capabilities. If they do their job well, they help the customer define its needs and how best to address them. Another avenue of information for companies is to hire consultants who, as unbiased experts, can assess and educate customers on their needs and possible solutions. Finally, the company must scan its own resources, including past purchase records, for relevant information.

Airbus was able to secure several very large sales in early 2013. Among the largest orders was from Nepal Airlines Corp, which contracted to purchase two of Airbus's A320 aircraft, equipped with Sharklet fuel-saving wing tip devices. The deal was valued at $183 million based on current list prices. Nepal, a landlocked country, recognized aviation as a good investment to connect to the world. The airline hopes that the addition of Airbus planes to its fleet will help grow tourism for the region as well as enhance the company's network through use of fuel-efficient aircraft. This deal came only days after an $8 billion, 60-plane deal with China Aviation Supplies Holding Co. for 42 A320 models and 18 A330 models. The reliability of the A320 model and its low operational cost has made it a popular choice for Chinese airlines. Airbus President and CEO Fabrice Bregier said, "These eco-efficient Airbus aircraft will contribute to the growth and success of China's aviation sector."[11]

BUYING CENTERS

As we discussed, business purchases are seldom made by just one person, particularly in modified rebuy and new purchase situations. A number of individuals with a stake in the purchase decision come together to form a **buying center** that manages the purchase decision process and ultimately makes the decision. The individuals included in the buying center may have direct responsibility over the decision (purchasing department) or financial control of the company (senior management). In other cases, the individuals might have a specific expertise helpful to the decision (engineer, consultant).[12]

LO 5-3

Understand the critical role of the buying center and each participant in the B2B process.

Buying centers usually are not permanent groups but are convened to make the decision and then disband. Also, individuals may participate in more than one buying center at any given time. Purchasing agents are apt to be members of several buying centers. In addition, while the vast majority of buying center participants work for the customer, others, such as outside consultants, are invited into the group because of their expertise. This happens, for example, in new purchases when a company believes it lacks sufficient internal knowledge and experience to make an informed decision. Most buying centers include a minimum of five people; however, they can be much larger. In larger multinational corporations, buying centers for companywide purchase decisions, such as a new corporate CRM system, can include dozens of people from all over the world.

Members of the Buying Center

Every participant in a buying center plays a certain role and some may play multiple roles (see Exhibit 5.4). In addition, an individual's role may change. As people move up in an organization, they can move from user to influencer and finally to a decider. These functions can be defined formally by the company or informally as a result of an individual's expertise or influence. Let's examine each of the five major roles.

User

Users are the actual consumer of the product and play a critical role. While typically not the decision makers, they do have a lot of input at various stages of the process. They are the first to recognize the problem based on a need, and they help define the product specifications. Finally, they provide critical feedback after the product purchase. As a result, their responsibility is enhanced in new purchase and modified rebuy situations when product specifications are being set for the purchase decision.

Initiators

The **initiator** starts the buying decision process usually in one of two ways. In one scenario the initiator is also the user of the product, as in the secretary who reorders when office supplies run low. A second scenario occurs when senior executives make decisions that require new resources (manufacturing sites, product development, and information technology). In these situations the executives act as initiators to the purchase decision process.

Influencers Individuals, both inside and outside the organization, with relevant expertise in a particular area act as **influencers**, providing information that is used by the buying center in making the final decision. Engineers are frequently called on to detail product requirements and specifications. Purchasing agents, based on their experience, are helpful in evaluating sales proposals. Marketing personnel can provide customer feedback. In all of these cases, the influencer's knowledge on a given topic relevant to the purchase decision can affect the purchase decision.

EXHIBIT 5.4 | Buying Center Participants

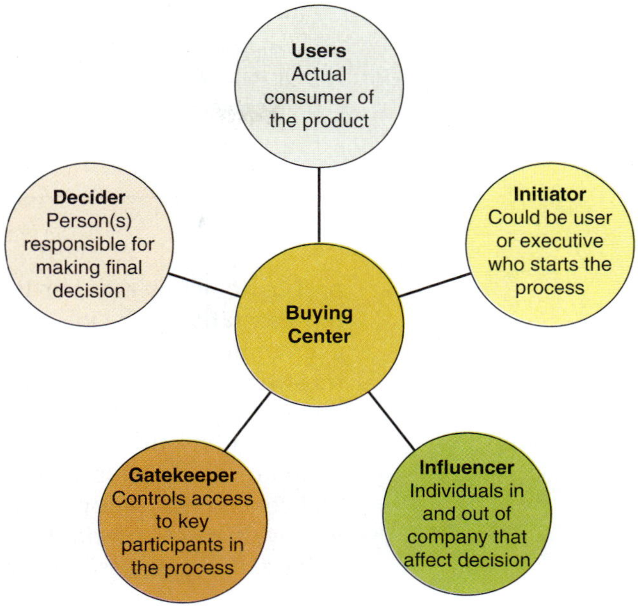

Gatekeepers Access to information and relevant individuals in the buying center is controlled by **gatekeepers**. Purchasing departments act as gatekeepers by limiting possible vendors to those approved by the company. Similarly, engineering, quality control, and service department personnel create product specifications that, in essence, limit the number of vendors. At the same time, basic access to key people is controlled by secretaries and administrative assistants. One of the toughest challenges facing salespeople in a new purchase or modified rebuy situation is getting access to the right people.

American Express communicates to business customers through many platforms.

Deciders Ultimately, the purchase decision rests with one or more individuals, **deciders**, in the buying center. Often it will be the most senior member of the team; however, it can also include other individuals (users, influencers), in which case the decision is reached by consensus. The more expensive and strategic the purchase, the higher in the organization the decision must go for final authority.[13] It is not uncommon for the CEO to sign off on major strategic decisions about technology, new manufacturing plants, and other key decisions that affect fundamental business processes. Costly capital equipment purchases often include the chief financial officer (CFO), who will most likely be a key decider. CFOs will employ a wide range of financial tools, including discounted cash flow analysis of the proposed investment, as they determine the most appropriate purchase decision.

Pursuing the Buying Center

Buying centers present marketers with three distinct challenges, as presented in Exhibit 5.5. First, who is part of the buying center? Simply identifying the members of a buying center can be difficult and is made more challenging by gatekeepers whose role, in

EXHIBIT 5.5 | Marketing Challenges in Buying Centers

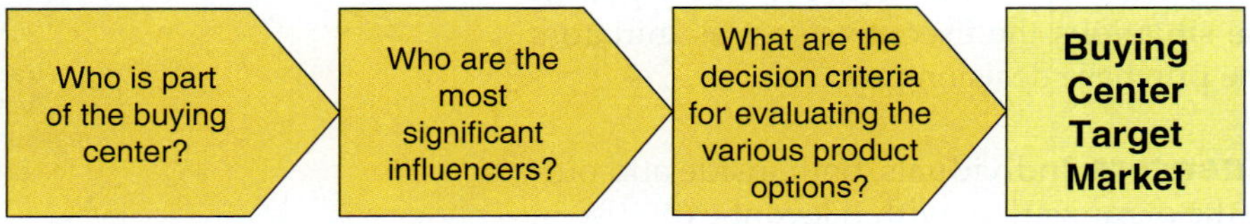

part, is to act as a buffer between buying center members and outside vendor representatives. The job of identifying membership in the buying center is made even more complex as participants come and go over time. Second, who are the most significant influencers in the buying center? This is critical in both preparing a sales presentation and following up. Targeting influencers is important in persuading the buying center to purchase the salesperson's product. Finally, what are the decision criteria for evaluating the various product options? A very real concern for salespeople is making sure their products perform well on critical evaluation criteria; however, without a good understanding of evaluation criteria, it is not possible to assess the probability of the product's success.

THE PLAYERS IN BUSINESS-TO-BUSINESS MARKETS

B2B markets are not homogenous. The complexity of business markets rivals that of consumer markets with more than 20 million small businesses in the United States alone. The number grows dramatically when you include large corporations, nonprofit institutions, and government entities. The diversity of businesses coupled with the unique characteristics of business-to-business markets means companies selling in B2B markets need to know their markets very well. Let's explore each of the major categories of business markets to better understand their similarities and differences.

The North American Industrial Classification System (NAICS)

Historically, the basic tool for defining and segmenting business markets was a classification system known as the Standard Industrial Classification (SIC) codes developed by the U.S. government in the 1930s. The SIC system organized businesses into 10 groups that further broke down business categories based on their output (what they produced or their primary business activity). For many years, it was the foundation for business segmentation in the United States.

The SIC codes were updated in the 1990s and are now called the **North American Industrial Classification System (NAICS)**. The system has been expanded to include businesses in Mexico and Canada. NAICS defines 20 major business sectors based on a six-digit hierarchical code. The first five digits are standardized across Mexico, Canada, and the United States, while the sixth digit enables countries to adjust the code to fit the country's own unique economic structure.[14]

The NAICS is not perfect; companies are classified on the basis of their primary output, which means that large companies with multiple businesses across different sectors are not accurately represented as they receive only one NAICS code. However, the system does offer a great starting point for researching a particular

EXHIBIT 5.6 | NAICS Example

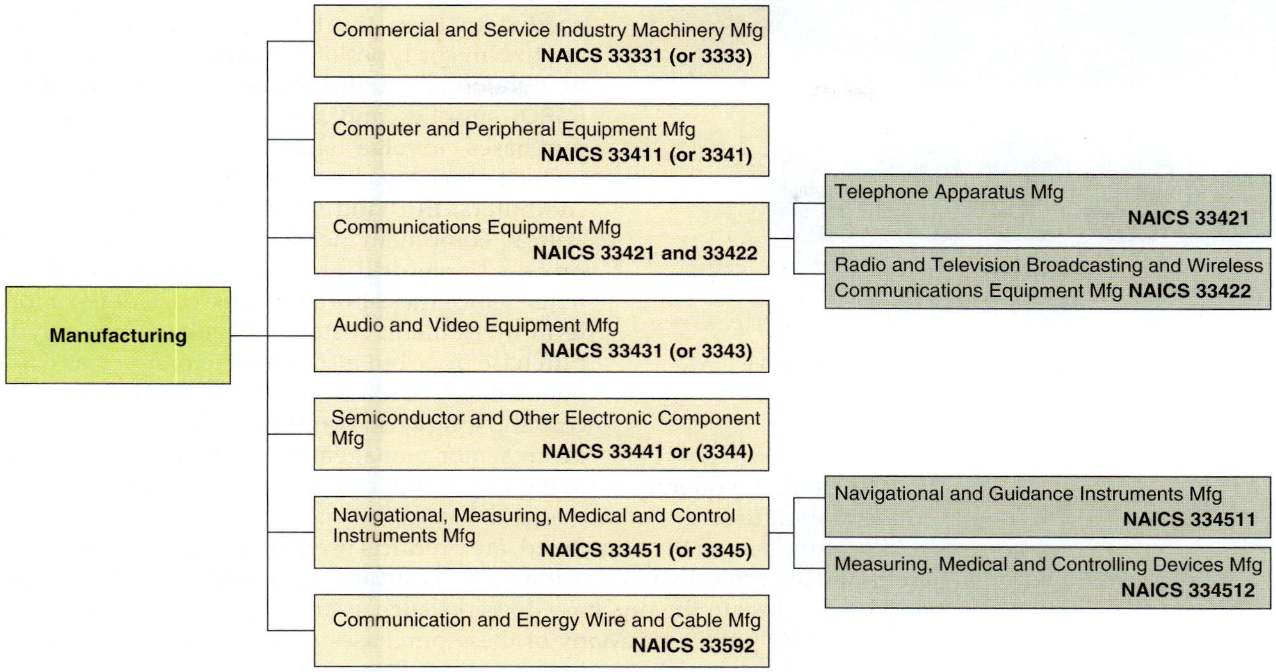

Source: NAICS, www.ic.gc.ca/eic/site/icgc.nsf/eng/home.

business market. It is possible to purchase detailed information on each of the codes in the system. This information includes data on companies listed in each code, number of employees, sales revenue, their location, and contact information. Exhibit 5.6 provides an example.

Manufacturers

One of the largest groups of business customers is manufacturers, which consume two types of products. First, components used in the manufacturing process are called **original equipment manufacturer (OEM)** purchases. Companies selling OEM products work to convince the OEM customer their products offer the best value (price and quality) to the OEM's customers. Intel's reputation for overall value among consumers has enabled the company to build a strong business with OEM computer manufacturers such as Lenovo to the point that Lenovo, and others, promote "Intel Inside."

OEM customers purchase in large quantities to support their own product demand. Two important outcomes result from this purchase power. First, OEM customers seek the very "best" prices from sellers. *Best* does not always mean lowest; other factors play an important role.[15] The assurance of product quality, ability to meet demand, just-in-time product delivery schedules, and other factors frequently figure into the final selection of product and vendor. The second result of large purchase quantities is the ability to dictate specific product specifications. OEM customers often compel suppliers to modify existing products and even develop new products. Sellers work closely with the OEM engineers and technicians to develop products that will fit the need of the OEM customer. The benefit is a high volume of product sales and the opportunity to develop a long-term strategic relationship.[16]

As an airplane manufacturer, Airbus must engage in elaborate PR campaigns.

A second category of products purchased by manufacturers are called **end user purchases** and represent the equipment, supplies, and services needed to keep the business operational. There are two major types of end user purchases: **capital equipment** and **materials, repairs, and operational (MRO)** supplies and services. Capital equipment purchases involve significant investments and include major technology decisions (mainframe computers, ERP and CRM software packages) or critical equipment needed in the manufacturing process (large drill presses, robotic assembly systems). Since these purchases are considered a long-term investment, customers evaluate not only the purchase price but also other factors such as cost of ownership, reliability, and ease of upgrading. The cost and long-term commitment of these purchases mean senior management is often involved in the final decision. Frequently a buying center will evaluate options and make a recommendation to senior management.

MRO supplies, on the other hand, are products used in everyday business operations and are typically not considered a significant expense. Purchasing agents or individuals close to the purchase decision, such as an office manager, are responsible for MRO purchases. Many of these purchases are straight rebuys; the individuals involved do not want to spend a lot of time making the purchase. Vendors in these industries are well aware that once they have a customer, the business is assured until the company does not perform up to customer expectations. Put another way, the business is theirs to lose.

Boeing struck a deal with the U.S. air force to deliver two Space Environmental NanoSat Experiment (SENSE) satellites to assess the value of small satellites in military space operations. The satellites weighed less than 9 pounds (4 kilograms) each and measured 30 × 10 × 10 centimeters in size. They were launched on the ORS-3 mission in the summer of 2013 to collect and transmit weather data. The satellites would be able to gather data to support weather prediction and assessments. Col. Scott Beidleman noted that the satellites provide a significant improvement in future air force space architecture, providing information to the warfighter. Director of Advanced Space & Intelligence Systems Bruce Chesley stated, "The SENSE nanosats offer customers an affordable, operationally robust option to conduct military missions using spacecraft no larger than a standard loaf of bread." Boeing worked with the Office of Naval Research, SRI International, The Aerospace Corp., and Atmospheric and Space Technology Research Associates to build, test, and integrate the NanoSats.[17]

Resellers

Companies that buy products and then resell them to other businesses or consumers are called **resellers**. Home Depot, for example, buys home products and then resells them to consumers, building contractors, and other professionals in the construction industry. Chapter 11 provides an in-depth discussion of consumer resellers, but it is important to note that resellers have unique needs when it comes to purchase decisions. Just as manufacturers need end user products, resellers also need equipment and supplies to run their businesses. Retailers need technology such as computers and checkout counters to keep track of sales and inventory. Distributors need stocking and inventory management systems to maintain their distribution centers and also have the same MRO needs.

Government

The single largest buyer of goods and services in the world is the U.S. government. Combined with state and local governments, the value of purchases is over $2 trillion. Local, state, and particularly federal **government** entities have unique and frequently challenging purchase practices. Detailed product specifications must be followed precisely, and the purchase process is often long. The purchase decision by the Department of Defense on the F-22A Raptor fighter took four and a half years and involved thousands of product specifications.[18] While the government is theoretically open to all vendors, the reality is that experience with the government purchase process is usually a prerequisite to success.

Federal and state governments make a number of resources available to potential vendors; it is possible to obtain guidelines from the federal government. Furthermore, some private companies exist to offer assistance in learning about the process. The National Association of State Purchasing Officials publishes information on selling products and services to each of the 50 states. In addition, small-business organizations, such as the Small Business Administration, provide information on federal government contracts and contact personnel at government agencies.

Institutions

Institutions such as nonprofits, hospitals, and other nongovernment organizations (NGOs) represent a large and important market that has some unique characteristics. First, profitability does not play as significant a role in many of these organizations; rather, the delivery of service to the targeted constituency is the primary objective. Profit, or surplus as it is often called in the nonprofit community, is important but is not the fundamental driver in decision making. For example, Adventist Health System, which owns and operates health care facilities in 12 states, is a large nonprofit health care provider that considers a range of priorities in making important strategic decisions.[19] A second unique characteristic is a limited number of resources. Even the largest NGOs, including the Red Cross, do not have access to the capital and resources of most large for-profit organizations.

THE BUSINESS MARKET PURCHASE DECISION PROCESS

LO 5-4

Learn the B2B purchase decision process and different buying situations.

In some respects business market purchase decisions follow the same basic process as consumer decisions. As presented in Exhibit 5.7, a problem is recognized, information is collected and evaluated, a decision is made, and the product experience is then evaluated for future decisions. However, there are also significant differences between business market purchase decisions and consumer purchase decisions. These differences make the process more complex and require the involvement of more people. One key difference is that, while consumer decisions often include an emotional component, business goals and performance specifications drive organizations toward a more rational decision process.

As we discussed, the process is not used for every purchase decision. In straight rebuy situations, the problem is recognized and the order is made. Defining

EXHIBIT 5.7 | Model of Business Market Purchase Decision Process

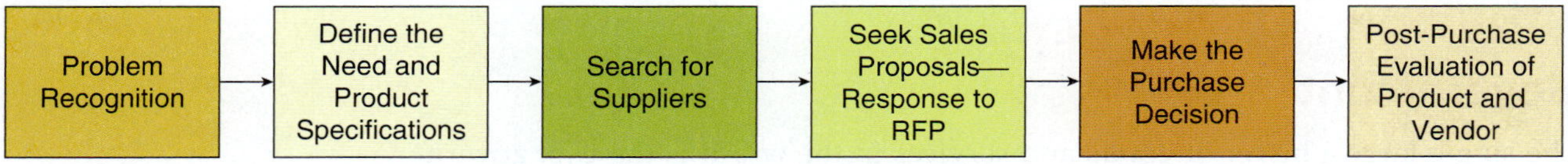

product specifications, searching for suppliers, and other steps in the process were probably done at one time, but, once a supplier is selected, the purchase decision process becomes more or less automatic. A selected or approved list of suppliers shortens the decision process dramatically. Buyers go to the targeted vendor or choose from a list of suppliers and make the purchase. This process is consistent across organizations. Modified rebuys, on the other hand, are much more organization and situation specific. In some situations, the process may be more like a straight rebuy with some changes to product specifications or contract terms. In other situations, it may resemble a new purchase with an evaluation of new suppliers and proposals. New purchases will include all the steps in the process. As a rule, a new purchase takes longer because going through each of the steps takes time. In some cases, the process may take years, as in the building of a new oil refinery or automobile assembly plant.

Problem Recognition

The business market purchase decision process is triggered when someone inside or outside the company identifies a need. In many cases, the need is a problem that requires a solution. The paper supply is running low and the office manager reorders more. A company's manufacturing facilities are at full capacity and it must consider options to increase production. In other situations, the need may be an opportunity that requires a new purchase. New technology can increase order efficiency or a new design of a critical component can improve the effectiveness of a company's own products, giving it an edge with consumers. As companies struggle to deal with higher energy prices, new alternative solutions, sometimes using older technologies, are being adopted for use in interesting ways.

Employees frequently activate the purchase process as part of their job. The office manager is responsible for keeping the office stocked with enough supplies. The vice president of strategic planning is tasked with planning for future manufacturing needs. However, salespeople from either the buying or selling company's sales force or channel partners also initiate the purchase process by helping identify a need or presenting an opportunity to increase efficiency or effectiveness. This is most likely to happen when the salesperson has established a trusted relationship with the company. Trade shows are also a source of new ideas; attendees often go to see what is new in the marketplace. Traditional marketing communications such as advertising and direct mail are less effective in business markets but are important in supporting the more personal communication efforts of salespeople.

Define the Need and Product Specifications

Once a problem has been identified, the next step is to clearly define the need. Individuals from across the organization clarify the problem and develop solutions. Not all problems lead to a new purchase. A vice president of information technology may notice an increase in call waiting times, but the issue could be

Badgeville Inc. develops gamification opportunities for companies. The company was founded in 2010 and has raised $40 million in capital through three rounds of financing. Its client list includes Deloitte, eBay Inc., EMC Corp., Oracle Corp., and Samsung Group. Kris Duggan, the co-founder and chief strategy officer, notes, "When the company started it was all about engagement. It consisted of techniques coming out of social gaming, and in the beginning was used to address enterprise software being purchased but not utilized to its full extent." The research shows that there has been $1 trillion spent on software from 2007–2013 and less than 50 percent of it is being used. Badgeville Inc. provides a method for companies to use gamification to get employees to use the software that's been purchased. The service offered helps train employees by including methods to get people to onboard the new software and as they complete tasks or complete a challenge, they earn points and potentially earn a reputation within their teams.[20]

a lack of training or a shortage of employees. The solution might include a new, expanded phone and call management system, but it will be up to management, working with other employees, to determine what is needed.

As part of describing the need, product specifications should be defined so that everyone inside and outside of the company knows exactly what is needed to solve the problem. This serves two important purposes. First, individuals inside the organization can plan for the future. Purchasing agents identify possible vendors while managers estimate costs and build budgets based on the specifications. Users plan how to assimilate the new purchase into existing work processes. The buying center will use the product specifications to help evaluate vendor proposals. Putting product specifications into a document for distribution is known as a **request for proposal (RFP)**. The second purpose of outlining product specifications is to guide potential suppliers. Product specifications as contained in the RFP become the starting point from which vendors put together their product solution. In the best-case scenario, there is a good fit between what the customer is asking for and the supplier's existing products.[21] Much more often, however, there are some specifications in which the potential products compare favorably and others where competitors excel. Exhibit 5.8 identifies the key sections of a request for proposal. RFPs generally require a great deal of information, and it takes a significant amount of time for a company to prepare a successful sales proposal.

The challenge for salespeople is to get involved in the purchase decision process as early as possible. If the salesperson, for example, has a strategic relationship with the customer, it may be possible to help define the product specifications. This is a real advantage because the vendor's salespeople can work to create specifications that present their products in the most favorable way. Product specifications are often written in such a way as to limit the number of vendors. Companies realize that not knowing the product specifications puts them at a disadvantage over other vendors. It is still possible to win the order, but the job becomes more difficult.

Search for Suppliers

Once the company's needs have been identified and product specifications have been outlined, business customers can identify potential suppliers. Two methods are commonly used to determine the list of vendors. First, companies create a list of preferred or approved suppliers and go to that list whenever a new purchase is being considered. The list can result from the company's cumulative experience. In this situation it is important to keep the list current with respect to existing vendors and also any new vendors.

EXHIBIT 5.8 | Sections of a Request for Proposal

1. ***Statement of Purpose:*** Describe the extent of products and services your organization is looking for, as well as the overall objectives of the contract.
2. ***Background Information:*** Present a brief overview of your organization and its operations, using statistics, customer demographics, and psychographics. State your strengths and weaknesses honestly. Don't forget to include comprehensive information on the people who will handle future correspondence.
3. ***Scope of Work:*** Enumerate the specific duties to be performed by the provider and the expected outcomes. Include a detailed listing of responsibilities, particularly when subcontractors are involved.
4. ***Outcome and Performance Standards:*** Specify the outcome targets, minimal performance standards expected from the contractor, and methods for monitoring performance and process for implementing corrective actions.
5. ***Deliverables:*** Provide a list of all products, reports, and plans that will be delivered to your organization and propose a delivery schedule.
6. ***Term of Contract:*** Specify length, start and end dates of the contract, and the options for renewal.
7. ***Payments, Incentives, and Penalties:*** List all the terms of payment for adequate performance. Highlight the basis for incentives for superior performance and penalties for inadequate performance or lack of compliance.
8. ***Contractual Terms and Conditions:*** Attach standard contracting forms, certifications, and assurances. You may include requirements specific to this particular contract.
9. ***Requirements for Proposal Preparation:*** A consistent structure in terms of content, information, and document types simplifies things for the people evaluating the proposals. Therefore, you should request a particular structure for the proposal and provide an exhaustive list of documents you want to receive.
10. ***Evaluation and Award Process:*** Lay down the procedures and criteria used for evaluating proposals and for making the final contract award.
11. ***Process Schedule:*** Clearly and concisely present the time line for the steps leading to the final decision, such as the dates for submitting the letter of intent, sending questions, attending the preproposal conference, submitting the proposal.
12. ***Contacts:*** Include a complete list of people to contact for information on the RFP, or with any other questions. Incorporate their name, title, responsibilities, and the various ways of contacting them into this list.

Source: *RFP Evaluation Centers*, www.rfp-templates.com.

A second, more complex method is to search for and identify potential suppliers. The Internet has become a valuable tool for companies in identifying potential suppliers. General search engines and even dedicated supplier search websites, such as Thomas Global Register, are easy to use and enable customers to identify specific potential vendors. Of course, companies still need to perform due diligence by checking vendor customer references, and in critical purchases it is advisable to research the vendor's financial stability and management capabilities.

> Potential suppliers employ sophisticated SEO (search engine optimization) tools to get listed on the critical "first page"—the most desired location on any search results page. For example, suppliers link to trade groups that drive traffic to their website and increase the probability of rising on the organic list. In addition, companies target keywords that minimize competitor access to first-page search results. Finally, it is possible to purchase keyword ads that test which phrases will drive the most web traffic.[22]

Seek Sales Proposals in Response to RFP

Communicating with business customers usually involves salespeople working directly with the individuals in the buying center to develop the best solution.

Companies frequently solicit proposals from a number of vendors for two reasons. First, even if there is a preferred vendor, getting more information about available options from other suppliers is a good idea. If it is an open vendor search, then the proposal becomes a valuable source of information as well as the primary evaluation tool. Second, getting additional proposals helps in negotiating with the preferred vendor. When a vendor is aware that other proposals are under consideration, that vendor works harder to meet the expectations of the customer.

Sales proposals, particularly those submitted in response to an RFP, are written so they can be studied and sent to various individuals inside the company. At this stage, vendors may or may not be invited to make a presentation. If they are, a copy of the presentation will usually be submitted as part of the proposal. Numerous software packages can help create sophisticated sales proposal packages. Oracle, for example, includes a sales proposal module in its CRM solutions software. In addition, many companies have created their own proprietary software to aid salespeople in creating a sales proposal. Putting together a template that is used throughout the company helps unify the content and look of a sales proposal.

However, this step is usually characterized by limited vendor contact. Again, many companies are asked to submit proposals from which a smaller set of potential vendors will be selected. As a result, the sales proposal plays a critical role in marketing to businesses. Most of the time it is the first and best chance to impress the customer. In general, proposals accomplish two objectives. First, the proposal clearly specifies how the company's products will meet the product specifications detailed in the RFP. Second, the proposal makes the case for selecting the company by presenting any additional information such as unique product features, service programs, or competitive pricing to help persuade the customer.

Make the Purchase Decision

Once the proposals are submitted, the next step is the purchase decision. Given the time and analysis companies put into the decision process one might think the decision is straightforward. The reality, however, is more complex, as detailed in Exhibit 5.9. Often the final decision involves trade-offs between equally important evaluation criteria and equally qualified vendors.

EXHIBIT 5.9 | Critical Choice in the Purchase Decision

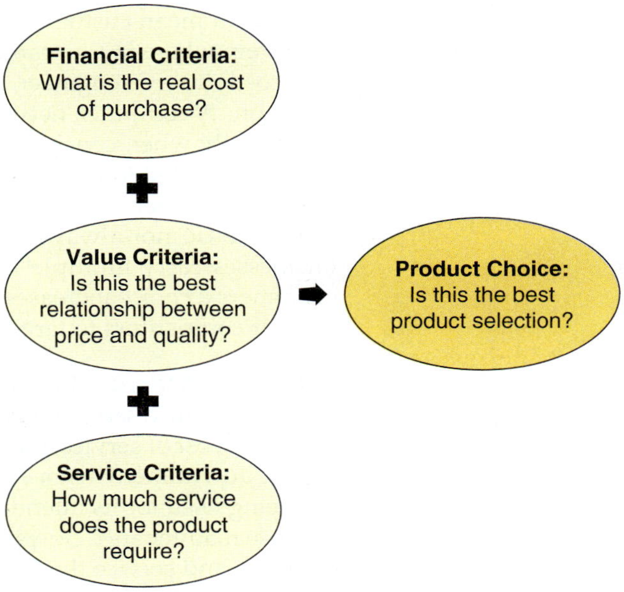
Financial Criteria:
What is the real cost of purchase?
Value Criteria:
Is this the best relationship between price and quality?
Service Criteria:
How much service does the product require?
Product Choice:
Is this the best product selection?

Product Selection The first purchase decision is the **product choice**. In many cases the product decision is based on a single criterion, for example, product cost (the office manager purchasing printer paper at the lowest price). Single-criterion decisions usually fall into a straight rebuy or very limited modified rebuy situation and do not require a buying center to assist in the new purchase decision. Much of the time, however, no one product fits all the product specifications exactly. As a result, the final decision assesses the product against the product evaluation criteria and determines the optimal solution.[23] Consider a company purchasing a new office copier. The first response might be, "pick the best copier," but what is the definition of "best"? One person might define best as most copies per minute, another as lowest cost per copy, and a third may consider the lowest maintenance costs to be the best. As a result, it is important to define the evaluation criteria and then follow a consistent and fair methodology in evaluating the sales proposals. Three primary criteria are used to evaluate the product choice.

Financial Criteria Financial criteria are a set of analyses and metrics grouped together to assess the cost of ownership. The actual purchase price is just one consideration in determining the real cost of a purchase. Maintenance and operating costs, repair charges, and supplies are all costs associated with ownership that can vary across product choices. These costs are then evaluated against the stated life of the product. This is important as some products with a higher initial price actually cost less over time because of the product's longer life. Financial analysis also evaluates the time it takes to break even on the investment. A company considering new equipment designed to lower manufacturing costs will want to know how long it will take to recoup the investment given the projected savings.

Business-to-business marketers understand that presenting a strong financial case for their products is an essential part of selling the product. As a result, many of these financial analyses are performed by the supplier and included in the sales proposal. Buyers then compare, and verify, the analyses across vendors.

For years sales of automobiles in Japan had been declining, so it seemed an odd time for Toyota to invest more than $1 billion in a new auto plant and related facilities in its home country. Then the giant earthquake of 2011 hit, destroying significant parts of central and northern Japan. The plant is now back up and running, and the investments have paid off as Toyota is now benefiting from greater plant efficiency and flexibility. In addition, Toyota also makes the point that the new facilities enable the company to test new manufacturing technologies that can be introduced at facilities around the world.[24]

Value Criteria Value is the relationship between price and quality and it is a significant facet of the purchase decision. B2B buyers are aware that the lowest-cost product may not be the right product, especially in critical OEM equipment where failure can mean customer dissatisfaction or in strategic purchases such as a new IT system where failure can cause serious business disruption. On the other hand, it is costly to overengineer a product and purchase more than is needed for the situation. A computer network that must work 100 percent of the time is much more costly when considering the backup systems and redundant hardware and software needed to maintain it than a system with 95 percent run time. It is up to the buying center to determine the specifications needed to do the job.[25]

Buyers do not always need the highest-quality product, which is why most businesses carry multiple lines with different quality and price levels. Offering customers a choice increases the likelihood of success and minimizes the opportunity for competitors to target gaps in a company's overall product line.[26]

Service Criteria Buyers are concerned with the service requirements of a product because servicing equipment costs a company in two ways. First, there is the direct cost of service, including labor and supplies. Second, there is the indirect cost of downtime when a system is out of service, which means the equipment is not being used for its intended purpose.[27] Southwest flies only Boeing 737s in part because maintenance crews need to know only one plane, which makes it easier to maintain and service the 737.

Products are designed, in part, to minimize service costs. There are trade-offs, however, as companies seek the best compromise between product performance and lower service costs. Knowing the buyer's specific priorities with regard to performance, service, and other critical criteria is essential to designing and building the product that best fits the product specifications.

John Deere is a longstanding supplier in the agriculture industry.

Supplier Choice Businesses buy not just a product; they also make a **supplier choice**. Often, multiple sellers will be offering the same product or very similar product configurations. As a result, supplier qualifications become part of the purchase decision. Decision makers know a purchase decision can turn out badly if the wrong vendor is selected, even if the product choice is correct.[28]

The most fundamental criterion in vendor selection is **reliability**, which is the vendor's ability to meet contractual obligations including delivery times and service schedules. Strategic business-to-business relationships are based, in part, on a high level of trust between organizations. In those situations, the supplier's reliability becomes an essential factor in the final selection. Furthermore, a judgment is often made about the seller's willingness to go above and beyond what is specified in the contract. All things being equal, the seller with the best reliability and intangibles, like a willingness to do a little more than required, usually gets the order.[29]

HP launched the world's first commercially available HP Moonshot system as a part of its Project Moonshot. It delivers new infrastructure economics using up to 89 percent less energy, 80 percent less space, and 77 percent less cost compared to traditional servers. The traditional mega data centers were nearing a breaking point that would hinder further growth due to their infrastructure. "With nearly 10 billion devices connected to the Internet and predictions for exponential growth, we've reached a point where the space, power, and cost demands of technology are no longer sustainable." Noted president and CEO Meg Whitman, "HP Moonshot marks the beginning of a new style of IT that will change infrastructure economics and lay the foundation for the next 20 billion devices." The system is a second-generation server. It was engineered to address IT challenges created by social, cloud, mobile, and big data. HP also announced a roadmap beginning in 2013 of workload-optimized HP ProLiant Moonshot servers incorporating processors from a broad ecosystem of HP partners including AMD, AppliedMicro, Calxeda, Intel, and Texas Instruments Incorporated.[30]

Personal and Organizational Factors Several additional factors affect product and supplier choices. Suppliers often find it difficult to understand the role these factors play in the final decision, but their influence can be profound. The first, **personal factors**, refers to the needs, desires, and objectives of those involved in the purchase decision. Everyone in the buying center comes with his or her own needs and goals. Someone might see this as an opportunity for promotion, another believes he will receive a raise if he can be successful, and a third may want to impress management. It is not possible to separate the individual agendas

EXHIBIT 5.10 | Post-Purchase Evaluation Criteria

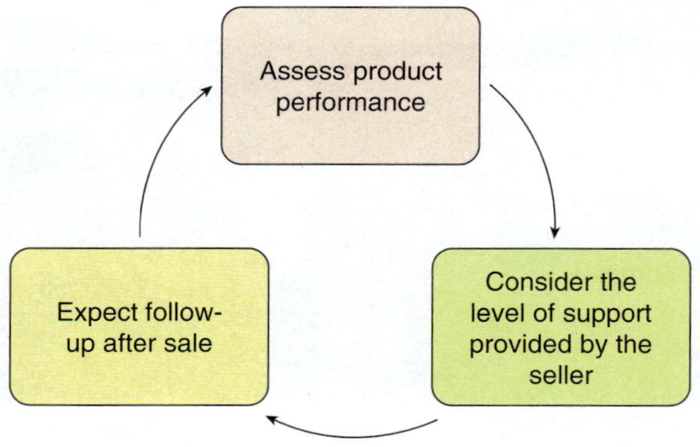

people bring to the buying center from the purchase decision. In addition, individuals in the buying center come to the group with their own perspective of the decision. Engineers, for example, tend to focus on product performance and specifications. Accountants often concentrate on the cost and other financial considerations. Purchasing agents give attention to vendor quality and ease of ordering. One reason buying centers are effective is their ability to bring individuals with different perspectives together to evaluate possible product options.

Another influence on the product and supplier choice is organizational factors. The primary **organizational factor** is risk tolerance. Individuals and companies all have a certain tolerance for risk. Their product decisions will be influenced by their aversion to or acceptance of risk.[31] Consider the IT manager looking to purchase a new network for his company. Two suppliers have submitted proposals that meet the product specification. One is a local vendor with an excellent reputation. This vendor has quoted a lower price and guaranteed better service. The other is Cisco Systems, the world leader in network equipment and software. The manager for the company with a low risk tolerance will probably choose Cisco Systems. It represents the "safe" choice. His superiors would never question purchasing from the market leader. If the same individual works for a risk-tolerant organization, the decision might be to go with the vendor offering better price and service. The cost of a mistake is high. If the network goes down and the company suffers a business disruption because the supplier has performed poorly, questions about the supplier selection arise. Risk tolerance does play a role as the buying center moves closer to a final decision.

Post-Purchase Evaluation of Product and Supplier

Once the purchase decision is made, buyers begin the process of evaluation (see Exhibit 5.10). Initially, they assess product performance and the seller's response to any problems or issues. A key for business marketers is to make sure the customer understands the proper operation and maintenance of the product. At the same time, buyers consider the level of support provided by the seller and expect follow-up after the sale to be sure there are no problems. Dealing with complaints, resolving customer problems, and making sure the company is meeting customer expectations are critical to ensuring customer satisfaction.

The evaluation process is designed, in part, to help customers make better purchase decisions in the future. Being the current seller is a distinct advantage because, if the customer evaluates the purchase decision positively, there is no need to change the decision next time. In essence, the evaluation process, if handled properly, can be the best sales tool for the seller when it comes time for the next purchase decision.

Naturally, the opposite is also true. If the product performs poorly or the seller does not meet customer expectations, competitors can use those mistakes to trigger a modified rebuy or even a new purchase decision process that increases their probability of success. Losing a customer is disappointing; however, it also represents an opportunity. By using well-developed service recovery strategies, companies can reacquire customers (Chapter 9 discusses service recovery strategies).

Navteq is a market leader in creating maps used in the navigation systems found on many luxury cars such as the Cadillac Escalade and BMW 7 series. However, the company realized it needed to expand beyond the OEM market in order to continue to grow. As a result, Navteq moved into new markets. In the early 2000s, onboard mapping was 100 percent of Navteq's revenue, but that number has dropped to less than 50 percent. The company realizes it is important to always be positioned for new market opportunities. Microsoft/Nokia realized the potential for growth and acquired Navteq to expand its reach in wireless mapping.[32]

THE ROLE OF TECHNOLOGY IN BUSINESS MARKETS

LO 5-5

Comprehend the role of technology in business markets.

Technology has transformed the business purchase decision process. From the Internet to portable handheld optical scanning devices, technology has made the purchase decision process more efficient and effective. Technology has also pushed the purchase decision process closer to the product user because front-line managers can now make purchases directly.[33]

Sophisticated programs manage inventories and automatically replenish supplies. By linking directly with **electronic data interchange (EDI)**, customer computers communicate directly with supplier computers to reorder as needed. Late deliveries, defective products, and other issues related to supplier performance can be identified and dealt with before they become a major problem. Collaboration between business buyers and sellers has increased significantly as a result of technology linkages.[34]

E-Procurement

B2B transactions have been growing at a phenomenal rate with online B2B commerce worldwide in excess of $1 trillion, a much larger amount than that generated by B2C online sales. The process of business purchasing online is referred to as **e-procurement**.[35] Let's examine the various e-procurement methods:

Industry purchasing sites: Industries have formed websites to streamline and standardize the e-procurement process. Steel, chemicals, paper, and automobile manufacturers have created integrated websites to assist their own purchasing departments in online purchasing and supplier selection.

Business function sites: Certain business functions have websites to standardize purchasing. For example, individual utilities used to negotiate by phone to buy and sell electricity with each other; however, today the purchase of electricity by utility companies is now done over a website dedicated to energy management.

Extranet to major suppliers: Many companies have set up direct links to approved suppliers to make the purchase easier and move it closer to front-line decision makers.[36] Office Depot, for example, has a number of direct relationships using EDI with thousands of companies.

Company buying sites: Many large companies have created their own websites to assist vendors. RFPs and other relevant supplier information as well as some contact information are accessible for review.

SUMMARY

Several significant characteristics differentiate business and consumer markets including the concentration and number of customers found in business markets. In addition, the buying process itself is often longer and more complex. The demand for products in B2B markets is also different, creating both a challenge and an opportunity for business sellers.

Different types of selling situations lead to very different types of customer decision processes. Business customers interact with their suppliers in very different situations from a straight rebuy to new purchases. The greatest opportunity for a business seller to win new business comes in modified rebuy and new purchase situations.

The buying center is a team of individuals, from inside and outside the organization, that engages in the purchase decision process and either makes or recommends to the decision maker the final product selection. It is essential for business sellers to identify and become familiar with the buying center involved in any purchase decision.

The purchase decision process includes six steps from problem identification through to purchase decision and post-purchase evaluation of the product and supplier. In a new purchase decision, the process can take months or even years and may involve dozens of individual customers inside the organization. The actual purchase decision involves two distinct decisions. Initially, based on an evaluation of product options against product specifications, the product choice decision is made. Often a second decision about the supplier is also required.

Technology is playing a major role in business-to-business marketing. The growth of online purchasing, also known as e-procurement, has transformed B2B alliances and made the process faster and more accurate.

KEY TERMS

B2B (business-to-business) markets 131
supply chain 134
product demand 135
derived demand 135
acceleration effect 135
inelastic demand 136
buying decision 136
straight rebuy 136
out supplier 137
modified rebuy 137
new purchase 137
buying center 138
users 138
initiator 138
influencers 139
gatekeepers 139
deciders 139
North American Industrial Classification System (NAICS) 140
original equipment manufacturer (OEM) 141
end user purchases 142
capital equipment 142
materials, repairs, operational (MRO) 142
resellers 142
government 143
institutions 143
request for proposal (RFP) 145
product choice 147
supplier choice 149
reliability 149
personal factors 149
organizational factors 150
electronic data interchange (EDI) 151
e-procurement 151

APPLICATION QUESTIONS

1. You are the marketing manager for Lenovo laptop computers. Identify and briefly discuss the differences between the consumer market for laptops and the business market. Then give an example of each difference using college students as the consumer market and defense-related companies as the business market.
2. You work for Siemens Power Generations Systems and are responsible for the sale of large, expensive ($2 million to $5 million) turbine generators to power utility companies. You have been contacted by the Ever-sure Utility Corporation in Anytown, USA. Identify the buying center you are likely to find inside the company and how you would market the generators to the buying center group.

3. You are vice president for information technology at your university. Recently you have been authorized to upgrade the network servers on campus. Draft an RFP that will be given to prospective vendors to help guide them in their sales process.
4. You are the primary sales representative for IBM calling on your university and are responsible for finalizing the sale of 20 new network servers. What is the most important factor you would focus on in making the sales presentation to the vice president of information technology and why? What other characteristics would you discuss and why?

MANAGEMENT DECISION CASE: Organizational Buying on a Grand Scale

Imagine that you work for a company producing a product that has only one buyer. The relationship between the buyer and your company has existed for decades and you have been supplying this buyer with products since the seemingly prehistoric late 1980s. Furthermore, imagine that this one buyer has only one supplier for the product your company produces and that your product is so important to this buyer's operations it would not be able to fulfill its mission as an organization without it. Thus, the importance of your company's product to the operations of the buying organization is enormous. As a result, the relationship between your company and members of the buying organization is extremely close—so close that sometimes your company hires employees away from the buying organization in an effort to stay current on that organization's requirements, better understand the extremely complex purchasing process they use, and further deepen the relationship between your two organizations.

In a relationship as described above, which organization do you think has an advantage when negotiating contracts for new purchases or extensions to existing contracts? Of course, it's a difficult question to answer unless you know exactly who the players are and what the product is. In this case, the seller is Northrup Grumman Corporation, the buyer is the U.S. Department of Defense (DOD), and the product is the B-2 Stealth Bomber. Were the paragraph above the entire information provided, it's fair to assume that most people would say when a product being sold is so vital to the buyer's operations the selling organization will have the advantage in purchase negotiations. However, the DOD is a quite unique entity and along the way the purchasing processes utilized therein can involve dozens if not hundreds of people, a labyrinth of regulations, potential testimony before a congressional committee, turnover in key personnel during the process, threats of funding cancellation by Congress, and many other contingency situations too numerous to mention. Whether it involves buying a B-2 Stealth Bomber ($2.1 billion per plane), the latest aircraft carrier (USS Gerald R. Ford, at $12.5 billion), or a contract for the provision of food service to hundreds of thousands of troops stationed in far-flung places around the globe, doing business with the DOD probably tops every other buying process in the world in terms of complexity. But as discussed in the chapter, when federal, state, and local governments combined spend over $2 trillion on an annual basis, it is worth it for companies like Northrup Grumman to expend the considerable extra effort to navigate the complexities and do business with those various government units.

Think of the differences between business and consumer markets and how those differences might apply to the DOD. The complexity of the buying process and the fact that it can take years for a project to be approved, funding to be provided, specifications to be written, contracts to be negotiated, prototypes to be developed and tested, and additional negotiations and more testing before the final product is actually deployed, all mean that the DOD is a buyer any seller must view as a *long-term partner*. Such complexity explains the tight and long-lasting relationships that exist between DOD entities and their venders. It also explains why many ex-military personnel go to work for suppliers—after all, who can maintain those close relationships and who knows the DOD buying procedures better than such people? Finally, given the massive buying power that exists at the DOD, it's no wonder that large defense contractors, Northrup Grumman being one, are located near the Pentagon in northern Virginia. Proximity, availability, and the potential to maintain a consistent presence are key ingredients to success when the buyer is as large and demanding as the DOD.

Questions for Consideration

1. Use the chapter discussion of various buying center roles to describe the potential members of the buying center for the air force when purchasing an item like the B-2 Stealth Bomber. Who should be included and what are their roles?

2. Assess the financial, value, and service criteria that a buying center at the DOD may consider when making purchases for both equipment (like the B-2 Stealth Bomber) and services (such as fuel transportation or food service). Also, what personal and organizational factors may influence a purchase decision at the DOD?
3. Contrast the buying process for the DOD with the buying process used by Target Corporation's procurement of laundry detergent from P&G for resale in Target Stores. What aspects of those buying processes are likely different and what aspects are likely similar?

Sources: Federation of American Scientists, "B-2 Spirit: Overview," www.fas.org/programs/ssp/man/uswpns/air/bombers/b2.html, accessed December 3, 2013; Todd Spangler, "Navy Set to Christen New Carrier USS Gerald R. Ford," *USA Today,* November 7, 2013, www.usatoday.com/story/news/nation/2013/11/07/navy-set-to-christen-new-carrier-uss-gerald-r-ford; Mac Thornberry "Reforming a Defense Acquisition System That Costs Money, Lives," Real Clear Defense, October 29, 2013, www.realcleardefense.com/articles/2013/10/29/reforming_a_defense_acquisition_system_that_costs_money_lives_106939.html.

MARKETING PLAN EXERCISE

ACTIVITY 5: Determine Business Market Relationships

This exercise has four primary activities:

1. Conduct an analysis of your key market opportunities to assess the fundamental nature of these markets. This analysis should include a description of:
   a. Who are the key companies in this market? How much business do you do with the industry leaders? What share of their total business do you have?
   b. Where are these companies located?
2. Identify the probable company structure and business center participants you would encounter in selling to your key business-to-business customer.
3. Put together a probable buying decision process for key B2B customers and discuss your internal process in selling to these customers in this process.
4. Develop a list of second-tier customers in key B2B markets that represent future potential customers.

NOTES

1. Oracle, "Oracle Invests in Proteus Digital Health and Its FDA-Approved Ingestible Sensor Platform," press release, May 1, 2013, www.oracle.com/us/corporate/press/1941306.
2. Thomas L. Powers and Jay U. Sterling, "Segmenting Business-to-Business Markets: A Micro-Macro Linking Methodology," *Journal of Business and Industrial Marketing* 23, no. 3 (2008), pp. 170–86.
3. Brian N. Rutherford, James S. Boles, Hiram C. Barksdale Jr., and Julie T. Johnson, "Buyer's Relational Desire and Numbers of Suppliers Used: The Relationship between Perceived Commitment and Continuance," *Journal of Marketing Theory and Practice* 16, no. 3 (2008), pp. 247–58.
4. Bradford Wernle and Mike Colias, "Ford, GM Work Together on New Nine-, Ten-Speed Transmissions," *AutoWeek,* April 15, 2013, www.autoweek.com/article/20130415/CARNEWS/130419905?utm_source=rss&utm_medium=feed&utm_campaign=.
5. Ruben Chumpitaz Caceres and Nicholas G. Paparoidamis, "Service Quality, Relationship Satisfaction, Trust, Commitment and Business-to-Business Loyalty," *European Journal of Marketing* 41, no. 7/8 (2007), pp. 836–48; and Papassapa Rauyruen and Kenneth E. Miller, "Relationship Quality as Predictor of B2B Customer Loyalty," *Journal of Business Research* 60, no. 1 (2007), pp. 21–35.
6. Srilata Zaheer and Shalini Manrakhan, "Concentration and Dispersion in Global Industries: Remote Electronic Access and Location of Economic Activities," *Journal of International Business Studies* 32, no. 4 (2001), pp. 667–87.
7. Tao Gao, M. Joseph Sirgy, and Monroe M. Bird, "Reducing Buyer Decision Making Uncertainty in Organizational Purchasing: Can Supplier Trust, Commitment, and Dependency Help?" *Journal of Business Research* 58, no. 4 (2005), pp. 397–409.
8. Rachel Smolker, "Go Ahead, Blame Biofuels," *BusinessWeek,* May 20, 2008, p. 24; and John Carey and Adrienne Carter with Assif Shammen, "Food vs. Fuel," *BusinessWeek,* February 5, 2007, pp. 58–61.
9. "OfficeMax Upgrades B2B Online Customer Experience on OfficeMaxWorkplace.com," *PR Newswire,* May 1, 2013, www.prnewswire.com/

news-releases-test/officemax-upgrades-b2b-online-customer-experience-on-officemaxwork-placecom-205572141.html.

10. Leonidas C. Leonidou, "Industrial Manufacturer-Customer Relationships: The Discriminating role of the Buying Situation," *Industrial Marketing Management* 33, no. 8 (2004), pp. 731–45.

11. Kelli Dugan, "Airbus Continues A320 Family Aircraft Surge with Nepalese Order," AL.com, April 29, 2013, www.al.com/business/index.ssf/2013/04/airbus_continues_a320_family_a.html.

12. G. Tomas M. Hult, David J. Ketchen Jr., and Brian R. Chabowski, "Leadership, the Buying Center, and Supply Chain Performance: A Study of Linked Users, Buyers, and Suppliers," *Industrial Marketing Management* 36, no. 3 (2007), pp. 393–408.

13. Marcel Paulssen and Matthias M. Birk, "Satisfaction and Repurchase Behavior in a Business to Business Setting: Investigating the Moderating Effect of Manufacturer, Company and Demographic Characteristics," *Industrial Marketing Management* 36, no. 7 (2007), pp. 983–95.

14. Marydee Ojala, "SIC Those NAICS on Me: Industry Classification Codes for Business Research," *Online* 29, no. 1 (2005), pp. 42–45; and Robert P. Parker, "More U.S. Economic Data Series Incorporate the North American Industry Classification System," *Business Economics* 38, no. 2 (2003), pp. 57–60.

15. Kun Liao and Paul Hong, "Building Global Supplier Networks: A Supplier Portfolio Entry Model," *Journal of Enterprise Information Management* 20, no. 5 (2007), pp. 511–23; and Chiaho Chang, "Procurement Policy and Supplier Behavior—OEM vs. ODM," *Journal of Business and Management* 8, no. 2 (2002), pp. 181–98.

16. Masaaki Kotabe, Michael J. Mol, and Janet Y. Murray, "Outsourcing, Performance, and the Role of E-Commerce: A Dynamic Perspective," *Industrial Marketing Management* 37, no. 1 (2008), pp. 37–48; and Bruno Schilli and Fan Dai, "Collaborative Life Cycle Management between Suppliers and OEM," *Computers in Industry* 57, no. 8/9 (2006), pp. 725–29.

17. Boeing, "Boeing Delivers 2 Nanosatellites to US Air Force: SENSE Vehicles Will Validate Nanosatellite Use in Military Space," news release, December 18, 2012, http://boeing.mediaroom.com/index.php?s=43&item=2535.

18. Robert S. Dudney, "Beyond the F-22 Problem," *Air Force Magazine* 91, no. 3 (2008), p. 2.

19. Diane Sears, "Joining Forces," *Florida Trend* 50, no. 13 (2008), p. 66.

20. Christopher Hosford, "Gamification: Finding the 'Softer' Ways to Incentivize Behavior," BtoB, May 1, 2013, www.btobonline.com/apps/pbcs.dll/article?AID=/20130501/SOCIAL05/304309976/gamification-finding-softer-ways-to-incentivize-behavior.

21. Jesus Cerquides, Maite Lopex-Sanchez, Antonio Reyes-Moro, and Juan A. Rodruguez-Aguilar, "Enabling Assisted Strategy Negotiations in Actual World Procurement Scenarios," *Electronic Commerce Research* 7, no. 3/4 (2007), pp. 189–221; and Mike Brewster, "Perfecting the RFP," *Inc.*, 2005, p. 38.

22. Stephen Copestake, "Getting Your Website Noticed," *Personal Computer World*, July 2008; and Marshall Lager, "The Dark Side of the Search Engine," *Customer Relationship Management* 11, no. 12 (2007), p. 50.

23. S. Y. Chou, C. Y. Shen, and Y. H. Chang, "Vendor Selection in a Modified Re-Buy Situation Using a Strategy Aligned Fuzzy Approach," *International Journal of Production Research* 45, no. 14 (2007), pp. 3113–24.

24. Reuters, "At Cautious Toyota, Low Risk Rules Even as Profit Booms," May 8, 2013, www.reuters.com/article/2013/05/08/toyota-earnings-dUSL3N0DP18R20130508.

25. S. Sen, H. Basligil, C. G. Sen, and H. Baracli, "A Framework for Defining Both Qualitative and Quantitative Supplier Selection Criteria Considering the Buyer-Supplier Integration Strategies," *International Journal of Production Research* 46, no. 7 (2008), pp. 1825–39.

26. Felix T. S. Chan and Niraj Kumar, "Global Supplier Development Considering Risk Factors Using Fuzzy Extended AHP-Based Approach," *Omega* 35, no. 4 (2007), pp. 417–31; and Donna Gill and B. (Ram) Ramaseshan, "Influences on Supplier Repurchase Selection of UK Importers," *Marketing Intelligence and Planning* 25, no. 6 (2007), pp. 597–611.

27. Ruth N. Bolton, Katherine N. Lemon, and Peter C. Verhoef, "Expanding Business to Business Customer Relationships: Modeling the Customer's Upgrade Decision," *Journal of Marketing* 72, no. 1 (2008), pp. 46–60; and James M. Barry, Paul Dion, and William Johnson, "A Cross Cultural Examination of Relationship Strength in B2B Services," *Journal of Services Marketing* 22, no. 2 (2008), pp. 114–31.

28. Maria Holmlund, "A Definition, Model and Empirical Analysis of Business to Business Relationship Quality," *International Journal of Service Industry Management* 19, no. 1 (2008), pp. 32–46.

29. Havard Hansen, Bendik M. Samuelsen, and Pal R. Siseth, "Customer Perceived Value in B-to-B Service Relationships: Investigating the Importance of Corporate Reputation," *Industrial Marketing Management* 37, no. 2 (2008), pp. 206–20; and Jeffrey E. Lewin and Wesley J. Johnston, "The Impact of Supplier Downsizing on Performance, Satisfaction

over Time, and Repurchase Decisions," *Journal of Business and Industrial Marketing* 23, no. 4 (2008), pp. 249–63.

30. Hewlett-Packard, "HP Launches New Class of Server for Social, Mobile, Cloud, and Big Data," April 8, 2013, press release www8.hp.com/us/en/hp-news/press-release.html?id=1389585#.UYF-K6V4gwF.
31. Wayne A. Neu and Stephen W. Brown, "Manufacturers Forming Successful Complex Business Services: Designing an Organization to Fit the Market," *International Journal of Service Industry Management* 19, no. 2 (2008), pp. 232–39.
32. Samantha Stainburn, "M&A Top Ten: Mapping a New Strategy," *Crain's Chicago Business* 31, no. 3 (2008), p. 25; and Alison Edwards, "The Map Knows All," *Calliope* 18, no. 3 (2007), pp. 48–50.
33. Blanca Hernandez Ortega, Julio Jimenez Martinez, and Ja Jose Martin De Hoyos, "The Role of Information Technology Knowledge, in B2B Development," *International Journal of E-Business Research* 4, no. 1 (2008), pp. 40–55.
34. Christian Tanner, Ralf Wolffle, Petra Schubert, and Michael Quade, "Current Trends and Challenges in Electronic Procurement: An Empirical Study," *Electronic Markets* 18, no. 1 (2008), pp. 8–19.
35. Juha Mikka Nurmilaakso, "Adoption of e-Business Functions Migration from EDI Based on XML Based e-Business Frameworks in Supply Chain Integration," *International Journal of Production Economics* 113, no. 2 (2008), pp. 721–41.
36. T. Ravichandran, S. Pant, and D. Chatterjee, "Impact of Industry Structure and Product Characteristics on the Structure of Be2 Vertical Hubs," *IEEE Transactions on Engineering Management* 54, no. 3 (2007), p. 506.

CHAPTER 06

Segmentation, Target Marketing, Positioning, and CRM

LEARNING OBJECTIVES

LO 6-1 Explain the criteria for effective segmentation.

LO 6-2 Identify the various approaches to market segmentation.

LO 6-3 Describe the steps in target marketing.

LO 6-4 Define positioning and link it to the use of the marketing mix.

LO 6-5 Use and interpret perceptual maps.

LO 6-6 Identify sources of differentiation.

LO 6-7 Avoid potential positioning errors.

LO 6-8 Define CRM and articulate its objectives and capabilities.

LO 6-9 Describe the CRM process cycle.

LO 6-10 Understand the concept of customer touchpoints and why touchpoints are critical in CRM.

FULFILLING CONSUMER NEEDS AND WANTS

EXHIBIT 6.1 | Market Segmentation, Target Marketing, and Positioning

Market Segmentation
Dividing a market into meaningful smaller markets or submarkets based on common characteristics.

↓

Target Marketing
Evaluating the market segments, then making decisions about which among them is most worthy of investment for development.

↓

Positioning
Communicating one or more sources of value to customers in ways that connect needs and wants to what the product has to offer. Positioning strategies are executed through the development of unique combinations of the marketing mix variables.

In one of the venerable band's most famous anthems, Rolling Stones front man Mick Jagger proclaims:

> You can't always get what you want.
> But if you try sometimes you just might find
> You get what you need.

Now, it's a safe bet that Mick Jagger wasn't thinking about needs and wants in the context of marketing and consumers when he and Keith Richards wrote that song in 1968, but the message resonates for marketing managers nonetheless. In fact, the triad of activities illustrated in Exhibit 6.1—market segmentation, target marketing, and positioning—get at the heart of marketing's ability to successfully create, communicate, and deliver value to customers and thus successfully fulfill their needs and wants.

In Chapter 1, you read about the evolution of marketing through a series of stages including pre-industrial revolution, focus on production and products, focus on selling, marketing concept, and post-marketing concept approaches. The last stage, which is really a more sophisticated extension of the original marketing concept, includes attention to multiple sources of differentiation, customer orientation, relationships, and mass customization and one-to-one marketing by which firms are capable of adding unique value to meet individual customer needs. This capability is enabled by CRM, which was introduced as a concept in Chapter 1 and will be developed further later in the chapter. What distinguishes much of marketing today from that of the past is this capability to more precisely home in on specific customers and customer groups and offer products or services that have a clear and compelling value proposition for those specific customers.[1]

Accomplishing this first requires the use of **market segmentation** to divide a market into meaningful smaller markets or submarkets based on common characteristics. Once a segmentation approach is developed, marketing managers engage in **target marketing**, which involves evaluating the segments and deciding which shows the most promise for development. In most ways, selecting target markets (also called market targets) is truly an *investment* decision. That is, a company must decide where to best invest its limited resources in developing markets for future growth. Everything else being equal, it should invest in the target markets that promise the best overall return on that investment over the long run.[2]

Finally, the way the firm ultimately connects its value proposition to a target market is through its positioning. **Positioning** relies on the communication of one or more sources of value to customers in a way that the customer can easily make the connection between his or her needs and wants and what the product has to offer. Execution of this approach is referred to as a firm's **positioning strategy.** Positioning strategies are executed through the development of unique combinations of the marketing mix variables, introduced in Chapter 1 as the 4Ps: product (or more broadly—the offering), price, place (distribution/supply chain), and promotion.[3]

The process of effective market segmentation, target marketing, and positioning is one of the most complex and strategically important aspects of marketing management. It bridges the overall process of creating, communicating, and delivering value to customers in that if the segmentation is flawed, target selection is incorrect, or positioning is unclear, there is no *value* because the customer doesn't connect with the product. Having a product whose value proposition is a well-kept secret is not a good thing in marketing—marketing managers want the right customers to clearly recognize their products' value-adding capabilities.[4]

Let's first take a closer look at segmentation. Then we will go on to gain an understanding of target marketing. Finally, we will introduce positioning as a lead-in to the marketing mix chapters that follow. These three concepts are equally relevant in both the consumer and business marketplaces. The criteria used for developing segments are somewhat different between the two markets, but the general concepts and importance of the process are similar.

WHAT IS SEGMENTATION?

LO 6-1

Explain the criteria for effective segmentation.

From a marketing manager's perspective, one way to think about markets is on a continuum that ranges from *undifferentiated,* where everybody essentially needs and wants the same thing, to *singular,* where each person has unique needs and wants. The territory between these two extremes is where segmentation approaches come into play.

Segmentation seeks to find one or more factors about members of a heterogeneous market that allow for dividing the market into smaller, more homogeneous subgroups for the purposes of developing different marketing strategies to best meet the segments' distinct needs and wants.[5] The operative word is *different,* as in **differentiation**, which means communicating and delivering value in different ways to different customer groups.[6] It is important to note that the basic logic and principles behind segmentation are sound, regardless of the basis on which a market is segmented:

- Not all customers are alike.
- Subgroups of customers can be identified on some basis of similarity.
- The subgroups will be smaller and more homogeneous than the overall market.
- Needs and wants of a subgroup are more efficiently and effectively addressed than would be possible within the heterogeneous full market.

Effective Segmentation

For years, L'Oréal targeted primarily women, but more recently men have become an increasingly valuable segment for skincare products.

Before developing and executing a segmentation approach, the marketing manager must be assured that several criteria for successful segmentation are met, as listed in Exhibit 6.2. The manager must satisfactorily answer these questions:

1. *Is the segment of sufficient size to warrant investing in a unique value-creating strategy for that segment as a target market?* Ultimately, there is no point doing market segmentation unless a positive return on investment is expected. Size of a segment doesn't necessarily mean number of customers—when Bombardier markets its small Learjets, it knows the number of potential buyers is limited. Yet, segmentation is still a valid approach because of differences in needs and wants among customers and the financial size of the transaction.
2. *Is the segment readily identifiable and can it be measured?* Effective segmentation relies on the marketing manager's ability to isolate members of a submarket to create a unique appeal. Segmentation most often requires data and if secondary data on the markets of interest aren't available or if primary data can't be easily collected, it may not be possible to do segmentation.

3. *Is the segment clearly differentiated on one or more important dimensions when communicating the value of the product?* For segmentation to work properly, it must allow for the creation and execution of different marketing strategies to the different submarkets identified. Segments should be expected to respond differently to different marketing strategies and programs. Otherwise, there is no reason to differentiate.
4. *Can the segment be reached (in terms of both communication and physical product) in order to deliver the value of the product, and subsequently can it be effectively and efficiently managed?* Barriers to reaching a segment might include language, physical distance, or, as in the case of some developing markets, transportation, technology, and infrastructure challenges. Firms have to be able to sustain their management of a target segment over time—if this activity becomes problematic, it can be a drain on resources and result in poor ROI.

EXHIBIT 6.2 | Criteria for Effective Segmentation

1. Segment is of sufficient size to warrant investing in a unique value-creating strategy for that segment as a target market.
2. Segment is readily identifiable and can be measured.
3. Segment is clearly differentiated on one or more important dimensions when communicating the value of the product.
4. Segment can be reached (in terms of both communication and physical product) to deliver the value of the product, and subsequently can be effectively and efficiently managed.

When considering segmentation, it is important to remember that an essential part of Marketing (Big M)—strategic marketing—is not just *identifying* existing segments but also *creating* new ones through product development strategies. The sensational initial introduction of Apple's iPhone stimulated needs and wants on the part of consumers in uncharted areas in terms of a single product's capabilities to fulfill, thus creating a new market by opening up new avenues of value-enhancing apps.[7]

SEGMENTING CONSUMER MARKETS

In the consumer marketplace, the categories of variables used by marketing managers to develop segments can be conveniently grouped into four broad categories as illustrated by Exhibit 6.3: geographic, demographic, psychographic, and behavioral. Let's consider each of these segmentation approaches in turn.

LO 6-2

Identify the various approaches to market segmentation.

Geographic Segmentation

One of the most straightforward approaches to segmentation is when evidence exists that consumers respond differently to marketing strategies and programs based on where they live. Thus, **geographic segmentation** divides consumer groups based on physical location. The key question is, do consumption patterns vary among the geographic submarkets identified? If so, firms can make tailored adjustments in their products to satisfy those regional differences in needs and wants.[8]

Within the United States, some of the more popular approaches to geographic segmentation include:

- *By region*—Northeast, Southeast, Midwest, and West, for example.
- *By density of population*—urban, suburban, exurban, and rural, for example.
- *By size of population*—Exhibit 6.4 shows the top 20 standard metropolitan statistical areas (SMSAs) in the United States.
- *By growth in population*—Exhibit 6.5 highlights the top 10 fastest-growing markets from 2010 to 2011, by number of people and percentage growth.
- *By climate*—colder Northern states versus warmer Southern states.

EXHIBIT 6.3 Consumer Market Segmentation Approaches

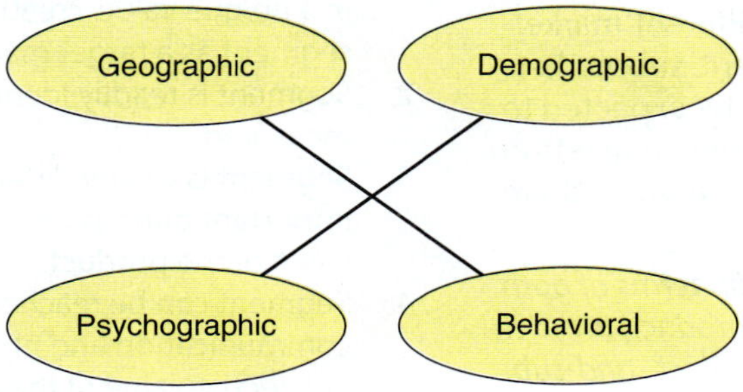

EXHIBIT 6.4 Top 20 U.S. SMSAs

Rank	SMSA	Pop. Millions	Rank	SMSA	Pop. Millions
1	New York	19	11	San Francisco	4.4
2	Los Angeles	12.9	12	Riverside, CA	4.3
3	Chicago	9.5	13	Detroit	4.3
4	Dallas	6.5	14	Phoenix	4.3
5	Houston	6	15	Seattle	3.5
6	Philadelphia	6	16	Minneapolis	3.3
7	Washington, D.C.	5.7	17	San Diego	3.1
8	Miami	5.7	18	Tampa	2.8
9	Atlanta	5.4	19	St. Louis	2.8
10	Boston	4.6	20	Baltimore	2.7

Source: U.S. Census Bureau, 2011 Census statistics posted April 2012. Largest city in each SMSA is listed.

Again, the key questions are whether segmenting by one or more of these geographic qualities means satisfying the criteria for effective segmentation and will it ultimately facilitate better communication and delivery of value to the submarkets than could be accomplished within the aggregate market? Target, for example, segments its target market by geographic climate. Starting in early September, Target begins marketing winter coats in its Minneapolis-area stores, an activity that won't begin until much later in Houston, where customers are still expecting several more months of 80 to 90 degrees. The chain's South Florida stores might never even stock traditional cold-weather apparel except in small quantities for travelers. Target wisely recognizes different customer needs across different climates and builds its marketing plans accordingly.

Geographic segmentation is useful but, in most instances, is an insufficient segmentation criterion in and of itself. Because people in the United States are extremely mobile and because the demand for many products is not determined by where a person lives, additional types of segmentation are needed to successfully target customers.

EXHIBIT 6.5 | Growth in U.S. Cities

10 U.S. Metro Areas with Highest Numerical Growth (April 1, 2010, to July 1, 2011)	
New York	69,777
Houston	45,716
San Antonio	32,152
Austin, TX	30,221
Los Angeles	27,077
Dallas	25,413
Phoenix	23,815
Denver	19,960
Charlotte, NC	19,663
San Diego	18,773

10 Fastest-Growing U.S. Large Cities (April 1, 2010, to July 1, 2011)	
New Orleans	4.9%
Round Rock, TX	4.8%
Austin, TX	3.8%
Plano, TX	3.8%
McKinney, TX	3.8%
Frisco, TX	3.8%
Dento, TX	3.4%
Denver	3.3%
Cary, NC	3.2%
Raleigh, NC	3.1%

Source: U.S. Census Bureau. Largest city in each SMSA is listed.

Demographic Segmentation

Another straightforward approach to segmentation is via demographic variables. In Chapter 4 you learned that demographics are the statistical characteristics of human populations such as age or income that are used to identify markets. **Demographic segmentation** divides consumer groups based on a variety of readily measurable descriptive factors about the group. Many different demographic variables are available for measurement including age, generational group, gender, family, race and ethnicity, income, occupation, education, social class, and geodemographic group. Demographic segmentation is one of the most popular segmentation approaches because customer needs and wants tend to vary with some degree of regularity based on demographic differences and because of the relative ease of measurement of the variables.[9] Let's look at the major demographic variables more closely (see Exhibit 6.6).

Age *Age segmentation* presumes some regularity of consumer needs and wants by chronological age.[10] It is important to make the distinction between

EXHIBIT 6.6 | Demographic Segmentation Variables

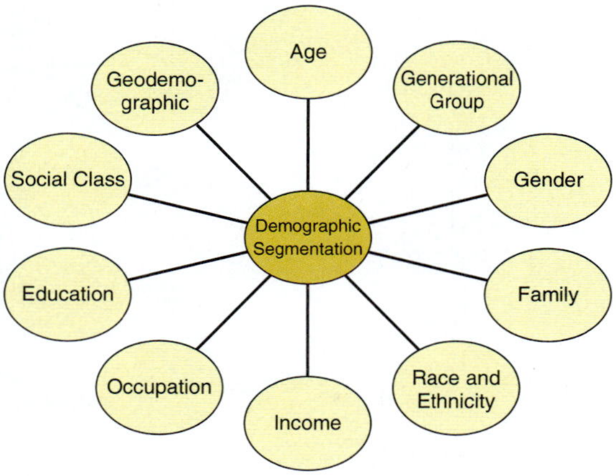

chronological age, actual age in years, and psychological or attitudinal age, which reflects how people see themselves.

McDonald's employs age segmentation to execute different marketing strategies to attract young children for a Happy Meal and older consumers for an early morning Egg McMuffin and coffee with friends. But marketers must take care to understand that age alone often is not sufficient for successful segmentation. Older consumers exhibit great differences from person to person on such things as income, mobility, and work status. In fact, marketing managers in companies ranging from travel to insurance to health care have come to realize that lumping older consumers into one group is not an effective segmentation approach because of the vast differences in other important variables.

Some very relevant issues related to age segmentation in home gaming are addressed in Ethical Dimension 6.

ETHICAL DIMENSION 6

Game On

Ask someone who is the typical video gamer and most people would describe a teenage boy locked in his room for hours with his eyes glued to a monitor that depicts him chasing, and being chased by, bad guys causing all kinds of mayhem. Although millions of young men fit this description, video gaming has also brought in new players, creating unique and vastly different market segments. The hard-core gamers are still predominantly men, but research suggests that more than 75 percent of *casual* gamers worldwide are women. Gamers still tend to be younger; nearly a quarter of the gamers in the United States are under 18 and three-quarters of all gamers are under 50 years old.

The video game industry has experienced dramatic changes in the last few years with a huge shift in gaming platforms from consoles to mobile devices and multiplayer online environments. Titles like "Madden Football" used to dominate the lists of popular video games, but those games have been replaced with titles like "BioShock Infinite" and "Tomb Raider." The largest titles can become billion-dollar brands and generate hundreds of millions in revenue.

As the market continues to expand, video and online gaming companies are seeking new business opportunities. With the broader demographic appeal, advertisers now consider video games a legitimate advertising channel, spending more than $500 million annually. Most of that money goes to put advertisers into the games. However, advertisers will spend $200 million to create "advergames," games designed specifically to promote a brand. Coca-Cola and other companies have created games to get young people connected to the brand. In addition, these companies have created Facebook pages and other social media sites to help generate interest and buzz about their products and brands.

Several key questions remain for the video gaming companies. Critics of violent video games suggest a harmful net effect on teenagers, primarily boys, acting out the violence. They reference the highly interactive, participative nature of the games that draws players into the violence. In addition, critics suggest the games reward the violent behaviors that players repeat over and over as they continue to play the game. Psychologists report that all these activities (1) thwart interactivity; (2) reward violent behavior; and (3) through repetition, lead to learned acceptance of violence as appropriate behavior. An example of this violence/reward mentality in gaming is the "Grand Theft Auto" game franchise.

A second issue for video game critics is the length of time children play the games. In a recent study, researchers reported teenage boys play video games on average 13 hours per week. When this much exposure is coupled with the dominance of violent games among this age group, psychologists and many parents get more and more concerned about the long-term effects.[11]

Ethical Perspective

1. **Video Game Developers:** They are meeting the needs of a target market by developing video games that appeal to that market. Is that a problem? What responsibility do they bear for the potential negative effects on young people?
2. **Parents:** If parents are aware of the violence, how should they handle the purchase and use of video games by their children?

Generational Group One approach to age segmentation that helps get at the heart of differences in needs and wants is *generational segmentation*. Much research has been done on understanding differences in groups of people by generation. What defines a generational group and how does one know when a new generational group is emerging? Sociologists look for defining events such as wars, major economic upheaval, or sociocultural revolution as triggers for generational change. As with other segmentation approaches, the notion that different positioning strategies can be developed and executed for different generational groups assumes some degree of homogeneity among the generational cohort.[12] The most recent generational groups, from oldest to youngest, along with their birth years are the GI Generation (1901–1924), Silent Generation (1925–1945), baby boomers (1946–1964), Generation X (1965–1977), Generation Y (1978–1994), and Millennials (1994 to present). It is important to recognize that because the Millennials are a "work in process" from a marketing perspective, a variety of other place-keeper names are also attached to them, including Generation Z and the Pluralist Generation ("Plurals"). It is way too soon to know what the next group after the Millennials might ultimately be like, although there is much speculation. Exhibit 6.7 describes each of these generational cohorts through the Millennials, including some of the core representative values of each.

In late 2012, American Express partnered with NBC Universal and Fox to create a system by which customers could purchase products "inspired by" their favorite shows from their mobile devices while the programs were airing. American Express members receive cash back when they purchase the products using American Express cards linked to their Facebook or Twitter accounts. At NBC, the plan makes use of Zeebo, an app that allows viewers to talk to friends watching the same show, and provides information on where to purchase products similar to those seen on the show. At Fox, the partnership used the Fox Now app to channel customer purchases of "New Girl" related products. In designing the programs, American Express and its partners had to take into account the demographics targeted—Gen X and Gen Y—and their shopping preferences. Gen Xers have more money, but Gen Y is more tech-savvy and more used to making purchases on mobile devices, while both generations share a distaste for extraneous advertising. The challenge has been designing a system that meets the needs of both.[13]

The generational group that has traditionally been the apple of the marketing manager's eye is the baby boomers. This is because there are so many of them and because they personify conspicuous consumption—acquiring products for the pure enjoyment of the purchase. An interesting aspect of boomers is that the oldest among the group have just entered their early 60s in age, and the majority of them will soon be facing decisions about retirement and beyond. Much of the research on baby boomers indicates that—at least in their minds—they don't age.[14] Recall that a marketer must be cognizant of the difference between chronological age and attitudinal age. It is anticipated that this forever-young generation will enter the segment we would traditionally label as "older consumer" without an old outlook on life and the future. This has profound implications for marketers in that it turns on end the stereotypical approaches to what products are marketed to them and how they are marketed.[15] Many boomers will become more active, spend more money, and want to experience more new things after retirement than they ever did while they were employed—that is, if you can get them to retire. Many smart marketers who happen

Converse appeals to the edgy and urban style of Gen Y.

EXHIBIT 6.7 | Generational Groups and Representative Values

GI (16 million born 1901–1924)
- Financial security and conservative spending (shaped by hard times and the economic depression of the 1930s)
- No such thing as problems—only challenges and opportunities
- Civic minded
- Duty to family, community, and country
- Unified and team oriented

Silent (35 million born 1925–1945)
- Strength in human relation skills
- Respectful of others' opinions
- Trusting conformists
- Health, stability, and wisdom
- Civic life and extended families

Baby boomer (78 million born 1946–1964)
- Forever young
- Individualistic
- Conspicuous consumption—great acquirers of goods and services
- Idealistic: value- and cause-driven despite indulgences and hedonism
- The end justifies the means

Generation X (57 million born 1965–1977)
- Lack of trust in society
- Cynical and media-savvy
- Entrepreneurial
- Accept diversity
- Environmentally conscious
- Work to live, not live to work

Generation Y (60 million born 1978–1994)
- Pragmatic
- Optimistic
- Team players
- Savvy consumers
- Edgy
- Focused on urban style
- More idealistic than Gen X
- Technology comes naturally

Millennial (42 + million born 1994 to present)
- Multicultural
- Highly tech-savvy
- Educated
- Grown up in affluence
- Big spending power

to be of Generation X or Y would do well to rethink the potential impact of successful strategies aimed at these ageless boomers.

Generation X is often thought of as a transitional generation. Its members are comfortable with much of the new-age technology but, unlike Gen Y, they didn't grow up with it, they had to learn it. Gen X is pegged as being a very entrepreneurial group, partly because many advancement opportunities in traditional firms have been thwarted by the overabundance of boomers who occupy those positions. It has been estimated that Gen X entrepreneurs are responsible for more than 70 percent of the new business start-ups in the United States. Gen X is not as consumption-crazed as the boomers, preferring more of a work-family life balance. For the marketing manager, this knowledge about the Gen X segment offers the opportunity to develop appeals to their independent spirit and practical nature.

Gen X is often referred to as the "baby bust" because it represents a natural cyclical downturn in birthrate. Because Gen X is such a small segment of the consumer market, many marketers have their eye squarely on the Gen Y and Millennial cohorts as the next great consumer frontier. Both of these groups are highly technology-savvy and don't balk at using any and every sort of communication medium to enhance their lives.[16]

Gender Target Corporation claims that about 80 percent of the dollar sales in its stores are made to women. Many firms note that men account for the majority of online purchases. Such knowledge provides evidence of the power of *gender segmentation,* which recognizes differences in needs and wants of men versus women. Certainly, a wide variety of products are clearly marketed for the primary consumption of either men or women, but not both—think Rogaine, cigars, and athletic supporters versus pregnancy tests, lipstick, and bras, for example. In such cases, marketers can concentrate on linking the product's value-adding properties to its corresponding gender segment. What about cases in which a product appeals to both men and women, but on the basis of satisfying different—maybe subtly different—needs and wants?[17]

Take, for example, razors. Gillette learned some years ago that, generally, women don't like to use a man's razor, which they had to do for decades because no thought was given to differences in gender usage preference. Research in the 1980s revealed that most women viewed men's razors as too bulky, with too many bells and whistles, and not feminine in color or design. Suddenly, Gillette found an underserved new submarket for segmenting its razor line: the female shaver! The result was a completely new brand and product line called Gillette Venus, whose tagline is "Reveal the Goddess in You." There are two main Venus lines: disposable and refillable razors. Between the two product lines there are more than 12 different razors, with everything from Simply Venus disposable razors, to Venus Spa Breeze (with built-in, white tea–scented shave gel), to the Venus & Olay Razor, which carries the tagline "A Match Made in Skin Heaven."[18]

When the Lego Group launched "Lego Friends" in December 2011, it was greeted with mass skepticism and protests (through #LiberateLEGO) against perceived sexism. The new Lego line features figurines that are taller and slimmer than traditional Legos, in a color palette that eschews the traditional bright solids for softer pastels. The new line is the result of years of study that focused on determining how children played with toys, and why the original lines of Lego toys didn't seem to appeal to girls. It seems that girls found the old designs unattractive, that (unlike boys) they usually preferred to use toys as avatars rather than as third-person characters, and that they preferred to be able to play with the toys before construction was complete. The resultant redesign was Lego Friends, which so far has been a resounding success. Already the company's fourth-bestselling line, it has helped Lego to increase its revenue by 25 percent globally. By adding a "girl's" line, Lego tripled the number of female Lego users.[19]

Family and Household In years past, the concepts of family and household were fairly easy for marketers to define—a married man and woman, likely with children, and sometimes with other relatives such as a grandparent who had moved back in. Now, *family and household segmentation* can be more complex. Marketing managers are cognizant of all kinds of different family arrangements including singles, unmarried cohabitating couples, gay and lesbian couples, parents with 30-something offspring who boomeranged back home, very large extended families living in one household, and so forth. Many of these changes in the concept of family have evolved based on changing economic realities, social norms, and cultural/subcultural mores.

Marketers who want to use family and household in segmentation need to understand the overall picture. One way to portray this variable is through the **family life cycle**, which was introduced in Chapter 4 and represents a series of life stages defined by age, marital status, number of children, and other factors.[20]

When Amana introduced the microwave oven in the 1960s, it started out as a product that was marketed to the busy homemaker as a way to supplement her (yes, it was marketed exclusively to women) food preparation and make her day at home more efficient. Now, most new microwaves are sold to singles, both men and women, who, in many instances, don't use or even own a traditional oven.

Race and Ethnicity *Race and ethnicity segmentation* has become of prime importance in the United States as the number of natural-born citizens of ethnic minorities grows and the number of immigrants has increased.[21] Exhibit 6.8 provides some important summary facts about the U.S. minority population.

In recent years, most firms have jumped on the bandwagon of segmenting by race and ethnicity, partly because many of these submarkets are growing quite

EXHIBIT 6.8 | Key Trends in the U.S. Minority Population

General Update

- At a population of nearly 50 million as of 2011, Hispanics remained the largest minority group, comprising 16.3% of the total U.S. population. African American was the second largest minority group, at 41.5 million (13.6% of total population). Asian comes in at third, with 14.3 million, or 4.8%. American Indians and Alaskan natives made up 1.7% of the population (although many listed this in conjunction with at least one other race), and Native Hawaiian or Other Pacific Islanders made up 0.4% of the total population.
- The Asian population grew the fastest between 2000 and 2010—by 45.6%. Hispanic growth rates were only slightly lower, at 43%. Overall, however, Hispanic population growth accounted for more than half of the total growth of the U.S. population.
- Four states and the District of Columbia are "majority-minority." Hawaii led the nation with a population that was 77.3% minority in 2000, followed by District of Columbia (65.2%), California (59.9%), New Mexico (59.5%), and Texas (54.7%).

Key Hispanic (Latino) Statistics

- Between 2000 and 2010, the Hispanic population grew by 15.2 million (or 43%)—more than half of the total population growth of the U.S. during that period.
- California had the highest Hispanic population of any state, as of the 2010 U.S. census (14.0 million), followed by Texas (9.5 million) and Florida (4.2 million). Texas saw the greatest numerical increase in Hispanic population between 2000 and 2010 (2.8 million), with Florida (1.5 million) and California (1.0 million) following. Hispanics comprised the highest percent of total population in New Mexico (46.3%), with California and Texas at almost the same level (37.6%).
- The Hispanic population is younger on average than the rest of the population, with 35% of the population 18 years old or younger, compared to only 24% for the rest of the population.

Key African-American Statistics

- The African-American population increased by 15% during the period from 2000 to 2010.
- In 2010, New York had the largest African-American population (3.3 million), followed by Florida and Texas (3.2 million each). African-American population increased the most in Florida (by 29%), Georgia (by 28%), and Texas (27%). In Mississippi, the African-American population comprised the highest percentage (37.3%); Louisiana (31.98%) and Georgia (30.02%) were next.

Key Asian Statistics

- The Asian population rose by 45.6% between 2000 and 2010, four times faster than the total U.S. population.
- In 2010 California had the largest Asian population by far (5.6 million), followed by New York (1.6 million) and Texas (1.1 million). The highest growth rates of Asian population between 2000 and 2010 were experienced in Texas and Florida (72% each), as well as in Virginia (62%). California has the highest Asian population by percentage of total population (33.1%); New York (9.7%) and Texas (6.6%) are second and third, respectively.

Source: U.S. Census Bureau.

rapidly in terms of both size and buying power and partly because they have historically been ignored by mainstream marketers.[22] African Americans account for slightly more than 12 percent of the U.S. population, a figure that has not been growing. In years past, very few products were marketed specifically to the African-American segment other than by firms specializing only in that segment. Hair and beauty product pioneer Johnson Products, founded in 1954, was an early believer in the power of developing products such as Ultra Sheen, Afro Sheen, Classy Curl, and others that brought the company consistently double-digit sales increases throughout the 1970s and 1980s. Ultimately, the product line became so attractive that it was acquired by mainstream beauty care manufacturer L'Oréal and eventually by Wella Corporation, another broad-line marketer of beauty care products. Today, almost all major cosmetic and beauty aid firms, from Avon to P&G, market products specifically designed to appeal to this vital market segment.

In contrast to the stability of the African-American segment, the Hispanic and Asian-American segments are both growing at a rapid rate. As Exhibit 6.8 demonstrates, Hispanics have overtaken African Americans as a percentage of the U.S. population. An obvious challenge with the Hispanic segment, at least from the perspective of recent immigrants, has been the language barrier.[23] In the past, marketers' use of the Spanish language and symbolism in communicating with customers has mostly been through tacky attempts at humor. Go to YouTube and take a look at the 1990s ads featuring Taco Bell's "Yo quiero Taco Bell"-uttering Chihuahua dog or the 1970s Frito-Lay ads featuring the Frito Bandito, for example. But today, marketers are taking Spanish-speaking Americans very seriously.[24] Compared to other groups, these segments are younger, are more oriented toward developing long-term relationships with people and brands, have more people per family and household, and have experienced a tantalizingly strong increase in disposable income.

Income *Income segmentation* is based on a very quantifiable demographic variable, and it is usually analyzed in incremental ranges. Until the Great Recession, that began in the late 2000s, the average income of U.S. families had been rising steadily, but at a declining rate of increase compared to prior decades. However, during the Great Recession, average household income dropped significantly and it is difficult to predict when and at what magnitude it may begin to rise.[25]

Marketers use income as a segmenting approach very frequently. Examples on the lower-income side include deep-discount retailers and dollar menus at fast-food restaurants. Examples at the higher end include luxury automobiles, gourmet restaurants, and exotic travel experiences. Interestingly though, there is not necessarily a direct correlation between income and price preferences. Southwest Airlines, for example, is a low-priced carrier yet maintains a certain cache with many high-income customers largely because of its fun style and spirit.[26]

Using income alone as a segmentation approach has some problems. First, many people either purposely misstate or refuse to reveal their income on questionnaires and in interviews used in collecting data for identifying segments. Second, with the readily available credit that is pervasive in the U.S. consumer marketplace, actual income may not necessarily drive one's ability to purchase products that in prior days were reserved for those with more income.[27] Cars costing tens of thousands of dollars can be had by nearly anyone nowadays by extending payments out six or more years. Even the old standby of income segmentation, home ownership, has fallen victim to wild mortgage schemes during many years of low initial interest, no-interest, and 40- and 50-year terms to entice buyers to go ahead and sign their financial lives away (which we now know had the unintended consequence of facilitating a meltdown of the mortgage banking industry).

Many luxury goods firms have been slow to move into the online retail space. Although online shopping represents more than $250 billion in sales annually, high-end retailers have tended to fear entering a space that might be seen to cheapen the brand. Givenchy, for example, was for years extremely cautious about opening the new channel. The brand is associated with the in-store shopping experience that results in a more personal relationship that is lost in online transactions. Givenchy, like other luxury brands such as Hermes, also feared that adding online retail would negatively affect brick-and-mortar sales. While Givenchy now has an online store, its slow adoption of this technology is typical of its segment, where customers are spending large amounts of money and have specific expectations and high standards in their interactions with the brand. So far, online shopping does not seem to have damaged Givenchy, and today there are very few luxury brands that do not have an online retail presence.[28]

Occupation *Occupational segmentation* recognizes that there may be a number of consistent needs and wants demonstrated by consumers based on what type of job they have. The U.S. Bureau of Census lists numerous standardized categories of occupations including Professional/Managerial, Technical, Government,

Trades, Agricultural, Educator, Student, and Unemployed.[29] In the United States, the workplace and our peer group of fellow workers is one of the strongest reference groups, and as you learned in Chapter 4, reference groups can be very powerful influencers on consumer behavior. All sorts of product lines are directly affected by occupation, including the clothing, equipment, and other personal support materials needed to fit in with the occupational peer group. Sometimes the employer influences purchase choice by offering tuition reimbursement, health care preferred provider networks, or discounts on products and services for employees. As a segmentation variable, occupation is very closely related to income, although the two are not perfectly correlated.[30] That is, many traditionally blue-collar jobs may pay higher wages than white-collar positions depending in part on the strength of the union within the firm and industry. Obviously, occupation is also related to education in that the latter usually enables the former.

Education In U.S. society, research consistently shows that education is one of the strongest predictors of success in terms of type of occupation, upward mobility, and long-term income potential. Everything else being equal, *educational segmentation* might lead a firm to offer its products based on some anticipated future payoff from the consumer. Take credit cards, for example. Why are credit card providers so eager to market themselves to college-bound high school seniors? Because they know that, even with low beginning credit limits, gaining usage early increases the chances of loyalty to the card over the long run—after the student finishes college, gains professional employment, and starts making a bigger salary. Unfortunately, educational segmentation works the other direction as well, which is a potential dark side of segmentation in general. Unscrupulous marketers have been accused of using educational segmentation (often combined with a language barrier) to intentionally take advantage of uneducated consumers in a host of ways including pushing unhealthy or untested products, encouraging bad financial investments, and promoting various illegal sales approaches such as taking the money for household or automobile repairs up front and employing illegal pyramid schemes.[31]

Social Class *Social class segmentation* involves grouping consumers by a standardized set of social strata around the familiar lower class, middle class, and upper class, and each of these contains several substrata. Exhibit 6.9 shows a traditional approach to segmentation by social class in the United States.

EXHIBIT 6.9 Traditional Social Class Strata in the United States

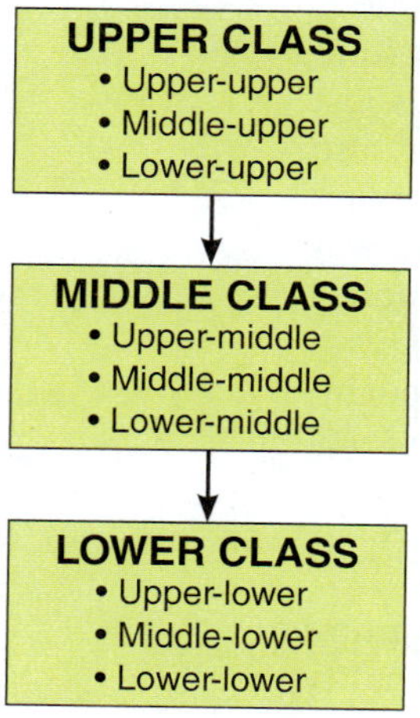

The composition of social classes takes into account several important demographic variables, including income, occupation, and education.[32] However, nowadays many mitigating factors might affect one's inclusion in one or the other of the class strata. Readily available credit has flattened the classes and made many luxury products affordable to a broad spectrum of consumers who in the past would not have been able to purchase them. And who doesn't know someone who is quite wealthy that also shops at Target for staple goods? Although the very upper and very lower strata are still potentially useful for segmentation, it has become increasingly difficult to segment among the groups within the big middle stratum. Because of this, most marketing managers today prefer either to defer to other demographic variables for segmentation or, more likely, to look at psychographics and behavioral segmentation approaches that capture much of what used to be evidenced by social class.[33]

Geodemographics A hybrid form of segmentation that considers both geographic and demographic factors is called *geodemographic segmentation.* Typically, marketers turn to firms that specialize in collecting such data on an ongoing basis to purchase data relevant to their geographic area of focus.[35] Let's say, for example, that you are interested in coming into the Orlando metropolitan area with a new upscale type of convenience store and gas station to compete for customers, especially females, who don't like the ambience at a typical convenience store. In fact, recently cutting-edge convenience and gas retailer WaWa did just that. Your research shows that it will be important to place your stores in neighborhoods trafficked by consumers who are more likely to be attracted to your upscale merchandise and more pleasant surroundings. Where do you turn for data on segments that might be a good match for your product?

Segmentation is not static. On the contrary, it is a powerful tool to help companies better understand their customers. Deciding how to best group customers and then what segments are priorities for pursuit is both an art and a science and is heavily reliant on solid data. H&R Block had an extensive system of customer segmentation in place, but the firm wasn't satisfied with the quality of its data for decision making. They reevaluated their system and added new and better data to create a more effective segmentation and targeting system. This allowed marketing to better prioritize different customer segments and target them more effectively. H&R Block is now much more effective in demonstrating where the priority new markets are and then providing marketing with better tools to approach these groups. The end result has been the opportunity to significantly increase the company's presence among Millennials, which have become a promising new segment for the company.[34]

One source is Nielsen's Claritas, which continually updates a large database called PRIZM-NE that is zip-code driven. PRIZM profiles every zip code in the United States by both demographic and lifestyle (psychographic) variables. Over time, PRIZM has discovered 66 "neighborhood types" into which all zip codes fall. Exhibit 6.10 describes several PRIZM clusters that might be potential customers for your new upscale convenience and gas store.

EXHIBIT 6.10 | Sample PRIZM Clusters

Winner's Circle

Among the wealthy suburban lifestyles, Winner's Circle is the youngest, a collection of mostly 35- to 54-year-old couples with large families in new-money subdivisions. Surrounding their homes are the signs of upscale living: recreational parks, golf courses, and upscale malls. With a median income over $100,000, Winner's Circle residents are big spenders who like to travel, ski, go out to eat, shop at clothing boutiques, and take in a show.

Money and Brains

The residents of Money and Brains seem to have it all: high incomes, advanced degrees, and sophisticated tastes to match their credentials. Many of these city dwellers are married couples with few children who live in fashionable homes on small, manicured lots.

Executive Suites

Executive Suites consists of upper-middle-class singles and couples typically living just beyond the nation's beltways. Filled with significant numbers of Asian Americans and college graduates—both groups are represented at more than twice the national average—this segment is a haven for white-collar professionals drawn to comfortable homes and apartments within a manageable commute to downtown jobs, restaurants, and entertainment.

Source: www.claritas.com.

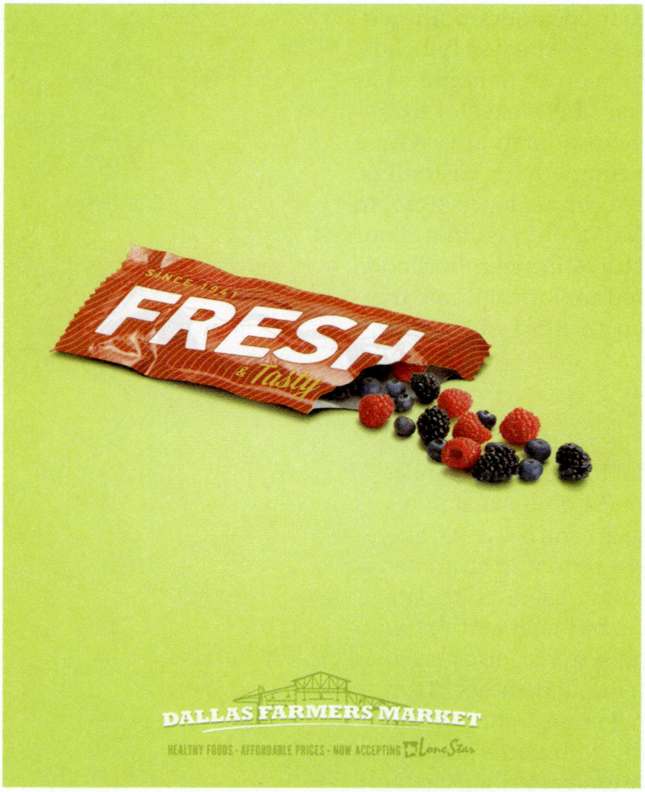

The Dallas Farmers Market is clearly messaging about a lifestyle in this ad, connecting with those consumers who value healthy foods but want affordable prices.

Judging from the description of the product, these PRIZM clusters seem to be likely segments of interest: Winner's Circle, Money and Brains, and Executive Suites. Certainly, other clusters not shown in Exhibit 6.10 might also fit your profile of assumed consumer needs and wants. The next step would be to seek zip codes whose location involves traffic patterns that will feed these consumer clusters into your convenience stores. These locations might involve being either close to housing additions or on key routes that members of these clusters take between home and work.

Psychographic Segmentation

Another approach to segmenting consumer markets is through **psychographic segmentation**, which relies on consumer variables such as personality and *AIOs* (activities, interests, and opinions) to segment a market. Psychographic segmentation is sometimes also referred to as segmentation by lifestyle or values. Psychographic segmentation builds on a purely demographic approach in that it helps flesh out the profile of the consumer as a human being and not just a location or demographic descriptor.[36] Psychographic segmentation brings individual differences into the profile along with the more readily measurable descriptive variables we have discussed so far.

An important challenge of using psychographic segmentation involves the reliability and validity of its measurement. Unlike geographic and demographic measures, which are relatively objective in nature, psychographic measures attempt to "get into the head" of the consumer. One way to better assure that such measures are reliable and valid is through the use of standardized questionnaires that reflect the experiences of a large number of users over an extended period. One popular psychographic instrument is **VALS™** (formerly known as **Values and Lifestyles**), a product of Strategic Business Insights (SBI). Want to know your own VALS™ type? Just go to www.strategicbusinessinsights.com/vals/presurvey.shtml, click on "Take the Survey," and complete a questionnaire.

Opened in the early 1990s, Volcom started out selling clothing and accessories for snowboarders, skateboarders, and surfers. Touting the slogan "Youth Against the Establishment," Volcom had a strong and established image and loyal customer base. Its acquisition in 2011 by PPR, a Paris-based department store chain, moved it toward an even stronger grounding as a lifestyle band. By branching into an entirely new line of footwear, Volcom is now offering a range from men's boots to ballet flats and wedges for women. The expansion out of the sports-centric brand origin provides an opportunity for customers to purchase Volcom products for a wider range of occasions. Senior VP of marketing Ryan Immegart, formerly a Volcom-sponsored snowboarder, admitted that not all of the styles can actually be skated in, but the line "really complements the lifestyle."[37]

VALS™ divides U.S. adults into eight groups that are determined both by primary motivation and by resources. Exhibit 6.11 portrays the basic VALS™ framework. Note that the key drivers in the system are the person's level of resources

EXHIBIT 6.11 | VALS™ Framework

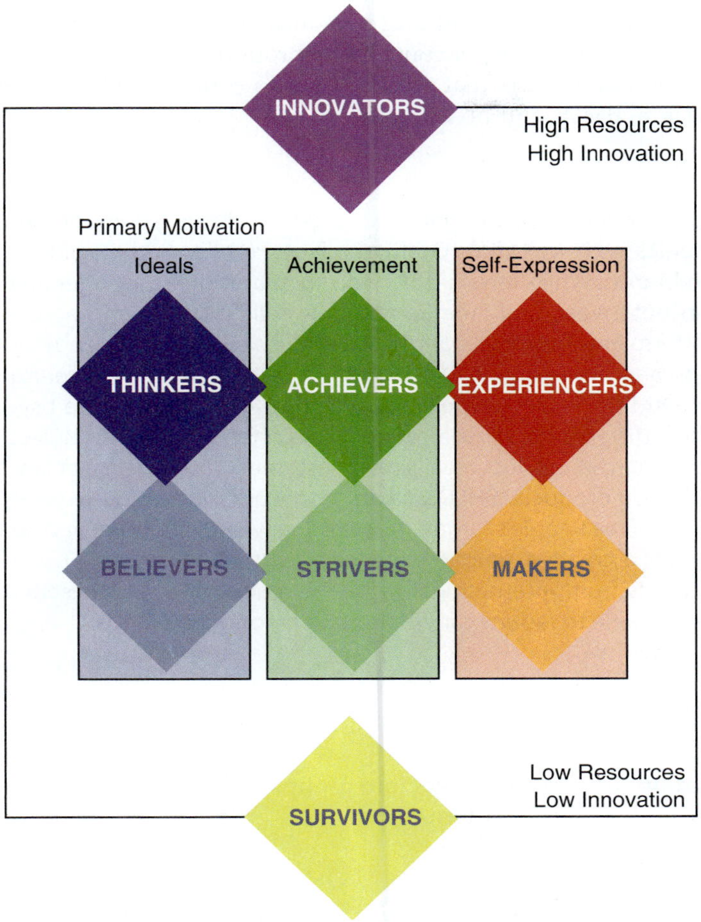

Source: Reprinted with permission from VALS™, Strategic Business Insights (SBI); www.strategicbusinessinsights.com/vals/

(high/low), innovation (high/low), and primary motivation (ideals, achievement, and self-expression). According to SBI, "Each of us is an individual. Yet each of us also has personality traits, attitudes, or needs that are similar to those of other people. VALS™ measures the underlying psychological motivations and resources that groups of consumers share that predict each group's typical choices as consumers." VALS™ has shown consistently strong evidence of reliability and validity.[38]

Again quoting SBI, "Consumers who are motivated primarily by ideals are guided by knowledge and principles. Consumers who are motivated primarily by achievement look for products and services that demonstrate success to their peers. And consumers who are motivated primarily by self-expression desire social or physical activity, variety, and risk." VALS™, or any similar psychographic instrument, works to help marketing managers successfully match people to products and helps focus the communication of value in ways that a particular VALS™ group is most likely to connect with. Product ownership, preferred media, hobbies, and so on are determined by integrating the VALS™ questionnaire into larger surveys such as GfK Mediamark Research & Intelligence (GfK MRI) or client private studies. Geographic concentrations of the VALS™ types are found using GeoVALS™ and SBI is internationalizing VALS™, having already developed systems for Japan, Venezuela, Dominican Republic, Nigeria, and China.

Exhibit 6.12 describes each of the eight VALS™ types.

Assume that you take the survey and discover you are an Achiever. Lots of hard-driving MBA students and undergraduate business majors are Achievers. The profile of Achievers shown in Exhibit 6.12 provides evidence of how a marketing manager might appeal to Achiever consumers through products that reflect status, prestige, and success. Brands that would seem to connect well with this type include Ritz-Carlton, BMW, and Bose.

Urban Outfitters, Inc., created hybrid concepts based on distinct demographics and psychographics with its Urban Outfitters, Free People, Anthropologie, BHLDN, and Terrain brands. While Terrain is very distinct, as it does not offer any clothing other than outerwear, and Free People only sells clothing and accessories, Urban Outfitters, Anthropologie, and BHLDN all have a broader array of clothing, accessories, and home goods. The brands are kept distinct by differing price points (Urban Outfitters is less expensive) and they focus on separate psychographics. Urban Outfitters caters to the young, and is often seen as the edgiest of the brands, with numerous product recalls after customers took offense at language or images used on products. BHLDN focuses on wedding and party-wear and related accessories. Free People's target market is the wealthy boho-chic. And Anthropologie markets a creative, unique experience with elaborate décor and handmade home goods from international artists. By cultivating such distinct images, the company is able to reduce cannibalization among the brands.[39]

Behavioral Segmentation

Behavioral segmentation divides customers into groups according to similarities in benefits sought or product usage patterns.

Benefits Sought Why do people buy? That is, what are the crucial value-adding properties of an offering? For many people, a Walmart Supercenter offers the ultimate in one-stop shopping. The idea of going to one store and getting everything from groceries to CDs to kitty litter has a lot of appeal, if the critical benefit sought is broad selection, low prices, and infrequent, extended trips to the store. On the other hand, in recent years Walgreens drugstores have been cropping up on corner after corner of high-traffic streets. Walgreens has been extremely successful in appealing to a shopper seeking a different set of benefits, namely less time in the store and a lower level of hassle. The chain caters to consumers for whom the convenience of having a store that is close to home or en route to work trumps other potential benefits such as selection and price.[40]

For many marketing managers, segmentation by benefits sought is the best place to start the process of market segmentation. You might begin by identifying groups interested in the specific bundle of benefits afforded by your offering and then move toward utilizing the other segmentation variables to further hone the profile of the core group that is attracted to your product's benefits.

Usage Patterns Segmentation by usage patterns includes usage occasions, usage rate, and user status. Occasions means specifically when the product is used. Why do you buy greeting cards? What causes you to take your significant other out for that special dinner? What makes you break down and rent that tux or buy that formal? Each of these purchases is driven by an occasion, and marketers are very savvy at playing to consumers' desires to use occasions as a reason to buy.[41]

Listerine in an example of usage-based segmentation. Back when Listerine was marketed as just a mouthwash, it tended to be used sporadically or in the morning as part of the day's hygiene routine. But now that the product also addresses such oral concerns as gingivitis and gum disease, the usage rate is way up with

EXHIBIT 6.12 | Description of the VALS™ Types

Innovators

Innovators are successful, sophisticated, take-charge people with high self-esteem. Because they have such abundant resources, they exhibit all three primary motivations in varying degrees. They are change leaders and are the most receptive to new ideas and technologies. Innovators are very active consumers, and their purchases reflect cultivated tastes for upscale, niche products and services.

Thinkers

Thinkers are motivated by ideals. They are mature, satisfied, comfortable, and reflective people who value order, knowledge, and responsibility. They tend to be well educated and actively seek out information in the decision-making process. They are well informed about world and national events and are alert to opportunities to broaden their knowledge.

Believers

Like Thinkers, Believers are motivated by ideals. They are conservative, conventional people with concrete beliefs based on traditional, established codes: family, religion, community, and the nation. Many Believers express moral codes that have deep roots and literal interpretation. They follow established routines, organized in large part around home, family, community, and social or religious organizations to which they belong.

Achievers

Motivated by achievement, Achievers are goal-oriented and deeply committed to career and family. Their social lives reflect this focus and are structured around family, their place of worship, and work. Achievers live conventional lives, are politically conservative, and respect authority and the status quo. They value consensus, predictability, and stability over risk, intimacy, and self-discovery.

Strivers

Strivers are trendy and fun loving. Because they are motivated by achievement, Strivers are concerned about the opinions and approval of others. Money defines success for Strivers, who don't have enough of it to meet their desires. They favor stylish products that emulate the purchases of people with greater material wealth. Many Strivers see themselves as having a job rather than a career, and a lack of skills and focus often prevents them from moving ahead.

Experiencers

Experiencers are motivated by self-expression. Young, enthusiastic, and impulsive consumers, Experiencers quickly become enthusiastic about new possibilities but are equally quick to cool. They seek variety and stimulation. Their energy finds an outlet in exercise, sports, outdoor recreation, and social activities. They are more "connected" through mobile technology than other consumer groups.

Makers

Like Experiencers, Makers are motivated by self-expression. They express themselves and experience the world by working on it—building a house, raising children, fixing a car, or canning vegetables—and have enough skill and energy to carry out their projects successfully. Makers are practical people who have constructive skills and value self-sufficiency. They live within a traditional context of family, practical work, and physical recreation and have little interest in what lies outside that context.

Survivors

Survivors live narrowly focused lives. Because they have few resources with which to cope, they often believe that the world is changing too quickly. They are comfortable with the familiar and are primarily concerned with safety and security. Because they must focus on meeting needs rather than fulfilling desires, Survivors do not show a strong primary motivation.

Source: Reprinted with permission from VALS™. Strategic Business Insights (SBI); www.strategicbusinessinsights.com/vals/ustypes.shtml.

many people developing a regular, twice-a-day regimen. This greatly enhanced the usage rate for the product.[42] Marketers often segment based on whether a consumer is a light, medium, or heavy user. Many firms subscribe to the concept of the *80/20 rule*—that 80 percent of the business is done by 20 percent of the users.

Degree of customer loyalty is another important focus for segmentation. Later in this chapter we comment on the capability of CRM to aid marketing managers in identifying, tracking, and communicating with especially loyal patrons so marketers can implement strategies to keep those patrons loyal and reduce temptation to switch. In practice, loyalty programs for airlines and hotels, as well as frequent shopper cards for supermarkets and other retailers, all play on the notion of keeping the segment of heaviest users satisfied and using the product and of building a relationship between the customer and the brand and company.[43]

Finally, segmenting users into groups such as former users, current users, potential users, first-time users, and regular users can be very advantageous. Often, firms will come up with extra incentives for former users to retry a product or for potential users to make that initial purchase. It is critical to influence the segment of first-time users to take the plunge and purchase. CRM programs enable marketing managers to customize the value offering, thus maximizing the appeal to each of these user status segments.

Firms Use Multiple Segmentation Approaches Simultaneously

We have seen that geographic, demographic, psychographic, and behavioral approaches to segmenting consumer markets all have strong potential. In practice, these approaches are not applied one at a time. Firms develop a profile of a segment that might include aspects of any or all of the segmentation approaches we have discussed. Exhibit 6.13 provides visual examples of a range of segmentation approaches, including combinations of several types of segmentation.

Developing the right segmentation strategy is one of the most important aspects of the marketing manager's role. Expertise in market segmentation is highly valued by companies across many industries because of the process's complexity and the potential for effective segmentation to have a major impact on a firm's success in the marketplace.[44]

Segmenting Business Markets

Chapter 5 provided an extensive treatment of the many important properties unique to business markets. The variables relevant to segmentation of business markets share some overlap with those in consumer markets, but it is worth highlighting several unique segmentation approaches here as well. Exhibit 6.14 summarizes several key approaches to business market segmentation.

EXHIBIT 6.13 | Examples of Segmentation Approaches

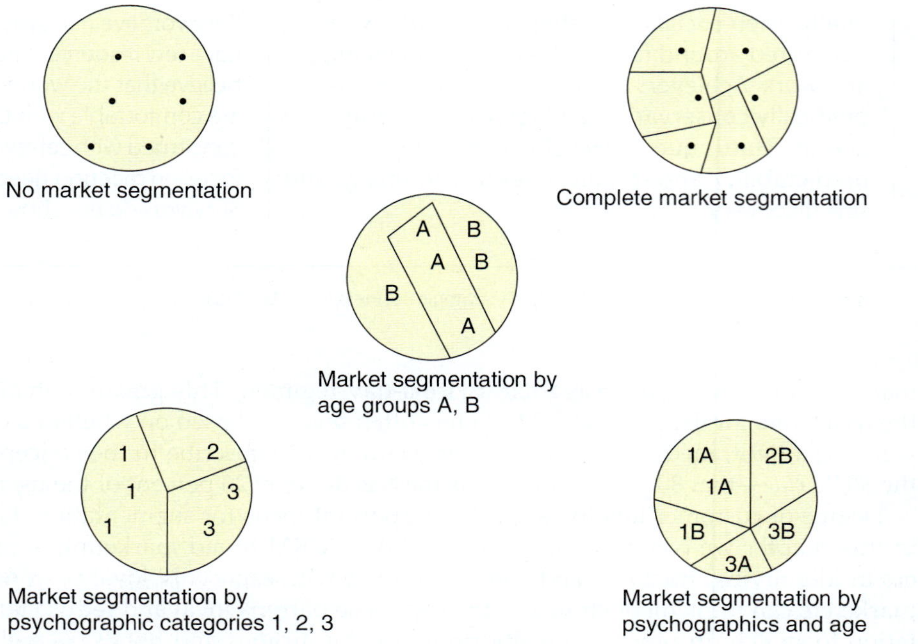

In some ways, business market segmentation is more straightforward than that of consumer markets. This is partly because there is often a more defined universe of potential customers.[45] For example, using one variable from each set in Exhibit 6.14, a firm might create a profile segment for focus that includes one industry, current nonusers, price-focused, large quantity, and strong loyalty. In any given industry in the business-to-business market, this segmentation profile would probably narrow the segment to include just a few firms. This would allow for a focused approach to communicating and delivering value to this profile of firms. Of course, as with consumer markets, segments must meet the criteria for effective segmentation and if the profile above appears too narrow, one or more of the variables can be removed.

TARGET MARKETING

LO 6-3

Describe the steps in target marketing.

Target marketing is the process of evaluating market segments and deciding which among them shows the most promise for development. The decision to invest in developing a segment into a target market represents an important turning point in the marketing planning process because, from this point forward, the direction of a firm's marketing strategies and related programs are set.[46] The three steps in target marketing are:

1. Analyze market segments.
2. Develop profiles of each potential target market.
3. Select a target marketing approach.

Analyze Market Segments

A number of strategic factors come into play when analyzing whether a segment is a good candidate for investment as a target market. Many different factors should be considered in the analysis. The goal is to determine the relative attractiveness of the various segments using an ROI (return on investment) approach. Everything else being equal, it is prudent to assign a high level of attractiveness to segments that provide the quickest, highest-level, and longest-sustaining anticipated ROI.[47]

Several factors should be considered when analyzing segment attractiveness. The following are among the most important: segment size and growth potential, competitive forces related to the segment, and overall *strategic fit* of the segment to the company's goals and value-adding capabilities.

EXHIBIT 6.14 | Key Business Market Segmentation Variables

- Demographic
  - Industry
  - Company size
  - Location
- Operating Variables
  - Technology
  - User status
  - Customer capabilities
- Purchasing Approaches
  - Purchasing function organization
  - Power structure
  - Nature of existing relationship
  - General purchasing policies
  - Purchasing criteria
- Situational Factors
  - Urgency
  - Specific application
  - Size of the order
- Personal Characteristics
  - Buyer-seller similarity
  - Attitudes toward risk
  - Loyalty

Source: This listing is derived from an influential early book on business markets—Thomas V. Bonoma and Benson P. Shapiro, *Segmenting the Industrial Market* (Lexington, MA: Lexington Books, 1983). The concepts are still fully valid today.

Segment Size and Growth Potential Reckitt Benckiser is a British consumer goods company known for brands such as Dettol (the best-selling antiseptic in the world), Veet (the best-selling depilatory brand globally), and smaller brands such as Clearasil, Lysol, and Varnish. Its biggest brands, however, are less well-known in the United States, so to move into U.S. markets, where it was not well represented, the company acquired Mucinex, Delsym, and eventually Cepacol, which positioned it squarely in the cough-and-cold market. With rising numbers of cases of the flu and a growing market for quick remedies, particularly with people more interested in dosing themselves (thanks in part to WebMD and other sites that allow sufferers to self-diagnose), the market was an attractive one, with a lot of growth potential and strong tie-ins to many of Reckitt Benckiser's other brands, particularly cleaners and disinfectants.[48]

Competitive Forces Related to the Segment In Chapter 2 we identified Michael Porter's competitive forces that firms must be cognizant of when considering investment in new target markets. For Reckitt Benckiser's cough-and-cold business, several of these forces predominate. First, rivalry among existing firms is fierce. Reckitt Benckiser entered a market dominated by Johnson & Johnson, but with fierce competition from brands like P&G as well. Second, a strong threat of substitute products is present in the form of a variety of cough-and-cold remedies, from homeopathic treatments to prescription medication to less conventional treatments like nasal irrigation (through neti pots and other sinus washes). New entrants are less of a threat, as patents and R&D make the barriers to entry high, and suppliers are not highly concentrated.

Strategic Fit of the Segment Strategic fit means there is a good match of a target market to the firm's internal structure, culture, goals, and resource capabilities. In the case of the Reckitt Benckiser acquisition of Mucinex and Delsym, the advantages and strategic fit were clear. The company already possessed similar international brands, and so it had experience with sourcing, production, and marketing. The brands also fit in well with the existing cleaning and disinfectant lines owned by Reckitt Benckiser, such as Lysol, since purchases of disinfectants often go hand-in-hand with purchases of cough or cold medication. The nature of the acquired brands was a great strategic fit for much of what Reckitt Benckiser already does in the market.

Develop Profiles of Each Potential Target Market

Once the market segments have been analyzed, marketing managers need to develop profiles of each segment under consideration for investment as a target market. Especially within the context of marketing planning, specifying the attributes of each segment and describing the characteristics of a "typical" consumer within that segment—from a geographic, demographic, psychographic, and behavioral perspective—are invaluable to gaining a better understanding of the degree to which each segment meets the criteria set out by a firm for segment attractiveness and target market ROI. Subsequently, a decision can now be made on prioritizing the segments for investment to develop them as target markets.[49]

Usually, this analysis results in segments that fall within four basic levels of priority for development:

1. **Primary target markets**—those segments that clearly have the best chance of meeting ROI goals and the other attractiveness factors.
2. **Secondary target markets**—those segments that have reasonable potential but for one reason or another are not best suited for development immediately.
3. **Tertiary target markets**—those segments that may develop emerging attractiveness for investment in the future but that do not appear attractive at present.
4. **Target markets to abandon for future development**.

EXHIBIT 6.15 | Continuum of Target Marketing Approaches

Very Broad			Very Narrow
Undifferentiated target marketing	Differentiated target marketing	Concentrated target marketing	Customized target marketing

Select a Target Marketing Approach

The final step in target marketing is to select the approach. Exhibit 6.15 portrays a continuum of approaches to target marketing from very broad to very narrow. Four basic options in target marketing strategy are undifferentiated, differentiated, concentrated (also called focus or niche), and customized (or one-to-one).

> ChristianMingle, a Christian online dating site, has been extremely successful by targeting a very specific—and growing—market. As of 2012, meeting online was second only to introductions by mutual friends as the way couples connect, with 23 percent of U.S. couples stating that they met digitally. ChristianMingle is owned by Spark Networks, a small player against mainstream competitors like Match.com, EHarmony, and OkCupid, but has avoided direct competition by focusing on more niche markets. With well over eight million users, ChristianMingle is the largest of Spark Networks' 28 sites, but the company also owns JDate (a Jewish dating site) and much smaller networks such as Silver Singles, Deaf Singles Connection, and LDS (Latter Day Saints) Singles. Although still relatively small, Spark Networks has experienced remarkable success so far and expects continued growth.[50]

Undifferentiated Target Marketing The broadest possible approach is **undifferentiated target marketing**—which is essentially a one-market strategy, sometimes referred to as an unsegmented *mass market*. Firms whose market approach is grounded in Porter's competitive strategy of low cost may use a relatively undifferentiated target marketing strategy based primarily on the resulting price advantage.[51] Southwest Airlines and Walmart are two firms that have built their businesses on their inherent internal cost advantages, passing along a price advantage to the mass market. But most firms don't have the kind of cost efficiencies it takes to operate such a target marketing approach and instead have to rely on developing sources of differentiation other than price.

As its tagline declares, Breitling markets "Instruments for Professionals"—not just ordinary watches—to its higher income target market.

Differentiated Target Marketing A differentiated target marketing approach, often referred to as simply *differentiation*, as you read earlier in this chapter, means developing different value offerings for different targeted segments. Possible sources of differentiation are many and include innovation/R&D, product quality, service leadership, employees, convenience, brand image, technology, corporate social responsibility, and many others. A significant challenge with differentiation as a core market strategy is that competitors are constantly coming to market with new differentiators that trump the efficacy of the current ones. Overnight a new technological innovation or other strategic shift by a competitor can doom a firm's current source of differentiation to the junk heap.[52]

FedEx famously differentiates based on speed of delivery and dependability of overall service to appeal to a target market willing to pay a price premium for these attributes. When UPS moved full force into the overnight package segment, its differentiating message was about full integration of services for the user through a smorgasbord of services including ground, overnight, and integrated supply chain solutions even for small-to-medium-size businesses. About the same time, FedEx entered UPS's lucrative over-the-road transport space with FedEx Ground. Initially, because of UPS's domination, FedEx had a difficult time differentiating itself in a meaningful way and only recently has FedEx Ground begun to gain widespread usage at a level that would even come close to affecting UPS's domination of that market.

Concentrated Target Marketing A **concentrated target marketing** approach, which Michael Porter refers to as a *focus strategy* and is also popularly called a *niche strategy,* involves targeting a large portion of a small market. Many start-up firms enter a marketplace as a focus player. Because they are not saddled with keeping up with competitive demands in the broader market, firms using concentrated target marketing can realize cost and operational efficiencies and better margins than many first positioned as differentiators.[53] The danger of being a focus player is that sometimes these firms get too successful and are no longer able to fly under the radar of the differentiators, especially if the niche they occupy is a growing niche within the larger market.

Customized (One-to-One) Marketing With the proliferation of CRM, firms are able to develop more customized approaches to target marketing. In Chapter 1 we said that **customized (one-to-one) marketing** advocates that firms should direct energy and resources into establishing a learning relationship with each customer and then connect that knowledge with the firm's production and service capabilities to fulfill that customer's needs in as custom a manner as possible.[54] The related approach of mass customization allows flexible manufacturing, augmented by highly efficient ordering and supply chain systems, to drive the capability for a consumer to essentially build a product from the ground up. Today, many online clothing retailers offer a high degree of customization in ordering. Consumers enjoy "building their own outfit" by completing a form that includes all the necessary body dimensions along with style and color choices, and within a few days a custom garment arrives via FedEx or UPS!

EasyJet is a British short-haul, low-cost airline headquartered in London. With profit per seat of just $8, the company is focused on controlling costs and increasing revenue wherever possible. The firm works to increase online check-in rates, which reduces the need for staff in airports, and it has "no frills" office spaces. Nonetheless, EasyJet uses customized marketing to increase sales. The "Inspire Me" tool on its website gives personalized destination recommendations to users based on responses to several questions about price range, timing, and destination preferences. The company also uses sophisticated, one-to-one e-mail campaigns. For example, the company sent e-mails to every passenger who had booked a trip during spring break but had not yet booked flights later in the year. Each e-mail included suggested trips with prices starting lower than what the customer had paid for the previous trip. For EasyJet, this type of customization has really paid off in higher revenues.[55]

POSITIONING

LO 6-4

Define positioning and link it to the use of the marketing mix.

Once market segments have been defined and analyzed and target markets have been selected for development, the firm must turn its attention to creating, communicating, delivering, and exchanging offerings that have value to the target markets—that is, positioning the product so that customers understand its ability to fulfill their needs and wants. The marketing mix of product, supply chain, price, and promotion is at the heart of positioning, and positioning strategies for a target market are executed through the development of unique combinations of these marketing mix variables.[56] Effective positioning is so important that the remaining chapters in this book are devoted to the various marketing mix elements.

Positioning doesn't occur in a vacuum; firms must position their offerings against competitors' offerings. Although McDonald's might like to think that their customers come because they're "lovin' it," the truth is that consumers of fast food can be fickle and they are constantly bombarded with the output of positioning strategies not just by direct hamburger competitors to McDonald's (such as Burger King and Wendy's) but also by many other types of quick-service restaurant cuisines.

In practice, much of the market research described in Chapter 3 is designed to facilitate successful positioning. Many positioning studies start with focus groups that allow participants to talk about aspects of their experiences with a product. From the focus groups, a set of attributes is developed for further analysis. Attributes of a product represent salient issues that consumers consider when evaluating the product. For quick-service restaurants like McDonald's, the set of relevant attributes includes items such as cleanliness of the restaurant, speed of service, breadth of menu offerings, healthy food options, prices, employee courtesy, and numerous others.

State Farm, which was founded in 1922, was known as a "quiet, reliable sort of brand," according to Tim Van Hoof, Assistant Vice President of Marketing Communications. While not necessarily a bad reputation, it didn't help the company connect with its target market. Furthermore, until recently the insurance giant still relied nearly totally on an agent model, while other companies like GEICO and Progressive aggressively pushed self-service options. The issue, according to Van Hoof, was to "be in the mind of the consumer" and offer the same core values in a way that is relevant—and more modern—so as to appeal to its audience more effectively. To that end, in 2011 the company retired the "Auto-Fire-Life" ovals from its logo since it now offers a much broader range of services, and began an ad campaign centered around Aaron Rodgers' "Discount Double Check" along with other clever ads like the now-famous "Jake from State Farm" and "Internet and the French Model" commercials. Interactive media campaigns have also helped boost customer interaction, with the result that State Farm, at over 90 years old, is more agile and more connected to its core customer base than ever.[57]

Typically, after a series of focus groups to develop or confirm the relevant attributes, the positioning research moves to a survey methodology in which respondents rate the importance of each attribute, as well as the degree to which each of several competitors' products exhibit the attributes of interest.[58] For example, McDonald's might survey consumers about how important cleanliness of the restaurant, speed of service, breadth of menu offerings, healthy food options, prices, and employee courtesy are, and then ask them to provide their perceptions of how well McDonald's, Burger King, and Wendy's stack up in actually delivering these desired attributes.

The results of such a survey can be analyzed through a gap analysis that shows not only gaps by attribute in importance versus delivery, but also gaps among the competitors in delivery. Perhaps the analysis would reveal that McDonald's excels at healthy food options and cleanliness of the restaurant, but Burger King excels at breadth of menu offerings and prices. If that's the case, each firm has to decide if it is comfortable continuing to invest in these elements of positioning or if investment in other elements is warranted. Recently, Burger King has deliberately invested in positioning itself as the "non-healthy menu" choice, blatantly featuring in ads its bigger and much more decadent food items in terms of fat and calorie content than either McDonald's or Wendy's advertises (although each certainly offers a fair share of unhealthy items).[59]

Perceptual Maps

LO 6-5

Use and interpret perceptual maps.

The data generated from the above analysis can be used to develop a useful visual tool for positioning called a **perceptual map**, which displays paired attributes in order to compare consumer perceptions of each competitor's delivery against those attributes.[60] Today this is usually accomplished by computer statistical software applications that plot each competitor's relative positioning on the attributes.

Exhibit 6.16 provides three different examples of paired attributes on a perceptual map. The first map shows a generic pairing of price and quality and identifies several quadrants of feasible positions based on price-quality pairings that result in positive perceived value by the customer. The logic is compelling as to why the other two quadrants are not feasible positioning. In the upper-left quadrant, marketing an inferior offering at a high price is the antithesis of good marketing management. It may seem that in the short run an opportunity exists to make a quick buck, but the approach runs counter to everything we've learned so far about value and building customer relationships as the core of successful marketing over the long run. The bottom-right quadrant's positioning of high quality at a low price seems attractive, but only firms that can legitimately sustain Porter's notion of low-cost strategy can reasonably consider such positioning. And even for those players, the idea of nurturing cost and efficiency savings in operations is not that you will take the entire savings to price; rather, Porter advocates that a low-cost strategy should afford the opportunity to take much of the savings to improved margins and increased reinvestment in product development, only reflecting perhaps a small price differential. Chapter 10 reveals the inherent dangers in positioning primarily based on low price.

EXHIBIT 6.16 Examples of Perceptual Maps Used in Positioning Decisions

Generic Price-Quality Perceptual Map

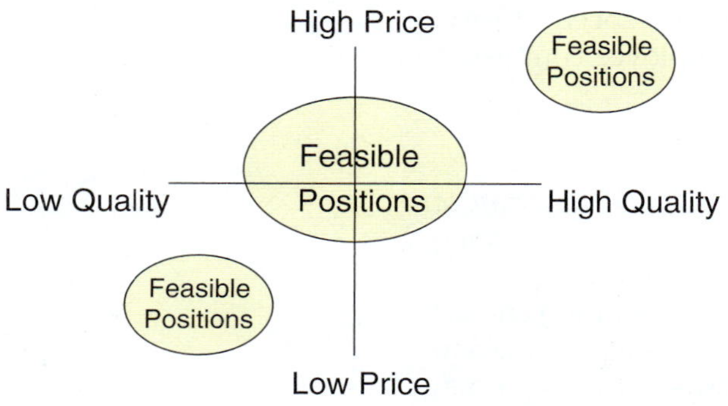

Perceptual Map for Hotel

Positioning involves trade-offs among other relevant attributes, not just price and quality.

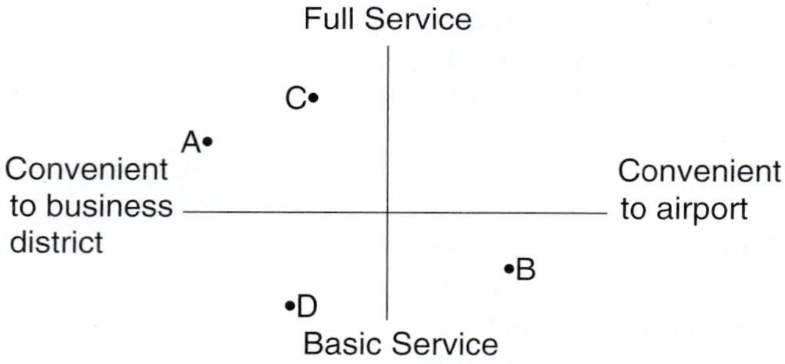

Perceptual Map for Automobile

Another example set of attributes.

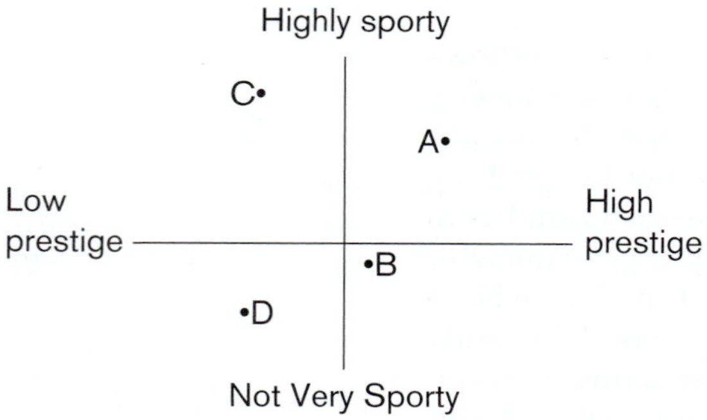

The other two perceptual maps in Exhibit 6.16 show where existing competitors are in the market based on the attributes reported. Such perceptual maps can be very useful in helping visualize where to make strategic changes to either move your product closer to the main market (clusters of competition) or further differentiate your product away from the competitive cluster and into more unique market space. In this way, perceptual maps aid in **repositioning** a product, which involves understanding the marketing mix approach necessary to change present consumer perceptions of the product. McDonald's has recently been engaged in a repositioning strategy into more healthy food options to appeal to an important target market of health-conscious consumers.

In actual practice, pairing just two attributes for consideration in making positioning decisions is overly simplistic. Data such as we described above are actually analyzed through a technique called multidimensional scaling that allows for interpretation of multiple attribute perceptions at the same time.

Sources of Differentiation

LO 6-6

Identify sources of differentiation.

Effective differentiation is absolutely central to successful positioning strategies. Michael Porter, in his classic book *Competitive Advantage,* explains differentiation as follows:

> When employing a differentiation strategy, the organization competes on the basis of providing unique goods or services with features that customers value, perceive as different, and for which they are willing to pay a premium.[61]

Marketing managers can seek to create differentiation for their offerings in a variety of ways. The following are some of the most often used sources of differentiation.

Innovative leadership: constantly developing the "next new thing." Example: Apple.

Service leadership: having an unusual and notable commitment to providing service to customers. Example: Ritz-Carlton.

Product leadership: performance, features, durability, reliability, style, and so on. Example: BMW.

Personnel leadership: hiring employees who are competent, reliable, courteous, credible, responsive, and able to communicate clearly. Examples: Chick-fil-A, Southwest Airlines.

Convenience leadership: making the product or service significantly easier to obtain. Example: Amazon.com.

Image leadership: symbols, atmosphere, and creative media. Example: Harley-Davidson.

Price leadership: Efficiencies in cost of labor, materials, supply chain, or other operational elements enabling the price leader to charge less. Example: Walmart.

It is important to note that firms and brands often rely on multiple sources of differentiation simultaneously. For example, Chick-fil-A likely stakes a claim to differentiation by service, product leadership, and convenience in addition to the aspect of personnel leadership noted above.

Jordache represents fashion and Walmart represents low price. Here, Walmart strengthens its price leadership while at the same time adding to its image based on the Jordache association and the connection to supermodel Heidi Klum.

Positioning Errors

LO 6-7

Avoid potential positioning errors.

Sometimes, positioning strategies don't work out as planned. The following positioning errors can undermine a firm's overall marketing strategy:[62]

- *Underpositioning:* when consumers have only a vague idea about the company and its products, and do not perceive any real differentiation. Until recently, both Audi and Volkswagen suffered from underpositioning as many consumers struggled to identify salient points of differentiation between those brands and their competitors. However, both brands have beefed up their marketing communication to better clarify exactly what each stands for in the marketplace.

- *Overpositioning:* when consumers have too narrow an understanding of the company, product, or brand. Dell became so entrenched as a brand of PCs that it has been a bit of a struggle to extend the brand into other lucrative product lines. In contrast, Apple and Samsung certainly are not overpositioned, having broadened the scope of their brands and products substantially during the same time frame.
- *Confused positioning:* when frequent changes and contradictory messages confuse consumers regarding the positioning of the brand. McDonald's found itself the victim of confused positioning as it moved out of the 1990s. It had tried (and failed) at so many diverse new product launches in the restaurants that many customers lost track of what the core of the brand was. Since then, under new top leadership, McDonald's has embraced its core differentiators of consistency of products and dependability of service, while growing new products at a much more conservative rate.
- *Doubtful positioning:* when the claims made for the product or brand are not regarded as credible by consumers. Sadly, firms that engage in unethical business practices often do not realize the magnitude of damage being done to their brand. Also, you will learn in the chapters on products and branding that trial is only the initial goal of marketing communication. After initial trial, firms need to ensure that the offering consistently meets or exceeds customer expectations so that repurchase—and loyalty—will occur, which is a process of customer expectations management. When FedEx promises 8 a.m. next-day delivery, it has to be sure its systems can actually produce such a level of performance all the time.

OBJECTIVES AND CAPABILITIES OF CRM

LO 6-8

Define CRM and articulate its objectives and capabilities.

We've mentioned CRM briefly in earlier chapters of this book. But what exactly is CRM? **Customer relationship management (CRM)** is a comprehensive business model for increasing revenues and profits by focusing on customers. Significantly, this definition does not speak to who should "own CRM" within the organization. In the mid-1990s, the introductory days of CRM systems, CEOs tended to relegate the operation of a firm's CRM system to the information technology group. After all, CRM is technology-based, isn't it? But legendary horror stories abound about CEOs who purchased multimillion-dollar CRM installations purely on the recommendation of the IT department, without any significant consultation with those in the firm who would be the system's primary *users,* such as salespeople, marketing managers, and customer service representatives. In the end, through the school of hard knocks, firms learned that no one group should have "ownership" of the CRM system. Positioning CRM as a comprehensive business model provides the impetus for top management to properly support it over the long run and for various internal stakeholder groups to have the opportunity to both use it and impact how it is used.[63]

Fortunately, with many of the initial CRM adoption misfires relegated to the past, most companies are now adopting CRM as a mission-critical business strategy. It is considered mission-critical largely because of competitive pressures in the marketplace; nobody can afford to be the lone wolf that does not have a handle on the customer side of an enterprise in a competitive space.

To optimize CRM's potential for contribution to the bottom line, companies are redesigning internal structures, as well as internal and external business processes and systems, to make it easier for customers to do business with them. Although marketing does not "own" CRM, because of CRM's focus on aligning the organization's internal and external processes and systems to be more customer-centric, marketing managers are a core contributor to the success of CRM by virtue of their expertise on customers and relationships.[64] And in particular, as Chapter 14 will discuss in detail, the sales force in CRM-driven organizations has taken center stage in executing a firm's customer management strategies, complete with new titles befitting the new sales roles such as "client manager," "relationship manager," and "business solution consultant."

Ultimately, CRM has three major objectives:

1. *Customer acquisition*—acquisition of the *right* customers based on known or learned characteristics that will drive growth and increase margins.
2. *Customer retention*—retention of satisfied and loyal profitable customers and channels, and thus to grow the business profitably over the long run.
3. *Customer profitability*—increased individual customer margins, while offering the right products at the right time.[65]

The Gerber Baby Grow-up Plan is an insurance program that allows parents to give their child security from the moment the child is born. The program itself doubles as a CRM initiative for Gerber, who benefits from this program as a way to reach its customers on a more in-depth level. It also ensures a constant basis of lifetime consumers who can serve as advocates for the brand. In exchange for the security that the plan provides enrollees, Gerber receives the opportunity to continually reach its most important demographic on a deeper level. As the child develops, so too does the relationship with the parents, and Gerber continually reaches out to the parents throughout the multiple growth stages of the child's life. Eventually, Gerber has an opportunity to reach the child directly in hopes of creating future business when the child eventually becomes a parent.[66]

To accomplish these objectives requires a clear focus on the product and service attributes that represent value to the customer and that create customer satisfaction and loyalty. **Customer satisfaction** means the level of liking an individual harbors for an offering—that is, to what level is the offering meeting or exceeding the customer's expectations? **Customer loyalty** means the degree to which an individual will resist switching, or defecting, from one offering to another. Loyalty is usually based on high satisfaction coupled with a high level of perceived value derived from the offering and a strong relationship with the provider and its brand(s). Customer satisfaction and loyalty are two extremely popular metrics used by marketing managers to gauge the health of their business and brands.[67]

All of this implies strong integration of CRM into the overall marketing planning process of a firm. Perusal of the elements of marketing planning presented in Chapter 2 reveals numerous points at which information derived from a CRM system can assist in the strategy development and execution process. Key parts of a marketing plan that rely on CRM-generated information include the situation analysis, market research, strategy development, implementation, and measurement phases of marketing planning. In fact, many of the metrics that marketing managers use to assess their success are derived directly from the firm's CRM system.[68]

One of the most important metrics in CRM is that of the **lifetime value of a customer**. Fredrick Reichheld in his books on customer loyalty has demonstrated time and again that investment in CRM yields more successful long-term relationships with customers, and that these relationships pay handsomely in terms of cost savings, revenue growth, profits, referrals, and other important business

EVERYONE LIKES MUSHROOMS IN THEIR OMELETTES, EXCEPT PEOPLE WHO DON'T.
Complimentary, cooked-to-order breakfast, two-room suites, open-air atriums and evening Manager's Reception.* These are just some of the ways Embassy Suites Hotels® puts extra thought into everything we do.
EVERYTHING FOR A REASON®
EMBASSY SUITES HOTELS®
TheHiltonFamily
For locations and reservations, please call 800-Embassy or visit embassysuites.com for Our Best Rates. Guaranteed.

Hoteliers such as Embassy Suites can customize offerings to loyal users by maintaining customer preference profiles.

success factors. It is possible to actually calculate an estimate of the projected financial returns from a customer, or **return on customer investment (ROCI)**, over the long run. This analysis provides a very useful strategic tool for deciding which customers deserve what levels of investment of various resources (money, people, time, information, etc.). Chapter 16 is devoted to identifying and exemplifying the use of marketing metrics. Many of the most useful marketing metrics derive their power and functionality from CRM.

Proliferation of ROCI analysis has raised the prospects of **firing a customer** who exhibits a low predicted lifetime value, and instead investing resources in other more profitable customers. Of course, such action assumes other more attractive customers exist.[69]

> A loyal customer spends more money with a company over time. Apple customers are among the most loyal and regularly jump on purchasing the newest version of each of Apple's many products. Of those who purchased an iPad Mini, only 47 percent were new to the iPad market. A high-functioning CRM system is vital to companies like Apple, where so many customers are repeat purchasers—information on those loyal customers is extremely important in order to make sure that everything possible is being done to retain them. For companies that don't quite engender the level of customer loyalty that top-of-field firms like Apple, Harley-Davidson, and Nordstrom do, the importance of CRM may be even greater, as they seek to create those high levels of loyalty that such firms enjoy.[70]

THE CRM PROCESS CYCLE

LO 6-9

Describe the CRM process cycle.

The process cycle for CRM may be divided into the following four elements: (1) knowledge discovery, (2) marketing planning, (3) customer interaction, and (4) analysis and refinement. Elements of the process cycle are portrayed in Exhibit 6.17 and discussed below.

EXHIBIT 6.17 | Process Cycle for CRM

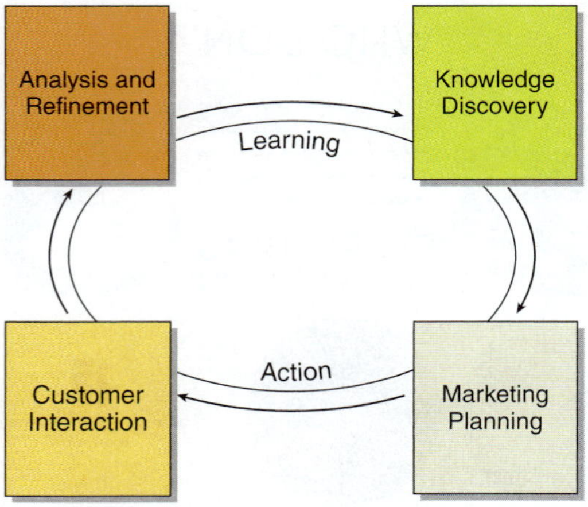

Source: Ronald S. Swift, *Accelerating Customer Relationships: Using CRM and Relationship Technologies,* 1st ed. (Upper Saddle River, NJ: Prentice Hall PTR, 2001), p. 40. Reproduced by permission of Pearson Education, Inc., Upper Saddle River, New Jersey.

Knowledge Discovery

Knowledge discovery is the process of analyzing the customer information acquired through various customer touchpoints. At their essence, **customer touchpoints** are where the selling firm touches the customer in some way, thus allowing for information about him or her to be collected. These might include point-of-sale systems, call-center files, Internet accesses, records from direct selling or customer service encounters, or any other customer contact experiences. Touchpoints occur at the intersection of a business event that takes place via a channel using some media, such as online inquiry from a prospect, telephone follow-up with a purchaser on a service issue, face-to-face encounter with a salesperson, and so on.[71]

A **data warehouse** environment is the optimal approach to handling all the customer data generated through the touchpoints and transforming those data into useful information for marketing management decision making and marketing planning. A data warehouse affords the opportunity to combine large amounts of information and then use data mining techniques to learn more about current and potential customers.[72]

Data mining is a sophisticated analytical approach to using the massive amounts of data accumulated through the CRM system to develop segments and micro-segments of customers for purposes of either market research or development of market segmentation and target marketing strategies. The knowledge discovery phase of the CRM process cycle becomes the focal point for many direct marketers. Direct marketing involves utilizing the data generated through this phase to develop "hit lists" of customer prospects, who are then contacted individually by various means of marketing communication. This activity is often referred to as **database marketing**.[73] Clearly, this knowledge discovery phase has much to do with the market research and the management of market information that you learned about in Chapter 3.

Marketing Planning

The next phase in the CRM process cycle is marketing planning, which represents a key use of the *output* from the knowledge discovery phase. That is, the information enables the capability to develop marketing and customer strategies and programs. CRM input into the marketing planning process is particularly useful in developing elements of the marketing mix strategies, including employing the marketing communication mix in integrated ways to customize approaches to different customer groups (issues of marketing communication will be discussed in Part Five of the book.).[74]

Customer Interaction

The customer interaction phase represents the actual implementation of the customer strategies and programs. This includes the personal selling effort, as well as all other customer-directed interactions. These must be aimed at all the customer touchpoints, or channels of customer contact, both in person and electronically.[75]

Analysis and Refinement

Finally, the analysis and refinement phase of the CRM process is where **organizational learning** occurs based on customer response to the implemented strategies and programs. Think of it as market research in the form of a continuous dialogue with customers, facilitated by effective use of CRM tools. With such an ongoing commitment and capability related to customer research, continuous adjustments made to the firm's overall customer initiatives should result in more efficient investment of resources and increasing ROCI.[76]

Salesforce.com (a.k.a., "Salesforce"), one of the world's most popular CRM systems, is betting that the future of CRM is online. The company is pushing into cloud computing and expanding into areas like human resources. CEO Marc Benioff explained in an interview with *Bloomberg Businessweek* that one of the reasons for the company's success is that its competitors really aren't in the cloud computing space at all—Salesforce is still the only company whose services do not require any purchases of hardware or software. The company originally facilitated information control for field sales teams, but expanded into customer relations tools and is now focusing new products on the marketing area. Benioff explains that the marketing tools are "the third leg of the stool" (of its strategy) because large customers need systems that can integrate all of their systems and information—a service that Salesforce intends to provide, demonstrating that CRM really does span the full scope of a company's operations.[77]

MORE ON CUSTOMER TOUCHPOINTS

LO 6-10

Understand the concept of customer touchpoints and why touchpoints are critical in CRM.

You have read that CRM initiatives depend heavily on interactions with customers, suppliers, or prospects via one or more touchpoints—such as a call center, salesperson, distributor, store, branch office, website, or e-mail. CRM entails both acquiring knowledge about customers and (where feasible) deploying information to customers at the touchpoint. Some touchpoints are *interactive* and allow for such two-way information exchange. That is, they involve *direct interface* between a customer and a firm's customer contact person in the form of a salesperson, telemarketer, customer service representative, interactive website, and so on. Other touchpoints are *noninteractive;* that is, the customer may simply provide information on a static website's data entry form or by mail, without the capability of simultaneous direct interface with a company representative. To maximize a firm's ability to successfully use touchpoints, an ongoing concerted effort must be undertaken to (1) identify *all* potential touchpoints, (2) develop specific objectives for what kind of information can be collected at each touchpoint, (3) determine how that information will be collected and ultimately integrated into the firm's overall customer database, and (4) develop policies on how the information will be accessed and used.

The aspect of CRM involving customer information collected through touchpoints raises substantial ethical and legal issues for the firm regarding privacy, particularly in the consumer marketplace. Clearly, a key component of a strong customer relationship with a firm is a high level of *trust*.[78] Customers must be absolutely certain that the information a firm collects and stores about them will not be used for unintended purposes. Often referred to as the "dark side of CRM," this issue has become so prominent in some industries that firms are beginning to publicly promote guarantees of nonabuse of stored customer information as a means of attracting customers.[79] It is a feature that resonates well with customers and likely provides a strong point of differentiation over competitors.

CRM Facilitates a Customer-Centric Culture

As you know, a firm that is customer-centric places the customer at the core of the enterprise including everything that happens, both inside and outside the firm. Customers are the lifeblood of any business—without them a firm has no sales, no profits, and ultimately no business. As such, marketing managers must approach their role with the attitude that customers are worth investing considerable resources against so long as an acceptable return on that investment can be anticipated.

At the strategic marketing level, a customer-centric culture includes, but is not limited to, the following major components:

1. Adopting a relationship or partnership business model overall, with mutually shared rewards and risk management.
2. Redefining the selling role within the firm to focus on customer business consultation and solutions.
3. Increasing formalization of customer analysis processes.
4. Taking a proactive leadership role in educating customers about value chain opportunities available by developing a business relationship.
5. Focusing on continuous improvement principles stressing customer satisfaction and loyalty.[80]

The effort a firm makes toward cultivating a customer-centric culture requires a high degree of formalization within the firm. **Formalization** means that structure, processes and tools, and managerial knowledge and commitment are formally established in support of the culture. With these elements in place, strategies and programs can be successfully developed and executed toward the goals related to customers, accompanied by a high degree of confidence they will yield the desired results. Today, the most prevalent formalization mechanism of a customer-centric culture is CRM.

As mentioned in Chapter 1, firms that are customer-centric have a high level of customer orientation. Organizations practicing a customer orientation place the customer at the core of all aspects of the enterprise and:

1. Instill an organization-wide focus on understanding the requirements of customers.
2. Generate an understanding of the customer marketplace and disseminate that knowledge to everyone in the firm.
3. Align system capabilities internally so that the organization responds effectively to customers with innovative, competitively differentiated, satisfaction-generating products and services.[81]

How do the concepts of customer centricity and customer orientation connect to the actions required by individual members of a firm? One way to think about how an organization member might exhibit a customer orientation is through a **customer mind-set**, which is a person's belief that understanding and satisfying customers, whether internal or external to the organization, is central to the proper execution of his or her job.[82] It is through organization members' customer mind-set that a customer orientation "comes alive" within a firm. Exhibit 6.18 provides example descriptors of customer mind-set in the context of both customers outside the firm as well as people inside the firm with whom one must interact to get the job done (internal customers). Concepts of internal customers and internal marketing are developed further in Chapter 9 on service as the core offering.

In the end, the software part of CRM will work, and can probably do far more for any firm than expected. CRM's real strengths, as well as its fragilities, rest with how the organization chooses to use CRM as a means of enabling a customer-centric culture and operationalizing a customer orientation as an ongoing driver of the enterprise. CRM across all dimensions—as a business strategy, set of processes, and analytic tools—has amazing potential to facilitate great marketing planning and management.

EXHIBIT 6.18 | Do You Have a Customer Mind-Set?

External Customer Mind-Set

I believe that . . .

- I must understand the needs of my company's customers.
- It is critical to provide value to my company's customers.
- I am primarily interested in satisfying my company's customers.
- I must understand who buys my company's products/services.
- I can perform my job better if I understand the needs of my company's customers.
- Understanding my company's customers will help me do my job better.

Internal Customer Mind-Set

I believe that . . .

- Employees who receive my work are my customers.
- Meeting the needs of employees who receive my work is critical to doing a good job.
- It is important to receive feedback from employees who receive my work.
- I focus on the requirements of the person who receives my work.

Score yourself from 1–6 on each item such that 1 = strongly disagree and 6 = strongly agree. Total up your score; a higher total score equates to more of a customer mind-set.

Source: Karen Norman Kennedy, Felicia G. Lassk, and Jerry R. Goolsby. Reprinted with kind permission from Springer Science + Business Media: *Journal of the Academy of Marketing Science,* "Customer Mind-Set of Employees Throughout the Organization," Vol. 30, 2002, pp. 159–171, by Karen Norman Kennedy, et al. Copyright ©2002.

SUMMARY

Effective segmentation, target marketing, and positioning are central to marketing management because these decisions set the direction for the execution of the marketing plan. First, potential appropriate segmentation approaches must be identified. Second, the segments must be evaluated and decisions made about which to invest in for the most favorable ROI—these become your target markets. Finally, sources of differentiation must be identified that will result in customers perceiving fulfillment of needs and wants based on the value proposition of the offering.

Customer relationship management (CRM) is a comprehensive business model for increasing revenues and profits by focusing on customers. CRM works effectively by focusing on acquisition and retention of profitable customers, thus enhancing customer satisfaction and loyalty. Successful CRM runs on information acquired through various customer touchpoints such as a salesperson, customer care representative, or website. Importantly, CRM facilitates a customer-centric culture and it is critical that all organization members exhibit a customer mind-set as they approach their jobs.

KEY TERMS

market segmentation 159
target marketing 159
positioning 159
positioning strategy 159
differentiation 160
geographic segmentation 161
demographic segmentation 163
family life cycle 167
psychographic segmentation 172
VALS™ (Values and Lifestyles) 172
behavioral segmentation 174
primary target markets 178
secondary target markets 178
tertiary target markets 178
undifferentiated target marketing 179
differentiated target marketing 179
concentrated target marketing 180
customized (one-to-one) marketing 180
perceptual map 182
repositioning 182
customer relationship management (CRM) 184
customer satisfaction 185
customer loyalty 185
lifetime value of a customer 185
return on customer investment (ROCI) 186
firing a customer 186
customer touchpoints 186
data warehouse 186
data mining 187
database marketing 187
organizational learning 187
formalization 188
customer mind-set 189

APPLICATION QUESTIONS

1. Go to the Nielsen/Claritas website (www.claritas.com/MyBestSegments/Default.jsp#) and click on "ZIP Code Look-Up" on the top bar. There you will find a demo that allows you to type in a zip code of your choice and find out what PRIZM clusters predominate in that geographic area.
   a. What do the findings tell you about the overall composition of potential customers within that zip code?
   b. Based on the array of clusters represented, what kinds of start-up businesses might flourish within the geographic area? Why do you believe those businesses in particular would be successful?
2. Go to the Strategic Business Insights website (www.strategicbusinessinsights.com) and click through to the section on VALS™. Find the VALS™ survey and complete the questionnaire.
   a. Are the results surprising? Why or why not? Do you see yourself as part of the identified VALS™ segment?
   b. If you are comfortable doing so, share your results with a few other people in the class and ask if they mind sharing their results with you. What is the consensus among the group about whether the survey actually captured a relevant profile about yourself and your classmates?

c. How might each of these brands benefit from the use of VALS™ as a psychographic segmentation tool:
   i. Ruth's Chris Steak House
   ii. Walt Disney World Theme Park
   iii. Target Inc.
   iv. Samsung
   v. Porsche

3. Assume for a moment that you are in marketing for Staples (the office supply company) and that the clients you are responsible for are business users (not end-user consumers). What five business market segmentation variables do you think will be most useful to consider as you move toward homing in on the Staples business target markets with the best ROI? Justify your choice of each.

4. Consider each of the brands below. Review the list of potential sources of differential competitive advantage (differentiation) highlighted in the chapter. For each: (*a*) indicate which one differentiation source you believe is most important to them currently and (*b*) indicate which other differentiation sources you believe might hold promise for development for them in the near future and *why.*
   a. Norwegian Cruise Line
   b. Sears Craftsman Tools
   c. Avon
   d. Lowe's Home Improvement Stores
   e. The Salvation Army

5. McDonald's is interested in your opinion of how it would stack up on a perceptual map against Burger King, Wendy's, Taco Bell, and Chick-fil-A on the attributes of convenience and product quality. Create the map by putting convenience as the vertical axis (high at the top and low at the bottom) and product quality as the horizontal axis (low on the left and high on the right). Then, indicate your perceptions of the five brands on these attributes by placing a dot for each in the spot that indicates your view (see chapter Exhibit 6.16 for examples).
   a. What does the result reveal about McDonald's current positioning on these attributes, based strictly from your perception?
   b. If possible, compare notes with others in your class. Do you find consistency?
   c. In general, what opportunities for repositioning do you see for any of the brands to take advantage of current perceptions revealed on the perceptual map? What would they have to do to accomplish this repositioning?

6. Consider each of the brands below. Assuming that a strong CRM system is in place in each brand's parent firm, what specific actions can marketing managers take in each case to ensure high satisfaction and loyalty among the most profitable customers?
   a. Aeropostale
   b. Wynn Las Vegas
   c. Your own college or university
   d. Subaru automobiles
   e. GE home appliances

7. Consider the CRM process cycle of knowledge discovery, market planning, customer interaction, and analysis and refinement. Pick a company of interest to you and identify one of its important brands or product lines (it can be a good or a service). Chart what you believe the CRM process cycle should be for that firm, paying particular attention to identifying the relevant customer touchpoints. Be as specific as you can in describing each of the cycle elements.

MANAGEMENT DECISION CASE: Hotel Choices and Their Appeal to Different Markets

When you are planning a trip and need to choose a hotel at your destination, how do you go about making that choice? For many people, the decision about which hotel to book depends on why they need it and what they want from the experience. For example, suppose you're headed on a big family beach summer vacation complete with multigenerational travelers including kids—clearly you'll want a choice location on or near the beach! But you'll also want other amenities such as free high-speed Internet, free Wi-Fi, spacious rooms (suites preferred), free breakfast, free parking, a swimming pool for when the beach gets "old" for the kids but they still want to get wet, a refrigerator, a microwave, and a location close to family restaurants and other family-friendly activities. Given this profile, a logical choice might be a hotel such as Fairfield Inn and Suites that is clearly positioned for low-priced but quality amenities and is highly family-centric.

Alternatively, what if you're a married person and want to get away to someplace a bit upscale to properly celebrate your 10th wedding anniversary? The grandparents are watching the kids for a couple days (lucky you) and you want a nice place in the city where you can enjoy some luxury and pampering that you do not often experience. In this case, your want room service, a full-service spa, a fitness center, a pool, high-speed Internet, a comfortable and spacious room with a nice view, a location with top restaurants and shops nearby, and a general attitude from hotel staff that "it's all about you." For an excursion like this, a JW Marriott in a downtown location like the one in Manhattan will fill those needs nicely.

But what if you instead are a frequent business traveler, traveling along and seeking the regularity of a business-focused hotel? Your needs will yet again be quite different from the two scenarios above. In this case you want a comfortable room, basic bar and food service on the premises, easy check-in and check-out, a business center with free printing, an exercise room, and meeting space for connecting with clients. Here, a Marriott Courtyard makes great sense.

In case you haven't guessed, each of the above hotel brands is operated by Marriott. In fact, Marriott has 18 different lodging brands, each of which targets its appeal to different market segments with different needs and wants with varying accommodations and amenities. The super-luxury market segment, where the hotel service staff call you by name and know whether you like a feather or foam pillow, is well-served by Ritz-Carlton and JW Marriott. Are you a meeting planner booking a large convention and meeting space along with enough guest rooms to accommodate your company's sales force for a national meeting? No problem—many of the full-service Marriott Hotels and Resorts will love to work with your market segment. On the other hand, perhaps you need a company that can provide accommodations for your employees that are relocating to a new location or are on a temporary assignment and need long-term housing of up to a month or more. For this market segment, Residence Inn by Marriott or Marriott Executive Apartments is a terrific option.

Bottom line, Marriott has done a superb job of recognizing the various market segments that exist in the lodging industry and developing brands and appeals to differentially target each of those segments. Such a strategy includes all types of differentiation—geographic, demographic, psychographic, and behavioral. Based on the needs and wants of the different segments, a positioning strategy is developed that communicates the distinctive features and value-added of each brand to its target consumers.

Despite Marriott's broad market coverage, they continue to look for opportunities to identify underserved markets. Indeed, they recently announced the introduction of one of their European-based properties, AC Hotels, to the United States. This hotel chain is designed to appeal to younger Gen Y and older Millennials, who are more technology and design savvy than any of Marriott's current market segments. Marriott expects to open 200 AC Hotels in the next 10 years. Those locations will feature an urban lifestyle environment where customers can stay constantly connected through social media in coffeehouse-like spaces—in short, a lodging experience designed to appeal to this important emerging target market. Since members of this segment are expected to spend $34 billion a year on hotel rooms in the near future, the time is ideal for Marriott to add this new edgy and urban brand to its lucrative line of properties.

Questions for Consideration

1. Go to Marriott's website (www.marriott.com) and peruse the different types of lodging brands offered. Select any three and based on the discussion of differentiation in the chapter, identify the relevant sources of differentiation offered by each.
2. Even with all of Marriott's brands, they still do not have any hotel properties in the truly "budget" category of lodging. That's a category occupied by properties such as Days Inn and Budgetel. Why do you think Marriott does not have a brand in this category of lodging? Do you think Marriott should enter this market segment, and, if so, provide an idea of what a budget Marriott brand might be like.

3. With 19 different lodging or extended-stay brands under the Marriott corporate umbrella, is Marriott at risk of making any positioning errors discussed in the chapter? That is, do they have too many choices? Justify your answer.

Sources: Marriott Hotel Brands, www.marriott.com/marriott-brands.mi, accessed December 6, 2013; Nancy Trejos, "New Hotel Brand to Check into USA: Marriott's European AC Hotels Target Millennials," *USA Today*, June 3, 2013, MONEY section, p. 1B.

MARKETING PLAN EXERCISES

ACTIVITY 6: Identifying Target Markets

In this chapter you learned that effective segmentation, target marketing, and positioning favorably impact marketing management. For purposes of your marketing plan, we'll leave the specifics of developing your overall positioning strategies to the upcoming chapters on the marketing mix. At this point, the following steps are needed.

1. Consider the various approaches to segmenting your market(s). What segmentation approaches do you recommend? Why do you recommend those approaches over other available approaches?
2. Evaluate your proposed segments against the criteria for effective segmentation. What does this evaluation lead you to conclude about the best way to proceed?
3. Systematically analyze each potential segment on your list using the three steps you learned in the chapter: (1) assess each in terms of segment size and growth potential, segment competitive forces, and strategic fit of the segment; (2) for the short set that emerges, develop profiles of each potential target market, then identify each of your final set as primary, secondary, tertiary, or abandoned; (3) select the target marketing approach for each of your primary targets.
4. Identify the likely sources of differential advantage on which you will focus later in developing your positioning strategies.

ACTIVITY 7: Plan for a CRM System

In this chapter, you learned about the value of CRM in fostering a customer-centric culture and establishing a relationship-based enterprise. At this point in the development of your marketing plan, the following steps are needed:

1. Establish the objectives of your CRM system with regard to customer acquisition, customer retention, and customer profitability. Pay particular attention to driving high customer satisfaction and loyalty among profitable customers.
2. Map out the CRM process cycle you will employ in your business. Identify all the relevant touchpoints you plan to utilize—both interactive and noninteractive.
3. Prepare a set of guidelines on the ethical handling of customer data, with a focus on avoiding misuse and theft.
4. Consider the reasons for CRM failure identified in the chapter. Develop an approach to ensure that each can be avoided in your firm.

NOTES

1. Nicole E. Coviello, Roderick J. Brodie, Peter J. Danaher, and Wesley J. Johnston, "How Firms Relate to Their Markets: An Empirical Examination of Contemporary Marketing Practices," *Journal of Marketing* 66, no. 3 (2002), pp. 33–57.
2. Jacquelyn S. Thomas and Ursula Y. Sullivan, "Managing Marketing Communications with Multichannel Customers," *Journal of Marketing* 69, no. 4 (October 2005), pp. 239–51; and Stephen L. Vargo and Robert F. Lusch, "Evolving to a New Dominant Logic for Marketing," *Journal of Marketing* 68, no. 1 (January 2004), pp. 1–17.
3. Javier Rodriguez-Pinto, Ana Isabel Rodriguez-Escudero, and Jesus Gutierrez-Cilian, "Order,

Positioning, Scope, and Outcomes of Market Entry," *Industrial Marketing Management* 37, no. 2 (April 2008), pp. 154–66.

4. Anders Gustafsson, Michael D. Johnson, and Inger Roos, "The Effects of Customer Satisfaction, Relationship Commitment Dimensions, and Triggers on Customer Retention," *Journal of Marketing* 69, no. 4 (October 2005), pp. 210–18; and Ajay Kalra and Ronald C. Goodstein, "The Impact of Advertising Positioning Strategies on Consumer Price Sensitivity," *Journal of Marketing Research* 35, no. 2 (May 1998), pp. 210–25.
5. Cenk Koca and Jonathan D. Bohlmann, "Segmented Switchers and Retailer Pricing Strategies," *Journal of Marketing* 72, no. 3 (May 2008), pp. 124–42.
6. Allan D. Shocker, Barry L. Bayus, and Namwoon Kim, "Product Complements and Substitutes in the Real World: The Relevance of 'Other Products'," *Journal of Marketing* 68, no. 1 (January 2004), pp. 28–40.
7. Arik Hesseldahl, "The iPhone Legacy: Pricier Smartphones?" *BusinessWeek,* November 1, 2007, www.businessweek.com/technology/content/oct2007/tc20071031_825744.htm?chan=search.
8. Leonard M. Lodish, "Another Reason Academics and Practitioners Should Communicate More," *Journal of Marketing Research* 44, no. 1 (February 2007), pp. 23–25.
9. Tat Y. Chan, V. Padmanabhan, and P. B. Seetharaman, "An Econometric Model of Location and Pricing in the Gasoline Market," *Journal of Marketing Research* 44, no. 4 (November 2007), pp. 622–35; and Jeff Wang and Melanie Wallendorf, "Materialism, Status Signaling, and Product Satisfaction," *Journal of the Academy of Marketing Science* 34, no. 4 (Fall 2006), pp. 494–506.
10. Subim Im, Barry L. Bayus, and Charlotte H. Mason, "An Empirical Study of Innate Consumer Innovativeness, Personal Characteristics, and New-Product Adoption Behavior," *Journal of the Academy of Marketing Science* 31, no. 1 (Winter 2003), pp. 61–74; and Sudhir N. Kale and Peter Klugsberger, "Reaping Rewards," *Marketing Management* 16, no. 4 (July/August 2007), p. 14.
11. "2007 Essential Facts about the Computer and Video Game Industry," *Sales, Demographic, and Usage Data,* Entertainment Software Association, www.theesa.com/facts/pdfs/ESA_EF_2007.pdf, accessed May 27, 2008.
12. Charles D. Schewe and Geoffrey Meredith, "Segmenting Global Markets by Generational Cohorts: Determining Motivations by Age," *Journal of Consumer Behaviour* 4, no. 1 (October 2004), pp. 51–64.
13. Brian Steinberg, "American Express Pushes E-Commerce to TV Commerce," *Advertising Age,* February 27, 2013, http://adage.com/article/media/american-express-pushes-e-commerce-tv-commerce/240048/.
14. Anne L. Balazs, "Expenditures of Older Americans," *Journal of the Academy of Marketing Science* 28, no. 4 (Fall 2000), pp. 543–46; and Christopher D. Hopkins, Catherine A. Roster, and Charles M. Wood, "Making the Transition to Retirement: Appraisals, Post-Transition Lifestyle, and Changes in Consumption Patterns," *Journal of Consumer Marketing* 23, no. 2 (2006), pp. 89–101.
15. Stuart Van Auken, Thomas E. Barry, and Richard P. Bagozzi, "A Cross-Country Construct Validation of Cognitive Age," *Journal of the Academy of Marketing Science* 34, no. 3 (Summer 2006), pp. 439–56.
16. Mark Andrew Mitchell, Piper McLean, and Gregory B. Turner, "Understanding Generation X . . . Boom or Bust Introduction," *Business Forum* 27, no. 1 (2005), pp. 26–31.
17. Qimei Chen, Shelly Rodgers, and William D. Wells, "Better Than Sex," *Marketing Research* 16, no. 4 (Winter 2004), pp. 16–22.
18. www.gillettevenus.com/us/, accessed May 29, 2008.
19. Brad Wieners, "For Lego, Pink Is the New Black," *Bloomberg Businessweek,* February 22, 2013, www.businessweek.com/articles/2013-02-22/for-lego-pink-is-the-new-black#r=hpt-ls; and Brad Wieners, "Lego Is for Girls," *Bloomberg Businessweek,* December 14, 2011, www.businessweek.com/magazine/lego-is-for-girls-12142011.html#p4.
20. Rex Y. Du and Wagner A Kamakura, "Household Life Cycles and Lifestyles in the United States," *Journal of Marketing Research* 43, no. 1 (February 2006), pp. 121–32.
21. Andrew Lindridge and Sally Dibb, "Is 'Culture' a Justifiable Variable for Market Segmentation? A Cross-Cultural Example," *Journal of Consumer Behaviour* 2, no. 3 (March 2003), pp. 269–87.
22. Frederick A. Palumbo and Ira Teich, "Market Segmentation Based on Level of Acculturation," *Marketing Intelligence & Planning* 22, no. 4 (2004), pp. 472–84.
23. Frederick A. Palumbo and Ira Teich, "Segmenting the U.S. Hispanic Market Based on Level of Acculturation," *Journal of Promotion Management* 12, no. 1 (2005), pp. 151–73.
24. Mark R. Forehand and Rohit Deshpande, "What We See Makes Us Who We Are: Priming Ethnic Self-Awareness and Advertising Response," *Journal of Marketing Research* 38, no. 3 (August 2001), pp. 336–48.
25. Carmen DeNavas-Walt, Bernadette D. Proctor, and Jessica Smith, "Income, Poverty, and Health Insurance Coverage in the United States: 2006," *U.S. Census Bureau* website, August 2007, www.census.gov/prod/2007pubs/p60-233.pdf.
26. C. B. Bhattacharya and Sankar Sen, "Consumer-Company Identification: A Framework for Understanding Consumers' Relationships with Companies," *Journal of Marketing* 67, no. 2 (April 2003), pp. 76–88.
27. Ben Levisohn and Brian Burnsed, "The Credit Rating in Your Shoe Box," *BusinessWeek,* April 10, 2008, www.businessweek.com/magazine/content/08_16/b4080052299512.htm?chan=search.

28. Lauren Sherman, "Why It Took So Long for Many Retailers to Embrace E-Commerce," *Advertising Age,* February 11, 2013, http://adage.com/article/digital/long-retailers-embrace-e-commerce/239686/.

29. www.census.gov.

30. Paul G. Patterson, "Demographic Correlates of Loyalty in a Service Context," *Journal of Services Marketing* 21, no. 2 (2007), pp. 112–21.

31. Madhubalan Viswanathan, Jose Antonio Rosa, and James Edwin Harris, "Decision Making and Coping of Functionally Illiterate Consumers and Some Implications for Marketing Management," *Journal of Marketing* 69, no. 1 (January 2005), pp. 15–31.

32. Charles M. Schaninger and Sanjay Putrevu, "Dual Spousal Work Involvement: An Alternative Method to Classify Households/Families," *Academy of Marketing Science Review* (2006), pp. 1–21.

33. Rob Lawson and Sarah Todd, "Consumer Lifestyles: A Social Stratification Perspective," *Marketing Theory* 2, no. 3 (September 2002), pp. 295–308.

34. Rich Beatty, "Data Guides, but the Gut Decides," *Advertising Age,* February 19, 2013, http://adage.com/article/cmo-strategy/data-guides-gut-decides/239894/.

35. David J. Faulds and Stephan F. Gohmann, "Adapting Geodemographic Information to Army Recruiting: The Case of Identifying and Enlisting Private Ryan," *Journal of Services Marketing* 15, no. 3 (2001), pp. 186–211.

36. Geraldine Fennell, Greg M. Allenby, Sha Yang, and Yancy Edwards, "The Effectiveness of Demographic and Psychographic Variables for Explaining Brand and Product Category Use," *Quantitative Marketing and Economics* 1, no. 2 (June 2003), pp. 223–44.

37. Lance Madden, "After 22 Years, Volcom Is Launching Its First Shoe Line," *Forbes,* February 14, 2013, www.forbes.com/sites/lancemadden/2013/02/14/after-22-years-volcom-is-launching-its-first-shoe-line/.

38. "VALS Survey," *Strategic Business Insights, www.strategicbusinessinsights.com/VALS.*

39. www.freepeople.com; www.urbanoutfitters.com; www.anthropologie.com; www.shopterrain.com; www.bhldn.com.

40. James Frederick, "Walgreens Leaders Reaffirm Strategy, Outlook," *Drug Store News,* February 16, 2004.

41. Florian V. Wangenheim and Tomas Bayon, "Behavioral Consequences of Overbooking Service Capacity," *Journal of Marketing* 71, no. 4 (October 2007), pp. 36–47; and Ruth N. Bolton, Katherine N. Lemon, and Peter C. Verhoef, "The Theoretical Underpinnings of Customer Asset Management: A Framework and Propositions for Future Research," *Journal of the Academy of Marketing Science* 32, no. 3 (Summer 2004), pp. 271–93.

42. Sarah Plaskitt, "Listerine Boosts Sales by 20%," *B&T Magazine,* May 22, 2003, www.bandt.com.au/news/49/0c016749.asp.

43. Yuping Liu, "The Long-Term Impact of Loyalty Programs on Consumer Purchase Behavior and Loyalty," *Journal of Marketing* 71, no. 4 (October 2007), pp. 19–35.

44. V. Kumar and J. Andrew Petersen, "Using Customer-Level Marketing Strategy to Enhance Firm Performance: A Review of Theoretical and Empirical Evidence," *Journal of the Academy of Marketing Science* 33, no. 4 (Fall 2005), pp. 504–20; and David Feldman, "Segmentation Building Blocks," *Marketing Research* 18, no. 2 (Summer 2006), p. 23.

45. Thomas L. Powers and Jay U. Sterling, "Segmenting Business-to-Business Markets: A Micro-Macro Linking Methodology," *Journal of Business & Industrial Marketing* 23, no. 3 (2008), pp. 170–77.

46. Peter R. Dickson, Paul W. Farris, and Willem J. M. I. Verbeke, "Dynamic Strategic Thinking," *Journal of the Academy of Marketing Science* 29, no. 3 (Summer 2001), pp. 216–38.

47. Eric Almquist and Gordon Wyner, "Boost Your Marketing ROI with Experimental Design," *Harvard Business Review* 79, no. 9 (October 2001), pp. 135–47.

48. Jack Neff, "Flu Gives Reckitt, Johnson & Johnson a Shot in the Arm," *Advertising Age* 14 (January 2013), http://adage.com/article/news/flu-reckitt-johnson-johnson-a-shot-arm/239156/.

49. Gary L. Frazier, "Organizing and Managing Channels of Distribution," *Journal of the Academy of Marketing Science* 27, no. 2 (Spring 1999), pp. 226–51; and Darren W. Dahl and Page Moreau, "The Influence and Value of Analogical Thinking during New Product Ideation," *Journal of Marketing Research* 39, no. 1 (February 2002), pp. 47–61.

50. Logan Hill, "At ChristianMingle and JDate, God's Your Wingman," *Bloomberg Businessweek,* February 28, 2013, www.businessweek.com/articles/2013-02-28/at-christianmingle-and-jdate-gods-your-wingman.

51. J. David Hunger and Thomas H. Wheelen, *Essentials of Strategic Management,* 4th ed. (Upper Saddle River, NJ: Prentice Hall, 2007).

52. Subin Im and John P. Workman Jr., "Market Orientation, Creativity, and New Product Performance in High-Technology Firms," *Journal of Marketing* 68, no. 2 (April 2004), pp. 114–32.

53. Bruce Buskirk, Stacy M. P. Schmidt, and David L. Ralph, "Patterns in High-Tech Firms Growth Strategies by Seeking Mass Mainstream Customer Adaptations," *The Business Review, Cambridge* 8, no. 1 (Summer 2007), pp. 34–40.

54. Don Peppers and Martha Rogers, *The One-to-One Manager: Real World Lessons in Customer Relationship Management* (New York: Doubleday Business, 2002).

55. Emma Hall, "How EasyJet Plans to Convert Web Surfers into Highfliers," *Advertising Age,* February 25, 2013, http://adage.com/article/

cmo-interviews/easyjet-plans-convert-web-surfers-highfliers/239955/.

56. David A. Schweidel, Eric T. Bradlow, and Patti Williams, "A Feature-Based Approach to Assessing Advertisement Similarity," *Journal of Marketing Research* 43, no. 2 (May 2006), pp. 237–43.

57. E.J. Schultz, "Agent of Change: How State Farm Used New Logo, Tagline to Stay Relevant at 90," *Advertising Age,* November 26, 2012, http://adage.com/article/special-report-marketer-alist-2012/state-farm-reinvents-90-logo-tagline-digital/238419/.

58. Andrew Curry, Gill Ringland, and Laurie Young, "Using Scenarios to Improve Marketing," *Strategy & Leadership* 34, no. 6 (2006), pp. 30–39.

59. "Burger King's Monster 923 Calorie Burger," *Metro News,* November 6, 2006, www.metro.co.uk/news/article.html?in_article_id=23982&in_page_id=34.

60. Detelina Marinova, "Actualizing Innovation Effort: The Impact of Market Knowledge Diffusion in a Dynamic System of Competition," *Journal of Marketing* 68, no. 3 (July 2004), pp. 1–20.

61. Michael E. Porter, *Competitive Advantage* (New York: Simon & Schuster, 1985).

62. David W. Cravens and Nigel F. Piercy, *Strategic Marketing,* 9th ed. (Boston: McGraw-Hill/Irwin, 2009).

63. Ronald S. Swift, *Accelerating Customer Relationships: Using CRM and Relationship Technologies* (Upper Saddle River, NJ: Prentice Hall PTR, 2001).

64. Stephen F. King and Thomas F. Burgess, "Understanding Success and Failure in Customer Relationship Management," *Industrial Marketing Management* 37, no. 4 (June 2008), pp. 421–31.

65. Stanley A. Brown, ed., *Customer Relationship Management: A Strategic Imperative in the World of E-Business* (Toronto: Wiley Canada, 2000), pp. 8–9.

66. "The Grow-Up Plan," *Gerberlife.com,* 2013, www.gerberlife.com/gl/view/guide_products/growup/index.jsp, accessed March 1, 2013.

67. Anders Gustafsson, Michael D. Johnson, and Inger Roos, "The Effects of Customer Satisfaction, Relationship Commitment Dimensions, and Triggers on Customer Retention," *Journal of Marketing* 69, no. 4 (October 2005), pp. 210–18.

68. Mohanbir Sawhney and Jeff Zabin, "Managing and Measuring Relational Equity in the Network Economy," *Journal of the Academy of Marketing Science* 30, no. 4 (Fall 2002), pp. 313–33.

69. Frederick F. Reichheld, *Loyalty Rules! How Leaders Build Lasting Relationships in the Digital Age* (Cambridge, MA: Harvard Business School Press, 2001).

70. Ken Layne, "Apple Customers Rich," *The Awl,* December 18, 2012, www.theawl.com/2012/12/apple-customers-rich.

71. Timothy W. Aurand, Linda Gorchels, and Terrence R. Bishop, "Human Resource Management's Role in Internal Branding: An Opportunity for Cross-Functional Brand Messaging Synergy," *Journal of Product and Brand Management* 14, no. 2/3 (2005), pp. 163–70; and Scott Davis, "Marketers Challenged to Respond to Changing Nature of Brand Building," *Journal of Advertising Research* 45, no. 2 (June 2005), pp. 198–200.

72. Sawhney and Zabin, "Managing and Measuring Relational Equity."

73. Werner Reinartz, Jacquelyn S. Thomas, and V. Kumar, "Balancing Acquisition and Retention Resources to Maximize Customer Profitability," *Journal of Marketing* 69, no. 1 (January 2005), pp. 63–79.

74. Nicole E. Coviello, Roderick J. Brodie, Peter J. Danaher, and Wesley J. Johnston, "How Firms Relate to Their Markets: An Empirical Examination of Contemporary Marketing Practices," *Journal of Marketing* 66, no. 3 (July 2002), pp. 33–47.

75. Peter C. Verhoef, "Understanding the Effect of Customer Relationship Management Efforts on Customer Retention and Customer Share Development," *Journal of Marketing* 67, no. 4 (October 2003), pp. 30–45.

76. Neil A. Morgan, Eugene W. Anderson, and Vikas Mittal, "Understanding Firm's Customer Satisfaction Information Usage," *Journal of Marketing* 69, no. 3 (July 2005), pp. 131–51.

77. Aaron Ricadela, "Salesforce Is a Cloud Computing King," *Bloomberg Businessweek,* February 14, 2013, www.businessweek.com/articles/2013-02-14/salesforce-is-a-cloud-computing-king.

78. James E. Richard, Peter C. Thirkell, and Sid L. Huff, "An Examination of Customer Relationship Management (CRM) Technology Adoption and Its Impact on Business-to-Business Customer Relationships," *Total Quality Management & Business Excellence* 18, no. 8 (October 2007), pp. 927–45.

79. Bob Lewis, "The Customer Is Wrong," *InfoWorld* 24, no. 2 (January 14, 2002), pp. 40–41.

80. George Day, "Capabilities for Forging Customer Relationships," *MSI Report* #00-118. Cambridge, MA: Marketing Science Institute, 2000.

81. Patricia Kilgore, "Personalization Provides a Winning Hand for Borgata," *Printing News,* December 11, 2006, pp. 7–8.

82. Karen Norman Kennedy, Felicia G. Lassk, and Jerry R. Goolsby, "Customer Mind-Set of Employees throughout the Organization," *Journal of the Academy of Marketing Science* 30 (Spring 2002), pp. 159–71.

PART 3

Develop the Value Offering–The Product Experience

chapter 07

PRODUCT STRATEGY AND NEW-PRODUCT DEVELOPMENT

chapter 08

BUILD THE BRAND

chapter 09

SERVICE AS THE CORE OFFERING

CHAPTER 07

Product Strategy and New-Product Development

LEARNING OBJECTIVES

LO 7-1 Understand the essential role of the product experience in marketing.

LO 7-2 Define the characteristics of a product.

LO 7-3 Recognize how product strategies evolve from one product to many products.

LO 7-4 Understand the life of a product and how product strategies change over time.

LO 7-5 Recognize the importance of new-product development to long-term success.

LO 7-6 Understand the new-product development process.

LO 7-7 Identify how new products become diffused in a market.

PRODUCT: THE HEART OF MARKETING

LO 7-1

Understand the essential role of the product experience in marketing.

As we discussed in Chapter 1, the primary function of marketing and, more broadly speaking, the entire organization is to deliver value to the customer. The essential component in delivering value is the product experience, which is why it is considered the heart of marketing. Consider the problems at General Motors that led to the $49.5 billion government bailout. Despite that decision, former CEO Dan Akerson stated just before his retirement that the company has made "great strides" since the bailout and will continue to do so by making well-designed and fuel-efficient vehicles.[1]

Instead of focusing solely on its product, Starbucks has been successful selling "the Starbucks experience" that extends beyond drinking coffee to social interaction and lifestyle. The company defines the "product" (coffee) and the coffee drinking experience in a way that delivers value to millions of customers around the world every day. Given the importance of the product experience in delivering customer value, it is not surprising that companies place a great deal of significance on getting the product experience right.

When the product is wrong, no amount of marketing communications and no degree of logistical expertise or pricing sophistication will make it successful. Apple is widely regarded as a product innovator with the iPod, iPhone, iPad, iMac, and other products. However, the company has also experienced some product missteps. One of the most notable was Newton, the first PDA, introduced in the early 1990s but discontinued after Palm brought out its line of smaller, more user-friendly products. While technically superior to Palm, Apple did not understand the key value drivers in the product. People wanted PDAs with connectivity to other computers, a reasonable combination of features, and a realistic price (early Newtons cost over $1,000).[2] Newton's failure highlights an interesting fact: the best product technically is not always the most successful product. People look for the product that delivers the best overall product experience.

The Apple Newton, while technically better than similar PDAs, failed in the marketplace because it did not deliver a better product experience than competitors such as Palm.

Product Characteristics

LO 7-2

Define the characteristics of a product.

Define the Product What does the term *product* mean? Most people define a product as a tangible object; however, that is not accurate. The product experience encompasses a great deal more, as we will learn over the next several chapters. Consider the customer walking into Starbucks; is he or she just buying a cup of coffee? Did the owner of a new Toyota Prius buy just a new car? Is a pair of Hollister jeans just a pair of jeans? The answer is that, while customers are buying a cup of coffee, a new car, and a pair of jeans, they are also buying a product experience. It is important for the marketer to understand exactly what the customer includes in that experience. This is a particularly difficult challenge because different target markets will view the same product in completely different ways. Parents buying their daughter a pair of jeans would probably consider Hollister jeans to be just another pair of jeans; however, to the teenager, the same purchase makes an important statement about herself and her choice of clothes.[3]

Product can be defined as anything that delivers value to satisfy a need or want and includes physical merchandise, services, events, people, places, organizations, information, even ideas. Most people have no problem considering a computer or car a product, but would these same individuals consider a get-away weekend at the Amelia Island Ritz Carlton in Florida a product? The Ritz-Carlton does and it develops a specific marketing strategy around the resort.

It is important to differentiate between a product and a product item. A product is a brand such as Post-it notes or Tide detergent. Within each product a company may develop a number of product items, each of which represents a unique size, feature, or price. Tide powder detergent offers 12 "scents," including fragrance-free, in a variety of sizes designed to reach a variety of target markets.[4] Each combination of scent and size represents a unique product item in the Tide product line and is known by a **stock-keeping unit (SKU)**. An SKU is a unique identification number used to track a product through a distribution system, inventory management, and pricing.

Essential Benefit Why does someone purchase a plane ticket? The answer quite obviously is to get from one place to another. Simply stated, the essential benefit of purchasing a plane ticket is getting somewhere else; therefore, the essence of the airline product experience is transporting people. Successful airlines, indeed all companies, understand that before anything else, they must deliver on the essential benefit.

The **essential benefit** is the fundamental need met by the product. No matter what other value-added product experiences are provided to the customer, the essential benefit must be part of the encounter. For example, an airline can offer low fares, an easy-to-navigate website, or in-flight Wi-Fi, but unless the customer receives the essential benefit (getting from Point A to Point B), the other items have very little meaning to the customer. Without the essential benefit, other benefits may actually increase the customer's dissatisfaction with the experience. What good are low fares if the customer doesn't arrive at the destination? Exhibit 7.1 illustrates four products and their essential benefits.

Core Product Aircraft, pilots, flight attendants, baggage handlers, reservation agents, managers, and an IT system are a few of the elements needed to get people and their luggage from one place to another. An airline brings all those pieces together to create a product that efficiently and effectively delivers the essential benefit, transporting someone from Point A to Point B.

Companies translate the essential benefit into physical, tangible elements known as the **core product**. Some companies do it better than others, making this critical challenge an important differentiator separating successful companies from their competitors.[5] Southwest Airlines, for example, has done a very good job of translating the essential benefits of air travel. By using one kind of airplane, identifying efficiencies in everything from reservations to flight routes, and taking care of employees, the company is the industry leader in low-cost air travel and, in the process, has revolutionized the entire airline industry. Contrast Southwest with the long list of carriers over the past 15 years that defined the core product experience in ways many customers found unsatisfying. Many of the "legacy" carriers such as United, American, and Delta experienced financial problems, even bankruptcy, in part because they did not adequately deliver a positive core product experience to the customer.

As a company creates the core product experience, it is vital to clearly understand customer expectations. Every aspect of the product experience is evaluated by the customer and then considered against a set of expectations. When an airline creates a flight, there is an expectation that the flight will arrive at its stated time. If the flight does not arrive on time, the passenger assesses the reasons. Was it the airline's fault, the weather, or something else? Airlines are sensitive about their on-time arrival percentage and where they rank relative to the competition because they know customers believe this is an important characteristic of the core product experience. The customer's evaluation of a product experience against a set of defined expectations is a critical element contributing to overall satisfaction or dissatisfaction with the product.[6]

Enhanced Product The core product is the starting point for the product experience. All cell phones deliver on the essential benefit of mobile communication,

EXHIBIT 7.1 | Four Products and Their Essential Benefits

Apple iPhone—making and receiving telephone calls

BMW 3 Series sedan—providing reliable transportation

Evian bottled water —quenching thirst

All detergent—cleaning laundry

but there is a vast difference between the introductory "free" phone offered by many service providers and the latest iPhone or Android. Features, cutting-edge designs and colors, connectivity to other digital devices, and new functionality (such as cloud storage) differentiate one product from another. As consumers around the world become more sophisticated, companies are required to look beyond delivering great core products to creating products that enhance, extend, and encourage the customer.

The **enhanced product** extends the core product to include additional features, designs, and innovations that exceed customer expectations. In this way, companies build on the core product, creating opportunities to strengthen the brand. Consider Southwest Airlines once again, which has done a good job of delivering people on time and meeting customer expectations regarding low-cost air travel. Southwest added features such as frequent flyer opportunities, Early-Bird Check-In, and Upgraded Boarding to further augment the customer's air travel experience. Exhibit 7.2 shows how the essential benefit, core product, and enhanced product are created for Southwest Airlines.

Motorola makes over 20 cell phone models with a wide range of features and benefits that compete against phones from LG Electronics, Samsung, Apple, and others. In an effort to offer consumer-enhanced benefits, the company introduced a phone, the Android, made of aluminum and scratch-resistant glass designed to be sturdy as well as operate as a fashion accessory. The "Droid," as it has come to be known, has been widely successful and one of the first to significantly challenge Apple's iPhone. The phone has several different models, but the same capabilities regardless of the version. Wi-Fi and Bluetooth technology are incorporated into the devices as well as high-resolution cameras. The GPS feature relies on Google Maps; the phones also have Google Voice Search, Voice Actions, and Voice Commands. All Android phones are equipped with technology that allows users to download and listen to music. Consumer expectations continue to increase and the cell phone manufacturers must continue to increase their offerings.[7]

Consider Sharp Electronics, which has developed a strong market position for its Aquos line of LED televisions. The company followed a strategy of developing and introducing enhanced versions of a successful core product. From its line of LCD display computer monitors, the company developed a new line of LED televisions (Aquos) ranging from 32 inches to more than 90 inches and costing as much as $11,000.[8]

Product Classifications

Products can be classified in four ways. Two of the four classifications define the nature of the product: tangibility and durability. The other two classification criteria deal with who uses the product: consumers or businesses. It is important to understand the nature and use of a product because marketing strategies differ among the various product classifications.

EXHIBIT 7.2 | Defining the Product at Southwest Airlines

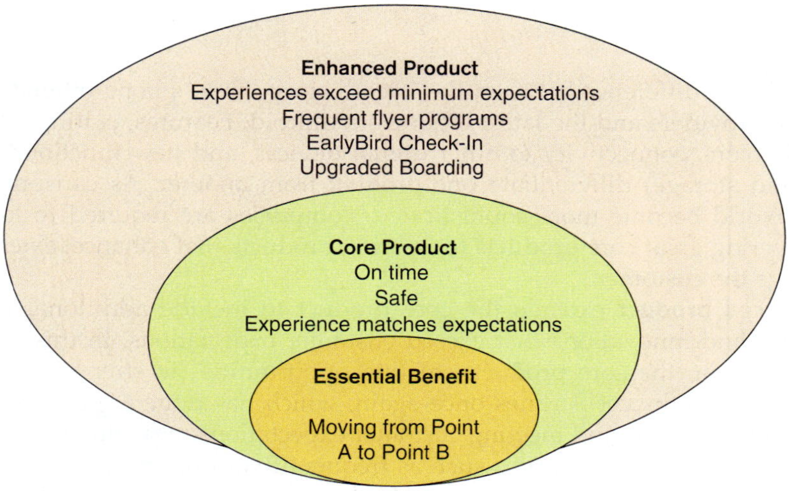

Tangibility: Physical Aspects of the Product Experience Products, as opposed to services, have a physical aspect referred to as **tangibility**. Tangible products present opportunities (customers can see, touch, and experience the product) and also some challenges (customers may find the product does not match their personal tastes and preferences). Services, which we will explore in Chapter 9, are intangible. A significant challenge for marketers today is that many tangible products have intangible characteristics.[9] For example a significant element in an individual's satisfaction with a new car is the customer service before and after the purchase. Intangible products, on the other hand, such as services have tangible characteristics. For example, airlines introduce new airline seats to create a competitive advantage.

Durability: Product Usage **Durability** references the length of product usage. **Nondurable products** are usually consumed in a few uses and, in general, cost less than durable products. Examples of consumer nondurables include personal grooming products such as toothpaste, soap, and shampoo, while business nondurables include office supplies such as printer ink, paper, and other less expensive, frequently purchased items. Because these products are purchased frequently and are not expensive, companies seek a wide distribution to make them as readily available as possible, create attractive price points to motivate purchase, and heavily advertise these products. **Durable products** have a longer product life and are often more expensive. Consumer durables include microwave ovens, washers/dryers, and certain electronics such as televisions. Business durables include products that may be used in the manufacturing process such as machine presses or IT networks, as well as equipment such as office furniture and computers to facilitate the running of the business.[10]

Consumer Goods Consumers purchase thousands of products from an assortment of millions of choices. On the surface it may seem difficult to develop a classification system for the variety of products consumers purchase, but the reality is that consumer purchase habits fall into four broad categories: convenience, shopping, specialty, and unsought.

Frequently purchased, relatively low-cost products for which customers have little interest in seeking new information or considering other options and rely heavily on prior brand experience and purchase behavior are called **convenience goods**. These products include most items people buy regularly such as toiletries, gasoline, and paper products and fall into four categories. Staples are usually food products people buy weekly or at least once a month such as Folgers coffee or Dannon yogurt. Impulse products, as the name implies, are purchased without planning. If you think about the products available in vending machines, you will have a good idea of an impulse product. Finally, there are a host of products people only purchase in times of emergency. For example, as hurricanes approach communities, people rush out to purchase extra supplies of food, gas, batteries, and other products. It is not uncommon to see occasional shortages of some products as distribution systems are strained to meet unplanned spikes in demand for these everyday products.

> Johnson's Baby Shampoo, Band-Aids, Listerine, Sudafed, Bengay, Rolaids, Neutrogena, and many other brands belong to Johnson & Johnson (J&J), a global leader in health care products. While J&J's other primary businesses including pharmaceutical drugs, such as Risperdal and Procrit, and medical devices such as stents (metal tubes that help clear arteries) are bigger, the consumer products division is the fastest-growing business unit and accounts for 25 percent of sales. J&J consumer products hold the market-leading position in 22 consumer categories.

Products that require consumers to do more research and compare across product dimensions such as color, size, features, and price are called **shopping goods**. Consumer products that fall into this category include clothes, furniture, and major appliances such as refrigerators and dishwashers. These products are purchased less frequently and are more costly than convenience goods. Price concerns, a variety of choices at various price levels, many different features, and a fear of making the wrong decision are among the factors that drive consumers to research these purchases. As a result, companies often develop product strategies that target product price points with particular features to appeal to the broadest range of consumers. For example, Whirlpool brand makes over 40 different electric dryers ranging in price from $549 to $1,649.

Specialty goods are a unique purchase made based on a defining characteristic for the consumer. The characteristic might be a real or perceived product feature such as Apple iPhone's easy user interface or brand identification like Porsche's reputation for building sports cars. Whatever the attribute(s), consumers apply decision rules that frequently minimize the number of different product choices and focus less on price. They are also more willing to seek out the product; however, expectations about product service, salesperson expertise, and customer service are higher. Bang and Olufsen's line of high-end electronic equipment is not available in regular retail outlets. Rather, the company has a limited number of retail stores in major cities. Consumers wanting to purchase Bang & Olufsen equipment must seek out those stores.

The final categories of goods, **unsought goods**, are products that consumers do not seek out and, indeed, often would rather not purchase at all. Insurance, particularly life insurance, is not a product people want to purchase. In general, customers do not want to purchase products or services related to sickness, death, or emergencies because, in part, the circumstances surrounding the purchase are not pleasant. As a result, companies have well-trained salespeople skilled in helping customers through the purchase process. These salespeople often must be supported by extensive marketing communications.

USAA provides a broad range of insurance and banking services products to military personnel and their families. USAA's success is due in large part to its understanding of the unique challenges of its military customers. For example, the company created a mobile website for military personnel in remote locations with access to the Internet. The focus on customer service has enabled this company to be consistently rated one of the best customer-focused companies in the world. Recently, customers were asked to rank their satisfaction levels with the company based on five metrics: customer service, claims satisfaction, value for price paid, percent who plan to renew, and percent who would recommend the company. USAA received an astounding 96 percent out of 100 in both the auto and home categories, propelling the company to status as the industry leader. Competitors look to the company for successful techniques to increase customer retention.[11]

Business Goods Businesses buy a vast array of products that can be classified into three broad areas based on two dimensions: (1) whether or not they are used in the manufacturing process and (2) cost. Goods incorporated into the company's finished product as a result of the manufacturing process are either materials or parts. **Materials** are natural (lumber, minerals such as copper) or farm products (corn, soybeans) that become part of the final product. **Parts** consist of equipment either fully assembled or in smaller pieces that will be assembled into larger components and, again, used in the production process.

In addition to the products that are used directly in the production process, companies purchase a number of products and services to support business operations. These can generally be placed on a continuum from low-cost/frequent purchases to very high-cost/infrequent purchases. **MRO (maintenance, repair, operating) supplies** are the everyday items that a company needs to keep running. While per unit cost is low, their total cost over a year can be high.

At the other end of the cost/purchase-frequency continuum are **capital goods**, which are major purchases in support of a significant business function. Building a new plant or a new IT network can require large equipment purchases that cost millions of dollars and require significant customization. These purchases are negotiated over a period of months, sometimes years. Consider that it takes 8 to 10 years to get a new large-scale oil refinery built and costs between $4 billion and $6 billion. Companies selling capital goods to businesses focus on personal selling and a high level of customer service with significant product customization.

Railcar users need to constantly replace older engines and cars with more reliable equipment incorporating the latest technologies. Long-term (standardizing maintenance programs) and short-term (quality decisions) efficiencies dictate the purchase decision, which can involve billions of dollars. Bombardier, a world leader in railcar manufacturing, has invested heavily in upgrading rail technology over the past 10 years. The most recent advancement has been electric transit technology targeted at electric light rail vehicles. It is designed to allow buses to be charged by underground induction stations when they stop to let passengers hop on and off. The first electric buses will be tested in Montreal during the winter. "We want to test the equipment in the most difficult conditions that you could have with our climate, meaning winter," said Bombardier spokesman Marc Laforge. The project would save an estimated $30 million per year given the price of crude oil.[12]

Product Discrimination: Create a Point of Differentiation

A fundamental question in the product purchase decision-making process is what makes this product different? As a result, marketing managers must identify important characteristics that successfully differentiate their product from others in the customer's mind. Then they must produce those elements in the product itself, balancing a number of factors including customer preferences, costs, and company resources. Exhibit 7.3 identifies product discriminators and gives an example.

Form The most elemental method of differentiating a product is to change its **form**—size, shape, color, and other physical elements. Many products considered very similar in functionality can be differentiated by variations in packaging or product delivery. Among the reasons cited for the growth in milk consumption over the past several years has been new packaging that delivers the product in smaller, more portable plastic containers that preserve freshness so the milk tastes better longer and is easier to use in more situations. Additionally, dairies have developed methods to extend shelf life, improving freshness and accessibility.

Bombardier builds a wide range of railcars and locomotives to meet transportation needs around the world. This train was designed for a transportation system in Nottingham, England.

Features When asked what makes a product different, many people will respond by talking about features.

EXHIBIT 7.3 | Product Discriminators

Form		With a large number of spray heads, ambient rain shower panels provide luxurious water delivery.
Features		The wealth of improvements and refinements in a TX4 sets it apart from any other taxi. New features include a Euro IV compliant engine—greener, cleaner, and delivering big torque at low speed— and an improved in-car entertainment system, with superior sound and MP3 compatibility.
Performance Quality		Oil companies produce several grades of gasoline to meet the demands of consumers.
Conformance Quality	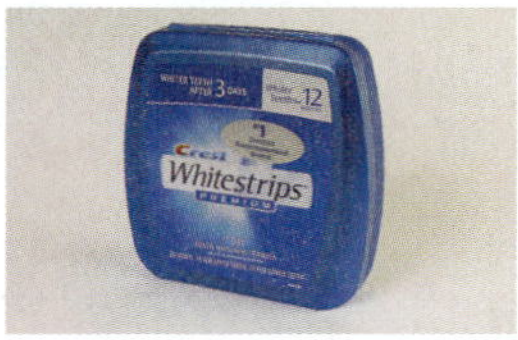	Crest Whitestrips are a good low-priced teeth whitener. The system also comes with a standard 60-day money-back guarantee, should you not care for the results.
Durability		Timberland has a reputation for building high-quality, durable products like these boots that come with a commitment to customer satisfaction.
Reliability		Carrier promotes the fact that its air conditioners are reliable. In addition, it provides different quality levels with varying warranties.

(cont.)

Repairability		Many bicycle manufacturers highlight the easy repair of the bikes. A key point is that anyone can fix most of the problems that may occur.
Style		*Style* magazine is all about promoting style in a person's life.

A **feature** is any product attribute or performance characteristic and is often added or subtracted from a product to differentiate it from competitors. However, while delivering consumer value is the primary driver in making product decisions, a company must balance the features customers want with what they will pay at a given quality level.[13]

Interestingly, based on their research, competitors often create products with very different feature configurations. Cell phone manufacturers, for example, are constantly assessing the feature mix across their product line. When comparing similar Samsung versus Microsoft/Nokia models, a number of feature differences will be easily identified. One of the great challenges for marketers is determining the feature mix that best satisfies the needs and wants of the target audience and at what price. No competitors ever arrive at the same feature mix, which means decisions about which features to include and exclude are critical to a product's success.

Commercial jet aircraft are among the most complex and challenging products to design and build. Two companies, Boeing and Airbus, have traditionally controlled the market. Airbus believed the future of commercial jets was in making a huge aircraft capable of carrying 600 people or more to large hubs around the world and created the A380. Boeing, on the other hand, believed airlines wanted jets that were more efficient, yet provided more room for passengers, and created the 787. However, Bombardier recently announced plans to challenge both companies by producing jets that are small but have features typically found on large aircraft. Bombardier hopes that by optimizing their line around two smaller sizes—with 110 and 130 seats, respectively, with a lighter body that seats five across instead of six in rival Boeing and Airbus aircraft—the jet can burn 20 percent less fuel and be 15 percent less expensive to operate.[14]

Performance Quality Should a company always build the highest-quality product? Some people would say the answer is yes. However, the answer is more complex than that. Essentially, companies should build products to the

EXHIBIT 7.4 | Form Variations for Coors Beer Products

performance quality level that their target audience is willing to pay for. Often this means a company will build products at multiple performance levels to meet demand at various price points. Keep in mind that the key is to deliver value to the customer. For many years, Sony Electronics has offered an extensive line of plasma televisions that can be purchased at stores such as Best Buy and Walmart. At the same time, the company also carries a more expensive line, XBR, that uses higher-quality materials and components. The XBR models are available only at high-end audio specialty stores.[15]

The market's perception of the company's performance quality is critical in defining its market space. Companies generally try to match product performance quality with the market's perception of the brand. Timex will not develop a $25,000 watch because the market would not expect, and may not accept, a watch with production quality at that level from Timex, although they do expect it from Rolex.[16] At the same time, companies need to be careful not to lower performance quality too dramatically in an effort to cut costs or reach new markets. Losing control of a quality image can do significant harm to a brand's image. For example, product safety remains a critical concern for consumers. Products that fail to meet quality standards can lead to a loss of consumer confidence. Ethical Dimension 7 discusses a growing concern about products shipped from China.

Conformance Quality An important issue for consumers is **conformance**, which is the product's ability to deliver on features and performance characteristics promised in marketing communications. The challenge for marketers and manufacturing is that every product must deliver on those promises. A product is said to have high conformance quality when a high percentage of the manufactured products fulfill the stated performance criteria.[17] If someone opened a Coke and there was no "fizz," it wouldn't be a Coke. The challenge for Coca-Cola and its bottlers is to ensure that every Coke has just the right carbonation when the consumer opens the can or bottle anywhere in the world.

Durability Consumer research and purchase patterns affirm that people find **durability**, the projected lifetime of the product under specific operating conditions, an important discriminating product characteristic and are willing to pay a premium for products that can demonstrate greater durability.[18] KitchenAid appliances have a reputation for durability that has translated into a price premium for their products.

Reliability A similar discriminator references the dependability of a product. **Reliability** is the percentage of time the product works without failure or stoppage. Businesses and consumers consistently report this is an important discriminator in their purchase decision; however, a product can be too reliable. While it is possible to build computers that will last for years and cost a premium, most computer manufacturers do not build them because computer technology

ETHICAL DIMENSION 7

That Garlic Came from Where?

Americans like fruits and vegetables; unfortunately, it is difficult to grow enough produce in the United States to meet the demand. This is particularly true for food manufacturers such as Kellogg, General Mills, and Kraft, which rely on imported produce from around the world to meet the demand. In addition, large retailers like Walmart are looking to stock fresh fruits and vegetables 365 days a year instead of having only a limited availability of the fresh produce that happens to be in season.

A small but rapidly growing source of fresh produce for American consumers is China. While total exports are a fraction of the total U.S. produce market, growth has been exponential. For example, in 2000, Chinese exports of fresh garlic amounted to 1 million pounds, or less than 1 percent of U.S. demand; however, in 2007 China exported 83 percent of U.S market demand and 90 percent in 2012.

As a consumer it is great to enjoy fresh garlic in January, especially since prices have not gone up dramatically despite the need to transport the produce long distances. Food experts, however, are becoming increasingly concerned about the quality of the produce coming out of China. The FDA recently reported that 107 food imports from China were detained in one month because the products were preserved with harmful chemicals and pesticides. This comes after the tainted pet food scandal in 2012 where pet food from China was laced with a harmful chemical.

Another issue driving the import of food products from China is the growth of organic foods. Dean Foods, Kellogg, and Walmart are importing organic strawberries, soybeans, mushrooms, and broccoli from China, and the same concerns about product quality exist, particularly since China didn't institute any organic food standards until 2005.

China is becoming a major exporter of food products worldwide, producing nearly half of the world's vegetables and 16 percent of the world's fruits. In addition, the nation is expanding the amount of land dedicated to vegetable and fruit farming. Currently, however, the quality-control standards established in the United States and other parts of the world to ensure product safety are not enforced. At the same time, consumers benefit from easy access to low-priced fruits and vegetables, and companies benefit from having product available for sale year-round. Yet the question still remains, is the garlic safe?[19]

Ethical Perspective

1. **American companies importing Chinese produce:** Should they stop importing fresh produce from China until product quality and safety standards match those in the United States? If consumers want fresh produce year-round, shouldn't companies seek out the lowest-cost provider?
2. **U.S. federal government:** Should it ban fresh produce from China until product quality and safety are assured? What responsibility does the government have in ensuring the quality and safety of Chinese produce?
3. **Consumers:** What role do consumers have in making sure the food products they consume are safe?

changes so quickly and product improvements happen so fast that people will not pay the premium for a computer that will last for many years.[20] They know that better, cheaper technology will be available before the computer actually malfunctions.

Repairability Increasingly, consumers and businesses evaluate the **repairability**, ease of fixing a problem with the product, as part of the product evaluation process. As a result, companies have built better diagnostics into their products to help isolate, identify, and repair products without the need for the costly repairs of a professional service.[21] Luxury cars such as the Chevy Corvette are available with tires that enable the driver to continue driving even after the tire has been damaged. At the same time and where appropriate, products are designed to "call in" to repair services online or on the phone. Cell phone manufacturers and service providers work together to build self-diagnostic phones that can be accessed in the field by service technicians. The technician can look at the phone's functionality and actually do minor software upgrades or repairs during a phone call.

Style One of the most difficult discriminators to accurately assess and build into a product is the look and feel of the product, or **style**. It is easy for someone to say a particular product has style, but designing it into a product can be a challenge. More than any other discriminator, style offers the advantage of being difficult to copy. While many companies from HP to Samsung have tried to copy the iPad, it still dominates the industry, although competitors such as Samsung continue to improve the look and feel of their products. Apple has a history of creating stylish products.

The real challenge is that style can be difficult to create consistently. Consumer tastes change over time, and what is considered stylish can quickly lose its appeal. Companies invest in information systems that help them spot trends. Once a trend is identified, product development teams must be able to translate it into design elements that can be incorporated into the product.[22] In some industries this is critical; for example, clothing manufacturers anticipate future trends, then use efficient production processes to design, build, and distribute their clothes while a particular style is still popular.

J.Crew is known for their classic lines and simple design. It prides itself on creating timeless clothing garments. However, the company felt its menswear line was becoming irrelevant and needed to be re-branded. The brand needed to connect with its consumers on a deeper level. It was decided that a warmer, more welcoming message would give the products a new context. The test store in Tribeca, known as the Liquor Store, showcased the work of local artists, photographers, and filmmakers. It helped build a really interesting environment for shoppers. J.Crew designers even went a step further and decided to write a book, *What a Man Should Know*, which discussed 50 semi-humorous, semi-useful things. At first it was only available at the Liquor Store. It gave people a reason to go there. The style of the store was critical to the company's growth. The re-branding has been successful making menswear more relevant to J.Crew's target market.[23]

Product Plan: Moving from One Product to Many Products

LO 7-3

Recognize how product strategies evolve from one product to many products.

Our discussion thus far has focused on a single product; however, companies generally create a range of products. These products can be variations or extensions of one basic product or completely different products. Most people would consider Post-it Notes, 3M's iconic brand of self-adhesive notes, a single product, but over 600 Post-it products are sold in more than 100 countries.[24] When you couple the extensive range of Post-it products with the thousands of products offered by 3M across more than 40 core product lines, it becomes apparent why management must understand how a product fits into the company's product strategy. Developing a plan sets strategy not only for a single product, but also for all the products in the company's catalog.

Product Line A **product line** is a group of products linked through usage, customer profile, price points, and distribution channels or needs satisfaction. Within a product line, strategies are developed for a single product, but also for all the products in the line. For example, 3M develops a strategy for each Post-it product, such as Post-it cards, that identifies possible product uses, different target markets, and marketing messages. At the same time, the company combines individual products for specific markets to create consumer-based solution catalogs. Students can find Post-it products targeted for them and teachers can find a separate listing of products.

The Campbell Soup brand was once the premier choice for canned soup. However, with the rise of brands such as Progresso and generic store brands, the company saw sales drop. Campbell's introduced its "Reduced Sodium" soup line that generated $100 million in sales in its first year. While this was a great success, it did not last. The company needed to modify its product line. CEO Denise Morrison believes that innovation requires an experimental mind-set. Some of the things the company learns from one product help with the next product. Campbell's decided to launch their Go Soup line, exotic-flavored soups packaged in pouches rather than cans to target the millennial generation. That generation is more focused on convenience and efficiency. It has proven successful, with net sales increasing 2 percent in early 2013. "It's starting to work. I'm not opening a bottle of champagne yet, but I'm encouraged by what I see," said Morrison.[25]

Companies must balance the number of items in a product line. Too many items and customers find it difficult to differentiate between individual products. In addition, cost inefficiencies involved in producing multiple products lower margins for the entire product line. Too few products and the company runs the risk of missing important market opportunities.

Product Mix Combining all the products offered by a company is called the **product mix**. Small, start-up companies frequently have a relatively limited product mix, but, as companies grow, their list of products grows as well. Developing strategies for the entire product mix is done at the highest levels of the organization.[26] Large companies, like 3M or GE, have widely disparate product lines that encompass hundreds of products and thousands of product items. Exhibit 7.5 lists some of the more than 55,000 products in 3M's product mix, which range from Post-it Notes to communication technology systems and a host of industrial applications.

Product Decisions Affect Other Marketing Mix Elements

Decisions about the product affect other elements of the marketing mix. Let's look at how two key marketing mix elements, pricing and marketing communications, are influenced by product decisions.

Pricing Pricing is one of the key marketing mix components and will be covered in detail in Chapter 10; however, several key issues related to product line pricing are appropriately covered here. Individual product pricing within the context of a broader product line requires a clear understanding of the price points for all the products in the line. Often multiple price points are targeted at specific markets with unique features following a "good, better, best" product line strategy. This strategy develops multiple product lines that include products with distinct features at each particular price point to attract multiple target markets. When new products are introduced, marketers carefully consider customer perceptions of the product's feature mix and price point to avoid customer confusion.

Technology companies, for many years, have faced the challenge of pricing new products that are less expensive but with more features than previous models. Dell and HP are sensitive to pricing new products because as new, more-powerful, less-expensive products come into the product mix, demand often drops for existing products. Dell prices new computer models to minimize

EXHIBIT 7.5 | 3M's Product Mix of 55,000 Products

Source: www.3m.com.
Reprinted courtesy of 3M Corporation.

Best Buy has been struggling to survive, as brick-and-mortar retailers such as Walmart and Target as well as online retailers such as Amazon offer lower prices on the same products. Knowing it had to make a drastic change, the company has instituted a price-matching strategy. This allows Best Buy the ability to match any product based on a competitor's price. Executives hope this will increase consumer demand for its products. In order to improve gross profit per square foot, the company will focus on stocking more items that generate higher margins. It will also aim to reduce costs through intelligent inventory management and supply chain optimization. In addition to the price-matching guarantee, Best Buy has created the "Renew Blue" program. The majority of the focus for this initiative is online growth. It will become a more interactive experience and mobile sites are currently being revamped. While it is not clear if the company's pricing strategy is a success, it is certainly a game changer in the industry.[27]

disrupting demand for its existing products while, at the same time, lowering prices of existing products to create greater separation between the new product and current products (see Exhibit 7.6).

Marketing Communications A key strategic decision for marketers is the degree to which marketing communications focuses on a single product item versus a product brand. Usually, companies do both, but the emphasis on one approach versus the other makes a big difference in the communications strategy. For example, 3M focuses much of its Post-it marketing communications on the Post-it product line, emphasizing the brand. Contrast that with Häagen-Dazs, which focuses on specific products (ice cream, sorbet, and yogurt) and specific product items within each product (chocolate, almond hazelnut swirl, pineapple coconut).

EXHIBIT 7.6 | Dell Offers a Wide Range of Products at Different Price Points

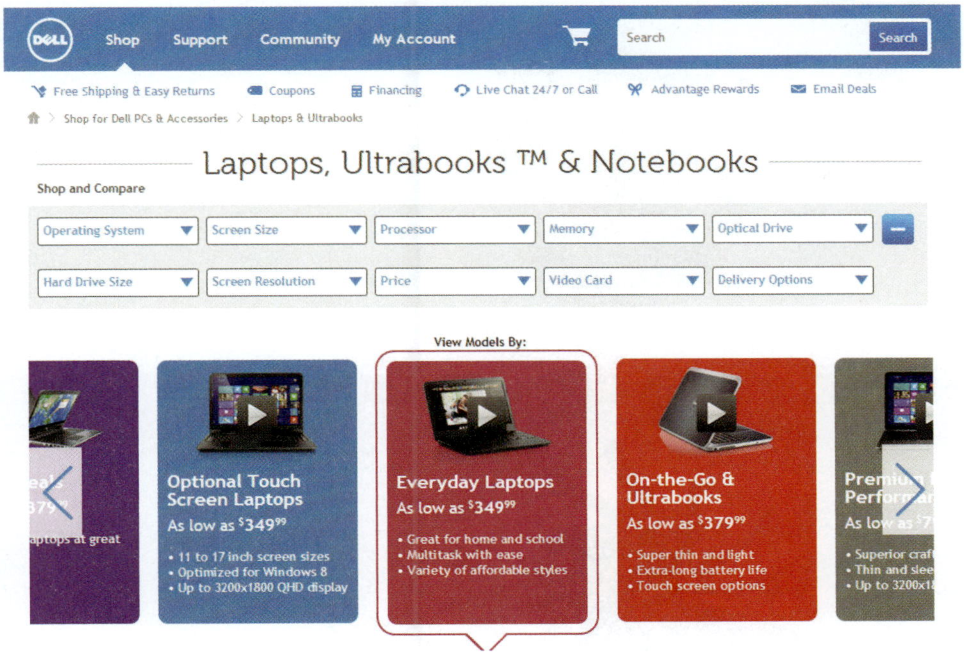

A second communications issue is the allocation of communications budget dollars across product items in a product line. Häagen-Dazs has more than 30 specific kinds of ice cream and dozens of other products across its entire product line. The company must make decisions about the allocation of budget dollars to each product, then each specific product item. This raises several challenges for marketing managers. Do they allocate dollars based on the most popular flavors like chocolate and vanilla? Or do they focus on new product items such as Mayan chocolate to build a competitive edge with products that are not offered by the competition? New products almost always have additional communication budgets to support the product's introduction. The assumption is that, once the product is established, it will be possible to cut back on the heavy expenditure of a new product communications campaign (see Exhibit 7.7).

THE LIFE OF THE PRODUCT: BUILDING THE PRODUCT EXPERIENCE

LO 7-4

Understand the life of a product and how product strategies change over time.

Companies create, launch, and transform products as market conditions change over time. This product evolution is referred to as the **product life cycle (PLC)** and defines the life of a product in four basic stages: introduction, growth, maturity, and decline (see Exhibit 7.8).[28]

The PLC generally refers to a product category (touring bicycles) rather than a product item (Giant Sedona bicycles), although companies often track their own product items against an industry PLC. The PLC is a useful tool because it (1) provides a strategic framework for market analysis, (2) tracks historical trends, and (3) identifies future market conditions. Giant Bicycles, for example, can evaluate the current touring bike market and then consider growth opportunities for the Sedona brand based on that product's position in the PLC.

EXHIBIT 7.7 | Häagen-Dazs Promotes One Product Item

made like no other
even more de lechable
Eager to surpass perfection, we took our original Latin-inspired blend of caramel and sweet cream and added a touch of the world's finest cinnamon. Surely your sweet tooth will dance the rumba with delight.
New Häagen-Dazs Cinnamon Dulce de Leche Ice Cream

Häagen Dazs has been successful building a product line that features old favorites but also frequently introduces new product flavors.

© HDIP, Inc.

EXHIBIT 7.8 | The Product Life Cycle

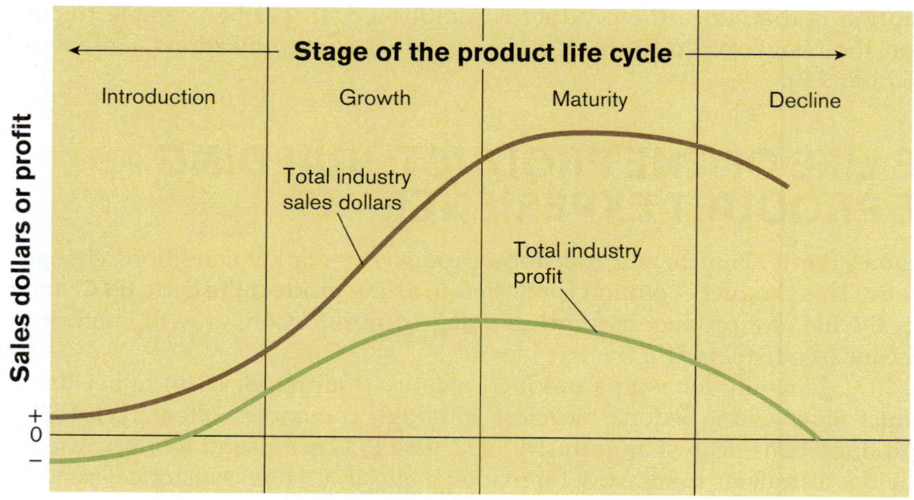

Stage of the product life cycle
Introduction
Growth
Maturity
Decline
Total industry sales dollars
Total industry profit
Sales dollars or profit

Reprinted from Roger Kerin, Steven Hartley, and William Rudelius, *Marketing,* 11th ed., 2013. Copyright © 2013 The McGraw-Hill Companies, Inc.

Product Life Cycle Sales Revenue and Profitability

Notice there are two lines on the PLC graph. The top line charts the industry sales revenue for the product over time. The sales revenue line increases dramatically in introduction and growth stages as the product moves through the consumer adoption process. At some point, sales begin to decline. However, a sales decline does not necessarily mean the death of the product. Companies may create new products or market conditions may change, which can reinvigorate the product and start a new growth phase. Bottled water was long considered a product in decline until Evian, Dasani, Zephyrhills, and others developed new packaging, added new flavors, and emphasized the healthy aspects of water. Now the product category is experiencing a period of significant growth around the world.

The second line on the PLC graph is the total profits from the companies that compete in that industry. When the product is introduced, the category pioneer, the company introducing the product, has incurred product development costs. At the same time, new companies entering the market also sustain product development and initial marketing costs associated with the product launch. As a result, the industry starts the PLC "in the red" (no profits). As the product category grows, successful companies recoup their initial costs and begin to realize a return on their investments.

Product Life Cycle Timeline

The speed at which products within a category move through the PLC is not consistent, and there is a great deal of variability across product categories. In some cases, a product moves through an entire cycle in a period of months and is replaced with the next product design. **Fads** come and go quickly, often reaching only a limited number of individuals but creating a lot of buzz in the marketplace.[29] Often, women's fashion is seasonal with a product line being introduced in the spring, moving through its growth cycle in the summer and fall, then finally going into decline by winter. The cycle takes one selling season, in this case, one year. With other products such as men's suits, it may take decades from introduction to decline. Men's classic two-piece suits experience incremental changes every season, but the same basic design has been around for many years. The functionality of the product has made it an enduring style for men.

Product Life Cycle Caveats

It is important to note several caveats about the product life cycle. The PLC is a helpful conceptual tool that works best when viewed as a framework for studying a product category. It can be difficult to know with certainty what stage a product is in, particularly at transition points in the PLC. Rather, the PLC enables marketing managers to assess historical trends in the category and track how the product has behaved over time. Naturally, there may be different interpretations of the same data as marketing managers in one company look at the numbers and arrive at one conclusion while managers in another company arrive at a different conclusion.

The PLC is also useful when marketing managers focus on historical precedent—Where has the product been?—and future possibilities—How do we plan now to be successful in the next stage? By using the PLC as a planning tool for developing new products, it is possible to avoid getting caught in the immediacy of volatile market fluctuations. Exhibit 7.9 summarizes the phases of the product life cycle.

Estée Lauder recently introduced Africa to its M•A•C cosmetics line by opening a store in Lagos, Nigeria. M•A•C has long catered to various ethnic groups, including American blacks. Estée Lauder sees the brand as the key to unlocking emerging markets. "The biggest play for the corporation, period, in terms of market development today, is the M•A•C brand," group president John Dempsey said. "It is the singular biggest source of growth for the company." The employees are critical to the brand's success, as they are the most trusted source of information among rural African consumers. After the company introduced the brand to Brazil in 2003, it took over distribution there. It can be assumed that a similar strategy is in the works should the African market prove to be successful. The brand's stores are a revelation in countries like Nigeria, where Western-style retailers are so scarce that wealthy shoppers are forced to search out upmarket brands on trips overseas.[30]

EXHIBIT 7.9 | Product Life Cycle

	Introduction Phase	Growth Phase	Maturity Phase	Decline Stage
Objective	Build market awareness for the product leading to trial purchase.	Differentiate product from those of new competitors, promoting rapid expansion.	Transition product from high growth to sales stability.	Determine the future of the product.
Profitability	Sales are low, typically high failure rate. High marketing and product costs.	Sales grow at increasing rate. Profits become healthier as operations are streamlined.	Sales continue to increase but at a decreasing rate. Cost minimization has reached full extent.	Long-run drop in sales. Profit margins dramatically reduced.
Market Conditions				
Market Segment	Nonexistent.	New market segment now established.	Market is approaching saturation.	Changing consumer tastes and substitute products eat away at market segment.
Targeted Consumers	Innovators and Early Adopters	Early Adopters to Majority Adopters	Majority Adopters	Laggards
Competitive Environment	Little competition.	Many competitors enter market.	Marginal competitors dropping out.	Falling demand forces many out of market.
Competitor Reaction	Market followers will release product similar to that of the pioneer.	Large companies may acquire small pioneering firms.	Typified by models of products with an emphasis on style over function.	Firms that remain focus on specialty products.

(cont.)

	Introduction Phase	Growth Phase	Maturity Phase	Decline Stage
Strategies				
Product	High-quality, innovative design providing new benefit to consumers.	More features and better design, learning from issues from first generation.	Product lines are widened or extended.	Consider product expenses in terms of return on investment.
	Features well-received and understood by target consumers.	Diversification of product and release of complementary products/services.	Work to further differentiate product from those of competitors.	Decide whether to invest further in product or allocate funding to new project(s).
Price	**Market penetration:** Attractive price point to gain market share and discourage competitors.	New and improved models sold at high price points.	Target high-end market with differentiated product and higher price point.	Offer product at low price point to try to stimulate any remaining demand.
	Market skimming: High initial price point targeting less price-sensitive consumers to recoup R&D costs before competitors enter market.	Existing models or earlier generations move down in price.	Established competition makes price pressures more pronounced, forcing lower-price strategy if product not well-differentiated.	Significant price pressures from both competitors and more price-sensitive consumers.
Marketing Communications	Inform and educate target audience about the product's features and benefits.	Link the brand with key product features and highlight differentiation between competitors.	Challenge of deciding between short-term sales promotions or investing more in the brand.	Cost of continued investment in marketing communications not justified by market conditions.
	Promotion focused on product awareness and to stimulate primary demand.	Promotion emphasizes brand advertising and comparative ads.		
Distribution	Wide distribution network with limited product availability: Create anticipation by promoting excitement and sense of scarcity.	Broaden distribution networks to keep up with expanding market demand.	Product has reached its maximum distribution.	Reduced distribution channels.
	Limit distribution but increase product availability: Release to limited number of target markets with high availability. Intensive personal selling to retailers and wholesalers.	Maintain high levels of product quality and boost customer service efforts to keep up with product.	Channel members identify weak products and begin dropping out if necessary.	Channel members cease to support the product.

NEW PRODUCTS—CREATING LONG-TERM SUCCESS

No matter how good a company's current products are, long-term growth depends on new products. This can be done in one of two basic ways: acquisition or internal development. Both approaches have their advantages and disadvantages.

"New" Defined

LO 7-5

Recognize the importance of new-product development to long-term success.

What does the term *new* mean? Everyday, consumers see or hear marketing communications that talk about "new and improved." At the same time, people speak about buying a new car (which may in fact be a used car) as well as a new TV (which may be last year's model). Let's look at how the term is defined by the product's manufacturer and customers.

Although 3D printing may sound like science fiction, it's been around for more than 25 years. Carmakers and aerospace companies have used industrial 3D printers to create prototype parts for vehicles. However, the industry is rapidly changing. According to Wohler Associates, the 3D printer industry was $1.7 billion in 2012 and forecasted to reach $3.7 billion by 2015. This growth can be attributed to the technology becoming more available to the masses. Companies such as MakerBot, Cube, and Autodesk are entering the market developing desktop-sized 3D printers that consumers can use at home to create anything from cups to bracelets. MakerBot Industries dominates the hobbyist consumer segment. It sold more than 10,000 of its Replicator printers for $1,749 to both companies and individuals. MakerBot's CEO Bret Pettis believes the future of the industry is the end of bland mass production; rather it is giving consumers the ability to customize or create a myriad of products. Time will tell whether consumers will embrace the rise of do-it-yourself product development.[31]

Company Perspective Most people would define *new* as a product that has not been available before or bears little resemblance to an existing product, and one type of new product is actually referred to as a **new-to-the-world product** because it has not been available before. Sometimes new-to-the-world products are so innovative they create a fundamental change in the marketplace and are known as *disruptive innovation.* They are called disruptive because they shift people's perspective and frequently alter their behavior by offering dramatically simpler, more convenient, and usually less-expensive products than currently exist. In the process they frequently make existing products less desirable. Desktop computers, cell phones, and tablet computers are examples of new-to-the-world products considered disruptive innovations.[32]

A second type of new-to-the-world product, *sustaining innovations,* are newer, better, faster versions of existing products that target, for the most part, existing customers. Sustaining innovations can be revolutionary by taking the market in a new direction. They can also be **upgrades or modifications to existing products** and represent incremental enhancements to current products.[33]

Once a product has been developed and is on the market, the company can extend the product by creating **additions to existing product lines**. For years, Coca-Cola has added new products to the Coke line, first with Diet Coke in the early 1980s and now with many different Coke-branded products including Coke Zero. These products are also available in various sizes and packaging, giving Coke many different product items.

Another "new" product approach is to **reposition existing products** to target new markets. The cell phone market used this strategy successfully to introduce cell phones in the mid-1990s. Originally cell phone service providers positioned the phones as a tool for businesspeople or as a safety tool targeting individuals such as working women and moms. As the product became more widely adopted, the positioning of the product changed to become an important work tool. As the market for cell phones has expanded, the positioning has evolved to include younger users. Cell phones are the dominant communication device for teenagers, and phones have been created for kids as young as seven.

Cost reduction, as the name implies, is a specific method for introducing lower-cost products that frequently focus on value-oriented product price points in the product mix. Generally this approach involves eliminating or reducing features, using less-expensive materials, or altering the service or warranty to offer the product at a lower price point to the market.[34]

Customer's Perspective While the company follows a specific strategy in creating a new product, the customer is unaware and, in reality, often does not really care about how the product arrived in the marketplace. The customer's perspective is much more narrow and self-directed. The customer is most interested in an answer to the fundamental question—is this product new to me? From the company's perspective it is important to realize that every customer approaches a new product a little differently. For example, an individual going in to buy his or her first cell phone from a service provider can find the process intimidating. As a result, cellular providers handle those customers carefully to reduce anxiety, concentrating on things like ease of use and simple service packages. Experienced cell phone users are interested in talking about the latest phone capabilities, packages, and technology. One challenge companies face is dealing with historical customer perceptions. BlackBerry has worked hard to change people's negative perceptions about the company with new product introductions and operating system. The company also dropped its old name (Research in Motion) for BlackBerry in an effort to create new, more-positive customer perceptions.

Reasons for New-Product Success or Failure

Since new-product development is such a critical factor in the long-term success of an organization, you might think companies are good at the development process. Unfortunately, this is not the case; 70 to 80 percent of all new products worldwide fail. While it is true that many of those products are developed by small entrepreneurs, no company is immune to product failure. Have you ever heard of Levi's business wear or Mr. Coffee coffee or Dunkin' Donuts cereal? Probably not, because each of these new products failed despite the fact they were introduced by companies with a track record of marketing success. The reasons vary, but it is possible to identify the role of the company, customers, and competitors in the success or failure of a new product.[35] Exhibit 7.10 summarizes the reasons for new product failure.

EXHIBIT 7.10 | Why Do Products Fail?

Company	Customers	Competitors	Environment
Inadequate value proposition	Change in purchase priorities	Aggressively attack new competition	Changes in government regulation or legislation
Poor marketing communications	Higher expectations		Changes in societal demands
Product does not meet customer expectations			Economic changes
Failure to fully develop product			

Environmentally friendly, luxury vehicle maker Tesla continues to face some tough challenges in the market. Hybrid vehicles have established a market, but electric vehicles are criticized on their performance and the lack of charging stations. With new Corporate Average Fuel Economy regulations, electric vehicle options may have an advantage. But given perceived limitations of electric vehicles, the question becomes how big is the market? The U.S. Department of Transportation collected data that showed 97 percent of vehicle trips are less than 50 miles and 88 percent are less than 20 miles. These data suggest that electric vehicles can meet the needs of the everyday driver and Tesla brings a new edge to the electric car market. Its Model S is comparable to an Audi A8 or BMW 7-Series. It is capable of traveling 200 miles on a single charge. Tesla provides the luxury that many consumers aspire to obtain.[36]

NEW-PRODUCT DEVELOPMENT PROCESS

The new-product development process consists of three main activities and eight specific tasks. Failure at any step significantly lowers the probability of long-term success. The three major activities in new-product development are to (1) identify product opportunities, (2) define the product opportunity, and (3) develop the product opportunity.

There is a great deal of variability in the new-product development timeline. Marketers must balance the product development process with the ever-changing demands of the marketplace. Take too long in product development and the market may have changed; rush the process and the product may be poorly designed or lack quality.[37]

Identify Product Opportunities

LO 7-6

Understand the new-product development process.

The first step in the new-product development process, identify potential product opportunities, has two specific tasks. First, companies must generate sufficient new-product ideas. Very few product ideas make it through the entire process and, as we have seen already, far fewer products actually become successful. As a result, it is important to have a steady flow of new ideas into the development process. Second, ideas need to be evaluated before resources are committed to development.

Generate New Ideas Product ideas are generated in one of two ways: internal or external to the firm. While companies develop a preference for one approach over the other, the reality is both internal and external sources produce good new-product ideas. A number of factors, including the company's commitment to innovation, the reputation of competitors for new-product development, and customer expectations, affect which approach a company prefers.[38]

Kimberly-Clark's Huggies brand of disposable diapers has developed dozens of different diaper products for newborns, older babies, and toddlers, as well as specialized products for extra comfort, overnight, and swimming diapers. K-C even manufactures six different kinds of baby wipes.

Internal Sources include employees from R&D, marketing, and manufacturing. Key employees know both the capabilities of the company and the needs of the market. Therefore, it is not surprising that internal sources are the single best source for new-product ideas. Funding product research is expensive; companies spend billions of dollars every year to generate product ideas.

People who work directly with customers are another source of ideas. As salespeople, customer service representatives, and others interact directly with customers, it is possible to identify new-product ideas. Often these ideas are incremental changes to existing products that solve a particular problem; however, occasionally the customer challenge requires a truly innovative solution.

Working with academia helps support the research activities of many organizations. This is particularly useful when companies engage in pure research, which looks at cutting-edge ideas that often do not have immediate market applications. Dedicated research labs such as Bell Labs drive product ideas and testing. As part of the old AT&T, Bell Labs was responsible for many of the most significant technology products of the 20th century. In many cases, such as the development of the transistor, the research was years ahead of market need. Now, while AT&T Labs still employs more than 4,500 scientists, the focus is identifying new-product ideas that are more market-focused and customer-driven.

3M has long focused on being a leader of innovation and recently recorded $30 billion in sales. The company's products sell in nearly 200 countries and it has made significant contributions to numerous industries including health care, communications, and office business products. The company created a corporate culture that fosters organic growth through inventing new products and dedicates 6 percent of its annual revenue to support its research and development. Aside from monetary investment in R&D, management encourages employees to spend time on products and research outside of their responsibilities. 3M often focuses on developing disruptive innovations outside of its current portfolio of more than 55,000 products. Since 1998, 3M has invested in other innovative companies through its New Ventures. The culture of open innovation allows unexpected connections to be made between industries and technologies that lead to increasingly more product innovations. Through its culture and top management's support, 3M has proven its long-term focus and sustainability in its innovations.[39]

External An excellent source of ideas comes from individuals and organizations not directly connected with the company. In some industries, such as Internet applications, small entrepreneurs drive innovation. Instagram is a popular Internet destination owned by Facebook. Started by entrepreneurs in 2010 who wanted to share files across social media platforms, the company has over 100 million registered users. The company's acquisition by Facebook in 2012 exemplifies how larger companies continue to grow by acquiring smaller companies with innovative products. Google, Microsoft, and Apple all maintain dedicated staff whose job it is to identify and acquire new start-up organizations with great product ideas.

Customers Customers are also an excellent source of product ideas. Solving their problems can lead to innovative solutions that have market potential beyond the immediate customer. Many companies encourage customer input directly online through e-mail and online discussion groups. Ford, BMW, Mercedes-Benz, and others sponsor user group bulletin boards that discuss improvements to existing products. While this will not likely lead to "new-to-the-world" products, it can lead to incremental or even substantial enhancements to existing products.

Distributors Distributors are a good source for new-product ideas, particularly when they are the primary link between the customer and the company. Small organizations generally do not have the resources for a national sales force and use distributors in many markets. Odyssey Software (a subsidiary of Symantec) is a developer of wireless business applications for the Windows platform that uses a network of global distributors to market its products.[40] The distributor network is a key partner in the development of new products for the company. In actuality, almost anyone outside the organization can generate a new-product idea.

Companies understand that even though the majority of ideas from external sources will not pass the screening process, they still want to encourage people to submit their product concepts. HP gets thousands of product ideas from a variety of individuals every year; however, very few are actually developed.

Screen and Evaluate Ideas Ideas need to be screened and evaluated as quickly as possible. The screening process has two primary objectives. The first objective is to eliminate product ideas judged unworthy of further consideration. New-product development is expensive and resources are scarce, so ideas are evaluated early to assess their viability. An idea is rejected for several reasons. Perhaps the proposal is just not very good or it may be reasonable but inconsistent with the company's overall business strategy. Evaluating ideas can sometimes create difficult choices for managers as they wrestle with broader societal issues.[41] Consider, for example, KidCare TV, which is a provider of useful "kid frendly" content via TV for pediatricians around the United States. KidCare TV provides the content free of charge but sells advertising that is delivered with the content. Critics argue the service simply reinforces the already negative practice of kids spending too much time watching television.

Two types of mistakes are associated with rejecting or moving forward with a new-product design, and both are potentially expensive for the company. The first is the **go-to-market mistake** made when a company fails to stop a bad product idea from moving into product development. This mistake runs on a continuum from very costly (the new product is not accepted and the company loses its initial investment) to not meeting targeted ROI projections (the product does not hit established benchmarks for profitability, or unit sales). Expensive mistakes often initiate a review of the screening process to figure out how the product made it through the development process. When the product fails to hit targeted benchmarks for success, the review may focus on errors in marketing strategy, target market adjustments, or competitive response to the product launch.

A **stop-to-market mistake** happens when a good idea is prematurely eliminated during the screening process. Almost every CEO can relate a story of the product success that got away. Most often companies are reluctant to talk about stop-to-market mistakes because it makes management uncomfortable and provides additional information about product development to competitors. For example, we have talked a lot about Apple, pointing out its wildly successful iPhone and iPad. But in addition to its failed Newton, which we discussed earlier, the company has also developed a number of other products that never made it to market. For example, the Macintosh PowerBook Duo Tablet was, arguably, the first tablet PC and was created in the early 1990s during the same period as Newton. Apple stopped development of the product, code-named PenLite, to avoid confusion with Newton. Among PenLite's many features was a wireless, full-function computer that connected with all PowerBook accessories.[42]

A second objective of the screening process is to help prioritize ideas that pass the initial screening and evaluation. All new-product concepts are not equal, and it is important to focus resources on those that best match the success criteria. The criteria used to prioritize the ideas vary by company but often include:

- Time to market (how long will it take to develop and get the product to market).
- ROI (what is the expected return for the dollars invested in the project).
- New product fit with overall company product portfolio.

This analysis includes an internal assessment by a team from specific areas across the company (finance, marketing, R&D, manufacturing, logistics).[43] Often these people are directly involved in new-product development and

Apple's iPad was a smash success, unlike the Newton.

have a thorough understanding of the success criteria and the company's overall product portfolio. Additionally, a relevant member of senior management provides continuity with long-term strategic goals and leadership in the screening process. Members of the team are rotated to ensure fresh ideas as there is often a significant time commitment required and members of the assessment team have other responsibilities in the company.[44]

Define the Product Opportunity

Ideas that pass through the screening process move into a development phase to define the product potential and market opportunity. Three specific tasks in this stage are to (1) define and test the product idea, (2) create a marketing strategy for the product, and (3) analyze the product's business case.

Define and Test Product Concept The product idea now needs to be clearly defined and tested. Ideas at this stage are frequently not fully developed or operational. At this point, depending on the concept, people and resources are allocated to move the product development forward and a budget is created to develop the product.

Product definition has three objectives. First, it defines the product's value proposition: what customer needs are being addressed and, in broad terms, at what price. Second, the definition briefly identifies the target market(s) and the purchase frequency. Third, the definition delineates the product's characteristics (look, feel, physical elements, and features of the product). As the product moves through development, the physical characteristics become more defined and particular features, often at different price points, are included in the prototypes.[45]

Target customers are useful in defining the product concept. Companies present models, limited prototypes, and verbal or written descriptions of the product concept to customers, individually or in focus groups. Computer graphics are also used to depict elements of the product and even functionality. For example, in the development of new jet airliners, Boeing and Airbus will develop sophisticated simulations that allow passengers to *virtually* sit in the airplane. In this way, customers get a more realistic perspective at a fraction of the cost to develop a full-scale working prototype.

During this phase, companies start getting market input to refine and develop the concept. Customers are asked about their attitudes toward the product idea and if they perceive the idea as different from other products on the market. Product developers want to know, Would you buy this product and how much are you willing to pay? The company needs to know if the product is appealing to the target audience. A second question is also essential in this testing: What would you like to change about the product concept? If customers suggest changes that are not feasible (too costly to implement, not technically possible), it dramatically reduces the viability of the project. Whenever possible, however, customer feedback is incorporated into the product's development. By making adjustments during this phase rather than waiting until after the launch, companies can increase the probability of success. Since the information is so critical, researchers use large samples of target customers to ensure confidence in the findings.

In creating an effective new product marketing strategy, it is important to clearly identify the product benefits to the target audience. Here the MINI is identifying a benefit: buy a MINI and you won't be bored. For someone in the MINI's target market, this benefit is attractive.

Create Marketing Strategy The product development process leads to a distinct set of physical characteristics and a detailed feature mix. As the product becomes better defined, marketing specialists develop a tentative, but detailed, marketing strategy. Even though the product is still under development, there are several reasons for preparing a marketing strategy now. First, defining the target market is helpful to the product developers. In addition to the basic market information (size, geography, and demographics), product developers appreciate knowing how the product will be used (context, environment) and the psychographics of the market (the market's activities, interests, and opinions). Marketers also assess the market share potential at critical points in time (how much market share can the new product get after one year?). At this point, tentative pricing, distribution, and marketing communications strategies are created that will be adapted as the product gets closer to rollout.[46] Often, as part of the initial marketing communications, appropriate publications will include articles about a new product. Finally, marketing managers begin to develop budgets for the product launch and estimates of the marketing communications budget, manufacturing capacity, and logistical needs.

Conduct Business Case Analysis As the product definition is developed and a tentative marketing strategy created, a critical "go–no go" decision is made before the next product development stage. At this point, the costs have been small relative to the cost of moving to full product development, market testing, and launch. There is a lot of pressure to get the decision right because a mistake is expensive. The **business case analysis** is an overall evaluation of a product and usually assesses the product's probability of success. It is often done when there are changes to an existing marketing plan, such as an increase in the marketing communications budget. The business case would assess the feasibility of increasing the communications budget.[47] In new-product development, the business case focuses on two key issues. First, the total demand for the product over a specified period of time, usually five years, is determined. Second, a cash flow statement is developed that specifies cash flow, profitability, and investment requirements.

Total Demand Sales are defined in two ways: revenue (unit sales × price) and unit sales. Each provides important information. Revenue is the top line number in a profitability analysis and is affected by price variations common to global products with substantial price differences around the world. Because currencies fluctuate, which can lead to wide variations in revenue, and price increases can also dramatically affect total revenue, unit sales is often considered a more realistic picture of product growth and represents the number of units sold, in various product configurations, around the world.

Estimating total demand is a function of three separate purchase situations.

- **New purchases**—first-time sales. With new products, these sales are called trial purchases. This is also calculated as the trial rate (how many individuals in a particular target market have tried the product).
- **Repeat purchases**—the number of products purchased by the same customer. This can be important with frequently purchased products such as convenience goods that rely on frequent repeat purchases for success.
- **Replacement purchases**—the number of products purchased to replace existing products that have become obsolete or have malfunctioned. Estimates are made on the number of product failures in any given year based on the expected product life. As more products are sold into a market through first-time and repeat purchases, the number of replacement sales will increase.

Profitability Analysis To this point, costs have been primarily in R&D and market research. However, at the next step, the company will incur manufacturing, marketing, accounting, and the logistical costs of bringing the product to market. As a result, a thorough analysis is conducted of the short- and long-term product profitability.

Develop the Product Opportunity

If the result of the previous analysis is a "go" decision, then the number of people and the resources allocated to the product's development increase substantially. For much of the 20th century, companies would move a substantial number of new-product concepts through to this stage and use product development and market testing to screen and eliminate ideas. That changed in the 1990s as the cost of taking products to market increased dramatically while failure rates remained high. Companies now screen product ideas much earlier in the development process. As a result, far fewer product ideas make it to this stage, and those products targeted for further development and market testing have a much higher probability of actually being launched in the marketplace.[48]

Develop the Product So far the product exists primarily as a concept, or, at most, a working prototype, but if the product idea is to go forward, it must move from viable product concept to a working product that meets customer needs profitably. The challenge for the development team is to design and build a product the customer wants to buy while hitting the company's success metrics—sales price, revenue, profit margins, unit sales, and cost to build.[49]

As part of the company's long-term growth strategy, Starbucks has made several acquisitions to diversify its product portfolio beyond coffee. For example, Starbucks purchased San Francisco company Bay Bread, LLC and its La Boulange brand for $100 million in cash. Starbucks' food portfolio is important for its future growth in multiple channels. The company has an ongoing strategy to improve its food offerings based on customer feedback. Revenue from food is now more than $1.5 billion per year in the U.S. company–operated stores and grew by double digits in recent years. Recognizing the customer's desire for higher-quality food options, it plans to integrate La Boulange products into Starbucks' product offerings. Customers have communicated a desire for products with fewer artificial ingredients and smaller portions. La Boulange fills this need using fresh ingredients, specialty grains, and locally sourced produce. Starbucks hopes the additional food products will also increase incremental sales and customer loyalty as well as grow the company through differentiated brand experiences.[50]

Previous research during concept testing provides substantial information about what customers are looking for in the product. Coupled with input from engineers, designers, and marketing specialists, the product definition developed earlier is operationalized. This process moves from a strategic understanding of the customer's basic needs to a specific operational definition of the product's characteristics. Following this process, the product's physical characteristics are defined by targeting the essential benefits delivered to the customer.[51]

There are two product development models. The first incorporates more planning and follows a sequential timeline with key process metrics being met at each stage before moving on through the process. In this scenario, product development spends a lot of time creating a product that is considered close to the final product that will be rolled out to customers. Consequently, product testing is used primarily to affirm the extensive development done earlier in the process.

The next approach encourages more prototypes that incrementally move the product through the development process. Here the product does not need to be "perfect" before testing; rather, the idea is to continuously test the product and use the testing process to enhance the product and solicit customer feedback. Through this process, the market becomes aware of the product, and if properly managed, interest in the product is increased during development.

In this second method, the goal is to shorten the time spent in development, moving from development to testing as quickly as possible to minimize cost and get the product in the hands of potential users. The longer a company takes at this stage, the greater the likelihood that competitors learn of the product, customer preferences change, or external environment conditions dictate further product adjustments.

Product Testing Generally a product undergoes two types of testing. As the product's characteristics are being finalized, most of the testing is done internally by engineers, product specialists, and other employees. This type of testing, called alpha testing, helps clarify the basic operationalization of the product such as the physical characteristics and features.

At some point, the company will want potential customers to begin testing the product. Beta testing encourages customers to evaluate and provide feedback on the prototype. The product may be close to the final configuration, but beta tests allow for further product testing and refinement.[52]

Test the Market Once the product has reached the point where the product development team is satisfied with its performance, physical characteristics, and features, it is ready to be tested in the marketplace. To maintain security, minimize product information leaks, and disrupt competitor intelligence, products are often given code names. Once the product moves to the marketplace testing stage, a marketing strategy is created for the test using the product's market name. Some elements of the strategy such as brand name and packaging will have been tested with consumers during product development.[53] For example, engineers work with package design professionals to ensure that, first, the product is protected and, second, the packaging maximizes marketing communications opportunities.

The amount of market testing is a function of several critical factors that are in conflict with one another. First, a company must evaluate the cost of being wrong. While a great deal of money has been spent to this point, the cost of launching a product failure is much higher. The greater the risk of failure, the more market testing a company will want to do before a full product launch.

At the same time, market testing takes time, and competitors can take advantage to enhance their product mix or develop marketing strategies to counter a successful product launch. In addition, depending on the product, the selling season may dictate faster product rollout because waiting too long may cost the company significant sales. Ultimately, management must balance these factors and choose the optimum market testing strategy.[54]

Consumer Product Market Tests In creating the market test, management must make four key decisions:

- *Where:* The location of the market test is based on how well it reflects the potential target markets. Most market tests involve somewhere between two and five cities to mitigate regional differences in purchase patterns (if there are any).
- *How long:* Most test markets run less than a year. The test should be long enough to include several purchase cycles. With many consumer products, purchase cycles are relatively short (days or weeks) so there is less need for a long market test.
- *Data:* Critical information needed to make necessary decisions must be identified. Management frequently wants to know how long it takes for the product to move through the distribution system, tracking the product from manufacturing plant through to the point of sale (matching inventory as it leaves the plant with store sales). In addition, buyers are interviewed on their product experience.

Trader Joe's conducts a great deal of analysis before it introduces a new product in its stores. The company considers hundreds of new products every year, but only a few make it onto store shelves.

- *Decision criteria:* Metrics for further action must be identified. At this stage it is difficult to pull a product, but if the product fails in the market test, management is faced with a difficult decision—drop the product or send it back for major redesign. If the product is a success, then the product launch decision is much easier. Exhibit 7.11 is a summary of the decision criteria used in market tests.

Consumer product market testing has two goals. First is to provide specific numbers to the business case estimates including new (trial purchases), repeat, and, if appropriate, initial replacement purchases. Additionally, information about buyer demographics is evaluated against earlier target market scenarios and is compared against company business case models and historical data. The company takes data from the market test and projects the future.

The second objective of market testing is to get feedback on the tactics that can be used to adjust the marketing plan before product launch. While a company will often hold back implementing the entire marketing plan for security reasons, input from customers, distributors, and retailers is helpful in adjusting the final marketing plan.

Business Product Market Test Products designed for business markets are tested differently than their consumer product counterparts. Essentially, the tests are smaller in scope and involve fewer individuals and companies; however, they are no less important in the new-product development process. Because business markets are smaller, beta testing often includes only a few key customers with a long-standing company relationship. If, on the other hand, the company has independent distributors, it identifies a limited number for the market test and provides additional support to them as the product is being tested.[55]

Often in parallel with beta testing, companies will use trade shows to solicit customer feedback. Trade shows are a cost-effective way to get customer input because they are an efficient and convenient location to introduce new products or test new product ideas.

EXHIBIT 7.11 | Summary of Decision Criteria in Market Tests

Category	Criteria
Financial	Gross margin
	Profit per unit shelf space
	Opportunity cost of capital needed to obtain the new item
Competition	Number of firms in the trading area
	Number of competing brands
Marketing strategy	Product uniqueness
	Vendor effort
	Marketing support
	Terms of trade: slotting allowances, off-invoice allowances, free cases, bill-back provisions
	Price
Other	Category growth
	Synergy with existing items

Source: www.emeraldinsight.com.

Product Launch At this point in the new-product process, it is time to implement the marketing plan. By now, considerable time, money, and human capital have been expended in the development of the product. Management has made the decision to launch the product. Now it is time to define the product's objectives (sales, target markets, success metrics), specify the value proposition, plan the marketing tactics, and implement the marketing plan. As we mentioned earlier, all of this will already have been done, but any necessary adjustments are made after the market test.

The product launch is critical to the long-term success of the product. Products that start poorly seldom recover from a poor launch. The pressure to create excitement, particularly for consumer products, leading to consumer trial purchase is a primary reason companies spend millions of dollars on a product launch. Microsoft spent in excess of $500 million to introduce Windows 8 in 2012 and that does not include the hundreds of millions spent by Microsoft partners (Intel, Dell, and others) in support of Windows 8. However, the product has met with mixed success, particularly among business users.[56]

Many marketing communication dollars are front-loaded at the product launch with the goal of creating sufficient product interest that will turn into repeat and replacement purchases later. If the product is not successful early, management is often unwilling to spend additional dollars as the product becomes widely distributed. The end result can be a downward spiral with low product interest generating fewer sales, which leads to more cutbacks in marketing support.[57]

CONSUMER ADOPTION AND DIFFUSION PROCESS

LO 7-7

Identify how new products become diffused in a market.

A target market consists of many people with different predispositions to purchase a product. Some will want to adopt a product early; others will wait until much later. The rate at which products become accepted is known as the adoption process. Marketers are interested in knowing the rate at which a product will be adopted into a market as well as the timeline (how long it will take for the product to move through the process). Of particular interest in a new-product launch are the groups at the beginning of the process, innovators and early adopters.[58]

A.C. Nielsen, one of the world's leading market research firms, reports that early buyers are critical in the success of a new product because they provide critical insights on the degree to which consumers will accept the product. People in this group are more likely to communicate their preferences (and dislikes) to others. They are also likely to influence the decisions of people who come later in the adoption process. As a result, companies such as Procter & Gamble and Electronic Arts spend a great deal of time learning about early buyers of their products.[59]

Consumer Product Adoption Process

As we have discussed, new products come in various forms, from new-to-the-world products to incremental changes to existing products, but the consumer adoption process is less concerned with the product definition and more concerned with the individual consumer's perception of the product. A product can be in the market for a long time and still be considered an innovation to an individual consumer. The **innovation diffusion process** is how long it takes a product to move from first purchase to last purchase (the last set of users to adopt the product). An individual moves through five stages before adopting a product:

1. **Awareness**—know of the product, but insufficient information to move forward through the adoption process.

2. **Interest**—receive additional information (advertising, word of mouth) and motivated to seek out added information for further evaluation.
3. **Evaluation**—combine all information (word of mouth, reviews, advertising) and evaluate the product for trial purchase.
4. **Trial**—purchase the product for the purpose of making a value decision.
5. **Adoption**—purchase the product with the intent of becoming a dependable user.

Marketers, particularly those involved in a new-product launch, want to move consumers through the process as quickly as possible. One reason to spend heavily at the product launch phase is to move people through awareness, interest, and evaluation, getting them to try the product quickly. Sales promotion tools (coupons, product sampling), endorsements, third-party reviews, and other marketing communications methods are all part of a strategy to move people toward trial purchase. Trial purchase is the focus of a product launch marketing plan because if you can get consumers to try the product, you can win them over with superior product design, features, and value.[60]

The Diffusion of Innovations

Everyone in a target market falls into one of five groups based on his or her willingness to try the innovation (see Exhibit 7.12). A person can be an innovator or early adopter in one product category and a laggard in another. However, marketers want to identify where individuals fall on the innovation curve for a particular product or product class. Interestingly, the process by which products become diffused in a market remains remarkably constant. Research into the adoption of the Internet in the United States found it very similar to the adoption of color television in the United States in the 1960s.

The process begins with a very small group who adopt the product, perhaps through targeted marketing (they are given the product to try, for example) or high involvement with the product. From there, larger numbers in the different groups move through the adoption process. Two-thirds of all adopters for a given product fall in the early and late majority. The final group, laggards, may not move into the adoption process until late in the product's life cycle.[61]

EXHIBIT 7.12 | Consumer Product Adoption Chart

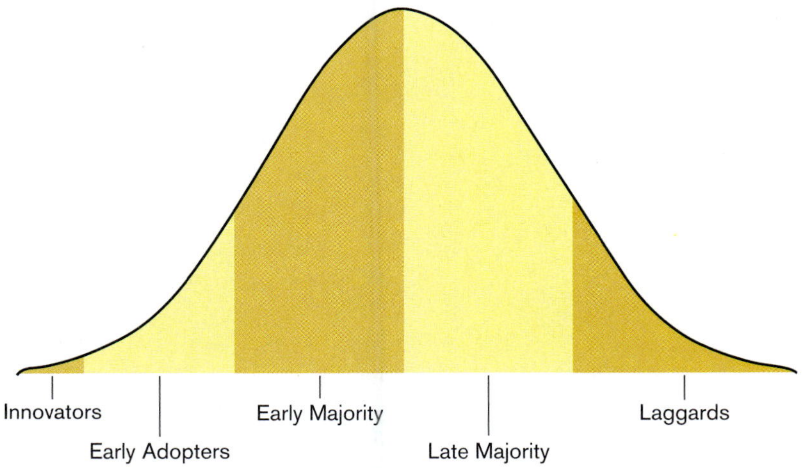

Source: www.rubiconconsulting.com.

- **Innovators** (2.5 percent)—Product enthusiasts enjoy being the first to try and master a new product. Individuals in this group are prime candidates for beta testing and represent a good source of feedback late in the product development process or early in the product launch phase.
- **Early Adopters** (13 percent)—Product opinion leaders seek out new products consistent with their personal self-image. This group is not price-sensitive and is willing to pay the price premium for a product. At the same time, early adopters demand a high level of personalized service and product features.
- **Early Majority** (34.5 percent)—Product watchers want to be convinced of the product's claims and value proposition before making a commitment. This group is considered critical to long-term success as they take the product into the main stream.
- **Late Majority** (34 percent)—Product followers are price-sensitive and risk-averse. They purchase older-generation or discontinued models with lower prices and fewer product features.
- **Laggards** (16 percent)—Product avoiders want to evade adoption as long as possible. Resistant to change, they will put off the purchase until there is no other option.

SUMMARY

The product experience is the essential element in delivering value to the customer. Organizations understand that, no matter what else happens in the customer experience, the product must deliver on its value proposition to the customer. Products have a detailed set of characteristics that include defined customer benefits as well as core and enhanced product attributes. Companies develop individual product strategies consistent with broader product line and category strategies that, in turn, achieve corporate goals and objectives. Products follow a product life cycle that includes introduction, growth, maturity, and decline. As a product moves through the cycle, marketing strategies change to meet new market conditions.

A key to the long term success of any company is the development of new products. New product development can take many forms from "new to the world" to variations of existing products. The new product development process has three elements, identify the product opportunity, define the product opportunity, and develop the product opportunity. A new product moves through a diffusion process with a market as different people purchase the product at different times.

KEY TERMS

product 199
stock-keeping unit (SKU) 200
essential benefit 200
core product 200
enhanced product 201
tangibility 203
durability 203
nondurable product 203
durable product 203
convenience goods 203
shopping goods 204
specialty goods 204
unsought goods 204
materials 204
parts 204
MRO supplies (maintenance, repair, operating) 205
capital goods 205
form 205
features 207
conformance 208
reliability 208
repairability 209
style 210
product line 210
product mix 211
product life cycle (PLC) 213
fads 215
market penetration 217
market skimming 217
new-to-the-world product 218
upgrades or modifications to existing products 218
additions to existing product lines 218
reposition existing products 218
cost reduction 219
go-to-market mistake 222
stop-to-market mistake 222
business case analysis 224
innovation diffusion process 228

APPLICATION QUESTIONS

1. You are a marketing manager for Starbucks. Describe the following as it relates to the product experience at Starbucks: essential benefit, core product, and enhanced product. Now imagine you are the marketing manager for Aquafresh Extreme toothpaste. Describe the product experience in terms of essential benefit, core product, and enhanced product.
2. Choose two comparable phones from Samsung and Microsoft/Nokia and examine each product. How does the product form differ between the two products? How are they the same? Now consider the features of the two products. What features are unique to each phone? Which phone, overall, appeals to you most and why?
3. One of the most difficult characteristics of a product to define is style. You are the marketing manager for Cadillac; define the product style for an Escalade. Compare and contrast that with product style for a Chevrolet Tahoe (another large SUV built on the same platform as the Escalade).
4. You are the marketing manager for Coca-Cola products in the United States. Describe the product line for Coke-branded products and briefly describe how each product differs from the other products in the Coke brand product line.

5. Motorola is introducing a new phone that incorporates Internet surfing capability using new LTE technology, a GPS program, and other new features that will greatly expand the features available on a cell phone. Develop a marketing strategy for the launch of the new product.

MANAGEMENT DECISION CASE: Product Development and Renewal in the Toy Market

Toy manufacturers have a tricky task. Each year they license images and characters from a new crop of TV shows and movies without actually knowing for sure which ones will be popular—hoping to sell enough product related to those characters to gain an acceptable ROI. In addition, they develop other nonlicensed product lines with the hope that those lines too will become wildly popular and create a positive cash flow and profits. Sometimes, a toy company gets lucky and really hits the jackpot. That's what happened with Mattel in the early years of its existence.

Mattel first started as a business making picture frames in 1945. With the war over and a desire to make the most of resources, one of Mattel's owners had the bright idea of building doll houses with the scrap wood that was left over from making the picture frames. The doll houses were an immediate success and quickly took over for the frames as the company's main focus. Fast-forward to 1959: Mattel introduces Barbie, an iconic brand that is sold in 150 countries. The Barbie line of products has since greatly expanded to include numerous friends such as Ken, Summer, Midge, Nikki, and Teresa, to name a few. In addition, she has had several occupations over the decades ranging from dentist to race car driver, and she and her friends have a multitude of accessories including a house, a cool car, and enough different clothing options that they never have to wear the same thing twice.

Despite Barbie's wild success (she currently has over 10.1 million Facebook friends), Mattel realized that she appealed to just half of the population (girls) and among that group, mainly to a narrow age band. To broaden out its overall appeal, Mattel developed the Hot Wheels, Tyco, and Fisher Price lines of products appealing to boys, preschoolers, and infants. In addition, the company has a strong relationship with the Walt Disney Company and produces toys for many of Disney's movies, including *Cars* and *Toy Story*.

All of this activity is emblematic of what it takes to develop a value-enhancing product that continues to provide positive returns to both Mattel and its customers. The essential benefit provided by Mattel's various product lines includes fantasy play and creativity. The core product includes the product form, which is the doll, the brand name Barbie, and all of the many accessories that provide the overall experience of playing with a Barbie doll. For Tyco the core product includes the remote-control vehicle, the vehicle's brand name, the remote controller itself, and a warranty for a specific time frame. In terms of the enhanced product, for Barbie it includes interactive play on the website, while for a Tyco remote-control vehicle it might include an owner's group in which people who own the same remote-controlled vehicle can exchange notes and comments about their experiences.

Despite all of Mattel's success, they continuously are looking for new market opportunities. Recently, they introduced a line of products called Monster High. This product line brings to life fashionable teenage descendants of famous monsters like Frankenstein and Dracula. As the line progresses through the life cycle of introduction, growth, maturity, and possibly decline, marketing managers at Mattel will continuously adjust their marketing strategy for Monster High in an effort to extend its product life cycle. At the same time, you can bet that product researchers will be hard at work developing the next potentially big toy sensation for Mattel.

Questions for Consideration

1. How would you classify Barbie as a product—as a convenience, shopping, or specialty product? Discuss why you chose that particular classification given the amount of shopping effort required by consumers to purchase a Barbie and the strategy utilized by Mattel to market Barbie.

2. American Girl, another line of popular dolls, also is manufactured and distributed by Mattel. Contrast the American Girl marketing strategy with that used by Mattel to market Barbie. Where do the strategies differ and where are they similar?

3. Discuss the various marketing strategies Mattel executives may use for Monster High as it progresses through the stages of the product life cycle. What aspects of the marketing mix should be emphasized at each stage and discuss why you believe those aspects are most important.

Sources: www.barbie.com/activities/friends/, accessed December 10, 2013; www.facebook.com/barbie, accessed December 10, 2013; Ian Shaffer, "Innovation Should Keep Mattel Ahead of the Pack; Not Content with Barbie Sale Alone," *The Montreal Gazette*, August 13, 2013 Business section, p. B2.

MARKETING PLAN EXERCISE

ACTIVITY 8: Define the Product Strategy

In this chapter we looked at the essential element in the marketing mix—the product. Developing an effective marketing plan begins with an understanding of your product, its role in the company's overall business strategy, and, more specifically, where it fits in the company's product mix. Additionally, it is important to establish a new-product development process that ensures a new-product pipeline of potentially successful new products. Your assignment in this chapter includes the following activities:

1. Define the product to include:
   a. Value proposition.
   b. Characteristics.
   c. Nature of product (consumer versus business product, and what type of product it represents).
2. Identify the product's position in the product line (if offered with other similar products) and, more broadly, the company's overall product mix. Address the following:
   a. How would this product differ from other products in the product line (if appropriate)?
   b. What price point would this product target and is there any conflict with existing products?
   c. How does the marketing message differ for this product from other products in the product line?

ACTIVITY 9: New-Product Development

In this chapter we looked at the essential element in the marketing mix—the product. Developing an effective marketing plan begins with an understanding of your product, its role in the company's overall business strategy, and, more specifically, where it fits in the company's product mix. Additionally, it is important to establish a new-product development process that ensures a new-product pipeline of potentially successful new products. Marketing plan activities in this section include the following:

1. Define a new-product development process for next-generation products. While the product may be new, it is important to have a plan in place for next-generation models.
   a. Do you want to expand existing products into new markets?
   b. Define expected features that will likely be added over the next 36 months and a timeline for introduction.
2. Does the company want to be known as innovative with regards to new-product development?
3. Chart the diffusion of the company's product into the market. Define each of the groups in the diffusion.

NOTES

1. Kaplan, D. (2013, March 7). Subject of Cars Revs Up GM's Chief. *Houston Chronicle.* Retrieved March 13, 2013, from www.houstonchronicle.com/business/article/subjuct-of-cars-revs-up-GM-s-chief-4334638.php.
2. Albert M. Muniz Jr. and Hope Jensen Schau, "Religiosity in the Abandoned Apple Newton Brand Community," *Journal of Consumer Research* 31, no. 4 (2005), pp. 737–48; and Hope Jensen Schau and Albert Muniz, "A Tale of Tales: The Apple Newton Narratives," *Journal of Strategic Marketing* 14, no. 1 (2006), pp. 19–28.
3. Hollister Jeans, www.hollisterco.com, January 2014.
4. Jack Neff, "Tide's Washday Miracle: Not Doing Laundry," *Advertising Age* 78, no. 45 (2007), p. 12.
5. Andreas B. Eisingerich and Tobias Kretschmer, "In E-Commerce, More Is More," *Harvard Business Review* 86, no. 3 (2008), pp. 20–35.
6. Lance A. Bettencourt and Anthony W. Ulwick, "The Customer-Centered Innovation Map," *Harvard Business Review* 86, no. 5 (2008), p. 109.
7. DROID RAZR M-4G LTE–Android Smartphone, Motorola Mobility LLC. USA. (n.d.), www.motorola.com/us/consumers/DROID-RAZR-M-BY-MOTOROLA/m-DROID-RAZR-M,en_US,pd.html?selectedTab=tab-2&cgid=mobile-phones#tab, accessed March 13, 2013.
8. Yukair Iwatani Kane, "Sony, Sharp Form Venture to Make LCD-TV Panels," *The Wall Street Journal,* February 27, 2008, p. B2; and Yukari Iwatani Kane and Evan Ramstad, "Sharp Grabs LCD-TV Sales Lead," *The Wall Street Journal,* November 2, 2007, p. B6.
9. Stephen L. Vargo and Robert F. Lusch, "From Goods Go Service(s): Divergences and Convergences of Logics," *Industrial Marketing Management* 37, no. 3 (2008), pp. 254–68.
10. Preyas S. Desai, Oded Koenigsberg, and Devarat Purohit, "The Role of Production Lead Time and Demand Uncertainty in Marketing Durable Goods," *Management Science* 53, no. 1 (2007), pp. 150–59.
11. M. W. Thomas, "USAA Has Top Scores in Customer Satisfaction Survey," *San Antonio Business Journal,* February 26, 2013, www.bizjournals.com/sanantonio/news/2013/02/26/usaa-has-top-scores-in-customer.html.
12. "Bombardier Electric Technology to Be Tested on Buses in Montreal, Germany," *The Canadian Press/Times Colonist,* February 13, 2013, www.timescolonist.com/life/driving/bombardier-electric-technology-to-be-tested-on-buses-in-montreal-germany-1.76067.
13. Marc Abrahams, "A Pointed Lesson about Product Features," *Harvard Business Review* 84, no. 3 (2006), pp. 21–23.
14. J. Ostrower and C. V. Hasselt, "Bombardier Challenges Boeing, Airbus," *The Wall Street Journal,* March 6, 2013, http://online.wsj.com/article/SB10001424127887323628804578344 68.
15. Sony Corp, www.sony.com, January 2014
16. Ben Levisohn, "Keep That Rolex Ticking," *BusinessWeek,* March 24, 2008, no. 4076, p. 21; and Stacy Meichtry, "How Timex Plans to Upgrade Its Image," *The Wall Street Journal,* June 21, 2007, p. B6.
17. Djoko Setijono and Jens J. Dahlgaard, "The Value of Quality Improvements," *International Journal of Quality and Reliability Management* 25, no. 3 (2008), pp. 292–306; and Gavriel Melirovich, "Quality of Design and Quality of Conformance: Contingency and Synergistic Approaches," *Total Quality Management and Business Excellence* 17, no. 2 (2008), pp. 205–20.
18. Rajeev K. Goel, "Uncertain Innovation with Uncertain Product Durability," *Applied Economics Letters* 13, no. 13 (2006), pp. 829–42.
19. Chuniai Chen, Jun Yang, and Christopher Findlay, "Measuring the Effect of Food Standards on China's Agricultural Exports," *Review of World Economics* 144, no. 1 (2008), pp. 83–107; and David Kesmodel and Nicholas Zamiska, "China Curbs Garlic, Ginger Exports to U.S.," *The Wall Street Journal,* September 18, 2007, p. D7.
20. Kamalini Ramdas and Taylor Randall, "Does Component Sharing Help or Hurt Reliability? An Empirical Study in the Automotive Industry," *Management Science* 54, no. 5 (2008), pp. 922–39; and Niranjan Pati and Dayr Reis, "The Quality Learning Curve: An Approach to Predicting Quality Improvement in Manufacturing and Services," *Journal of Global Business Issues* 1, no. 2 (2007), pp. 129–41.
21. Bimai Nepal, Leslie Monplaisir, and Nanua Singh, "A Framework to Integrate Design for Reliability and Maintainability in Modular Product Design," *International Journal of Product Development* 4, no. 5 (2007), pp. 459–674.
22. Ravinda Chitturi, Rajagopal Raghunathan, and Vijar Mahajan, "Delight by Design: The Role of Hedonic versus Utilitarian Benefits," *Journal of Marketing* 72, no. 3 (2008), pp. 48–61.
23. A. Sperduti, "Anthony Sperduti on Rebooting J.Crew Retail," *Bloomberg Businessweek,* January 24, 2013, www.businessweek.com/articles/2013-01-24/anthony-sperduti-on-rebooting-j-dot-crew-retail.
24. Penelope Green, "While You Were Out, the Post-it Went Home," *New York Times,* June 28, 2007, p. F1.

25. J. Goudreau, "The Campbell Soup Turnaround Is Heating Up. Will It Sizzle or Fizzle Out?," *Forbes,* February 21, 2013, www.forbes.com/sites/jennagoudreau/2013/02/21/the-campbell-soup-turnaround-is-heating-up-will-it-sizzle-or-fizzle-out/.
26. Muhammad A. Noor, Rick Rabiser, and Paul Grunbacher, "Agile Product Line Planning: A Collaborative Approach and a Case Study," *Journal of Systems and Software* 81, no. 6 (2008), pp. 868–81.
27. Trefis Team, "Best Buy's Price Matching Strategy Helps as Turnaround Efforts Drag On," *Forbes,* March 13, 2013, www.forbes.com/sites/greatspeculations/2013/03/06/best-buys-price-matching-strategy-helps-as-turnaround-efforts-drag-on/.
28. Peter N. Golder and Gerald J. Tellis, "Growing, Growing, Gone: Cascades, Diffusion, and Turning Points in the Product Life Cycle," *Marketing Science* 23, no. 2 (2004), pp. 207–21.
29. Kate Niederhoffer, Rob Mooth, David Wiesenfeld, and Jonathon Gordon, "The Origin and Impact of CPG New Product Buzz: Emerging Trends and Implications," *Journal of Advertising* 47, no. 4 (2007), pp. 420–36.
30. Bloomberg, "Estee Lauder Puts on Right Strategy for Africa," Gulfnews.com, March 18, 2013, http://gulfnews.com/business/retail/estee-lauder-puts-on-right-strategy-for-africa-1.1159643.
31. Ashley Vance, "3D Printers: Make Whatever You Want," *Bloomberg Businessweek,* April 26, 2012, www.businessweek.com/articles/2012-04-26/3d-printers-make-whatever-you-want#p1.
32. Glen M. Schmidt and Cheryl T. Druehl, "When Is a Disruptive Innovation Disruptive?," *Journal of Product Innovation Management* 25, no. 4 (2008), pp. 347–62; and Lee G. Demuth III, "A Viewpoint on Disruptive Innovation," *Journal of American Academy of Business* 13, no. 1 (2008), pp. 86–92.
33. Geoffrey A. Moore, "Darwin and the Demon: Innovating within Established Enterprises," *Harvard Business Review* 82, no. 7/8 (2005), pp. 86–98.
34. Kenneth J. Petersen, Robert B. Handfield, and Gary L. Ragatz, "Supplier Integration into New Product Development: Coordinating Product, Process and Supply Chain Design," *Journal of Operations Management* 23, no. 3/4 (2003), pp. 371–89.
35. Cornelia Droge, Roger Calantone, and Nukhet Harmancioglu, "New Product Success: Is It Really Controllable by Managers in Highly Turbulent Environments?" *Journal of Production Innovation Management* 25, no. 3 (2008), pp. 272–90.
36. Mark Rogowsky, "Are Tesla's Electric Cars 'Niche Vehicles'? Is Your Gas-Powered Car One Too?," *Forbes,* February 19, 2013, www.forbes.com/sites/markrogowsky/2013/02/19/are-teslas-electric-cars-niche-vehicles-is-your-gas-powered-car-one-too/.
37. "Eclipse 500 Wins Export Approvals," *Flight International* 173, no. 5137 (2008), p. 12; and Bruce Nussbuam, "The Best Product Design of 2007," *BusinessWeek,* no. 4044 (2007), p. 52.
38. Rajesh Sethi and Zafar Iqbal, "State Gate Controls, Learning Failure, and Adverse Effect on Novel New Products," *Journal of Marketing* 72, no. 1 (2008), pp. 118–32.
39. Robert F. Brands, "Innovation: 3M's Lessons to Be Learned," *Huffington Post,* May 16, 2012, www.huffingtonpost.com/robert-f-brands/innovation-3ms-lessons-to_b_1515768.html.
40. "Odyssey Software's Athena Add-In for Microsoft's System Center Configuration Manager 2007 Names 'Best of Tech Ed 2008 IT Professional Awards, Finalist," *PR Newswire,* June 3, 2008.
41. John Saunders, Veronica Wong, Chris Stagg, and Mariadel Mar Souza Fontana, "How Screening Criteria Change during Brand Management," *Journal of Product and Brand Management* 14, no. 4/5 (2005), pp. 239–50.
42. "Apple Prototypes: 5 Products We Never Saw," *Applegazette,* June 20, 2008, www.applegazette.com/mac.
43. Raul O. Chao and Stylianon Kavadias, "A Theoretical Framework for Managing the New Product Development Portfolio: When and How to Use Strategic Buckets," *Management Science* 54, no. 5 (2008), pp. 907–22.
44. Dean Richard Prebble, Gerritt Anton De Waal, and Cristiaan de Groot, "Applying Multiple Perspectives to the Design of a Commercialization Process," *R&D Management* 38, no. 3 (2008), pp. 311–27.
45. Karan Girotra, Christian Terwiesch, and Karl T. Ulrich, "Valuing R&D Projects in a Portfolio: Evidence from the Pharmaceutical Industry," *Management Science* 53, no. 9 (2007), pp. 1452–66.
46. Lenny H. Pattikawa, Ernst Verwaal, and Harry R. Commandeur, "Understanding New Product Project Performance," *European Journal of Marketing* 40, no. 11/12 (2006), pp. 1178–93.
47. Nukhel Armancioglu, Regina C. McNally, Roger J. Calantone, and Serdar S. Durmusoglu, "Your New Product Development (NPD) Is Only as Good as Your Process: An Exploratory Analysis of New NPD Process Design and Implementation," *R&D Management* 37, no. 95 (2007), pp. 399–415.
48. Glen L. Urban and John R. Hauser, "Listening In to Find and Explore New Combinations of Customer Needs," *Journal of Marketing* 68, no. 2 (2004), pp. 72–90.
49. B. Sorescu and Jelena Spanjol, "Innovation's Effect on Firm Value and Risk: Insights from Consumer

Packaged Goods," *Journal of Marketing* 72, no. 2 (2008), pp. 114–31.

50. "Starbucks Announces Agreement to Acquire La Boulange Bakery to Elevate Core Food Offerings and Build Premium, Artisanal Bakery Brand," *Starbucks News,* http://news.starbucks.com/article_display.cfm?article_id=661, accessed March 12, 2013.
51. J. Brock Smith and Mark Colgate, "Customer Value Creation: A Practical Framework," *Journal of Marketing Theory and Practice* 15, no. 1 (2007), pp. 7–24.
52. Sanjiv Erat and Stylianos Kavadias, "Sequential Testing of Product Designs: Implications for Learning," *Management Science* 54, no. 5 (2008), pp. 956–69.
53. Wei-Lun Chang, "A Typology of Co-Branding Strategy: Position and Classification," *Journal of the Academy of Business* 12, no. 92 (2008), pp. 220–27.
54. Sharan Jagpal, Kamel Jedidi, and M. Jamil, "A Multibrand Concept Testing Methodology for New Product Strategy," *Journal of Product Innovation Management* 24, no. 1 (2007), pp. 34–51.
55. Destan Kandemir, Roger Calantone, and Rosanna Garcia, "An Exploration of Organizational Factors in New Product Development Success," *Journal of Business and Industrial Marketing* 21, no. 5 (2006), pp. 300–18.
56. Lance Whitney, "Windows 8.1 Closes in on Vista among Desktop OS Users," CNET, January 2, 2014, http://news.cnet.com/8301-10805_3-57616441-75/windows-8.1-closes-in-on-vista-among-desktop-os-users/
57. Henrik Sjodin, "Upsetting Brand Extensions: An Enquiry into Current Customer Inclination to Spread Negative Word of Mouth," *Journal of Brand Management* 15, no. 4 (2008), pp. 258–62; and Niederhoffer et al., "The Origin and Impact of CPG New Product Buzz."
58. Christophe Van Den Butte and Yogesh V. Joshi, "New Product Diffusion with Influentials and Imitators," *Marketing Science* 26, no. 3 (2007), pp. 400–24.
59. Joe Wilkie and Nick Sorvillo, "Targeting Early Adopters: A Means for New Product Survival," A.C. Nielsen, June 23, 2008.
60. Kapil Bawa and Robert Shoemaker, "The Effects of Free Sample Promotions on Incremental Brand Sales," *Marketing Science* 23, no. 3 (2004), pp. 345–64.
61. Morris Kalliny and Angela Hausman, "The Impact of Cultural and Religious Values on Consumer's Adoption of Innovation," *Journal of the Academy of Marketing Studies* 11, no. 1 (2007), pp. 125–37; and Stacy L. Wood and C. Page Moreau, "From Fear to Loathing? How Emotion Influences the Evaluation and Early Use of Innovations," *Journal of Marketing* 70, no. 3 (July 2006), pp. 44–60.

CHAPTER 08

Build the Brand

LEARNING OBJECTIVES

LO 8-1 Recognize the essential elements in a brand.

LO 8-2 Learn the importance of brand equity in product strategy.

LO 8-3 Explain the role of packaging and labeling as critical brand elements.

LO 8-4 Define the responsibility of warranties and service agreements in building consumer confidence.

BRAND: THE FUNDAMENTAL CHARACTER OF A PRODUCT

LO 8-1

Recognize the essential elements in a brand.

Why does someone purchase an $85 Ralph Lauren Polo shirt instead of a $10 Walmart pullover polo shirt? In part, the quality is better, but something else is also driving the purchase—a complex relationship between the individual purchasing the shirt and the brand Polo. Why do Ralph Lauren and other manufacturers such as Lacoste and Tommy Hilfiger prominently display their logo on merchandise? Because people who buy those products want others to know who manufactured the shirt, jacket, or pants. Equally important, the manufacturers want everyone to see the logo. Both customers and manufacturers realize the importance of the brand.

If asked, you could probably identify the logo for Ralph Lauren Polo, but how would you define the Polo brand? Exhibit 8.1 highlights some of the different ways Ralph Lauren translates his brand into products and services. A **brand,** as defined by the American Marketing Association, is "a name, term, sign, symbol, or design, or a combination of them, intended to identify the goods or services of one seller or groups of sellers and to differentiate them from those of competitors." While the "Polo Pony" is a recognizable symbol of Polo products, customers and noncustomers assign a much deeper meaning to the brand.[1] In this chapter we'll focus on branding and critical elements in the branding process to learn more about this essential product building block. First we will discuss the many roles of a brand, including those assigned by customer, company, and competition as well as potential problems for a brand. Next, we'll examine an important concept—brand equity—which is used to frame the relationship of the brand to the customer. In addition, we examine four branding strategies. Finally, two other key elements of a customer's overall perception of a brand are examined: packaging and labeling as well as warranties and service agreements.

The importance of branding is not limited to consumer products. Business-to-business customers also consider brands when making purchase decisions. As we will see in this chapter, brands are important for customers and companies, which is why marketing managers are vitally interested in learning as much as possible about their customers' brand perceptions when developing effective branding strategies.

Brands Play Many Roles

Brands take on different roles for customers, manufacturers, even competitors. No other single product element conveys more information about the company. **Branding strategy** is an integral part of the product development process because companies know that successful new products result from a well-conceived branding strategy. At the same time, established products are defined, in large measure, by their brand, and companies work very hard to protect this critical asset. Let's examine brand roles.

Customer Brand Roles Whether the customer is a consumer or another business, brands have three primary roles. First, the brand conveys information about the product. Without any additional data, customers construct expectations about quality, service, even features based on the brand. Years after ending the marketing communications campaign, many customers see the FedEx logo and still think, "Absolutely, positively, overnight." The logo itself creates an expectation of service though FedEx now offers many delivery options and products.

Scent-Air Technology is one of several companies that will custom-design a fragrance to help consumers connect with a brand. For example, the St. Louis Rams U.S. football team pump a candy cane smell into its stadium and the team was so pleased with the results that it intends to expand the program next year, pumping different scents into different parts of the stadium. A wide range of companies from Bloomingdale's to General Dynamics are using "scent technology" in their offices and stores. These companies and others understand that scent plays a significant role in the overall brand experience. Products that smell good sell better.[2]

Brands also educate the customer about the product. People assign meaning to their product experiences by brand and, over time, make judgments about which brands are best at meeting their needs and which are not. As a result, product evaluations and purchase decisions become less formidable as the customer relies on

EXHIBIT 8.1 | The Polo Brand

the cumulative brand experience to simplify the purchase process.[3] The thought process works something like this: "I have had great product experiences with Brand X in the past. I will purchase Brand X again, making this purchase decision easier and faster." In essence the customer's "brand education" helps make the purchase decision with less effort. For many, home repair is daunting, so hardware retailers like Lowe's provide as much information as possible to reduce anxiety about the process. Indeed, Lowe's has worked hard to develop a reputation for making the home repair process easy for everyone.

A third brand role is to help reassure the customer in the purchase decision.[4] For many years there was a phrase in IT, "No one ever got fired for buying IBM." IBM's reputation and market dominance in the large computer and network server market meant that even if the product did not meet performance expectations, the customer felt more secure and less anxious about choosing IBM equipment. Older, established brands like Lysol provide a sense of security and reduce concerns about product quality (see Exhibit 8.2).

An increasingly important element of consumers' evaluation of brands is the degree to which they feel that brand shares the same values. Panera Bread focuses on creating this sense of shared value by promoting the brand as socially and environmentally responsible. With slogans like "Live consciously. Eat Deliciously." Panera makes an explicit connection between the value of the products it offers and the values important to its customers. The company focuses on its commitment to preparing fresh bread daily and using fresh ingredients such as antibiotic-free chicken, making it a good choice for customers' health, but also for their consciences, as natural or organic ingredients become more popular with Panera's target demographic. The risk with such branding is that any company action seen as contrary to the stated mission or perceived brand will create a sense of betrayal in customers. Nevertheless, for Panera Bread and other companies reaching out to the socially conscious consumer, understanding and using such branding effectively is crucial.[5]

EXHIBIT 8.2 | Consumer Brand Roles

Convey information: FedEx

Educate the customer: Lowe's

Help reassure the customer

Company Brand Roles Brands also perform important roles for the brand's sponsor (manufacturer, distributor, or retailer). They offer legal protection for the product through a trademark. By protecting the brand, the company is able to defend essential product elements such as its features, patentable ideas in manufacturing or product design, and packaging.[6] A second critical role is that brands offer an effective and efficient methodology for categorizing products.[7] Samsung has thousands of products across many product categories and branding helps keep track of those products.

Competitor Brand Roles Market-leading brands provide competitors with a benchmark against which to compete. In industries with strong market-leading brands, competitors design and build products targeted specifically at the market leader. In these situations, the competitor leverages its product strength against the market-leading brand's perceived weakness. For years, pleasure motorboat manufacturers would

Microsoft's Windows operating system is on the vast majority of computers around the world and is the standard operating systems for business, consumers, and governments. Now Microsoft has moved into a new market—mobile devices and more specifically tablet computers with its Surface line of tablets. But in the tablet computer market, Microsoft is not the market leader; indeed, companies like Apple and Samsung dominate the market. In addition, it competes against companies like Dell and HP that manufacture tablet computers with Microsoft's own Windows operating system.

frame their sales message with, "we are just as good as Sea Ray (the market leader) but less expensive." Sea Ray enjoyed a price premium in the market and competitors such as Regal, Chaparral, Rinker, and others would target their price points and feature mix against Sea Ray boats.

The Boundaries of Branding

While branding can have a strong effect on the product experience, it is not all-powerful. A good branding strategy will not overcome a poorly designed product that fails to deliver on the value proposition.[8] Too frequently companies

ETHICAL DIMENSION 8

Baileys' and the Digital Bar

While you may not be familiar with the company Diageo, you are almost certainly familiar with its brands, which hold dominant positions in their respective markets—Smirnoff (the No. 1 vodka in the world), Johnnie Walker (the No. 1 Scotch whisky in the world), Guinness (the No. 1 stout in the world), Captain Morgan (the No. 2 rum), Bailey's (the top liqueur), Jose Cuervo (the No. 1 tequila in the world), and Tanqueray (the No. 1 imported gin in the United States). The company's impressive list of brands is sold in more than 180 countries and dominates the premium spirit market with sales in excess of $16 billion.

Diageo, like many consumer product companies, is moving dramatically into digital marketing as it targets younger customers (millenials). However, unlike Procter & Gamble or Lever Brothers, Diageo and other alcohol companies must adhere to ethical standards on product usage. More specifically, the company is responsible for making sure it targets young people of legal drinking age. This creates a particular challenge in digital marketing as it is difficult, if not impossible, to know with certainty who is receiving the message. For example, a visit to a Diageo brand website will ask for the individual's birthday and location. If the visitor is from the United States, the individual must be over 21 to access the site; however, it is possible for someone to type in any date.

In an effort to more effectively target its younger customers, Diageo has created Facebook pages for many of its popular brands (Bailey's, Captain Morgan, Smirnoff). The company's market research suggests that this is one of the critical access points to its younger customers, while traditional marketing communications such as print do not work as well with this group. The company tailors each page to the interests of its followers. For example, the Smirnoff page focuses on recipes whereas Captain Morgan features photos.

Managers at Diageo watch the Facebook pages very closely and acknowledge that embracing new technologies creates some challenges as they remain concerned about underage access to adult content and violating ethical codes of conduct.

Ethical Perspective

1. **Diageo:** The company faces a challenge—to find effective digital technologies that connect with younger customers while maintaining ethical standards regarding underage drinking. How should the company deal with this challenge? If you were CEO at Diageo, how would you manage the company's Facebook pages? Would you limit access? Why or why not?
2. **Customers:** Do younger customers have a responsibility to voluntarily not participate in adult activities on Facebook?
3. **Government:** Given the growth of virtual communities, should the government create stricter guidelines for underage access to adult content?

put a good brand on a bad product, which often leads to erosion of the brand's value. Years before the iPod there was the Rio, the first commercially successful MP3 player introduced in 1998. Unfortunately, it suffered from a number of problems (small capacity, high price) and was not able to compete against the iPod that addressed those issues better. While highly regarded with an easy-to-use customer interface, the product, company, and brand were overwhelmed by other competitors and changing customer preferences.

A brand must also be protected. Counterfeit products or illegal activities conducted under the name of another company's brand can do significant damage to the brand.[9] This is why companies aggressively protect their brands around the world. Read Ethical Dimension 8 to find out more about the challenge Diageo, a leading spirits manufacturer, confronts in using digital marketing strategies while it protects the company's brands by maintaining ethical guidelines on product usage and access to confidential company data.

Finally, there must be real, identifiable, and meaningful differences among products. If all products are perceived to be equal, then it is more difficult to create a **brand identity,** which is a summary of unique qualities attributed to the brand.[10] Commodities are difficult to brand because customers often fail to perceive a difference among products. Major oil companies such as ExxonMobil, Shell, and BP want to differentiate their gasoline from competitors' but find it difficult because most people do not perceive a difference. Despite all their efforts, companies still find it difficult to overcome perceptions about a brand.

BRAND EQUITY—OWNING A BRAND

LO8-2

Learn the importance of brand equity in product strategy.

Equity is about ownership and value. For example, people often think of their homes when they consider the term *equity*. Home equity is the difference between the price of the home (asset) and the mortgage (liability). The larger the difference between the value of the property and the mortgage loan value, the more equity is accrued to the homeowner.

In a very real sense the same is true of brand equity. Every brand has positives—for example, Mercedes-Benz has a reputation for high-quality cars—and negatives—Mercedes also has a reputation for being expensive. The greater the perceived difference between the positives and negatives, the more a customer will develop equity in the brand. When customers take "ownership" of a brand, they make an "investment" that often extends beyond a financial obligation and includes emotional and psychological attachment. Then the company can realize a number of benefits, which we discuss in the next section; however, if the company does a poor job of managing the brand, such as lowering the product quality, those same customers may become negative. As a marketing manager, you want to learn about the brand equity of your product to better understand the relationship of your product to target markets and create more effective marketing strategies.[11]

Defining Brand Equity

Brand equity can be defined as "a set of assets (and liabilities) linked to a brand's name and symbol that adds to (or subtracts from) the value provided by a product or service to a firm or that firm's customers." This definition, developed by David Aaker, can be broken into five dimensions:[12]

- **Brand awareness:** The most basic form of brand equity is simply being aware of the brand. Awareness is the foundation of all other brand relationships. It signals a familiarity and *potential* commitment to the brand.
- **Brand loyalty:** This is the strongest form of brand equity and reflects a commitment to repeat purchases. Loyal customers are reassured by the brand and are often ambassadors to new customers. Loyal customers enable a company

to reduce marketing costs, leverage trade relationships, and speak to competitive threats with greater success.

- **Perceived quality:** Brands convey a perception of quality that is either positive or negative. Companies use a positive perceived quality to differentiate the product and create higher price points. Rolex watches have been able to sustain a price premium long into their life cycle because of the perceived quality in design and performance of the product.
- **Brand association:** Customers develop a number of emotional, psychological, and performance associations with a brand. In many cases, these associations become a primary purchase driver, particularly with brand loyal users. Dell has a reputation as a mass-market computer company with reasonably good-quality products but poor customer service. As a result, competitors, such as Hewlett-Packard, have been able to create market opportunities by associating their brand with higher levels of product support and customer service.
- **Brand assets:** Brands possess other assets such as trademarks and patents that represent a significant competitive advantage. Google is very protective of its search algorithm intellectual property, which, in the view of the company, gives the company a significant advantage over other search engines.

Let's consider the implications of these dimensions for marketing managers. First, moving customers from brand awareness to loyalty requires a thorough understanding of the target market and a successful marketing strategy. This is accomplished by developing a strong value offering and then communicating that to the target market. This is an essential element of the marketing manager's job.[13] Second, as we discussed in Chapters 4 and 5, customers develop perceptions about a product and associate it with attitudes and even emotion that are encompassed in a product's brand equity. By learning how customers view competitors' as well as their own brand, managers seek to affect people's perceptions and attitudes about their product.[14] Finally, managers protect their brands because they represent a vital asset for the company. They are vigilant about how they are portrayed in the marketplace, particularly by competitors.

Coca-Cola has created one of the most powerful global brands and its logo, displayed on a Coke truck in India, is recognized around the world.

Both the customers and the company have a stake in the brand's success. People do not want to purchase a brand if there is a question about quality, performance, or some other dimension of the product experience. They seek to maximize the benefits of the purchase and minimize the disadvantages. At the same time, companies understand every brand has liabilities that must be overcome to enhance the customer's perceived equity in the product. As a result,

The Carnival *Triumph* was the third Carnival cruise ship to experience serious problems in three years when a fire broke out onboard in February 2013. The fire, caused by a fuel line leak, damaged the ship's engine room and left the ship of 4,200 passengers with no power, little food, and few working bathrooms. Four days later the ship was finally towed into port, but the damage had been done. Although the company bounced back well after the 2010 fire on the Carnival *Splendor* caused the ship to lose power, and again after the Costa *Concordia* capsized in 2012, killing more than 30 people onboard, the third accident on a Carnival cruise made some investors, as well as the general public, lose confidence in the cruise line, and has tarnished the brand further. Although the brand may still recover, lower consumer perceptions can be extremely damaging in the short run.[16]

marketing managers constantly battle to increase brand equity or the customer's perception that the product's positive elements are greater than the negative elements. Brands do have real value and represent a significant company asset.[15] Exhibit 8.3 lists the most valuable brands in the world as measured by Brand Z. Note the value of these brands runs into the billions of dollars and changes are based on a number of things including changes in company strategy, brand success or failure, competitive pressures, and consumer acceptance.

Benefits of Brand Equity

Building brand equity takes time and money. Given the necessary commitment of resources required to build brand equity, it is reasonable to question whether it is worth the investment. High brand equity delivers a number of benefits to the customers and manufacturers, retailers, and distributors or brand sponsors who control the brand. Three benefits are perceived quality, brand connections, and brand

EXHIBIT 8.3 | The Most Valuable Brands in the World

	Category	Brand	Brand value 2013 SM	Brand contribution	Brand value % change 2013 vs 2012	Rank change
1	Technology		185,071	4	1%	0
2	Technology	Google	113,669	3	5%	1
3	Technology	IBM	112,536	3	−3%	−1
4	Fast Food	McDonald's	90,256	4	−5%	0
5	Soft Drinks	Coca-Cola	78,415	5	6%	1
6	Telecoms	at&t	75,507	3	10%	2
7	Technology	Microsoft	69,814	3	−9%	−2
8	Tobacco	Marlboro	69,383	3	−6%	−1
9	Credit Card	VISA	56,060	4	46%	6
10	Telecoms	中国移动通信 CHINA MOBILE	55,368	3	18%	0

Source: www.millwardbrown.com, June 21, 2013, http://www.millwardbrown.com/brandz/2013/Top100/Docs/2013_BrandZ_Top100_Chart.pdf.

loyalty. Let's consider each of these benefits from two perspectives, the customer and the company managing the brand or the brand sponsor. Many of these benefits are difficult to quantify but dramatically affect the success or failure of the brand.

Perceived Quality

Customers All things being equal (value proposition, product features), the *branded product gives customers a reason to buy.* This is a big advantage over unbranded products because customers will infer a level of quality from the branded product that facilitates their purchase decision.[17]

Brand sponsor The perceived quality of a brand provides three distinct benefits to the company. First, the perception of a brand's quality enables companies to extend the product range. Despite the economic slowdown of recent years, Ford's overall brand remains strong, which has been an important factor in building consumer interest and confidence in the C-Max, Ford's answer to the challenge of Prius's domination of the hybrid market. Second, the perception of quality can lead to a price premium opportunity.[18] P&G and other consumer products companies, for instance, enjoy consistently higher prices (and margins) than generic and other locally branded products in the same category. Finally, the perception of quality is an excellent differentiator in the market. For example, Ray-Ban was among the first to successfully brand sunglasses. Its branding strategy positions the sunglasses in the high-quality, premium-priced segment of the market and has been successful for more than 60 years.

Linking Benefit to Strategy Successful marketing strategy builds quality into the entire customer experience—product, service, and any interaction with the company. As companies extend their product lines, they must ensure the customer's brand experience remains positive; put simply, get it right before you introduce new products and services.[19] Quality can create a price premium, but managers understand that to validate that price premium they must constantly validate the value proposition for the customer and answer the customer question, "what makes this product different?"[20]

Brand Connections

Customers Two primary customer advantages result from brand associations. First, customers process, store, and retrieve product information by brand, which is a big advantage for strong brands. People are more likely to connect information with a brand they know rather than sort through information on unfamiliar brands. For example, consumers generally don't consider checking accounts from all banks; rather, they consider the branded product such as Bank of America's checking or another brand they know. A second benefit is that strong brands generate a more positive attitude toward the product.[21] Customers generally have more upbeat thoughts about a powerful brand than a weak brand or generic product. Cisco network servers are an industry leader with an excellent reputation supported by IT professionals, who use a wide range of other manufacturers.

Brand Sponsor When customers identify with a brand and then transfer that loyalty to the product, it creates an additional barrier to entry for new brands,[22] particularly for smaller firms that lack brand recognition. The default choice for network servers is Cisco in many corporate IT departments because executives have heard of Cisco even if they are not familiar with the product itself, thus making it harder for other servers to enter the market.

Linking Benefit to Strategy Because of customer brand connections, marketing managers generally want to extend the brand to new products. However, extending a brand needs to fit the target market's perception of the brand. When Toyota, Honda, and Nissan created luxury cars, they realized the need to create a new brand because the target markets would be less willing to accept their current brands in a luxury automobile. It is also important for strong brands to reinforce their market presence because it helps maintain a barrier to entry.

Brand Loyalty

Customers Brand loyal customers do not spend as much time searching for new information and, as a result, generally spend less time in the purchase decision process.[23] Motorcycles have experienced a high degree of brand loyalty among the major competitors such as BMW, Honda, and Harley-Davidson. It is not unusual to find owners across all three brands that are driving their third or fourth motorcycle.

Brand Sponsor Loyalty to the brand offers four distinct benefits that represent real market advantages to the brand sponsor. A well-executed branding strategy helps reduce long-term marketing costs, giving the brand sponsor more flexibility in the marketing budgets. Starbucks has a relatively small advertising budget because it is so well known that it doesn't need to spend much money raising brand awareness. Branded products give sponsors additional channel leverage.[24] Walmart's ability to extract lower prices from suppliers is legendary, but companies understand the importance of having their products in the world's largest retailer. Brand-loyal customers are vocal and tell others about their experiences, which attracts new customers. Disney has a loyal base of guests who visit the parks every year and become excellent ambassadors for the company. The company offers loyal users specific benefits to cultivate continued loyalty and encourage them to bring new guests. Finally, brand-loyal customers are forgiving, which enables companies to respond to a negative experience. Frequent guests to the Disney parks are not shy about voicing their opinions about everything from rides to the cleanliness of the parks. This creates a sense of ownership (equity) and loyalty.

Linking Benefit to Strategy Because of customer loyalty, marketing managers with a strong brand have greater flexibility in their marketing budgets. For example, Starbucks spends very little on paid advertising because customers already have brand equity. At the same time, Intel, which makes a product most people never see, spends a great deal of money building its brand and now people ask for "Intel Inside." Marketing managers know that loyal customers are great advocates for a brand. As a result, blogs and other online communities have become excellent tools for marketers to reinforce the brand's message.[25]

Companies continue to assess the effectiveness of social media as an advertising and brand promotion tool, with some opting to forgo advertising on social media platforms such as Facebook. The primary question is the benefits vis-à-vis the cost of paying for ad space. A Nielsen survey found several other key trends in social media. First, the vast majority of advertisers (89 percent) use free social media platforms such as Twitter, Pinterest, and Facebook as a way to interact with customers directly. Second, third-party social media platforms remain popular, as brands pay for blog posts or outside production of YouTube content in the hope of creating the next viral sensation. Spending on social media remains high as well, with 70 percent of the advertisers surveyed by Nielsen stating that up to 10 percent of their budgets went to such efforts—a number that continues to increase.[26]

BRANDING DECISIONS

Branding is a complex concept that brings together all the elements of a product into a single, focused customer idea. As a result, the branding decision is among the most important in marketing. Four basic strategic decisions in defining a brand are (1) stand-alone or family branding, (2) national or store branding, (3) licensing, and (4) co-branding.

Stand-Alone or Family Branding

Does the brand stand alone or exist as part of a brand family? Each choice has advantages and disadvantages. **Stand-alone brands** separate the company from the brand, which insulates the company if there is a problem with the brand. But stand-alone brands are expensive to create and maintain as there is little or no synergy between company brands. **Family branding** advantages and disadvantages are just the opposite. There is synergy among members of a brand family, but a negative event with one product often leads to negative publicity for the entire brand family.[27]

Lever Brothers, a worldwide leader in consumer products, follows a stand-alone brand strategy in its personal care division with nine brands that operate independently of each other (AXE, Dove, Lifebuoy, Lux, Ponds, Rexona, Sunsilk, Signal, and Vaseline) (see Exhibit 8.4). Heinz, on the other hand, uses a family branding strategy with all products introduced under the Heinz brand (ketchup and other condiments).

Companies also use branding to extend a line. For example, White Wave Foods, manufacturer of International Delight coffee creamers, frequently adds

EXHIBIT 8.4 | Sample of Branding Decisions

Lever Brothers

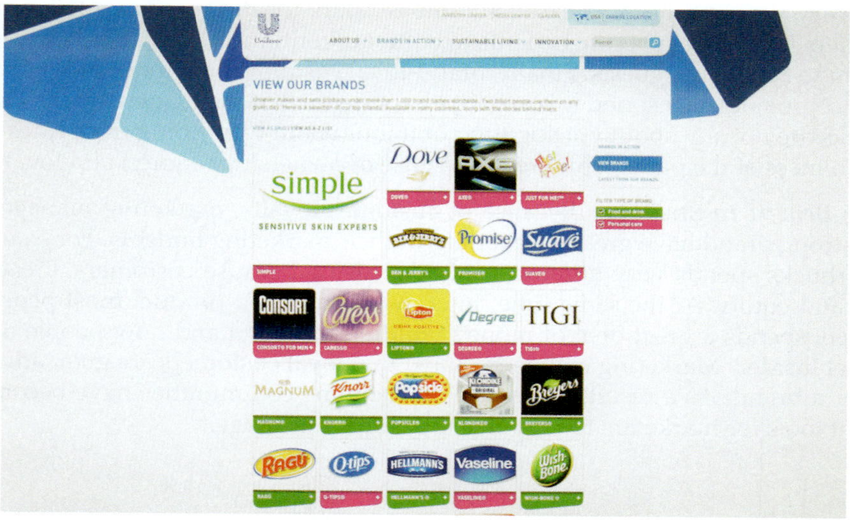

Heinz

new flavors to the line. Each new product extends the line of International Delight creamers. Increasingly, as companies seek new, creative ways to connect with customers, they are including them in the brand building process.[28] Also, a company can use its brand to expand into new product categories, known as a **category extension.**[29] Dell used its brand to expand into new product categories, including printers and consumer electronics such as LCD and plasma televisions. Exhibit 8.5 illustrates product extensions through brand, line, and category.

Pepsi is consistently one of the most effective brands in maximizing its social media marketing strategy. For several years they have developed creative social media campaigns around their advertising campaign, such as the Super Bowl, with great success. The company carefully monitors its social media communication with followers. Pepsi wants to engage its followers but not become too "hard sell" in the process. They believe in engaging Pepsi in social media such as Facebook because they want to know more about the product, but they don't want to be sold on Pepsi. The company believes this builds a stronger relationship between Pepsi drinkers and the Pepsi brand.[30]

EXHIBIT 8.5 | Brand, Line, and Category Extensions

Brand Extension: AXE

Line Extension: International Delights

Category Extension: Dell

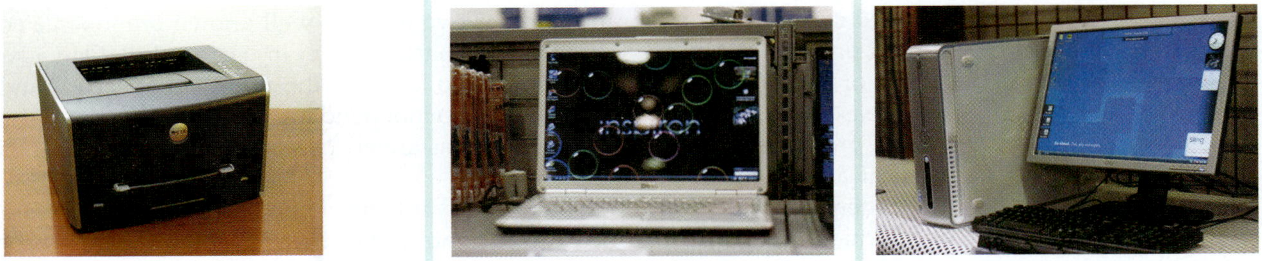

Yet another option is combining family brands with a more distinct individual product brand. Many companies follow a variation of this strategy. American Express introduced the One card that incorporates the American Express brand as well as its own stand-alone brand One.

National or Store Branding

Another decision is whether the product should adopt a national or store brand strategy. Large consumer products companies such as Procter & Gamble create **national brands** that are sold around the country under the same brand. Gillette Fusion, Crest toothpaste, and many others are national brands that can be found anywhere. National brands enable manufacturers to leverage marketing resources by creating efficiencies in marketing communications and distribution.[31] In addition, national brands generally have a higher perceived quality and, as a result, enjoy a price premium. However, developing a national brand is costly and lower-priced store brands are strong competitors in many product categories.[32]

An alternative to creating a national brand is a **store brand.** Many large retailers create a store brand to market their own products. For example, Target has a number of store brands including "Up & Up," which includes a broad range of household commodities (including everything from contact solution to laundry detergent to paper plates). Often contracting with the large manufacturers such as Procter & Gamble, retailers are able to compete directly with national brands by offering lower prices.

Licensing

Companies can also choose to extend their brand by **licensing**—offering other manufacturers the right to use the brand in exchange for a set fee or percentage of sales. There is very little risk to the brand sponsor, and licensing can generate incremental revenue. In addition, it can extend the brand and build more brand associations among new users, creating additional benefits.[33] The brand sponsor does need to monitor the licensees to assure product quality and proper use of the brand. Finally, license partners should fit the company's overall marketing strategy for the brand.[34] Among the best followers of the license strategy are movies, which license their brand (the movie) to a wide range of companies (restaurants, toy manufacturers, and others). *The Avengers* broke box office records with $1.5 billion in global box office revenue, but license agreements will keep making money for the franchise for years. Not only does Disney sell merchandise through the Marvel division, it has licensing agreements with Acura, Wyndham Hotels, and Hasbro, among many others.

Co-Branding

Frequently a company discovers advantages to linking its products with other products inside the company or externally with products from other companies, called **co-branding.** Co-branding joins two or more well-known brands in a common product or takes two brands and markets them in partnership. One advantage of co-branding is the opportunity to leverage the strengths of each brand to increase sales beyond what they could do independently. In addition, it may open each product up to new markets as well as lower costs by sharing marketing communications expenses.[35]

There are also several potential disadvantages. First, companies that co-brand externally give up some measure of control over their brand; by joining brands each company sacrifices some control to market the co-branded product. If one of the brands encounters a problem, for example, a quality issue, it can have a negative effect on the co-branded product. Another potential disadvantage is overexposure; a successful product does not want too many co-branded relationships because it can dilute the brand's image.[36]

Successful co-branding relationships work best when both brands come together as equals that make sense in the marketplace. Costco and American Express joined together to offer a Costco-American Express card that allows users to get rebates on their purchases at Costco while expanding the reach of American Express to Costco members. Critical decisions in the process revolve around resource commitments, which company is spending what, and what other resources are asked of each company. In addition, it is important for each company in the relationship to understand the performance objectives and expected benefits of each partner.

Generally, co-branding involves one of four relationships. The first is a joint venture between two companies; for example, American Express uses this model frequently, partnering with a variety of third-party financial institutions that issue the Amex-branded cards and are responsible for customer service and billing, but the credit card company supplies the transaction processing and merchant network. A second type of co-branding affiliation happens when a company combines two of its own products. Procter & Gamble combined its Crest toothpaste and Scope mouthwash to create Crest + Scope Outlast—a toothpaste that combines teeth cleaning properties with a "fresh breath feeling." A third type of co-branding relationship involves bringing multiple companies together to form a new branded product. For instance, Moxy Hotels is a joint venture effort from Marriott Hotels and Inter IKEA, the parent company of Swedish furniture company IKEA. The JV will be Marriot's first line of budget hotels in Europe, and is designed specifically to appeal to millennials. A final co-branding relationship involves retailers that share the same retail location. One example of this type of relationship in the United States is Barnes & Noble and Starbucks; the brands have similar target markets, so bringing Starbucks cafes under Barnes & Noble roofs strengthens the appeal.

PACKAGING AND LABELING: ESSENTIAL BRAND ELEMENTS

LO8-3

Explain the role of packaging and labeling as critical brand elements.

The product package and label must perform several critical roles in support of the brand. As a result, marketers, product developers, and package design specialists are involved in package design early in product development. Then, as product updates occur, the package is reconfigured to accommodate product modifications.

Until 2013, Doritos, the world's largest brand of tortilla chips, used different packaging for its chips in most of the 37 countries in which they were sold. While the designs were customized by country or region, Doritos executives felt that the lack of a unified brand was ultimately having a negative effect on customers' ability to connect to the product. According to Doritos's parent company PepsiCo Frito-Lay, Doritos customers globally have similar interests, and were often connected across borders through social media, but they lacked a "consistent way of speaking about the brand" as a result of the inconsistent branding. The new logo and bag designs are therefore meant to be a unifying force, giving a consistent, international face to the brand. The Doritos repackaging followed similar moves by Quaker, another PepsiCo brand, and by Pepsi itself, which has also been moving to consolidate its brand positioning around the world.[37]

Package Objectives

Protect Above all, the package must protect the product. The challenge is defining how much protection is necessary and cost-effective. In some cases, as in a can of Coke, the package is a significant component of the product's overall cost so there is concern about any increases in package cost. However, the can of Coke must be strong enough to hold the carbonated beverage under variations in temperature and other use conditions. Additionally, Coca-Cola must consider a variety of package materials (plastic, metal), sizes, and shapes (regular can, Coke's classic "contour" design), and it must design each to operate more or less the same under a variety of situations (see Exhibit 8.6).

Protecting customers from unauthorized access to the product is also part of package design. Prescription bottles and most over-the-counter medicines are required to be tamper-proof and child-proof to protect customers. Package safety seals provide a layer of security and verification to the customer that the product has not been altered before purchase. Finally, a growing concern is product theft, particularly in the retail store.[38] As a result, the package design should include anti-theft methodology, such as bar coding or magnetic stripes, that discourages shoplifting.

IDEO, a leading design firm, is working with other design companies, SmartDesign and Continuum, as well as the two largest professional associations, AIGA and Industrial Designers Society of America, to create a greener, more environmentally sensitive approach to package design. The goal is to create packaging that not only protects the product but also minimizes the environmental effects of the packaging.[39]

Communicate Packages communicate a great deal of information about the product. Some of that information is designed as marketing communications. At the point of sale, the package is the last marketing communication the customer will see before the purchase. Consequently, packaging plays a critical role in the company's overall marketing communications strategy, particularly for consumer products. Coke's distinctive contour bottle design (pictured in Exhibit 8.6) is so unique the package can be identified in the dark. Additionally, packaging offers the brand sponsor the opportunity to present the trademark, logo, and other relevant information in an appealing and persuasive manner. As the customer stands in front of a shelf full of products in a store, the marketer wants the brand to be clearly visible to the buyer. This means packaging must be designed to easily communicate critical brand messages quickly through color or design cues.[40] The familiar Coke swirl logo is among the most recognized brand symbols in the world and is easily identified on a store shelf or in a vending machine.

Unique package design can create a distinctive competitive advantage. Coke's contour bottle and L'eggs' egg-shape package for hosiery are important components of the overall brand image for those products. Their distinctive package design increases brand awareness at the point of sale where the customer makes the final purchase decision (see Exhibit 8.7).

EXHIBIT 8.6 | Various Coke Package Designs, Shapes, and Sizes

EXHIBIT 8.7 | Innovative Package Designs

Chewy Chips Ahoy bag

GOAL: Improve freshness and convenience

BACKSTORY: After months of in-home research, Kraft discovered that its customers often transferred Chips Ahoy cookies to jars for easy access and to avoid staleness. The company solved both problems by creating a patented resealable opening on the top of the bag.

BOTTOM LINE: Since launch, sales have nearly doubled from the older packaging.

Kleenex Tissues oval box

GOAL: Make a common household product unique

BACKSTORY: Americans spend more on home decor during the holidays than at any other time, so Kimberly-Clark introduced an oval-shape Kleenex box that was a clear departure from its usual rectangular shapes. The goal was to position the product as a must-have accessory rather than a functional item.

BOTTOM LINE: It was the company's best-selling holiday line in history and Kimberly-Clark has followed it with designs for each season of the year.

Crest Vivid White toothpaste package

GOAL: Stand out on store shelves

BACKSTORY: When Procter & Gamble's Crest set out to develop a premium whitening product, designers avoided creating yet another horizontal, graphics-heavy toothpaste box. Instead, they turned to the beauty aisle for inspiration. "We drew upon the vertical packaging and the deep metallic blue used to convey 'premium,'" says design manager Greg Zimmer.

BOTTOM LINE: Crest toothpaste sales have risen while competitor Colgate's sales have fallen, according to IRI.

(cont.)

EXHIBIT 8.8 | Kashi Good Friends Cereal Box

Promote Usage Package design also encourages product use. It does this in several ways. First, packages frequently show the product being used by a happy customer (Kashi Good Friends shows a couple enjoying a box of cereal), which supports the overall marketing message (see Exhibit 8.8). This connects the product to the target customer. Second, in many cases, packages visually demonstrate a product. Avery Paper shows each product clearly on the box; for example, a box of clear white mailing labels shows the label and how it can be used. Third, marketers and package designers make extensive use of blister packs (products encased in clear plastic) and other package designs to visibly present and protect the product. When buying a SanDisk Cruzer flash drive, it is much easier to visualize using it when you can see the product and have key features highlighted on the package.

EXHIBIT 8.7 | Innovative Package Designs *(cont.)*

Mazola Pure bottle

GOAL: Communicate a brand identity

BACKSTORY: Mazola shook up the pan-spray market with the debut of its alcohol-free oil, which aimed to profit from the growing trend in organic cooking. But the company knew that shoppers wouldn't discover the health-conscious brand if it encased the product in another steel cylinder. After considering hair spray and deodorant bottles, Mazola's designers settled on a curvy plastic container with an eye-catching iridescent finish.

BOTTOM LINE: The item overtook established brands to become the No. 2 spray.

Heinz Ketchup upside-down bottle

GOAL: Increase functionality

BACKSTORY: Heinz revolutionized the 170-year-old industry when it introduced its inverted bottle (consumers had complained for years about how hard it was to squeeze out that last bit of ketchup). The Pittsburgh-based company spent three years designing the convenient container, which is equipped with a vacuum cap that stops crustiness from forming around the lid.

BOTTOM LINE: Since the product's introduction, Heinz ketchup sales consistently beat the industry average sales growth.

Domino Sugar four-pound canister

GOAL: Create a more user-friendly package

BACKSTORY: To boost flat sales, Domino replaced the ubiquitous paper packaging for sugar. The easy-to-store plastic canister enables the Yonkers, New York, company to charge a premium for a package that actually contains less sugar.

BOTTOM LINE: The canister has become one of Domino's best-selling retail items.

Heineken is hoping that new packaging will help make its beer more recognizable globally. The traditional green beer bottles have gotten an update in the form of longer necks. The logo stayed the same to help keep the bottles recognizable: the same green oval, black scroll with "Heineken" across the center, and red star. The new bottles also have a thumb groove intended to help keep the drink colder by subtly encouraging drinkers to grip the bottle at a lower point. While these seem like minor changes, Heineken saw positive changes in drinker attitudes during initial market testing—the new bottles were perceived as more modern and progressive than the old. And Heineken is not the only beer manufacturer to bet that changing packaging will boost sales and improve customer perception of the brand: Miller Lite released new bottles for sale in restaurants and bars, and Budweiser is issuing "bow-tie" cans that are a play on the company's logo.[41]

Effective Packaging

Effective packaging accomplishes the objectives noted above in a persuasive, interesting, and visually appealing manner consistent with the target market's expectations. Materials, shape, colors, graphics, indeed all the design elements are used to create an aesthetically appealing package for the customer.

EXHIBIT 8.9 | The Meaning of Color in Package Design

Source: Portions reproduced from Capital Books, *Colors for Your Every Mood* with the permission of author and publisher, June 2013.

Color plays an important role in package design. Each color conveys a different mood.

Aesthetics Color plays a significant role in package design, indeed, in the entire branding strategy.[42] It is no accident that Coke's packaging has red as the dominant color (red connotes active and energetic) while Pepsi uses blue (fresh and relaxed). The colors reflect the brand and are carried through in the package design. Exhibit 8.9 relates the aesthetics of color to package design.

A visually appealing package, however, is not enough. It must be directed at the target audience to be successful. In most retail environments, a package has very little time to connect with the customer at the point of purchase. As a result, designs that are appropriate, interesting, and persuasive to the target market are critical.

Harmonizes with All Marketing Mix Elements A successful product package coordinates with all other marketing mix elements and is an extension of the product's marketing strategy. At the point of purchase, the package reinforces marketing communications by connecting advertising images (logo, pictures on the package) to the customer. As a result, package designers frequently work closely with advertising and other marketing communications specialists to orchestrate an integrated message and look throughout the marketing communications process. Canon digital cameras are packaged in a small box dominated by a picture of the camera. The boxes stand alone as a promotional tool that includes the logo, camera model number, and picture. In addition, the package design and logo are coordinated with other collateral marketing literature as well as the website.

Labeling

The package label is an important and valuable location. Often there is not enough space to accommodate all the information relevant parties would like to include on the label. Consider, for example, that government agencies require certain information on almost every label while company attorneys want disclaimers to limit product liability. Also, marketing managers want promotional messages and brand information, while product managers would like product use instructions.

Legal Requirements Labels must meet federal, state, even local rules and regulations. The Food and Drug Administration (FDA) requires all processed-food

Although wine consumption has grown steadily in the United States in the last 40 years, consumption of box wine has fallen behind as tastes have become more sophisticated. Synonymous with cheap, poor-quality wine, the box wine industry hardly seems to be an ideal market for innovation. Constellation Brands, however, is challenging this with Black Box, the first premium box wine. Indeed, Black Box uses the traditional "cheap" box to its advantage. Although still cardboard, with the twist-off cap expected on box wine, the package design emphasizes the quality of the product, touting the awards Black Box has received, and making use of simple, elegant colors, lines, and scripts. Black Box also touts the benefits of the box as opposed to traditional bottles: the wine stays good for four to six weeks, rather than just a few days, after opening; the packaging is biodegradable and therefore more eco-friendly; and the 500-mL version is more portable than traditional wine bottles.[43]

companies to provide detailed nutritional information clearly identifying calories, fats, carbohydrates, and other information. Other products must have warnings of a certain size that are easily read and understood by the customer.[44] Hazardous materials such as cleaning products, pesticides, and many other items require 14 different pieces of information be included on the label. It is easy to understand why space on the label is at such a premium.

Consumer advocacy groups and government agencies evaluate labels to identify misleading or mislabeled products and there is a long history of legal prosecution for inappropriate, unethical, even illegal product labeling. In 1914, the federal government, through the Federal Trade Commission, first ruled misleading or blatantly phony labels were illegal and represented unfair competition. Since then, additional legislation has been passed by the federal government such as the Fair Packaging and Labeling Act (1967). States have also passed legislation, which, in most cases, supports federal legislation but also extends specific rules and policies (for example, the Michigan Food Label Law of 2000).

Pharmaceutical companies must be especially careful with labeling because of the extensive legal ramifications of any problems with packaging. FDA regulations do not allow generic drug makers to update their labeling, even if new risks associated with the drug become clear, until they receive FDA approval, so generics are only responsible for the warnings available for the branded drug at the time the generic is released. As a result, Pfizer and other pharmaceuticals have heretofore been responsible only for their own branded drugs. A 2013 ruling by the Alabama Supreme Court, however, puts Pfizer and others at risk by ruling that Pfizer can be sued by a man who claims to have been harmed by taking a generic version of Pfizer's Reglan. While the case is working its way through the appeals process, the ramifications of this ruling for Pfizer and other drug makers is immense: they can be held responsible for not just the labeling of their drugs, but that of the generics they do not actually manufacture.[45]

Consumer Requirements Consumers want to use products out of the box and package labeling is the most convenient place for initial use instructions. Additionally, product precautions, simple assembly information, and appropriate age for product use may also be included on the package. Essentially, any information the consumer needs to make a product choice, particularly at the point of purchase, needs to be on the package.

Marketing Requirements Since package labeling represents the last marketing opportunity before the purchase decision, as much label space as possible is allocated to marketing communications. Brand, logo, product image, and other relevant marketing messages take up the dominant space on the label. On a box of Procter & Gamble's Bounce fabric softener sheets, the brand name "Bounce" is approximately 50 percent of the space on the front panel and the rest of the space is a bright color (orange) with clean fresh images of a sun rising and a green field. P&G uses the entire front panel of the box to support the marketing efforts of the brand (see Exhibit 8.10).

EXHIBIT 8.10 | Bounce Fabric Softener Packaging

WARRANTIES AND SERVICE AGREEMENTS: BUILDING CUSTOMER CONFIDENCE

LO8-4

Define the responsibility of warranties and service agreements in building consumer confidence.

Part of the customer's overall perception of a brand is the seller's commitment to the product. This commitment is most clearly articulated in the product's warranties and service agreements.[46] As part of the purchase contract with the customer, manufacturers are required by law to state the reasonable expectations for product performance. If the product does not meet those reasonable performance expectations, the customer has the legal right to return the product to the appropriate location for repair, replacement, or refund.

The two kinds of warranties are general and specific. **General warranties** make broad promises about product performance and customer satisfaction. These warranties are generally open to customers returning the product for a broad range of reasons beyond specific product performance problems. Many companies have adopted lenient policies that allow a product return without even asking the customer for a reason. Others require a reason, although there is often a great deal of latitude in what is an acceptable justification. **Specific warranties,** on the other hand, offer explicit product performance promises related to components of the product. Automobile warranties are specific warranties covering various components of the product with different warranties. The warranty for tires is by the tire manufacturer while warranties for the power train (engine, drive system) are generally different from those for the rest of the automobile.

Warranties Help Define the Brand

The manufacturer's promise of performance helps define the brand for the customer. Victorinox, maker of the famous Swiss Army knife, states its warranty as follows: "Swiss Army Brands, Inc., warrants its Victorinox Original Swiss Army Knives to be free from defects in material and workmanship for the entire life of the knife." Swiss Army Knives have the reputation of being among the best knives in the world, and the company's warranty supports that perception. A company willing to stand behind its product for life provides a lot of reassurance to the customer. In addition, there is an implied quality perception about a product warranted for life.

Cost versus Benefit Honoring a warranty incurs costs. At one level, the company must be competitive and offer warranties consistent with the industry. However, companies constantly evaluate their warranties (length of time, return/replacement/refund policies, nature of product performance) to consider whether the benefits of the warranty exceed the costs.[47] This is particularly true when companies offer warranties above the industry average. For years, luxury carmakers such as Lexus, Mercedes-Benz, BMW, Audi, and others offered warranties (four years or 50,000 miles bumper to bumper) beyond those provided by other manufacturers (GM, Ford, and Chrysler, which offered three years or 36,000 miles).

Offering longer warranties helped validate the perception of a luxury, quality automobile manufacturer. Recently, however, Mercedes-Benz has quietly reduced its warranty coverage by eliminating some free scheduled maintenance because the costs were too high. At the same time, Hyundai and others have expanded their warranties to build consumer confidence in their cars. They realize that extending the period of warranty coverage demonstrates they are making better cars in a very tangible way.

Convey a Message to the Customer Warranties convey a powerful message to the customer about perceived product quality and manufacturer commitment to customer satisfaction. Particularly with expensive products or purchase decisions in which the customer has anxiety, the warranty can play a significant role in the final product choice. As a result, companies focus a lot of time not only creating the warranty but also considering how best to communicate it to the customer. In some cases, as in FedEx's classic tag line "absolutely, positively overnight," the warranty becomes part of the advertising campaign. With most products, however, companies take a lower profile and build warranty statements into the overall marketing communications strategy and product information.[48]

SUMMARY

An essential element in any product is its brand. The brand conveys a great deal of information about the product and the customer experience. Powerful brands enjoy benefits in the market that other products do not. As a result, companies carefully consider a product's branding strategy in creating an overall marketing plan. Packaging and labeling are also critical brand elements that convey a lot about the product to the customer. Finally, customers attach great importance to the sellers' commitment to the products as conveyed in the product's warranties and service agreements.

KEY TERMS

brand	239	perceived quality	244	national brands	250
brand strategy	239	brand associations	244	store brands	250
brand identity	243	brand assets	244	licensing	250
brand equity	243	stand-alone brands	248	co-branding	250
brand awareness	243	family branding	248	general warranty	257
brand loyalty	243	category extensions	249	specific warranty	257

APPLICATION QUESTIONS

1. You are the product manager for Ralph Lauren's Polo shirts. What specific information are you trying to convey in the brand's iconic polo pony logo? For example, what does the Polo brand say about quality, features, style relative to the Tommy Hilfiger and Lacoste brands?
2. Johnson & Johnson has been able to establish strong brand equity for its line of baby products. What benefits does J&J have because of its brand equity for these products?
3. You have been asked by Coca-Cola's product manager to present the arguments for and against extending the Coke brand to a new cola drink. What would be the arguments for and against extending the Coke brand to a new cola drink?
4. SanDisk is introducing a new MP3 player and you are responsible for creating the package design. What key information and other creative elements would you include on the package?

MANAGEMENT DECISION CASE: Developing and Growing Brand Equity in an Iconic Brand

Quick Quiz: Each year, brand equity consultancy Interbrand publishes its Top 100 List of Best Global Brands. Which brand do you think recently finished behind Porsche but ahead of Ferrari in the personal transportation category? Here's a hint for you in the form of a quote from the company's chief marketing officer (CMO) that describes the company's essence and its importance to its customers: "We're really not about transportation; it's not about getting from Point A to Point B. It's about living in the way you choose." Obviously, that quote would have to come from a CMO whose firm views itself as adding value far more than getting from one place to the other. Instead, it's about a lifestyle. Give up? Well, the answer is Harley-Davidson!

Think about it. What is the *purpose* of a Harley motorcycle? For one thing, it's about the strong sense of community among owners as they partake in the loudest, toughest, most eye-catching ride imaginable. That telltale engine roar—you can hear one coming blocks away—is even featured in a "flash" on the homepage of Harley's website. The truth is, the roar itself fulfills one of the essential roles of a brand—instant recognition and connection. One does not need to physically see a motorcycle to know if it's a Harley or not. For many long-time loyalists, the sound evokes a sense of nostalgia and a time when life was less complicated and free of responsibility (*Easy Rider*, anyone?). The Harley logo evokes the same emotions and serves as a constant reminder of the quality and reputation of the product. For years, Harley maintained a strategy that customers would usually have a wait for delivery of their purchase of its most popular models, which they gladly did in order to own just that right bike to enhance their image and street cred. It's been said that while many weekend Harley riders might look the part of a motorcycle gang member, an incredible number of them are top-earning professional people (decoded: Harleys don't come cheap).

Interbrand's recent estimate of Harley's brand equity is $4.2 billion. That's a balance sheet asset that has no physical form! Such value is largely a result of the loyalty Harley owners have to the company and the close association they feel for the brand. A display of this loyalty took place in 2013 when over 100,000 Harley owners from all over the world, including a large number from China, traveled to Milwaukee in celebration of the company's 110th anniversary. Another display of affinity for the brand is through membership in the Harley Owners Group (H.O.G. for short), where owners can interact with one another in an online or in-person community of like-minded people. As a result of this loyalty, the reputation for quality, and the affinity Harley owners feel for the brand, the company is able to ask for and receive the premium prices it commands.

As with many popular brands, Harley has learned to capitalize on its brand name and iconic brand symbol by putting it on a variety of other products. Leather coats with the symbol embossed across the back are a natural brand extension for Harley. Doing a quick search on Amazon.com for Harley items, tens of thousands of products are identified. Those products include more clothing items ranging from adult t-shirts, hoodies, and boots to infant wear; accessories like iPhone cases and guitar straps; and other memorabilia like eyewear, jewelry, salt and pepper shakers, children's toys, bed sheets, and even dog collars and leashes, to name a few. Harley is a master at branding, and when you own a brand name this powerful, you want to put it into circulation on as many different products as you can, for which the branding association makes sense to a customer. It's one of the rare breed of brands that is an undisputed icon.

Questions for Consideration

1. For the past several years, in order to sustain sales and profit growth, Harley has relied heavily on baby boomers to buy a motorcycle in an effort to recapture their youth and rebelliousness. However, that market segment is quickly aging out of mainstream motorcycle-buying consumers. Identify one other market segment that you believe Harley should target more strongly in the future. What product modifications or other changes do you recommend to make the brand even more valuable to this new target market?
2. Licensing the brand name and symbol is an important source of revenue for Harley. What types of products do you think do not fit with the Harley image and therefore are not good candidates for licensing by Harley? Develop a list and discuss your selections.
3. Warranties and service agreements play an important role in communicating a company's willingness to stand behind its products. Research the warranty coverage and how well the Harley dealership network stands behind the product. How do the warranty coverage and service provided by dealers enhance the brand value of Harley?

Sources: Amazon.com, www.amazon.com/s/ref=nb_sb_ss_i_0_7?url=search-alias%3Daps&field-keywords=harley+davidson&sprefix=harley+%2Caps%2C258, accessed December 12, 2013; "Best Global Brands 2013," www.interbrand.com/en/best-global-brands/2013/Best-Global-Brands-2013-Brand-View.aspx, accessed December 12, 2013; "Loud, Proud and Lots of Leather; Thousands of Harley Riders Head 'Home' to Milwaukee to Mark 110th Anniversary," *The Toronto Star*, September 7, 2013, WHEELS section, p. W14.

MARKETING PLAN EXERCISE

ACTIVITY 10 Define the Branding Strategy

As we have learned in this chapter, building a strong brand is critical to a product's long-term success. At the same time, it is important to understand how a product's position in its life cycle influences marketing mix decisions.
Specific activities include:

1. Create a package design for the product. Specifically, the design should include necessary legal statements, marketing communications, and other information considered important for the package.
2. Develop a warranty for the product. What elements are specifically covered in the warranty? Does the warranty meet, equal, or fail to meet market expectations and competitor warranties?

3. Create a branding strategy to include
   a. National/store branding.
   b. Stand-alone/family branding.
   c. Possible licensing considerations.
   d. Co-branding opportunities.

NOTES

1. Jonathan Birchall, "Ralph Lauren Aims to Double Sales in Asia and Europe," *Financial Times,* May 29, 2008, p. 17; and John Brodie, "It's Ralph's World," *Fortune* 156, no. 6 (2007), pp. 64–68.
2. DeWayne Bevil, "Simpsons Ride Opens at Universal," *Orlando Sentinel,* April 29, 2008, p. B1; and Kara Newman, "How to Sell with Smell," *Business 2.0,* April 2007, p. 36.
3. Arch G. Woodside, Suresh Sood, and Kenneth E. Miller, "When Consumers and Brands Talk: Storytelling Theory and Research in Psychology and Marketing," *Psychology & Marketing* 25, no. 2 (2008), pp. 97–111.
4. Franz Rudolf Esch, Tobia Langner, Bernd H. Schmitt, and Patrick Gaus, "Are Brands Forever? Brand Knowledge and Relationship Affect Current and Future Purchases," *Journal of Product and Brand Management* 15, no. 2 (2006), pp. 98–105.
5. Stuart Elliot, "Selling Products by Selling Shared Values," *New York Times,* February 13, 2013, www.nytimes.com/2013/02/14/business/media/panera-to-advertise-its-social-consciousness-advertising.html?ref=business&_r=1&.
6. William Kingston, "Trademark Registration Is Not a Right," *Journal of Macromarketing* 26, no. 1 (2006), pp. 17–26.
7. Madhubalan Viswanathan and Terry L. Childers, "Understanding How Product Attributes Influence Product Categorization: Development and Validation of Fuzzy Set–Based Measures of Gradedness in Product Categories," *Journal of Marketing Research* 36, no. 1 (1999), pp. 75–95.
8. Pamela Miles Homer, "Perceived Quality and Image: When All Is Not 'Rosy,'" *Journal of Business Research* 61, no. 6 (2008), pp. 715–30.
9. Julie Manning Magid, Anthony D. Cox, and Dena S. Cox, "Quantifying Brand Image: Empirical Evidence of Trademark Dilution," *American Business Law Journal* 43, no. 1 (2006), pp. 1–43.
10. Bing Jing, "Product Differentiation Under Imperfect Information: When Does Offering a Lower Quality Pay?" *Quantitative Marketing and Economics* 5, no. 1 (2007), pp. 35–62.
11. William B. Locander and David L. Luechauer, "Building Equity," *Marketing Management* 14, no. 3 (2005), pp. 45–48.
12. David Aaker, *Managing Brand Equity* (New York: Free Press, 1991).
13. Saikat Banerjee, "Strategic Brand-Culture Fit: A Conceptual Framework for Brand Management," *Journal of Brand Management* 15, no. 5 (2008), pp. 312–22.
14. "The New Brand Landscape," *Marketing Health Services* 28, no. 1 (2008), p. 14; and Helen Stride and Stephen Lee, "No Logo? No Way, Branding in the Non-Profit Sector," *Journal of Marketing Management* 23, no. 1/2 (2007), pp. 107–22.
15. Matthew Yeung and Bala Ramasamy, "Brand Value and Firm Performance Nexus: Further Empirical Evidence," *Journal of Brand Management* 15, no. 5 (2008), pp. 322–36.
16. Christopher Palmeri and Margaret Newkirk, "Will Carnival Recover from the Latest Cruise Ship Mishap?," *Bloomberg Businessweek,* February 21, 2013, www.businessweek.com/articles/2013-02-21/will-carnival-recover-from-the-latest-cruise-ship-mishap.
17. B. Ramaseshan and Hsiu-Yuan Tsao, "Moderating Effects of the Brand Concept on the Relationship Between Brand Personality and Perceived Quality," *Journal of Brand Management* 14, no. 6 (2007), pp. 458–67; and Joel Espejel, Carmina Fandos, and Carlos Flavian, "The Role of Intrinsic and Extrinsic Quality Attributes on Consumer Behavior for Traditional Food Products," *Managing Service Quality* 17, no. 6 (2007), pp. 681–99.
18. Keith Walley, Paul Custance, Sam Taylor, Adam Lindgreen, and Martin Hinghley, "The Importance of Brand in the Industrial Purchase Decision: A Case Study of the UK Tractor Market," *Journal of Business & Industrial Marketing* 22, no. 6 (2007), pp. 383–99.
19. Karen E. Klein, "A Practical Guide to Branding," *BusinessWeek,* June 9, 2008, www.businessweek.com/print/smallbiz/content/jun2008/sb2008069_694225.htm.
20. Natalie Mizik and Robert Jacobson, "The Financial Value Impact of Perceptual Brand Attributes," *Journal of Marketing Research* 45, no. 1 (2008), pp. 15–31.
21. David Ballantyne and Robert Aitken, "Branding in B2B Markets: Insights from the Service Dominant

Logic of Marketing," *Journal of Business & Industrial Marketing* 22, no. 6 (2007), pp. 363–81.

22. Avinash V. Mainkar, Michael Lubatkin, and William S. Schulze, "Toward a Product-Proliferation Theory of Entry Barriers," *Academy of Management Review* 31, no. 4 (2006), pp. 1062–79.
23. Rong Huang and Emine Sarigollu, "Assessing Satisfaction with Core and Secondary Attributes," *Journal of Business Research* 61, no. 9 (2008), pp. 942–59.
24. Suraksah Gupta, Susan Grant, and T. C. Melewar, "The Expanding Role of Intangible Assets of the Brand," *Management Decision* 46, no. 6 (2008), pp. 948–61.
25. Brad D. Carlson, Tracy A. Suter, and Tom J. Brown, "Social versus Psychological Brand Community: The Role of Psychological Sense of Brand Community," *Journal of Business Research* 61, no. 4 (2008), pp. 284–301.
26. Tanzina Vega, "Report Gauges Companies' Approach to Advertising on Social Media," *New York Times,* January 29, 2012, http://mediadecoder.blogs.nytimes.com/2013/01/29/report-gauges-companies-approach-to-advertising-on-social-media/.
27. Jing Lei, Niraj Dawar, and Jos Lemmink, "Negative Spillover in Brand Portfolios: Exploring the Antecedents of Asymmetric Effects," *Journal of Marketing* 72, no. 3 (May 2008), pp. 111–29.
28. Satish Nambisan and Priya Nambisan, "How to Profit from a Better 'Virtual Customer Environment,' *MIT Sloan Management Review* 49, no. 3 (2008), pp. 53–70.
29. Ingrid M. Martin, David W. Stewart, and Shashi Matta, "Branding Strategies, Marketing Communication, and Perceived Brand Meaning: The Transfer of Purposive, Goal Oriented Brand Meaning to Brand Extensions," *Journal of the Academy of Marketing Science* 33, no. 3 (2005), pp. 275–95.
30. Jim Edwards, "Pepsi Social Media Chief Sums Up His Strategy in One Word: 'Homophily,'" *Business Insider,* September 27, 2012, http://finance.yahoo.com/news/pepsi-social-media-chief-sums-200040989.html.
31. N. Amrouche, G. Martin-Herran, and G. Zaccour, "Pricing and Advertising of Private and National Brands in a Dynamic Marketing Channel," *Journal of Optimization Theory and Applications* 137, no. 3 (2008), pp. 465–84.
32. Tsung-Chi Liu and Chung-Yu Want, "Factors Affecting Attitudes toward Private Labels and Promoted Brands," *Journal of Marketing Management* 24, no. 3/4 (2008), pp. 283–99; and Kyong-Nan Kwon, Mi-Hee Lee, and Yoo Jin Kin, "The Effect of Perceived Product Characteristics on Private Brand Purchases," *Journal of Consumer Marketing* 25, no. 2 (2008), pp. 105–22.
33. Najam Saqib and Rajesh V. Manchanda, "Consumers' Evaluations of Co-Branded Products, the Licensing Effect," *Journal of Product and Brand Management* 17, no. 2 (2008), pp. 73–89.
34. Klaus-Peter Wiedmann and Dirk Ludewig, "How Risky Are Brand Licensing Strategies in View of Customer Perceptions and Reactions?" *Journal of General Management* 33, no. 3 (2008), pp. 31–50.
35. Alokparna Basu Monga and Loraine Lau-Gesk, "Blending Co-Brand Personalities: An Examination of the Complex Self," *Journal of Marketing Research* 44, no. 3 (2007), pp. 389–402.
36. Wei-Lun Chang, "A Typology of Co-Branding Strategy: Position and Classification," *Journal of the American Academy of Business* 12, no. 2 (March 2008), pp. 220–27.
37. E. J. Schultz, "Doritos Launches First Global Campaign," *Advertising Age,* March 6, 2013, http://adage.com/article/news/doritos-launches-global-campaign/240173/.
38. Pinya Silayoi and Mark Speece, "The Importance of Packaging Attributes: A Conjoint Analysis Approach," *European Journal of Marketing* 41, no. 11/12 (2007), pp. 1495–1508.
39. Jessie Scanlon, "Pushing the Boundaries of Design," *BusinessWeek,* June 12, 2007, pp. 38–39.
40. Ulrich R. Orth and Keven Malkewitz, "Holistic Package Design and Consumer Brand Impressions," *Journal of Marketing* 72, no. 3 (2008), pp. 64–81.
41. E. J. Schultz, "Why Your Heineken Bottle Now Has a Long Neck," *Advertising Age,* March 8, 2013, http://adage.com/article/news/heineken-touts-big-u-s-bottle-update-1946/240235/.
42. Thomas J. Madden, Kelly Hewett, and Martin S. Roth, "Managing Images in Different Cultures: Across National Study of Color Meanings and Preferences," *Journal of International Marketing* 8, no. 4 (2000), pp. 90–108.
43. Avi Dan, "Constellation Transforms the Wine Market with Inside the Box Thinking," *Forbes,* February 26, 2013, www.forbes.com/sites/avidan/2013/02/26/constellation-transforms-the-wine-market-with-inside-the-box-thinking/.
44. Eric F. Shaver and Curt C. Braun, "Caution: How to Develop an Effective Product Warning," *Risk Management* 55, no. 6 (2008), pp. 46–52.
45. Ed Silverman, "Pfizer Wants Court to Rehear Generic Labeling Case and Avoid Tort Hell," *Forbes,* February 25, 2013, www.forbes.com/sites/edsilverman/2013/02/25/pfizer-wants-

court-to-rehear-generic-labeling-case-and-avoid-tort-hell/.

46. Rebecca J. Slotegraaf and J. Jeffrey Inman, "Longitudinal Shifts in the Drivers of Satisfaction with Product Quality: The Role of Attribute Resolvability," *Journal of Marketing Research* 41, no. 3 (2004), pp. 269–83.

47. D. N. P. Murthy, O. Solem, and T. Roren, "Product Warranty Logistics: Issues and Challenges," *European Journal of Operational Research* 156, no. 1 (2004), pp. 110–25.

48. Shallendra Pratap Jain, Rebecca J. Slotegraaf, and Charles D. Lindsey, "Towards Dimensionalizing Warranty Information: The Role of Consumer Costs of Warranty Information," *Journal of Consumer Psychology* 17, no. 1 (2007), pp. 70–88.

CHAPTER 09

Service as the Core Offering

LEARNING OBJECTIVES

- **LO9-1** Understand why service is a key source of potential differentiation.
- **LO9-2** Explain the characteristics that set services apart from physical goods.
- **LO9-3** Explain the service-profit chain and how it guides marketing management decisions about service.
- **LO9-4** Describe the continuum from pure goods to pure services.
- **LO9-5** Discuss the elements of service quality and gap analysis.
- **LO9-6** Measure service quality through use of SERVQUAL.
- **LO9-7** Understand service blueprinting and how it aids marketing managers.

WHY SERVICE IS IMPORTANT

LO 9-1

Understand why service is a key source of potential differentiation.

There's no debate that today we operate in an economy that is increasingly focused on intangible offerings—services—instead of just physical goods. A **service** is a product in the sense that it represents a bundle of benefits that can satisfy customer wants and needs, yet it does so without physical form. As such, the value a customer realizes from purchasing a service is not based on its physical attributes, but rather on some other effect the service has on him or her in fulfilling needs and wants. And differences in the quality of a service can be profound; just think for a moment about the best and worst experiences you've had with a server in a restaurant. Even if the food itself is good, it is the service aspect of a meal out that everyone remembers most. All the data suggest that we now live in a predominantly **service economy**. More than 80 percent of jobs in the United States are service-related. Compare that to 55 percent of jobs in 1970. The Bureau of Labor Statistics expects service jobs to account for *all* new domestic job growth for the foreseeable future, partly because the number of jobs outside the service sector is actually declining. Jobs represented in the **service sector** of the economy include such important categories as intellectual property, consulting, hospitality, travel, law, health care, education, technology, telecommunications, and entertainment—all high-growth job categories. In terms of U.S. gross domestic product, services account for more than 75 percent and that number is growing. The long-term shift from goods-producing to service-producing employment is expected to continue. Service-providing industries are expected to account for about 16.8 million new wage and salary jobs generated from 2008 to 2018, while goods-producing industries will see overall job loss. In today's workplace everyone is involved in service in some way; everyone has customers either outside or inside the firm, or both.

Changing U.S. demographics represent a major driver for why the service sector is thriving. For example, as baby boomers begin to retire and spend their discretionary income on travel and entertainment, firms in those industries will prosper. As the baby boomers continue to age, health services will begin to predominate their spending. In the meantime, the fixation of Generation Y and millennials toward all things technological will continue to drive impressive growth in gaming, music, computing, cellular phone, and other technological industries.

Service as a Differentiator

In Chapter 6, we mentioned that service leadership and personnel leadership are two important sources of differentiation for a company. Recall that differentiation means communicating and delivering value in different ways to different customer groups. Presumably these groups are segments that show the most promise for return on marketing investment. As a marketing manager, a significant challenge with using differentiation as a core market strategy is that competitors are constantly coming to market with new differentiators that trump the efficacy of the current ones.

In his book *On Great Service,* Leonard Berry, a leading expert in the field of services marketing, advocates that a focus on service and on enabling employees to effectively deliver service can be one differentiator that is hard for the competition to replicate. Many firms are reluctant to invest in great service, largely because it takes time and patience before a return on the investment may be noticeable. But Berry's point is that although the payback might take time, once a firm is able to deliver great service as a core differentiator, it is much more likely to provide a sustainable competitive advantage than are most other sources of differentiation.[1]

A New Dominant Logic for Marketing

That service is central to marketing management today is embodied in an important article that appeared in one of the field's leading journals, the *Journal of Marketing,* titled "Evolving to a New Dominant Logic for Marketing."

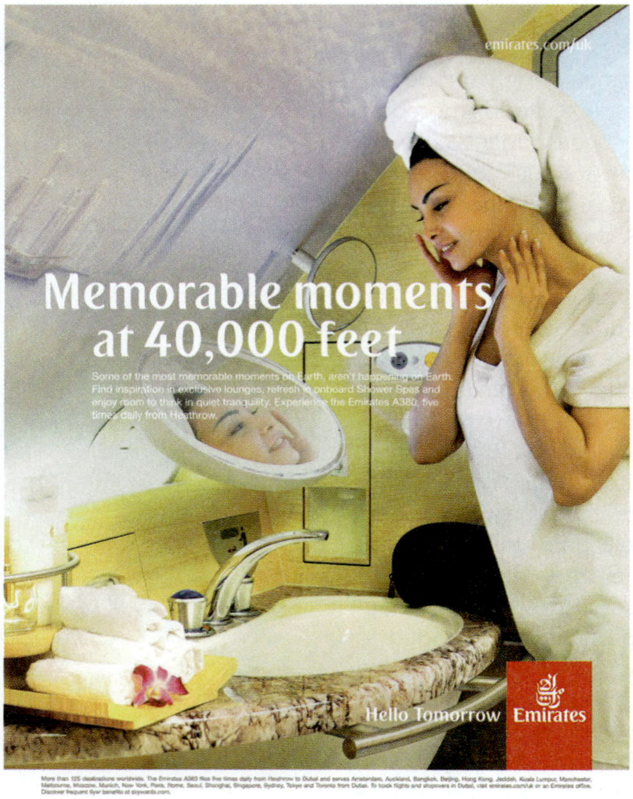

Emirates Air provides an onboard shower spa as one way to differentiate itself as a premium provider of air travel.

The **new dominant logic for marketing** implies a shift in worldview from the traditional goods versus services dichotomy to recognition of the following:

> Customers do not buy goods or services: [T]hey buy *offerings* which render services which create value . . . . The traditional division between goods and services is long outdated. The shift in focus to services is a shift from the means and the producer perspective to the utilization and the customer perspective.

In a service-centered view, tangible goods serve as "appliances" for service provision rather than ends in themselves such that in some ways the product becomes secondary or incidental to the service it propagates. This perspective has profound implications for how marketing managers approach their business in a world of increasingly commoditized physical goods. The most fundamental question is "Just *what is it* that we are marketing?" Or, put another way: What is the product and where does its value come from? A service-centered perspective is very consistent with a customer-centric approach in which people, processes, systems, and other resources are to be aligned to best serve customers. It disposes of the limitations of thinking about marketing in terms of goods taken to the marketplace and instead leads to opportunities for expanding the market by assisting the customer in the process of specialization and value creation.[2]

An overall service-centered view is fundamental to successful marketing management today. The remainder of this chapter is devoted to providing insights for effectively capitalizing on the service opportunities associated with an offering. First, unique characteristics of services are described that set services apart from physical goods for marketing managers. Second, the concept of the service-profit chain is introduced. Third, service attributes are discussed along with a continuum of products from pure goods to pure services. Fourth, the concept of service quality is introduced along with its measurement and uses by management. Finally, service blueprinting is introduced as a way for a marketing manager to map out the overall service delivery system for a business.

CHARACTERISTICS OF SERVICES

Services possess several distinct characteristics different from physical goods. As illustrated in Exhibit 9.1, these are intangibility, inseparability, variability, and perishability. We'll discuss each one and its impact on customers and marketing.

EXHIBIT 9.1 | Characteristics of Services

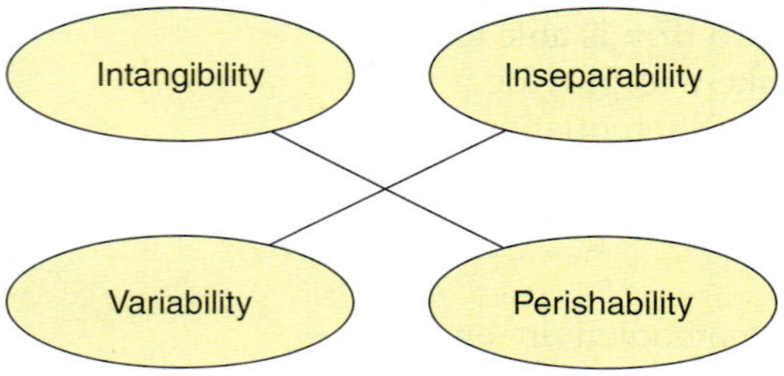

Intangibility

A service cannot be experienced through the physical senses. It cannot be seen, heard, tasted, felt, or smelled by a customer. This property represents the **intangibility** of services versus goods; goods can easily be experienced through the senses. A State Farm Insurance agent issues a policy for an automobile. Yes, the customer will receive a written policy document. But the policy itself is not the product in the sense of a physical good such as a box of cereal or a bottle of shampoo. Instead, the product is the sense of financial security the insurance policy provides to the customer. It is the confidence that if something dire happens to the car, State Farm will fix it or replace it.

So how do customers draw conclusions about a brand such as State Farm if they can't actually try the product before purchase? This is one of the challenges of intangibles. Strong branding can be an important way to make a service seem more tangible. Service firms such as State Farm use strong imagery to send out signals about their products, increase trust, and ease customer uncertainty about what is being purchased. Ever see the ads saying, "Like a good neighbor, State Farm is there"? This phrase and the accompanying visual images provide cues about the dependability of the service, replacing to an extent the ability customers have to try physical products in advance of purchase. When it comes to making purchase decisions about services, customers draw conclusions from what tangibles they can experience—things like the company's people, website, marketing communications, office ambience, and pricing. In a service setting, the importance and impact of marketing are heightened considerably because in many cases there's little else tangible for the customer to experience before purchase.[3]

LO 9-2

Explain the characteristics that set services apart from physical goods.

One way that Intuit handles the intangibility of its TurboTax and other financial software is through its website. The site helps potential customers and users understand the software. The site includes multiple forums to facilitate discussion between users and bloggers alike. Intuit also solicits customers for text and video content. Customers are invited to engage with the company on social media websites such as Twitter, Facebook, and YouTube. "With one or two clicks, you can make a call or chat and, if you allow it, we can share your screen and see the return," says Dan Maurer, the head of Intuit's consumer business. On the TurboTax website, users can input their information and the website will automatically save the data. Customers do not have to worry about losing their information. As a service provider, Intuit separates itself from its competitors by understanding the importance of providing a tangible connection from the company to the customer.[4]

Sometimes it is possible to enhance tangibility of a service through a bit of customer trial. For example, MBA programs often encourage prospective students to come to open houses or visit classes to gain a sense of how the school they are considering approaches teaching and learning. Vacation ownership companies such as Hilton Grand Vacations Club and Marriott Vacation Club actively solicit guests for tours of their facilities while they are visiting an area to allow them to experience a taste of what the location is like as a regular vacation destination. And advertising agencies make portfolios of past work available to prospective clients as a sampling of the firm's creative capabilities.[5]

Inseparability

Even with the best efforts at enhancing a service's tangibility, a customer still can't really experience it until it is actually consumed. This characteristic represents the **inseparability** of a service—it is produced and consumed at the same time and cannot be separated from its provider. With physical goods, the familiar process is production, storage, sale, and then consumption. But with services, first the service is sold and then it is produced and consumed at the same time. Perhaps it is more accurate to think of a service as being *performed* rather than produced.[6] In a theatrical play or an orchestral concert, many individuals have a part in the performance. Similarly, the quality of a service encounter is determined in part by the interaction of the players. Most elegant restaurants structure their customer encounters as elaborate productions involving servers, the wine steward, the maître d', the chef, and, of course, the table of diners. Benihana restaurants take the concept of service as drama to truly new heights of customer involvement and excitement—the company's tag line is "an experience at every table."

Boston Market is a fast-casual dining restaurant that understands the importance of the guest experience. Prior to 2010, customers were served on plastic plates and provided plastic cutlery. The management team recognized that its guests wanted a more high-end experience so all the restaurants were modernized and real plates and cutlery were introduced. The ambiance of the stores needed to match customer perception. This tied into customer service as well. "What we have found is that the key is to engage our people. So we went out and met with all our employees and all our general managers and talked about what we need to change. We now have a new attitude toward our customers," said CEO George Michel. Customer feedback resulted in another, more portable way to serve the food that is now implemented at the drive-through windows. The mantra of the chain is "love to serve" and Michel intends for every guest to feel the love when he or she enters one of Boston Market's establishments.[7]

The inseparability of performance and consumption of services heightens the role of the human service providers in the customer's experience. It also leads to opportunities for considerable customization in delivering the service. Finicky customers in the hair stylist's chair can coax just the right cut. Want two scoops of cinnamon ice cream instead of one on that apple tort? Just ask the server.

In the financial services industry, for example, customization of services is prominent. Bank tellers are empowered to take a quick look at your account record when you are at the window to make a deposit and might very likely suggest you do something different with your money if you're not currently optimizing your returns.[8] And cellular service providers know that if they don't proactively suggest updating rate plans, customers will be more likely to walk away once their contracted years are fulfilled.

Variability

An offshoot of the inseparability issue, **variability** of a service means that because it can't be separated from the provider, a service's quality can only be as good as that of the provider him-/herself.[9] Ritz-Carlton, Nordstrom, Disney, and Southwest Airlines have become iconic firms in their industries largely by focusing on their people—hiring, training, keeping, and promoting the very best people they can get. Legendary Southwest Chairman Herb Kelleher built a business in part around ensuring that his people were *different* from typical airline employees—more engaged, fun, and fiercely loyal to the company.[10] The same can be said for the other firms above. Focusing on employees as a source of differentiation in marketing is usually a smart move, mainly because so many firms just can't seem to pull it off very well. The point is to remove much of the variability of customers' experiences with your service and instead provide a more dependable level of quality. Go into any Nordstrom and work with any of Nordstrom's sales associates and you will very likely experience the same high level of satisfaction with the service. The same is true for Ritz-Carlton, and any of the great service organizations.[11]

Goods, in general, tend to be much more standardized than services because, once a firm has invested in continuous process improvement and quality control in its manufacturing operations, products flow off the line with very little variation. With services, continual investment in training, retraining, and good management of people is required if variability is to be consistently low. It is in this area where the disciplines of marketing, operations, leadership, and human resource management probably have their closest intersection. What makes Ritz-Carlton great? A quick answer is: its people. But what makes its people great? World-class operations, leadership, and HR practices. And the net effect for Ritz-Carlton is that its branding and market positioning are largely defined by its wonderful people and the way they handle each customer as a valued guest. For service firms, great marketing cannot take place without a strong overarching culture that values employees.

Perishability

If you schedule an appointment for a routine physical with your physician and then simply don't show up, the doctor loses the revenue from that time slot. That's **perishability**—the fact that a service can't be stored or saved up for future use.[12] Perishability is a major potential problem for service providers, and explains why, under the circumstances above, many physicians have a policy of charging the patient for the missed appointment. Ever wonder why an airline won't issue a refund or let you change your super-low-fare ticket after the door closes and the plane leaves without you? It's because the value of that empty seat—its ability to generate incremental revenue for the airline—dropped to zero when the door closed and the plane backed away from the gate.

Fluctuating demand is related to perishability of services.[13] Consider rental car firms such as Hertz, Avis, and the like in a city such as Orlando, which brings in both tourists and conventions. If demand were relatively constant, the rental car companies could keep the same basic inventory on the lot at all times. However, in the case of both individual vacationers and conventioneers, demand for cars varies considerably by season, and for the latter is driven by the size of the convention. The worst scenario is for the city to attract a huge convention and for the rental firms not to have sufficient cars available. No cars, no revenue for Hertz and Avis. Not to mention, the convention organizers would likely think twice before scheduling their event in Orlando again.

Because demand for most goods tends to be more stable and because they can generally be stored for use after purchase, this critical issue of synchronizing supply and demand is easier to deal with for goods than for services. Hertz and Avis don't want to maintain huge extra inventories of vehicles on off-peak periods; hence they might use price incentives to promote more rentals during those times. Or they might literally move cars around—pulling in massive numbers of extra vehicles from other nearby markets such as Miami or Tampa to take care of high-demand periods. One thing they know for sure is that if there are no cars on the lot, any opportunity for revenue perishes.

THE SERVICE-PROFIT CHAIN

LO 9-3

Explain the service-profit chain and how it guides marketing management decisions about service.

In a now-famous *Harvard Business Review* article and follow-up book, James Heskett and his colleagues proposed a formalization of linkages between employee and customer aspects of service delivery called the **service-profit chain**. Because of the inseparability and variability of services, employees play a critical role in their level of success. The service-profit chain, which is portrayed in Exhibit 9.2, is designed to help managers better understand the key linkages in a service delivery system that drive customer loyalty, revenue growth, and higher profits.

Internal Service Quality

This aspect of the service-profit chain includes elements of workplace design, job design, employee selection and development processes, employee rewards and recognition approaches, and availability of effective tools for use by employees in serving customers. Considerable evidence exists that **internal marketing**, treating

EXHIBIT 9.2 | The Service-Profit Chain

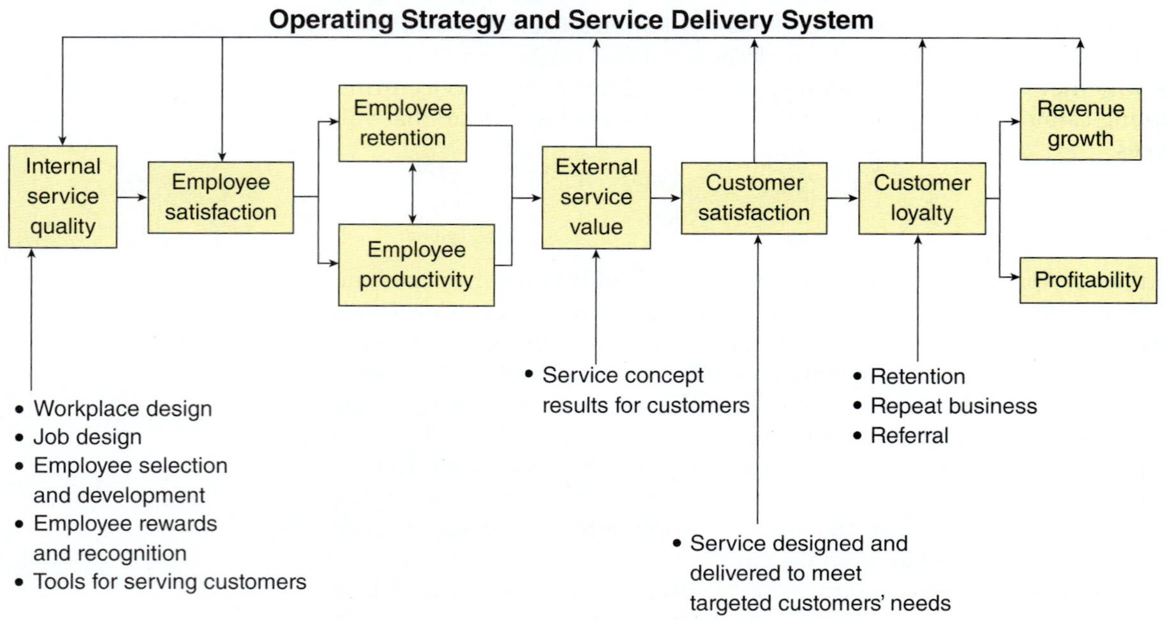

employees as customers and developing systems and benefits that satisfy their needs, is an essential element of internal service quality. Firms practicing internal service quality are **customer-centric**—they place the customer at the center of everything that takes place both inside and outside the firm. Firms that are customer-centric exhibit a high degree of customer orientation, which means they do the following:

1. Instill an organization-wide focus on understanding customers' requirements.
2. Generate an understanding of the marketplace and disseminate that knowledge to everyone in the firm.
3. Align system capabilities internally so that the organization can respond effectively with innovative, competitively differentiated, satisfaction-generating goods and services.

Employees can be a great resource for companies to improve their service experience. Canadian Tire Corp. understands this and implements employee engagement programs regularly. A company rollout started in January of 2013 and has seen great success. "The initiative is a recognition that Canadian Tire needs to have a fully committed workforce to compete in an increasingly competitive retail landscape," said Doug Nathanson, Canadian Tire's senior vice president and chief human resources officer. Employee engagement directly contributes to the company's bottom line. A study of more than 7,000 organizations by HR consulting firm Aon Hewitt found that each disengaged employee costs an organization an average of $10,000 in profit annually. Canadian Tire believes it is important not only to celebrate employee success, but also to actively listen to their suggestions and implement them. "Ultimately it's about attracting and retaining employees, and improving customer service to really drive results," Nathanson said.[14]

In the context of internal service quality, it is assumed that a firm's culture, business philosophy, strategy, structure, and processes will be aligned in order to create, communicate, and deliver value to customers. Finally, a focus on internal service quality implies that employees hold a **customer mind-set**, meaning that employees believe that understanding and satisfying customers, whether internal or external to the firm, is central to doing their job well.[15]

RBS
RBS
It's in the blood
Success at any Grand Slam depends on focus and determination, but playing at Wimbledon in front of an expectant home crowd provides an even greater challenge.
At The Royal Bank of Scotland we believe that you're born with these qualities. You've either got them or you haven't. We know Andy and Jamie have what it takes.
rbs.com/sport
Make it happen
RBS
The Royal Bank of Scotland

Having pro tennis siblings Andy and Jamie Murray as symbols for Royal Bank of Scotland adds a strong sense of pride to the organization, and of course also captures the attention of prospective customers.

Satisfied, Productive, and Loyal Employees

Great service doesn't happen without great people. A big part of making the service-profit chain work is creating an environment in which all employees can be successful. Internal marketing is an integral element of this, and Caesars' Entertainment is a great example of a firm that almost obsessively focuses on facilitating the success of its people, regardless of their position, and especially if they are in direct contact with customers. It's not surprising Caesars has such a zest for internal marketing and enablement of employee success. Gary Loveman, one of the original authors of the service-profit chain concept, went on to become chairman, CEO, and president. During his tenure, the company became the most successful hotelier/casino in Las Vegas and continues to expand elsewhere as well. Caesars' stable of brands includes Caesars Palace, Bally's, Paris, Rio, Flamingo, Harrah's, and others.[16]

To be executed effectively, internal marketing must include the following critical elements: competing for talent, offering an overall vision, training and developing people, stressing teamwork, modeling desired behaviors by managers, enabling employees to make their own decisions, measuring and rewarding great service performance, and knowing and reacting to employees' needs. Perhaps most important of all, employees must have a deep understanding of the brand and must be able to consistently articulate a clear, concise message to customers that reflects the firm's service strategy and branding.[17] At Caesars, Loveman points with pride to the fact that everyone in the firm understands and can articulate its branding and values.

DeSantis Breindel, a leading B2B branding and marketing firm, frequently publishes a blog focusing on the importance of advocating for the brand within a corporation—one of the most important elements of internal marketing. The company stands by the idea that "[employees] must be empowered with the right tools to communicate the brand externally—whether at a social gathering or a business function, through e-mail, social media, or a phone call. This is where employee communications and internal branding plays[sic] a critical role in maximizing the value of a brand." Organizations should rely on employees who have a strong bond to and a thorough understanding of the brand to be their most valuable brand ambassadors. To foster this internal marketing strategy, the business must create a sense of unity within all of its business units. Employees must feel a sense of shared purpose; a fundamental connection to the company's mission, vision, and values; and an understanding of how they contribute to the company's success.[18]

Greater Service Value for External Customers

There is strong evidence that attention to internal service quality and to employee satisfaction, productivity, and retention results in stronger value to external customers of a service. Remember that when the concept of value was introduced in Chapter 1 we discussed it as a ratio of what a customer gives versus what he or she gets in return from a purchase. Importantly, the customer inputs are not just financial—customers give up time, convenience, and other opportunities in making a purchase choice. Customers set their expectations for the value they hope to derive from a service based largely on the evidence provided by the marketer before the purchase. A fundamental rule in marketing is to not set customer expectations so high that they cannot be effectively met on a consistent basis.[19] This is because it is always better to underpromise and overdeliver than the reverse scenario. This concept is often called **customer expectations management**.

What does Southwest Airlines promise the flyer? The airline doesn't have traditional assigned seating, a first-class cabin, or even "real food" on flights. But it doesn't promise any of these things. In fact, it has built a business out of snubbing the other big airlines' approaches (and made a lot of money doing so). What Southwest *does* promise is a fun, on-time flight. So long as it can continue to deliver against that message, customers will likely continue to see Southwest as a great travel value.

Customer Satisfaction and Loyalty

In the service-profit chain, meeting or exceeding customer expectations leads to customer satisfaction, since the service was designed and delivered in a manner that added value. A strong correlation exists between satisfied and loyal customers. Loyalty sparks high **customer retention**—low propensity to consider switching to other providers—as well as repeat business, referrals, and **customer advocacy**, a willingness and ability on the part of a customer to participate in communicating the brand message to others within his or her sphere of influence.[20] Why do customers consider switching from one service provider to another? Reasons run the gamut from low utility to various forms of service failure to concerns about a firm's practices. A summary of causes of switching behavior is presented in Exhibit 9.3.

Caesars Entertainment understands the strong linkage between high customer satisfaction and loyalty and invests heavily in its most highly satisfied customers to ensure their loyalty and advocacy. Exhibit 9.4 portrays this relationship.

CRM and database marketing are key tools that allow Caesars Entertainment, as well as any firm interested in increasing satisfaction and loyalty and improving retention, to use the concepts in Exhibit 9.4 to focus on serving the most profitable customers. For the various Caesars casino brands, this approach manifests itself through the Total Rewards loyalty program. Caesars has found that its ROI for customers in the "Zone of Affection" is considerably higher than in the other zones ("Indifference" and "Defection"). Very satisfied customer "apostles" are the ones that Caesars wants to develop to the fullest extent to keep them coming back and spending money in its hotels and casinos. Research indicates that, although investing in indifferent customers to improve their satisfaction may yield some returns, only when customers reach the "Zone of Affection" do they truly maximize their profitability to the brand.

Revenue and Profit Growth

In the context of Exhibit 9.4, customers that are "satisfied" and "very satisfied" are identified through Caesars' Total Rewards loyalty program cards, which they

EXHIBIT 9.3 | Causes of Switching Behavior

Pricing

- High price
- Price increases
- Unfair pricing
- Deceptive pricing

Inconvenience

- Location/hours
- Wait for appointment
- Wait for service

Core Service Failure

- Service mistakes
- Billing errors
- Service catastrophe

Service Encounter Failures

- Uncaring
- Impolite
- Unresponsive
- Unknowledgeable

Response to Service Failure

- Negative response
- No response
- Reluctant response

Competition

- Found better service

Ethical Problems

- Cheating
- Hard sell
- Safety concerns
- Conflict of interest

Involuntary switching

- Customer moved
- Provider closed

Source: Susan M. Keaveney, "Customer Switching Behavior in Service Industries: An Exploratory Study," *Journal of Marketing,* April 1995, pp. 71–82. Reprinted with permission of the American Marketing Association.

EXHIBIT 9.4 | Focus on the Most Satisfied Customers

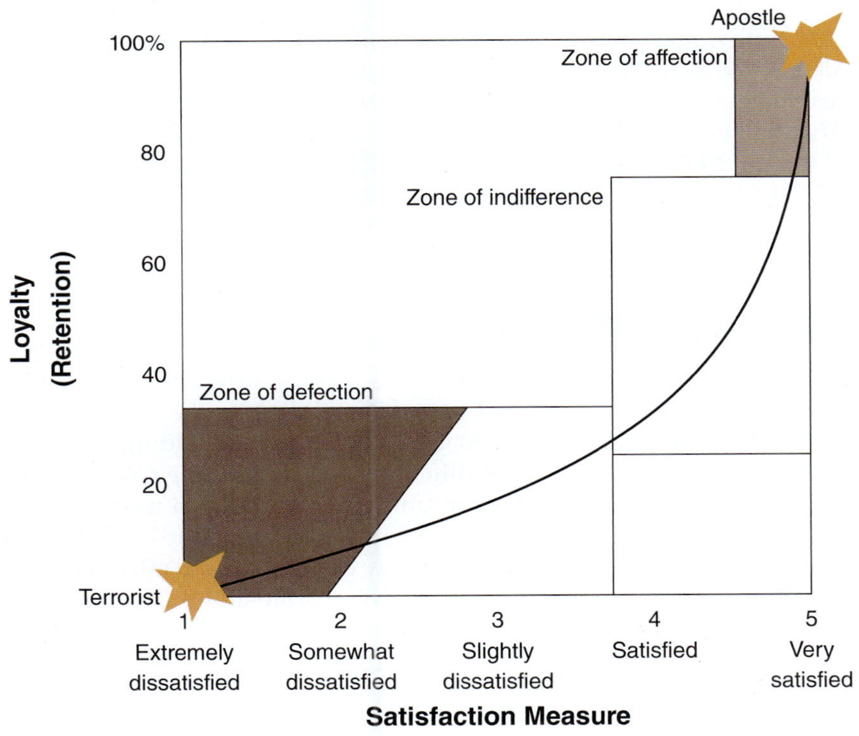

Source: Reprinted by permission of *Harvard Business Review,* from "Putting the Service-Profit Chain to Work", by James L. Heskett, Thomas O. Jones, Gary W. Loveman, W. Earl Sasser Jr., and Leonard A. Schlesinger, March/April 1994. Copyright © 1994 by the Harvard Business School Publishing Corporation, all rights reserved.

use at hotel check-in, in slot machines, and at all gaming tables. They truly are the apple of the eye of Caesars' employees while they are on the property, and more broadly they represent the total focus of Caesars' marketing efforts—largely through direct marketing approaches with customized offers. Like slots? You'll get an invitation to a slot tournament. Poker's your thing? Look for an invitation to a poker tournament. It's not that Caesars is disinterested in or doesn't want the money of the other customers, but it has learned from its research that customers in the "Zone of Affection" spend considerably more money and provide a substantially greater return on customer investment than others.[21]

Caesars embraces customer satisfaction measurement and it segments markets based on satisfaction score groups. The ultimate Caesars customer is the "apostle"—highly satisfied, fiercely loyal, a frequent Caesars guest who serves as a strong advocate for the Caesars experience to friends and acquaintances. For the service-profit chain to provide insight for marketing managers into how to best develop and execute service strategies, a variety of metrics must be in place with measures taken continually. In fact, all aspects of the chain—from internal service quality to employee issues to value to satisfaction and loyalty to financial performance—must be quantified and used for marketing management decision making. Chapter 16 provides a detailed treatment of marketing metrics, and many of the measures developed and exemplified in that chapter relate directly to executing the service-profit chain.

The Oklahoma City Thunder, an NBA basketball team, started building their franchise in 2008. The owners understood the importance of personalizing their fan base and invested in a CRM system to help them achieve this goal. "Our vision was to make the Thunder the most fan-centric organization in professional sports," said Scott Loft, Vice President of Ticket Sales, Retention, and Database Operations for the Thunder. "When fans enter the Chesapeake Energy Arena for a Thunder home game, we want them to feel like guests rather than customers or numbers." The CRM system helps to standardize the organization's guest care practices. According to the team's Net Promoter Score, a system that helps businesses measure customer satisfaction, the Thunder has an NPS of 91.2 percent. This figure is more than twice as high as the NBA average. Additionally, the Thunder has been ranked the top NBA team in terms of the overall fan experience: 99 percent of guests have rated their overall experience as "good" or "excellent."[22]

SERVICE ATTRIBUTES

LO 9-4

Describe the continuum from pure goods to pure services.

So far we've looked at why service is at the core of firm success, identified characteristics of services, and gained an understanding of the linkages in the service-profit chain. We're now ready to gain a better understanding of how services fit within the broader context of different types of offerings. A useful way to approach answering this question is through consideration of a continuum of goods and services that range from easy to evaluate to difficult to evaluate based on three major types of attributes relevant to any offering: search attributes, experience attributes, and credence attributes. Exhibit 9.5 illustrates exemplar goods and services across a continuum of these attributes.

Search Attributes

Depending on the type of offering, consumers may engage in a search for various alternative products to find the one that most closely meets their decision criteria for purchase. With physical goods, such comparison is usually relatively simple as there are many **search attributes**, which are aspects of an offering that are physically

EXHIBIT 9.5 | Continuum of Evaluation for Different Types of Offerings

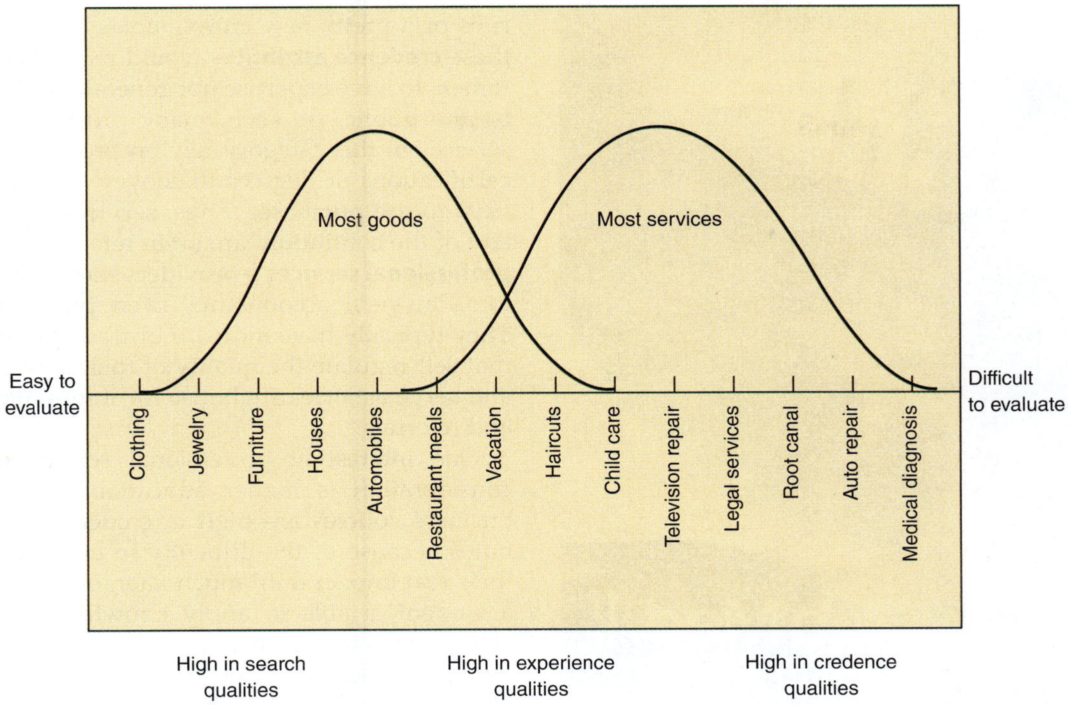

Source: Valarie A. Zeithaml, "How Consumer Evaluation Processes Differ between Goods and Services," in *Marketing of Services*, James H. Donnelly and William R. George, eds., 1991. Reprinted with permission of the American Marketing Association.

observable before consumption. For example, a shopper can compare the picture quality, price, and warranty of several high-definition televisions right on the Best Buy showroom floor. Because of the intangibility aspect of services, however, it is much more difficult to do such direct comparisons during a search process. Try comparing the performance of one mutual fund over another; the exercise gives new meaning to the old phrase "comparing apples and oranges." The bottom line is that services are low in search qualities because it is difficult to evaluate many aspects of them before purchase. Usually the customer doesn't truly know how the service performs until *after* the sale—that's the inseparability aspect of services.[23]

Experience Attributes

Experience attributes are aspects of an offering that can be evaluated only during or after consumption. Many services fit this category, including restaurants, vacations, hair cuts, and child care. They tend to have both tangible and intangible aspects; for example, a dining-out experience includes a physical good, the meal, as well as the service portion. Based on the level to which customer expectations were met, a decision will be made about whether or not to repeat the purchase another time.[24]

Credence Attributes

In many cases, a customer cannot make a reasonable evaluation of the quality of a service even after use. Services such as television repair, legal services, dentistry,

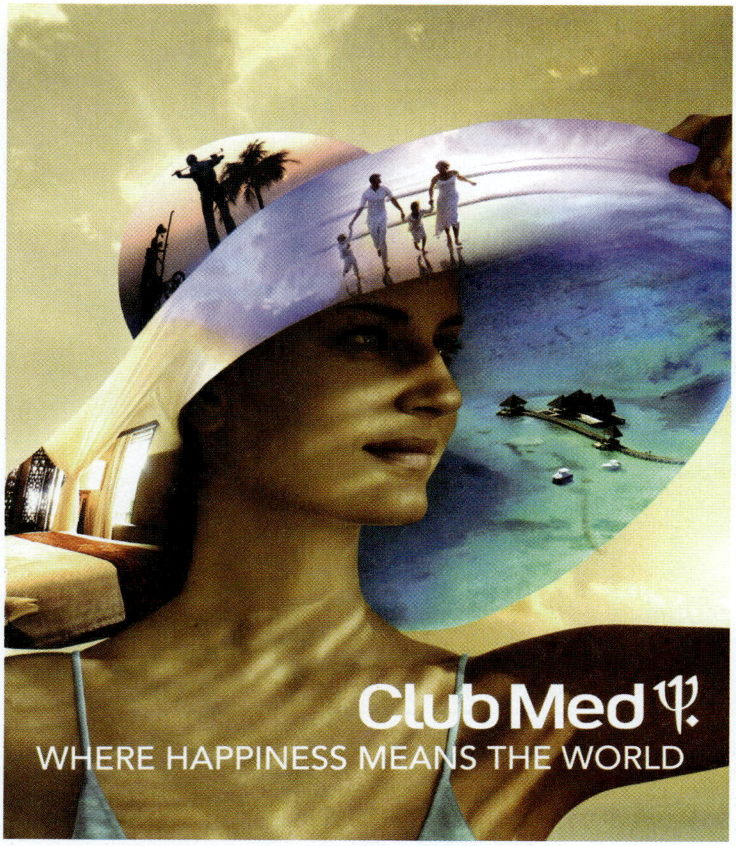

Club med presents imagery and a tag line that are clearly reflective of a service heavy in experience attributes.

auto repair, and medical services require specialized training to deliver. The customer may only know the desired end state—a car that runs or a pretty new crown molar. To assess these **credence attributes** would require customers to have expertise not generally shared by the public. As such, many providers of services in this category rely on professional certifications or degrees to convey a level of trust to the purchaser. Thus, services at this end of the continuum are often referred to as **professional services**—providers such as doctors, lawyers, accountants, even plumbers. They typically have industry or trade groups that self-regulate the quality of their services and serve as a clearinghouse for information and referrals.

One interesting professional service for consideration is higher education. College business courses are high in credence attributes because of the difficulty in evaluating their real impact until much later, often after a student is able to apply knowledge and skills gained to a particular job situation. The perennial question in business education is, "Who is the customer?" One approach frames the companies that hire a business school's students as the primary customer, which would seem to imply the students are a product of the business school rather than its customer. Employing a marketing metaphor, this approach puts the professor in the role of product development and branding—positioning the student for success in the marketplace. This overall approach may be appropriate because business education is high in credence attributes. Understandably, however, all students want to be treated as "customers" too.

Like higher education, physicians and professional health care service providers in general exhibit some unique characteristics. Ethical Dimension 9 provides an example of one challenging issue in modern health care—patients who travel globally to seek treatments that are banned inside the United States.

Working with a home builder can be a very scary experience. It is challenging to know ahead of time if the builder will construct a good house. That is why potential customers rely on word-of-mouth (WOM) recommendations from friends or relatives who have had firsthand experience with the company. Pulte Homes is one of the top builders in the nation when it comes to satisfaction of existing customers, which through WOM drives new customers to Pulte Homes. Communities built by Pulte Homes are designed to deliver the best quality of life for home owners. By combining innovative designs, an unwavering commitment to quality, and attention to detail, the company has become one of the nation's premier brands for upwardly mobile home buyers.[25]

Importance of Understanding Service Attributes

Because services tend to exhibit high experience and credence attributes, marketing strategies must be developed that consider the implications of these characteristics. As we've discussed, services customers tend to take their cues on what to purchase from whatever evidence they can gather to make up for the lack of ability to try the service beforehand. Word-of-mouth referrals, physical cues such as the ambience of the physical location, functionality of the website, and professionalism of the employees operate as a surrogate for trial. Because of the higher risk involved in purchasing a service versus a good, once a customer begins to have a positive experience with a service provider and build a relationship with the firm, customer loyalty to services tends to be greater than loyalty to goods. Of course, the flip side of that for the marketing manager is that if your competitor offers great service and people as a key differentiator, and you can't match it, it can be very difficult to get customers to switch to or even try a new provider.[26]

ETHICAL DIMENSION 9

The Service of Medicine—U.S. Consumers' Global Search for a Cure

One of the most important global service industries is the delivery of health care. In the United States, for example, health care represents 16 percent of GDP, totaling nearly $2 trillion, and is projected to be 20 percent of GDP by 2021. Despite the United States' extensive health care system and the dramatic changes brought about by the Patient Protection and Affordable Care Act, the search for medical help by U.S. citizens in need has become a *global* effort. Each country has its own medical testing policies and protocols, which means drugs and medical procedures not permitted in one country might be available in another country. For example, patients often purchase drugs in Canada and Mexico that are not available in the U.S. and travel to Europe for medical procedures that are not authorized to be performed in the U.S.

One medical issue, stem cell medicine, has generated serious political and social debate around the world. Medical researchers have reported significant benefits using stem cells across a wide range of medical issues. Although stem cells can be obtained from several sources, it is the use of embryonic stem cells taken from a fetus that causes significant moral concern for some. At present, stem cell research and the use of stem cells in therapy is more limited in the U.S. than in many other parts of the world such as Europe and Asia, where it is much more widely accepted and available.

China has been especially aggressive in allowing stem cell medical therapy on humans. Patients can seek treatment in Chinese clinics across a broad spectrum of medical issues such as severe spinal injuries, ataxia, cerebral palsy, and multiple sclerosis. In many cases, their U.S. doctors point out that the procedures have not been properly tested and discount the medical claims reported by the Chinese clinics. But patients who do make the trip to China feel they have exhausted their medical options in the U.S., see little hope in continuing their current treatments, and are looking for other options. Extensive U.S. medical research and testing protocols mean that many of these procedures are years away from approval and will not benefit patients that are currently in need.

The average stem cell treatment in China costs $17,000, a fee obviously not covered by medical insurance. Further compounding the problem is the short-term beneficial nature of the treatments, which means therapy must likely be repeated for continued relief. In China, patients receive a variety of other treatment therapies including physical therapy, acupuncture, massage, and electrical stimulation in addition to the stem cell treatment. This makes isolating the benefits of the stem cell portion of the treatment very difficult.

It is not clear how changes in U.S. health care as a result of the Affordable Care Act will impact this type of experimental procedure. However, the moral and ethical implications of seeking this type of health care will continue to be an important issue for the medical community and patients.[27]

Ethical Perspective

1. **U.S. Physician:** Many doctors in the United States cite a lack of valid research and no evidence of long-term health benefits related to Chinese stem cell therapy. At the same time, patients who go to China often report benefits from the treatment. Once a patient has exhausted existing treatments in the U.S., should a doctor recommend the patient consider Chinese stem cell treatment?
2. **U.S. Patient:** As a patient, would you consider traveling to China for stem cell therapy? If so, would you wait until all U.S. treatments had been exhausted?

There are thousands of reasons to see a dermatologist. What's yours?
dryness and redness... itching is healed
crow's feet and laugh lines... aging concealed
Whether your skin needs medical, surgical or cosmetic treatment, trust the expert care of a board-certified dermatologist.
AAD
Physicians Dedicated to Excellence in Dermatology™
www.aad.org

More and more professional associations such as the American Academy of Dermatology are marketing themselves and their members' services directly to end user consumers.

SERVICE QUALITY

Earlier we mentioned the importance of managing customer expectations—the notion that underpromising and overdelivering is powerful because it contributes to a high level of customer satisfaction. Exceeding customer expectations is often referred to as **customer delight**, which has been shown to correlate highly with loyalty and high return on customer investment.[28] Firms practicing great service often build in **delightful surprises** for their customers as part of their service experience—the warm chocolate chip cookie you get at Doubletree on every stay was originally conceived as a delightful surprise, a fairly inexpensive way to make a memorable impact on weary travelers. Although Doubletree patrons have now come to expect their cookie, this little extra has become a part of the firm's branding and image, and customer surveys regularly indicate it is one of the most-loved aspects of the Doubletree experience.

Just what is service quality? In many respects, **service quality** represents a formalization of the measurement of customer expectations of a service compared to perceptions of actual service performance. The playing field for service quality is the **service encounter**, which is the period during which a customer interacts in any way with a service provider. This can be in person, by phone, or through other electronic means. While much of the actual service delivery might occur behind the curtain—consider the tax preparer who works on your IRS return or the travel agent who spends hours pulling together your extreme sport trip to Reykjavík—customer evaluations of a service tend to be based on the behaviors of the service provider and the accompanying physical surroundings during the service encounter itself. This is why the face-to-face time between customer and service provider is often called the **moment of truth**. Most customer judgments take place at that moment.[29]

Gap Analysis

LO 9-5

Discuss the elements of service quality and gap analysis.

Review the Gap Model of Service Quality, presented in Exhibit 9.6. The basis of the **gap model** is the identification and measurement of differences in five key areas of the service delivery process. Notice how the model is divided by a horizontal line, with the area below the line representing the provider side of the service encounter and the area above the line representing the customer side. For marketing managers, ongoing use of the gap model to identify emerging problems in service delivery is an important way to ensure service quality.

Let's take a closer look at each of the gaps. To illustrate the power of the analysis, we will develop a threaded example involving Outback Steakhouse, one of the restaurant brands owned and operated by Bloomin' Brands, Inc. of Tampa, Florida. Their other brands include Carrabba's Italian Grill, Bonefish Grill, Roy's Restaurant, and Fleming's Prime Steakhouse & Wine Bar. From a surface viewpoint, most people might assume that the founders of Outback—the original restaurant was in Tampa, Florida—built their differentiation primarily on the Australian theme and hearty portions at moderate prices. However, that is only part of their original success formula. From the beginning, Outback's founders relied heavily on its service delivery system to set it apart from other mid-priced, family-style restaurants. Their success is undeniable, with Outback units

EXHIBIT 9.6 | Gap Model of Service Quality

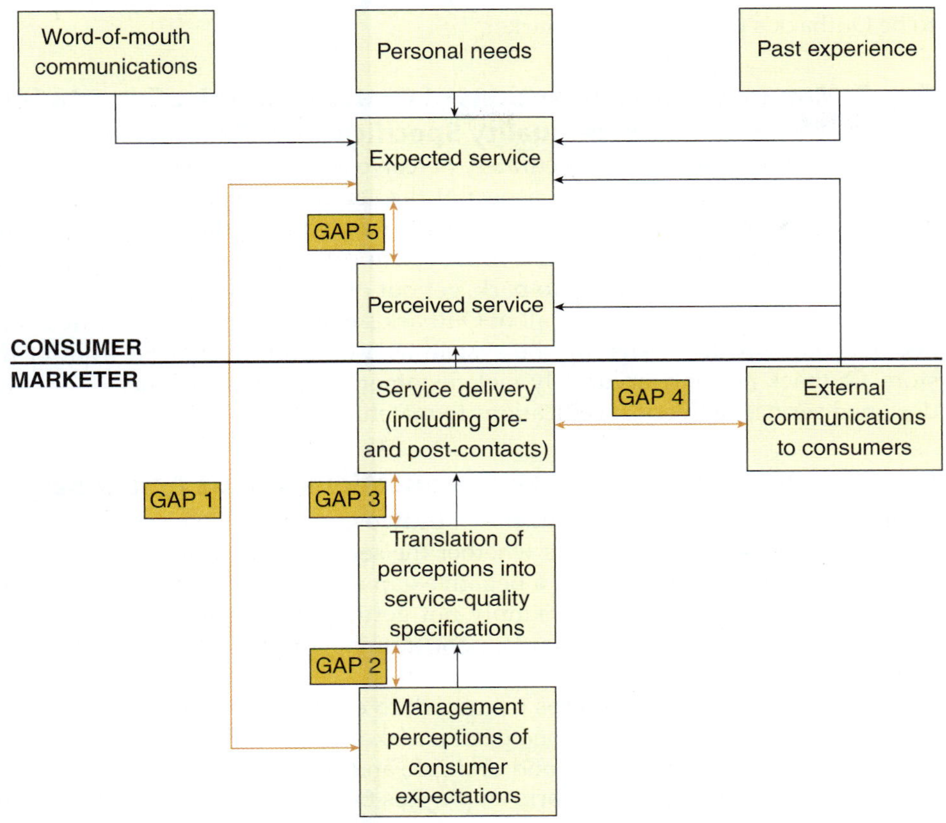

Source: A. Parasuraman, Valarie A. Zeithaml, and Leonard L. Berry, "A Conceptual Model of Service Quality and Its Implications for Future Research," *Journal of Marketing,* Fall 1985, pp. 41–50. Reprinted with permission of the American Marketing Association.

consistently leading their segment of the industry in customer turns per table, revenue and profit per square foot, and the all-important metrics of customer satisfaction. Using a service-profit chain approach to the business, Outback's founders focused strongly on its people, assuring that every store manager is a proprietor/owner of the business. Servers, even college students, tend to stay much longer than the industry average due to higher tips generated by more rapid table turnover.[30]

Gap 1: Management's Perceptions of Customer Service Expectations versus Actual Customer Expectations of Service In Chapter 3 you learned about the importance of ongoing, well-executed market research to provide input for marketing management decision making. Gap 1 is where a lack of the right customer data can wreak havoc on service delivery. Unfortunately, firms all too often make unfounded assumptions about customers' wants and needs and translate them into product offerings. Then management is surprised when new products fail or customers begin to switch to other providers.

Outback Steakhouse was an early leader in providing convenient phone-ahead curbside service for customer pickup. Although it varies by location, some stores do as much as 15 to 20 percent of their revenue in customer takeout. This is especially profitable because it requires little extra server labor to fill these pickup orders. How did Outback know to add this new service? Not surprisingly, it was through market research that showed customers were increasingly disappointed with traditional fast-food drive-throughs and were willing to pay more for a quality, convenient meal they could enjoy at home. Convenience and time utility are two major drivers of busy young professional families today, which just happens to be Outback's primary target market.[31]

Gap 2: Management's Perceptions of Customer Service Expectations versus the Actual Service Quality Specifications Developed In Gap 2, management may or may not accurately perceive actual customer expectations of service, but regardless builds an aspect of the service delivery system that does not meet customer wants and needs. A perfect example of this would be if Outback had designed its curbside carryout system differently. Customers grabbing takeout after work do not want to park, get out of the car, and go into the restaurant to pick up the food. Almost all of Outback's competitors originally designed takeout that way. By designing the system as a curbside pickup in front of the store, Outback not only accurately met customer expectations of service but also designed service delivery specifications to match.

Gap 3: Actual Service Quality Specifications versus Actual Service Delivery Interestingly, unlike the previous two gaps, this one has no element of perception—this gap strictly asks whether the service is provided in the manner intended. As such, when there is a negative gap at Gap 3, it nearly always points to management and employees simply not getting the job done. This could be due to vague performance standards, poor training, or ineffective monitoring by management.

Like many firms, Outback uses teamwork to enhance its service delivery system. Ever notice that more than one person makes contact with you at your table, asks how you are doing, brings food or drink, and so forth? To make the curbside pickup system work like clockwork, employees from the phone order-taker to the cooks to the car-runner must be in sync. If cars back up, employees are trained to go down the line to make contact, provide estimated remaining wait times, and even handle payment so that when the food does come out the customer can immediately depart. You may wait a while to get your table at an Outback restaurant on a peak evening (if it's a nice night, you can sit outside and sip a beverage), but once you're seated the restaurant has aggressive standards for wait times for getting your meal at the table. When these wait times are significantly exceeded, the employees are trained to apologize, not offer lame excuses, and then offer something extra like a free dessert or a coupon for a free Bloomin' Onion next time.

This process is called **service recovery** and is actually a very strategic aspect of marketing management. Much research in services marketing has shown that **service failure**, when properly handled through service recovery, does not necessarily impact customer satisfaction, loyalty, or retention unless service failures become habitual.[32] All firms employing service as a marketing strategy must plan ahead for the eventuality of service failures and train employees to properly execute service recovery.

Sometimes a service failure can be quite severe. A classic example occurred in February 2007 when JetBlue Airways found itself the victim of a major winter storm at New York's JFK International Airport. Word quickly spread via media stories, blogs, and word of mouth that many hundreds of JetBlue passengers were left stranded on airplanes that had pulled away from their gates but were not allowed to take off or return to the gate for up to 12 hours. By the next day, then-CEO David Neeleman had declared publicly that the airline had suffered an operational meltdown and that a series of bad decisions compounded with an already bad situation to make it even worse.[33]

Is service recovery even possible given the magnitude of the service failure that JetBlue's customers experienced at JFK? Neeleman certainly can't be faulted for lack of trying. Immediately after the incident, he sent out an apology letter electronically to every customer in the company's database, backed up by a video message posted on the company website. This was followed by a new JetBlue Airways Customer Bill of Rights, which received press for being industry-leading. Neeleman's letter is presented in Exhibit 9.7, and the current version of JetBlue's Customer Bill of Rights can be reviewed on the company's website. Apparently JetBlue's customers believe this service recovery was appropriate and effective. JetBlue's customer ratings of quality have continued to be among the highest in the industry, ranking in the top three every year for the past five years![34]

Gap 4: Actual Service Delivery versus What the Firm Communicates It Delivers This gap fundamentally represents customer expectations management

EXHIBIT 9.7 | JetBlue Airways Service Recovery Letter

jetBlue AIRWAYS

An Apology from JetBlue Airways

Dear JetBlue Customers,

We are sorry and embarrassed. But most of all, we are deeply sorry.

Last week was the worst operational week in Jet Blue's seven year history. Following the severe winter ice storm in the Northeast, we subjected our customers to unacceptable delays, flight cancellations, lost baggage, and other major inconveniences. The storm disrupted the movement of aircraft, and, more importantly, disrupted the movement of JetBlue's pilot and inflight crewmembers who were depending on those planes to get them to the airports where they were scheduled to serve you. With the busy President's Day weekend upon us, rebooking opportunities were scarce and hold times at 1-800-JETBLUE were unacceptably long or not even available, further hindering our recovery efforts.

Words cannot express how truly sorry we are for the anxiety, furstration and inconvenience that we caused. This is especially saddening because JetBlue was founded on the promise of bringing humanity back to air travel and making the experience of flying happier and easier for everyone who chooses to fly with us. We know we failed to deliver on this promise last week.

We are committed to you, our valued customers, and are taking immediate corrective steps to regain your confidence in us. We have begun putting a comprehensive plan in place to provide better and more timely information to you, more tools and resources for our crewmembers and improved procedures for handling operational difficulties in the future. We are confident, as a result of these actions, that JetBlue will emerge as a more reliable and even more customer responsive airline than ever before.

Most importantly, we have published the JetBlue Airways Customer Bill of Rights—our official commitment to you of how we will handle operational interruptions going forward—including details of compensation. I have a video message to share with you about this industry leading action.

You deserved better–a lot better–from us last week. Nothing is more important than regaining your trust and all of us here hope you will give us the opportunity to welcome you onboard again soon adn provide you the positive JetBlue Experience you have come to expect from us.

Sincerely,

David Neeleman
Founder and CEO
JetBlue Airways

JETBLUE AIRWAYS CUSTOMER BILL OF RIGHTS

Courtesy of JetBlue Airways.

through marketing communications. Part Five of this book will familiarize you with different ways to communicate the value offering to customers. The messages the marketing manager puts out through various communication vehicles are in large measure what sets the expectations for the customer. Thus, deceptive advertising, overly zealous sales pitches, and coupon promotions backed by too little stock to handle demand all create a negative gap at Gap 4. In the case of Outback's curbside pickup, although it has done some advertising over the years, most of Outback's media ads focus more on special occasions and the fun theme of the restaurant. Because much of Outback's product is the experience provided the diner inside the restaurant, it has allowed the pickup business to grow more through word of mouth and in-store signage. Outback has not set any unrealistic expectations about its curbside takeout via its marketing communications.

Gap 5: Perceived Service by Customers versus Actual Customer Expectations of Service Finally, Gap 5 represents the core issue of expectations versus perceptions and is the only gap that occurs exclusively in the customer's space. This is the gap between the service a customer expects to receive and the customer's perceptions of the level of service actually received. The score for this gap, which can be positive or negative, is the manifestation of a firm's customer expectations management strategy and the efficacy of its service delivery system.[35] For Outback Steakhouse, as well as most other firms, these scores are a direct flow-through into customer satisfaction measurement. Occasionally after eating at Outback, you might get a special receipt that has a toll-free number to call at Outback to answer a brief telephone questionnaire about your service encounter. Outback might offer some free food for completing the survey by providing you with an activation number. Almost always such survey research efforts are aimed at measuring importance scores (how important various aspects of a service are to the customer) versus actual performance scores (how well did we do on delivering against these service aspects during your last service encounter with us).

To provide an example of Gap 5 in practice, Exhibit 9.8 lists 14 hypothetical attributes that a restaurant like Outback might consider for analysis in terms of customer perceptions of their importance. Then, Exhibit 9.9 portrays a matrix based on a hypothetical analysis of importance perceptions versus performance perceptions for those 14 attributes, showing areas where the restaurant can invest in service improvement, areas where it needs to simply keep up the current service, areas of low priority for attention, and areas where too much emphasis is being placed on service aspects. One other analysis could be easily added—comparative matrices for several of Outback's closest competitors so the chain can easily see how well the competition is doing in delivering against the same attributes. Such analytical approaches are invaluable in allowing marketing managers to know how to best invest in service quality.

EXHIBIT 9.8 | Example Attributes

1. Healthy food options.
2. Convenient locations.
3. Quick to-go pickup outside.
4. Clean restrooms.
5. Variety of menu items.
6. Friendly and courteous staff.
7. Children's food choices.
8. Fun ambience.
9. Accurate order fulfillment.
10. Speed of service.
11. Senior discounts.
12. Accommodating hours of operation.
13. Children's play area.
14. Innovative new menu items.

Customers would likely be surveyed on the attributes with questions such as the following, using an appropriate rating scale:

Rate the importance of each attribute to your decision to dine at _____ restaurant.
Rate how well _____ restaurant provides each attribute.

Any airline will face service gaps, such as from a flight delay or lost luggage. What distinguishes a company is how it handles that service failure. Southwest Airlines has been recognized by customers for its superior service recovery process. Jonathan Clarkson, director of the Southwest Airlines Rapid Rewards Loyalty program, believes employees are the key differentiators for positive customer experiences. "Our customer relations specialists are empowered to do more than other call center agents," said Clarkson. "For example, we empower them to make flight changes or put points back into customers' accounts if the situation warrants." Ensuring that the customer is pleased with the outcome is essential to increasing loyalty. Customer satisfaction increased 6 percent in one year and customer loyalty jumped 4 percent within the first three months of 2013. "From my perspective, it's all about whether you're willing to make a commitment to the [customer experience] or not. At Southwest, we've had an unwavering commitment to our customers for over forty years," said Clarkson.[36]

SERVQUAL: A Multiple-Item Scale to Measure Service Quality

LO 9-6

Measure service quality through use of SERVQUAL.

Marketers didn't separate out services for separate study from goods until the early 1980s. The movement toward a focus on service as a core differentiator was driven, in part, by a team of professors: Leonard Berry, Valarie Zeithaml, and A. Parasuraman. Much of their work resulted in the gap analysis approach described in the prior section.[37] But another important aspect of their research was determining what service quality really means from the perspective of customers. Their work uncovered five **dimensions of service quality**, illustrated by Exhibit 9.10 and described below.

Tangibles

Tangibles are the physical evidence of a service or the observable aspects that help customers form advance opinions about the service despite its general intangibility. Examples of tangibles include appearance of service providers, website, marketing communications materials, and the ambience and look of the office or retail store. Such tangibles send cues to the customer about the quality of the service.

Reliability

Reliability is the ability to provide service dependably and accurately and thus to deliver what was promised. Reliability means performing the service right the first time and every time. Research has consistently demonstrated that reliability tends to be one of the most important aspects of service quality.

Responsiveness

Responsiveness is the willingness and ability to provide prompt service and to respond quickly to customer requests. Customers often complain about a lack of responsiveness on the part of service providers. Service providers exhibit poor responsiveness when they create difficulty making contact, exhibit poor follow-up, make excuses for poor service, and generally act as though they are doing the customer a favor.

EXHIBIT 9.9 | Importance–Performance Analysis Matrix

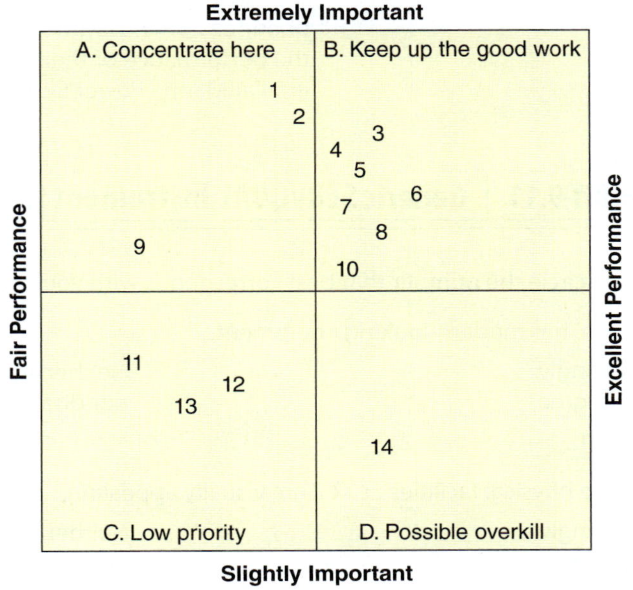

EXHIBIT 9.10 | Dimensions of Service Quality

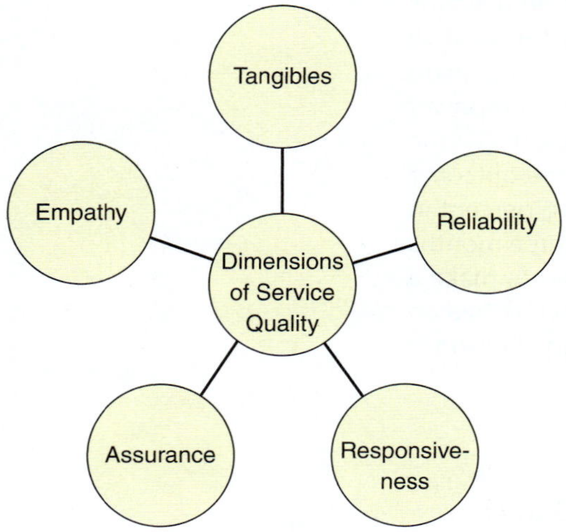

Assurance **Assurance** is the knowledge and courtesy of employees, and the ability to convey trust and build a customer's confidence in the quality of the service. Service providers often provide assurance primarily through their own competence in the job.

Empathy **Empathy** is the caring and individual attention a service provider gives to customers. Empathy means considering things from the customer's point of view.

The SERVQUAL Instrument

Parasuraman, Zeithaml, and Berry developed a measurement instrument called **SERVQUAL** to reflect these five dimensions.[39] The scale has been applied in tens of thousands of service settings across all types of industries. It can be adapted to most any application in which the marketing manager wishes to gain customer input about the importance and performance of a firm against the five dimensions of service quality. Companies track SERVQUAL scores over time to understand how their service quality is tracking so that marketing managers can create approaches to improve areas as needed.[40] Exhibit 9.11 provides a generic version of the SERVQUAL scale.

Caterpillar sells heavy equipment. You've seen its familiar yellow bulldozers and trucks on construction sites. Caterpillar customers rely on the equipment to keep working—if a bulldozer breaks down, all work comes to a halt. That is why Caterpillar differentiates itself through fast, responsive service. Caterpillar will ship spare parts to a customer anywhere in the world, from Alaska to Timbuktu, in just 24 hours. Furthermore, it is important to the company that its customers know they are being heard. Recently, the "We Listened" initiative was launched, targeted at the marine industry's needs. Caterpillar created the Marine Resource Center on its website as a way to enhance customer communication. "We realize our customers have varying levels of communication with their local dealer, but the most basic premise of the 'We Listened' campaign is to ensure that each one of our customers knows that we care about their business and want to optimize the performance of their Cat products through education and training," said Caterpillar Marine Power Systems product support director Jaime Tetrault.[38]

EXHIBIT 9.11 | Generic SERVQUAL Instrument for XYZ Company

Please circle the number that best corresponds with your view related to XYZ.

1. XYZ has modern-looking equipment.

Strongly disagree			Neither agree nor disagree			Strongly agree
1	2	3	4	5	6	7

2. The physical facilities at XYZ are visually appealing.

Strongly disagree			Neither agree nor disagree			Strongly agree
1	2	3	4	5	6	7

EXHIBIT 9.11 | Generic SERVQUAL Instrument for XYZ Company *(cont.)*

3. Employees at XYZ appear professionally dressed.

Strongly disagree			Neither agree nor disagree			Strongly agree
1	2	3	4	5	6	7

4. Materials associated with XYZ (website, promotional brochures, service tracking documents, invoices, etc.) are visually appealing.

Strongly disagree			Neither agree nor disagree			Strongly agree
1	2	3	4	5	6	7

5. When employees at XYZ promise to do something by a certain time, they do so.

Strongly disagree			Neither agree nor disagree			Strongly agree
1	2	3	4	5	6	7

6. When a customer has a problem, employees at XYZ show a sincere interest in solving it.

Strongly disagree			Neither agree nor disagree			Strongly agree
1	2	3	4	5	6	7

7. XYZ employees perform the service right the first time.

Strongly disagree			Neither agree nor disagree			Strongly agree
1	2	3	4	5	6	7

8. XYZ employees provide their services at the time they promise to do so.

Strongly disagree			Neither agree nor disagree			Strongly agree
1	2	3	4	5	6	7

9. XYZ insists on error-free records.

Strongly disagree			Neither agree nor disagree			Strongly agree
1	2	3	4	5	6	7

10. Employees at XYZ tell you exactly when services will be performed.

Strongly disagree			Neither agree nor disagree			Strongly agree
1	2	3	4	5	6	7

11. Employees at XYZ give prompt service to you.

Strongly disagree			Neither agree nor disagree			Strongly agree
1	2	3	4	5	6	7

12. Employees at XYZ are always willing to help you.

Strongly disagree			Neither agree nor disagree			Strongly agree
1	2	3	4	5	6	7

(cont.)

EXHIBIT 9.11 | Generic SERVQUAL Instrument for XYZ Company *(concluded)*

13. Employees at XYZ are never too busy to respond to your requests.

Strongly disagree			Neither agree nor disagree			Strongly agree
1	2	3	4	5	6	7

14. The behavior of employees at XYZ instills confidence in you.

Strongly disagree			Neither agree nor disagree			Strongly agree
1	2	3	4	5	6	7

15. You feel safe in your transactions with XYZ.

Strongly disagree			Neither agree nor disagree			Strongly agree
1	2	3	4	5	6	7

16. Employees at XYZ are consistently courteous to you.

Strongly disagree			Neither agree nor disagree			Strongly agree
1	2	3	4	5	6	7

17. Employees at XYZ have the knowledge to answer your questions.

Strongly disagree			Neither agree nor disagree			Strongly agree
1	2	3	4	5	6	7

18. XYZ employees give you individual attention.

Strongly disagree			Neither agree nor disagree			Strongly agree
1	2	3	4	5	6	7

19. XYZ has operating hours convenient to all its customers.

Strongly disagree			Neither agree nor disagree			Strongly agree
1	2	3	4	5	6	7

20. XYZ has employees who give you personal attention.

Strongly disagree			Neither agree nor disagree			Strongly agree
1	2	3	4	5	6	7

21. XYZ employees have your best interests at heart.

Strongly disagree			Neither agree nor disagree			Strongly agree
1	2	3	4	5	6	7

22. XYZ employees understand your needs.

Strongly disagree			Neither agree nor disagree			Strongly agree
1	2	3	4	5	6	7

Key to the instrument by SERVQUAL dimension: Tangibles = Questions 1–4; Reliability = Questions 5–9; Responsiveness = Questions 10–13; Assurance = Questions 14–17; Empathy = Questions 18–22.

SERVICE BLUEPRINTS

LO 9-7

Understand service blueprinting and how it aids marketing managers.

Earlier in the chapter, you read that from its inception Outback Steakhouse conceived of its service delivery system as an important source of differentiation in its positioning against other mid-priced family restaurants. How does a marketing manager conceive of such a system, lay it out, and then implement it so that everyone in the firm can follow it and play their part? The answer is through **service blueprints**, which borrows concepts from manufacturing and operations management to actually map out (likely through the use of computer software) a complete pictorial design and flow chart of all the activities from the first customer contact to the actual delivery of the service.

A simple example of a service blueprint for a floral delivery service is mapped out in Exhibit 9.12.

Note in tracking through the floral delivery service blueprint that activities are divided between those above the **line of visibility** (or those activities directly involving the customer that the customer sees) and those below the line of visibility to the customer (in this case, backstage operations and processing activities). The "moments of truth" we discussed earlier occur above the line of visibility.

A service blueprint is invaluable as a tool for marketing managers, especially for service encounters that are more complex than floral delivery, restaurants, and the like. First, the mere creation of the document serves to uncover potential bottlenecks in the service delivery system before it goes operational. Second, it represents a tremendous training device for employees involved in service delivery. Especially in a teamwork environment such as Outback Steakhouse where servers, cooks, and bartenders are so dependent on each other's performance to maximize the customer's positive experience overall, familiarizing each person involved in service delivery with exactly how his or her role fits into the entire system helps everyone take on a customer mind-set—even employees who ordinarily don't directly interface with the external customers such as the cooks.[41] Finally, using a service blueprint provides managers with an important way to integrate service topics into the performance evaluation process for all employees. Smart firms that rely on service for differentiation such as Outback, Ritz-Carlton, and Southwest Airlines provide incentives to their people who consistently contribute to the delivery of great service.

EXHIBIT 9.12 | Service Blueprint for Floral Delivery

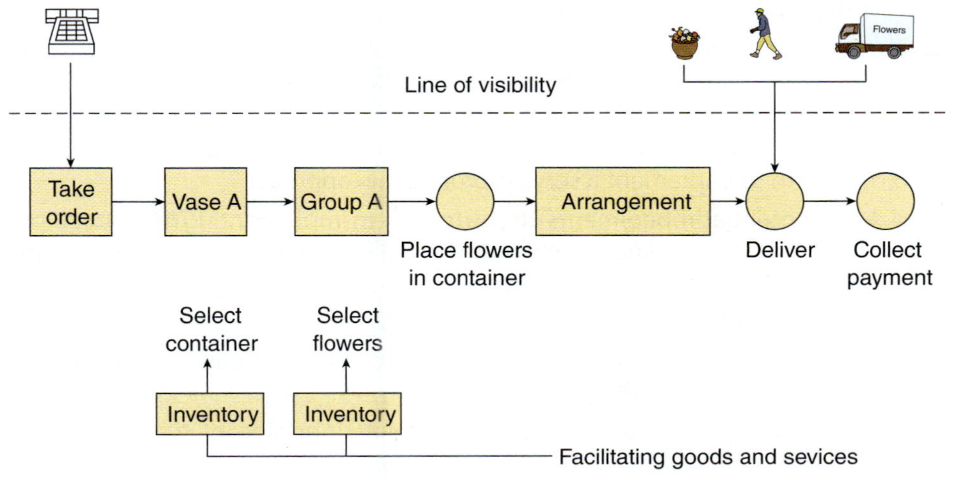

SUMMARY

In today's competitive marketplace, service is an important source of differentiation. But services have unique characteristics that must be understood as well as attributes that make services quite different from goods. An important concept for marketing managers to master is the service-profit chain, which provides a framework for linking elements of the service delivery system that drive customer loyalty, revenue growth, and higher profits. Key tools for establishing and measuring effective service include gap analysis, SERVQUAL, and service blueprints.

KEY TERMS

service 265
service economy 265
service sector 265
new dominant logic for marketing 266
intangibility 266
inseparability 267
variability 268
perishability 269
fluctuating demand 269
service-profit chain 269
internal marketing 269
customer-centric 270
customer mind-set 271
customer expectations management 272
customer retention 272
customer advocacy 272
search attributes 274
experience attributes 275
credence attributes 276
professional services 276
customer delight 278
delightful surprises 278
service quality 278
service encounter 278
moment of truth 278
gap model 278
service recovery 280
service failure 280
dimensions of service quality 283
tangibles 283
reliability 283
responsiveness 283
assurance 284
empathy 284
SERVQUAL 284
service blueprints 287
line of visibility 287

APPLICATION QUESTIONS

1. Marketing managers must be cognizant of the unique characteristics of services: intangibility, inseparability, variability, and perishability.
   a. How does each of these characteristics potentially impact the development and execution of marketing plans?
   b. What might a manager do to mitigate any negative consequences of each characteristic on the delivery of his or her firm's service?
   c. Come up with an example of a service encounter you have had as a customer (either in the B2C or B2B market) in which each of these characteristics came into play in how the service was delivered.
2. The service-profit chain guides managers toward understanding and facilitating successful linkages in the service delivery system to drive loyalty, revenue growth, and higher profits.
   a. What functional areas of a firm must a marketing manager effectively interface with to implement a service-profit chain approach?
   b. What potential impediments do you foresee in implementing the service-profit chain in an organization? How might these impediments best be overcome?
   c. What do you believe are the key advantages in implementing a service-profit chain approach?
3. Review Exhibit 9.5 and the accompanying discussion on search, experience, and credence attributes of offerings.
   a. Why are the types of offerings on the far right side of the continuum—professional services—difficult for customers to evaluate?
   b. What challenges does this difficulty create for marketing managers in professional services firms? Why?

4. Review the Gap Model of Service Quality (Exhibit 9.6). Consider each of the five gaps where customer expectations might not be met. Select a firm of your choice and for each potential gap list specific actions that the firm could take to improve the likelihood that customer expectations will be met on a regular basis.
5. Consider the five dimensions of service quality: tangibles, reliability, responsiveness, assurance, and empathy.
   a. Identify a recent service encounter you have experienced as a customer (either B2C or B2B) that you would classify as a generally bad experience. In what ways specifically did each of the five service quality dimensions contribute to your perceptions of poor service? Be as specific with your examples as you can. What could the service provider have done to improve each of the relevant dimensions and thus improve your experience?
   b. Repeat the above process but instead of a bad service experience this time identify a generally good service experience. For each relevant dimension, specifically what did the service provider do really well? Did you experience any delightful surprise? If so, what?

MANAGEMENT DECISION CASE: Service and the Story of Netflix

As mentioned at the top of this chapter, services account for over 75 percent of U.S. gross domestic product (GDP), which means the service sector amounts to almost $13 trillion! Given that kind of economic impact, it's no wonder the new thinking in business is that everything is related to service and how one company distinguishes itself from its competitors will largely depend on the services that are offered and how they are performed in conjunction with any physical product. In a classic article in *Fortune* over 20 years ago, the gauntlet for service was thrown down: "It matters not whether a company creates something you can touch . . . . what counts more is the service built into that something—the way the product is designed and delivered, billed and bundled, explained and installed, repaired and renewed." With this philosophy in mind, let's consider Netflix.

Netflix got its start in 1997 as a company providing DVDs to customers through the mail. Its then-novel business model differed from other DVD rental outlets in that Netflix did not have any physical locations. This allowed the company to save money on lease payments to building owners and on wages for employees to staff stores. Another key to their early success was that they eliminated a particular customer annoyance when renting DVDs from more traditional locations like Blockbuster—late fees for DVDs returned to the store after their due date. Also, the low monthly subscription price hit a sweet spot with Netflix customers—the subscription was lower than what many people had been paying Blockbuster monthly in late fees alone! But attractive pricing by itself rarely guarantees success—the *service* provided by Netflix also had to be right.

The DVD rental and online video streaming service provided by Netflix exemplifies the four distinct characteristics of services quite well: intangibility, inseparability, variability, and perishability. The service is intangible in that a customer cannot experience what Netflix provides without actually signing up for the service. Because of this intangibility aspect, Netflix offers a 30-day free trial, thus giving potential customers an opportunity to experience the service before they actually have to start paying for it. Of course, the free trial also helps with overcoming the inseparability aspect of services. Because services are produced and consumed at the same time, a free trial is a great incentive to entice customers to experience the service to see if it is as good as claimed. One thing that Netflix had to get right from the beginning was consistent, high-quality delivery of the service—that is, stamp out variability. Variability in the wrong DVD showing up in the mailbox or with the online streaming service shutting down haphazardly had to be eliminated for Netflix to retain customers and enhance their subscriber base. Finally, perishability impacts Netflix in that not many people are interested in streaming a movie on Monday morning at 10:00 a.m. However, the number of people wanting to stage their own weekend-at-home *Breaking Bad* marathon from the first to the last season could be significant. As a result, Netflix had to ensure that their infrastructure could accommodate this fluctuating demand.

Given their most recent success, Netflix clearly has struck a chord with customers. The company has surpassed the 40-million subscriber mark and its stock price went from less than $92 per share at the beginning of 2013 to over $380 per share by mid-October of that same year. However, for a company that has been planning for the demise of the DVD roughly since its founding in 1997, Netflix is not likely to sit back and rely on the past to project it into the future. The extent to which Netflix succeeds going forward depends in large measure on how well it creatively executes its service strategy for the benefit of customers.

Questions for Consideration

1. Netflix started out as a DVD rental company but has since added online video streaming to their service offerings. Also, in recent years they began developing their own content, which reduces their reliance on other production companies to provide the shows customers watch. What other innovative offerings do you recommend Netflix investigate for the future (think "outside the box" on this)?
2. Over its history, Netflix has done a great job of utilizing the elements of the marketing mix to enhance its success. Describe Netflix's marketing mix—what product, pricing, distribution, and promotion strategies have contributed to its popularity with customers?
3. The chapter identifies five dimensions of service quality. Considering these with respect to Netflix, how does the firm stack up on each of these dimensions to set itself apart from competitors and other providers of entertainment content?

Sources: Alexandra Frean, "Netflix Storms Past 40 Million Subscribers as Shares Soar," *The Times*, October 22, 2013; Ronald Henkoff, "Service Is Everybody's Business," *Fortune* 29, no. 13, (June 27, 1994), pp. 48–60; "National Income and Product Accounts," http://bea.gov/newsreleases/national/GDP/GDPnewsrelease.htm, accessed December 16, 2013; Nick Wingfield, "Netflix Boss Plots Life after the DVD," *The Wall Street Journal*, June 23, 2009, p. A1.

MARKETING PLAN EXERCISE

ACTIVITY 11: Differentiating via Service Quality

In your marketing plan, consider how you might effectively use service as a source of differentiation for your offering(s). As you learned in this chapter, to successfully accomplish this, you must be sensitive to nuances of services versus goods and also be able to ensure that the people and processes in your firm are able to properly support the service.

1. Evaluate the opportunity to utilize service as an important differentiator.
2. Employ a service-profit chain approach to identify people and operational aspects of your plan to support service differentiation.
3. Develop specific action plans and metrics in support of your service differentiation approach.

NOTES

1. Leonard L. Berry, *On Great Service: A Framework for Action* (New York, The Free Press, 1995).
2. Stephen L. Vargo and Robert F. Lusch, "Evolving to a New Dominant Logic for Marketing," *Journal of Marketing* 68, no. 1 (January 2004), pp. 1–17.
3. Michael K. Brady, Brian L. Bourdeau, and Julia Heskel, "The Importance of Brand Cues in Intangible Service Industries: An Application to Investment Services," *Journal of Services Marketing* 19, no. 6/7 (2005), pp. 401–11.
4. A. Vance, "Intuit's TurboTax: File from the Bath but Not the Shower," *Bloomberg Businessweek*, March 20, 2013, www.businessweek.com/articles/2013-03-20/intuits-turbotax-evolves-to-make-filing-taxes-easier.
5. Harvir S. Bansal, Shirley F. Taylor, and Yannik St. James, "'Migrating' to New Service Providers: Toward a Unifying Framework of Customers' Switching Behaviors," *Journal of the Academy of Marketing Science* 33, no. 1 (Winter 2005), pp. 96–116.
6. Jeremy J. Sierra and Shaun McQuitty, "Service Providers and Customers: Social Exchange Theory and Service Loyalty," *Journal of Services Marketing* 19, no. 6/7 (2005), pp. 392–401.
7. "Boston Market Is Now Serving Ribs," *Fox News*, April 4, 2013, www.foxnews.com/leisure/2013/04/04/boston-m.
8. Don Kuehnast, "Customer Relationship Management Solution Energizes Bank Sales Environment," *Microsoft Business Solutions CRM Customer Case Study*, 2004.

9. Christian Homburg, Wayne D. Hoyer, and Martin Fassnacht, "Service Orientation of a Retailer's Business Strategy: Dimensions, Antecedents, and Performance Outcomes," *Journal of Marketing* 66, no. 4 (October 2002), pp. 86–102; and Medhi Mourali, Michael Laroche, and Frank Pons, "Individualistic Orientation and Customer Susceptibility to Interpersonal Influence," *Journal of Services Marketing* 19, no. 3 (2005), pp. 164–74.
10. William J. Holstein, "At Southwest, the Culture Drives Success," *BusinessWeek*, February 21, 2008, www.businessweek.com/managing/content/feb2008/ca20080221_179423.htm?chan=search.
11. Jena McGregor, "Customer Service Champs," *BusinessWeek*, March 3, 2008, pp. 37–50.
12. Rajshekhar G. Javalgi, Thomas W. Whipple, Amit K. Ghosh, and Robert B. Young, "Market Orientation, Strategic Flexibility, and Performance: Implications for Services Providers," *Journal of Services Marketing* 19, no. 4 (2005), pp. 212–22.
13. Kenneth J. Klassen and Thomas R. Rohleder, "Combining Operations and Marketing to Manage Capacity and Demand in Services," *Service Industries Journal* 21, no. 2 (April 2001), pp. 1–30.
14. S. Bourette, "Why You Want Your Employees to Be Committed and Proud," *The Globe and Mail,* April 4, 2013, www.theglobeandmail.com/report-on-business/careers/career-advice/life-at-work/why-you-want-your-employees-to-be-committed-and-proud/article10784222/?cmpid=rss1.
15. D. Todd Donovan, Tom J. Brown, and John C. Mowen, "Internal Benefits of Service-Worker Customer Orientation: Job Satisfaction, Commitment, and Organizational Citizenship Behaviors," *Journal of Marketing* 68, no. 1 (January 2004), pp. 128–46.
16. Margaret Littman, "Playing for Keeps," *ABA Journal* 91 (June 2005), pp. 71–72.
17. Ceridwyn King and Debra Grace, "Exploring the Role of Employees in the Delivery of the Brand: A Case Study Approach," *Qualitative Market Research* 8, no. 3 (2005), pp. 277–96.
18. "From Employee to Brand Ambassador: Maximiz ing the Value of the Professional Services Brand," DeSantis Breindel, January 17, 2013, www.desantisbreindel.com/maximizing-the-value-of-the-professional-services-brand/.
19. Deepak Sirdeshmukh, Jagdip Singh, and Barry Sabol, "Customer Trust, Value, and Loyalty in Relational Exchanges," *Journal of Marketing* 66, no. 1 (January 2002), pp. 15–38.
20. Lawrence A. Crosby and Brian Lunde, "Loyalty Linkage," *Marketing Management* 16, no. 3 (May/June 2007), p. 12; and James H. McAlexander, John W. Schouten, and Harold F. Koening, "Building Brand Community," *Journal of Marketing* 66, no. 1 (January 2002), pp. 38–55.
21. Sudhir N. Kale and Peter Klugsberger, "Reaping Rewards," *Marketing Management* 16, no. 4 (July/August 2007), p. 14.
22. J. LeClaire, "Microsoft Dynamics CRM Heads to the NBA," *Sci-Tech Today,* April 4, 2013, www.sci-tech-today.com/news/Microsoft-Dynamics-CRM-Heads-to-NBA/story.xhtml?story_id=01000147A2KG&full_skip=1.
23. Anita Goyal, "Consumer Perceptions towards the Purchase of Credit Cards," *Journal of Service Research* 6 (July 2006), pp. 179–91.
24. Minakshi Trivedi, Michael S. Morgan, and Kalpesh Kaushik Desai, "Consumer's Value for Informational Role of Agent in Service Industry," *Journal of Services Marketing* 22, no. 2 (2008), pp. 149–59.
25. G. Arnold, "Anguilla Single-Family Neighborhood in Sandoval Sells Out," *Naples Daily News* (User Story from GravinaSmithMatteArnold), March 8, 2013, www.naplesnews.com/news/2013/mar/08/anguilla-single-family-neighborhood-in-sandoval-se/.
26. Frances X. Frei, "The Four Things a Service Business Must Get Right," *Harvard Business Review* 86, no. 4 (April 2008), pp. 70–80.
27. "Update on Health Care Reform," *Consumer Reports*, March 2013, www.consumerreports.org/cro/2012/06/update-on-health-care-reform/index.htm; and Frei, "The Four Things a Service Business Must Get Right."
28. Kevin M. McNeilly and Terri Feldman Barr, "I Love My Accountants—They're Wonderful: Understanding Customer Delight in the Professional Services Arena," *Journal of Services Marketing* 20, no. 3 (2006), pp. 152–59.
29. Kenneth R. Evans, Simona Stan, and Lynn Murray, "The Customer Socialization Paradox: The Mixed Effects of Communicating Customer Role Expectations," *Journal of Services Marketing* 22, no. 3 (2008), pp. 213–23; and Amy K. Smith and Ruth N. Bolton, "The Effect of Customers' Emotional Responses to Service Failures on their Recovery Effort Evaluations and Satisfaction Judgments," *Journal of the Academy of Marketing Science* 30, no. 1 (Winter 2002), pp. 5–23.
30. Chris T. Sullivan, "A Stake in the Business," *Harvard Business Review* 83, no. 9 (September 2005), p. 57.
31. "Takeout Trend," *BusinessWeek,* August 24, 2007, www.businessweek.com/mediacenter/video/businessweektv/f3dcbeb754a244fb3ad7082bfe62af0362e7d167.html?chan=search.
32. "Is Customer Delight a Viable Goal?" *Businessline,* March 23, 2007, p. 1.

33. Jena McGregor, "An Extraordinary Stumble at JetBlue," *BusinessWeek,* March 5, 2007, pp. 58–59.
34. Brent D. Bowen and Dean E. Headley (2013), *Airline Quality Ratings 2013*, Purdue University Advanced Aviation Analytics Institute for Research, http://docs.lib.purdue.edu/cgi/viewcontent.cgi?article=1024&context=aqrr, accessed January 13, 2014.
35. Teck H. Ho and Yu-Sheng Zheng, "Setting Customer Expectation in Service Delivery: An Integrated Marketing-Operations Perspective," *Management Science* 50, no. 4 (April 2004), pp. 479–89.
36. J. Dasteel, "Getting on Board with Customer Experience," *Forbes*, March 26, 2013, www.forbes.com/sites/oracle/2013/03/26/getting-on-board-with-customer-experience/2/.
37. A. Parasuraman, Valarie A. Zeithaml, and Leonard L. Berry, "A Conceptual Model of Service Quality and Its Implications for Future Research," *Journal of Marketing, Fall* 1985, pp. 41–50.
38. "Caterpillar Goes Back to Basics of Service Excellence with 'We Listened' Initiative," 4-Traders.com, February 28, 2013. www.4-traders.com/CATERPILLAR-INC-4817/news/Caterpillar-Inc-Caterpillar-Goes-Back-to-Basics-of-Service-Excellence-with-We-Listened-Initiati-16372638/.
39. A. Parasuraman, Leonard L. Barry, and Valarie A. Zeithaml, "SERVQUAL: A Multiple-Item Scale for Measuring Consumer Perceptions of Service Quality," *Journal of Retailing* 64, no. 1 (1988), pp. 12–40; and A. Parasuraman, Leonard L. Barry, and Valarie A. Zeithaml, "Refinement and Reassessment of the SERVQUAL Scale," *Journal of Retailing* 67, no. 4 (1991), pp. 420–50.
40. A. Parasuraman, Leonard L. Berry, and Valarie A. Zeithaml, "Perceived Service Quality as a Customer-Based Performance Measure: An Empirical Examination of Organizational Barriers Using an Extended Service Quality Model," *Human Resource Management* 30, no. 3 (Fall 1991), pp. 335–42.
41. Pao-Tiao Chuang, "Combining Service Blueprint and FMEA for Service Design," *Service Industries Journal* 27, no. 2 (March 2007), pp. 91–105.

PART 4

Price and Deliver the Value Offering

chapter 10

MANAGE PRICING DECISIONS

chapter 11

MANAGE MARKETING CHANNELS AND POINTS OF CUSTOMER INTERFACE

CHAPTER 10

Manage Pricing Decisions

LEARNING OBJECTIVES

LO 10-1 Understand the integral role of price as a core component of value.

LO 10-2 Explore different pricing objectives and related strategies.

LO 10-3 Identify pricing tactics.

LO 10-4 Describe approaches to setting the exact price.

LO 10-5 Determine discounts and allowances to offer to channel members.

LO 10-6 Understand how to execute price changes.

LO 10-7 Examine legal considerations in pricing.

PRICE IS A CORE COMPONENT OF VALUE

LO 10-1

Understand the integral role of price as a core component of value.

You have learned that *value* is a ratio of the bundle of benefits a customer receives from an offering compared to the costs incurred by the customer in acquiring that bundle of benefits. From the customer's perspective, many but not all of those costs are reflected within the price paid for the offering. There are other types of costs, such as time invested in the purchase process or the opportunity costs of choosing one offering over another. But for most purchasers, regardless of whether the setting is B2C or B2B, the vast majority of costs are associated with the purchase price. As such, price—or, more specifically, the customer's *perception* of the offering's pricing—is a key determinant of perceived value. When customers exhibit strongly held beliefs that a firm's offerings provide high value, they are much more likely to remain loyal to the firm and its brands as well as actively tell others about their favorable experiences. Thus, marketing managers must take pricing decisions very seriously.[1]

From a marketing planning and strategy perspective, Michael Porter has consistently advocated that firms that are able to compete based on some extraordinary efficiency in one or more internal processes bring to the market a competitive advantage based on **cost leadership**. And although firms competing on cost leadership will likely also engage in one of Porter's other competitive strategies (differentiation or focus/niche), their core cost advantages translate directly to an edge over their competitors based on much more flexibility in their pricing strategies as well as their ability to translate some of the cost savings to the bottom line.[2]

For example, Southwest Airlines is widely regarded as a cost leader in its industry, which has become a critical factor in this era of high fuel costs. Southwest's internal process efficiencies stem from several important sources. First, it flies mostly the same type of plane—various series of the Boeing 737. This makes the maintenance process much more efficient than carriers whose fleet includes multiple types of aircraft. Second, Southwest has a very simple process of booking passengers and does not offer assigned seats. Finally, it avoids many of the delay-prone hubs used by most of its competitors, instead often opting for smaller airports in major metropolitan areas (Midway in Chicago instead of O'Hare, for example). These and other internal efficiencies translate into a cost structure second to none in the industry.

But what does such cost leadership mean for Southwest's pricing decision making? A knee-jerk response might be to simply lower fares to match the level of cost advantage. That might increase sales volume, but it also might start a price war with other airlines that have cost advantages (JetBlue, for instance). A more strategic approach—and the approach Southwest actually uses—is to translate part of its cost advantage into a more transparent, mileage-driven pricing structure for customers but at the same time take a portion of the cost advantage to increase the firm's profit margins, partly to reward shareholders and partly to reinvest for the firm's growth.

The UK's biggest electronics retailer, Dixons Retail Plc, through its chain Currys, encourages an obsession with price checking by its customers. Currys promises if customers find the same product cheaper at another store, it will beat the competitor's price by 10 percent of the difference. This is valid with in-store comparisons within 30 miles, as well as online with a select group of online retailers. Despite touting lower-priced goods, Currys is able to beat retailers such as Amazon in profitability as its stores encourage customers to purchase product extras. For example, salespeople in Currys' stores typically sell an additional two items each time a customer purchases a washing machine, namely home delivery and installation. Those add-ons boost overall margins. Despite these additional costs to consumers, they'll often choose the convenience provided by Currys over the do-it-yourself price savings on Amazon.[3]

Most importantly, Southwest's pricing model not only contributes to its financial performance but also is an integral part of its overall value proposition and provides a valuable lesson for the way a marketing manager should approach pricing decisions—that is, pricing decisions cannot be made in a vacuum but rather must consider the whole of the firm's offering, especially the concurrent decisions the firm is making about branding and products, service approaches, supply chain, and marketing communication. For the marketing manager, pricing is much more than an economic break-even point or a cost-plus accounting calculation. Price is a critical component that plays into a customer's assessment of the value afforded by a firm and its offerings. As such, managerial decisions about pricing should be undertaken methodically and always with a focus on how price impacts the all-important cost-versus-bundle-of-benefits

ETHICAL DIMENSION 10

Is Goodwill Good or Just Good Business?

A small school 90 minutes from Mexico City is so poorly funded that it cannot afford toilet paper for the lavatories, but, thanks to Intel, an eighth-grade class is searching the Internet on new laptops. Intel, one of the largest technology companies in the world, has a program called "Classmate" that offers laptop computers for educational systems in poorer countries for around $300 each. While still expensive for the poorest nations, the company has pledged to lower costs even further and plans call for a $200 model.

At the same time, Dr. Nicholas Negroponte, professor at the Massachusetts Institute of Technology and co-founder of the MIT media lab, has been working on the XO computer through his One Laptop per Child (OLPC) foundation, whose mission is to deliver computers to kids around the world for $100. OLPC has enlisted the help of Google, eBay, and Advanced Micro Devices (AMD)—AMD just happens to be Intel's major competitor in the chip market.

Although both organizations seek a similar goal—getting inexpensive laptops into the hands of poorer students—their approaches are very different. Negroponte has created a new device with a specially designed interface that represents a dramatic departure from the world standard Microsoft Windows/Intel operating environment. Intel, on the other hand, is using its substantial leverage with suppliers to drive costs out of a standard laptop, preferring to work within existing hardware including its own chips and software products. Intel and OLPC have introduced their products in more than 35 countries.

Critics of Intel's approach suggest that, rather than goodwill, the company's focus on delivering low-cost computers to schoolchildren is designed to create a new market for its own products. As the world moves from desktop computers to laptops and, of more concern to Intel, to mobile devices such as smartphones, the company has experienced slower growth and greater competition. Intel does not dominate the market for mobile-device computer chips in the same manner it does the computer market. Some experts believe that although the margins are low, the market for very-low-cost computers is huge and represents a key growth opportunity for Intel.

Negroponte and OLPC have accused Intel of trying to drive the XO computer project out of business and suggest this is because OLPC buys its chips from AMD. Negroponte also argues that, although Intel's computers are inexpensive, the company views low-end computers as a market and not a human right.[4]

Ethical Perspective

1. **Intel:** Is it unethical for Intel to pursue the Classmate project if its primary purpose is to target a new market? Should the company be encouraged to develop the Classmate computer without a profit incentive; that is, should it offer the product for sale at its cost?
2. **Governments:** Should governments support the OLPC project with its nonprofit perspective and low-cost computer over Intel's for-profit Classmate project?

assessment that equates to customer perceived value.[5] Ethical Dimension 10 evaluates some of these pricing concepts in terms of social responsibility.

The rest of this chapter details the important pricing decision-making process from a marketing manager's perspective: establish pricing objectives and related strategies; select pricing tactics; set the exact price; determine channel discounts and allowances; execute price changes; and understand legal considerations in pricing. Exhibit 10.1 protrays these elements of pricing decisions.

EXHIBIT 10.1 Elements of Pricing Decisions

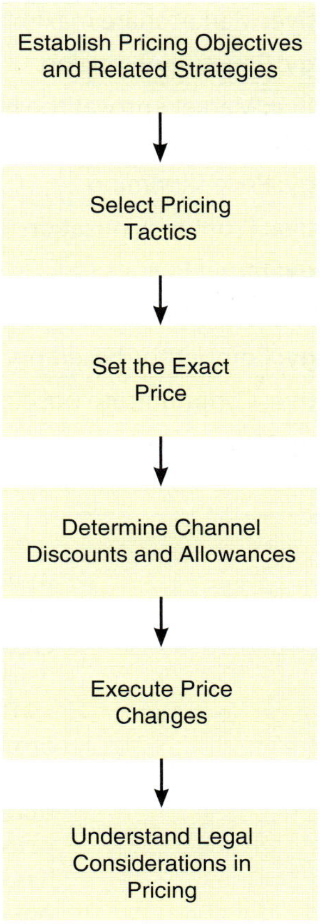

ESTABLISH PRICING OBJECTIVES AND RELATED STRATEGIES

As illustrated in the Southwest Airlines example, pricing objectives are but one component leading to an overall value proposition. However, a product's price tends to be so visible and definitive that customers often have trouble moving past price to consider other critical benefits the product affords. This characteristic puts pressure on marketing managers to establish pricing objectives that best reflect and enhance the value proposition, while at the same time achieving the firm's financial objectives. Striking a balance between these two forces sometimes makes pricing an especially challenging part of marketing.[6]

Pricing objectives are the desired or expected result associated with a pricing strategy. Pricing objectives must be consistent with other marketing-related objectives (positioning, branding, etc.) as well as with the firm's overall objectives (including financial objectives) for doing business.[7] Exhibit 10.2 portrays several of the most common pricing objectives, along with their related strategies.

The decision of which pricing objective or objectives to establish is driven by many interrelated factors. As you learn about each of the approaches, keep in mind that most firms attempt to balance a range of issues through their pricing objectives, including internal organization-level goals, internal capabilities, and a host of external market and competitive factors.

LO 10-2

Explore different pricing objectives and related strategies.

Dunkin' Donuts' pricing strategy is based on its positioning relative to rivals McDonald's and Starbucks in the breakfast market. Rather than engage in a price war with McDonald's, Dunkin' Donuts has tried to close the gap between itself and Starbucks. Although Dunkin' Donuts makes more money on breakfast sales overall than Starbucks, its average customer check is much lower. Additionally, Panera Bread Co. and Starbucks have seen an impressive sales boost due to their loyalty programs that offer deals to customers after a certain amount of money has been spent. In 2011, Dunkin' Donuts launched a program that gave customers $1 for every $20 spent on their Dunkin' Donuts card and has recently launched an updated program using a smartphone app to more closely compete with Starbucks. Fortunately for Dunkin' Donuts, to date McDonald's does not feature a consumer loyalty program.[8]

EXHIBIT 10.2 | Pricing Objectives and Related Strategies

Objective: Market share maximization	**Strategy:** Penetration pricing
Objective: Market entry at the highest possible initial price	**Strategy:** Price skimming
Objective: Profit maximization	**Strategy:** Target ROI
Objective: Benchmark the competition	**Strategy:** Competitor-based pricing
Objective: Communicate positioning through price	**Strategy:** Value pricing

Penetration Pricing

Market share is the percentage of total category sales accounted for by a firm. When a firm's objective is to gain as much market share as possible, a likely pricing strategy is **penetration pricing**, sometimes also referred to as pricing for maximum marketing share. In markets where customers are sensitive to price and where internal efficiencies lead to cost advantages allowing for acceptable margins even with aggressive pricing, a penetration objective can create a powerful barrier to market entry for other firms, thus protecting market share.

Sometimes penetration pricing is used as part of a new-product introduction. In both the B2C and B2B markets, it is common for prices to be set low initially to ward off competition and then for prices to creep up over time.[9] Such pricing is built into the product's budget over the life cycle of the item. Recall from Chapter 7 that as a product progresses through the product life cycle, margins tend to be at their highest during the maturity stage. This is partly because weaker competitors tend to drop out due to penetration pricing earlier in the cycle (introduction and growth stages), which creates the potential for remaining firms to decrease spending and raise prices during the maturity stage.

Be careful with a penetration pricing strategy. Because price is a cue for developing customer perceptions of product quality, the value proposition may be reduced if a low price belies the product's actual quality attributes.[10] An axiom in marketing is that customers always find it more palatable when a firm reduces a price than when it raises a price, and a corollary to the axiom is that once a price has been changed (one way or the other), changing it back creates confusion about positioning and brand image.

The global market for multiple sclerosis (MS) medication is worth $14 billion, with the U.S. market alone worth $8.5 million. The revenue in the U.S. market has continued to grow through recent years, but the growth is almost all due to continually increasing prices of existing medication. Biogen Idec Inc. has released a new pill, Tecfidera, into the market at a lower price than its major competitors. Novartis AG makes the closest competing MS therapy. Biogen hopes its pricing strategy will result in the classic marketing axiom "reduce price and increase volume"—realizing a net revenue increase. The price difference will be about $4,700 annually, but despite this advantage, Biogen faces challenges entering the market. Although the market is large, it is already crowded with competitors and the patient population is often reluctant to switch therapies. Biogen's hope is that the convenience and effectiveness Biogen offers coupled with its lower price will be a powerful enough combination to entice customers to switch from their current method of treatment.[11]

Price Skimming

A strategy of **price skimming** addresses the objective of entering a market at a relatively high price point. In proposing price skimming, the marketing manager usually is convinced that a strong price-quality relationship exists for the product. This might be done to lend prestige to a brand, or skimming is sometimes used in a new-product introduction by a firm with a first-mover advantage to skim early sales while the product has a high level of panache and exclusivity in the marketplace.[12]

Major developers of gaming consoles, including Nintendo, Microsoft, and Sony, always introduce a new platform with the objective of price skimming. Plasma televisions all started with very high price points and have gradually inched pricing downward as more and more customers began to purchase. Pharmaceutical companies justify very high introductory prices for new medications based on a necessity to recoup exorbitant R&D costs associated with their industry. Those same drugs steadily decline in price as more advanced competitive drugs come along, and, when patent protection runs out, the price drops precipitously as generic versions of the drug flood the market.

Game console makers must continually reevaluate their pricing strategy for their older technologies. As Microsoft anticipated the release of its Xbox 720, it subsequently lowered the prices of Xbox 360s. As a part of a new promotion, Microsoft announced that customers could purchase a 250GB Xbox 360 for $99 and the 250GB Xbox 360 with Kinect for $149. Otherwise these would have retailed for $299 and $399, respectively. However, those prices would only have been available if the customer also purchased Xbox Live Gold membership for two years. That service itself cost $14.99 per month. For those who play video games online, this may be a worthy deal, but for the casual gamer it's an extra $180 per year in additional cost. In the past, Microsoft has sold consoles at a single price point, so this approach was a change in strategy to sell hardware at a discount with the aim of gaining more revenue through its backend services. At times in which consumers are looking for deals, creative pricing strategies such as this may prove a winner.[13]

Regardless of the motivation for a price skimming strategy, as with penetration pricing, when multiple-year budgets are developed, marketing managers must consider the likelihood of competitive entry and adjust pricing projections accordingly. An initial pricing objective of skimming will require modification over time based in part on the rate of adoption and diffusion by consumers.

In general, skimming can be an appropriate pricing objective within the context of a focus (niche) strategy. By definition, such an approach positions a product for appeal to a limited (narrow) customer group or submarket of a larger market. Because niche market players typically attract fewer and less-aggressive competitors than those employing differentiation strategies within the larger market, a focus strategy can usually support higher prices and the potential for skimming can be extended. The ability to use price skimming declines precipitously, however, if the product migrates from a niche position to that of a differentiated product within the larger market.[14]

Profit Maximization and Target ROI

Pricing objectives very frequently are designed for profit maximization, which necessitates a **target return on investment (ROI)** pricing strategy. Here, a bottom-line profit is established first and then pricing is set to achieve the target. Although this approach sounds straightforward, it actually brings up an important reason pricing is best cast within the purview of marketing instead of under the sole control of accountants or financial managers in a firm. When pricing decisions on a given product are made strictly to bolster gross margins, bottom-line profits, or ROI without regard to the short- and long-term impacts of the pricing strategy on other important market- and customer-related elements of success, the product becomes strategically vulnerable. Marketing managers are in the best position to take into account the competitor, customer, and brand image impact of pricing approaches.[15]

Still, in preparing product budgets and forecasts, marketing managers are expected to pay close attention to their organization's financial objectives. During the research that leads to a decision to introduce a new product or modify an existing one, one key variable of interest is whether the market will bear a price point that enhances the firm's overall financial performance. Often, **price elasticity of demand**—the measure of customers' price sensitivity estimated by dividing relative changes in quantity sold by relative changes in price—becomes central to whether a product can even be viably introduced within the context of a firm's financial objectives.[16] The basic price elasticity (e) equation is portrayed below:

$$e = \frac{\%\ \text{change in quantity demanded}}{\%\ \text{change in price}}$$

Unfortunately, price sensitivity is notoriously one of the most difficult issues to determine through market research. Sometimes, historical records or secondary data can provide evidence of pricing's impact on sales volume. When primary research methods are used to ask customers about pricing—whether through survey, focus group, experiments, or other methodology—they most often place the respondents into a hypothetical "what if" mode of thinking in which they are asked to predict how one price or the other might impact their decision to buy. This is a very difficult assertion for a person to make and can lead to bad data and ultimately poor pricing decisions. Importantly, in many instances, much of a customer's reaction to pricing is more psychological or emotional in nature than rational and logical.[17]

Finally, the idea of pricing based on purely economic models and solely for profit maximization raises important ethical concerns, especially in cases where essential products are in short supply. The latest wonder drugs, building materials after a major disaster, and new technologies needed for emerging markets are but three examples in which pricing for pure profit motive can damage both a firm's image and ultimately its relationships with customers. And as oil prices have soared over recent years, more and more consumer groups have been actively calling for investigation of the pricing practices of the big oil companies, and Congress has periodically called in the CEOs to testify about their profits. At the same time, independent distributors, gasoline retailers, and end-user consumers of gasoline have all struggled because of the high prices.[18]

Competitor-Based Pricing

Gaining a thorough understanding of competitors' marketing practices is a key element of successful marketing planning and execution. A competitor's price is one of the most visible elements of its marketing strategy, and you can often infer the pricing objective by carefully analyzing historical and current pricing patterns. Based on such analysis, a firm may develop **competitor-based pricing** strategies. This approach might lead the marketing manager to decide to price at some market average price, or perhaps above or below it in the context of penetration or skimming objectives.

The logic of competitor-based pricing is quite rational unless *(a)* it is the *only* approach considered when making the ultimate pricing decisions or *(b)* it leads to exaggerated extremes in pricing such that on the high end a firm's products do not project customer value or on the low end price wars ensue. A **price war** occurs when a company purposefully makes pricing decisions to undercut one or more competitors and gain sales and net market share.[19] Such was the case in the early 1990s when Sears embarked on a short-lived "low-price" strategy to compete with Walmart on certain high-profile goods, sparking a major price war. Sears management, concerned at the time about losing the Gen X market to Walmart and other discounters, fired the first salvo by publicly announcing a list of items on which it would not be undersold. One of these items, branded disposable diapers such as Pampers and Luvs, led the way in Sears' ads nationwide at prices well below cost.

Unfortunately for Sears, management grossly underestimated the power of Walmart to thwart such competitive threats. First, Walmart's chairman went public in the press by reiterating that Walmart was the true low-price king in retailing (the company's tagline at the time was "Low Prices . . . Always") and assuring customers Walmart would match any advertised Sears price. Then, within days and in market after market, Walmart took to the newspapers with full-page ads discounting diapers to ridiculous levels never before seen, thus negating Sears' approach. This price war was short-lived and forced Sears to immediately rethink its pricing strategy.

Stability Pricing A potentially more productive strategy related to competitor-based pricing is **stability pricing**, in which a firm attempts to find a neutral *set point* for price that is neither low enough to raise the ire of competition nor high enough to put the value proposition at risk with customers. Many factors go into selecting a specific product's stability price point. In markets where customers typically witness rapidly changing prices, stability pricing can provide a source of competitive advantage.[20] Southwest Airlines employs a stability pricing strategy by displaying only five or six fares to a particular destination, with price points based on when the ticket is purchased and the days of the week the customer will be traveling. Unlike most other domestic carriers, Southwest actually prices based on the distance of the trip and is less tied to load-maximization formulas in which a fare can change minute by minute depending on ticket sales. The airline's stability pricing approach has proved highly popular with customers, and it's been successful for the firm as its seat occupancy rate continues to be among the highest in the industry.

Value Pricing

Firms that have an objective of utilizing pricing to communicate positioning use a **value pricing** strategy. Value pricing overtly attempts to consider the role of price as it reflects the bundle of benefits sought by the customer. Because value is in the eyes of the beholder, affected by his or her perceptions of the offering coupled with the operative needs and wants, pricing decisions are strongly driven by the sources of differential advantage a product can realistically deliver. Effectively communicating a product's differential advantages is at the heart of positioning strategy, and exposure to these elements spurs the customer to develop perceptions of value and a subsequent understanding of the value proposition.[21]

Value pricing is complex and overarches the other pricing objectives discussed so far. Through value pricing, a marketing manager seeks to ensure that the offering meets or exceeds the customer's expectations—that is, when he or she does the mental arithmetic that calculates whether the investment in the offering is likely to provide sufficient benefits to justify the cost. Put another way, value pricing considers the whole deliverable and its possible sources of differential advantage—image, service, product quality, personnel, innovation, and many others—the whole gamut of elements that create customer benefit. For instance, Toyotas and Hondas cost more to purchase initially than other comparable vehicles, but they last longer, require fewer repairs, are

The Butlins Hotel in the UK sends a strong value pricing signal by showing all the great extra activities you can engage in if you stay at their property.

EXHIBIT 10.3 | Generic Price-Quality Positioning Map

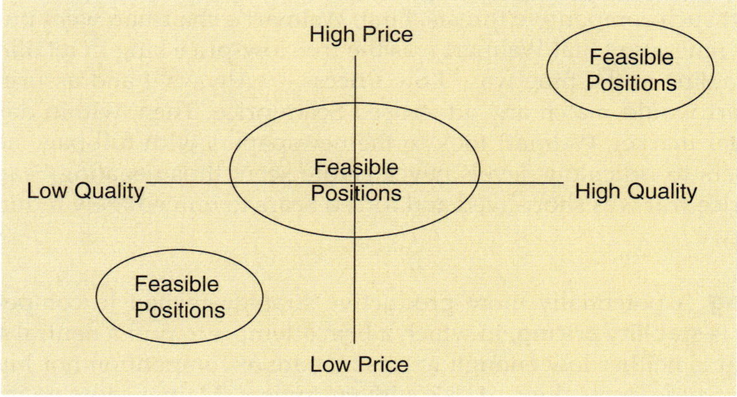

more fuel-efficient, and hold their resale value much better; overall, they have a lower lifetime cost of ownership.

From this assessment, the marketing manager makes a pricing decision that best reflects that product's capacity to be perceived as a good customer value. This high-impact decision helps frame customers' reactions and their relationship with the product and the company. Not surprisingly, Toyota and Honda drivers tend to be very brand loyal, with a very high repeat purchase rate, and many multiple-car families of one or the other.

Would a firm ever benefit from pricing without regard to value? This is an intriguing question that can best be illustrated through the example of a positioning map like the one in Chapter 6. Exhibit 10.3 provides a positioning map with price on one axis and quality on the other. In this instance, we're using the term *quality* rather generically to simply connote a range of differential advantages that might comprise the perceived bundle of benefits for the offering.

Notice in Exhibit 10.3 that a diagonal range of feasible positioning options exists based on matching price to the benefits achieved. For most products, as long as the customer perceives the ratio of price and benefit to be at least at equilibrium, perceptions of value will likely be favorable. Thus, a poorer-quality product offset by a super-low price can be perceived as a good value just as a higher-quality product at a high price can be.

The key lesson marketing managers should draw about value pricing goes back to a key point about managing customer expectations in Chapter 9: Overpromising and underdelivering is one of the quickest ways to create poor value perceptions and thus alienate customers. Marketers will do well to not overpromise benefits, but rather should communicate and deliver a realistic level of benefits for a price.[22]

But what happens when one strays off the favorable diagonal of price/benefit harmony? In the lower-right quadrant—high quality/low price—a penetration strategy might be in play. Or perhaps a firm is taking advantage of its cost leadership by offering a somewhat reduced price. However, over the long run, reducing price too much based on either of these pricing strategies can unnecessarily damage both margins and brand image. Penetration is usually intended to be a temporary strategy, giving the product a chance to gain a strong foothold in market share while warding off competition for a time. Michael Porter has long advocated that cost leadership based on value chain efficiencies should not be wholesale translated to low prices—the reason the approach is called *cost* leadership, not *price* leadership. Successful cost leaders tend to offer a somewhat lower price in the marketplace, but they also translate a substantial portion of their efficiencies to margin, thus enhancing the long-term growth and performance of the firm. Bottom line, it may be all right to play in the bottom-right quadrant temporarily in the case of penetration or to creep slightly into that quadrant over the long haul with a properly executed cost leadership approach.

Clearly, operating in the upper-left (high price/low benefits) quadrant can be problematic. Some firms utilize price skimming strategies, especially on product introductions, even when all the bugs have yet to be worked out of the product. New technology products are notorious for having surprises in quality, functionality, and reliability crop up soon after introduction. When this happens, it can be extremely damaging to the value proposition and to the brand. In such cases, from an ethical perspective, one could question the firm's intent. Did the company rush a product to market to beat an impending entry by competition, pricing it high due to first-mover advantage, all the while knowing that serious quality problems existed? Firms and brands that continually attempt to operate in the high-price/low-benefits quadrant do not survive over the long run as customer trust is damaged. Unfortunately, some highly unscrupulous companies perpetuate their operations in this quadrant by constantly changing company name, location, and brand names. Stories of customer rip-offs are particularly prolific in the service sector (from construction to financial services to health care) because in this sector the offering is inextricably linked to the provider and it's difficult to assess quality until after the service is rendered.

Like many off-airport parking facilities, theParkingSpot features much lower prices than on-airport parking but hopefully (because of their shuttles) without a concurrent loss of convenience.

SELECT PRICING TACTICS

LO 10-3

Identify pricing tactics.

Once management establishes the overall pricing objectives and strategies, it's time to develop and execute the pricing tactics in the marketplace that will operationalize the strategies. Exhibit 10.4 summarizes tactical pricing approaches.

As with establishing pricing strategies, for a variety of reasons firms frequently rely on combinations of pricing tactics in the marketplace rather than putting all their eggs in one basket. As you read about each approach, don't think of it as a stand-alone strategy but instead consider how it might work in tandem with other approaches that a marketing manager might decide to employ.

EXHIBIT 10.4 | Tactical Pricing Approaches

Product Line Pricing

As you have learned, firms rarely market single products. Most products are part of an overall product line of related offerings; and this is true whether the product is in the B2C or B2B marketplace, or in the realm of goods or service. **Product line pricing** (or **price lining**) affords the marketing manager an opportunity to develop a rational pricing strategy across a complete line of related items. As a customer is evaluating the choices available within a firm's product line, the **price points** established for the various items in the line need to make sense and reflect the differences in benefits offered as the customer moves up and down the product line.

EXHIBIT 10.5 Product Line Pricing by Room Type at the Fairmont Kea Lani on Maui

Room Type	Description of View	Price
Fairmont	Neighborhood side streets and landscaping	$ 559
Fairmont Mountainside	Upcountry/Haleakala	$ 649
Fairmont Garden View	Tropical gardens and resort landscaping	$ 684
Partial Ocean View	Partial ocean view from outside the room	$ 729
Ocean View	Angled ocean view from within the room	$ 874
Deluxe Ocean View	Full ocean view	$ 949
Poolside	Upper lagoon pool/garden	$ 969
Signature Kilohana	Panoramic ocean view	$1,149

Source: www.fairmont.com/kea-lani-maui/, accessed May 4, 2013, for reservation dates in August 2013.

Consider the different types of rooms offered by a resort hotel on Maui. At top properties such as the Fairmont Kea Lani in Wailea, even a room on a lower floor with a limited view might easily run well over $500 per night during peak season. Exhibit 10.5 shows the array of room types and prices across the product line—the different grades of guest room.

In price lining, the escalation of product prices up the product line has to consider factors such as real cost differences among the various features offered, customer assessments of the value added by the increasing level of benefits, and prices competitors are charging for similar products. Price lining can greatly simplify a customer's purchase decision making by clearly defining a smorgasbord of offerings based on different bundles of benefits at different prices. Regardless of the product category, customers often approach a purchase with some preconceived range of price acceptability in mind, and product line pricing helps guide them toward the best purchase match to their needs while facilitating easy comparison among offerings.[23]

Price is obviously an important consideration when breaking into a new market. Google Chromebook launched focusing on the consumer segment, but has increasingly been taken on by businesses. The laptops, made by Acer and Samsung, are priced between $199 and $249 in the U.S. market. This super low pricing has made the devices very attractive for businesses and schools. However, these devices are useless without an Internet connection since their software is a cloud-based application. Businesses such as Egan Construction, which works on the Minnesota light rail project, have seen the value in such devices. "Employees are not afraid to use [Chromebooks] on the job [and] if one does get damaged, we can swap it out with another in a matter of minutes with zero time wasted or data lost," says Egan Construction CIO Jim Nonn. "We've saved so much in moving forward with Chromebooks instead of Windows laptops—about $200 per machine."[24]

Price lining can occur at a level much broader in scope than individual products. For example, Marriott has branded its entire family of accommodations based on different value propositions, supported by clearly delineated pricing strategies. Its offerings include Ritz-Carlton and JW Marriott for the most discriminating patron, Marriott and Renaissance at the next level of full service, and an array of differentially positioned brands such as Courtyard, Residence Inn, SpringHill Suites, Fairfield Inn, and TownPlace Suites. Marriott clearly communicates the differences and value in each of these brands, partly by how each is priced in relation to the others. By now you should have a strong sense of how strategically important price is within the marketing mix as a cue for the customer's perceptions of value.[25]

Here HP offers a substantial rebate on a choice of two laptops with Beats audio when customers trade in their old laptop.

Captive Pricing

Captive pricing, sometimes called **complementary pricing**, entails gaining a commitment from a customer to a basic product or system that requires continual purchase of peripherals to operate.[26] What is the most *profitable* part of Hewlett-Packard's office products business: printers or ink cartridges? It's the cartridges. And although other sources for replacement cartridges exist for HP machines, the company does a great job of convincing users that only genuine HP cartridges can be depended on for high-quality performance.

Like HP in printers, Gillette built its business in razors by hooking customers on the latest and greatest new multiblade system through every type of promotion possible from Super Bowl ads to free samples. Gillette counts on the fact that we will go back time and again to repurchase the replacement blades that carry the real margins the company is after.

Captive pricing is just as common in the service sector, where it is sometimes called two-part pricing. Any firm that charges a monthly access fee, membership, retainer fee, or service charge and then bills by the specific service provided is using this pricing approach.

Price Bundling

When customers are given the opportunity to purchase a package deal at a reduced price compared to what the individual components of the package would cost separately, the firm is using a **price bundling** strategy.[27] Cable television providers want you to buy the full gamut of entertainment products from them, and the more you add to your bundle—digital television, premium channels, downloadable movies, local and long-distance phone service, cellular service, gaming, high-speed Internet—the better the deal becomes compared to the total of the individual prices of each piece of the bundle.

One company considering a new price bundling strategy is HBO. HBO's core business is being an add-on to basic cable packages through traditional cable providers. HBO's distributors include Time Warner Cable, Comcast, Bright House, Cox, and Verizon FiOS among others. In 2010, HBO GO was launched, which allows subscribers to access content over the Internet via personal computers and tablet devices. Of the 29 million HBO subscribers, by early 2013 only 6.5 million had registered to use HBO GO. CEO Richard Plepler announced that the company was considering partnering with broadband Internet providers to expand HBO's reach. Customers could pay $50 a month for Internet plus $10–$15 for HBO.[28]

A potential dark side to price bundling is that, in some industries, it can become unclear just what the regular, or unbundled, price is for a given component of a package. The cable/telecommunications industry is regulated to the point that this is less an issue, but in unregulated industries, unscrupulous firms sometimes set artificially high prices for the sake of pushing customers into buying a package. Later in the chapter we will review several of the most important legal considerations related to pricing.

Beyond legalities, ethical issues sometimes arise with regard to price bundling. For example, car shoppers often find every car on the lot within a given model has many of the same features automatically bundled as add-ons. How many of those features would you buy if you had a choice? The extra features being bundled typically carry much larger margins than the margin on the core vehicle itself. If you special order a car without the bundle, chances are you will be waiting months for it to be delivered to the lot—*if* the dealer will even order it for you.

Reference Pricing

As in price bundling, it can be useful for customers to have some type of comparative price when considering a product purchase. Such a comparison is referred to as **reference pricing** and, in the case of price bundling, the reference price is the total price of the components of the bundle if purchased separately versus the bundled price. The savings would be expected to stimulate purchase of the bundle so long as the perceived value realized is sufficient.

Reference pricing is implemented in a number of ways. Sometimes a product catalog might show a manufacturer's suggested list price next to the actual price the product is offered for in the catalog. In retail stores, in any given product category a private-label product (say, the Walgreens brand for instance) is often purposely displayed on a shelf right next to its national brand equivalent. The retailer hopes the savings realized by the direct price comparison of a bottle of Walgreens' mint mouthwash versus the bottle of Scope next to it will be enough to stimulate purchase. Reference pricing is very heavily used in B2B price lists, often reflecting price level differences depending on how many items are purchased or reflecting the amount saved by a firm's special "contract rate" with a vendor versus what a noncontract rate would be.

Clearly, reference pricing can create a powerful psychological impact on a customer by virtue of the savings (real or imagined) demonstrated by the comparison. Ever have a salesperson tell you that a price increase is imminent and if you don't purchase today you'll pay more tomorrow? Customer hedging behaviors against pricing uncertainty are driven by referencing projected prices in the future. And, of course, a sale or promotional price provides a strong reference point and, if the comparative difference is great enough, shoppers flock to the store as if going into battle to take advantage of temporary price reductions while they are in effect.[29]

Prestige Pricing

As mentioned earlier, one rationale for establishing a price skimming objective is **prestige pricing**—lending prestige to a product or brand by virtue of a price relatively higher than the competition. With prestige pricing, some of the traditional price/demand curves cannot properly predict sales or market response because it violates the common assumption that increasing price decreases volume. From the perspective of financial returns, prestige pricing is a phenomenal approach because, everything else being equal, commanding a premium price reflects directly on margins and bottom line.[30]

Prestige pricing plays on psychological principles that attach quality attributions to higher-priced goods—a typical response to some higher-priced products is that they must be better than their competitors; otherwise the price would be lower. When the Norwegian glacier water Voss entered the U.S. market in 2002, it entered with a prestige pricing strategy that helped create a whole new category of ultra-premium bottled waters. Order Voss in a chic restaurant and you can expect to pay a double-digit price per bottle. What's the value proposition that would support such a high price? The exclusivity of distribution, unique cylinder shape of the bottle, and exotic glacial imagery all combine so that a premium price actually enhances the customer's feelings of experiencing something really special (yes, water can be an experiential purchase). Promotion of Voss water has included numerous product placements showing celebrities and others among the rich and famous partaking of the brand. Had Voss entered the market without such a prestige pricing strategy, it is highly unlikely it would have achieved the buzz and early cult status it did.

Price changes can be challenging for businesses, potentially affecting consumer perceptions of product quality. Kiehl's, a 161-year-old cosmetics brand, was purchased by L'Oréal. Although Kiehl's is a relatively inexpensive brand in the United States, L'Oréal positioned the products as luxury goods in the European market. A bottle of Cucumber Herbal Alcohol-Free Toner was sold for £18, compared to it a third of that price in the United States. In the past Europeans were willing to pay extra for a hip American imported product, but after the economic crisis hit in 2008, the brand was suffering. L'Oréal used a strategy that is usually avoided in luxury markets and cut the price of Kiehl's products by 20 percent in 21 of its markets. This approach makes Kiehl's an outlier in an industry in which consumers strongly relate quality to price. Despite its efforts to regain market share and lost customers, Kiehl's may be doing harm to its overall image as it's becoming perceptually equated with mass-market brands.[31]

Odd/Even Pricing

Odd pricing simply means that the price is not expressed in whole dollars, while **even pricing** is a whole-dollar amount ($1.99 versus $2.00, for example). Odd pricing originally came about before the advent of sales taxes and widespread credit card use to bolster cash register security and reduce theft. That is, if a customer brings a $5.00 item to a clerk and presents a $5.00 bill for payment, it was believed that the temptation would be greater for the clerk to simply pocket the bill and not record the sale. It was reasoned that if the clerk had to make change—say a nickel if the item were priced at $4.95—the likelihood was higher that the sale would actually be rung into the cash register.[32]

Now, the rationale for odd pricing is very different and it is often regarded as a key element of **psychological pricing**, or creating a perception about price merely from the image the numbers provide the customer. Studies indicate that at certain important price breaks—$9.99 versus $10.00, $99.95 versus $100.00, and so on—customers mentally process the price as significantly lower because of the reduced digit count in the price point.[33] However, odd pricing can backfire if misapplied. For example, it seems acceptable for a bottle of Voss to be prestige priced at $12.95 instead of $13.00, but a physician, management consultant, or CPA wouldn't want to charge a client $195 instead of simply $200 for services rendered.

One-Price Strategy and Variable Pricing

An ethnocentric aspect of the U.S. marketplace is the nearly total reliance by marketers on a **one-price strategy** with end-user consumers. That is, except for temporary price reductions for promotional or clearance purposes, the price marked on a good is what it typically sells for. The Snicker bar at the convenience store is 99 cents regardless of whether you are a schoolchild or corporate CEO, and the clerk doesn't want to bargain with you about the price. A one-price strategy makes planning and forecasting infinitely easier than the alternative approach, **variable pricing**, which is found in many other countries and cultures but is relatively rare in the U.S. With variable pricing, customers are allowed—even encouraged—to haggle about prices. Ultimately, *the* price is whatever the buyer and seller agree to—a marked price is nothing more than a starting point for negotiation. Variable pricing is traditional in the U.S. with a few consumer goods—cars, boats, houses, and the like. But it is the pervasive way of doing business with all sorts of products across large parts of the globe.

In the U.S. service sector, variable pricing is much more common. It is also more common in B2B in general versus B2C. When variable pricing is used in the United States, in some cases it carries legal limitations. Many pricing laws have been enacted specifically to protect both channel purchasers and end-user consumers from a variety of unfair pricing practices.

Everyday Low Pricing (EDLP) and High/Low Pricing

The rise of Walmart as one of the world's largest corporations has brought the concept of **everyday low pricing (EDLP)** to the forefront of global consumer consciousness. EDLP is not an option just for retailers; it's an important strategic choice for nearly any firm. The fundamental philosophy behind EDLP is to reduce investment in promotion and transfer part of the savings to lower price. Thus, firms practicing an EDLP strategy typically report substantially reduced promotional expenditures on their financial statements. They instead rely much more on generating buzz in the market about the EDLP to create and maintain customer traffic and sales volume. EDLP, when successfully implemented, has a strong advantage of reducing ups and downs in customer traffic, thus making forecasting more accurate.

The antithesis to EDLP is a **high/low pricing** strategy, in which firms rely on periodic heavy *promotional pricing,* primarily communicated through advertising and sales promotion, to build traffic and sales volume. The promotional investment is offset by somewhat higher everyday prices. Why would a firm elect high/low pricing instead of EDLP? Usually, the firm has little choice because of what competitors are doing. It takes a long time for any product or service provider to convince the market that it has EDLP. Most often, firms use various elements of promotion to build sales of new products, shore up sales of declining products, or combat competitors' promotional activity in the same marketplace. Some industries truly are over the top in employing high/low pricing strategies—airlines, auto dealerships, and personal computers are a few that run so many price promotions that customers are conditioned to wait and rarely purchase a product at full price. When high/low pricing reaches this fevered pitch in an industry, it almost always hurts the bottom line of all firms.[34]

TARGET.
Walmart
Save money. Live better.

Target and Walmart have historically used different pricing tactics—Target relies more on high/low pricing with heavy promotion while Walmart relies more heavily on everyday low pricing (EDLP).

Logos reprinted Courtesy of Target Brands, Inc. and Walmart Stores, Inc.

Industry competitors may have very different pricing strategies. In early 2013, Japanese brands like Toyota and Nissan were wooing customers with temporary discount pricing and incentives for customers, but Korean brand Kia Motors was not. Japanese companies were experiencing a weakening yen, which gave them more leeway to offer discounts. This was making competition fiercer for a brand like Kia that was trying to reposition away from being a purely bargain-priced brand. As of March 2013, new Kia cars in the U.S. were discounted $1,300 for each purchase, which was much lower than Nissan's $2,500 and Toyota's $1,800 discounts. Kia's president, Lee Soon-am, said the company will keep pricing at the current levels in the U.S. as part of its evolving brand strategy. Their market has been further bolstered by the introduction of three new models, including a new Forte compact, a Cadenza midsize sedan, and an all-new Soul utility vehicle. Kia aimed to sell over 2.75 million vehicles in 2013, an ambitious number that would be an all-time record for the firm.[35]

Auction Pricing

Auctions have been around for centuries. In an auction, in which individuals competitively bid against each other and the purchase goes to the high bidder, the market truly sets the price (although some minimum bid amount is often established by the seller). As a strategy, **auction pricing** has gained in prominence as Internet commerce has come of age. The most famous example of auction pricing is eBay. Whereas in the past prices at auction were wholly dependent on the level of demand represented by a fairly small number of people either physically gathered at the auction location or connected through traditional telecommunication, today the Internet provides a vast electronic playing field for customers to participate in the auction on a real-time basis.

This phenomenon has resulted in a marketplace in which auction prices can be considerably more reflective of the real value of an offering versus other static price purchase environments. Besides standard auction approaches (buyers bid for a seller's offering), online **reverse auctions** are now very common in which sellers bid prices to capture a buyer's business. Priceline.com is a prominent example of a reverse auction firm that serves as a clearinghouse for extra capacity from airlines, hotels, and cruise lines.[36]

Flash sales have created buzz in Internet retailing. Wayfair is one of the largest privately owned e-commerce companies with $600 million in sales in 2012. CEO Niraj Shah wanted to provide unique products that its consumers could afford that were differentiated from mass-market outlets like Bed Bath & Beyond and Target. Wayfair launched its first flash sales through its Joss & Main line in 2011, and noticed that the line outpaced overall Wayfair sales. Daily Fair was developed as a response to this issue to become the anchor for sales. The site offers 72-hour sales on a limited number of different brands and product lines showcasing collections of inventory with the added benefit of urgency of the sale. Flash sales capture the attention of the impulse shopper, who is enticed by the discounted price and urgency of both time and limited inventory.[37]

SET THE EXACT PRICE

LO 10-4

Describe approaches to setting the exact price.

To set an exact price for an offering, be it a good or service, marketing managers should consider several calculations to arrive at the optimal price. We will discuss four methods here that are frequently used: cost-plus pricing/markup on cost, markup on sales price, average-cost pricing, and target return pricing.

Cost-Plus Pricing/Markup on Cost

Cost-plus pricing is really just a general heuristic that builds a price by adding a standardized markup on top of costs for an offering, hence the term **markup on cost.**[38] First an estimate of costs involved must be developed. In accounting courses, you learn that determining costs is no easy task. For example, many different types of costs can be considered, including fixed and variable costs, direct costs and indirect costs, and shared or overhead costs, which might be allocated to the offering on some prorated basis. Nevertheless, once a cost has been established, cost-plus pricing requires the predetermination of some standardized markup percentage that is to be applied based on company guidelines. Often, managers will receive a list of standard markup amounts by product line. Easy pricing decision making is the advantage of cost-plus pricing, but for most firms it is too simplistic.

Consider the following example. Assume the firm desires a standard markup of 50 percent over cost. Thus:

$$\begin{aligned} \text{Cost} &= \quad \$\ 7.00 \\ \text{Markup on cost } (.50 \times \$7.00) &= +\ \$\ 3.50 \\ \text{Price} &= \quad \$10.50 \end{aligned}$$

Markup on Sales Price

In determining markup, one approach is to use the sales price as a basis. Consider the following example:

$$\begin{aligned} \text{Sales price} &= \$12.00 \\ \text{Cost} &= \$\ 7.00 \\ \text{Markup} &= \$\ 5.00 \end{aligned}$$

The markup percentage is \$5.00 ÷ \$12.00 = 41.7 percent. That is, the \$5.00 markup is 41.7 percent of the sales price. In most applications, when a marketing manager simply refers to "markup," he or she is referring to this calculation—**markup on sales price**, which uses the sales price as a basis of calculating the markup percentage. This is because most important items on financial reports (gross sales, revenue, etc.) are sales, not cost, figures.[39]

All else being equal, calculating a markup on cost makes the markup appear higher than a markup on price even though the dollar figures are identical. For the above example, the markup on cost is \$5.00 ÷ \$7.00 = 71.4 percent, which seems more attractive than the 41.7 percent we calculated above. Sometimes marketers will refer to "100 percent markup," usually meaning they are simply doubling the cost to establish a price.

Average-Cost Pricing

Often pricing decisions are made by identifying all costs associated with an offering to come up with what the average cost of a single unit might be.[40] The basic formula for **average-cost pricing** is:

$$\text{All costs} \div \text{Total number of units} = \text{Average cost of a single unit}$$

To make this calculation requires predicting how much of the offering will be demanded. Assuming total costs of \$100,000 and forecasted total number of units of 250, the average cost of a single unit is:

$$\$100{,}000 \div 250 = \$400$$

One can then add a profit margin to the total cost figures to calculate a likely price for a unit of the offering:

$$\$100{,}000 \text{ total cost} + \$25{,}000 \text{ profit margin} = \$125{,}000$$

Thus, the average price of a single unit based on the above profit margin is:

$$\$125{,}000 \div 250 \text{ units} = \$500$$

Caution is warranted in employing average-cost pricing, as it is always possible that the quantity demanded will not match the marketing manager's forecast. Let's assume that instead of 250, the actual number of units in the above example turns out to be only 200. Revenue would drop to \$100,000, but total costs would not drop proportionately because many of the costs are incurred regardless of sales volume. This example vividly illustrates the point made earlier in the chapter that it is unwise to base pricing decisions on costs alone. Market and customer factors must also be carefully considered in establishing a price.

Target Return Pricing

To better take into account the differential impact of fixed and variable costs, marketing managers can use **target return pricing**. First, a few definitions are in order. Fixed costs are incurred over time, regardless of volume. Variable costs fluctuate with volume. And total costs are simply a sum of the fixed and variable costs.[41] To use target return pricing, one must first calculate total fixed costs. Second, a target return must be established. Let's assume that total fixed costs are $250,000 and the target return is set at $50,000 for a total of $300,000.

Next, a demand forecast must be made. If demand is forecast at 1,500 units:

$$(\text{Fixed costs} + \text{Target return}) \div \text{Units} = (\$250{,}000 + \$50{,}000) \div 1{,}500 = \$200 \text{ per unit.}$$

Suppose the variable costs per unit are $50. This results in a price per unit of:

$$\$200 + \$50 = \$250$$

As with average-cost pricing, the effectiveness of target return pricing is highly dependent on the accuracy of the forecast. In the example above, if customer demand comes in at 1,000 units instead of 1,500, at a price of $250 the marketing manager will experience a $50 per unit loss!

DETERMINE CHANNEL DISCOUNTS AND ALLOWANCES

LO 10-5

Determine discounts and allowances to offer to channel members.

Discounts are direct, immediate reductions in price provided to purchasers. **Allowances** remit monies to purchasers after the fact. In general, in B2B transactions, marketing managers must be cognizant of several types of discount and allowance approaches that essentially amount to price adjustments for channel buyers. While the pricing discounts and purchasing allowances mentioned in this section primarily pertain to B2B, in some instances, end-user consumers may be offered some of the same price adjustments.

Sellers offer discounts and allowances for a variety of reasons. Paying a bill early, purchasing a certain quantity, purchasing seasonal products during the off-season, and experiencing an overstock on certain products are common rationales for offering various discounts and allowances. At its essence, the approach hopes to impact purchaser behavior in directions that benefit the selling firm by sweetening the buying organization's terms of sale.

Cash Discounts

Sellers offer **cash discounts** to elicit quicker payment of invoices. The rational purchaser weighs the discount offered for early payment versus the value of keeping the money until it is due. Ideally the cash discount results in financial advantage for both parties. Cash discounts are stated in a typical format such as 2%/10, Net/40, which translates to the buyer receiving 2 percent off the total bill if payment is received within 10 days of the invoice date, but after that point there is no discount and the whole invoice is due within 40 days of the invoice date.

Trade Discounts

Trade discounts, also sometime called functional discounts, provide an incentive to a channel member for performing some function in the channel that benefits the seller. Examples include stocking a seller's product or performing a service related to that product, such as installation or repair, within the channel. Trade discounts are normally expressed as a percentage off the invoice price.

Companies like YO! Sushi frequently use discounts to get consumers to try their product for the first time. Text and mobile discounts are increasingly popular for use by marketers.

Quantity Discounts

Quantity discounts are taken off an invoice price based on different levels of product purchased. Quantity discounts may be offered on an order-by-order basis, in which case they are noncumulative, or they may be offered on a cumulative basis over time as an incentive to promote customer loyalty. From a legal standpoint, it is essential that quantity discounts are offered to all customers on an equally proportionate basis so that small buyers as well as large buyers follow the same rules for qualification. The later section on legal considerations in pricing extends the discussion about fairness in pricing practices.[42]

Seasonal Discounts

Firms often purchase seasonal products many months before the season begins. For example, a retailer might purchase a winter apparel line at a trade show a year before its season, accept delivery in August, begin displaying it in September, yet cold weather may not hit until November or December. To accommodate such lengthy sales processes, firms offer **seasonal discounts**, which reward the purchaser for shifting part of the inventory storage function away from the manufacturer.[43] Seasonal discounts are often expressed as greatly extended invoice due dates. In the winter clothes line example, terms of 2%/120, Net 145 would not be unusual.

Promotional Allowances

Within a given channel, sellers often want purchasers to help execute their promotional strategies. A consumer products marketer like P&G, for example, depends heavily on wholesalers, distributors, and retailers to promote its brands. When a retailer runs an ad for a P&G brand such as Crest toothpaste, it is nearly always in response to **promotional allowances** provided by the manufacturer. Ordinarily, upon proof of performance of the promotion, the retailer will receive a check back from the manufacturer to compensate for part of the promotional costs. The allowance might be calculated as a percentage of the invoice for Crest purchased from P&G or it might be a fixed dollar figure per dozen or per case.[44]

Geographic Aspects of Pricing

A variety of geographically driven pricing options are common within a channel. Among those most used are FOB pricing, uniform delivered pricing, and zone pricing.

FOB Pricing The initials **FOB** stand for free on board, meaning that title transfer and freight paid on the goods being shipped are based on the FOB location. For example, FOB-origin or FOB-factory pricing indicates that the purchaser pays freight charges and takes title the moment the goods are placed on the truck or other transportation vehicle. The greater the distance between shipper and customer, the higher the freight charges to the customer. In contrast, FOB-destination indicates that until the goods arrive at the purchaser's location, title doesn't change hands and freight charges are the responsibility of the seller.[45]

Uniform Delivered Pricing Many direct-to-consumer marketers such as Amazon and Lands' End practice **uniform delivered pricing**, in which the same delivery fee is charged to customers regardless of geographic location within the 48 contiguous states.[46] Pricing rates are quoted for other locations, and expedited delivery is generally available for a higher fee.

Zone Pricing In a **zone pricing** approach, shippers set up geographic pricing zones based on the distance from the shipping location. The parcel post system of the U.S. Postal Service is set up this way.[47] Rates are calculated for the various combinations of sending and receiving zones.

EXECUTE PRICE CHANGES

LO 10-6

Understand how to execute price changes.

Over time, price changes are inevitable. A marketing manager may want to raise or lower a price for competitive or other reasons, or competitors may make price changes that require a considered pricing response from your own firm. Among the marketing mix variables, price is the easiest and quickest to alter, so sometimes firms overrely on price changes to stimulate additional sales or gain market share. You've already seen that establishing pricing objectives and strategies and implementing pricing tactics are complex and entail important managerial decisions. It is important to also recall that in the overall scope of marketing planning and strategy, pricing does not take place in a vacuum. That is, a change in an offering's price—either up or down—can dramatically impact the effectiveness of the overall marketing mix variables in reflecting your offering's positioning in the eyes of customers.

It is important for marketing managers to conduct appropriate market research in advance of major price changes to try to determine the likely impact of a price change on customer perceptions of the offering and likelihood to purchase. Both qualitative research approaches, such as focus groups, and quantitative approaches, such as surveys and experiments, can be designed to determine the degree to which an anticipated price change might influence customer response. Ideally, price changes upward will reflect the **just noticeable difference (JND)** in a price, which is the amount of price increase that can be taken without affecting customer demand.

If a potential upward price change is being driven by pressure on margins, creative marketers often look for ways to save margin without increasing price. Over the years, candy manufacturers have been severely affected by swings in the price of sugar. As the sugar price has gone up, a good portion of the profit margin of a candy bar has been preserved by simply reducing the size of the bar. Today's chocolate lovers would be amazed at seeing how much larger a Snickers bar was in 1970 versus today. At the same time, the basic bar size has shrunk multiple times during that period, including a 10-percent reduction (and concurrent 30-calorie reduction) in early 2013. While the price of a bar has also risen dramatically during the same period (an average of four times the 1970 price), the price increase would have been even more dramatic without the reduction in ounces.

In addition to reducing the offering in terms of size or quantity, other nonprice approaches to mitigating the pressure to maintain margins include altering or reducing discounts and allowances, unbundling some services or features from the original offering, increasing minimum order quantities, or simply reducing product quality. However, marketing managers should be cautious when they begin to consider altering the product itself to retain margins; customer response to such tinkering might be negative.

A worst-case scenario occurs when a firm takes a price decrease on an offering to stimulate volume and grow share, only to have one or more competitors immediately and aggressively jump in to meet or beat the price decrease, resulting in a price war. Price wars are the quickest way to destroy margins and bottom-line profit. The old marketing adage "We'll price our product lower but make it up on volume" doesn't work when competitive price pressure forces prices below cost!

Assume that you, as a marketing manager, just found out that a competitor has taken a price increase or decrease. You must evaluate the change and select the appropriate response for your product line. The basic principles and cautions about competing on price are the same, regardless of whether your firm or a competitor fires the first shot. If your firm is the market leader, you may find that competitors tend to create similar but somewhat inferior offerings at attractive prices in an attempt to knock you off as leader.

When formulating a response to a competitor's price reduction, remember to consider your offering from the perspective of its overall value proposition to customers and not be too quick to react in kind with a price decrease. In the case of a competitor's price increase, perhaps based on escalating costs or margin pressure, analysis may reveal the increase is an opportunity to both gain a price advantage and perhaps increase your volume and share, especially if you are a cost leader and can maintain desired margins at your current price. Or you may simply wish to take a concurrent price increase and enjoy the related margin enhancement. Remember, a cost leadership strategy does not necessarily imply price leadership; rather, the best cost leader firms take a portion of their cost leadership to margin and perhaps a portion to price advantage.

UNDERSTAND LEGAL CONSIDERATIONS IN PRICING

LO 10-7

Examine legal considerations in pricing.

In the process of setting pricing objectives and developing and implementing pricing strategies and tactics, marketing managers must be aware that some aspects of pricing decision making can be very sensitive legally. Laws at the national, state, and local levels are in place that impact a firm's pricing practices. Federal legislation includes the Sherman Antitrust Act (1890), Clayton Act (1914), Robinson-Patman Act (1936), and Consumer Goods Pricing Act (1975). The Federal Trade Commission (FTC) actively monitors and enforces federal pricing laws. Several of the more important legal considerations in pricing and their associated regulatory bases are discussed below.

Price-Fixing

Companies that collude to set prices at a mutually beneficial high level are engaged in **price-fixing**. When competitors are involved in the collusion, horizontal price-fixing occurs.[48] The Sherman Act forbids horizontal price-fixing, which could result in overall higher prices for consumers since various competitors are all pricing the same to maximize their profits.

When independent members of a channel (for example, manufacturers, distributors, and retailers) collude to establish a minimum retail price, referred to as retail price maintenance, vertical price-fixing occurs. Vertical price-fixing is illegal under the Consumer Goods Pricing Act, and for good reason. Vertical price-fixing assures everybody in the channel is satisfied with their "cut" of the profits, but the profit boost is achieved by increased prices to consumers.

Price Discrimination

Price discrimination occurs when a seller offers different prices to different customers without a substantive basis, such that competition is reduced. The

Robinson-Patman Act explicitly prohibits giving, inducing, or receiving discriminatory prices except under certain specific conditions such as situations where proof exists that the costs of selling to one customer are higher than to another (such as making distributions to remote locations) or when temporary, defensive price reductions are necessary to meet competition in a specific local area.[49]

Deceptive Pricing

Knowingly stating prices in a manner that gives a false impression to customers is **deceptive pricing**. Deceptive pricing practices are monitored and enforced by the FTC. Deceptive pricing may take several forms. Sometimes, firms will set artificially high reference prices for merchandise just before a promotion so that an advertised sale price will look much more attractive to customers.[50] Or a seller may advertise an item at an unbelievably low price to lure customers into a store, and once the customer arrives refuse to sell the advertised item and instead push a similar item with a much higher price and higher margin. When this occurs and it can be demonstrated that a seller had no true intent to actually make the lower-priced item available for sale, the practice is called **bait and switch** and is illegal. Finally, the ubiquitous reliance of retailers on scanner-based pricing has opened a plethora of stealth pricing fraud schemes, perpetrated by dishonest retailers who label an item on the shelf sign at a lower price than it is actually priced within the scanner database. For certain, some of the scanner errors result from mistakes and not fraud, but the nontransparent nature of scanner pricing puts a burden on the customer to return to the days of "buyer beware."

Predatory Pricing

A strategy to intentionally sell below cost to push a competitor out of a market, then raise prices to new highs, is called predatory pricing. Predatory pricing is illegal but prosecuting it can be very tricky because intent must be proved. Other plausible explanations exist for drastic price reductions including inventory overstocks, so proving that predatory pricing has occurred is difficult.

Fair Trade and Minimum Markup Laws

Fair trade laws were popular in the past because they allowed manufacturers to establish artificially high prices by limiting the ability of wholesalers and retailers to offer reduced or discounted prices. Fair trade laws varied greatly from state to state, depending largely on how strong the independent retailer and wholesaler lobby was in a particular locale. These laws protected mom-and-pop operators from the price discounting by chain stores.[51]

Closely associated with fair trade laws are **minimum markup laws**, which require a certain percentage markup be applied to products. In one extreme case in the early 1970s, the State of Oklahoma took legal action against Target Corporation to force the discounter to obey Oklahoma's minimum markup law that prohibited advertising a wide variety of merchandise for less than a 6 percent profit. This effectively shut down Target's ability to advertise **loss leader products**, items (typically paper towels, toilet paper, toothpaste, and the like) sacrificed at prices below cost to attract shoppers to the store.[52] Target fought back by creating special versions of its famous full-color Sunday advertising inserts for Oklahoma shoppers that showed in very large type the nationally advertised sales price accompanied by a disclaimer clearly showing a much higher "in Oklahoma" price. In effect, the ads told Oklahomans they couldn't get the same prices as the rest of the country, and it didn't take long for Oklahoma consumers to come to their senses and realize that the state's fair pricing law might protect small retailers, but it hurt everyday shoppers. In 1975, the federal Consumer Goods Pricing Act repealed all state fair trade laws and minimum markup laws.

SUMMARY

Clearly, price is a critical element in an offering's perceived value. Marketing managers must establish clear pricing objectives and related strategies, supported by well-executed pricing tactics. In setting the exact price, it is best to compare several approaches before making a decision. Several channel discounts and allowances are available that can impact purchaser behavior in ways that benefit the selling firm. Price changes are inevitable and marketing managers must anticipate customer and competitor responses. Finally, marketing managers must be sensitive to legal ramifications of certain pricing practices.

KEY TERMS

cost leadership 295
pricing objectives 297
market share 298
penetration pricing 298
price skimming 298
target return on investment (ROI) 299
price elasticity of demand 300
competitor-based pricing 300
price war 300
stability pricing 301
value pricing 301
product line pricing (price lining) 303
price points 303
captive pricing (complementary pricing) 305
price bundling 305
reference pricing 306
prestige pricing 306
odd pricing 307
even pricing 307
psychological pricing 307
one-price strategy 307
variable pricing 307
everyday low pricing (EDLP) 308
high/low pricing 308
auction pricing 309
reverse auctions 309
cost-plus pricing 309
markup on cost 309
markup on sales price 310
average-cost pricing 310
target return pricing 311
discounts 311
allowances 311
cash discounts 311
trade discounts 311
quantity discounts 312
seasonal discounts 312
promotional allowances 312
FOB 312
uniform delivered pricing 313
zone pricing 313
just noticeable difference (JND) 313
price-fixing 314
price discrimination 314
deceptive pricing 315
bait and switch 315
fair trade laws 315
minimum markup laws 315
loss leader products 315

APPLICATION QUESTIONS

1. Why might penetration pricing potentially negatively impact brand image and product positioning in the long run? Given this risk, why would a marketing manager use penetration pricing? Identify a brand (other than the examples in the chapter) that you believe is engaged in penetration pricing.
2. Pricing against competitors is common. Yet, the approach carries some significant problems.
   a. What are the advantages of competitor-based pricing?
   b. What are the risks of using competitor-based pricing exclusive of other approaches?
   c. Identify a few industries in which taking competitor-based pricing into account might be especially beneficial when developing an overall pricing strategy. What caused you to select the industries you did?
3. Review Exhibit 10.3 on price-quality positioning along with the accompanying discussion.
   a. Consider the low quality/high price quadrant. Identify a brand (other than the examples in the chapter) that you believe presently resides in this quadrant. How is it able to command a high price? Do you believe the pricing strategy is sustainable for that brand? Why or why not?

b. Consider the high quality/low price quadrant. Identify a brand (other than the examples in the chapter) that you believe presently resides in this quadrant. In your opinion, why has the brand undertaken this pricing strategy? Do you believe there are risks to the brand in remaining too long in that quadrant? Why or why not?

4. Select any three of the pricing tactics identified in the chapter. For *each* tactic:
   a. Identify a brand (other than the examples in the chapter) that you believe is currently employing that tactic.
   b. Provide evidence to support the use of that tactic.
   c. Is the use of the tactic effective? Why or why not?
   d. What factors might cause a need to abandon this tactic in favor of another?
5. Assume that you are a marketing manager for Pantene shampoo and conditioner, two of Procter & Gamble's star products. Several competitors have recently begun to cut prices to retailers and also to offer more aggressive channel allowances to boost sales and market share.
   a. What options do you have as a response to the competitive price declines?
   b. What are the risks associated with each of the options?
   c. Assuming Pantene is the market leader in its category, what response to the price cuts do you recommend?

MANAGEMENT DECISION CASE:
Price Unbundling: An Uncommon Word Leading to Very Nice Financial Returns

Up until 2008, when a person bought an airline ticket, the price of the ticket included all kinds of nice services. Back in the "dark ages" (that is, pre-2008), that airline ticket would have included the ability to check a bag and, depending on the length of the flight, it may have included any or all of the following: a meal, headphones, the ability to store a carry-on in the overhead bin, and as much legroom as everyone else who had not forked over the cost of a first-class or business-class ticket. However, nowadays airlines have discovered the joys of "unbundling." This practice, which is leading to some hefty extra fees for travelers, is generating revenue for airlines to the tune of $27.1 billion in the most recent period with data available. That number represents a huge increase of nearly 20 percent over the fee revenue generated by airlines the previous year.

In a competitive environment in which airlines were faced with high operating costs, intense competition, and a customer base that can compare prices instantly on the many online travel sites, something had to be done that allowed airlines to increase their revenue streams. That "something," airline executives decided, was to unbundle many of the services customers expected with the purchase of an airline ticket from the price of the fare itself.

Think of the many services and nice-to-haves that exist when one travels via air to a particular destination. If you are tall and would like the extra legroom that an emergency exit row may provide, how much are you willing to pay to sit in that row? Some airlines are beginning to charge people an extra fee for not only the exit row seat but also large blocks of other seats near the front of the plane designated by names such as "main cabin extra"—extra meaning a few extra inches of legroom. If you are not checking a bag to avoid the "checked bag fee," which really kicked off the whole unbundling phenomenon, how confident are you that you can find a space in the overhead bin? Many airlines recognize that the overhead bin space is a piece of real estate that can be rented for a fee. However, since "overhead bin charges" or "carry-on bag charges" are not fully accepted by most air travel customers (yet), airlines have to get creative in how they will monetize that space. Thus, "priority boarding" is invented for an extra fee. Yes, you can now pay an extra fee for priority boarding that virtually guarantees your bag space in the overhead bin. Elect not to pay the fee and you run the risk of the bins being full when you board the plane and having to check your bag at the cabin door.

Priority boarding and premium seat location fees are just two of the many fees airlines are now charging. Others include reservation change fees, overweight and oversize bag fees, in-flight meal fees, "stand-by flier" fees, Internet access fees, and 50-percent-more-frequent-flier-miles fees, to name a few. All of these fees have proven crucial to airlines realizing operating income in the past few years. In fact, in 2012 airline revenue per passenger exceeded costs by just 37 cents.

That number includes $8.49 per passenger in additional fees. To put it another way, without the additional revenue airlines realized on fees, their costs would have exceeded revenues to the tune of $8.12 per passenger. Clearly, regardless of how passengers feel about paying for services previously included with the price of a ticket, airline fees are here to stay and likely will be expanded in the future.

Questions for Consideration

1. What type of pricing strategies and tactics are airlines using given their base ticket price for the seat plus additional fees for everything else? What other creative additional fees might they charge in the future?
2. Southwest Airlines prides itself on allowing passengers to check bags for free. Given that virtually all of Southwest's competitors have started charging these extra fees, do you think it will continue to hold out before it too has to charge extra fees? Why should it? How does the pricing strategy that Southwest Airlines employs differ from that of its competitors and what competitive advantage does Southwest enjoy by not charging extra fees?
3. What kind of unbundled pricing strategies or fees would you recommend for other service industries like hotels, restaurants, or cruise lines given the relative success of such fees in the air travel industry?

Sources: Christopher Elliott, "Don't Fall for the 'Unbundling' Ploy; Airlines Have Fliers Fooled That Paying a la Carte Makes Sense;" *USA Today*, September 16, 2013, MONEY section, p4B. Susan Carey, "Airline Fees Keep Climbing; Some Carriers Bundle Charges for Former Freebies, Framing Them as a Service," *The Wall Street Journal*, July 4, 2013.

MARKETING PLAN EXERCISE

ACTIVITY 12: Price Your Offering

As you learned in this chapter, your approach to pricing is an integral aspect of positioning your offering. Price sends a signal to customers about the offering's quality and other characteristics. At the same time, effective pricing ensures margins and profits needed for continued success.

1. Review the options for pricing objectives and strategies and establish an appropriate set for your offering.
2. Review the various available pricing tactics and select a mix of tactics that you believe is most appropriate for your offering.
3. Consider the methods of establishing an exact price presented in the chapter. Use these approaches to develop a comparative set for review. Select a final price for the offering.
4. What channel discounts and allowances will you provide on your offering?

NOTES

1. Richard G. Netemeyer, Balaji Krishnan, Chris Pullig, and Guangping Wang, "Developing and Validating Measures of Facets of Customer-Based Brand Equity," *Journal of Business Research,* 57, no. 2 (February 2004), pp. 209–24.
2. Richard J. Speed, "Oh Mr. Porter! A Re-Appraisal of Competitive Strategy," *Marketing Intelligence & Planning,* 7, no. 5/6 (1989), pp. 8–11.
3. S. Shannon, "Dixon CEO Says Profitability Beats Amazon as Stores Sell Extras," Bloomberg.com, March 14, 2013, www.bloomberg.com/news/2013-03-14/dixons-ceo-says-profitability-beats-amazon-as-stores-sell-extras.html.
4. Anna Helm, "Uruguay's One Laptop per Child Program, Impact and Numbers," The Next Web, April 7, 2013, http://thenextweb.com/la/2013/04/07/uruguays-one-laptop-per-child-program-impact-and-numbers/; Bruce Einhorn, "Intel Inside the Third World," *BusinessWeek,* July 9 and 16, 2007, pp. 38–40; and Reena Jana, "Behind the Intel/OLPC Breakup," *BusinessWeek*, January, 8, 2008, www.businessweek.com/print/innovate/content/jan2008/id2008018_145303.htm.
5. Roy W. Ralston, "The Effects of Customer Service, Branding, and Price on the Perceived Value of Local Telephone Service," *Journal of Business Research* 56, no. 3 (March 2003), pp. 201–13.

6. Kent B. Monroe, "Pricing Practices That Endanger Profits," *Marketing Management,* 10, no. 3 (September/October 2001), pp. 42–46.
7. George J. Avlonitis and Kostis A. Indounas, "Pricing Objectives and Pricing Methods in the Services Sector," *Journal of Services Marketing,* 19, no. 1 (2005), pp. 47–57.
8. T. Gara, "Your Donut Loyalty Will Soon Be Rewarded," *The Wall Street Journal,* January 31, 2013, http://blogs.wsj.com/corporate-intelligence/2013/01/31/your-donut-loyalty-will-soon-be-rewarded/.
9. Yikuan Lee and Gina Colarelli O'Connor, "New Product Launch Strategy for Network Effects Products," *Journal of the Academy of Marketing Science,* 31, no. 3 (Summer 2003), pp. 241–55.
10. Angel F. Villarejo-Ramos and Manuel J. Sanchez-Franco, "The Impact of Marketing Communication and Price Promotion on Brand Equity," *Journal of Brand Management,* 12, no. 6 (August 2005), pp. 431–44.
11. "Biogen Prices Multiple-Sclerosis Drug below Rivals," Fox Business, March 29, 2013, www.foxbusiness.com/news/2013/03/29/biogen-prices-multiple-sclerosis-drug-below-rivals/.
12. Ana Garrido-Rubio and Yolanda Polo-Redondo, "Tactical Launch Decisions: Influence on Innovation Success/Failure," *Journal of Product and Brand Management,* 14, no. 1 (2005), pp. 29–38.
13. D. Reisinger, "Now You Can Get Discounts on All Xbox 360 Models . . . for a Price," *CNET,* October 23, 2012 http://news.cnet.com/8301-10805_3-57538024-75/now-you-can-get-discounts-on-all-xbox-360-models.-for-a-price/.
14. Ioana Popescu and Yaozhong Wu, "Dynamic Pricing Strategies with Reference Effects," *Operations Research,* 55, no. 3 (May/June 2007), pp. 413–32.
15. Mark Burton and Steve Haggett, "Rocket PLAN," *Marketing Management,* 16, no. 5 (September/October 2007), p. 32.
16. Tulin Erdem, Michael P. Keane, and Baohong Sun, "The Impact of Advertising on Consumer Price Sensitivity in Experience Goods Markets," *Quantitative Marketing and Economics,* 6, no. 2 (June 2008), pp. 139–76.
17. Harun Ahmet Kuyumcu, "Emerging Trends in Scientific Pricing," *Journal of Revenue and Pricing Management,* 6, no. 4 (December 2007), pp. 293–99.
18. Tina Seeley, "CFTC Targets Shipping, Storage in Oil Investigation (Update2)," *Bloomberg,* May 30, 2008.
19. Tridib Mazumdar, S. P. Raj, and Indrajit Sinha, "Reference Price Research: Review and Propositions," *Journal of Marketing,* 69, no. 4 (October 2005), pp. 84–102; and Xueming Luo, Aric Rindfleisch, and David K. Tse, "Working with Rivals: The Impact of Competitor Alliances on Financial Performance," *Journal of Marketing Research,* 44, no. 1 (February 2007), pp. 73–83.
20. Marc Vanhuele and Xavier Dreze, "Measuring the Price Knowledge Shoppers Bring to the Store," *Journal of Marketing,* 66, no. 4 (October 2002), pp. 72–85.
21. Kusum Ailawadi, Donald R. Lehmann, and Scott A. Neslin, "Market Response to a Major Policy Change in the Marketing Mix: Learning from Procter & Gamble's Value Pricing Strategy," *Journal of Marketing* 65, no. 1 (January 2001), pp. 44–61.
22. Stephan Zielke and Thomas Dobbelstein, "Customers' Willingness to Purchase New Store Brands," *Journal of Product and Brand Management,* 16, no. 2 (2007), pp. 112–21.
23. Michaela Draganska and Dipak C. Jain, "Consumer Preferences and Product-Line Pricing Strategies: An Empirical Analysis," *Marketing Science,* 25, no. 2 (March/April 2006), pp. 164–75.
24. C. Fitzsimmons, "Chromebook and the Low Cost of Being Accessible," *BRW,* March 26, 2013, www.brw.com.au/p/techgadgets/chromebook_and_the_low_cost_of_being_lLOk43JPUrljd5tK7Zh7KL.
25. Baba Shiv, Ziv Carmon, and Dan Ariely, "Placebo Effects of Marketing Actions: Consumers May Get What They Pay For," *Journal of Marketing Research* 42, no. 4 (November 2005), pp. 383–93.
26. Michael Levy, Dhruv Grewal, Praveen K. Kopalle, and James D. Hess, "Emerging Trends in Retail Pricing Practice: Implications for Research," *Journal of Retailing,* 80, no. 3 (2004), pp. 13–21.
27. Chris Janiszewski and Marcus Cunha Jr., "The Influence of Price Discount Framing on the Evaluation of a Product Bundle," *Journal of Consumer Research* 30, no. 4 (March 2004), pp. 534–46.
28. A. Barr and L. Baker, "HBO CEO Mulls Teaming with Broadband Partners for HBO GO," Reuters, March 21, 2013, www.reuters.com/article/2013/03/21/hbo-streaming-idUSL1N0CD7WP20130321.
29. Daniel J. Howard and Roger A. Kerin, "Broadening the Scope of Reference Price Advertising Research: A Field Study of Consumer Shopping Involvement," *Journal of Marketing,* 70, no. 4 (October 2006), pp. 185–204.
30. James McClure and Erdogan Kumcu, "Promotions and Product Pricing: Parsimony versus Veblenesque Demand," *Journal of Economic Behavior & Organization* 65, no. 1 (January 2008), pp. 105–17.
31. A. Roberts, "Price Cuts Hit Kiehl's Luxury Image in Europe," *Bloomberg Businessweek,* December 20, 2012, www.businessweek.com/articles/2012-12-20/price-cuts-hit-kiehls-luxury-image-in-europe#r=com-ls.

32. Robert M. Schindler and Alan R. Wiman, "Effects of Odd Pricing on Price Recall," *Journal of Business Research*, 19, no. 3 (November 1989), pp. 165–77.
33. John Huston and Nipoli Kamdar, "$9.99: Can 'Just-Below' Pricing Be Reconciled with Rationality?," *Eastern Economic Journal*, 22, no. 2 (Spring 1996), pp. 137–45.
34. Kathleen Seiders and Glenn B. Voss, "From Price to Purchase," *Marketing Management*, 13, no. 6 (November/December 2004), pp. 38–43.
35. Kyong-Ae Choi, "Kia Sticks to U.S. Pricing Strategy Despite Competition," *The Wall Street Journal*, March 28, 2013, http://online.wsj.com/article/SB1000142 4127887324685104578387843053206894.html.
36. Christian Terwiesch, Sergei Savin, and Il-Horn Hann, "Online Haggling at a Name-Your-Own-Price Retailer: Theory and Application," *Management Science* 51, no. 3 (March 2005), pp. 339–52.
37. J. J. Colao, "Flash Sales Work: Wayfair, the $600 Million Ecommerce Behemoth, Launches Daily Fair," *Forbes*, February 20, 2013, www.forbes.com/sites/jjcolao/2013/02/20/flash-sales-work-wayfair-the-600-million-ecommerce-behemoth-launches-daily-fair/.
38. Chris Guilding, Colin Drury, and Mike Tayles, "An Empirical Investigation of the Importance of Cost-Plus Pricing," *Managerial Auditing Journal*, 20, no. 2 (2005), pp. 125–37.
39. J. Isaac Brannon, "The Effects of Resale Price Maintenance Laws on Petrol Prices and Station Attrition: Empirical Evidence from Wisconsin," *Applied Economics*, 35, no. 3 (February 2003), pp. 343–49.
40. Chuan He and Yuxin Chen, "Managing e-Marketplace: A Strategic Analysis of Nonprice Advertising," *Management Science*, 25, no. 2 (March/April 2006), pp. 175–87.
41. Ben Vinod, "Retail Revenue Management and the New Paradigm of Merchandise Optimisation," *Journal of Revenue and Pricing Management*, 3, no. 4 (January 2005), pp. 358–68.
42. George J. Avlonitis and Kostis A. Indounas, "Pricing Practices of Service Organizations," *Journal of Services Marketing*, 20, no. 5 (2006), pp. 346–57.
43. Keith S. Coulter, "Decreasing Price Sensitivity Involving Physical Product Inventory: A Yield Management Application," *Journal of Product and Brand Management* 10, no. 4/5 (2001), pp. 301–17.
44. Kusum L. Ailawadi and Bari Harlam, "An Empirical Analysis of the Determinants of Retail Margins: The Role of Store-Brand Share," *Journal of Marketing* 68, no. 1 (January 2004), pp. 147–65.
45. Fred S. McChesney and William F. Shughart II, "Delivered Pricing in Theory and Policy Practice," *Antitrust Bulletin*, 52, no. 2 (Summer 2007), pp. 205–28.
46. Hiroshi Ohta, Yan-Shu Lin, and Masa K. Naito, "Spatial Perfect Competition: A Uniform Delivered Pricing Model," *Pacific Economic Review*, 10, no. 4 (December 2005), pp. 407–20.
47. Pradeep K. Chintagunta, Jean-Pierre Dube, and Vishal Singh, "Balancing Profitability and Customer Welfare in a Supermarket Chain," *Quantitative Marketing and Economics*, 1, no. 1 (March 2003), pp. 111–46.
48. John M. Connor, "Forensic Economics: An Introduction with Special Emphasis on Price Fixing," *Journal of Competition Law & Economics*, 4, no. 1 (March 2008), pp. 21–59.
49. Siva Viswanathan, Jason Kuruzovich, Sanjay Gosain, and Ritu Agarwal, "Online Infomediaries and Price Discrimination: Evidence from the Automotive Retailing Sector," *Journal of Marketing*, 71 no. 3 (July 2007), pp. 89–107.
50. Allan J. Kimmel, "Deception in Marketing Research and Practice: An Introduction," *Psychology & Marketing*, 18, no. 7 (July 2001), pp. 657–61.
51. Jules Stuyck, Evelyne Terryn, and Tom van Dyck, "Confidence through Fairness? The New Directive on Unfair Business-to-Consumer Commercial Practices in the Internal Market," *Common Market Law Review*, 43, no. 1 (February 2006), pp. 107–52.
52. Patrick DeGraba, "The Loss Leader Is a Turkey: Targeted Discounts from Multi-Product Competitors," *International Journal of Industrial Organization*, 24, no. 3 (May 2006), pp. 613–28.

CHAPTER 11

Manage Marketing Channels and Points of Customer Interface

LEARNING OBJECTIVES

LO 11-1 Define a value network and how organizations operate within this approach.

LO 11-2 Identify various types of intermediaries and distribution channels.

LO 11-3 Understand the impact of intermediary contributions via physical distribution functions, transaction and communication functions, and facilitating functions.

LO 11-4 Explain the different types of vertical marketing systems.

LO 11-5 Utilize suitable criteria to select appropriate channel approaches.

LO 11-6 Identify the logistics aspects of supply chain management.

LO 11-7 Understand the role of retailing in delivering the value offering to the customer.

LO 11-8 Recognize the characteristics and types of store retailers.

LO 11-9 Recognize the characteristics and types of non-store retailers.

LO 11-10 Describe the evolving role of e-commerce.

THE VALUE CHAIN AND VALUE NETWORKS

LO 11-1

Define a value network and how organizations operate within this approach.

The concept of the value chain, which was introduced in Chapter 2, is worth revisiting at this point. The value chain portrays a synthesis of primary and support activities utilized by an organization to design, produce, market, deliver, and support its products (see Exhibit 11.1).

EXHIBIT 11.1 | Porter's Generic Value Chain

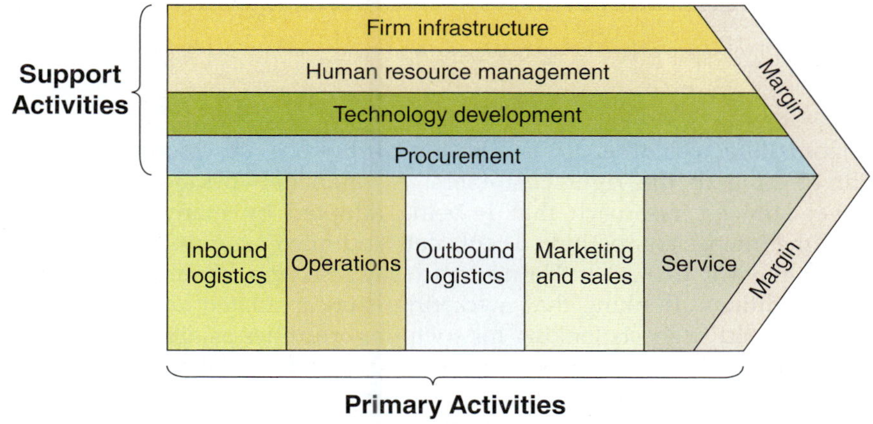

Source: Reprinted with permission of the Free Press, a Division of Simon & Schuster Adult Publishing Group, from *Competitive Advantage: Creating and Sustaining Superior Performance*, by Michael E. Porter. Copyright © 1985, 1988 by Michael E. Porter. All rights reserved.

Several of the value chain activities are directly relevant to what you will read about in this chapter, including inbound and outbound logistics, operations issues, and procurement. A **supply chain** represents all organizations involved in supplying a firm, the members of its channels of distribution, and its end-user consumers and business users. The goal is coordination of these value-adding flows among the entities in a way that maximizes overall value delivered and profit realized.[1] The management of this process is called **supply chain management**. Emblematic of the central role that channel and supply chain issues play in forming the value proposition of modern firms, it is telling that today more and more marketing managers are turning to elements of the "place P" within the 4Ps of the marketing mix for sources of differential competitive advantage.[2] How value is added by successfully managing a firm's channels and the supply chain is the central topic of this chapter.

At the broadest level, a firm might view itself as an integral part of a **value network**, which may be thought of as an overarching system of formal and informal relationships within which the firm participates to procure, transform and enhance, and ultimately supply its offerings in final form within a market space. Value networks are fluid and complex. They are composed of potentially numerous firms with which a company interacts vertically within its channel of distribution

Toshiba adds value to customers in many ways through innovation, technology, and great marketing, service, and logistics.

EXHIBIT 11.2 | Elements of a Value Network

- The overarching process focus is on value co-creation.
- A shared vision exists within the network with a common aim of fostering value co-creation.
- Value co-creation is viewed as emanating from the expertise and competencies of all parties within the network.
- Network and team *relationships* are key elements in the co-creation of the value.
- This value is viewed as *network value.*
- Relationship conflicts are viewed as potential barriers to the creation of network value and a process for conflict co-management is essential.

Source: Derived from Stephen L. Vargo and Robert F. Lusch, "Evolving to a New Dominant Logic for Marketing," *Journal of Marketing* 68 (January 2004), pp. 1–17.

and horizontally across other firms whose contributions are essential to getting the right offering to the right customers. A value network perspective is a macro-level strategic approach that is being adopted by many firms in part because of the intense competition to cut costs and maximize process efficiencies every step of the way to market. The approach suggests opportunities for breaking outside of traditional thinking that marketing is encapsulated *within* an organization, and instead suggests looking for such opportunities as alliances, strategic partnerships, nontraditional channel approaches, episodic collaborations, and outsourcing opportunities to provide unique sources of competitive edge.[3]

At its core, a value network exists to co-create value. The aim is **value co-creation** by the participating suppliers, customers, and other stakeholders in which the members of the network combine capabilities according to their expertise and the competencies required from the situation.[4] The key elements of a value network are portrayed in Exhibit 11.2.

Based on the concept of value networks, a whole new breed of organization is arising called a **network organization**, or **virtual organization**, because it eliminates many in-house business functions and activities in favor of focusing only on those aspects for which it is best equipped to add value.[5] Such approaches are often pursued to provide quicker market response and to free resources to focus on the firm's core deliverables. Network firms usually formalize contracts with suppliers, distributors, and other important partners to contribute the aspects of the value chain those entities do best, then draw on their own internal capabilities to focus on core internal sources of value. Some network organizations operate much like a shell in which most or all of the actual manufacturing, distribution, operations, and maybe even R&D and marketing execution are outsourced to efficient experts.[6] Ethical Dimension 11 provides an interesting look at global outsourcing at Apple.

Scotts Miracle-Gro Company, which markets weed control and other lawn- and garden-care products, outsources the management of its warehouses. The warehouses are run by seven third-party logistics providers (3PLs). To oversee and evaluate how the warehouses are run, Scotts developed a 12-point fleet vehicle performance management program for its 3PLs. "By comparing the performance of vehicles in different plants and with different operators, we believe we will be able to identify best practices and change the habits of people, which can reduce maintenance costs," said Matthew Chute, senior buyer of indirect sourcing. Eight of the performance points emphasize improvements in staff behaviors, three focus on processes, and one spotlights technology. The warehouse management team developed specific expectations, procedures, and metrics that its 3PLs must meet to remain Scotts's partners. "We have a short window to ship our product, and we operate in a demanding environment," says John Smith, manager of global raw materials. "Prior to putting in the fleet management program, it wasn't uncommon to have two or three lifts a day down for repairs."[7]

ETHICAL DIMENSION 11

Outsourcing "Cool"

The Apple iPhone 5 is an undeniable success, as were the prior versions. A "game changer," the iPhone has taken the lowly simple cell phone to a whole new level by offering a wide range of features (digital music player, Internet surfing, PDA, e-mail) in an elegant touch-screen device. More that six years since it was introduced, the product continues to incorporate a number of innovative designs that require integration of sophisticated products from companies all over the world including Samsung and Qualcomm chips, SanDisk flash memory, and Sony batteries.

Apple did not invent the smartphone but improved the product by creating innovative features in the iPhone and changing the market perception. However, Apple does not assemble the iPhone because the challenges of handling the thousands of sensors, chips, and other parts is labor-intensive as well as technologically challenging. Instead, they use foreign manufacturers, mostly in Asia, because of their ability to handle complex technology manufacturing and lower labor costs.

Apple chose Hon Hai Precision Industry in Taiwan to manufacture the iPhone 5. Operating under the trade name Foxconn, the company is one of the largest technology companies in the world with sales exceeding $40 billion. Hon Hai Precision Industry has been criticized for using sweatshop labor conditions in China to increase productivity. This has resulted in widely publicized stories about suicides due to the working conditions at Foxconn facilities. Hon Hai has sued Chinese reporters who file negative reports about the company's labor practices.

Apple's response has been to send teams to China to investigate various allegations and has reported that, while there were some abuses, overall the company was a good employer. Hon Hai has not experienced significant problems as a result of questions about its labor policies; however, the company has kept a very low profile and that is the way Apple prefers it. Negative publicity about events such as the working conditions in China can potentially damage Apple's carefully developed brand image in the same way that similar practices by its outsourced Asian shoe manufacturers have plagued Nike's reputation for decades.

Apple's brand image as a maker of cool, innovative products appeals to a broad range of consumers. Part of that image is based on the perception that Apple is a responsible corporation that is environmentally concerned and labor friendly.[8]

Ethical Perspective

1. **Apple:** How aggressive should Apple be in making sure its suppliers follow strict labor rules and policies? Should the company enforce U.S. labor standards or simply the standards of the local country?
2. **Consumers:** If you were aware that Apple was using a supplier that violated established labor practices, would you buy an Apple product? Do you research a company's policies about supplier labor practices or environmental policies before buying a product? If you don't, should you?

In the future, more firms, and especially start-ups, entrepreneurial organizations, and those whose core products are in the critical introduction and growth phases, will opt for a network organization approach to take advantage of the value network concept. This prediction is based on a competitive need for firms to be **nimble** in all aspects of their operation—that is, to be in a position to be maximally flexible, adaptable, and speedy in response to the many key change drivers affecting business today such as rapidly shifting technology, discontinuous innovation, fickle consumer markets, and relentless market globalization.[9] Taking a value network approach frees up internal resources so a firm can be more nimble in addressing external uncontrollable opportunities and threats, thus yielding a potential competitive advantage over firms that have high costs associated with performing many of the value chain functions themselves. A network organization facilitates concentration on one's own distinctive competencies while efficiently gathering value from outside firms that are concentrating their efforts in their own areas of expertise within your value network.

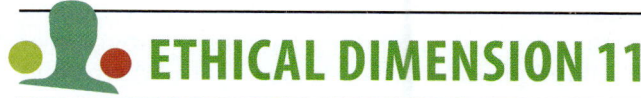

Many organizations are beginning to consider their customers—both end users and within a channel—as important members of a value network. As you learned in Chapter 9, firms cultivate customer involvement in various aspects of product and market development to enable customer advocacy, which is a willingness and ability on the part of a customer to participate in communicating the brand message to others within his or her sphere of influence. There are several potential value-adding ways to involve customers, in both B2B and B2C settings, including participation in ongoing research and customer advisory panels and provision of recognition, rewards, and delightful surprises for customers that participate in the relationship at a high level.

Overall, managing marketing channels and the supply chain is a fruitful area of concentration for marketing managers because of its potential to enhance the value of the firm's goods and services in a variety of ways. As you read further about the various specific components of the "place P" in the marketing mix, keep in mind that in today's business environments, the boundaries of just *how* these value-adding activities are delivered and *by whom* within the value network is a very open opportunity. As we have learned, these decisions are made with the knowledge that intelligent investment in the primary and support activities within the value chain should positively enhance profit margin through more efficient and effective firm performance.

CHANNELS AND INTERMEDIARIES

LO 11-2

Identify various types of intermediaries and distribution channels.

A **channel of distribution** consists of interdependent entities that are aligned for the purpose of transferring possession of a product from producer to consumer or business user. Put another way, a channel is a system of interdependent relationships among a set of organizations that facilitates the exchange process.[10] Most channels are not direct from producer to consumer. Instead, they contain a variety of **intermediaries**, formerly called middlemen, that play a role in the exchange process between producer and consumer.[11] A wide variety of types of

EXHIBIT 11.3 | Major Types of Intermediaries

MIDDLEMAN: Independent business entity that links producers and end-user consumers or organizational buyers.

MERCHANT MIDDLEMAN: Middleman that buys goods outright, taking title to them.

AGENT: Business entity that negotiates purchases, sales, or both but does not take title to the goods involved.

MANUFACTURERS' AGENT: Agent that usually operates on an extended contract, often sells within an exclusive territory, handles noncompeting but related lines of goods, and has limited authority to price and create terms of sale.

DISTRIBUTOR: Wholesale middleman, found especially when selective or exclusive distribution is common and strong promotional support is needed. Sometimes used synonymously for a wholesaler.

WHOLESALER: Entity primarily engaged in buying, taking title to, storing (usually), and physically handling goods in large quantities. Wholesalers resell the goods (usually in smaller quantities) to retailers or to organizational buyers.

JOBBER: Middleman that buys from manufacturers and sells to retailers. This intermediary is sometimes called a "rack jobber" to connote the service of stocking racks or shelves with merchandise.

FACILITATING AGENT: Entity that assists in the performance of distribution tasks other than buying, selling, and transferring title (examples include trucking companies, warehouses, importers, etc.).

RETAILER: Entity primarily engaged in selling to end-user consumers.

Source: *Dictionary of Marketing Terms,* 2nd ed., Peter D. Bennett, ed. (Chicago: American Marketing Association, 1995).

intermediaries exist, and they usually fall within two principal categories: **merchant intermediaries**, who take title to the product, and **agent intermediaries**, who do not take title to the product.[12] Agent intermediaries perform a variety of physical distribution, transaction and communication, and facilitating functions that make exchange possible. Exhibit 11.3 provides further insight about major types of intermediaries.

The majority of L.L. Bean's sales are through its online and catalog direct channels. But they also have a channel intermediary in the form of their own retail stores.

On the surface, intermediaries seem unnecessary. Wouldn't it be much more efficient for all channels to be direct from producer to consumer like Dell or Avon? The answer goes back to what we learned in Chapter 2 about the different types of utilities—form, time, place, and ownership. Sometimes you might hear a phrase such as, "We save you money by cutting out the middleman!" But, in reality, cutting out intermediaries is not a guarantee of saving consumers money. In the long run, channel intermediaries tend to continue to participate in a channel only as long as their value added to the channel supports their inclusion. If an intermediary of any of the types shown in Exhibit 11.3 doesn't carry its weight, the channel structure eventually will change accordingly to maximize efficiencies across the utilities. Thus, channel members add their value by bridging gaps in form, time, place, and ownership that naturally exist between producers and consumers.

Exhibits 11.4 and 11.5 illustrate examples within two distinct channel situations: one with end-user consumers as the final element in the channel and one ending with an organizational buyer in which the product is used within the business. The exhibits call attention to the fact that channels are distinguishable based on the number of intermediaries they contain—the more intermediaries that are involved, the longer the channel. A **direct channel**, portrayed as the first example in each exhibit, has no intermediaries and operates strictly from producer to end-user consumer or business user. An **indirect channel** contains one or more intermediary levels, as represented by all the other examples within each exhibit.[13]

EXHIBIT 11.4 | End-User Consumer Channels

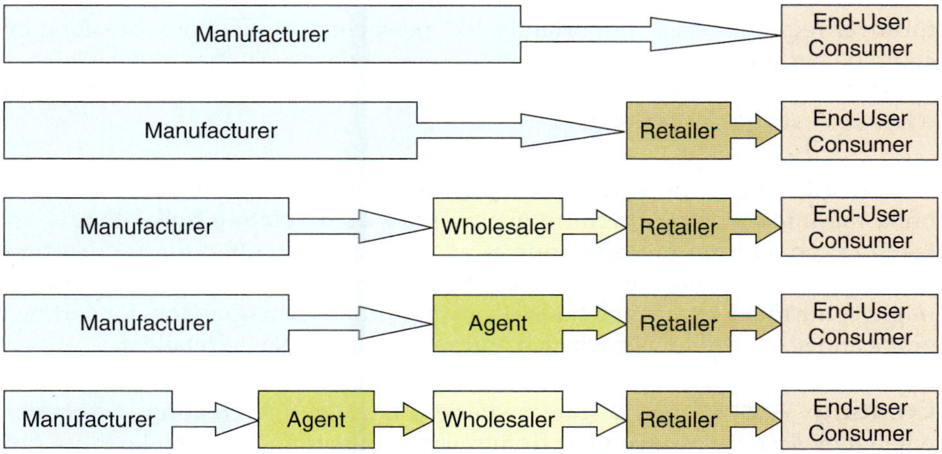

EXHIBIT 11.5 | Organizational Channels

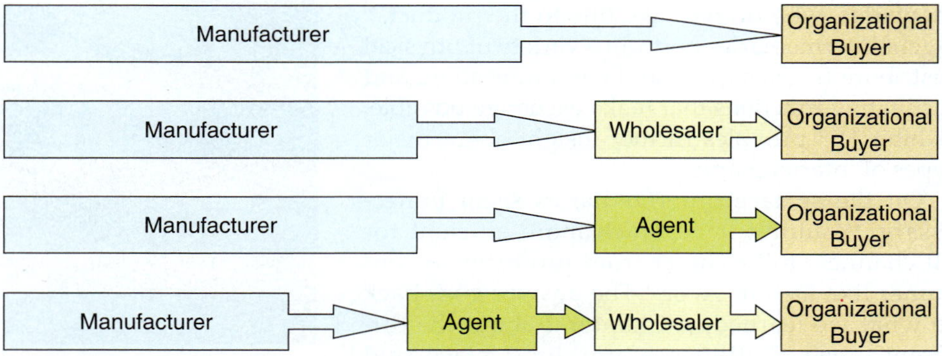

FUNCTIONS OF CHANNEL INTERMEDIARIES

LO 11-3

Understand the impact of intermediary contributions via physical distribution functions, transaction and communication functions, and facilitating functions.

Channel intermediaries enhance utilities by providing a wide array of specific functions. Their contributions can be classified into physical distribution functions, transaction and communication functions, and facilitating functions.

Physical Distribution Functions

One function of channel intermediaries is **physical distribution**, or **logistics**, which is the integrated process of moving input materials to the producer, in-process inventory through the firm, and finished goods out of the firm through the channel of distribution. Let's examine how channel intermediaries contribute to the physical distribution function.

Breaking Bulk In many industries, such as consumer health products, when finished goods come off a firm's production line, the manufacturer packages the individual pieces into large cartons for shipping into the channel of distribution. This is a convenient way for manufacturers to ship out the product. However, consumers shopping in a drugstore, whether a national chain such as Walgreens or an independent pharmacy in your hometown, don't need to see 144 units of a shampoo or deodorant on a store shelf. The function of **breaking bulk** occurs within a channel to better match quantities needed to space constraints and inventory turnover requirements.[14] Importantly, like most channel functions, breaking bulk could be performed by different types of intermediaries, in the case of Walgreens by the retailer's own warehouse and in the case of the local pharmacy by a drug wholesaler such as McKesson.

Accumulating Bulk and Sorting In some industries, rather than breaking bulk, the intermediaries perform a process of **accumulating bulk**—that is, they take in product from multiple sources and transform it, often through **sorting** it into different classifications for sales through the channel.[15] Eggs, for example, might come into a processing house from individual farm operators for sorting by grade and size, then to be packaged and sent on their way to retailers.

Creating Assortments Intermediaries engage in **creating assortments** when they accumulate products from several sources and then make those products available down the channel as a convenient assortment for consumers.[16]

Assume for a moment you are looking for a new high-definition television (HDTV). With no channel intermediaries you would have to review the entire line of HDTVs from each manufacturer to truly understand the different product features offered across their product lines. But walk into Best Buy or go to the retailer's website and an assortment across those manufacturers is already waiting for your review, selected by Best Buy's expert buying staff based on features and value. Most consumers appreciate the convenience associated with having an assortment of choices available for review.

QVC expands the assortment available to its customers by offering a wider variety of products on its website. The website must work in tandem with the on-air network and serve as the "anytime assortment." While online presence is critical to success, having a mobile presence can make an even greater impact on today's consumer. Orders made through QVC's website and via smartphone apps accounted for 26 percent of net revenue during 2012, and are projected to continue to rise. Dermot Boyd, CEO of QVC UK, said: "Mobile is the fastest growing platform and that includes tablets. But TV viewing has gone up too. The important thing is we can be on both screens: TV and tablets. Tablets and mobiles reinforce the TV platform, and we are streaming on the web too. Often, when people see something on QVC, it drives in-store sales of that product as well. And, through our website, QVC also allows brands to expand. At the end of the day, we're a retailer too."[17]

Reducing Transactions We've already seen how the introduction of even one intermediary into a channel can contribute to greatly **reducing transactions** necessary to complete an exchange. While it might seem counterintuitive to those who are not studying marketing management, channels with intermediaries actually tend to save end-user consumers money over what most direct producer to consumer distribution approaches would cost, given the same product.[18] Manufacturers' costs would skyrocket if they held the responsibility for interfacing with and delivering product to every one of their end users. Consider that conveniently located retailers save consumers a lot of money by reducing travel costs versus buying directly from a manufacturer. As mentioned earlier, in the long run, channel intermediaries remain in the channel only as long as they are adding efficiencies, reducing costs, and adding value within that channel.

Transportation and Storage Relatively few producers operate their own transportation networks or provide warehousing facilities. Producers make money by pushing finished goods out the door and into the channel of distribution. As such, **transportation and storage** functions are among the most commonly provided channel intermediary activities. In the publishing industry, Amazon.com and other online booksellers play an invaluable role to both publishers and consumers by ensuring that sufficient inventories of the right books are available for shipping across a variety of transportation choices, from UPS ground to next-day air depending on the urgency of the order.

Transaction and Communication Functions

Another category of intermediary contribution within a channel is the performance of transaction and communication functions. These functions include:

- *Selling.* Often, intermediaries provide a sales force to represent a manufacturer's product line. This could take the form of manufacturers' representatives, or brokers, that represent a product line down the channel. Alternatively, the salespeople might work for a wholesaler or retailer.[19]

- *Buying.* Both wholesalers and retailers perform an important function by evaluating products and ultimately simplifying purchase decisions by creating assortments.[20]
- *Marketing communications.* Intermediaries frequently receive incentives from manufacturers to participate in helping promote products in the channel.[21] When a Target ad features Tide laundry detergent, it's a safe bet that Target has received a promotional allowance from P&G to feature the brand. Likewise, that shelf tag in your neighborhood pharmacy featuring a special price on Rolaids very likely was placed there by the pharmacy's wholesaler as part of a promotion by McNeil Consumer Healthcare, a subsidiary of J&J.

Facilitating Functions

In a channel, **facilitating functions** performed by intermediaries include a variety of activities that help fulfill completed transactions and also maintain the viability of the channel relationships. These include:

- *Financing.* Without readily available credit at various stages in the distribution process, many channels could not operate. In any given channel, when credit is required by one channel member, it may be facilitated by another channel member such as a producer, wholesaler, or retailer, depending on the situation. Alternatively, credit may be facilitated by outside sources such as banks and credit card providers.[22]
- *Market research.* Because intermediaries are closer to end-user consumers and business users than manufacturers, they are in an ideal position to gather information about the market and consumer trends. Collecting and sharing market and competitive information helps members of the channel continue to offer the right product mix at the right prices.[23]

The H-E-B supermarket chain has a store in the northern Houston suburb of Conroe, Texas, that focuses primarily on offering customers a high-end shopping experience. The store has a very different product mix compared to stores elsewhere in the country. The H-E-B store collects consumer data at the store level to ensure a great match of products to its customer base. "Everything about the new store, from its design to its fresh offerings, was specifically tailored to meet the needs and desires of this community," said George Kaehler, unit director for H-E-B'S Conroe Market. "We know our customers will enjoy the endless product selection and fresh offerings." As one example of this customization, the company has designed a fresh guacamole bar, where a trained chef makes the guacamole to order from ripe avocados using fresh lime juice, cilantro, tomatoes, and onions. Through this overall approach, H-E-B is catering directly to its clientele in the area.[24]

- *Risk-taking.* A big part of how an intermediary can add value is by reducing the risk of others in the channel. Any of the major physical distribution functions described above that are assumed by a channel member come with potential risks and liabilities.[25] For example, accumulating bulk in perishable goods comes with a risk of spoilage if customer demand estimates are inaccurately high. Also, when product liability lawsuits are filed, the defendants named are nearly always anyone within the distribution channel that played a part in getting the product to market.
- *Other services.* Services performed by intermediaries run a gamut of activities such as training others in the channel on how to display or sell the products,

performing repair and maintenance of products after a sale, and providing customized software for inventory management, accounting and billing, and other operational processes.

GENCO provides product repair services for retailers and for consumer goods and electronics manufacturers such as Philips Consumer Electronics. GENCO inspects all the returned goods at scanning stations in a central returns center to determine whether the products can be repaired. Products that cannot be repaired may be reclaimed or sent to liquidators. GENCO maintains a global network of liquidation channels that includes salvage buyers, online auction partners, B2B exchanges, fixed-price offerings, and category and bulk salvage. Liquidation is especially important for electronics stores that sell the latest smartphones, computers, and tablets. [26]

DISINTERMEDIATION AND E-CHANNELS

Driven largely by the advent of electronic commerce and online marketing, **disintermediation**, or the shortening or collapsing of marketing channels due to the elimination of one or more intermediaries, is common in the electronic channel. In the early days of e-commerce, many entrepreneurs rushed to market with a website to sell their favorite products. This dot-com boom quickly turned to a bust, however, in part because many of these new-age marketers didn't understand the basics of distribution channels. Simply opening a website that features a product is one thing, but it's another thing entirely to invest in the infrastructure and capabilities needed to consistently fulfill orders in a timely and accurate manner. Most postmortems on the cause of the dot-com bust point to poor channel and supply chain practices as the No. 1 reason so many of those initial e-marketers failed. That is, customer expectations were peaked by the novelty and convenience of buying online only to be dashed by delays and errors in product fulfillment after the sale.[27]

The Internet disintermediated thousands of travel agencies. In many cases, travel agents became unnecessary as people booked their own travel online. Other intermediaries, such as financial services and investment counselors, real estate agents, and insurance brokers, likewise have had to contend with customers accessing information on the Internet. However, Chris Nicholas, vice president of client development at CI Travel in Norfolk, said recent articles in *The Wall Street Journal, USA Today,* and elsewhere document customer dissatisfaction with online travel agencies. Customers also are often put off by the overwhelming number of travel options offered online. "There is only one advantage of booking online—price," Nicholas said. "And often travel professionals match or beat a price. Every other advantage goes to the travel management company that exists to make sure you are delighted with your choices and offers to help when something goes awry."[28]

Today, electronic commerce has settled into a more rational position as one of several approaches within marketing management for distributing and promoting goods and services. E-marketers are much more savvy about how they set up and manage their channels and realize that disintermediation may not improve aggregate channel performance. The trend toward more stability in online shopping was facilitated in large measure by the entry of firms such as UPS and FedEx into the market of providing a broad range of integrated supply chain solutions.

Recently, many e-commerce (and other) firms are finding that handing over one or more of their core internal functions, such as most or all of their supply chain activities, to other (third-party) companies that are experts in those areas allows the firm to better focus on its core business. This approach, which is referred to as **outsourcing** or **third-party logistics (3PL)**, is attractive for many firms whose own core competencies do not include these elements. The trend has opened up opportunities for firms such as UPS and FedEx, as well as a host of other smaller firms, to change their business focus from mere shippers into broad-based logistics consultancies that handle all aspects of clients' supply chain functions.[29]

VERTICAL MARKETING SYSTEMS

Whereas standard marketing channels are comprised of independent entities, a **vertical marketing system (VMS)** consists of vertically aligned networks behaving and performing as a unified system.[30] A VMS can be set up in three different ways: corporate systems, contractual systems, and administered systems. At its essence, in a VMS a channel member *(a)* owns the others, *(b)* has contracts with them, or *(c)* simply forces cooperation through sheer clout within the channel.

Corporate Systems

LO 11-4

Explain the different types of vertical marketing systems.

In **corporate VMS**, a channel member has invested in backward or forward **vertical integration** by buying a controlling interest in other intermediaries. In the Midwest, what is now the Braum's Ice Cream and Dairy Store chain started in the 1930s as a family dairy farm in Kansas. Over time the Braum family acquired almost every aspect of its distribution channel—milk processing, other product manufacturing, transportation, warehousing, and the Braum's stores. An owned, or corporate, VMS such as that practiced by Braum's creates a powerful competitive advantage in the marketplace due to cost and process efficiencies realized when a channel is strictly controlled by one entity.

Contractual Systems

A **contractual VMS** consists of otherwise independent entities that are bound together legally through contractual agreement. The most famous example of this arrangement is a **franchise organization**, which is designed to create a contractual relationship between a franchisor that grants the franchise and the franchisee, or the independent entity entering into an agreement to perform at the standards required by the franchisor.[31] *Entrepreneur* magazine reports that franchising remains the highest-potential start-up and growth mechanism for small-business owners, and it's an effective way to expand a distribution channel quickly and efficiently. Subway, the world's largest franchise system, has over 40,000 outlets in over 100 countries.

Another common contractual VMS is the **retailer cooperative**, or co-op. In this era of chain stores, independent retailers across a variety of product categories have banded together to gain cost and operating economies of scale in the channel. Associated Grocers is a retailer-owned co-op of more than 2,900 stores in 24 states that, through enhanced buying and distribution power, can better compete with supermarket chains than if the stores were buying separately.[32] A variation on this concept is the **wholesaler cooperative**, such as Ace Hardware, in which retailers contract for varying degrees of exclusive dealings with a particular wholesaler.[33]

Administered Systems

In an **administered VMS**, the sheer size and power of one of the channel members place it in a position of channel control. The lead player in such situations may be referred to as the **channel captain** or **channel leader**, signifying its ability to control many aspects of that channel's operations.[34] For years, P&G was the channel captain in every channel in which it was a member based on the clout of its extensive stable of No. 1 brands. It became notorious for dictating terms of sale, limiting quantities of promotional goods to intermediaries, and steamrolling uncooperative wholesalers and retailers into submission. But the rise of giant retailers—Walmart, in particular—shifted the power in the channel and forced P&G to become more customer-compliant.

It is possible that an administered VMS can be more formally structured through strategic alliances and partnership agreements among channel members that agree to work in mutual cooperation. P&G and Walmart have a longstanding strategic alliance that includes connectivity of inventory, billing systems, and market research. The result is improved inventory management, more efficient invoice processing, and product development that better serves the consumer marketplace. Approaches such as this are often referred to as **partner relationship management (PRM) strategies**. The goal of PRM is to share resources, especially knowledge-based resources, to effect optimally profitable relationships between two channel members.[35]

CHANNEL BEHAVIOR: CONFLICT AND POWER

The very nature of channels, especially traditional channels composed of independent entities, fosters differences in channel power among members. **Channel power** is the degree to which any member of a marketing channel can exercise influence over the other members of the channel. As we saw with the administered VMS, power can directly influence the relationships within the channel. Ultimately, **channel conflict** can occur in which channel members experience disagreements and their relationship can become strained or fall apart. Unresolved channel conflict not only can result in an uncooperative and inefficient channel, but it also can ultimately impact end-user consumers through inferior products, spotty inventory, and higher prices.

Danskin sells activewear through 3,000 retail locations nationwide. When the company decided to launch its website, it was very mindful of potential channel conflict. Thus, the company initially offered only plus-sized products on the web so that it would not compete directly with the retail stores. When Danskin's retail customers did not show resistance to the website, the company slowly expanded its online presence, adding regular-sized apparel and more fashion styles. To avoid competing with its retail customers on price, Danskin's online merchandise was offered at the manufacturer's suggested retail price. The brand has done exceedingly well for its parent company, Iconix. Recently, Danskin has been relying on celebrity endorsements to drive consumers to the website. These celebrities do not appear in the actual retail stores; instead, they have a strictly online presence. Web prices are still higher than the in-store prices in order to continue to give Danskin's valued retailers that advantage over direct-to-customer online purchases.[36]

French and Raven have identified five important sources of power that are relevant in a channel setting. Those power sources are illustrated in Exhibit 11.6 and explained below.

- *Coercive power.* **Coercive power** involves an explicit or implicit threat that a channel captain will invoke negative consequences on a channel member if it does not comply with the leader's request or expectations. Walmart has exceedingly tight standards for how shippers must schedule delivery appointments at a Walmart distribution center. If the truck misses the appointment by even a few minutes, the error results in punitive financial consequences for the vendor. If the problem becomes repetitive, a vendor will be placed on probation as an approved source.

EXHIBIT 11.6 | Sources of Channel Power

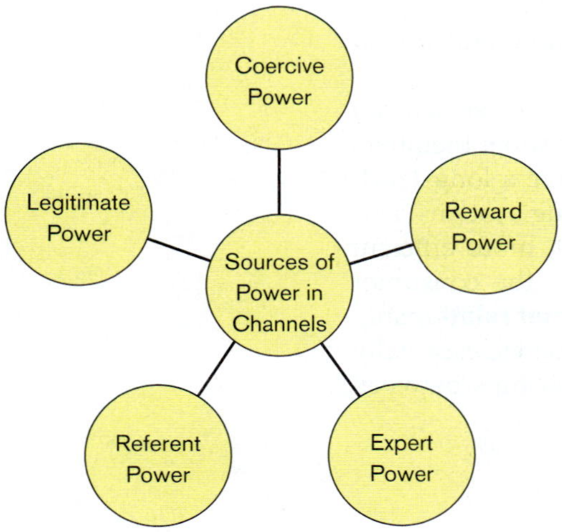

- *Reward power.* Despite Walmart's ability to coerce, few vendors will turn up their nose at potential business from the retailing giant just because they can be difficult to work with. Naturally, the motivating force is Walmart's huge **reward power** in the form of writing big orders.
- *Expert power.* Often, channel members adopt an approach of utilizing their unique competencies to influence others in the channel. **Expert power** might take the form of sharing important product knowledge, such as a representative from Clinique setting up a demonstration for cosmetic consultants in a Nordstrom store to stimulate sales expertise. Or it might involve sharing of information such as Kroger Supermarkets providing consumer preference data to Frito-Lay to get it to produce a special flavor of chips for a specific geographic area that Kroger serves.
- *Referent power.* When a channel member is respected, admired, or revered based on one or more attributes, that member enjoys **referent power** within the channel. Only the best of the best brands can rely on this power source. In frozen foods, Stouffer's (a unit of Nestlé) commands a level of respect well above the competition because of its outstanding quality standards, successful marketing and branding strategies, and cooperativeness with retailers. When frozen-food sections of supermarkets are reset to accommodate new-product entries and remove discontinued items, Stouffer reps are often trusted to help store clerks reset the shelves and in many instances Stouffer's is given prime display space in the freezer case.
- *Legitimate power.* **Legitimate power** results from contracts such as franchise agreements or other formal agreements. When McDonald's requires franchisees that want to participate in the latest iteration of their famous Monopoly scratch-off game to sign an agreement as to how the game will be promoted and administered in the store, it is exercising legitimate power to control misuse of the promotional activity.[37]

SELECTING CHANNEL APPROACHES

LO 11-5

Utilize suitable criteria to select appropriate channel approaches.

Given the plethora of choices of channel intermediaries and channel structures that we've reviewed, marketing managers have a lot to consider when designing or selecting the channel approach that will best meet their needs. When marketing planning, a good channel decision can be one of the most important within the entire planning process and can lead to market advantage over competitors. Among the issues for consideration are:

1. What is the level of distribution intensity sought within the channel?
2. How much control and adaptability are required over the channel and its activities?
3. What are the priority channel functions that require investment?

Distribution Intensity

Distribution intensity refers to the number of intermediaries involved in distributing the product. Distribution strategies can be intensive, selective, or exclusive.

Intensive Distribution When the objective is to obtain maximum product exposure throughout the channel, an **intensive distribution** strategy is designed to saturate every possible intermediary and especially retailers. Intensive distribution is typically associated with low-cost **convenience goods**. **Impulse goods** are also appropriate for intensive distribution, as their sales rely on the consumer seeing the product, feeling an immediate want, and being able to purchase now.

Selective Distribution **Shopping goods**, goods for which a consumer may engage in a limited search, are candidates for **selective distribution**. Examples of goods that fit this approach include most appliances, midrange fashion apparel, and home furnishings. A selective distribution strategy may require that intermediaries provide a modicum of customer service during the sale and, depending on the type of good, follow-up service after the sale. Intermediary reputation, especially of the retailers, can be an asset in selective distribution. For example, selecting a retailer whose brand connection enhances and is compatible with the product is essential. Distributing a Kenneth Cole watch or accessory at either Kmart or Tiffany & Company is not a good fit, but gaining distribution in Dillard's and Macy's makes a lot of sense.

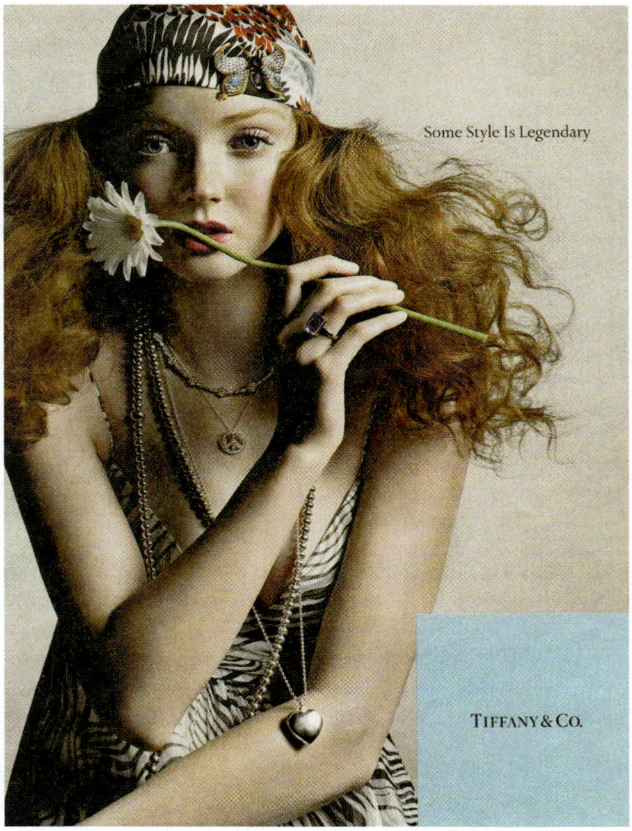

Tiffany & Company benefits from exclusive distribution as it plays up the luxurious benefits of its products.

Exclusive Distribution When a manufacturer opts for **exclusive distribution** in a channel, it is often part of an overall positioning strategy built on prestige, scarcity, and premium pricing. In Chapter 10 you read about Voss Water's highly successful entry into the ultra-premium bottled water market. Voss's prestige was greatly enhanced by a distribution strategy that involved only one wholesale distributor per state, which had to be a liquor, wine, and spirits wholesaler with relationships already built among the exclusive restaurants and hotels that Voss was targeting. Exclusive distribution also often arises because a significant personal selling effort is required with the consumer before product purchase. Products that possess complex or unique properties that only a one-to-one in-person interaction with a customer can explain are often best served by intermediaries with specialized sales capabilities.[38]

Luxury brand Chanel keeps its exclusivity by selling its products through upscale department stores such as Neiman Marcus and Saks Fifth Avenue and independent high-end boutiques like Jeffrey's in New York. When the company decided to enter the Chinese market, it was extremely particular about the stores it contracted with. Chanel's president of fashion, Bruno Pavlovsky, said, "We try to get the best three boutiques in Shanghai instead of having 10 boutiques." It is their number one priority. "We try to bring through the boutiques the best value of the brand . . . our idea is not to open lots of boutiques but to be able to give, through the existing ones, the best value and the best service to our customers." The brand firmly believes that exclusivity is the best way to ensure customers keep coming back for more, and that it is essential not to overwhelm any markets it enters with too many outlets.[39]

Channel Control and Adaptability

Review of the types of intermediaries in Exhibit 11.3 and channel examples in Exhibits 11.4 and 11.5 reveals a variety of options that can lead to more or less control and adaptability over the channel. Hiring an in-house sales force, investing in a fleet of trucks, building a warehouse facility, pursuing a corporate VMS through vertical integration, and engaging in a contractual VMS with other intermediaries each would increase a firm's control of the channel but at the same time limit its flexibility to change if the competition and other external forces require it. Other options such as brokers, manufacturer's agents, and common carriers have the opposite effect in that a firm's influence and control in the channel are minimized but great flexibility is attained to dramatically and quickly alter aspects of the channel if needed.

In deciding on the right balance between control and flexibility in a channel, marketing managers must consider the type of products involved, cost issues among the various options, strength of belief in the accuracy of the sales forecast, and likelihood that major changes will occur in the customer or competitive marketplace that would necessitate restructuring the channel. Often, customers drive the ultimate choice a marketing manager makes about a channel, as flexibility or control differentially impact the value proposition from one customer to the next.

Prioritization of Channel Functions—Push versus Pull Strategy

The third aspect of channel decisions by marketing managers relates to what channel functions are most important to the success of the particular products. In large measure, this decision is framed by whether the general approach is a push strategy or a pull strategy. A **push strategy** means that much of the intensive promotional activities take place from the manufacturer downward through the channel of distribution. Think of this approach as an investment by the manufacturer in intermediaries so that they will have a maximal incentive to stock, promote, sell, and ship the firm's products. Push strategies usually are supported by heavy allowance payments to intermediaries for helping accomplish the manufacturer's goals. Examples include funding an extra incentive to a wholesale drug salesperson for pushing a particular medication to an independent pharmacy, or paying a **slotting allowance** or **shelf fee** to secure distribution in an intermediary's inventory listing and warehouse or onto a retail shelf.[40]

In contrast, a manufacturer employing a **pull straegy** focuses much of its promotional investment on the end-user consumer. In this case, heavy advertising in mass media, direct marketing, couponing, and other direct-to-consumer promotion are expected to create demand from intermediaries from the bottom of the channel upward. A pull strategy doesn't mean a manufacturer wouldn't engage in any channel incentives, but rather that the incentives would likely be greatly reduced versus a push strategy.[41]

Obviously, a number of important marketing management decisions about channel structure and types of intermediaries to best utilize are influenced by the degree to which the channel intermediaries are relied on to help create and support demand. The degree of push versus pull used is fundamental in framing the channel structure and relationships that are likely to optimize a product's success.

LO 11-6

Identify the logistics aspects of supply chain management.

LOGISTICS ASPECTS OF SUPPLY CHAIN MANAGEMENT

Physical distribution, or logistics, is the integrated process of moving input materials to the producer, in-process inventory through the firm, and finished goods out of the firm through the channel of distribution. Traditionally, logistics was thought of as an internal flow going one direction—**outbound logistics**. That is, it was thought that logistics started with production and ended with receipt of the finished good by the end-user consumer or business user. From a supply chain perspective, logistics professionals today tend to take a more holistic view of physical distribution. Thus, along with outbound logistics, it is important to consider **inbound logistics**—sourcing materials and knowledge inputs from external suppliers to the point at which production begins.

Today, the concept of reverse logistics must also be taken into account. **Reverse logistics** deals with how to get goods back to a manufacturer or intermediary after purchase. Product returns result for many reasons including spoilage and breakage, excess inventory, customer dissatisfaction, and overstocks.[42] In particular, online sellers in both the B2C and B2B space recognize that an inherent aspect of electronic commerce is the increased likelihood of product return. Returns are higher in this channel in large part because of the inability to physically examine the merchandise before purchase. Smart online sellers build return allowances—either free, with shipping charges, or with a restocking fee—into their pricing model. To do this, the seller must work out an efficient and customer-friendly procedure for how merchandise is to be returned. In many cases, the selling firm partners with one logistics company to handle the reverse logistics. For example, Zappos partners with UPS and the USPS and provides its customers the convenience of printing a free return label online at the Zappos website.

Several logistics aspects of supply chain management require close attention by marketing managers. These are order processing, warehousing and materials handling, inventory management, and transportation.

Fidelitone Logistics handles reverse logistics for companies. Consumer goods are returned for many reasons, and Fidelitone inspects the returns to determine if the shipment was wrong, if it was the wrong color or wrong size, or if the returned item is defective. Recently, it was announced that the company merged with TechniPak, a Tennessee-based company that provides order fulfillment services for a variety of online direct-to-consumer retailers. Josh Johnson, president of Fidelitone Logistics, said, "This partnership not only strengthens a core service offering, but provides a great deal of industry expertise and a strong history of delivering client satisfaction." Returns have become a major aspect of customer service and bring with them costs such as additional paperwork and distribution centers to handle the goods. That's why companies use intermediaries that are more efficient to provide these services.[43]

Order Processing

Receiving and properly processing customer orders is a critical step in getting product moving through the supply chain. It is also a point at which mistakes can easily occur, and when a mistake occurs in the order, it usually carries through the whole fulfillment system. If the item ordered is in stock, outbound processing from inventory occurs. If the item is not in stock, referred to as a **stock-out**, then inbound replenishment processes are triggered.

Fortunately, in many modern organizations, order processing has become highly mechanized. Sophisticated and integrated **enterprise resource planning (ERP) systems** now manage much of the logistics and other processes for many firms. ERP is a software application designed to integrate information related to logistics processes throughout the organization. Once data are entered, they

Logistics issues are obviously critical in shipping food products such as produce. Exposure to too much heat or cold can ruin the inventory in transit.

are automatically linked through internal systems and become available for use with all relevant decisions that rely on the ERP information. ERP enables employees throughout the system, whether in sales, billing, customer service, or some other group, to take ownership of their piece of the supply chain and to accurately communicate order status both to the customer and among themselves.[44]

Warehousing and Materials Handling

In an ideal supply chain, materials of all kinds are handled as few times as possible. Any warehouse needs to be designed so that after goods are received and checked in, they move directly to their designated storage locations. Efficient, orderly, clean, and well-marked warehouses enhance the flow of goods.

Decisions must be made about the optimal size for a warehouse, how many warehouses to have, and where they should be located to minimize transportation costs. The last point is especially important if the warehouse serves as a distribution center in which functions such as breaking and accumulating bulk occur for ultimate reshipping to customers.

Inventory Management

To ensure that inventories of both raw materials and finished goods are sufficient to meet customer demand without undue delay, firms utilize sophisticated **just-in-time (JIT) inventory control systems**. A JIT system's goal is to balance the double-edge sword of potentially having too many goods on hand and creating unnecessary warehousing costs, with the chance of having so little inventory in stock that stock-outs occur, requiring expensive rush production and express delivery situations.[45]

PRM arrangements often open up their collective IT systems for data sharing toward more reliable JIT inventory management. Walmart's legendary capability of real-time analysis and data transmission to vendors about inventories at any store or distribution center location has created a substantial competitive advantage over many other retailers. In any industry, customers expect product to be in stock and available, and when it's not they quickly become prone to switching to competitors. One component of ERP systems is usually **materials requirement planning (MRP)**. MRP guides overall management of the inbound materials from suppliers to facilitate minimal production delays.[46]

Transportation

With the cost of fuel today, it is not unusual for transportation costs to run as much as 10 percent of cost of goods sold. Effective transportation management is one way that many firms keep a lid on costs while also optimizing delivery options for customers. Exhibit 11.7 provides a comparison of several transportation options on a variety of criteria such as dependability, cost, speed, and suitable products. The decision about which one or what mix of these transportation options to choose will have a major impact on a firm's bottom line.

EXHIBIT 11.7 | Comparative Attributes across Different Transportation Modes

Low Cost	Speed	Reliability of Delivery	Flexibility of Delivery	Reputation for Delivering Undamaged Goods
1. Pipeline	1. Air	1. Pipeline	1. Motor	1. Pipeline
2. Water	2. Motor	2. Air	2. Rail	2. Water
3. Rail	3. Rail	3. Motor	3. Air	3. Air
4. Motor	4. Pipeline	4. Rail	4. Water	4. Motor
5. Air	5. Water	5. Water	5. Pipeline	5. Rail

Note: Numbers indicate relative ranking based on general trade-offs of cost versus other attributes of each mode.

DHL Supply Chain, one of the leading logistics and third-party providers, has launched the SmartPOD app. It is a solution that provides DHL's drivers and third-party haulers with a simple way of capturing real-time data and electronic proof of delivery (POD) information. This was designed in response to rising transportation costs and a demand for instantaneous vehicle location data, such as departure and arrival times. Openfield, an agribusiness company, subcontracts up to 100,000 loads of grain to third-party haulers annually, and was one of the first companies to roll out the app. Jim Hotchin, director of operations at Openfield, said, "With our drivers on the road Monday through Friday, it was taking up to two weeks to process information, resulting in delayed cash flows and supply shortages. Using the SmartPOD app, we get delivery information in real time, thus significantly impacting efficiency and achieving cost savings."[47]

LEGAL ISSUES IN SUPPLY CHAIN MANAGEMENT

As with pricing practices, a variety of laws impact the decision making about channels and logistics. Among others, the Sherman Antitrust Act (1890), Clayton Act (1914), and Federal Trade Commission Act (1914) provide much of the basis for legislation impacting supply chains. Three key legal issues related to distribution are exclusive dealing, exclusive territories, and tying contracts.

Exclusive Dealing

When a supplier creates a restrictive agreement that prohibits intermediaries that handle its product from selling competing firms' products, **exclusive dealing** has occurred. Whether a particular arrangement is legal depends on whether it interferes with the intermediary's right to act independently or the rights of competitors to succeed—that is, is competition lessened by the arrangement? Exclusive dealing lessens competition if it (1) accounts for substantial market share, (2) involves a substantial dollar amount, and (3) involves a big supplier and smaller intermediary, which sets up a case for coercion.

Exclusive dealing may be legal if the parties show exclusivity is essential for strategic reasons, such as to maintain product image. High-fashion brands often engage in exclusive dealing with retailers so that their image is not sullied by being merchandised in the store next to step-down labels. Also, if limited production capacity on the part of the supplier legitimately restricts its sales capabilities, exclusive dealing may also be legal. In this case, the point of the exclusive deal is to try to ensure the limited quantities of product have the best possible chance of being "sold through" to end users.[48]

Exclusive Territories

An **exclusive territory** protects an intermediary from having to compete with others selling a producer's goods. Can a producer always grant an intermediary an exclusive territory for sales purposes? Not necessarily. For this practice to be legal, it would have to be demonstrated that the exclusivity doesn't violate any statutes on restriction of competition. This issue often manifests itself in the context of suppliers limiting the number of retail outlets within a certain geographic area. One possible defense of exclusive territories might be that the costs of a new store (restaurant, retailer, dealer, etc.) entering the market are so great that the nature of the market and risks involved demand an opportunity for exclusivity.[49]

Tying Contracts

If a seller requires an intermediary to purchase a supplementary product to qualify to purchase the primary product the intermediary wishes to buy, a **tying contract** is in place. Example: "You can buy my printer, but to do so you *must* sign a contract to buy my ink"—thus, the products are "tied together" as terms of sale. Tying contracts are illegal, but historically it has often been difficult to prove in a court of law whether an agreement is or isn't a tying contract.[50]

RETAILING

LO 11-7

Understand the role of retailing in delivering the value offering to the customer.

You have learned that retailers are one form of channel intermediary. In this section we will focus a bit more on them as they tend to be the type of intermediary that most people encounter most frequently. **Retailing** is any business activity that creates value in the delivery of goods and services to consumers for their personal, nonbusiness consumption and is an essential component of the supply chain. As we discussed in earlier in the chapter, an efficient, effective supply chain moves materials from manufacturer to consumer. Retailing, in whatever form, is the point of contact in the supply chain with the consumer of the product. Put another way, retailing in its various forms represents a very important point of customer interface.

The retail sector plays a fundamental role in terms of employment and economic activity for any economy. In the United States, for example, retailing accounts for nearly 15 percent of all employment and generates over 6 percent of the gross domestic product. More importantly, it provides a vital connection between companies and customers. Retailing, however, plays a critical role in economies around the world and is growing in a number of emerging countries (See Exhibit 11.8).

In an inscreasingly interconnected world where consumers communicate directly with manufacturers, some question the long-term viability of retailing. Some suggest that retailing, at least traditional store-based retailing, will give way to Internet-based shopping experiences like Amazon. However, despite predictions about the demise of traditional retailing in the late 1990s, the retail sector continues to grow.[51] While the Internet has definitely altered the retail landscape, retailers still perform four critical functions that add value for companies and consumers. That is,

Most people know Walmart is the world's largest retailer, but the world's second largest retailer—Carrefour, based in France—is also very powerful with thousands of different retail formats around the world.

EXHIBIT 11.8 | Top 10 Global Retail Market Opportunities

2012 Rank	Country	Region	Market Attractiveness	Country Risk	Market Saturation	Time Pressure	GRDI Score
		Weight	*25%**	*25%*	*30%*	*20%*	
1	Brazil	Latin America	100	85.4	48.2	61.6	73.8
2	Chile	Latin America	86.6	100	17.4	57.1	65.3
3	China	Asia	53.4	72.6	29.3	100	63.8
4	Uruguay	Latin America	84.1	56.1	60	52.3	63.1
5	India	Asia	31	66.7	57.6	87.9	60.8
6	Georgia	Central Asia	27	68.7	92.6	54	60.6
7	United Arab Emirates	Mid. East/ N. Africa	86.1	93.9	9.4	52.9	60.6
8	Oman	Mid. East/ N. Africa	69.3	98.3	17.4	50.4	58.9
9	Mongolia	Asia	6.4	54.4	98.2	75.1	58.5
10	Peru	Latin America	43.8	55.5	62.9	67.2	57.4
			0 = low attractiveness 100 = high attractiveness	*0 = high risk 100 = low risk*	*0 = saturated 100 = not saturated*	*0 = no time pressure 100 = urgency to enter*	

* These percentages refer to the weighting of each factor. That is, GRDI = 25% (Market Attractiveness) + 25% (Country Risk) + 30% (Market Saturation) + 20% (Time Pressure).

Source: A. T. Kearney, "2012 Global Retail Development Index," www.atkearney.com/consumer-products-retail/global-retail-development-index/full-report/-/asset_publisher/oPFrGkblkz0Q/content/global-retail-development-index/10192, accessed May 2013.

they (1) offer variety for consumers, (2) separate large product volume into consumer purchase quantities, (3) maintain inventory levels, and (4) make additional services available to consumers. Let's examine each of these functions.

Offer Variety for Consumers

Retailers create an assortment of products that fit the consumer's needs. Some retailers define their assortment of products very broadly and offer a wide variety of products to consumers. Walmart and Target carry everything from food, clothing, hardware, and garden to automotive products. Grocery chains like H-E-B, Kroger, and Wegmans want to become "one-stop shops" offering consumers so many choices they will consider it their first choice when shopping.[52]

A typical supermarket carries between 20,000 and 30,000 product items. While that may seem like a large number, it is only a small fraction of all the products available. As a result, it is critical to select the right variety of products based on the demographics of the store's shoppers. The single college student shopping at a supermarket close to campus does not likely require the large economy box of detergent that the homemaker across town needs. Keep in mind that manufacturers make dozens of sizes and formats of each product. P&G makes over 45 different Tide products, not including the various box sizes. An individual store will likely carry three to five different Tide products in a couple of box sizes.[53]

Separate Large Product Volume into Consumer Purchase Quantities

You learned earlier in the chapter that chains work most efficiently and effectively when producing large volumes of products and moving them through the distributions system in bulk. However, consumers don't need or want the quantities produced by manufacturers. Retailers play a vital role assimilating the large quantities produced by manufacturers and offering smaller, more consumer-friendly quantities for the consumer.[54] For example, Sharp produces hundreds of 80-inch AQUOS LCD TVs each day, but an individual consumer needs only one at any given time. So retailers enable Sharp to manufacture in efficient product volume then transport the televisions from plants outside the United States to any retailer in the United States where it is possible to purchase a single TV at a competitive price.

Maintain Inventory Levels

One of the most important retailer functions is holding inventory in advance of a consumer purchase. Consumers around the world want to purchase when they are ready and expect the product to be available on demand. However, there is a cost of keeping products close to the customer. Products move through the supply chain in large quantities and are stored in warehouses that can be owned by manufacturers, distributors, or the retailer. It is from these warehouses that online retailers often ship directly to the consumer.

Many consumers, however, want to see the product in person before purchasing it. Additionally, in many cases, they want to take the product home for immediate consumption. As a result, retailers provide a valuable service to the consumer by keeping the product in inventory ready for purchase. At the same time, the retailers' inventory helps manufacturers because it stores the product close to consumers and makes it easier for them to purchase.[55]

Zara, the Spanish-based fashion retail outlet, focuses on moving its inventory quickly. The retailer's model attracts young, fashion-conscious shoppers who want the latest runway looks at attainable prices. To that end, Zara employs over 300 designers and produces over 30,000 items annually. Collections are refreshed as often as twice weekly to keep customers coming back to the store regularly in search of new items. Recently the chain has also rearranged stores so that there are fewer racks on the floor, giving Zara the feel of a more upscale designer location. Zara has also reduced the amount of inventory displayed on each rack so that customers have the sense that if they don't purchase immediately, they may miss the opportunity to do so. The chain also moves inventory very quickly from production to store floors so that products are always up-to-date and customers see runway looks faster at Zara than at competitors.[56]

Make Additional Services Available to Consumers

Retailers offer additional services that facilitate the purchase for the consumer. Financing and purchase options (cash, credit card, checks) are important financial services consumers expect, but they require a significant investment by the retailer. In many retail environments, consumers want advice in evaluating product options, which means having trained personnel available to answer questions and provide customer service. The opportunity to test product before purchase enhances the purchase experience but requires retailers to plan for the service and allocate resources.[57] Clothing stores, for example, allocate space for dressing rooms to allow people to try on the product before purchase.

These critical functions add value to the purchase for the consumer and provide an effective customer interface for the supply chain. As a result, retailing, despite profound changes, remains critical to the supply chain and consumer marketing.

Characteristics of Store Retailers

With more than 1.5 million store-based retailers in the United States, it may seem impossible to identify a classification system that would be useful for all retailers. While there is certainly great variety in the number and type of retailers, there are four specific characteristics that define store retailers: type of merchandise, assortment, services imparted to consumers, and differences in the value proposition. Understanding these characteristics is essential because they define the retail competitive environment, which allows marketing managers to develop strategies and tactics. Let's consider each element.

LO 11-8

Recognize the characteristics and types of store retailers.

Type of Merchandise One of the most fundamental characteristics used to classify retailers is by type of merchandise. Several years ago the United States, Canada, and Mexico created a unified classification system for all business activity that was based on a system from the 1920s developed by the U.S. Census Bureau. As discussed in Chapter 5, remember that the North American Industry Classification System (NAICS) assigns a hierarchical six-digit code based on the company's products and services. The first two digits of the code identify the business sector while the last four categorize a specific business subdivision. Most merchandise retailers fall into the 44 and 45 sectors, while services are in 71 (arts, entertainment, and recreation) and 72 (accommodation and food services).[58]

Assortment Even within a particular product category, the variety and assortment of products carried by retailers can be very different. **Variety** is the number of product categories offered by a retailer and is referred to as **breadth of merchandise**. **Assortment** is the number of different product items within a product category and is referred to as the **depth of merchandise**.[59]

It is possible, for example, to purchase a briefcase from a department store, warehouse club or superstore, or luggage store. Wilson's Leather Stores is a specialty clothing and accessories retailer specializing in leather products. Its primary product lines include women's and men's clothing as well as travel and business-related leather merchandise. The company carries an extensive line of leather briefcases. Costco, the successful warehouse club, also carries briefcases. However, Wilson's Leather has less variety across product lines but more assortment within a few product lines focused on leather products than Costco, which has a large variety of product categories but very little assortment within each product category. Despite the fact they both carry briefcases, target market differences as well as distinct variations in the products offered suggest the two companies do not compete directly.

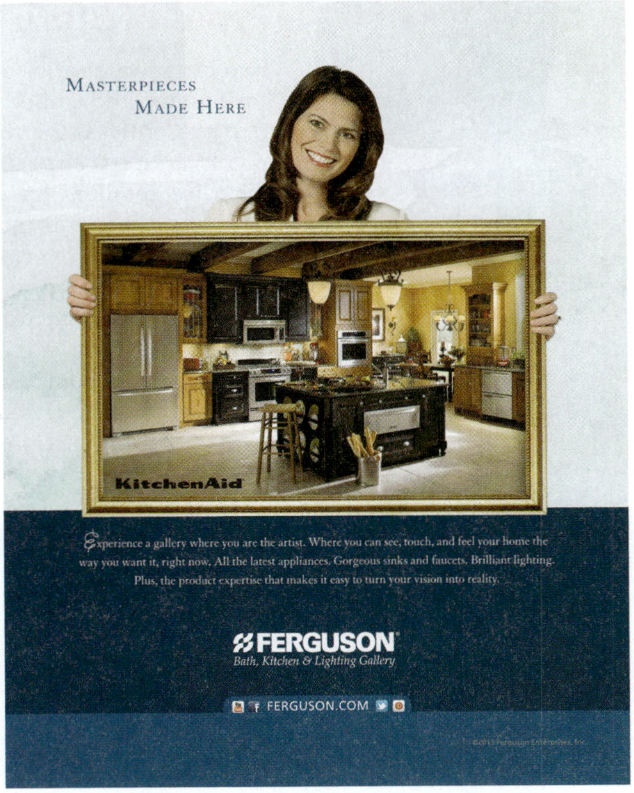

Ferguson is a specialty retailer that offers a variety of products for the bath and kitchen. The company has salespeople that work with builders, contractors, and consumers.

Services Imparted to Consumers Consumers expect a minimum level of services from all retailers that generally includes flexible payment options, proper merchandise display, convenient store hours, and easy access. However, beyond the basic services, retailers have a wide range of options based on their market strategy and consumer needs.[60] Most pharmacies, for example, do not deliver prescriptions to the home. A few local pharmacies in many markets, however, do provide home delivery, and consumers in those markets find the service helpful. While the average supermarket carries thousands of products, some differentiate themselves by providing a little extra service. When a customer does not find the product desired, chains such as Publix will order and store the product for a customer even if it is not part of their normal inventory.

Differences in the Value Propostion The value proposition, as we have discussed, defines value in terms of price and delivered benefits to the customer. Retailers make critical decisions about each of these elements in the value proposition. A general rule in retailing is that broader, deeper product assortments and expanded service options require a higher price to cover increased costs. In other words, carrying more inventories or providing additional services has a cost that ultimately must be covered by the consumer. At the same time, the growth of warehouse clubs (Costco, Sam's Club) and discount stores (Walmart, Target) reflects a strong consumer focus on lower prices, which means fewer services and limited assortments and variety. Essentially, those retailers are making the decision to focus on price as the driver in the value proposition.

Specialty retailers, on the other hand, focus on value-added benefits such as greater product selection, more experienced service personnel, and other services. For those retailers, the focus is on the delivered benefits and, as a result, prices are higher. The trade-off between delivered benefits and price is a critical decision for retailers, and they are constantly evaluating their mix of product/service benefits and pricing strategy based on internal company objectives and comparison shopping against the competition.[61]

Types of Store Retailers

Two broad categories define traditional store retailing in industrialized countries, particularly the United States: food and general merchandise retailers.

As recently as 20 years ago virtually all food sales in the United States were at conventional supermarkets; today that figure is only 61 percent. General merchandise retailers have become **food retailers** and conventional supermarkets carry more general merchandise. Indeed, the largest food retailer in the world is Walmart with over $100 billion in food and related sales. Exhibit 11.9 lists the world's largest food retailers.

Food retailers occupy a unique retail space and face a number of specific challenges. Much of the food retailer's product mix is perishable (dairy, meat, fruits, vegetables) so companies develop sophisticated supply chains that keep products moving into the store while carefully balancing inventory levels to reduce spoilage. Another unique challenge for food retailers is that profit margins are low relative to other retailing concepts, with net margins averaging 1 percent of sales.[62]

The growth of low-cost alternatives to conventional supermarkets has created a dramatic shift in the food retail market space. Conventional supermarkets are responding to new competitors with

- Greater emphasis on freshness—using just-in-time delivery and maximizing the advantage of their established supply chain.
- Targeting new markets such as health-conscious consumers—incorporating more organic, low-fat, high-quality food into their product mix.
- Creating a neighborhood atmosphere and upgrading facilities—maximizing the location advantage (being close to the consumer) they have in many communities.[63]

EXHIBIT 11.10 | Growth of Electronic Retailing

U.S. E-Commerce Spending (Excludes Auctions and Large Corporate Purchases)

	Jan–Oct 2011 (in millions)	Jan–Oct 2012 (in millions)	Percent Change
Total	$161,826	$186,100	15%
Non-Travel (Retail)	67,376	83,149	24
Travel	94,450	102,951	9

Source: www.marketingcharts.com/wp/topics/e-commerce/consumers-spent-more-than-100-billion-online-on-travel-last-year-27203/attachment/comscore-online-travel-spending-in-2012-feb2013/ and www.marketingcharts.com/wp/topics/e-commerce/final-tally-us-retail-e-commerce-spend-up-15-in-2012-26847/attachment/comscore-retail-ecommerce-q1-2007-q4-2012-feb2013-2/, accessed March 5, 2013.

The greatest success in electronic retailing has been in products where convenience and price are key drivers in the purchase decision. People do enjoy shopping at Barnes & Noble, but they also appreciate the convenience of shopping online for books. Companies such as e-Trade and traditional financial organizations such as Merrill Lynch are successful offering low-cost trading options and other services online. As consumers become more comfortable evaluating products and making purchase decisions online, they expand their electronic shopping experience. Apple's iTunes redefined the retail music industry with online music downloads accounting for over 26 percent of all music purchased, surpassing even large retail outlets like Walmart as early as 2008.[76] This change has been relatively fast and dramatic as music companies develop new business models to accommodate the changes in the marketplace.

Click-only retailers produce a lot of their revenue from non-retail operations. Amazon, for example, actually generates a significant portion of its revenue acting as the "back office" e-commerce fulfillment and website development for large retailers such as Target and numerous others. Another high-profile online-only consumer website is eBay, which, as we all know, is far from a traditional retailer even in an e-commerce context.[77]

Advantages of Electronic Retailing

Extensive Selection No other channel offers the breadth and depth of selection. From information search to purchase, the Internet gives consumers greater access to more choices and different product options. In the time it takes someone to drive to Barnes & Noble and find a book, it is possible to visit the Barnes & Noble website, order the book (probably at a lower price), and have it shipped for next-day delivery.[78]

Considerable Information Available for Product Research and Evaluation The Internet dramatically expands consumers' knowledge, offering an almost unlimited number of websites that research, evaluate, and recommend products and services. From retailers (Best Buy in electronics) to independent testing organizations (CNet in technology), consumers can find information on anything.[79] For example, if a consumer wants to find out more about a 1958 John Deere 420T tractor, all he or she has to do is visit www.antiquetractors.com. If a consumer wants a 1935 Whittall Bird of Paradise rug, he or she can simply check out eBay. Additionally, many sites offer additional tools such as side-by-side product comparisons, video product reviews, or three-dimensional interactive product displays that educate consumers in an entertaining and visually informative manner.

Online retailers like eBay have moved into mobile apps for easier customer access.

Build Product Communities The Internet brings together groups of individuals with a shared interest to create virtual communities. These communities share information, ideas, and product information. Babycenter.com offers parents a one-stop source for information about babies, children, and parenting. These sites are an excellent communication channel for companies marketing products to relevant target markets. Johnson & Johnson is a primary sponsor of Babycenter.com and refers to the site as a "trusted partner" on its own baby products website.[80]

Individualized Customer Experience The Internet allows a great deal of personalization for both the consumer and the company. Consumers can get one-on-one interaction from a customer service representative and create their own web content based on personal preferences. At the same time, companies can tailor messages and web content by analyzing consumer web history. The end result is a more customized, personal experience for the consumer.

Disadvantage of Electronic Retailing Electronic retailing has a number of advantages; however, there are several drawbacks.

Easier for Customers to Walk Away The customer is in total control of the web experience and has the opportunity to walk away at any time. In sharp contrast to a personal-selling situation or even a retail store, the customer can simply click to another site. This puts additional pressure on the website to attract and then hold on to visitors. In evaluating a website, one of the key measures is its "stickiness," which refers to the amount of time visitors remain at the site. A good website not only attracts a lot of visitors, but it also gets them to remain and explore the site.

Reduced Ability to Sell Features and Benefits Websites now incorporate sophisticated tools to display and highlight critical features and benefits. However, unless the customer initiates additional contact via web live chat, phone, or e-mail, it is not possible to engage the customer to answer questions or deal with objections.

Security of Personal Data While companies work hard to make their websites secure and keep personal data such as credit card numbers private, many consumers still have concerns about the security of their data. These concerns lead some consumers to limit their electronic purchases.[81]

Business-to-Business Electronic Commerce

Although the Internet has reshaped the way businesses and consumers interact, it has had a much more significant role in the business-to-business customer interface. B2B electronic commerce now accounts for over $300 billion in sales—50 percent more than the revenue for retail.[82] Exhibit 11.11 highlights the growing importance of digital versus traditional advertising, particularly in the B2B sector, where spending on traditional advertising is dropping the most.

Many companies now require their vendors to do business online. Disney suppliers become part of Disney's EDI (electronic data interchange) network and process orders via the Internet. This requires an initial investment of thousands of dollars to get the infrastructure (hardware and software) to connect with Disney.

EXHIBIT 11.11 **Change in Digital and Traditional Ad Spending by Sector, 2012–2013**

	Digital	Traditional
B2C—Product	+14.60%	−0.60%
B2C—Service	+10.40	−2.20
B2B—Product	+ 8.20	−4.10
B2B—Service	+10.50	−2.20

Source: www.emarketer.com/Article/Traditional-Media-Ad-Spend-Dips-Lower-More-Dollars-Shift-Digital/1009727, accessed March 11, 2013.

As mentioned earlier in the chapter, Walmart, a pioneer in the application of technology into business processes, directly connects its large suppliers such as P&G with its IT network so that stock replenishment is fast and seamlessly accurate.

The Internet has also increased the efficiency of B2B relationships through dedicated B2B sites that facilitate the exchange of products and services. This has made many markets, such as the wholesale distribution of electricity, more efficient as buyers and sellers get together quickly. Known as **market makers**, these sites (such as Lendingtree.com for mortgage and other loans) bring buyers and sellers together.[83]

Customer communities are, as the name suggests, sites where customers come and share stories about their vendor experiences. These sites enable customers to evaluate vendors and then make better product decisions. Nortel Networks sponsors a customer community program to encourage customer dialogue and deliver the most current information and education on its portfolio of products, solutions, and enabling technologies. The company's goal is to offer customers insight into Nortel while providing a forum for feedback and commentary.[84]

SUMMARY

Channel and supply chain decisions are central to creating a firm's value proposition. Competitive advantage can be gained through effective and efficient channel management, physical distribution, and logistics. Vertical marketing systems and partner relationship management strategies add attractive levels of integration among channel members. The aim of such value networks is value co-creation by the participating suppliers, customers, and other stakeholders in which the members of the network combine capabilities according to their expertise and the competencies required from the situation.

Retailers are the type of channel intermediary that most people encounter most frequently. Technology has dramatically changed how, where, and when consumers choose to interact with retailers. But despite the growth of electronic retailing, traditional retailing—when it clearly adds value—continues to flourish and non-store retailing also continues to grow. And although the growth of B2C e-retailing has certainly been impressive, B2B e-commerce actually has grown even faster and now accounts for considerably more revenue than B2C.

KEY TERMS

supply chain 323
supply chain management 323
value network 323
value co-creation 324
network organization (virtual organization) 324
nimble 325
channel of distribution 326
intermediaries 326
merchant intermediaries 327
agent intermediaries 327
direct channel 327
indirect channel 327
physical distribution (logistics) 328
breaking bulk 328
accumulating bulk 328
sorting 328
creating assortments 328
reducing transactions 329
transportation and storage 329
facilitating functions 330
disintermediation 331
outsourcing (third-party logistics, 3PL) 332
vertical marketing system (VMS) 332
corporate VMS 332
vertical integration 332
contractual VMS 332
franchise organization 332
retailer cooperative 332
wholesaler cooperative 332
administered VMS 332
channel captain (channel leader) 332
partner relationship management (PRM) strategies 333
channel power 333
channel conflict 333
coercive power 333
reward power 334
expert power 334
referent power 334
legitimate power 334
distribution intensity 334
intensive distribution 335
convenience goods 335
impulse goods 335
shopping goods 335
selective distribution 335
exclusive distribution 335
push strategy 336
slotting allowance (shelf fee) 336
pull strategy 336
outbound logistics 337
inbound logistics 337
reverse logistics 337
stock-out 337
enterprise resource planning (ERP) system 337
just-in-time (JIT) inventory control system 338
materials requirement planning (MRP) 338
exclusive dealing 339
exclusive territory 340
tying contract 340
retailing 340
variety 343
breadth of merchandise 343
assortment 343
depth of merchandise 343
food retailer 344
showrooming 346
non-store retailer 346
catalog retailer 346
direct selling 347
television home shopping 348
vending machine retailing 348
electronic commerce (e-commerce) 348
electronic retailing (e-retailing or e-tailing) 348
market makers 351
customer communities 351

APPLICATION QUESTIONS

1. Consider the concept of value co-creation.
   a. In your own words, explain the concept of value co-creation.
   b. What are some specific ways value can be co-created?
   c. Provide an example of a specific value network you believe results in a high level of value co-creation.
   d. Provide an example of a specific firm or firms that could benefit by establishing a value network and engaging in value co-creation. In what ways would this approach be an improvement over their existing business approach?
2. The chapter discusses the importance of being "nimble" in all aspects of a firm's operation—that is, to be in a position to be maximally flexible, adaptable, and speedy in response to change.
   a. Identify two firms in two different industries that you believe exhibit a nimble nature in their operations.
   b. What specific evidence leads you to believe these firms are nimble, especially in their channel and supply chain activities?
3. Consider the issue of disintermediation in electronic channels.
   a. Do you believe that *all* channels will disintermediate down to simple direct channels over time? Why or why not?
   b. Does your opinion change if the question is asked only about B2C channels? Only for B2B channels? Why?
4. Consider this statement: "It's important in business today for all firms to work to cut out the middleman. Intermediaries represent costs that can be saved by finding ways to cut them out of the system. Down-channel buyers always benefit when this happens." Do you agree with this statement? Why or why not? Be specific in arguing your point based on what you learned in the chapter.
5. Exhorting firms to develop networks and alliances for purposes of value co-creation sounds like a good idea. However, is there a point at which such approaches can be taken too far *(a)* from a legal perspective, *(b)* from an ethical perspective, and *(c)* from a strategic perspective? Explain your viewpoint.
6. Consider your school's e-commerce capabilities.
   a. From a student's perspective, what e-commerce functions are available on your campus website (for example, class registration, payment, delivery of course materials)?
   b. How would you rate the website's ease of use for the functions you identified?
   c. What functions does the campus website perform well and what functions does it perform poorly? Explain.
   d. What e-comerce functions do you think should be added to the website's capabilities that are not presently offered?

MANAGEMENT DECISION CASE: Pushing Supply Chain Efficiencies to the Maximum in Retailing

To effectively and consistently compete, major retailers like Macy's, Kohl's, Sears, and JCPenney need stylish, high-quality, yet affordable merchandise available at all times. Customer appetites for fashion necessitate that these and other stores develop strong partnerships with suppliers from around the world, expanding their network for sourcing the right goods quickly. One supplier, Li & Fung, has filled the need for retailer inventory considerably better than most others and, as a result it has become "the most important company most American shoppers have never heard of." It does a great job of enhancing supply chains to deliver affordable, high-quality merchandise on time and in large quantities. Providing such capabilities to almost a third of retailers found in most American shopping malls, including those listed above plus others like Walmart, Target, and Kmart, has allowed Li & Fung to achieve an incredible $20+ billion in revenue over the last several years.

Li & Fung achieves this success despite not owning any clothing factories, sewing machines, or fabric mills. Instead, the company's main assets are its relationships with more than 15,000 suppliers in over 60 countries. Those relationships allow Li & Fung to reduce the time to market from six months to an incredible six weeks on large-scale orders. For example, an order for 500,000 specially designed skirts can now go from the drawing board to the store shelf in less than half the time it takes a student to complete one semester at college! If a rush order is needed, the company is well known for making it happen—for example it might turn to a Mexican port that can accept a shipment faster than could some different port of entry. Suffice it to say, Li & Fung has made itself virtually indispensable to many of its retail customers.

As an intermediary, Li & Fung performs many physical distribution functions, leverages its connections with those 15,000+ suppliers to drastically reduce the number of transactions a retailer like Macy's has to engage in to procure its inventory, and provides transportation and storage. The ability to store inventory and then transport goods to a specific retailer's warehouse location at a specific time is crucial to the retailer's strategy of just-in-time inventory control and gives Li & Fung a strong competitive advantage that is difficult for its competitors to duplicate.

Because Li & Fung is so successful at providing its retail customers with affordable and stylish clothing in a reduced time frame, some have labeled it the "Walmart of purchasing," which is intended as a supreme compliment. Unfortunately, certain aspects of its business practices also have earned it the moniker of "the garment industry's sweatshop locator." In fact, the list of employee safety incidents involving suppliers to Li & Fung is quite long and includes a fire at a factory in Bangladesh producing clothing for Kohl's in which 29 people died, an explosion and stampede where 50 were injured and 2 were killed at a factory producing clothing for Tommy Hilfiger, and a fire that killed 112 workers after many of them were ordered to continue working even though fire alarms were blaring. In addition, the company has been accused of cheating workers at a factory in Turkey out of wages and contracting with a factory in Cambodia where conditions caused several hundred workers to become ill. All of this has occurred despite Li & Fung proclaiming that it conducts rigorous safety audits to ensure the company does business only with factories that adhere to its safety standards.

Bottom line, the pressure to find low-cost suppliers in the retail industry is relentless and every few pennies saved on the cost of production oftentimes results in lax safety and employee welfare practices. The challenge for Li & Fung going forward will be to continue providing its well-known American retail customers with high-quality merchandise at attractive price points and in a timely manner while also making sure that workers engaged within the overall supply chain are not exposed to dangerous conditions.

Questions for Consideration

1. What type of intermediary is Li & Fung for its customers? Is it an agent, a wholesaler, a manufacturer's agent, jobber, or some other choice? What evidence can you offer to support your choice?
2. Some critics have said that American consumers ultimately are to blame for a lack of safety precautions at factories utilized by Li & Fung because they are addicted to low-cost merchandise and generally refuse to pay higher prices for items. What is your reaction to this statement? Are you willing to pay an extra $5 or $10 for a pair of jeans, for example, if that additional money is used to enhance employee safety?
3. Retailers Nordstrom and Walmart are positioned very differently in the marketplace. Using the characteristics of store retailers addressed in the chapter, which includes merchandise assortment, level of service, and retail value proposition, compare the retail strategy implemented by Nordstrom to that utilized by Walmart.

Source: Ian Urbina and Keith Bradsher, "Linking Factories to Malls, Middleman Pushes Low Costs," *New York Times*, August 8, 2013, p. A1.

MARKETING PLAN EXERCISE

ACTIVITY 13: Establishing Distribution Channels for Your Offering

Selecting the most appropriate channels of distribution for your offering and then working out the overall best approach to establishing and operating your supply chain is a critical element of your marketing plan.

1. Define and describe the value network within which you will operate. Develop an approach to ensure that your supply chain operation is a nimble as possible.

2. Decide what type of channel configuration is optimal for you and what intermediaries should be part of the channel.
3. Select what physical distribution functions you will accomplish in-house and how these will be set up. Then, select what physical distribution functions you will outsource and to whom.
4. Identify what aspects of e-channels you must address.
5. Decide:
   a. What level of distribution intensity you seek within each channel.
   b. How much control and adaptability are required over the channel and its activities.
   c. The priority channel functions that require investment.
6. Develop your plans for the following logistics functions:
   a. Order processing.
   b. Warehousing and materials handling.
   c. Inventory management.
   d. Transportation.

NOTES

1. Aksel I. Rokkan, Jan B. Heide, and Kenneth H. Wathne, "Specific Investments in Marketing Relationships: Expropriation and Bonding Effects," *Journal of Marketing Research,* 40, no. 2 (May 2003), pp. 210–24.
2. Sjoerd Schaafsma and Joerg Hofstetter, "Raising the Game to a New Level," *ECR Journal: International Commerce Review* 5, no. 1 (Summer 2005), pp. 66–69.
3. Lee G. Cooper, "Strategic Marketing Planning for Radically New Products," *Journal of Marketing* 64, no. 1 (January 2000), pp. 1–16.
4. Bernard Cova and Robert Salle, "Marketing Solutions in Accordance with the S-D Logic: Co-creating Value with Customer Network Actors," *Industrial Marketing Management* 37, no. 3 (May 2008), pp. 270–77.
5. Jennifer Rowley, "Synergy and Strategy in E-Business," *Marketing Intelligence & Planning* 20, no. 4/5 (2002), pp. 215–22.
6. Ravi S. Achrol and Michael J. Etzel, "The Structure of Reseller Goals and Performance in Marketing Channels," *Journal of the Academy of Marketing Science* 31, no. 2 (Spring 2003), pp. 146–63.
7. B. Trebilcock, "Scotts Miracle-Gro: The Grass Is Greener . . . Thanks to Lift Trucks," *Modern Materials Handling,* April 1, 2013, www.mmh.com/article/scotts_miracle_gro_the_grass_is_greenerthanks_to_lift_trucks.
8. David Barboza and Charles Duhigg, "China Contractor Again Faces Labor Issue on iPhones," *New York Times,* September 10, 2012; and "Tie Your Own Bow Tie; How to Make Smart Product Management Decisions," *Strategic Direction* 23, no. 5 (2007), pp. 5–8.
9. "Tie Your Own Bow Tie:.
10. Stephen Keysuk Kim, "Relational Behaviors in Marketing Channel Relationships: Transaction Cost Implications," *Journal of Business Research* 60, no. 11 (November 2007), pp. 1125–34.
11. Junhong Chu, Pradeep K. Chintagunta, and Naufel J. Vilcassim, "Assessing the Economic Value of Distribution Channels: An Application to the Personal Computer Industry," *Journal of Marketing Research* 44, no. 1 (February 2007), pp. 29–41.
12. Daniel C. Bello and Nicholas C. Williamson, "The American Export Trading Company: Designing a New International Marketing Institution," *Journal of Marketing* 49, no. 4 (Fall 1985), pp. 60–69.
13. Alberto Sa Vinhas and Erin Anderson, "How Potential Conflict Drives Channel Structure (Direct and Indirect) Channels," *Journal of Marketing Research* 42, no. 4 (November 2005), pp. 507–15.
14. Michael Ketzenberg, Richard Metters, and Vicente Vargas, "Quantifying the Benefits of Breaking Bulk in Retail Operations," *International Journal of Production Economics* 80, no. 3 (December 2002), pp. 249–63.
15. E. Bashkansky, S. Dror, R. Ravid, and P. Grabov, "Effectiveness of Product Quality Classifier," *Quality Engineering* 19, no. 3 (July 2007), p. 235.
16. Jason M. Carpenter, "Demographics and Patronage Motives of Supercenter Shoppers in the United States," *International Journal of Retail & Distribution Management* 36, no. 1 (2008), pp. 5–16.
17. R. Sembhy, "Celebrating Two Decades in the UK's Living Rooms," *Express,* April 28, 2013, www.express.co.uk/finance/personalfinance/395429/Celebrating-two-decades-in-the-UK-s-living-rooms.

18. Devon S. Johnson and Sundar Bharadwaj, "Digitization of Selling Activity and Sales Force Performance: An Empirical Investigation," *Journal of the Academy of Marketing Science* 33, no. 1 (Winter 2005), pp. 3–18; and Xueming Luo and Naveen Donthu, "The Role of Cyber-Intermediaries: A Framework Based on Transaction Cost Analysis, Agency, Relationship Marketing, and Social Exchange Theories," *Journal of Business & Industrial Marketing* 22, no. 7 (2007), pp. 452–58.
19. Joseph Pancras and K. Sudhir, "Optimal Marketing Strategies for a Customer Data Intermediary," *Journal of Marketing Research* 44, no. 4 (November 2007), pp. 452–58.
20. Virpi Havila, Jan Johanson, and Peter Thilenius, "International Businessrelationship Triads," *International Marketing Review* 21, no. 2 (2004), pp. 172–86.
21. Kevin Lane Keller, "Building Customer-Based Brand Equity," *Marketing Management* 10, no. 2 (July/ August 2001), pp. 14–19.
22. Phillip Bond, "Bank and Nonbank Financial Intermediation," *Journal of Finance* 59, no. 6 (December 2004), pp. 2489–530.
23. Pancras and Sudhir, "Optimal Marketing Strategies for a Customer Data Intermediary."
24. "H-E-B Conroe Market Opens May 8," *Courier of Montgomery County,* April 26, 2013, www.yourhoustonnews.com/courier/news/h-e-b-conroe-market-opens-may/article_b668f9cc-3511-5f5e-8843-3ef46269472b.html.
25. Amal R. Karunaratna and Lester W. Johonson, "Initiating and Maintaining Export Channel Intermediary Relationships," *Journal of International Marketing* 5, no. 2 (1997), pp. 11–32.
26. "Liquidation Helps Add Value to Supply Chains," GENCO, January 8, 2013, www.genco.com/resources/logistics-article.php?aid=800940728.
27. Bert Rosenbloom, "The Wholesaler's Role in the Marketing Channel: Disintermediation vs. Reintermediation," *International Review of Retail, Distribution, and Consumer Research* 17, no. 4 (September 2007), pp. 327–39.
28. L. Artis, "Despite Online Competition, Travel Agencies See a Return of Customers," *Inside Business: The Hampton Roads Business Journal,* June 29, 2012, http://insidebiz.com/news/despite-online-competition-travel-agencies-see-return-customers.
29. Kenneth K. Boyer and G. Tomas M. Hult, "Extending the Supply Chain: Integrating Operations and Marketing in the Online Grocery Industry," *Journal of Operations Management* 23, no. 6 (September 2005), pp. 642–61; and Thomas L. Friedman, *The World Is Flat 3.0: A Brief History of the Twenty-First Century* (New York: Picador, 2007).
30. Achrol and Etzel, "The Structure of Reseller Goals and Performance in Marketing Channels."
31. Gilles Corriveau and Robert D. Tamilla, "Comparing Transactional Forms in Administered, Contractual, and Corporate Systems in Grocery Distribution," *Journal of Business Research* 55, no. 9 (September 2002), pp. 771–73.
32. L. Lynn Judd and Bobby C. Vaught, "Three Differential Variables and Their Relation to Retail Strategy and Profitability," *Journal of the Academy of Marketing Science* 16, no. 3/4 (Fall 1988), pp. 30–37.
33. Tim Burkink, "Cooperative and Voluntary Wholesale Groups: Channel Coordination and Interim Knowledge Transfer," *Supply Chain Management* 7, no. 2 (2002), pp. 60–70.
34. Corriveau and Tamilla, "Comparing Transactional Forms in Administered, Contractual, and Corporate Systems in Grocery Distribution."
35. Nancy Nix, Robert Lusch, Zach Zacharia, and Wesley Bridges, "Competent Collaborations," *Marketing Management* 17, no. 2 (March/April 2008), p. 18.
36. "Danskin Womens Activewear, Loungewear & Everyday Essentials," www.Danskin.com, accessed April 29, 2013.
37. John R. P. French and Bertram Raven, *The Bases of Social Power* (Ann Arbor: University of Michigan Press, 1959).
38. Boonghee Yoo, Naveen Donthu, and Sungho Lee, "An Examination of Selected Marketing Mix Elements and Brand Equity," *Journal of the Academy of Marketing Science* 28, no. 2 (Spring 2000), pp. 195–211.
39. Wire Staff, "Chanel's Exclusivity Keeps It a Cut Above," *CNN,* November 8, 2012, http://edition.cnn.com/2012/11/08/business/chanel-targets-china.
40. P. Rajan Varadarajan, Satish Jayachandran, and J. Chris White, "Strategic Interdependence in Organizations: Deconglomeration and Marketing Strategy," *Journal of Marketing* 65, no. 1 (January 2001), pp. 15–28.
41. Frederick E. Webster Jr., "Understanding the Relationships among Brands, Consumers, and Resellers," *Journal of the Academy of Marketing Science* 28, no. 1 (Winter 2000), pp. 17–23.
42. Vaidyanathan Jayaraman and Yadong Luo, "Creating Competitive Advantages through New Value Creation: A Reverse Logistics Perspective," *Academy of Management Perspectives* 21, no. 2 (May 2007), pp. 56–73.
43. "Fidelitone Logistics Expands Order Fulfillment Services by Merger with TechniPak LLC," *PRWeb,* January 15, 2013, www.prweb.com/releases/2013/1/prweb10320602.htm.
44. Stanley C. Gardiner, Joe B. Hanna, and Michael S. LaTour, "ERP and the Reengineering of Industrial Marketing Processes: A Prescriptive Overview for the

New-Age Marketing Manager," *Industrial Marketing Management* 31, no. 4 (July 2002), pp. 357–65.

45. Dale G. Sauers, "Evaluating Just in-Time Projects from a More Focused Framework," *Quality Process* 34, no. 1 (January 2001), p. 160.
46. Alan D. Smith, "Effective Supplier Selection and Management Issues in Modern Manufacturing and Marketing Service Environments," *Services Marketing Quarterly* 29, no. 2 (2007), pp. 45–65.
47. N. Matthews, "DHL Supply Chain Launches Real Time Data Tracking Mobile App," *SHD Logistics News,* April 29, 2013, www.shdlogistics.com/news/view/dhl-supply-chain-launches-real-time-data-tracking-mobile-app.
48. Richard J. Gilbert, "Exclusive Dealing, Preferential Dealing, and Dynamic Efficiency," *Review of Industrial Organization* 16, no. 2 (2000), pp. 167–84.
49. Howard P. Marvel and Stephen McCafferty, "Comparing Vertical Restraints," *Journal of Economics and Business* 48, no. 5 (December 1996), pp. 473–86.
50. Alan J. Meese, "Tying Meets the New Institutional Economics: Farewell to the Chimera of Forcing," *University of Pennsylvania Law Review* 146, no. 1 (November 1997), pp. 1–98.
51. Stuart E. Jackson, "Making Growth Make Sense for Retail and Franchise Businesses," *Journal of Business Strategy* 29, no. 3 (2008), pp. 48–64.
52. Kirthi Kalyanam, Sharad Borle, and Peter Boartwright, "Deconstructing Each Item's Category Contribution," *Marketing Science* 26, no. 3 (2007), pp. 327–44.
53. Andrew Baxter, "Profile: Tide and Ariel Clean Up," *Financial Times,* April 21, 2008, p. 6; and Robert Berner, "How P&G Pampers New Thinking," *BusinessWeek,* no. 4079 (2008), p. 73.
54. Chandra K. Jaggi, S. K. Goyal, and S. K. Goel, "Retailer's Optimal Replenishment Decisions with Credit Linked Demand under Permissible Delay in Payments," *European Journal of Operational Research* 190, no. 1 (2008), pp. 130–48; and R. Glenn Richey Jr., Mert Tokman, and Lauren R. Skinner, "Exploring Collaborative Technology Utilization in Retailer-Supplier Performance," *Journal of Business Research* 61, no. 8 (2008), pp. 842–60.
55. Martin A. Koschat, "Store Inventory Can Affect Demand: Empirical Evidence from Retailing," *Journal of Retailing* 84, no. 2 (2008), pp. 165–81.
56. Tim Chilcott, "The Magic Formula That Makes Zara Millions," *Bloomberg Businessweek,* December 7, 2012, www.businessweek.com/videos/2012-12-07/the-magic-formula-that-makes-zara-millions; and Lorna Hall, "How Zara Gets Shoppers in the Door," *Bloomberg Businessweek,* March 13, 2013, www.businessweek.com/videos/2013-03-13/how-zara-gets-shoppers-in-the-door.
57. James G. Maxham III, Richard G. Netemeyer, and Donald R. Lichtenstein, "The Retail Value Chain: Linking Employee Perceptions to Employee Performance, Customer Evaluations and Store Performance," *Marketing Science* 27, no. 2 (2008), pp. 147–69; and Aron O'Cass and Debra Grace, "Understanding the Role of Retail Service in Light of Self-Image Store Image Congruence," *Psychology and Marketing* 25, no. 6 (2008), pp. 521–39.
58. Christina M. L. Kelton, Margaret K. Pasquale, and Robert P. Rebeliein, "Using the North American Industry Classification System (NAICS) to Identify National Industry Cluster Templates for Applied Regional Analysis," *Regional Studies* 42, no. 3 (2008), pp. 305–20.
59. Jie Zhang and Aradhna Krishna, "Brand Level Effects of Stockkeeping Unit Reductions," *Journal of Marketing Research* 44, no. 4 (2007), pp. 545–61; and Felipe Caro and Jeremie Gallien, "Dynamic Assortment with Demand Learning for Seasonal Consumer Goods," *Management Science* 63, no. 2 (2007), pp. 276–83.
60. Dan Padgett and Micahael S. Mulvey, "Differentiation via Technology: Strategic Positioning of Services Following the Introduction of Disruptive Technology," *Journal of Retailing* 83, no. 4 (2007), pp. 375–91.
61. G. H. Griffiths and A. Howard, "Balancing Clicks and Brands—Strategies for Multichannel Retailers," *Journal of Global Business Issues* 2, no. 10 (2008), pp. 69–74.
62. Sameer Kumar, "A Study of the Supermarket Industry and Its Growing Logistics Capabilities," *International Journal of Retail & Distribution Management* 36, no. 3 (2008), pp. 192–210.
63. Susan Reda, "Wegman of My Dreams," *Stores* 90, no. 3 (2008), p. 10; and "Tesco's American Dream: Doing It Differently," *Strategic Direction* 24, no. 2 (2008), p.11.
64. Lydia Dishman, "Why Walmart Is Betting Big on Small Stores," *Forbes,* March 6, 2013, www.forbes.com/sites/lydiadishman/2013/03/06/why-walmart-is-betting-big-on-small-stores.
65. Haiyan Hu and Cynthia R. Jasper, "Social Cues in the Store Environment and Their Impact on Store Image," *International Journal of Retail and Distribution Management* 34, no. 1 (2006), pp. 25–49.
66. Peter J. McGoldrick and Matalie Collins, "Multichannel Retailing: Profiling the Multichannel Shopper," *International Review of Retail, Distribution and Consumer Research* 17, no. 2 (2007), pp. 139–52.
67. Asim Ansari, Carl F. Mela, and Scott A. Neslin, "Customer Channel Migration," *Journal of Marketing Research* 45, no. 1 (2008), pp. 60–77.
68. Bill Merrilees and Tino Fenech, "From Catalog to Web: B2B Multichannel Marketing Strategy," *Industrial Marketing Management* 36, no. 1 (2007), pp. 44–61.

69. Ruby Roy Dholakia, Miao Zhao, and Nikhilesh Dholakia, "Multichannel Retailing: A Case Study of Early Experiences," *Journal of Interactive Marketing* 19, no. 2 (2005), pp. 63–75.

70. Dennis L. Duffy, "Direct Selling as the Next Channel," *Journal of Consumer Marketing* 22, no. 1 (2005), pp. 43–46.

71. Jack Neff, "Direct-Selling Giant Amway Quietly Builds Brands, Racks Up Sales," *Advertising Age*, February 18, 2013, http://adage.com/article/cmo-strategy/amway-quietly-builds-brands-racks-sales.

72. Clyde A. Warden, Stephen Chi-Tsun Huang, Tsung Chi Liu, and Wann-Yih Wu, "Global Media, Local Metaphor: Television Shopping and Marketing as Relationship in America, Japan and Taiwan," *Journal of Retailing* 84, no. 1 (2008), pp. 119–34; and Enrique Bigne Alcaniz, Silvia Sanz Blas, and Francisco Toran Torres, "Dependency in Consumer Media Relations: An Application to the Case of Teleshopping," *Journal of Consumer Behavior* 5, no. 5 (2006), pp. 397–411.

73. "Vending Machine Operators in the US: Market Research Report," IbisWorld, September 2013, www.ibisworld.com/industry/default.aspx?indid=1113.

74. Eliot Maras, "In the Face of Challenge, Opportunity Beckons," *Automatic Merchandiser* 50, no. 5 (May 2008), p. 6; and Eliot Maras, "Badly Needed Consumer Research Is Here, So Use It," *Automatic Merchandiser* 49, no. 1 (January 2007), p. 4

75. "Online Sales to Climb Despite Struggling Economy," *National Retail Federation*, April 8, 2008, www.nrf.com/modules.php?name=news&sp_id=499.

76. Jim Dalrymple, "Apple Is Number Two Music Retailer in the United States," *MacWorld* 25, no. 5 (2008), p. 28.

77. "Business: The Three Survivors: Yahoo, eBay, and Amazon," *The Economist* 387, no. 8585 (2008), pp. 69–90.

78. Pearl Pu, Li Chen, and Pratyush Kumar, "Evaluating Product Search and Recommender Systems for E-Commerce Environments," *Electronic Commerce Research* 8, no. 1/2 (2008), pp. 1–28.

79. Andreas B. Eisingerich and Tobia Kretschmer, "In E-Commerce, More Is More," *Harvard Business Review* 86, no. 3 (2008), pp. 20–38; and Amanda Spink and Bernard J. Jansen, "Trends in Searching for Commerce Related Information on Web-Search Engines," *Journal of Electronic Commerce Research* 9, no. 2 (2008), pp. 154–60.

80. Christy M. K. Cheung, Matthew K. O. Lee, and Neil Rabjohn, "The Impact of Electronic Word-of-Mouth: The Adoption of Online Opinions in Online Customer Communities," *Internet Research* 18, no. 3 (2008), pp. 229–41; Dina Mayzlin, "Promotional Chat on the Internet," *Marketing Science* 25, no. 2 (2006), pp. 155–65.

81. Kyosti Pennanen, Tarja Tiainen, and Harri T. Luomala, "A Qualitative Exploration of a Consumer's Value Based e-Trust Building Process: A Framework Development," *Qualitative Market Research* 10, no. 1 (2007), pp. 28–42.

82. "2012 B2B E-Commerce Survey: Results and Trends," Oracle, February 2012, www.oracle.com/us/products/applications/b2b-ecommerce-trends-2012-1503041.pdf.

83. Myonung Soo Kim and Jae Hyeon Ahn, "Comparison of Trust Sources of an Online Market Maker in the E-Marketplace: Buyer's and Seller's Perspectives," *Journal of Computer Information Systems* 47, no. 1 (2006), pp. 84–95.

84. Rene Algesheimer and Paul M. Dholakia, "Do Customer Communities Pay Off?" *Harvard Business Review* 84, no. 11 (2006), pp. 26–41.

PART 5

Communicate the Value Offering through the Elements of Integrated Marketing Communications

chapter 12
PROMOTIONAL STRATEGY AND NEW MEDIA

chapter 13
ADVERTISING, SALES PROMOTION, AND PUBLIC RELATIONS

chapter 14
PERSONAL SELLING AND DIRECT MARKETING

CHAPTER 12

Promotional Strategy and New Media

LEARNING OBJECTIVES

LO 12-1 Explain integrated marketing communications (IMC) concepts and their role in marketing management.

LO 12-2 Identify the elements of the promotion mix and the pros and cons of each element.

LO 12-3 Connect communication models to real-world challenges in promotional strategy.

LO 12-4 Describe in detail the marketing manager's role in promotional strategy.

LO 12-5 Explain key concepts of interactive communications.

Integrated marketing communications (IMC) is the strategic approach companies use to communicate to their target customers. As we have discussed throughout the book, massive changes are taking place in marketing and marketing managers must adapt to those changes; however, nowhere are those changes more evident than in marketing communications. In this chapter we first examine the complex concept of IMC. Then we discuss the new wave of interactive communication tools that have changed—and will continue to change—the customer relationship through the ways companies communicate with customers.

ESSENTIALS OF PROMOTION AND INTEGRATED MARKETING COMMUNICATIONS (IMC)

Marketing managers communicate with customers through promotion. **Promotion** involves several forms of communication to inform, persuade, or remind. This communication is accomplished through specific elements of the **promotion mix—advertising**, **sales promotion**, **public relations (PR)**, **personal selling**, **direct marketing**, and **interactive marketing**. Exhibit 12.1 sketches out these elements, also called the *marketing communications mix*. The first three—advertising, sales promotion, and PR—tend to be relatively less personal in nature than the next two—personal selling and direct marketing. The larger an audience a communication tool must reach, the less personal it will be. New media (interactive marketing), the last element in the mix, shares some elements of both.

LO 12-1

Explain integrated marketing communications (IMC) concepts and their role in marketing management.

EXHIBIT 12.1 | Definitions of Elements of the Promotion Mix

Advertising	Paid form of relatively less personal marketing communications, often through a mass medium to one or more target markets. Example media include television, radio, magazines, newspapers, and outdoors.
Sales Promotion	Provides an inducement for an end-user consumer to buy your product or for a salesperson or someone else in the channel to sell it. Designed to augment other forms of promotion; rarely used alone. Example sales promotion tools for customers are coupons, rebates, and sweepstakes. Inducements for channel members often involve special monies or prizes for pushing a particular offering.
Public Relations (PR)	Systematic approach to influencing attitudes, opinions, and behaviors of customers and others. Often executed through publicity, which is an unpaid and relatively less personal form of marketing communications usually through news stories and mentions at public events.
Personal Selling	One-to-one personal communication with a customer by a salesperson, either in person or through another manner that provides two-way dialogue (phone, messaging, e-mail).
Direct Marketing	An interactive marketing system that uses one or more advertising media to effect a measurable response and/or transaction at any location. Direct marketing involves personal communication with a customer by means other than a salesperson. Most often this involves receiving materials in the mail, but increasingly it could include targeted e-mails as well.
Interactive Marketing	An Internet-driven relationship between companies, their brands, and customers. Interactive marketing enables customers to control information flow and encourages customer-company interaction as well as a higher level of customer service. The company's website is the most common interactive marketing tool, but the increased use of mobile devices (phones, tablet computers, laptops) has created other interactive marketing opportunities (apps).

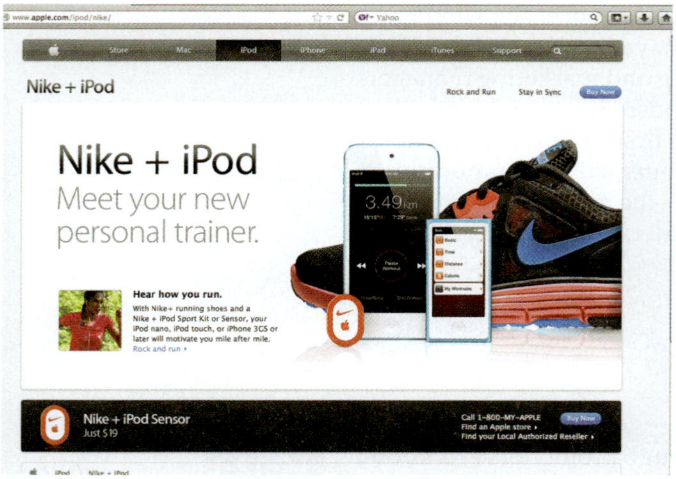

Nike+ utilizes a variety of outlets to reach customers and add value to their experience.

The promotion mix is vital to marketing planning. The development of **promotion mix strategies**, or simply *promotional strategies,* involves decisions about which combination of elements in the promotion mix is likely to best communicate the offering to the marketplace. The mix is designed to achieve an acceptable ROI for the marketer, given the product and target markets involved. For ongoing planning purposes, much of marketing communications operates on a campaign-to-campaign basis. A **promotional campaign** for a particular product or product line tracks the effectiveness and efficiency of promotional strategies as it allocates expenditures to a specific creative execution over a given time period.

Sometimes several media vehicles are used within one campaign. For example, a co-promotion between Nike shoes and Apple's iPhone uses both TV and the web to drive sales. Called Nike Plus, the project uses the iPhone as a tool for monitoring a runner's pace and style. Customers can go to a website that gives them more information as well as a sense of community *and* the opportunity to buy more products! The purpose of the TV commercial is to drive traffic to the website.[1]

When Cinco de Mayo was falling on a Sunday in 2013, Dos Equis recognized an opportunity. In order to get a Dos Equis in consumers' hands sooner, the company created the Dos de Mayo campaign. Dos Equis utilized its famed spokesman, "The most interesting man in the world," to create consumer awareness of this event. It began with an online video asking fans to mobilize and create word-of-mouth buzz. Second, an online infographic was released that displayed interesting Cinco de Mayo and Dos Equis facts referring readers to go to the company's Dos de Mayo website as well as its own hashtag for social media. Finally, Dos Equis threw a Dos de Mayo party in Los Angeles. The company, along with Maxim, held a sweepstakes in which fans won a chance to attend the sponsored party. In its campaign creation, not only has Dos Equis targeted its consumers using its beloved spokesman, but it also found social media outlets to engage its fans and to reach its ultimate goal of large-scale consumer buzz.[2]

The Rise of IMC

Electronic marketing channels, sophisticated research, customer database management, and integrated customer relationship management (CRM) systems allow for accurate management of customer relationships and communication with customers, creating less and less dependency on traditional promotion through mass media. At the same time, various traditional media outlets are now quite fragmented; we have literally thousands of cable and satellite dish television channels, hundreds of specialty magazines, micro-specialty genres in radio programming, and instant access to news, information, and entertainment online. How do we do promotion within today's environment? IMC is the strategic approach to communicating the brand and company message to targeted customers in ways that are clear, concise, and consistent and yet are customizable as needed to maximize the impact on a particular audience.[3]

Think of the difference in IMC versus more traditional promotion mix strategies as shown in Exhibit 12.2. A traditional promotion mix decision is effectively a separate assessment of whether to invest in promoting the offering through one or more of the elements of the promotion mix. In contrast, an integrated decision is a *holistic and interrelated decision process* that is connected to the overall brand message; it is fully customizable to different customer groups.

EXHIBIT 12.2 | Traditional Promotion Mix vs. IMC Decision Making

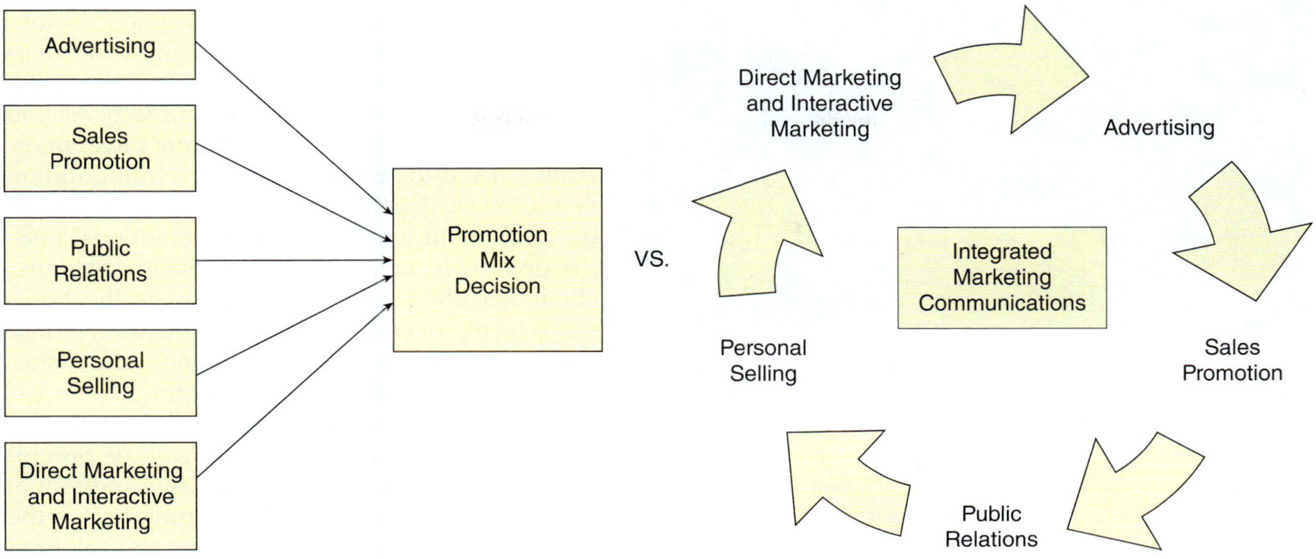

IMC Decision Making

LO 12-2

Identify the elements of the promotion mix and the pros and cons of each element.

An IMC approach means *integration of communication elements*. Exhibit 12.2 highlights the holistic decision process. Each element impacts the others, and the whole becomes more than the sum of the parts. A strong focus on a unified branding message and theme occurs throughout the process. In traditional methods the elements are developed separately; and while they do combine later to provide a promotional mix strategy, they are not necessarily viewed holistically as central to the brand. Because an IMC approach is an inherently more strategic approach to communicating with customers, managers who use it are much more likely to consistently communicate the right brand messages to the right customers at the right time through the right media.

Companies find that old strategies connecting customers to the company can still be successful. In a significant update to its traditional home party, Tupperware has created the TupperClub, which brings friends together for a social evening. Gone are the burping containers and money saving recipes; in their place are dinner and conversation. What is interesting is that the TupperClub concept is moving "uptown," becoming more accepted among the wealthy.[4]

Social commerce has become the next level of word-of-mouth marketing. Companies are rewarding brand advocates, who go online to recommend products and services with cash, discounts, and other offers. The boutique jewelry brand Stella & Dot is taking the direct selling model to the next level. Stella & Dot "stylists" promote and sell the products in at-home trunk shows, but also give guests access to their personalized social commerce platform, where products can be purchased at any time. The stylists are able to promote their site to friends via Facebook, Twitter, and Pinterest. In return, the stylist earns up to 30 percent commission for sales generated. UK managing director Kathleen Mitchell says, "it's essential to have these third-party advocates for our selling model. We have independent stylists who run their own business, but they sell through e-commerce platforms . . . If you don't involve the consumer and create a truly social enterprise, your business will be on one side and your customers on another because everyone is engaging in this way."[5]

Entertainment companies like Cirque du Soleil recognize the importance of strong IMC. Here Cirque du Soleil presents an interactive website for its show "Movi Kanti Revo."

IMC and the Promotion Mix

What kinds of decisions are involved in developing and executing IMC strategy? Consider Exhibit 12.3, which compares the impact of marketing management factors in an IMC approach with those of a personal selling approach. As you can see, a gamut of critical issues from buyer information needs to purchase size to the configuration of the marketing mix elements all influence the decision about where to invest promotional budget dollars. In fact, in many marketing-planning situations, the promotional budget is the lion's share of the overall marketing budget—typically surpassing packaging, distribution, and other marketing elements by a wide margin.

The allocation of the promotional marketing budget across the various elements of the promotion mix is a complex decision. Each promotional form has its own individual pros and cons, as Exhibit 12.4 shows. Again, within the IMC approach, it is the integration of the elements—not just each individual element—and the resulting synergies of the branding message that make the strongest sustainable impact on customers.

Push and Pull Strategies

Two fundamental approaches to promotional strategy are *push* and *pull* strategies. These are depicted in Exhibit 12.5. The specific promotion mix elements selected for investment will vary depending on the relative degree of push or pull desired.

In a **push strategy**, the focus is on the channel of distribution, and in getting the offering into the channel. Members of the channel are targeted for promotion and are depended on to then push the offering into the hands of end users. A push strategy typically relies on a combination of personal selling and sales promotion directed toward channel members.[6] In a **pull strategy**, the focus shifts

EXHIBIT 12.3 | Illustrative Factors Influencing IMC Strategy

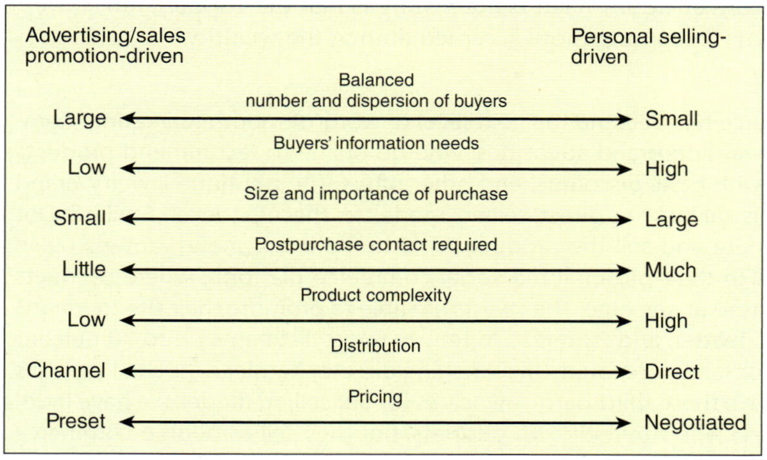

Source: Reprinted from David W. Cravens and Nigel F. Piercy, *Strategic Marketing,* 10th ed., 2013. Copyright © 2013 The McGraw-Hill Companies, Inc.

EXHIBIT 12.4 | Selected Pros and Cons of Individual Promotion Mix Elements

Promotion Mix Element	Pros	Cons
Advertising	• Many media choices • Efficiently reaches large numbers of customers • Great creative flexibility	• Shotgun approach reaches many outside the target • Oversaturation of ads lessens impact • High production costs
Sales Promotion	• Stimulates purchase directly through incentive to buy • Serves as an effective accompaniment to other promotion forms	• Can lead customers to continually wait for the next coupon, rebate, etc. • Brand may be impacted by price-cutting image
Public Relations	• Unpaid communication seen as more credible than paid forms • Association of offering with quality media outlet enhances brand	• Low control of how the message turns out • Highly labor intensive cost of mounting PR campaigns
Personal Selling	• Strong two-way communication of ideas • Directly eases customer confusion and persuades purchase	• Very expensive cost per customer contact • Salesperson may go "off message" from brand to secure the sale
Direct Marketing and Interactive Marketing	• Message customization without high costs of personal selling • Strong relationship building, especially when customer can control the interaction	• Spam and other unwanted correspondence when targeting is poorly executed • Reliance on CRM and database marketing requires constant updating

to stimulating demand for an offering directly from the end user. Advertising, consumer-directed sales promotion, PR, or direct and interactive marketing can be combined in various ways to target end users, creating demand that results in the channel making an offering available for purchase. In practice, push and pull strategies are rarely used mutually exclusively.[7] Rather, a promotional strategy is developed that strikes the best balance of investment of promotional funds in both push and pull strategies that make sense for the product and market involved.

EXHIBIT 12.5 | Push and Pull Promotional Strategies

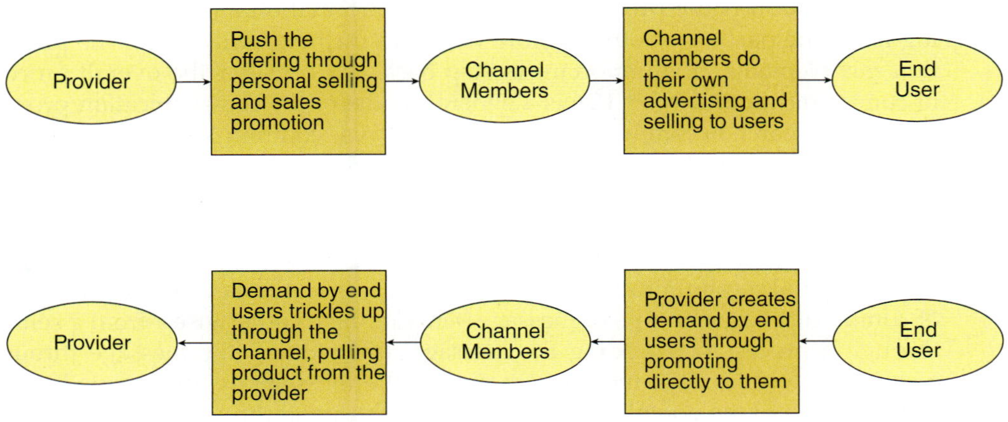

Internal Marketing and IMC

A final critical aspect of IMC is *internal marketing*. **Internal marketing** is the application of marketing concepts and strategies inside an organization. A great deal of research has shown that if members of an organization aren't knowledgeable about its offerings, don't understand who the customers are, and can't effectively articulate the branding message, successful marketing management is very difficult. The firm's employees are potentially its best and most trusted brand and message ambassadors. Properly armed, they can articulate what the firm and its offerings stand for in ways that nobody else can.[8]

Great brand marketers today pay a lot of attention to ensuring that *everybody* in the firm has pride of ownership in its brand, products, and services. From Southwest Airlines to Caterpillar to Apple, companies that do great marketing are placing a high priority on enabling each and every employee to communicate the marketing message. Most firms successful in internal marketing enlist the help of the human resources department to communicate the brand messages to all employees, beginning with employee orientation programs and continuing when new products are introduced or new markets are entered.

Looking Ahead

Taken together the three chapters on integrated marketing communications provide a managerially relevant overview of issues involved in promotion mix decision making. In the remainder of this chapter, you will learn about two models—the communication process model and a hierarchy of effects model—in promotional strategy development, as well as the marketing manager's role in promotional strategy. Then we examine the vital importance of interactive communications. Chapter 13 looks at the promotional mix elements that deliver the message to large groups of people and includes an introduction to advertising, sales promotion, and PR, while Chapter 14 details those tools that take a more personal approach and covers personal selling and direct marketing.

Perhaps more than any other area of marketing management, IMC promotion as a topic is incredibly broad in its strategy yet specialized in its tactics. Each of the elements of the promotion mix is often a separate course of study in college, and sometimes even more than one course. Your task as a student of marketing management is to not only gain an understanding of the process of promotional strategy decision making, but to know the promotional tools and decision options available for marketing planning in practice. An appropriate place to begin is by introducing a general model of communication.

COMMUNICATION PROCESS MODEL

Communication is the process of exchanging information and conveying meaning from one party to another. Before we begin further discussion of the promotion mix elements, it is important to step back and consider the overall process of communication. Exhibit 12.6 is a general model of the communication process based on research in communication theory. Because communication is an integral aspect of a marketer's charge in any organization, it is important to understand the fundamentals of the process. To achieve the desired effect, the marketing manager must consider all of the communication elements in developing the firm's promotional strategies.

The general communication process model identifies the elements in the process of communicating any type of message—marketing or otherwise—from a sender through a process of encoding the message, transmitting the message through a channel, decoding the message, receipt of the message by an intended target (hopefully), and the potential for a response by the target through a feedback loop. Surrounding the entire communication process is noise, or other messages and

EXHIBIT 12.6 | General Communication Process Model

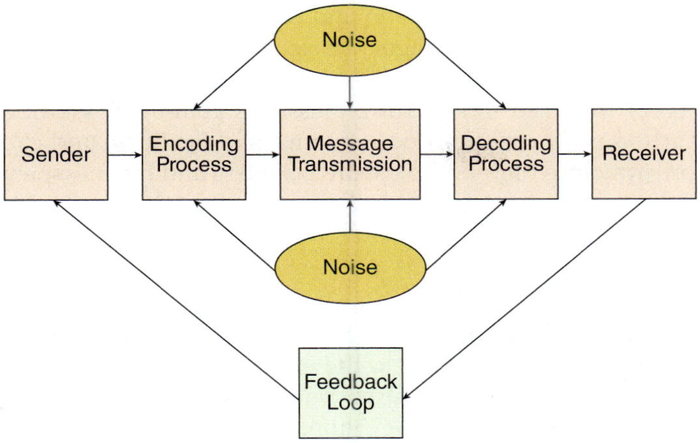

distractions that reduce the impact and effectiveness of the communication process on the intended target.

Let's translate the elements of the communication process into a marketing management situation.

Sender

LO 12-3

Connect communication models to real-world challenges in promotional strategy.

The **sender** is the source of the message. In a marketing context, the source is generally the organization whose offerings are the subjects of the communication. Often, the identification of the sender is connected more to a brand than to an organization. For example, although some people are aware that Kimberly-Clark markets Huggies disposable diapers, because of the company's individual branding strategy, the message source is intentionally tied to that brand and not to the corporation. However, the issue of **corporate identity** and its impact on customer attitudes and responses toward product offerings now is receiving heightened attention. Research indicates that a growing number of customers pay attention to what organization is behind the message and what its values are, especially in terms of sustainability and social responsibility, when making their purchase decisions.[9]

Importantly, sometimes the sending firm and its brands or product offerings affect the range of choices for managers throughout the remainder of the communication process model. Consider Marriott International, which has a wide range of brands from Fairfield Inn (budget focus) to Ritz-Carlton (luxury focus). When executing its marketing communications, to effectively position each of these brands uniquely in the mind of the consumer, Marriott must carefully choose distinct messages for each. This may or may not involve including highlighting the word *Marriott* in the communication; for example, Ritz-Carlton never mentions the Marriott brand, but the lower-end offerings do.

Encoding Process

Through the **encoding process**, the sender translates an idea to be communicated into a symbolic message consisting of words, pictures, numbers, and gestures in preparation for transmittal to a receiver. For brands that have developed strong imagery, the encoding process is helped along dramatically. Think about the symbolism of the brand logos for McDonald's, Boeing, and Apple, for example. For many customers, each logo conjures up instant feelings and thoughts about the brands, product line, and company. In this way, branding and marketing communications are inextricably linked—that is, strong investment in brand building almost always pays off through more effective and efficient marketing communications.

The encoding of messages about Fairfield Inn and Ritz-Carlton results in quite a different imagery. Fairfield Inn projects imagery of clean, functional, yet comparatively frugal accommodations. To many, Fairfield Inn equates to business travel on a budget. The imagery involved in encoding messages about Ritz-Carlton is very different. Ritz-Carlton portrays sumptuous rooms, spa facilities, and exotic locations in its focus on attracting high-end pleasure travelers and businesspeople for whom travel budgets are not an issue.

Message Transmission

After encoding, **message transmission** places the communication into some *channel* or *medium* so that it can make its way to the intended receiver. Think of a **channel** or **medium** as the conduit by which the encoded message travels. Options are wide ranging and include the Internet, television, radio, magazines, newspaper stories, and salespeople. The message arrives at the receiver via some communication channel, but that doesn't necessarily mean that every potential receiver will be equally receptive to the message. Thus, it is the sender's job to select the channel(s) that will reach a maximum number of targeted receivers and a minimum number of nontargeted receivers.

Decoding Process

The message arrives and is sensed (viewed, heard) by the receiver. But communication does not actually occur until the receiver *decodes* it. The **decoding process** takes place when the receiver interprets the meaning of the message's symbols as encoded by the sender. A typical challenge for marketers at this stage of the communication process is that different receivers are likely to interpret the message differently based on their own backgrounds and biases. This phenomenon results in **selective perception**—different meanings assigned to the same message by different receivers, based on an array of individual differences.[10]

The potential for selective perception is ubiquitous; to mitigate its impact, marketers try mightily to develop messages that are as consistent and unambiguous as possible. To one viewer, an ad for Fairfield Inn intended to feature imagery and words about the brand's economically thrifty qualities might get translated into "cheap motel." To another, the message might be received as "clean, reasonably priced, with free Internet." Obviously, Marriott is hoping the majority receive the second message.

Receiver

The intended **receiver** is the individual who is the target of the communication. Marketers work hard through research to ensure proper identification of target customers who are expected to have a high likelihood of connecting with the message based on their needs and wants. Obviously, in a personal selling or direct marketing context, the receivers are identified individually for contact. In the case of less personal marketing communications forms—advertising, sales promotion, and PR—marketing managers attempt to select communication channels and create messages that will have the greatest chance of actually being decoded, and acted upon, by the target receivers.[11]

Feedback Loop

The communication model provides opportunity for two-way communication through a **feedback loop**, in which the receiver can communicate reactions back to the sender. In a personal selling situation, the potential for customer feedback is instantaneous and direct.[12] In fact, one of the most important characteristics of successful salespeople is effective listening skills, or the ability to take in even subtle customer feedback and respond in ways that bring value back to the customer. Similarly, interactive marketing provides a clear two-way electronic conduit for information flow between company and customer. But compared to personal selling and interactive marketing, feedback on marketing communications delivered through advertising, sales promotion, PR, and noninteractive direct marketing is harder to come by. In those cases, marketers have to work hard to solicit customer responses.

For marketers, facilitating the ability of customers to provide feedback is important to success. As you read in Chapter 9 on service, a critical success factor in retaining loyal, satisfied customers is the ability to continually receive information back from customers on their experiences—good, bad, or ambiguous—with a firm and its offerings. Investment in ongoing efforts to promote two-way communication between firm and customer makes sense, especially given the temptations in today's hyper-competitive marketplace for customers to switch brands at the drop of a hat.

Uncle Ben's cuts through the noise with the eye-capturing and daring ad.

Noise

Most adults remember the child's game of telephone, where a circle of children gather and whisper a message into each other's ears. The last child to receive the message says it out loud, and usually laughter erupts. It's a safe bet that what comes out the back end of that communication process is very different from what went in. The *distortion* or interference that can occur at any stage of a communication process is referred to as **noise**, and the potential for noise is insidious in marketing communications.[13]

In a perfect world of communication, a decoded message would enter the mind of the receiver exactly the same as the one encoded by the sender. However, it is inevitable that noise will interfere with the purity of the process in the form of conflicting messages, misunderstood terminology, problems or errors in the channel or media used for the communication, or simply the overwhelming din (or clutter) of modern hyper-communication. Too many messages, too many competing media, and too many alternative activities for today's customers to partake—all of these factors contribute to a general degrading of the effectiveness of marketing communications. The result is that marketers must be smarter than ever about the way they develop and execute their communications. The ability of DVR to wipe out an entire genre of advertising is emblematic of the challenges facing marketers' promotional strategies. And the fact that Gen Yers and millennials tend to shun many traditional promotional forms in favor of communications *they* can control ensures that the noise problem is going to get worse before it gets better.[14]

The existence of DVR has hit broadcast cable companies hard as viewers both avoid commercials by recording shows and delay viewership. With live viewership decreasing, revenue through advertising sales was decreasing as well. However, the industry has had to make adjustments to account for viewers' tuning in using Video on Demand (VOD) features and DVR services. "Live+7" has saved some shows themselves from cancellation, such as NBC's *Smash*, as ratings increase over that period. However, the advertising standard has adjusted to "commercial+3" rating, which is how many viewers watched the commercials within three days of a show's first broadcast, although some NBC executives now believe ad sales should be calculated on+7 terms as well. That remains to be resolved as DVR users often skip over commercials. However, there is growth in the use of VOD where viewers order episodes they have missed. This trend may help broadcasters command more revenue from ad sales as VOD can include commercials that cannot be skipped.[15]

HIERARCHY OF EFFECTS MODEL

Buyers pass through purchase decision processes in three steps: cognitive (learn), affective (feel), and behavioral (do). Various models support our understanding by illustrating these stages as a hierarchy of effects in the context of customer response to marketing communications. Here we illustrate one popular version of such models, the **AIDA model**, so named because the effects (or steps) build in this order: **A**ttention (or **A**wareness), **I**nterest, **D**esire, and **A**ction. The attention stage correlates to the cognitive step of buyer decision making, the interest and desire stages to the affective step, and the action stage to the behavioral step.[16] Exhibit 12.7 portrays the AIDA model.

Where target customers fit on the model is critically important to effective selection and execution of the promotion mix. As in the general communication model, various mixes of messages and media are required to ensure that the different targets are likely to decode and process the communication successfully. Below are tips for maximizing success in promoting across the stages of the AIDA model. Exhibit 12.8 rates the general appropriateness of applying each of the promotion mix elements in coordination with each stage of the hierarchy of effects of the targets.

Attention

If target customers are essentially unaware of an offering, most of the investment in communication must be in raising awareness and gaining their attention. Depending on the situation, this may involve developing the customer's awareness for a whole new set of customer needs and wants as well as revealing that your product exists to address those needs and wants. In the initial introduction of the Prius, Toyota put much effort into building awareness of the emerging need for hybrid cars and also into educating potential customers about what a hybrid car actually is. Essentially, the automaker created a product category from scratch, and for a while there was little return on the promotional investment. However, when gas prices began to soar and environmental issues became more prominent, Prius was in a prime position to become the leader in its product category, gaining a first-mover advantage and making it difficult for competitors to catch up. Now, every major car manufacturer is jumping into the category.

EXHIBIT 12.7 | AIDA Model

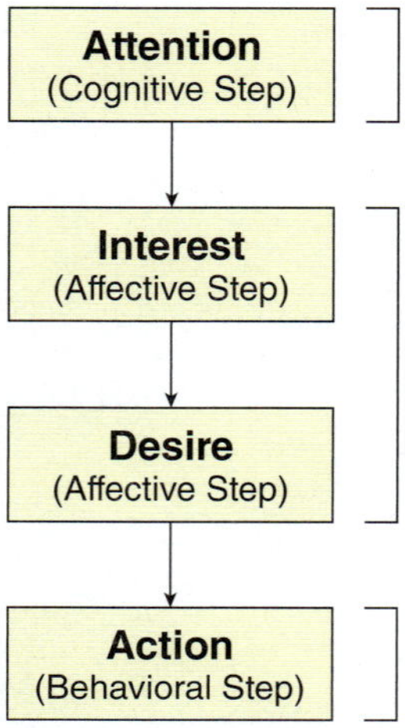

Gaining attention and building initial awareness can be a daunting task for marketers. Tremendous expenditures may be required to establish a foothold with customers, especially when a brand is relatively unknown or a product category is in its infancy. Chapter 4 covered different categories of adopters depending on how willing a potential customer is to try and buy a new product. At the attention stage of the AIDA model, marketing managers hope to use promotions to gain awareness of their offering with the innovators and early adopters. If marketers can influence these groups to purchase, innovators and early adopters can get others to jump on the bandwagon.

In many cases, gaining attention requires investment in mass appeal forms of promotion, especially advertising and PR. When ultra-premium

Voss water was introduced in the United States, marketers relied heavily on PR to create awareness, connecting the water to celebrities and gaining product placements in movies and in magazines sold in outlets frequented by the target customers.

Interest

To translate customer attention into interest requires persuasive communication. For more technical or complicated products, this means beginning to inform customers more specifically about what a product offering can do for *them*—how it helps fulfill needs and wants. To stimulate interest, the promotion must begin to touch a customer's hot buttons.

For example, generating awareness about the iPhone is not a problem for Apple; the buildup in the media is always gargantuan for months before the initial product introduction. But what would stimulate a person to move beyond inevitable awareness to interest in possibly purchasing? Apple masterfully uses its early promotion to cleverly point out new features and convince customers that any ordinary cell phone simply would not do. Interest is peaked by the communication of product features such as Siri, iPhone's personal assistant, and benefits, the ability to perform a number of tasks using your voice, and also by the imagery suggesting that each new iPhone is something really different.

artesian
VOSS
water
from
norway
sparkling
Splendidly Still and Luxuriously Sparkling
VOSS
facebook.com/vossworld

As a high-end water brand, Voss keeps its print advertising sleek.

Desire

Moving from interest to desire means that a customer has to move past a *need* and begin to really *want* that specific product. Promotion feeds desire through strong persuasive communication. At this stage, salespeople and customized direct and interactive marketing enter the promotion mix. Messages are altered to influence customers to feel that they simply can't do without the item. The innovators and early adopters show off their purchases to holdouts, and the ball is rolling.

EXHIBIT 12.8 | Appropriateness of Promotion Mix Elements at AIDA Stages

Promotion Mix Element	Attention Stage	Interest Stage	Desire Stage	Action Stage
Advertising	↑↑↑	↑↑↑	↑↑	↑↑
Sales Promotion	↑↑	↑↑	↑↑↑	↑↑↑
Public Relations	↑↑↑	↑↑↑	↑↑	↑
Personal Selling	↑	↑	↑↑↑	↑↑↑
Direct Marketing and Interactive Marketing	↑	↑↑	↑↑↑	↑↑

↑ = Generally least appropriate for use
↑↑↑ = Generally most appropriate for use

Such is certainly the case with the iPhone. Many people undoubtedly let their friends and co-workers see and touch their prized possession—sharing the experience of its functionality and form. Apple wisely drives the momentum through targeted direct mailings and e-mailings, inviting potential customers into Apple stores so that salespeople could fully demonstrate the broad spectrum of product virtues. The interest stage of the hierarchy is generally where the emotional part of buyer decision making peaks, and much of the promotional message is centered on creating positive feelings for the brand and product.

Action

The action stage is the purchase itself. To stimulate ultimate purchase, marketers often rely on salespeople, accompanied by some form of sales promotion, to close the sale. Sales promotion, by its nature, stimulates purchase. For the customer, it can be a coupon, rebate, or other special extra that pushes him or her over the edge to buy. Sales promotion can serve as *the close.* The reason sales organizations put so much emphasis on training salespeople in closing techniques is that they are seen as the final stimulant to purchase.

Growing evidence suggests that Gen Yers and millennials may respond differently to promotional strategies than prior generations. These differences may be attributable to the hierarchy of effects they go through in making purchase decisions. Previous generations, which have been the focus of marketing for years (i.e., Gen X and older), did not grow up with the same level of information availability and access as the younger groups. As a result, marketers have traditionally been placed in the pivotal role of outbound information providers for these customers, largely through promotion. This is true not only in the B2C marketplace, but also in B2B markets where organizational buyers have traditionally relied on their salespeople for information about products and markets. Gen Yers and millennials have experienced a very different set of circumstances related to information. With today's Internet-based communications, they are accustomed to doing their own research on products, developing their own opinions, and then taking action with less influence from traditional promotional approaches (including salespeople).

This is not to say that the role of the marketing manager in developing promotional strategy is less important when it comes to the younger generation. Rather, the caution is that the response of younger generations to different promotional approaches is not the same as that of previous generations. They are much less likely to want to be "sold to," are generally disinterested in mass advertising, and tend to place high value on objective information for decision making, likely from sources outside of traditional promotion. For example, communication going on in Facebook, blogs, message boards, chat rooms, and other forms of virtual communities carry much more weight than other communication forms. Although in some ways these qualities make marketing to the younger generations different than to previous generations, their unique attitudes toward marketing also create important opportunities for marketers. For example, they are generally very tuned in to brands, thus affording an opportunity for marketing managers to smartly integrate branding into promotional themes.

In doing marketing planning in the 21st century, the marketing manager who addresses these preferences among the important Gen Y and millennial markets will gain a competitive edge over marketers that attempt to capture this business through more traditional promotion forms.

LO 12-4

Describe in detail the marketing manager's role in promotional strategy.

THE MARKETING MANAGER'S ROLE IN PROMOTIONAL STRATEGY

As mentioned at the beginning of the chapter, the field of promotion is very broad and requires a good understanding in many distinct areas to execute effectively. As a part of the marketing field, the area of promotion more than any other tends to be heavily outsourced. Creative companies such as advertising and PR agencies have the focus and expertise to add substantial value to the execution of a marketer's promotional planning. And because of the unique nature of personal selling, most firms set up the sales organization as a separate entity from marketing or outsource it in the form of external distributors or brokers that represent a company's offerings to customers within the channel. But the proliferation of outsourcing of marketing communications and separation of sales from marketing do not absolve the marketing manager from the need to understand the basics of promotion so that the agency's contributions, as well as those of the sales force, can be properly integrated into the marketing planning process.

> The Chrysler Group LLC created a yearlong campaign entitled "The Year of the Farmer." It debuted the campaign during the Super Bowl with its spot for Ram trucks, recreating Paul Harvey's 1978 speech "So God Made a Farmer" using images of the truck along with rural fields, and working farmers, arranged as a slideshow. The company commissioned 10 notable photographers to capture the images. Chrysler is seeking to raise awareness of the importance of farming in America. Now, a larger collection of photographs is being used for a commemorative book. The book and a portion of its proceeds will go to local chapters of the National FFA Organization to help fight hunger. Aside from its charitable contributions, Chrysler is pushing its association with industries in agriculture and farming with its heavy-duty truck lines. The ad generated millions of views on YouTube and increased traffic on the Ram website. Daily page views reached 330,000 the day after the Super Bowl aired, up from its 40,000 prior to the spot airing.[17]

The seven major elements of the marketing manager's role in managing promotion are identified in Exhibit 12.9 as follows: identify targets for promotion, establish goals for promotion, select the promotion mix, develop the message, select media for use in promotion, prepare promotion budget, and establish measures of results.

EXHIBIT 12.9 | **Elements of the Marketing Manager's Role in Promotional Strategy**

Identify Targets for Promotion
↓
Establish Goals for Promotion
↓
Select the Promotion Mix
↓
Develop the Message
↓
Select Media for Use in Promotion
↓
Prepare Promotion Budget
↓
Establish Measures of Results

Identify Targets for Promotion

You learned in Chapter 6 that target marketing is a process of evaluating market segments and deciding which are most attractive for investment in development. We also discussed that positioning involves communicating one or more sources of value to customers in ways that the customer can easily make the connection between his or her needs and wants and what the product has to offer. The promotional mix strategy is a crucial element in positioning a firm's offerings effectively. It is not possible for the marketing manager to make sense of developing a promotional strategy until the targets are selected.[18]

Establish Goals for Promotion

Before moving forward to develop a promotion mix, the marketing manager must establish goals for promotion. Having a great product but being a best-kept secret is not a favorable position. Earlier we defined promotion as the means by which various forms of communication are used to inform, persuade, or remind potential customers. Exhibit 12.10 summarizes these essential goals of promotion and how each might be achieved.

Goal One: To Inform How does a customer know that Hilton is running a temporary special on room rates in its Orlando hotels? Or what the store hours are for Macy's annual white sale? Or that a $100 rebate is available on that Canon digital camera you've had your eye on? Or that the next-generation iPhone is about to be released? One important goal of promotion is providing information—about a firm, brand, and product offerings. Unless you are fortunate enough to be in the position where the media start clamoring months in advance for a glimpse of the next new product, chances are you will have to resort to paid forms of promotion to get your information across to potential customers.

Goal Two: To Persuade Rarely is the simple communication of facts sufficient for marketers to effectively make their case to potential customers, who are faced with many competing brands and product options. Promotion provides the opportunity to state your offering's advantages and to give the customer a reason to select you over the competition. Why should a construction project lease Caterpillar equipment instead of Kamatsu? What are the advantages of the Toyota Camry over the Honda Accord, and vice versa? Can a person *really* get a healthy meal at McDonald's? Persuasive communication is at the core of marketing and affords companies the chance to put their best foot forward for customers. Of course, persuasion can be taken to extremes, and the potential for crossing an ethical or legal line in promotion is a constant problem for marketers.

The downsides of crossing that line can be severe. In the 1970s, Listerine, playing on its "kills germs" theme, advertised that regular use could "reduce the number and severity of colds," a product claim that was blatantly untrue. The federal government forced the manufacturer to run high-profile retraction ads for several months, severely damaging the public trust and costing substantial revenue and market share to archrival Scope. In promotion, a certain degree of **puffery**, or relatively minor embellishments of product claims to bolster the persuasive message, generally is legal. However, in today's litigious environment, determining the fine line between puffery and making a false claim is best left to the legal department, not marketers.

Goal Three: To Remind For brands that are already top-of-mind for many customers, a primary goal of promotion is to keep the brand and its imagery at the forefront. Essentially, Coca-Cola has 100 percent brand awareness among U.S.

EXHIBIT 12.10 | Goals for Promotion

Goal One: To Inform
- Indicate features when introducing new products or making product modifications
- Provide explanation of product functionality
- Articulate what a company and its brands stand for in order to develop a clear image
- Discuss various uses and applications for the product

Goal Two: To Persuade
- Impact customer perceptions of a product, especially in comparison to competitor's products
- Get customers to try a product, hopefully resulting in a more permanent switch from a competitor
- Influence customers to purchase right now due to some strong benefit or need
- Drive customers to seek more information online or through a salesperson

Goal Three: To Remind
- Maintain a customer relationship with a brand
- Provide impetus for purchase based on some impending event

consumers (as well as in many other parts of the globe). So why does Coke need to invest in promotion? Marketers must constantly communicate with customers to maintain brand loyalty and reduce the tendency to switch to other brands. For example, the income tax preparation firm Jackson Hewitt starts reminding Americans through a fall promotion that income tax season is right around the corner. Jackson Hewitt wants to plant the seed early so that after the first of the year you will pull together your papers and make an appointment to have your tax return prepared. Reminding customers is a key goal of promotion and often stimulates direct purchase.

As a new product, the Samsung Ecobubble aims to inform and capture the attention of new customers.

Select the Promotion Mix

Promotion mix decisions are dependent on several factors. These include the nature of the offering, stage of the offering in the product life cycle, nature of the market, and available budget.

Nature of the Offering Some key questions must be answered about the product itself. You learned in Chapters 4 and 5 that B2C products and markets differ in important ways from B2B products and markets. Often, goods and services offered in the B2B marketplace tend to be more complex than those sold to end-user consumers. Also, you learned in Chapter 9 that services possess several distinct characteristics different from physical goods. Whether in the B2B or B2C space, the more complex, intangible, unique, and new an offering, the more challenging the communication about it will be and the more likely that relatively more personal forms of promotion will have to be relied on. In such cases, personal selling and direct or interactive marketing afford a greater opportunity for potential customers to become educated about the offering.[19]

Another related issue to consider is the strength of the brand. Promotion of brands that are already well known and that carry high positive brand equity allow for more reliance on relatively less personal forms of promotion such as advertising, sales promotion, and PR. The brand itself often carries the day in such communication; for example, when BMW introduced the new edition of their very successful 3-series cars, the equity built up among loyal BMW owners made purchase nearly a fait accompli.

Stage of the Offering in the Product Life Cycle Chapter 7 introduced you to the concept of the product life cycle (PLC). Now it is important to make a connection between the PLC and promotion mix decision making. Exhibit 12.11 portrays the PLC and associated promotion mix considerations.[20]

Nature of the Market Whether in the B2B or B2C space, the nature of the market served affects promotion mix decisions. Among the important factors:

- *Level of heterogeneity of target customers.* The more target groups and the more diverse the targets, the wider array of promotion mix applications to be developed.[21]
- *Level of geographic dispersion of target customers.* Obviously, online interactive approaches permeate geographic borders much more efficiently than traditional advertising. Geographic constraints are especially challenging for using face-to-face personal selling, since buyers and sellers have to physically get together.
- *Type of purchase decision to be made.* Is the purchase typically a routine, low customer involvement purchase or is it a specialized purchase with higher customer involvement?[22]

EXHIBIT 12.11 | Promotion Mix Decisions across the PLC

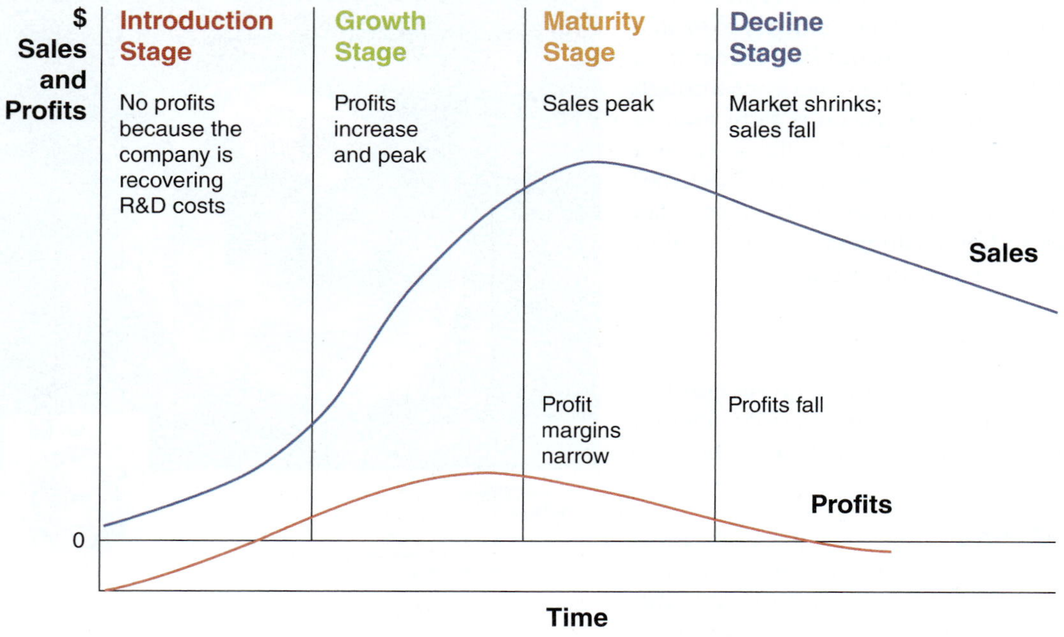

To stimulate primary demand, focus on gaining attention and awareness through PR and advertising. In this stage of the PLC, investment in promotion has little ROI to show for it.	Advertising tends to increase and eventually peaks. Focus on brand and brand comparisons. Sales promotion used to gain trial. Personal selling is active in the channel. Direct marketing and interactive marketing build share.	Advertising may begin to decrease. Direct and interactive marketing used to keep customers loyal. Sales promotion props up volume. Reduced promotional expenditures allow for an increase in the bottom line.	Further into decline, little or no promotion. Occasional "fire sales" to keep the brand in front of remaining users. Heavy use of direct and interactive marketing to ensure remaining loyal users stay supplied—and at a heavy profit margin.

- *Level and type of competition.* If there are many competitors in the same market space, and especially if they are also actively engaged in promoting their offerings, consideration must be given to ensuring your promotion stands out from those of the competition. This may entail going with a promotion mix that seems unusual for the situation but assures notoriety. For example, CUTCO promotes its cutlery only through direct personal selling to consumers. All of its major competitors use more traditional forms of promotion, such as advertising and sales promotion through retail channels.[23] On many occasions CUTCO's management has been asked why it doesn't adopt more traditional promotional forms for household products. The simple answer is that it is the most profitable company in the industry and it wants neither to increase promotional expenditures by turning to advertising nor to risk getting lost among a sea of other brands in department stores.

Available Budget Ultimately, the budget can constrain decisions about the elements of the promotion mix in which to invest. Costs of different media vary widely. At the high end, costs of making a single face-to-face sales call can easily cost $500 to several thousand dollars depending on the industry. Prime 30-second ads during the Super Bowl go for more than $2.5 million. It is very common for firms, and especially start-up firms, to find they are undercapitalized and to begin to cut their promotion budget during the critical introductory and growth phases of the PLC. This action tends to direct their promotional activities in ways that minimize the cost per customer contact, not necessarily toward the most effective or appropriate promotional approaches for their target customers.

Personal selling, some types of sales promotion (big rebates and product sampling, for example), and labor-intensive PR initiatives have very high costs per contact. Advertising, on the other hand, generally has much lower cost per contact. Unfortunately, low cost per contact is not the whole story, and marketing is littered with failed promotion plans that tried to squeeze an underfunded promotion budget by chasing low-cost-per-contact options.[24] A central aspect of the marketing manager's role when developing a promotion mix is consideration of trade-offs among the available budget, the nature of the market, the stage in the PLC, and the nature of the offering.

Promotion in general should be viewed as an *investment,* not a cost. From an accounting statement perspective, promotional expenses will show up as costs. But the budget for promotion dollars should be developed as an investment to grow a brand rather than as an afterthought of last year's revenues. We will discuss several approaches to promotion budgeting later in the chapter.

Develop the Message

This task is a very common one for outsourcing by a marketing manager, especially in larger organizations. Much of the message design process requires strong creative energy to come up with a **promotional appeal** that is appropriate for the offering and market, connects well with the brand, and has a high likelihood of ultimately taking the target through the AIDA steps toward purchase.[25] Three broad categories of promotional appeals are rational appeals, emotional appeals, and moral appeals.

Rational Appeals A **rational appeal** centers on benefits an offering can provide to a customer. Quality of the product, associated service, low price, good value, dependability, and performance are potential benefits that can be communicated.[26] The iconic ads featuring the Maytag repairman, who never had anything to do because a Maytag simply doesn't break down, is a rational appeal (tempered with a good dose of humor) pointing out that nobody likes having to pay to fix an appliance. It is interesting to note that Maytag has updated its focus on dependability by creating a Facebook page that encourages people to identify others they find dependable.

Emotional Appeals In contrast, an **emotional appeal** plays on human nature using humor, drama, joy, adventure, sorrow, love, surprise, guilt, shame, fear—the whole gamut of human emotions and aspirations—in developing promotional messages. Effectively crafted, such message approaches can have a high impact on target customers and can contribute a great deal to defining a brand's personality.[27] The Aflac duck with its humorously timed quacks and physical comedy has done wonders for a previously obscure insurance company whose brand used to be virtually invisible. Advertisers also use the negative end of the emotional spectrum to tell us about all sorts of things we should *not* want to have—stained teeth,

Tropicana uses an emotional appeal for its orange juice.

high-interest mortgages, insufficient education, 20 extra pounds—you name it, and there's a marketer communicating an emotional appeal and offering you a solution (for the right price).

Looking at the perception of their brand, BMW set out to create a campaign based soley on emotion: The "Designed for Driving Pleasure" campaign. The goal of the campaign was to convey to consumers that BMW is more than just an automotive company; they create "driving pleasure" through their cars. From car enthusiasts who love BMW for the sportslike feel to soccer moms who want a sleek yet safe car, the power of driving pleasure is a universal feeling. BMW's campaign was to entwine exhilaration and driving; from the efficient dynamic technologies that make BMW the most efficient luxury car brand in America to speed to green technology, the feeling of being behind BMW is pure pleasure.[28]

As consumer interest in health and wellness continues, Weight Watchers is facing more competition from start-ups and mobile apps. The company has begun to shift its focus from messages of diet to messages of health. Weight Watchers Senior VP–Marketing Cheryl Callan said, "We try and take the high ground. [Weight loss is] a highly emotional issue and there are enormous barriers for people to take action and do something. There's shame, there's guilt, and there's all sorts of feelings that you are dealing with." The company itself is altering its vision of itself to be a health care company. Consumer marketing is using its "360" program, which adds lifestyle and environment management to its food-tracking point system. The aim is to help the user establish skills that allow him or her to live in a consistently healthier way. CEO David Kirchhoff believes that the advertisements have not been resonating with consumers. The company is working on creating a compelling message to appeal to the consumer. As the $38 billion industry is becoming increasingly competitive, effective messaging is even more critical.[29]

WE COMBAT NATURAL DISASTERS WITH ACTS OF GOD.
When catastrophe strikes, your generosity strikes back. Thanks to your help. The Salvation Army serves disaster survivors from the moment of impact until the healing is complete. Proving that while disasters may be unpredictable, the good of people is not. Thank you for your continued giving at 1-800-SAL-ARMY or at salvationarmyusa.org.
THE SALVATION ARMY
DISASTER RELIEF EMERGENCY RESPONSE REHABILITATION HUMAN TRAFFICKING ABOLITION YOUTH SERVICES EVANGELISM
DOING THE MOST GOOD

The Salvation Army frequently uses moral appeals.

Moral Appeals A **moral appeal** in promotional messaging is used to strike a chord with a target customer's sense of right and wrong.[30] Many charities, cause-related marketers, and politicians use moral appeals to elicit support. The Salvation Army uses a tagline "Doing the Most Good" to reflect its reputation of providing more benefits out of donation dollars than many other charities.

Select Media for Use in Promotion

Media selection decisions involve making specific choices about the media, or channel, for the message within each element of the promotion mix selected. Each of the elements of the promotion mix—advertising, sales promotion, PR, personal selling, direct marketing, and interactive marketing—has a variety of media choices available. Attention will be given to those in sections that follow.

Prepare Promotion Budget

As mentioned previously, establishing an appropriate promotion budget sets the stage for a successful promotional strategy. The promotion budget is usually part of the overall marketing budget because the promotion

Promotion must create a call to action in the viewer. In honor of its centennial anniversary, the Anti-Defamation League launched the "Imagine a World Without Hate" campaign. The video depicts images of iconic role models such as Martin Luther King Jr., Anne Frank, Daniel Pearl, and Harvey Milk while John Lennon's "Imagine" plays in the background. Each of the individuals shown had him- or herself been a victim of violence and hate crimes. ADL's purpose for the video is to imagine what these individuals could have continued to contribute to the world had they lived. The contributions featured in the spot refer to topical issues at debate. Aside from noting historical figures, the spot reinforces the mission ADL has to fight bigotry and foster respect. It is noted that relatives of those shown in the video had given their consent and a donation to aid in its creation, most notably from the Estate of John Lennon. The organization is using a moral appeal to entice individuals moved by the 80-second video to donate to its cause.[31]

plan is a subset of the overall marketing plan. A variety of typical approaches to promotion budgeting are used. We focus on four types of promotional budgets: the objective-and-task method, percent-of-sales method, comparative parity method, and the all-you-can-afford method.

Objective-and-Task Method The **objective-and-task method** of promotion budgeting takes an investment approach in that goals are set for the upcoming year and then promotional dollars are budgeted to support the achievement of those goals. Here, the horse is properly before the cart, since the goals drive the budget and the budget enables the execution of the necessary strategies and tactics to achieve those goals. Put another way, the task at hand drives the budget. This approach is very consistent with a market-driving approach to strategic marketing, since investment in opportunistic product and market development requires the support of sufficient and appropriate promotional strategies.

Unfortunately, although this is a superior approach to developing a promotion budget, it is not the most widely used. Many firms are locked into arcane approaches to budgeting that have been in place for years in their firms. Marketing managers must argue the case for objective-and-task-driven promotion budgeting. Although it is much more challenging to implement than other methods, the payoff of viewing promotional dollars as an investment rather than an expense opens the door to growing a firm's brands exponentially. Like any investment, the method is not without its risks; there is always the chance that sufficient ROI will not be achieved on the promotional strategy. But in the long run, the objective-and-task approach affords the best opportunity for marketing success.

Percent-of-Sales Method The **percent-of-sales method** is the most popular approach to promotion budgeting but it is a very constraining model for a firm. There is an undeniable appeal in building a budget off a convenient percentage of revenue, allocated by product or by product line. Product X deserves $500,000 worth of promotion next year because it is forecast to do $10 million in revenue and our firm allocates 5 percent of revenue to promotion expense. The actual percentages of promotional budget to sales employed vary widely by industry and, in fact, vary quite a bit among firms in a particular industry. For example, Walmart has historically spent a far lower percentage of revenues on promotion than Target—less than 2 percent versus close to 5 percent—because their business models and target customers are very different. Firms like the percent-of-sales method because it is considered to be a conservative approach, is easy to administer, and affords maximal budgetary control at higher levels.[32]

But the disadvantages of the percent-of-sales method are compelling. First and foremost, promotion dollar investment should lead to sales; promotion should not be the *result* of sales. Under this method, problems arise when sales are declining because promotion expenditures decline in lockstep, thus exacerbating the downward sales trend and often dooming the product. A firm doesn't really need a professional marketing manager to execute promotional strategy under this budget scenario because the true product-market possibilities will never be achieved.

Comparative-Parity Method In the **comparative-parity method** of promotion budgeting, the marketing manager focuses on the competitive marketplace and specifically on comparing promotion expenditures across all key competitors in the market to find a budget number that matches. Typically, competitive information is obtained from industry sources, from trade association estimates of promotional spending, or from the public records of the other firms. A budget may be set based on some industry average, on the expenditures of the leading firm, or on the expenditures of the firm most like your own.[33]

This approach does offer some advantage in that it forces a firm to analyze how its competition is developing promotional strategy. But the notion of developing competitor-driven promotion budgets is as flawed and constraining as the percent-of-sales method. In this case, the firm is limiting itself to merely reacting to competitors instead of proactively developing its own strategy. Much research indicates that competitor-driven strategy development almost always leads to missed market opportunities, as the firm is so focused on the competition that it overlooks important changes in the customer marketplace that deserve opportunistic investment of promotion dollars.

An additional problem with the comparative-parity method is its inherent assumption that all the competitive firms are basically apples-to-apples comparatively when it comes to their promotions. Companies differ substantially in how they execute the promotion mix, and these differences are not effectively captured in the firm's raw budget numbers.

All-You-Can-Afford Method With the **all-you-can-afford method**, a firm simply sets its promotion budget as whatever funds are left over after everything else that's considered a necessity is paid for.[34] Many small business owners and entrepreneurs find themselves using this approach, and it is maximally self-defeating. For years, the Small Business Administration (SBA) has published data on key reasons that business plans fail to gain funding and also key reasons for start-up failures. Consistently, one of the major reasons for both is a poorly conceived and underfunded promotion budget. Such business owners tend to grossly underestimate what it takes to communicate their offering to target customers. The SBA advises that start-ups should capitalize to a level at which they can *comfortably* continue to invest heavily in promotion for the first three to five years of the business, at least. During this early time frame in a business life cycle, most firms do not turn any profit.

Establish Measures of Results

A final role for the marketing manager in promotional strategy is the development of appropriate metrics to determine the success of the promotion plan. The topic of marketing metrics is covered in detail in Chapter 16 with example metrics for various aspects of the marketing planning process including promotion. For now, it is important to note that decisions about which metrics to employ to assess the efficiency and effectiveness of promotion must be selected in the context of the specific goals established for the promotion plan. It is likely that measurement will occur on two levels: first, at the strategic level to determine incremental progress at designated time intervals toward achieving the promotional goals; and second, on a tactical level to assess the effectiveness of various forms of media and the creative execution.

NEW MEDIA

The Internet has redefined the relationship between companies and customers. In less than 20 years, it has established a powerful new communication channel. **Interactive marketing** is an Internet-driven relationship between companies, their brands, and customers. It enables customers to control information flow and encourages customer–company interaction as well as a higher level of customer service.[35] Even though it represents about 30 percent of U.S. commerce and less than 20 percent of global business, the Internet and, more broadly, interactive electronic marketing are the future. In both B2C and B2B markets, electronic interactive channels are considered essential elements in an overall marketing communications strategy. Indeed, many companies including P&G and General Motors are shifting communication budgets to Internet marketing and away from traditional communication channels, particularly network television.

Customers drive interactive marketing, controlling when, where, and how they interact. While companies expand access to information and explore new methods to facilitate the exchange process, customers define the relationship on their terms. The speed of this transformation has caught many companies by surprise. Finding what works, and equally important what doesn't work, presents a number of challenges. For example, as customers become more connected to a company, their expectations about service and the customer–company relationship also increase. In addition, combining traditional marketing communications channels with online, interactive media has proven to be a challenge. Communicating with customers is faster using e-marketing media, which often creates a challenge coordinating online and traditional marketing messages.

In the following chapters we will explore the unique challenges of creating marketing communications directed to markets (Chapter 13) versus individuals (Chapter 14); however, one of the interesting elements of interactive marketing communications is that various tools have elements of both market and individual focused communications. For example, a company's website is available to anyone with an Internet connection but also allows for personalization. In this section we examine interactive communications separately from other market and individual focused marketing communications for two reasons. First, as just noted, interactive communications are difficult to classify as market or individual focused communications; they contain elements of both. Second, interactive communications are growing at a phenomenal rate and represent the future of marketing communications. As a result, we need to look at it as a package of marketing communications tools. However, while interactive communications encompass a powerful set of marketing communications tools, it still must be part of a broader integrated marketing communications strategy. The discussion is divided into three sections: Online Communication Decisions, Mobile Growth Opportunities, and Social Media Change the Conversation.

LO 12-5

Explain key concepts of interactive communications.

Online Communication Decisions

This category encompasses website presentation and online advertising decisions.

Website Presentation A firm's website is the primary point of connection with the online customer. Customers visit a website to get information, ask questions, register complaints, develop a sense of community with other users, and purchase the product. As a result, it must do a number of things well. Performing the traditional role of retail storefront, the website conveys the company's value

WWF employs a simple yet effective, call to action on its website.

proposition to anyone who visits the site. Effective sites are able to draw new potential customers "inside" to check out the company's products and services.

At the same time, the website must service existing customers by providing access to customer service and information in an efficient and effective manner. Several researchers define the website interface on seven dimensions (see Exhibit 12.12).

Context Context refers to the overall layout, design, and aesthetic appeal of the site. Broadband and high-speed Internet have led to more graphics, video, and interesting design features that make the website more appealing. The challenge for the web designer is balancing the aesthetic appeal of high graphic content with the download time for graphics and other complex visual elements. The look and feel of the site must be consistent with the company or product's overall brand image. For example, visit the Zappos website and then go to Lucky Brand jeans to see how different companies approach the layout and design of a website.

Content In the past companies put their existing print materials (catalogs, for example) on the website and there was little in the way of original web content. Today, companies' websites incorporate a great deal of web-specific content. Volkswagen creates ads that run only on its website, while Costco and Best Buy have a specific web strategy that displays products not available in stores. Text, photos, charts, and graphics are all part of web content.

Community A key advantage of web-based communication is the opportunity to create a community of users or visitors to the site. Blogs and company bulletin boards encourage a sense of community that enhances the customer's company and product experience. Companies are still learning how to effectively harness

EXHIBIT 12.12 | Summary of Seven Design Elements of the Customer Interface

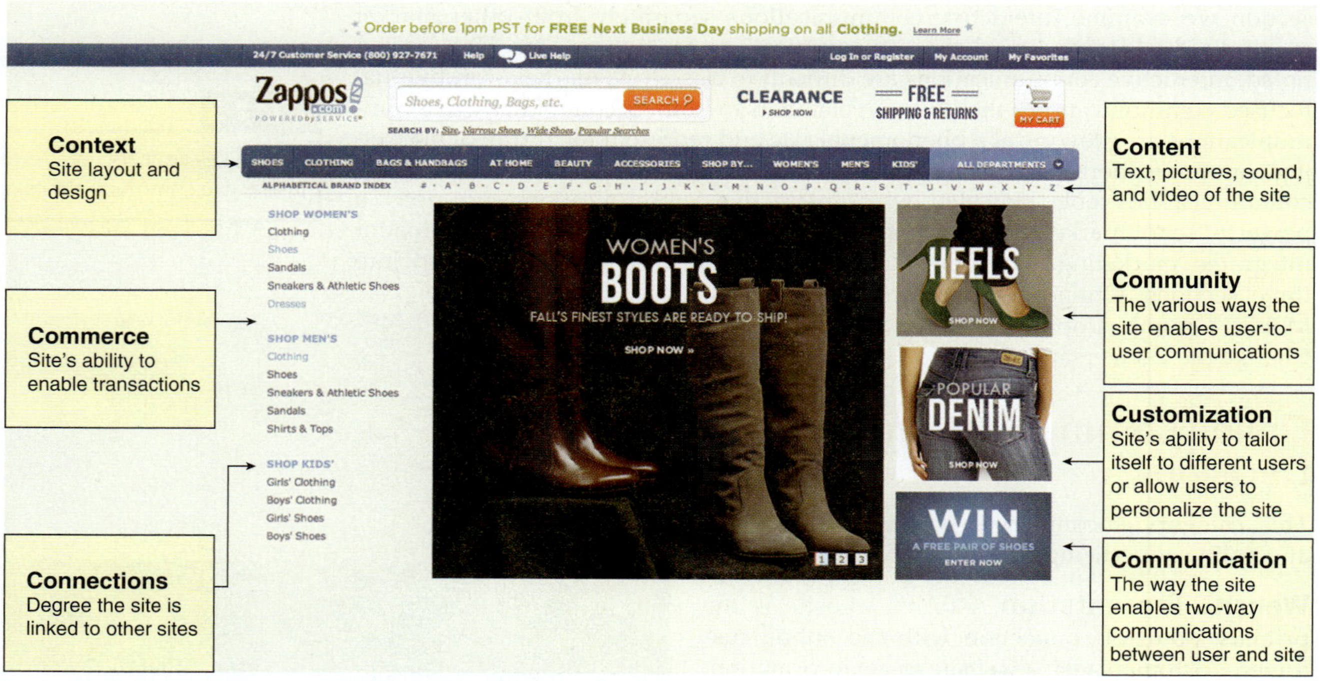

Reprinted courtesy of Zappos.

the power of community for their products. In many cases, third parties such as Kelly Blue Book, an auto industry site, have established the most powerful online communities. These communities bring users (or car owners in the case of Kelly Blue Book) together to discuss a variety of topics. These communities provide solutions (generated by members of the commuity) to problems, discuss the advantages/disadvantages of product features, and encourage people interested in the product to connect.

Customization The ability to create a unique individual experience with a company website adds great value to the customer interface. Customers appreciate and expect customization of their website experience. Simple customization includes turning off the sound to the site and reducing the graphic interface (html versus flash sites). More customized sites enable customers to choose content and context. Yahoo, for example, allows users to create their own Yahoo experience, defining the look and content of their Yahoo web page.

Communication The interactive channel allows companies to communicate with customers in three ways. First, companies communicate to customers and visitors to the website one-on-one through the Contact feature or e-mail. Second, customers and interested visitors communicate directly with the company through customer service requests. Finally, companies use instant messaging for customer service requests and sales inquiries. Symantec software, for example, has representatives available online to walk customers through questions about service or products.

Connection The web allows for communication among many sources. Information sites such as Edmunds.com (automobiles) and CNET.com (electronics) offer a lot of information at the site but also allow users to access company and retailer websites when they need more information or wish to make a purchase. This kind of connectivity greatly expands the usefulness of the site for the user.

Commerce The number of products purchased online has grown dramatically over the last five years. Some products, music for one, are now purchased primarily over the Internet through either music download sites such as iTunes or retail sites such as Amazon. Web designers know that creating a simple, easy-to-understand, and secure purchase experience is essential for success in online commerce. Customers are still concerned with online purchase security; however, the convenience, pricing, and selection of the online purchase experience have led to significant growth in consumer online purchasing.

Microsites In addition to the company's primary site, many companies create smaller, more focused sites that deal with specific topics such as new product introductions or targeted products within a large product portfolio known as **microsites**. For example, Audi, Mercedes Benz, and Sony create smaller sites to highlight certain products. In another scenario, banks create microsites to help customers work through specific issues such as home financing (value of current home, links to real estate sites like Zillow) or information about cars (reviews, getting a loan).

Online Advertising Decisions Internet advertising is growing and there is no indication the demand is slowing. Costs are still low relative to other advertising channels such as television, and, since it is much more targeted and measured, advertisers appreciate the ability to know exactly how well their dollars are working on the Internet.

The web offers companies a wide range of advertising options. Companies create sophisticated analysis programs that review an individual's web traffic, how long people remain on the page, their web browsing history, and many other characteristics to target specific ads. As a result, companies are changing their advertising strategies to include more interactive electronic media, including display ads, sponsorships, search ads, and e-mail options.

Display Ads These include banner ads and interstitials. **Banner ads** are boxes containing graphics and text and have a hyperlink embedded in them. Clicking on a banner ad will take you to the company's website. In a response similar to the reaction to telemarketing, there is a growing negative perception toward banner ads. While still prevalent throughout the Internet, the click-through rate is very low and companies have expanded to other forms of Internet advertising. **Interstitials** are more graphic, visually interesting ads that move across the web page. As with banner ads, people find these ads distracting, and antivirus software from Norton, McAfee, as well as Windows enables users to block them.

Sponsorships High-traffic websites sell **sponsorships** that enable companies to subsidize some section of the web page on the site. Edmunds.com offers a number of sponsorship opportunities. For example, as customers evaluate vehicles, they are made aware of a "premier dealer" in their area that is helping to sponsor the site.

Search Ads Most web searches (35 percent at last count) are for products and services, and **search ads** have shown the greatest growth in the last several years. Companies pay to be included on the page as the results of the search inquiry come up. Complex algorithms developed by Google, Yahoo, and others place ads based on an analysis of keywords. Advertisers pay based on the position of the ad on the search results page as well as the number of click-throughs. While the response rate is low, around 2 percent, the cost is also low (less than $.50 per click-through) compared to more than $1 per lead from an ad in the telephone directory.

E-Mail Not to be overlooked, e-mail still offers some real advantages over direct mail and other forms of communication. First, it is targeted and can be customized to the individual. Second, it is immediate so companies can offer coupons, or other promotions, quickly and expect results. Third, it allows for additional personalization as individuals can opt for specific messaging that increases the likelihood it will be read. At the same time there are some disadvantages. The most significant disadvantage is, like regular direct mail, it can be deleted easily. Moreover, most people are inundated with e-mail today and incorporate spam filters and other tools to limit the e-mails they receive. E-mail works best when it is part of a broader communications strategy that includes both traditional communications tools (advertising) and interactive communications.

Mobile Growth Opportunities

While the Internet has fundamentally changed the way companies and customers interact, there is a new equally important change taking place: the growth of mobile communication devices (smartphones, tablets, and notebook computers). A recent study found there were close to 5.5 billion mobile subscribers around the world and the number is increasing every day, with China and India leading the growth. As consumers move to a "post-pc" world, they create new opportunities for marketers to target them with relevant options on the go. Let's consider some of the most powerful mobile tools, at least as they exist today.

Text Messaging Nearly 41 billion SMS messages were sent *every day* in 2013. People are communicating with each other from anywhere and many companies have embraced text messaging as a useful communication tool. Perhaps it should not be a big surprise that one of the activities where people do a great

HSN may have started with home shopping, but CEO Mindy Grossman says the current shopping experience is "boundary-less retail." HSN is number 26 in the Internet Retailer Top 500 guide. The company is removing silos from its shopping experience. Instead, it intends to utilize portable devices, desktop, and television. The goal is to create an immersive shopping experience. HSN will offer programming, videos, and product information for TV, computers, tablets, and smartphones. A community aspect will be utilized in which customers can discuss pre- and post-purchase information. Their digital commerce will be enhanced to include mobile and e-commerce. Mobile commerce has been integral in new customer capture for the company. Its mobile sales totaled more than $100 million in the first three quarters of 2012, comprising 10.1 percent of overall e-commerce sales of $990.5 million. Mobile accounts for 20 percent of new HSN customers. Jill Braff, executive vice president of digital commerce, notes, "a multichannel shopper is more engaged and spends more money."[36]

deal of messaging is shopping. In addition, consumers are adopting other related technologies like IM (instant messaging) and mobile e-mail (e-mail, contacts, and calendars that are able to follow the individual). Finally, with the growth of smartphones a new technology called A2P (application to person) enables companies to send messages from automated applications to people on everything from alerts from their banks to special offers from retailers. Customers can even make purchases.

Mobile Payments and M-Commerce While not widely available in the United States, mobile purchasing is expanding rapidly and already exceeds $200 billion a year. Japan leads the world in mobile purchasing, but the United States and China are expected to see big increases in mobile purchases. In addition, new technologies such as NFC (near field communication) have the ability to turn your mobile device into a credit card. One of the challenges with NFC is the close cooperation between handset manufacturers, banks, and the retailing industry. Some companies, like Starbucks, have worked to create an NFC-type app for smartphones, but the potential for this to allow users a better shopping experience is significant.

M-commerce, sales generated from a mobile device, is undeniably a growing component of the consumers' mobile experience. Amazon reported more than $5 billion in mobile sales in 2013 and eBay's mobile payment volume was over $13 billion. The merging of various activities on a single device changes the relationship between the company and its customers. Increasingly, if a company does not a have a strong mobile strategy, it will be at a disadvantage with its tech savvy customers.

Geo-Location Marketing Smartphones have the ability to track the individual's location. Not surprisingly, marketers are considering ways to incorporate location-based marketing into a marketing communications strategy. **Geo-location marketing** is the use of geographic data to drive marketing messaging and other marketing decisions. Companies such as Sonic and Starbucks have created strategies to target customers when they are near one of their stores. In addition to the technical challenges of effectively marketing to someone in a specific location at a specific time, serious questions about privacy surround this technology. At this point, only a limited number of companies use geo-location technology in their marketing communications and they require a customer to opt in to the service. One of the complaints of traditional couponing has been the low response rate and, even in early stages of adoption, geo-location marketing has demonstrated the ability to increase the response rate.

Social Media Change the Conversation

Perhaps no change has had a greater impact on marketing communications than the growth of social media. The ability for people to come together online has moved the conversation about a product or company away from the company. Customers can speak directly to each other about the good and bad of their product experiences. This has created both opportunities and threats for companies as they look to first understand the impact of social media on their business, then develop effective marketing strategies to manage it. When it is done well, a company's social media presence can reinforce existing marketing messaging as well as give the company a more community-focused, tech-savvy presence. In addition, the immediacy of social media forces companies to stay connected to their customers. Facebook pages are frequently updated during the day; people have a reason to visit often (more on this below). At the same time, an ineffective or poorly executed social media strategy can very quickly damage a company's image and reduce the effectiveness of other marketing communications. There are three forms of social media that most impact marketers: social networks, product review sites, and online communities (forums).

In order to provide more useful information for businesses, Klout released an analytics dashboard to help brands identify key influencers. "This is really the first step but a meaningful step towards a set of tools that will enable brands to more effectively understand and engage with their influencers," noted Klout CEO Joe Fernandez. Klout for Business aims to tell businesses who their influencers are among their Twitter followers and Facebook fans. This information includes the influencers by age groups, gender, location, and what topics influence them. Klout rewrote its topic analysis system to allow companies to search their influencers' interests and influences. Prior to the Klout for Business rollout, companies can use Klout's insights to run Klout Perks campaigns including VIP Perks products. Mobile VIP Perks step up the physical customer service experience by geofencing locations to alert businesses of Klout users in the vicinity. The recognition of social influencers important in social media campaigns and brand advocacy leaves room for companies like Klout to develop more business-related software to interact with high-scoring Klout users.[37]

Social Networks As the name implies social networks are about connecting people through friendship, mutual interest, or some other characteristic. The concept of a social network goes back to the 1800s, when it referred to a collection of people who developed a relationship based on some unifying element. A modern interpretation refers to groups of people connected through technology. Today, there are hundreds of social networks that encompass a variety of topics from broad-based collections of people (Facebook) to very specialized sites that focus on specific topics: photo sharing (Flickr), movies (Flixster), healthy and green lifestyle (Care2), and motherhood (CafeMom). Some of the largest social network sites are targeted at non-English-speaking countries such as Qzone (China) and Vkontakte (Russian-speaking areas).

Social networks present marketers with some real challenges. As the conversation moves to a community focus, companies lose the ability to control the

American Express wants consumers to share with their network just how they use American Express. It's part of the new way to advertise to consumers, called the "Social Currency" campaign that invites consumers to trade in rewards points in a less conventional way than before, including buying concert tickets and electronics on Amazon.com, with the stories being directly linked to social networking sites like Facebook and Twitter. American Express has also linked with Twitter.[38]

message and yet they cannot ignore online communities. Their customers are discussing their products; in addition, their competitors are engaging their customers in social networks so a company fails to participate in social networks at its own peril. Let's examine three of the more popular: Facebook, Twitter, and LinkedIn.

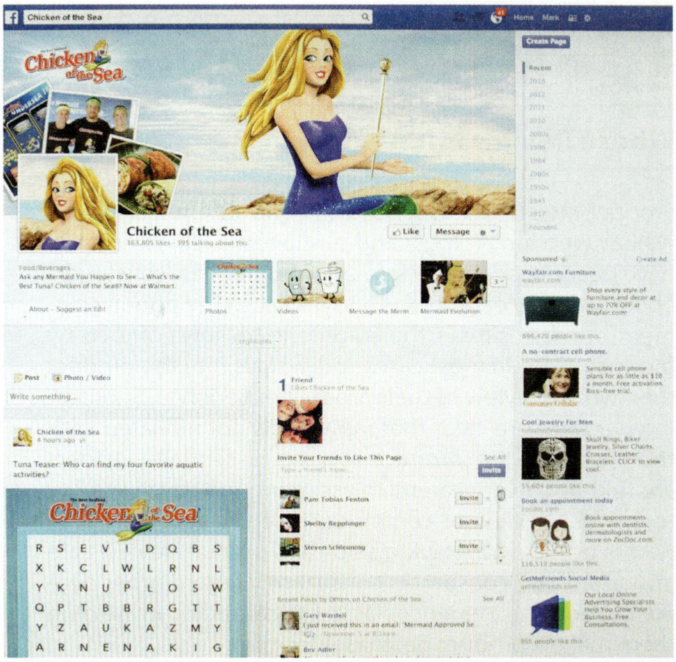

It is essential for most companies to have a Facebook presence. Chicken of the Sea runs its own Facebook fan page.

Facebook Facebook is the largest social networking site in the world with roughly one billion users. Originally started as a site for college students to connect with each other, Facebook has grown to include a broad base of different users from grandparents to kids, large companies (P&G, Dell) to small entrepreneurs. For marketers, Facebook represents one of the best opportunities to engage a social network; its open access and broad appeal can translate to a large number of Facebook friends. Some companies like Dell, with nearly 1 million friends, have embraced Facebook with a strategy designed to offer unique offers and information. Other companies like Apple take a more conservative approach with minimal presence on Facebook. One of the challenges for companies is the immediacy of social network sites. Creating a Facebook page may not cost money, but making it interesting and, more importantly, giving people a reason to come back requires a *significant* commitment. In addition, as individuals post comments, the company must dedicate resources to make sure those posting feel connected to the company.

Brands like Gillette have been quick to realize the power of social media like Twitter.

Twitter Twitter is a micro-blogging site with close to 600 million users. It is a different experience than Facebook—shorter and more immediate. Users are limited to 140-character *tweets* that offer immediate insight on how someone is feeling or what he or she is thinking. Research suggests that 20 percent of all tweets are related to a product or service, making it an important source of feedback about customers' product experiences. At a minimum, companies need to monitor Twitter for customer insights. A more expanded strategy, uses Twitter to broadcast messages out to users. Dell, again, has adopted an aggressive Twitter strategy, sending out Tweets about online specials (available only to those on Twitter). In addition, it creates accounts to offer technical support and support to individuals living in various countries around the world such as Germany and France.

LinkedIn Targeted at working professionals, LinkedIn has a membership of over 120 million users and offers some distinct advantages in terms of a professional calling card. Key features include the ability

Companies have turned to Twitter to increase sales. Using web intents on their articles, ESPN makes it very easy for users to quickly share information. When they click on the Twitter bird logo, a web intent window pops up with a preloaded, custom tweet, making it very easy for users to share content with their followers. In one 30-day period, ESPN noted 1,250 tweets per day with over 15 clicks per tweet back to the ESPN site. Making it easy for users to tweet information from ESPN led to increased traffic at the site.[39]

ETHICAL DIMENSION 12

Whose Review Is It Anyway?

Product sites such as CNET.com and Edmunds.com as well as web logs (blogs) and e-retailers such as Amazon have become popular information sources for consumers about a variety of products and services. One popular element of these sites is the comments/reviews offered by product users. In most cases, individuals rate the product then write a review of their product experience. Sponsoring websites are clear that individuals not affiliated with the site offer the product reviews. Essentially, readers are told to be very careful in assigning too much validity to any one review or comment since the veracity of the post is not known. Having said that, product reviews are important and consumers consistently regard other people's product experiences as a critical factor in helping them make a product purchase decision.

Until a few years ago, the assumption was that product users wrote reviews with no connection to the company or the website. However, that is not always the case. A number of companies have been caught paying bloggers to post positive reviews and other information. Indeed, the practice has become so widespread that several companies are now in the business of linking advertisers with bloggers willing to post information about a company's products. One of those companies, PayPerPost, reports over 8,700 advertisers and 50,000 bloggers. Bloggers earn between $5 and $100 per post depending on the length of the post and popularity of the blog. Advertisers with PayPerPost include large companies such as Hewlett-Packard and *Sports Illustrated;* however, smaller companies also use the service. Wallhogs.com, a small manufacturer of life-size wall cutouts and prints, believes the positive feedback created by bloggers hired through PayPerPost had a significant effect on the company's initial success. Another example is a company called VIP Deals that sold a black leather case for the Amazon Kindle Fire. The product received an unusually high number of 5-star ratings on Amazon (310 out of 355); however, upon further investigation, some buyers of the product were told in a letter that if they posted a review of the case, the company would refund the purchase price. Since the practice was revealed, Amazon removed the product, but the practice of linking the company to the product review is much more common than many people know.

Critics charge the process is deceptive by giving the impression that a posting is from a legitimate blogger instead of a paid endorsement. In addition, they argue that the paid blog postings artificially inflate advertiser rankings, a key metric used by Google to list sites in the search engine. In an effort to counter claims that the postings are deceiving, PayPerPost has changed its policies and now requires bloggers to include a disclosure badge to identify the post as company-sponsored.[40]

The ability of individuals to share product experiences is an important and evolving part of the Internet. Does the use of bloggers paid by advertisers damage the credibility of product-experience posts?

Ethical Perspective

1. **Advertisers:** Should advertisers hire bloggers to post positive product experiences? Should they require bloggers to indicate whether or not they have been paid to post their review?
2. **Consumers:** Should bloggers post whether or not an advertiser pays them? Does it make any difference whether bloggers are being paid to post reviews to "neutral" product websites and blogs?

to create a contact network of people that allows individuals to stay in touch with each other as well as offer introductions. People opt in to an individual's contact network by being asked to join and responding affirmatively. Companies are making extensive use of LinkedIn for recruiting. As a result, students are being encouraged to create LinkedIn accounts that take on many of the characteristics of a resume. Salespeople have quickly adopted LinkedIn as a communication tool for their customers. Many business cards make note of the individual's LinkedIn account.

Product Review Sites A particular type of social media, product review sites, offers individuals the chance to (1) provide feedback on their product experience and (2) search for information before a purchase. In both cases, marketers need to be monitoring relevant sites for their products. Examples of some well-known product review sites include the following:

- CNET is one of the most popular sites for individuals interested in electronics. CNET posts professional product reviews across a wide range of electronics products. At the same time, it encourages individuals to provide their own feedback on these products. Taken together it provides a great deal of information for anyone looking to purchase any technology.

- Urbanspoon is a user-generated product review site of local restaurants. Urbanspoon creates a local community of users (supported by professional critical reviews from local media) providing restaurant reviews by location, price, cuisine, and features.
- Consumersearch acts as an aggregator of reviews across a wide range of products, everything from home and garden to automotive. While it offers its own reviews of many products, the site also includes reviews from other sources as well as customer reviews from Amazon.

How important are product reviews to consumer-purchase decisions? Consider the following: over 70 percent of Americans consult product reviews before a purchase, a high product rating increases the likelihood of purchase by over 50 percent, and nearly half of all retail sales are influenced by web research. These statistics strongly suggest that companies should have a strategy for monitoring relevant product review sites. Ethical Dimension 12 discusses one of the ethical issues companies run into trying to influence product review sites. Specifically, the issue is the use of company-sponsored web bloggers to present information about a product, which has come under criticism for misrepresenting the nature of the relationship between the company and the blogger.

Online Communities Many companies have realized the positive results of creating online communities within their own websites. While it is certainly true that people will share negative as well as positive feedback, it is also true that companies providing an open forum encourage customers to stay connected to the company and give the company a chance to respond directly to customer concerns. Naturally, for the site to be effective, it must be perceived as "honest"; in other words, the company must not delete negative posts but rather allow participants to share a wide range of views. Apple is one company that has embraced this strategy with thousands of communities built around their products and customers (consumers versus professionals). These forums offer customers important product support, deal with customer concerns, and build a strong sense of community among Apple customers.

Social networking sites such as Reddit.com have created a new generation of influencers. Reddit is the self-proclaimed front page of the Internet. The company has been growing ever since it was acquired in 2006. At that time it had 700,000 page views a day. In 2011, when it was spun off from its owner Condé Nast, it was getting 1.6 billion page views a month. As of October 2012 the site reported more than 3.8 billion monthly page views and more than 46 million unique visitors in the same time frame. The site had a total of 400 million unique users in 2012. With its immense viewership, Reddit is seeking investors. It continues to drive more traffic to its site by hosting "ask me anything" events. Such events have featured high-profile individuals, including President Obama, the Mars Curiosity rover team, and U.S. Representative Zoe Lofgren. The site allows users to create subcategories and moderate content, some of which have become influencers even within the site.[41]

Viral Marketing The immediacy and personalization of social networks and, more broadly, the web itself set up the environment for *viral marketing*. The American Marketing Association defines **viral marketing** as a "marketing phenomenon that facilitates and encourages people to pass along a marketing message." Nicknamed viral because the number of people exposed to a message mimicks the process of passing a virus or disease from one person to another. Viral marketing (or buzz marketing) is the process of creating a video clip, image, message, e-book, or some other content in an effort to have the media passed on by individuals in a social network or by word-of-mouth.

When it works, it has the ability to spread very quickly (go viral) and generate a tremendous amount of buzz or awareness around the product. As we discussed earlier, when Ram was ready to introduce a new edition of its pickup trucks, the company decided to create a commercial around the theme of farmers. The commercial ran during the 2013 Super Bowl and it became the most watched ad of the Super Bowl with over 18 million views.[42] Interest in the trucks was heightened beyond what would normally be generated spending money on traditional advertising tools. By the end of 2013, that commercial had been viewed over 35 million times on YouTube.

Marketing managers have known how valuable strong word-of-mouth can be in a product's success. However, with the growth of social networking on the Internet and the ability of marketers to target individuals more carefully, it is now possible to create marketing communication campaigns that simulate a word-of-mouth, one-on-one methodology on the Internet. P&G has a community called Vocalpoint that focuses on the health, nutritional, and personal needs of women. One of the keys to the site is that participants are invited to join based on their preference for social connectedness, or their willingness to reach out to other women (research suggests that participants speak to more than 20 women a day), which serves to build additional buzz for the company.

Viral Marketing Guidelines In many respects, successful viral marketing requires a very different approach to marketing communications than, for example, advertising or personal selling. When it works, it can be possible to connect the success of the viral marketing with sales success. One successful viral marketing effort was the Mentos-Diet Coke "geyser" ad, which showed the effect of dropping several Mentos in a bottle of Diet Coke. The Mentos ad generated 5 million views in three months. People viewing the ad were encouraged to participate in "Make Your Own Mentos Geyser" competitions and the company distributed thousands of product samples. The result was a 20 percent sales increase, which it attributes to the ad. However, the link between a viral marketing campaign and sales is often not that easy to establish. Let's consider some guidelines.

Measuring Success One of the biggest challenges marketing managers face in viral marketing is measurement. While it is certainly easy to know how many hits there are to a particular website, translating that into marketing metrics, such as higher unit sales, is more difficult. As a result, marketers often define broad goals for a viral campaign. Another viral campaign started by Mentos, the Mentos Intern, encourages website visitors to assign tasks to a 19-year-old student intern named Trevor. Success for the campaign was not defined in terms of sales but "how well the campaign can integrate the idea of Mentos into pop culture." This more broadly defined goal may be appropriate since more defined metrics such as unit sales are difficult to identify.

Connecting People to the Experience One key to a successful campaign is enabling participants to be part of the experience. Ranked as one of the most successful viral marketers over the last several years, Old Spice highlights its men's products through its own creative viral videos on its websites and encourages visitors to stay connected with its products by including ringtones, screensavers, and wallpapers that are updated. Giving people a reason to come back and become engaged connects people to the product.

Targeting a Younger Demographic Viral marketing works well with a younger demographic and enables marketers to reach out to a different market segment. And yet there are good examples of creative stretch. For example, Folgers's "Happy Morning" viral video campaign focused primarily on an older market segment. The video, a funny send-up on happy morning commercials, was widely distributed to video websites and represented Folgers' first significant attempt to reach younger audiences using a viral marketing strategy. The ability to target younger audiences without offending existing target markets that are not likely to be part of the same social networks gives companies the freedom to experiment.

SUMMARY

Developing promotional strategies is an integral part of marketing management and marketing planning. A firm's investment in promotion often involves a substantial amount of money. Fostering an integrated marketing communications (IMC) approach in an organization ensures consistency in communication of the brand and promotional messages across all internal and external communication channels. Although marketing managers are rarely experts in all areas of promotion, they must be well versed in the process of IMC and how it connects to the overall marketing plan.

The communication process model demonstrates the complex process of creating a message and the many challenges marketers face in making sure the message is received correctly. The hierarchy of effects model, on the other hand, focuses on the internal process people work through in seeing, understanding, and developing an interest in a message, then moving to action. Marketing managers must understand both these models to create an effective marketing communications model.

Marketing managers have a variety of tools available for them including advertising, sales promotion, direct marketing, personal selling, public relations, and interactive communications. These tools all have advantages and disadvantages; the goal is to align the right tool with the right objective. For example, if the goal is to increase awareness of the product, traditional advertising (radio, TV, print) may offer the best option; however, if the goal is to deal with specific customer issues before the purchase, then a personal selling strategy can work well.

The role of the marketing manager in the marketing communications process begins with a good understanding of the product's target markets. From there the marketing manager creates a set of objectives for the campaign, identifies the specific elements of the promotion mix, develops the message, and selects the media. At this point the marketing manager has sufficient information to formulate the budget and implement the campaign. Finally, and this is critical, the campaign must be measured to determine how well it is working.

Interactive marketing communications has fundamentally changed the relationship between the company and its customers. From direct communication (e-mail, mobile communications) to promotional opportunities (website), the ability of interactive communications to connect with the customer and for customers to connect with each other creates some significant opportunities to strengthen the relationship or, if managed poorly, the ability to weaken or even destroy the relationship.

KEY TERMS

integrated marketing communications (IMC) 361
promotion 361
promotion mix 361
advertising 361
sales promotion 361
public relations (PR) 361
personal selling 361
direct marketing 361
interactive marketing 361
promotion mix strategies 362
promotional campaign 362
push strategy 364
pull strategy 364
internal marketing 366
communication 366
sender 367
corporate identity 367
encoding process 367
message transmission 368
channel or medium 368
decoding process 368
selective perception 368
receiver 368
feedback loop 368
noise 369
AIDA model 370
puffery 374
promotional appeal 377
rational appeal 377
emotional appeal 377
moral appeal 378
objective-and-task method 379
percent-of-sales method 379
comparative-parity method 380
all-you-can-afford method 380
interactive marketing 381
microsites 383
banner ads 384
interstitials 384
sponsorships 384
search ads 384
M-commerce 385
geo-location marketing 385
viral marketing 389

APPLICATION QUESTIONS

1. Consider the concept of integrated marketing communications (IMC). Select a company and investigate its use of IMC in developing and executing promotional strategies. Look for evidence through its media and messages.
   a. What evidence leads you to conclude the company is or is not successfully practicing an IMC approach? Be specific and connect the evidence to the discussion of IMC in the chapter.
   b. Is there evidence that the firm practices internal marketing? If so, please share what leads you to this conclusion. If not, speculate on how internal marketing would be of value to the organization.
   c. For this or any firm, what are the major advantages of taking an IMC approach? What are the downsides of not practicing IMC?
2. Think of a situation you've experienced in which some communication process you were involved in did not go as well as it might have (it doesn't have to be marketing communications). Using the communication process model (Exhibit 12.6) and accompanying discussion as a guide, systematically retrace the steps of that communication experience through the elements of the model and identify *(a)* where the problems occurred and *(b)* what could have been done differently at each problem step to make the communication experience better.
3. Consider a major purchase you have made recently. Review the AIDA model (Exhibit 12.7) and accompanying discussion.
   a. Think back on the process that led up to your purchase and reconstruct the types of promotion that you experienced during each stage of the AIDA model. Which of the promotional forms was most effective in your situation, and why?
   b. As you reconstruct this purchase experience and the promotional messages you received during it, what other promotion mix elements that you did *not* experience at the time might have been effective in convincing you to make the purchase? At what stage of the AIDA model would they have been helpful, and in what ways do you believe they might have impacted your decision process?
4. The chapter discusses the role of the marketing manager in promotional strategy (Exhibit 12.9 and accompanying discussion). The trend today in both large and small firms is for much of the promotion function to be outsourced.
   a. Comment on this outsourcing trend. What are the major reasons for the trend? What are the pros and cons? What is your personal view about outsourcing all or part of promotion?
   b. Assume you are a marketing manager for a firm that outsources promotion to a creative agency. In what ways does this arrangement impact your job? In particular, concentrate on how it impacts your marketing planning (being mindful that promotion planning is a key element). How would you interact with the agency as a manager representing your firm (assume you have responsibility for the agency relationship with your company)? That is, what are the key things you should do to ensure a productive relationship?
5. You are the marketing manager for the Toyota Highlander SUV and have been tasked with creating an effective social media strategy. Review the discussion about interactive marketing and consider the following:
   a. Develop a social media strategy targeted at Toyota Highlander buyers incorporating all elements of interactive media.
   b. Identify specific social media you would use in the strategy and develop a social media campaign.

MANAGEMENT DECISION CASE:
Water is Life: Attracting Attention to a Cause through Guerilla Tactics

A worker in New York City is waiting for a subway train during her morning commute when she notices a paper cup dispenser hanging on the wall in the subway station. It's an unusual location for a paper cup dispenser and it is not one she has noticed any other morning (or evening for that matter) during her routine commute. Another odd aspect of the cup dispenser's location is that there is no water dispenser in the area—no water fountain, no sink, no source where someone could get a drink of water to use in the cup. In fact, the only water visible anywhere is coming from a leak in the sidewall of the commuter station that forms a small puddle on the floor before it runs into the area where the train tracks are located. On further inspection of the cup, the commuter finds these words: "Ingredients: Cholera, Hepatitis, Typhoid, Fecal Matter, Salmonella, E. coli," inviting her to "drink up." Another thing the commuter notices is a website for an organization called Water is Life, which has as its mission to provide clean drinking water, sanitation, and education programs to schools and villages in developing countries.

The out-of-place cup dispenser and the message provided on the cups provide a clear example of *guerilla marketing,* which more and more charitable organizations are using to attract attention to their cause. Guerilla marketing has been around since the mid-1980s and it involves using comparatively few resources for promoting products and services to achieve specific goals. Such tactics appeal to small businesses and charities because, if done well, much awareness can be achieved without spending large sums of money on traditional advertising campaigns. In addition, guerrilla marketing tactics can be effective because they catch consumers at unsuspecting times and places (such as the subway station) and in unusual ways when their normal "guard" against advertising is down. Think of it as a street-level intervention that sparks consumer notice.

Charitable organizations use unconventional promotional tactics to their advantage to break through the clutter and noise of all other promotional activity. Individuals are exposed to between 2,000 and 3,000 messages on a daily basis, which creates a "din" of noise for the receiver. Consequently, the sender of any message promoting a product (or cause) must be very careful to encode that message so that it communicates exactly what is intended. For example, with the cup dispenser and the simple writing on the cup, Water is Life hopes to communicate a lack of safe drinking water in many parts of the world. But since the decoding process depends heavily on the target audience it is possible that the only message communicated was that water leaking out of the subway wall was contaminated! Hence, unless the cup contains an invitation to visit the Water is Life website to learn more about its efforts to provide safe drinking water to developing countries, it is possible the target audience would not be inspired to actually take any action. That is, the consumer may become somewhat aware but not achieve interest, desire, or action toward Water is Life.

The number of nonprofit organizations has risen by over 20 percent in the last decade to well over 1.5 million in the United States, so expect more of them to experiment with reaching out to their potential donor base through guerilla and other unconventional means. As one public relations advisor recently commented, "If you don't have a good first five seconds, it's over." Guerrilla marketing is likely to be employed more often because of its low cost and the potential to go viral, thus exposing the message to perhaps millions of people through social media.

Questions for Consideration

1. What elements of the promotion mix do you think guerrilla marketing relies on the most to be successful?

2. Doritos used a guerrilla marketing campaign in which product images were projected on the sides of buildings while inviting viewers to text message their flavor preference. How do such tactics fit within an overall integrated marketing communications approach to the brand's target audience? What other IMC approaches might best complement the Doritos strategy.

3. According to the AIDA model, buyers pass through different decision processes on their way to making a decision. Assuming the cups in the dispenser contain a message to visit the organization's website, what are the promotional steps needed to take individuals through the AIDA model to the point where people are willing to donate money or their time to the cause promoted by Water is Life.

Sources: Dava Flavelle, "Marketing Outside the Box; Guerrilla Ads: Hitting the Mark, or a Shot in the Foot?" *Toronto Star*, August 22, 2009, Business section, p. B01; David Wallis, "Charities Try Provocative Ads to Attract Attention," *New York Times*, November 8, 2013, p. F8; WATERisLIFE mission, http://waterislife.com/about/water-is-life-mission/, accessed December 19, 2013.

MARKETING PLAN EXERCISE

ACTIVITY 14: Promoting Your Offering

The promotion plan is an integral part of any marketing plan, and often carries a significant portion of the marketing budget. Develop the following elements for promoting your offering:

1. Review the promotion mix elements and begin to develop goals for promotion and a promotional strategy utilizing the elements of the mix that are most appropriate for your offering.
2. Link the promotional strategy to PLC stages as well as the stages your customers will go through on the AIDA model.
3. Decide how you intend to manage promotion for the offering. Decide on outsourced elements versus elements that will be handled in-house. Establish a structure and process for promotion management.

NOTES

1. Bob Garfield, "The Post Advertising Age," *Advertising Age,* March 26, 2007.
2. "Dos Equis Moves Cinco De Mayo to May 2," *Advertising Age*, April 4, 2013, http://adage.com/article/creativity-pick-of-the-day/dos-equis-moves-cinco-de-mayo-2/240714/.
3. Don E. Schultz and Phillip J. Kitchen, "Integrated Marketing Communications in U.S. Advertising Agencies: An Exploratory Study," *Journal of Advertising Research* 37, no. 5 (September/ October 1997), pp. 7–18.
4. Tim Parry, "Get in on the Party," MultichannelMerchant.com, January 1, 2007, http://multichannelmerchant.com/crosschannel/marketing/party_2/, accessed June 19, 2008.
5. M. Chahal, "The New Word of Mouth," *Marketing Week*, August 23, 2012, www.marketingweek.co.uk/trends/the-new-word-of-mouth/4003281.article.
6. P. Rajan Varadarajan, Satish Jayachandran, and J. Chris White, "Strategic Interdependence in Organizations: Deconglomeration and Marketing Strategy," *Journal of Marketing* 65, no. 1 (January 2001), pp. 15–28.
7. Frederick E. Webster Jr., "Understanding the Relationships among Brands, Consumers, and Resellers," *Journal of the Academy of Marketing Science* 28, no. 1 (Winter 2000), pp. 17–23.
8. Emim Babakus, Ugar Yavas, Osman M. Karatepe, and Turgay Avci, "The Effect of Management Commitment to Service Quality on Employees' Affective and Performance Outcomes," *Journal of the Academy of Marketing Science* 31, no. 3 (Summer 2003), pp. 272–86.
9. C. B. Bhattacharya and Sankar Sen, "Consumer-Company Identification: A Framework for Understanding Consumers' Relationships with Companies," *Journal of Marketing* 67, no. 2 (April 2003), pp. 76–88.
10. Charles R. Taylor, George R. Franke, and Hae-Kyong Bang, "Use and Effectiveness of Billboards," *Journal of Advertising* 35, no. 4 (Winter 2006), pp. 21–34.
11. Ibid.
12. Susan Powell Mantel, Ellen Bolman Pullins, David A. Reid, and Richard E. Buehrer, "A Realistic Sales Experience: Providing Feedback by Integrating Buying, Selling, and Managing Experiences," *Journal of Personal Selling & Sales Management* 22, no. 1 (Winter 2002), pp. 33–40.
13. Bob T. Wu and Stephen J. Newell, "The Impact of Noise on Recall of Advertisements," *Journal of Marketing Theory and Practice* 11, no. 2 (Spring 2003), pp. 56–65.
14. Brian Steinberg, "NBC Turns 'Fresh Eyes' to Its Ad Sales," *The Wall Street Journal*, February 12, 2007, p. B5.
15. B. Carter, "NBC Series Saved by Delayed Viewership," *New York Times*, June 24, 2012, www.nytimes.com/2012/06/25/business/media/nbcs-smash-owes-renewal-to-power-of-delayed-viewership.html?_r=2&.
16. Yu-Shan Lin and Jun-Ying Huang, "Internet Blogs as a Tourism Marketing Medium: A Case Study," *Journal of Business Research* 59, no. 10/11 (October 2006), pp. 1201–05.
17. C. Rogers, "Chrysler 'Farmer' Ad Was a Hit—Soon It Will Be a Book," *The Wall Street Journal*, February 11, 2013, http://blogs.wsj.com/drivers-seat/2013/02/11/chrysler-farmer-ad-was-a-hit-soon-it-will-be-a-book/.
18. Thomas Reutterer, Andreas Mild, Martin Natter, and Alfred Taudes, "A Dynamic Segmentation Approach for Targeting and Customizing Direct Marketing Campaigns," *Journal of Interactive Marketing* 20, no. 3/4 (Summer/Fall 2006), pp. 43–57.

19. Subimal Chatterjee, Yong Soon Kang, and Debi Prasad Mishra, "Market Signals and Relative Preference: The Moderating Effects of Conflicting Information, Decision Focus, and Need for Cognition," *Journal of Business Research* 58, no. 10 (October 2005), pp. 1362–70.
20. Mark Burton and Steve Haggett, "Rocket PLAN," *Marketing Management* 16, no. 5 (September/October 2007), p. 32.
21. David A. Schweidel, Peter S. Fader, and Eric T. Bradlow, "Understanding Service Retention within and across Cohorts Using Limited Information," *Journal of Marketing* 72, no. 1 (January 2008), pp. 82–94.
22. Brian Wansink, Robert J. Kent, and Stephen J. Hoch, "An Anchoring and Adjustment Model for Purchase Quantity Decisions," *Journal of Marketing Research* 35, no. 1 (February 1998), pp. 71–81.
23. "Illinois State Continues Sales Curriculum Incorporating Cutco, Vector Marketing Program," *PRWeb*, March 4, 2008, www.prweb.com/releases/cutco/vector/prweb741974.htm.
24. John I. Coppett and Roy Dale Voorhees, "Telemarketing: Supplement to Field Sales," *Industrial Marketing Management* 14, no. 3 (August 1985), pp. 213–16.
25. Joo-Gim Heaney, Ronald E. Goldsmith, and Wan Jamaliah Wan, "Status Consumption among Malaysian Consumers: Exploring Its Relationships with Materialism and Attention-to-Social-Comparison-Information," *Journal of International Consumer Marketing* 17, no. 4 (2005), pp. 83–98.
26. Hae-Kyong Bang, Mary Anne Raymond, Charles R. Taylor, and Young Sook Moon, "A Comparison of Service Quality Dimensions Conveyed in Advertisements for Service Providers in the USA and Korea: A Content Analysis," *International Marketing Review* 22, no. 3 (2005), pp. 309–27.
27. Kathleen Mortimer, "Identifying the Components of Effective Service Advertisements," *Journal of Services Marketing* 22, no. 2 (2008), pp. 104–13.
28. Van Bojovic, "BMW Makes It Clear: It Is 'Designed for Driving Pleasure,'" *Branding Magazine*, February 21, 2013, www.brandingmagazine.com/2013/02/21/bmw-designed-for-driving-pleasure/.
29. E. J. Schultz, "Weight-Watchers, Slim-Fast Ditch Diet-Only Focus in Ads," *Advertising Age*, April 1, 2013, http://adage.com/article/news/weight-watchers-slim-fast-ditch-diet-focus-ads/240629/.
30. Ziad Swaidan, Mohammed Y. A. Rawwas, and Scott J. Vitell, "Culture and Moral Ideologies of African Americans," *Journal of Marketing Theory and Practice* 16, no. 2 (Spring 2008), pp. 127–37.
31. "ADL Launches Major Centennial Year Public Awareness Campaign," Anti-Defamation League, www.adl.org/press-center/press-releases/miscellaneous/adl-launches-major-centennial-campaign-imagine-a-world-without-hate.html, accessed April 5, 2013.
32. David C. Carlson and Paul McDevitt, "Budgeting Promotional Expenditures: Theory and Practice," *Managerial Finance* 11, no. 1 (1985), pp. 1–4.
33. Boonghee Yoo and Rujirutana Mandhachitara, "Estimating Advertising Effects on Sales in a Competitive Setting," *Journal of Advertising Research* 43, no. 3 (September 2003), pp. 310–21.
34. Nicolaos E. Synodinos, Charles F. Keown, and Laurence W. Jacobs, "Transnational Advertising Practices: A Survey of Leading Brand Advertisers in Fifteen Countries," *Journal of Advertising Research* 29, no. 2 (April/May 1989), pp. 43–50.
35. George M. Zinkhan, "The Marketplace, Emerging Technology and Marketing Theory," *Marketing Theory* 5, no. 1 (2005), pp. 105–16.
36. K. Woodward, "HSN Outlines an Increasingly Social and Mobile Marketing Strategy," *Internet Retailer*, November 27, 2012, www.internetretailer.com/2012/11/27/hsn-outlines-social-and-mobile-marketing-strateg.
37. T. Peters, "Klout for Business Is Only First Step to a Serious Marketing Platform: Company Could Add Social Ad Buying, Customer Data to Product," *Adweek*, March 20, 2013, www.adweek.com/news/technology/klout-business-only-first-step-serious-marketing-platform-148063.
38. Dennis Williams, "Twitter with Amex in Sync for Social Currency," *Geek Insider*, February 24, 2013, www.geekinsider.com/2013/02/24/twitter-x-amex-in-sync-for-social-currency/.
39. https://business.twitter.com/success-stories/espn.
40. Dee Gill, "Blogging Ethics 101," *Crain's Chicago Business* 30, no. 46 (2007), p. 33; and Jon Fine, "Polluting the Blogosphere," *BusinessWeek*, July 10, 2006, www.businessweek.com/magazine/content/06_28/b3992034.htm.
41. D. Kerr, "Reddit Reportedly Seeks Investors with Influence," CNET, January 9, 2013, http://news.cnet.com/8301-1023_3-57563179-93/reddit-reportedly-seeks-investors-with-influence/.
42. Rogers, "Chrysler 'Farmer' Ad Was a Hit—Soon It Will Be a Book."

CHAPTER 13

Advertising, Sales Promotion, and Public Relations

LEARNING OBJECTIVES

LO 13-1 Understand the key types of advertising and the role of the creative agency.

LO 13-2 Identify various approaches to sales promotion and how each might be used.

LO 13-3 Describe the activities and aims of public relations.

In this chapter we explore critical marketing communication tools directed at broad or mass markets—advertising, sales promotion, and public relations (PR). These are three vital elements of integrated marketing communications (IMC). In Chapter 12 you learned that advertising is a paid form of relatively less personal marketing communications, often through a mass medium to one or more target markets. To much of the general public, advertising is synonymous with marketing because advertising is a very visible side of marketing—not surprising, since advertising is one of the dominant forms of marketing communication.

Beyond advertising, marketers have additional promotional tools—sales promotion and PR—to facilitate communication with their broad target markets. Recall from Chapter 12 that sales promotion provides an inducement for an end-user consumer to buy your product or for a salesperson or someone else in the channel to sell it. It is rarely used as the sole promotional method; instead it usually augments other forms of promotion. And PR is a systematic approach to influencing attitudes, opinions, and behaviors of customers and others. PR is often executed through publicity, which is an unpaid and relatively less personal form of marketing communications usually through news stories and mentions at public events.

Let's take a look at each of these three approaches to marketing communications to broad markets in greater detail.

ADVERTISING

LO 13-1

Understand the key types of advertising and the role of the creative agency.

To most of the general public, advertising is synonymous with marketing. Advertising is what most people see as the visible side of marketing—not surprising, since the amount of money spent by firms on advertising is staggering. According to *Ad Age,* in 2012 (the most recent year for which full data are available) spending by the top 100 U.S. advertisers was an estimated $104.5 billion, up just 2.8 percent from 2011, and the smallest increase since the economic recovery began. However, this figure comes with an important caveat: these numbers track more traditional forms of advertising that are considered "measured media"—magazine, newspaper, TV, radio, outdoor, and display advertising on the Internet. Not included are so-called unmeasured media such as direct marketing, promotion, Internet paid search, social media, and others.

Who are the biggest company spenders on advertising? Exhibit 13.1 shows the top 20 U.S. advertisers and data on their total spending on advertising (measured media) in 2012. It is noteworthy that each of the top 20 U.S. advertisers operates in the *consumer* marketplace, although several also have significant B2B operations, but the key issue is that big national advertising tends to be dominated by B2C firms. Advertising is ubiquitous promotion, and because it is so visible and seemingly easily understood, many turn to advertising as their promotion mix element of first choice.

There is a danger in overrelying on advertising to the exclusion of other promotional choices. Customers can quickly and easily become bored with any given advertising campaign, a concept referred to as **advertising wearout.** This phenomenon necessitates a constant creation of new ads with new or adjusted themes, resulting in a constant churn of messages.[1] When Wendy's announced a few years ago that it was pulling its long-running campaign featuring the young girl in red-haired pigtails, it said the decision was made because the advertisements had run their course. Viewers were "over it." However, after a several-year break, in 2011 not only did Wendy return, but it was the real Wendy in the flesh—the daughter of Wendy's founder Dave Thomas. Since then, the character has morphed into a modern-looking new icon just right for the next generation of hamburger lovers. The need for constant renewal of ads is great for advertising agencies, which get paid to create them, but incredibly expensive for marketing managers.

Another problem with advertising is that beyond a certain ad spending level, diminishing returns tend to set in. That is, market share stops growing—or

EXHIBIT 13.1 | Top 20 U.S. Advertisers

Rank 2012	Rank 2011	Advertiser	Total U.S. Ad Spending in 2012 (billions)	Percentage Spending Change versus 2011
1	1	P&G	$ 4.8	−1.0
2	3	General Motors	3.1	8.9
3	4	Comcast	3.0	8.2
4	2	AT&T	2.9	−7.2
5	5	Verizon	2.4	−5.6
6	7	Ford Motor	2.3	6.3
7	9	L'Oréal	2.2	5.4
8	6	JPMorgan Chase	2.2	−11.3
9	8	American Express	2.1	−2.6
10	26	Toyota Motor	2.0	14.8
11	15	Fiat (Chrysler)	1.9	10.1
12	10	Walt Disney	1.9	−11.1
13	14	Walmart	1.8	0.0
14	12	Time Warner	1.7	−16.4
15	19	Target	1.7	4.0
16	13	Johnson & Johnson	1.7	−14.9
17	11	Pfizer	1.6	−21.0
18	17	Bank of America	1.6	−5.3
19	20	Macy's	1.6	6.4
20	23	Berkshire Hathaway	1.6	13.1
Total			$ 44.1	

Source: Reprinted with permission (100 Leading National Advertisers 2012, *Ad Age*). Copyright Crain Communications Inc.

even begins to decline—despite continued spending. This effect is known as the **advertising response function** and leads marketing managers to rely more heavily on advertising early in the product life cycle (PLC), as well as to focus on it during target customers' initial stages of the AIDA model that we presented in Chapter 12.[2] Spending higher dollars, in this case on advertising, on the promotional goals of *informing* and *persuading* is likely to pay back at a higher level than spending equal dollars on the promotional goal of *reminding*.

Despite these challenges, advertising is not only a potentially highly effective promotional vehicle (when applied properly), but it is also a part of the very fabric of the U.S. culture and, increasingly, of the global culture. The craze associated with the annual Super Bowl advertisements is a testament to the power of advertising to excite the masses.

Types of Advertising

There are two major types of advertising: institutional advertising and product advertising. The choice of which approach to use depends on the promotional goals and the situation.

Institutional Advertising The goal of **institutional advertising** is to promote an industry, company, family of brands, or some other issues broader than a specific product. Institutional advertising is often used to inform or remind, but to a lesser degree to persuade. Earlier you read about the concept of corporate identity in the context of the sender of communication.[3] Many customers pay a great deal of attention to the organization behind an advertising message, how socially responsible the company is, and what values it stands for. Institutional advertising can help build and enhance a corporate brand or family brand. For instance, P&G runs institutional ads about a charitable cause it supports—the Special Olympics. Certain families of P&G brands (Crest, Pampers, etc.) generally are featured as well. Such an approach helps build the corporate identity of P&G and can enhance its brands through positive association.

Sometimes entire industries will run institutional advertising. For example, the California Milk Advisory Board runs a major national television campaign featuring "happy cows." The Board's website has provided a selection process for voting on the next cow "stars" for commercials, complete with audition videos (and the requisite "bloopers"), and recently heavily promoted "Ice Cream Month" as a way to increase dairy purchases. Their logo of "Real California Milk" is intended to encourage consumers to seek out California-produced brands, a bit like the famous "Intel Inside" branding on computers. Consider these additional examples of industry-sponsored institutional advertising, manifest through catchy taglines:

- Cotton, the fabric of our lives.
- The incredible edible egg.
- Pork, the other white meat.
- Beef, it's what's for dinner.

Institutional advertising is a particularly smart strategy during the early phases of the PLC and AIDA model in that it can enhance feelings of trust in potential customers with a message that is broader than just "buy me." Institutional advertising is also often employed when a company or industry has a PR problem to dig out from. Recall from Chapter 9 that when JetBlue experienced its operational meltdown at JFK International Airport in February 2007, leaving hundreds of passengers stranded on their planes on the tarmac for up to 12 hours during a snowstorm, within a few days the firm had already begun a massive service recovery effort, including an institutional advertising campaign hawking its commitment to a new Passengers' Bill of Rights.

One area of advertising other types of promotion that garners a fair amount of attention is the targeting of teenagers and children. Ethical Dimension 13 poses some interesting issues for consideration in this regard.

Product Advertising The vast majority of advertising is **product advertising,** designed to increase purchase of a specific offering (good or service). Three principal types of product advertising are available: pioneering advertising, competitive advertising, and comparative advertising. The decision on which to employ often depends on the stage of the PLC.

Taco Bell does a great job of product advertising by showing appealing photos of its food surrounded by bright colors.

ETHICAL DIMENSION 13

The Resourceful Teen and Promotional Ethics

Today's teenagers are more plugged in than any other generation in history. Facebook, text messaging, and a never-ending cacophony of marketing communications enable teens to connect with each other and experience marketing messages virtually nonstop. More than any other generation, teens have made instant communication and, more broadly, an online lifestyle a significant part of their world. Their online experiences coupled with the ability of new media to track and store user information offer innovative opportunities for marketers to target advertising messages and monitor the results. Marketers are empowered as never before by the ability to track individual activities, analyze large amounts of data (big data), and then develop unique, individually targeted messaging and offerings to teens. For example, Facebook allows advertisers to create display ads using information from individual users that is posted in their profiles.

Given this environment, two critical questions for marketers to teens are (1) How much information should we collect and use to develop marketing messaging and (2) What are the most appropriate online marketing strategies from both an ethical and a business strategy perspective? Although the Children's Online Privacy Protection Act (COPPA) requires marketers to get parental consent to collect personal information on anyone younger than 13, no law regulates advertising or direct marketing to individuals over the age of 13. Marketing managers face difficult and strategic questions as they learn to operate in this brave new world of marketing to teenagers.

A key issue for both marketers and teenagers is the degree to which companies should use information that is readily available online. Private details about teens are available for analysis, but how much and to what degree should marketers use the information to create individual-specific promotional messaging? In addition, much of the individual data is self-generated (i.e., posted on social media sites by consumers) and there are few checks and balances to validate the information. Companies have the ability to connect a sophisticated understanding of teenagers with an individual's personal data to develop highly targeted marketing communications.

How reliable and valid is the posted information? People on the Internet often make themselves a few years younger (or older in the case of teenagers), several inches taller, and maybe a few pounds lighter. Of most concern, today's resourceful teenagers can create identities that allow them access to age-restricted websites such as eBay, which requires a buyer or seller to be 18. Because of this, marketers end up presenting messaging to youngsters that may not be appropriate for the age group—for example, someone under 21 may indicate a different age online and receive liquor or beer advertising.

There's no doubt that teenagers appreciate brands and marketing and at the same time marketers appreciate greater access to those teens. On the surface, it would appear easier than ever to find and speak to the teen market, but things are not always as they seem.

Ethical Perspective

1. **Marketers:** Should a marketer be allowed to use information from an individual's social networking profile like Facebook to develop promotional messages? Is targeted messaging to teens based on analysis of personal information ethical?
2. **Teenagers:** What is your opinion of teenagers providing false information to gain access to websites restricted by age or some other characteristic? How much of this is the marketer's responsibility and how much responsibility falls to the parents?

Pioneering advertising stimulates primary demand. Hence, it tends to be used during the introductory and early growth stages of the PLC when it is important to gain purchase by innovators and early adopters. From an AIDA model perspective, pioneering advertising seeks to gain awareness and initial interest. Marketing managers introducing new products almost always focus advertising on this form, letting potential customers know what the product is and how it is used. The appeal is usually more rational than emotional.[4]

Marketing managers employ **competitive advertising** to build sales of a specific brand. Here, the appeal often shifts to more emotion and the goal is persuasion as well as providing information. Building a positive customer attitude toward the brand is a key component of competitive advertising, and this approach is heavily used during the growth and early maturity stages of the PLC. Triggering the desire and action stages of the AIDA model is a focus of the message.[5]

In **comparative advertising,** two or more brands are directly compared against each other on certain attributes.[6] Comparative advertising is common during the maturity stage of the PLC, as attempts at shaking out weaker competitors are generally part of a marketing strategy. Obviously, a key to successfully employing this approach is having one or more legitimate claims about your brand that put it in a favorable position against the competition. For example, Samsung has done a great job of whittling away at Apple's market share in the smartphone category through its strong comparative approach to touting the advantages of its Galaxy line over the iPhone.

Comparative advertising works especially well when you are not No. 1 in a product category because you can put the market leader on the defensive. Examples of comparative advertising by a No. 2 brand include Pepsi versus Coke, Avis versus Hertz, and Burger King versus McDonald's. However, it is a very risky advertising approach when you *are* the top brand. Customers may perceive that you are on the defensive, when in reality you are not. The psychology of a top brand stooping to comparisons with a lower brand usually does not make sense. Most experts recommend avoiding comparative advertising if your brand is the leader.

This comparative ad by Reddi Wip takes on rival CoolWhip by pointing out that Reddi Wip always uses real dairy cream, not hydrogenated oil.

Advertising spots featuring humorous hyperbole, which are exaggerated statements or claims not meant to be taken literally, are entertaining for consumers, but do they serve their purpose? DIRECTV aired a series of "It's more annoying than" spots to discuss its services in comparison to its rivals on the cable TV side. The spots featured situations such as getting attacked by turtles, clowns, and a pedestrian bothered by an inflatable balloon. Advertising often makes overstated promises or exaggeration of a product or service (technically referred to as "puffery"). There are regulations and cultural norms that restrain advertising from wilder or inaccurate claims. Although hyperbole ads can be clever and funny, little research exists on the actual effectiveness of such advertising. Though the audience may enjoy the spot, liking may not necessarily translate into purchase, let alone long-term loyal customer relationships.[7]

Advertising Execution and Media Types

In selecting which types of advertising media to employ, the marketing manager must consider reach and frequency. **Reach** measures the percentage of individuals in a defined target market that are exposed to an ad during a specified time period. **Frequency** measures the average number of times a person in the target market is exposed to the message. Obviously, the greater the reach and the higher the frequency, the more expensive the overall advertising campaign will be. As you might imagine, because advertising budgets are not unlimited, trade-offs are usually required in balancing reach and frequency within budgetary constraints. Goals are generally set and budgeted based on a desired level of reach and frequency. During the course of a campaign, the marketing manager

The Role of the Creative Agency

Advertising and PR are among the most outsourced functions in marketing, and with good reason. Most organizations naturally focus on their own product or service expertise; thus, developing sufficient internal expertise in the creative side of promotion would be extremely costly and could reduce their focus on their core business. For many marketing managers, the relationship with their firm's creative agency is an important part of the job. Agencies vary , with some being specialized firms that focus on an industry or on a particular area of promotion, such as print media or product placement. Others are full-service shops that manage all aspects of their clients' integrated marketing communications (IMC) strategy. Because of the proliferation of an IMC approach in many firms today, the trend is toward more full-service creative agencies and even toward integration of marketing planning and branding services with traditional agency tasks. Almost always a client is billed an hourly rate, plus the costs of media purchases.

Over the past several years, another major trend has been the development of strategic partnerships between creative agencies and full-service web builders. For many marketers, the website is the core of their marketing communications strategy. Often a new-product introduction or rebranding initiative focuses largely on the website, with print and other media types used primarily to drive customers to the web. Some of the very largest agencies have even established their own comprehensive web operations and are able to perform a full gamut of web services for clients including website building and maintenance, hosting, management of direct e-mail correspondence with customers, and management of the client's overall CRM system.

It is likely that the importance of the outsourced full-service marketing agency will continue to grow into the next decade. As marketing itself becomes more strategic within organizations, more and more of the tactical or programmatic aspects of marketing that were formerly handled in-house will be outsourced. In such a scenario, the importance of the marketing manager role is heightened, as that individual will be the frontline person in a firm that is charged with managing all aspects of the outsourced agency relationship.

With the advent of Big Data and CRM, new challenges have emerged with direct e-mail marketing. Quantity and complexity of information may result in a retailer having data on your preferences and buying habits that may not be reflected in the e-mails you receive. Many organizations seem overwhelmed about Big Data and entire marketing conferences are organized to teach firms how to effectively use it to improve customer engagement, the customer experience, content targeting, and predictive analytics. Learning the ins and outs of handling Big Data needs to be a top priority for all marketers today, and in no area of marketing is the potential for benefit higher than in advertising and promotion.[9]

SALES PROMOTION

LO 13-2

Identify various approaches to sales promotion and how each might be used.

Sales promotion was defined in Chapter 12 as a promotion mix element that provides an inducement for an end-user consumer to buy a product or for a salesperson or someone else in the channel to sell it. Sales promotion is designed to augment other forms of promotion and is rarely used alone. This is because sales promotion initiatives rely on other media forms such as advertising and direct or interactive marketing as a communication vehicle. Think of sales promotion as prompting a "buy now" response; that is, it is squarely aimed at the action (behavior) stage of the AIDA model.

Sales promotion can be aimed directly at end-user consumers, or it can be targeted to members of a channel on which a firm relies to sell product. In the latter case, sales promotion is an important element of a push strategy. One additional potential target for sales promotion is a firm's own sales force. Bonus payments, prizes, trips, and other incentives to induce a salesperson to push one product over another are forms of internal sales promotion. Salesperson incentives will be discussed further in Chapter 14. For now, let's look at sales promotion to consumers and to channel members.

During the economic downturn many consumers came to really appreciate deals and value-added extras. Weening them away from these goodies post-recession is proving to be difficult! Chase Bank has focused on adding value for its small business owners by enhancing its loyalty rewards for the Ink credit card, which has special small business-centric features. It offers owners restriction-free travel, the chance to earn more points faster, and cash back—three highly sought-after benefits. To put its money where its mouth is for the small business owner, a part of the market that can be easily overlooked by other big banks, Chase has increased lending by over 70 percent and given credit to over 300,000 small businesses.[10]

Sales Promotion to Consumers

When a firm is looking to gain product trial, spike distribution, shore up sagging quarterly sales, or rekindle interest in a waning brand, sales promotion can be an appropriate choice for investment of promotional dollars. Exhibit 13.4 summarizes nine popular consumer sales promotion approaches.

As with most promotional elements, marketing managers rarely select only one form of consumer sales promotion for execution. Many of the sales promotion options complement each other and all are potentially complementary of the overall promotion mix. One potential downside to sales promotion is a tendency by some firms and industries to overrely on sales promotion to bring in sales on a regular basis. This occurs because of sales promotion's power to elicit an actual purchase. Consider the proliferation of rebates on new-car purchases. Car manufacturers essentially "train" car shoppers not to look for a new vehicle unless a rebate is being offered. Ultimately, if sales promotion becomes institutionalized in such a manner, firms simply build in a hefty cushion into the "everyday" price of the product, thus negating any real benefit to the customer of the promotion. Overuse of sales promotion is not a good promotional strategy and can lead to a general cheapening of brand image and distrust by customers.

In this sales promotion, Michelin offers a $70 reward card to customers who purchase any set of four new passenger or light truck tires.

Sales Promotion to Channel Members

Several sales promotion approaches are available for use with members of a firm's channel of distribution. Typically, these channel members would be distributors, brokers, agents, and other forms of middlemen.

EXHIBIT 13.4 | Consumer Sales Promotion Options

Sales Promotion Approach	Description	Comments	Example
Product sampling	A physical sample of the product is given to consumers.	Excellent for inducing trial. Sample can be received by mail or in a store.	Gillette sends out a free razor to induce switching from an older model.
Coupons	An instant price reduction at point of sale, available in print media, online, or in-store.	Coupon usage is generally down among consumers. Still a good inducement to "buy now."	Inside the free razor from Gillette is a coupon for $1.00 off the purchase of a pack of blades.
Rebates	A price reduction for purchase of a specific product during a specific time period.	Possibly instant at point of sale, but more frequently requires submission and delay in processing.	Sharp offers a $100 rebate through Best Buy for purchase of a flat-screen television during February.
Contests and sweepstakes	Appeal to consumers' sense of fun and luck. May suggest a purchase but legally must be offered without a purchase requirement.	Contests require some element of skill beyond mere chance. Sweepstakes are pure chance.	McDonald's famous Monopoly game—the more you eat, the more you play (and vice versa!).
Premiums	Another product offered free for purchasing the brand targeted in the promotion.	Gives the customer a bonus for purchase. Products may be complementary or unrelated.	Burger King offers the latest movie hero toy with purchase of a meal.
Multiple-purchase offers	Incentive to buy more of the brand at a special price.	Typically "buy 2, get 1 free" or similar.	Centrum Vitamin offer—buy a bottle of 100, get an extra mini-bottle of 20.
Point-of-purchase materials	Displays set up in a retail store to support advertising and remind customers to purchase.	Especially good at driving purchase toward a featured brand in a product category at the store aisle.	Dr. Scholl's FootMapping Center kiosk at Walgreens.
Product placements	Having product images appear in movies, on television, or in photographs in print media.	Strong connections with the show or story, as well as to any associated celebrities.	Apple appeared in 8 of 34 Number 1 films in 2012.
Loyalty programs	Accumulate points for doing business with a company. Designed to strengthen long-term customer relationships and reduce switching.	Especially popular among the airline and hospitality industry. Credit card providers often facilitate.	American Airlines AAdvantage program, facilitated by Citi and MasterCard.

The purpose is to stimulate them to push your product, resulting in more sales in the channel and ultimately to end users.

Trade shows can be a very fruitful form of sales promotion. A **trade show** is an industry- or company-sponsored event in which booths are set up for the dissemination of information about offerings to members of a channel. Sometimes actual sales occur at a trade show, but often the primary purpose is promotion to attendees. Sales leads are obtained and passed along to the firm's sales organization for follow-up after the trade show.[11]

Another form of sales promotion to a channel is **cooperative advertising and promotion.** In cooperative advertising, a manufacturer provides special incentive money to channel members for certain performances such as running advertisements for one of the manufacturer's brands or doing product demonstrations with potential customers. The idea of cooperative advertising and promotion is that the manufacturer shares promotional expenses with channel members in the process of marketing to end-user consumers.[12]

Sometimes money is made available for a channel member in the form of a special payment for selling certain products, making a large order, or other specific performance. This form of channel-focused sales promotion is called an **allowance.** In addition, as with the consumer market, contests and displays with point-of-purchase materials are also frequently used as sales promotion approaches in the channel.[13]

PUBLIC RELATIONS (PR)

LO 13-3

Describe the activities and aims of public relations.

In Chapter 12 we defined public relations (PR) as a systematic approach to influencing attitudes, opinions, and behaviors of customers and others. PR is often executed through **publicity,** which is an unpaid and relatively less personal form of marketing communications usually through news stories and mentions at public events.[14]

PR is a specialized field. Usually, undergraduate and graduate marketing programs do not include training in PR. Many PR professionals receive specialized training in communication, and outstanding PR people are highly sought after. Some firms have in-house PR departments, while others outsource much or all of the PR function to external agencies. Major responsibilities of a PR department might include any of the following activities:

- Gaining product publicity and buzz.
- Securing event sponsorships (for the company and its brands).
- Managing a crisis.
- Managing and writing news stories.
- Facilitating community affairs.
- Managing relationships with members of the local, national, and global media (media relations).
- Serving as organizational spokesperson.
- Educating consumers.
- Lobbying and governmental affairs.
- Handling investor relations.

However, few PR departments perform all of these functions; some of the above functions are often spread across other areas of a firm, such as investor relations to the finance department and lobbying and governmental affairs to the legal department.

We'll focus on the three core functions of PR that are most closely aligned with the role of the marketing manager: gaining product publicity and buzz, securing event sponsorships, and crisis management.

Gaining Product Publicity and Buzz

Especially when it comes to new product offerings, gaining publicity in news outlets and other public forums can provide a major boost to sales. During the introductory phase of the PLC, communication of information is a central promotional goal. The most credible and trusted information sources for potential customers are those that write or tell about a product for free. Newspaper and magazine articles, web postings and blogs, social marketing websites, news stories on television and radio—all of these forms of communication can be cultivated through an active PR program. Many new products have benefited from the initial awareness generated by a well-placed story in a publication or on a website frequented by targeted customers.

Although the media employed are free, by no means is the process of securing the story placements free. In fact, PR can account for a great deal of money in a promotion budget due to the work hours required to constantly be writing stories and cultivating media outlets. But the payoff on that investment can be substantial due to the buzz generated among everyday consumers about a brand. **Buzz,** or word-of-mouth communication, is consumer-to-consumer communication generated about a brand in the marketplace. The impact of buzz is not limited to current customers or even potential customers. When buzz about a brand hits the marketplace and especially when it sweeps through social media, it can quickly become a cultural phenomenon. This is a key reason why, as you read in Chapter 12, so many firms today are shifting much of their marketing communications to New Media!

One way to gain media attention is to tie your promotion to a topic people are interested in. Recently, corporate social responsibility has become a topic of increased interest to the general public. Kellogg's partnered with Action for Healthy Kids to announce the "Share Your Breakfast" campaign. The aim is to share 1 million breakfasts with kids across the country who would otherwise go without. Senior Vice President of Marketing Doug Van De Velde stated, "At Kellogg's, we believe a great breakfast, like a bowl of cereal with milk, can lead to a great day. Unfortunately many children do not have access to this important meal, which is why our partnership with Action for Healthy Kids and the support of people across the country are so critical. Together we can make a difference and help ensure kids start the day strong." The company gained national attention for this campaign as congressional leaders in Washington, D.C., officially celebrated National Breakfast Week.[15]

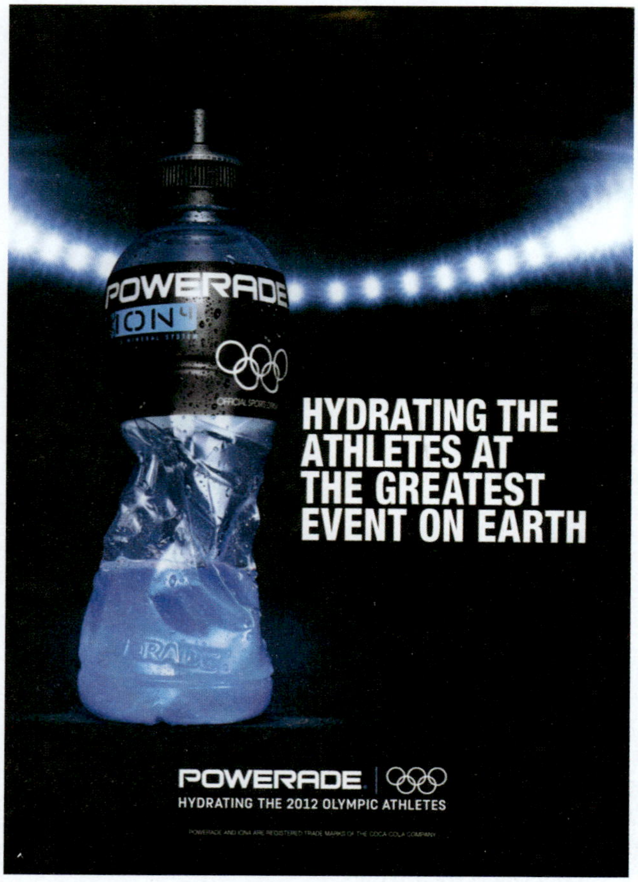

One of the world's biggest sponsorship opportunities is the Olympics.

Securing Event Sponsorships

Event sponsorships, having your brand and company associated with events in the sports, music, arts, and other entertainment communities, can add tremendous brand equity and also provide substantial exposure with the right target customers. Event sponsorships have become a mainstay of promotional strategy. A huge success story for marketers in event sponsorship is NASCAR, which appeals to millions of loyal and passionate racing fans. Consumers transfer the loyalty and passion about NASCAR directly to the brands represented by the sponsorships. No wonder NASCAR cars are referred to as "speeding billboards."[16]

Closely related to event sponsorship is issue sponsorship, in which a firm and its brands connect with a cause or issue that is especially important to its customers. Ever since the movie *Super Size Me* railed on McDonald's unhealthy menu items, the venerable chain has been under fire for not taking a lead in nutrition education. In 2012, the firm got major kudos when it decided to take a stand by posting the calorie counts of all items right on the menu boards. Sure, you can still eat your burger and fries there, but at least consumers can now compare those calories with the counts of several less-fattening items now available. Like publicity, the right sponsorships can generate positive buzz in the marketplace that enhances brand image.

Deloitte and the British Paralympic Association (BPA) have had a long-standing relationship. Their association began in 2006, with the development of Parasport, a website to provide individuals with information on disability sports and locations to play them. During the London 2012 Games, the organizations partnered to support the Paralympics UK team, including fund-raising through Deloitte's "Ride across Britain." Ride across Britain has raised over £1 million since 2010. CEO of BPA Tim Hollingsworth said, "Deloitte is a fantastic long term supporter of BPA and we are delighted that we will continue to work together. Their support in the buildup to London 2012 truly made a difference both in how we were able to support the team and how we are able to leverage the inspiration of the games to promote opportunities at grassroots levels. They are a great partner for any business and so we are really pleased that they will continue to be a part of our Paralympic family through Rio 2016."[17]

Crisis Management

Crisis management is a planned, coordinated approach for disseminating information during times of emergency and for handling the effects of unfavorable publicity.[18] When Hurricane Charley hit Orlando, Florida, in 2004, the Orlando Utility Commission (OUC), Orlando's main electric provider, mobilized its crisis management team immediately, putting into action a plan team members had practiced many times. Although power was out for some residents for more than a week, customer feedback on how OUC handled the crisis was far superior to that of other utilities and governmental entities in the region. Roseanne Harrington, vice president for marketing, communications, community relations, and web strategy at OUC—The Reliable One, attributes the positive customer attitude to constant updates provided to patrons, being truthful and realistic in setting expectations for return of service (not overpromising), and diligent attention to getting customers back in service as quickly as possible—hence, "The Reliable One" tagline that the firm proudly communicates. All firms should have a crisis management plan in place for contingencies that are relevant to their industry and customers.

SUMMARY

Advertising is a paid form of relatively less personal marketing communications, often through a mass medium to one or more target markets. Two major forms of advertising are institutional and product advertising. For marketing managers, creative agencies play an important role due to the proliferation of outsourcing of advertising initiatives in firms. A variety of types of advertising media are available—a key to success is knowing when and how to apply each type of those approaches. Sales promotion is a promotion mix element that provides an inducement for an end-user consumer to buy a product or for a salesperson or someone else in the channel to sell it. Thus, sales promotion is relevant in both B2C and B2B settings, but the approaches used are quite different between the two. Sales promotion is designed to augment other forms of promotion and is rarely used alone. Public relations (PR) is a systematic approach to influencing attitudes, opinions, and behaviors of customers and others. PR is often executed through publicity, which is an unpaid and relatively less personal form of marketing communications usually through news stories and mentions at public events. Buzz, or word-of-mouth communication, is the consumer-to-consumer communication generated about a brand in the marketplace.

KEY TERMS

advertising wearout 397
advertising response function 398
institutional advertising 399
product advertising 399
pioneering advertising 400
competitive advertising 400
comparative advertising 401
reach 401
frequency 401
advertising execution 402
clutter 402
trade show 406
cooperative advertising and promotion 406
allowance 407
publicity 407
buzz 408
event sponsorship 408
crisis management 409

APPLICATION QUESTIONS

1. Consider the concept of advertising wearout.
   a. What is advertising wearout?
   b. What do you think are some causes of the wearout?
   c. Come up with as many ads as you can that, for you, are "worn out"? Can you recall how long each ad interested you before wearout began to set in?
2. Review Exhibit 13.1 on the Top 20 U.S. Advertisers.
   a. Look at those whose advertising went down by double digits from the prior year. Speculate about what might have caused those advertisers' expenditures to decline.
   b. Do the same analysis of those whose advertising went up by double digits from the prior year. What do you suppose might have caused each to go up?
3. Review the Common Approaches to Advertising Execution (Exhibit 13.2) and Pros and Cons of Key Advertising Media (Exhibit 13.3). Review some ads in any three of the seven different types of media identified, watching for examples of the different execution approaches.
   a. Make notes about the ads you reviewed and the different types of media execution you witnessed. Which ads do you think were the most effective? Why?

b. For the same ads, based on the chapter's list of pros and cons for each, identify specific examples of ads for which one or more of the pros and cons apply.

c. Share your findings with another student or with the class.

4. Exhibit 13.4 presents some of the most common consumer sales promotion approaches. Select any three of the approaches and think of a purchase you have made in response to each. How important was the availability of the sales promotion to your ultimate decision to buy?

   a. Crisis management is a very important function of any type of organization including for-profit firms, nonprofits, governmental entities, and others. Identify with an example of an organization that faced a crisis of some type that was highly publicized. This could be a product recall that challenged a firm, a management or financial scandal, a natural disaster faced by a governmental body or charitable agency, or any other such issue.

   b. How did the organization address the crisis? What specifically did they do once it was evident a crisis was afoot?

   c. Give your opinion of how they handled the crisis. What would recommend that they could have done better?

MANAGEMENT DECISION CASE: Advertising to Gain or Keep Market Share in the Hypercompetitive Insurance Space

When you think about it, insurance is a product that most people would just as soon avoid, as the basic purpose of the product is to protect a consumer from some type of harm (whether a hurricane in Florida or a fender bender on the 405 in LA). The big job of the insurance marketer is to convince consumers that they not only *need* it, but that they *want* it! Thus, if you watch television or engage with other forms of media, you no doubt know that insurance companies are some of the biggest spenders on advertising—did you know that GEICO, Progressive, State Farm, and Allstate all rank in ad spending ahead of consumer product giants like Budweiser, Coca-Cola, and Home Depot? In fact, ad spending among auto insurers has increased 60 percent just since 2007. Because of this huge investment in ad spending, importance is heightened that insurers get it right and experience a return on advertising investment.

What does it take to get insurance advertising right? In the auto insurance market, in recent years the answer to that question apparently is humor. All of the companies listed above use a humorous approach to execute their advertising strategy. GEICO is the humor king, with the familiar gecko and his amorphous accent, Maxwell the pig (his favorite line—"Wheeee"), and the "happier than" ads showing such things as an animated camel happily proclaiming to office cubicle dwellers that it's "hump" day or a body builder happy to be directing traffic at a busy city intersection. Progressive has the ubiquitous Flo as a spokesperson helping customers name their own price. State Farm has featured Green Bay Packers quarterback Aaron Rodgers and friends making sure you get your discount double check, while Allstate's "Mayhem" line of commercials shows all kinds of calamities that their insurance will cover. And who doesn't know that "Nationwide is on your side"? J. K. Simmons (you know, the guy from *Law & Order, Spider-Man, Juno, The Closer, I Love You, Man . . .*) appears in the role of Professor Nathanial Burke, the advice-doling academic in Farmers Insurance Group's "University of Farmers" campaign in which he teaches prospective Farmers agents about the dangers lurking just around the corner—laundry fires, hailstones, flying farm animals—which are played out in rather over-the-top fashion for your viewing amusement. Finally, Liberty Mutual's line of "Human" (thank you, Human League) commercials show people making mistakes leading to property damage that a Liberty Mutual claims representative is more than happy to correct.

Despite the overwhelming rush to insurance humor, some firms actually have decided to buck the trend and go with a different executional style. In a recent twist, Nationwide has shifted a good portion of its ad dollars into its "Join the Nation" campaign using a slice-of-life style to generate an emotional connection with the company. They provide a special website where folks can "join the Nation." Another company, USAA, has a reputation for catering to military personnel, veterans, and their families. In USAA's first-ever national advertising campaign, they used real customers and a mood-based appeal to set a more serious tone. The implication is that buying an insurance product is a serious decision and one that impacts greatly a person's family members. These two approaches set a stark contrast to the majority of "wacky" humor insurance ads like Maxwell and Flo.

Much advertising, no matter what type, has as one of its goals the communication of a message designed to persuade people to consider the company, its brand, and its products when making a purchase decision. Unfortunately, in the insurance world, it is extremely difficult to get customers to change from one provider to an other. Nationwide has lost 9 percent of its market share since 2009 despite spending roughly $200 million annually on advertising. That's a lot of investment for negative results. Some industry experts estimate that only about one in ten drivers actually switches car insurance policies after a big ad push. The reality is that many people doing business with more traditional insurers like State Farm, Farmers Insurance Group, and Allstate have a relationship with their current agent—a real person whom they know by name and talk to in person—making it difficult to decide to break up that relationship and change firms. As a result, it's much easier to simply renew your existing policy when the statement arrives in the mail. One huge exception is USAA—who, by the way, does 100 percent of its business by phone or online—which has seen an 8 percent increase in market share since beginning its most recent advertising campaign. In this hypercompetitive market, the challenge going forward for all insurance companies will be to avoid losing market share, and hopefully gain a little share, while maximizing the effectiveness of their ad spending.

Questions for Consideration

1. What types of advertising are being used by these insurance companies? Pick two of the insurance companies listed, go online and review their current ad campaign, describe their ads, and then indicate if they are using product, institutional, pioneering, or comparative advertising. Be sure to justify your selection.
2. Many of the ads for insurance referred to in the case are primarily transmitted to the target audience using television as the medium. However, the proliferation of DVRs means that fewer people are actually watching the ads in real time and instead are fast-forwarding through them to get to the show content. With that in mind, what other media do you recommend that these companies use to reach their target audience? That is, how should they *integrate* the marketing communications?
3. Take a closer look at State Farm. What advertising strategy do you recommend it follow to distinguish itself from its competitors? Be sure you discuss the type of advertising, the executional style, and the type of media along with a justification for your choices.

Source: Gary Strauss, "The Joke's on Insurers; Funny Ads, Cute Critters Aren't Exactly Paying Off, so Expect Some Changes," *USA Today*, July 26, 2012 Money section, p. 1B.

MARKETING PLAN EXERCISE

Activity 15: Building the Promotional Elements

Building on Activity 14 in the last chapter, continue to build your promotion plan as an integral part of your marketing plan.

1. What approaches to advertising will you take? Select and justify the media types to be used and discuss how you will execute each.
2. Make a decision on whether some forms of sales promotion will be part of your promotion plan to consumers and/or channel members. If so, select the sales promotion approaches you will employ and justify each.
3. Develop your PR plan.
4. Decide how you intend to manage promotion for the offering. Decide on outsourced elements versus elements that will be handled in-house. Establish a structure and process for promotion management.

NOTES

1. Margaret Henderson Blair, "An Empirical Investigation of Advertising Wearin and Wearout," *Journal of Advertising Research* 40, no. 6 (November/December 2000), pp. 95–100.
2. John R. Hauser and Steven M. Shugan, "Defensive Marketing Strategies," *Marketing Science* 27, no. 1 (January/February 2008), pp. 88–112.
3. Janas Sinclair and Tracy Irani, "Advocacy Advertising for Biotechnology," *Journal of Advertising* 34, no. 3 (Fall 2005), pp. 59–63.
4. Glen L. Urban, Theresa Carter, Steven Gaskin, and Zofia Mucha, "Market Share Rewards to Pioneering Brands: An Empirical Analysis and Strategic Implications," *Management Science* 32, no. 6 (June 1986), pp. 645–59.
5. Peter J. Danaher, André Bonfrer, and Sanjay Dhar, "The Effect of Competitive Advertising Interference on Sales for Packaged Goods," *Journal of Marketing Research* 45, no. 2 (April 2008), pp. 211–25.
6. Chingching Chang, "The Relative Effectiveness of Comparative and Noncomparative Advertising: Evidence for Gender Differences in Information Processing Strategies," *Journal of Advertising* 36, no. 1 (Spring 2007), pp. 21–35.
7. Jonathan Salem Baskin, "Hyperbole in an Ad Makes an Impression, but Does It Work?," *Advertising Age,* April 3, 2013, http://adage.com/article/cmo-strategy/hyperbole-work-advertising/240658/.
8. J. Berkowitz, "Do You Lean Left or Right? Exploring the Explosive Rivalry between Twix Bars," *Fast Company: Co.CREATE,* July 16, 2012, www.fastcocreate.com/1681193/do-you-lean-left-or-right-exploring-the-explosive-rivalry-between-twix-bars.
9. R. Salkowitz, "How Big Data Makes Sloppy Marketing Look Dumber," *Fast Company,* March 12, 2013, www.fastcompany.com/3006858/how-big-data-makes-sloppy-marketing-look-even-dumber.
10. "Ink from Chase Enhances Rewards Program for Small Business Cardholders," *MarketWatch,* November 28, 2011, www.marketwatch.com/story/ink-from-chase-enhances-rewards-program-for-small-business-cardholders-2011-11-28.
11. Li Ling-yee, "The Effects of Firm Resources on Trade Show Performance: How Do Trade Show Marketing Processes Matter?," *Journal of Business & Industrial Marketing* 23, no. 1 (2008), pp. 35–47.
12. Salma Karray and Georges Zaccour, "Could Co-op Advertising Be a Manufacturer's Counterstrategy to Store Brands?," *Journal of Business Research* 59, no. 9 (September 2006), pp. 1008–15.
13. Sang Yong Kim and Richard Staelin, "Manufacturer Allowances and Retailer Pass-through Rates in a Competitive Environment," *Marketing Science* 18, no. 1 (1999), pp. 59–77.
14. Hyun Seung Jin, Jaebeom Suh, and D. Todd Donavan, "Salient Effects of Publicity in Advertised Brand Recall and Recognition: The List-Strength Paradigm," *Journal of Advertising* 37, no. 1 (Spring 2008), pp. 45–57.
15. "Kellogg's Rallies Americans to Share the Power of Their Breakfast," *PR Newswire,* March 5, 2012, www.prnewswire.com/news-releases/kelloggs-rallies-americans-to-share-the-power-of-their-breakfast-141408843.html.
16. "Win Sunday, Sell Monday," *LoganRacing.com,* www.loganracing.com/Marketing/NASCAR_General.html, accessed June 10, 2008.
17. "Deloitte Confirms Another 4 Years of Deloitte Rides across Britain," Deloitte, February 27, 2013, www.deloitte.com/view/en_GB/uk/news/newsreleases/d2b4fbe643a1d310VgnVCM3000003456f70aRCRD.htm.
18. Joseph Eric Massey and John P. Larsen, "Qualitative Research—Case Studies—Crisis Management in Real Time: How to Successfully Plan for and Respond to a Crisis," *Journal of Promotion Management* 12, no. 3/4 (2006), pp. 63–97.

CHAPTER 14

Personal Selling and Direct Marketing

LEARNING OBJECTIVES

LO 14-1 Understand the role of personal selling in an integrated marketing communications strategy.

LO 14-2 Learn the process of relationship selling.

LO 14-3 Understand the major job responsibilities of sales management.

LO 14-4 Identify the role of direct marketing in integrated marketing communications (IMC).

This chapter will focus on personal communication methods—specifically, personal selling and direct marketing. These tools have the potential to connect the company with the customer as well as encourage the customer to interact with the company in a way that significantly strengthens the relationship between the two. However, if managed poorly, personal selling and direct marketing can profoundly harm the relationship with the customer. Companies know that personal communication is critical to long-term success and dedicate resources to ensure the quality of the relationship between them and the customer.

TOWARD A MORE PERSONAL COMMUNICATION WITH THE CUSTOMER

Interactive communications enable companies to create a conversation with their customers. As we discussed in Chapter 12, these tools offer some powerful advantages over traditional integrated marketing communications, while still connecting to broader IMC strategies. Advertising, sales promotion, and public relations are essential IMC tools, but unidirectional for the most part. In other words, the company communicates with the customer, but the customer has limited ability to provide feedback. Companies know how important it is to communicate directly with the customer and, in turn, receive direct feedback from the customer. Effective integrated marketing communications therefore incorporates personal communication elements.

Mindshare, an advertising agency, has launched a mobile application to help managers stay connected to customer feedback. Customer feedback is an important tool for companies to use and allows companies to better manage customer relationships. As soon as a customer gives feedback, the Mindshare application connects to the location-specific retail managers and will instantly alert managers to address problems and track data effectively. "With the Mindshare App, we have taken feedback management to the next level, by making customer comments even more actionable. Not only is the customer feedback available at the manager's desktop computer, but also it is now available directly on the manager's mobile device.[1]

LO 14-1

Understand the role of personal selling in an integrated marketing communications strategy.

PERSONAL SELLING—THE MOST PERSONAL FORM OF COMMUNICATION

With the average cost of a sales call exceeding $500 and the Internet's interactive capabilities, some people have predicted the decline of personal selling as an effective marketing communications tool. However, this has not been the case. While there is no question that selling is among the most expensive forms of marketing communication, personal selling offers three distinct advantages over other marketing communications methods:

- *Immediate feedback to the customer.* Customers don't want to wait for information. They demand accurate information quickly, putting pressure on companies for immediate, personal communication with a salesperson or customer service representative.[2]
- *Ability to tailor the message to the customer.* No other marketing communication method does a better job of creating personal, unique customer messages in real time. Salespeople generate distinctive sales messages that directly address customer problems and concerns.[3]
- *Enhance the personal relationship between company and customer.* Salespeople and the personal selling function

Brands like GAP are expected to maintain constant contact with customers through social media and other web services anywhere in the world.

are the single most effective approach for establishing and enhancing the personal relationship between company and customer. In particular, business-to-business (B2B) customers appreciate the efficiency of the Internet and other communication tools but expect a personal relationship with their suppliers. There is no substitute for a salesperson working with the customer one-on-one to solve problems.[4]

Social media changed the landscape of today's selling market. Customers now expect to be able to interact with sales representatives at any given moment. Prom season is a particularly busy time for Men's Warehouse as young men scramble to rent tuxedos. The company sponsored a "Prom Nation" contest with prizes such as $500 toward limo rentals. It promoted the contest via Facebook, Twitter, Pinterest, and Instagram. "It's our goal to create lifelong customers," says Sam Stogner, vice president of Men's Wearhouse formalwear. "Young men are finally dressing up more," said James Martin, store operations manager for Men's Wearhouse. "Fashion goes through cycles. Years ago, everything was baggy with underwear exposed. Now, the emphasis is on more fitted garments, which are more flattering." Communicating through the appropraite avenues will drive sales for companies like Men's Warehouse. In a market where parents expect to spend over $1,000 on prom-related items alone, this is an extremely attractive market.[5]

Activities in Personal Selling

Personal selling is a two-way communication process between salesperson and buyer with the goal of securing, building, and maintaining long-term relationships with profitable customers. To be successful in this process, salespeople need a variety of skills that change all the time. Research suggests salespeople today

EXHIBIT 14.1 | Matrix of Selling Activities

	Communicate	Sell	Build Customer Relationships	Manage Information
Technology	1. E-mail 2. Make telephone calls/leave voice-mail messages	1. Script sales pitch 2. Create customer-specific content 3. Provide relevant technology to customer	1. Create useful company web page content 2. Develop good team skills inside the company	Develop database management skills to manage customer database
Nontechnology	1. Enhance language and overall communication skills 2. Develop effective presentation skills	1. Learn relationship-selling skills 2. Conduct research of customer's business 3. Define and sell value-added services to customer 4. Follow up after customer contact 5. Identify and target key customer accounts 6. Listen effectively	1. Develop strong supplier alliances 2. Build rapport with all members of the customer's buying center 3. Network inside the company and throughout the customer's business 4. Build trust 5. Coordinate customer relationships inside the company	1. Develop time management skills 2. Organize information flow to maximize the effectiveness and reduce irrelevant data

are expected to be more skilled, available, and better communicators than ever before. Four basic selling activities composed of dozens of individual tasks define the salesperson's job: communicate, sell, build customer relationships, and manage information. The challenge for many companies is defining the correct mix of activities and then adapting the activities as the selling environment changes.[6] Exhibit 14.1 identifies the four major selling activities and specific tasks associated with each activity.

Communicate Effective communication is an essential selling activity. As the point of contact between customer and company, a salesperson must communicate effectively with both. With the customer, the salesperson needs good verbal communication skills to present the sales message. Equally important are good presentation skills and tools that incorporate technology (PowerPoint, social media) into the sales presentation. Finally, customers expect near constant access to the company so the salesperson must also have mobile communications skills.[7]

Communication with the company is also important. As discussed in Chapter 3, salespeople represent an excellent source of market information; they are familiar with customers and their needs. Customer feedback is also an excellent source of new-product ideas. Finally, field salespeople frequently find out about competitor or marketplace changes before anyone else in the company. All this information needs to be collected, analyzed, and disseminated to appropriate marketing managers.

Sell Selling requires a specific, complex set of tasks to reach the point where the customer agrees to purchase the product. From customer research early in the process through the sales presentation and customer support after purchase, the sales process is difficult.[8]

Build Customer Relationships Customers demand a close, strategic relationship with suppliers, and, as the primary point of contact with the company, salespeople are expected to build and support the customer relationship. This means spending time with the customer, developing excellent customer relationship management skills, and ultimately building trust with a customer.[9]

Information Management Salespeople today must be excellent information managers, collecting information from a variety of sources (their own company, customers, competitors, and independent information sources), determining what is relevant, and then presenting it to the customer. For example, managing the flow of customer information inside the company to ensure the right people get the right information at the right time takes time and follow-up. Often, information is collected from customers and other external sources such as transportation companies to facilitate an order inside the company. Customers will have preferred shipping times that need to be coordinated with transportation companies to ensure on-time arrival. At the same time, being sensitive to customer security concerns means controlling access to information.[10]

It is often assumed that the best salespeople have the most outgoing personalities. However, research has recently dispelled this myth. Tim Geisart, chief marketing officer for IBM's Kenexa unit, told *The New York Times* that according to Kenexa's research, which is based on millions of worker surveys, tests, and manager assessments, the most important characteristic for sales success is emotional courage or a persistence to keep going even after initially being told no. In fact, other companies have found that the most innovative workers (also the happiest by the company's definition) are those with a strong sense of mission about their work who also feel they have a great deal of personal autonomy. Emotional intelligence will continue to play a critical role in the workplace in the future. Employers are placing greater emphasis on these skills than ever before. Hiring managers are changing the ways they evaluate and screen potential candidates as well.[11]

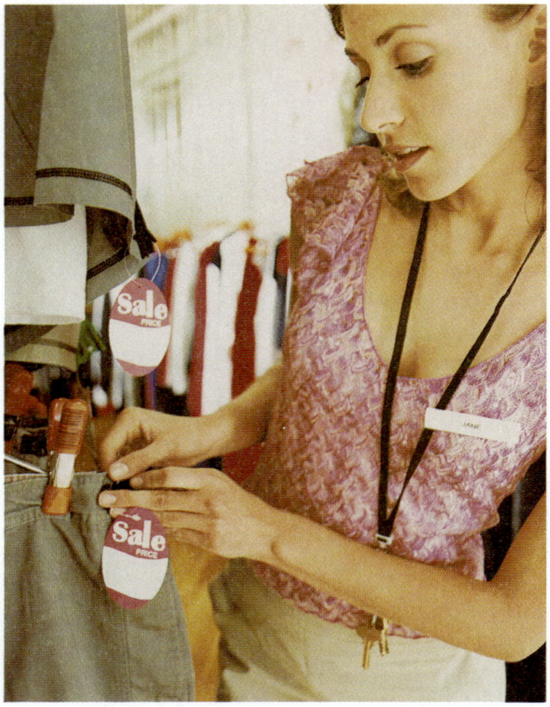

Though we typically think of business-to-consumer salespeople in retailing, a great deal more selling occurs between businesses.

Sales in B2C versus B2B Markets

In terms of sheer numbers, most salespeople are employed in various kinds of retail selling, or B2C. These jobs involve selling products to end users for their personal use. Examples of these types of sales positions are direct sellers such as Mary Kay and Tupperware, residential real estate agents, and retail store salespeople. However, salespeople in B2B markets do much more relationship selling.

Some personal characteristics and sales activities are similar across both B2C and B2B markets. Good interpersonal and communication skills, excellent knowledge of the products being sold, and an ability to discover customer needs and solve their problems are common characteristics to both sales environments. Similarly, managers must recruit and train appropriate people no matter what the sales job, provide them with objectives that match the firm's overall marketing program, then supervise, motivate, and finally evaluate their performance.[12]

But B2C and B2B selling also differ in some important ways. Many of the goods and services sold by B2B salespeople are more expensive and technically complex than those in B2C. In addition, B2B customers tend to be larger and engage in extensive decision-making processes involving many people.

Classifying Sales Positions

While retail selling employs more people, personal selling plays a more important and strategic purpose in business-to-business markets. Because of the important strategic function of personal selling in B2B markets, our discussion of sales positions will focus on various sales positions in this arena. There are many different types of sales jobs that require a variety of specific and unique skills. However, no matter what the job title, the salesperson's primary responsibility is to increase business from current and potential customers by providing a good value proposition to customers and effectively dealing with their concerns. The four major types of sales positions are trade servicer, missionary seller, technical seller, and solutions seller.

Trade Servicer **Trade servicers** are the group of resellers such as retailers or distributors with whom the sales force does business. Their primary responsibility is to increase business from current or potential customers by providing them with merchandising and promotional assistance. For example, the P&G salesperson selling soap products to individual store managers in a large grocery chain is an example of a trade servicer.

Missionary Seller **Missionary salespeople** often do not take orders from customers directly but persuade customers to buy their firm's product from distributors or other suppliers. Anheuser-Busch does missionary selling when its salespeople call on bar owners and encourage them to order a particular brand of beer from the local distributor. One of the best examples of missionary salespeople is a pharmaceutical rep, or detailer, who calls on doctors as a representative of the pharmaceutical manufacturers. When Pfizer introduced Lyrica, a top-selling anti-inflammatory drug, its salespeople communicated with physicians to alert them to the efficacy of the product, explain its advantages over other pain medication, and influence them to prescribe it to their patients. Keep in mind that the Pfizer salesperson does not "sell" any product directly to the patient.[13]

Technical Seller An example of **technical selling** is the sales engineer from General Electric who calls on Boeing to sell the GE90 jet engine to be used in Boeing aircraft. The trend is for most technical selling to be done in cross-functional teams. The complexity of many of the products and associated services involved in technical selling makes it difficult for any one salesperson to master all aspects of the sale. Cross-functional teams often include someone who is technically competent in the product (engineer), a customer service specialist, a financial analyst, and an account manager responsible for maintaining the customer-company relationship.

Anheuser-Busch uses missionary selling to get its Budweiser beer into stores.

Solution Seller More and more customers look for strategic partners who provide comprehensive solutions to their business problems. **Key account salespeople,** those responsible for managing large accounts, are skilled in developing complex solutions to a particular customer problem.[14] In addition, in industries such as information technology, customers look to suppliers for wide-ranging solutions from IT infrastructure design to defining product specifications, to purchase and installation of equipment or software, and support after the sale. A Cisco Systems or IBM salesperson, for example, needs to know not only a great deal about hardware and software but also the customer's business in order to develop a solution to the customer's IT problems.

The Personal Selling Process

LO 14-2

Learn the process of relationship selling.

Because personal selling is so important in establishing and maintaining customer relationships, particularly in B2B markets, many companies create a separate personal selling function that operates independently from the rest of marketing. As a result, marketing managers often do not have salespeople reporting directly to them. However, marketing managers need to understand the personal selling process for two reasons. First, in companies where salespeople play an important role, personal selling is the single most critical connection to the customer. From selling to customer service, salespeople are often the customer's primary contact point with the company. Marketing managers need a clear understanding of the selling process because it has such a profound effect on the customer relationship. Second, a number of marketing activities such as customer service and marketing communications will be affected by the personal selling function. Understanding the selling process helps marketing managers better plan a marketing communications strategy and coordinate other marketing activities such as customer service.

Exhibit 14.2 shows the six stages in the personal selling process. Although the selling process involves only a few steps, the specific activities involved at each step vary greatly depending on the type of sales position and the firm's overall customer relationship strategy. Marketing managers must ensure that a firm's sales program incorporates sufficient policies to guide each salesperson while at the same time coordinating the selling effort with the firm's marketing and relationship strategy. B2C and B2B salespeople use the same selling process, although how the process works varies greatly between the two environments. For example, B2C salespeople generally do not actively prospect for customers, since the customer is visiting the store, or follow up with the customer after the sale.

Prospecting for Customers Prospecting is critical because recruiting new customers is an essential element in a company's growth strategy. Marketing managers encourage salespeople to use a variety of sources to identify prospects,

EXHIBIT 14.2 | The Personal Selling Process

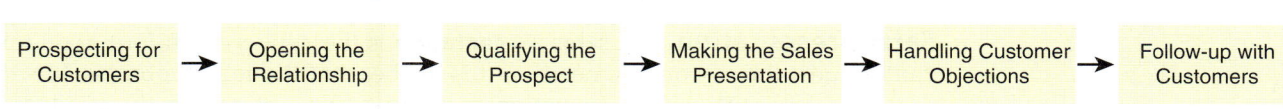

Prospecting for Customers → Opening the Relationship → Qualifying the Prospect → Making the Sales Presentation → Handling Customer Objections → Follow-up with Customers

including trade association and industry directories, other customers and suppliers, and referrals from company marketing efforts.

Telemarketing and other direct marketing efforts, which we will discuss in the next section, are also used to generate prospective customers. **Outbound telemarketing** involves calling potential customers at their home or office, either to make a sales call via telephone or to set up an appointment for a field salesperson. **Inbound telemarketing,** where prospective customers call a toll-free number for more information, is also used to identify and qualify prospects. When prospects call for more information, a telemarketing representative determines the extent of interest and assesses the prospect qualifications, then passes the contact information on to the appropriate salesperson. The Internet has the ability to generate potential new customer leads and a number of companies have dedicated teams to manage their Internet lead generation and customer inquiries. In addition, many companies, particularly those selling complex products, provide technical product information to customers. Salespeople, assigned in some firms specifically for Internet customers, follow up on legitimate inquiries with a traditional sales call. Hubspot is a software service company that allows its users (companies) to use its inbound marketing techniques to build up businesses, which is great news for smaller companies that don't have the marketing budgets of larger companies. Not only does Hubspot offer inbound marketing techniques, but it itself practice what it preaches, using inbound marketing techniques to attract new customers with great success.[15]

In coordinating the marketing effort, marketing managers must understand how much emphasis salespeople give to prospecting for new customers versus calling on existing customers. The appropriate policy depends on the selling and customer relationship strategy of the company, the nature of the product, and the firm's customers. Working with sales managers, the marketing manager considers the right mix of activities for the salesperson. For example, firms that have established customer relationships or products that require substantial service after the sale like Epic Healthcare encourage salespeople to devote most of their effort to servicing existing customers.[16]

Opening the Relationship In the initial approach to the prospective customer, the sales representative should try to determine who has the greatest influence or authority in the purchase. For example, when the firm's product is inexpensive and purchased routinely, salespeople are frequently instructed to deal with the purchasing department. At the other end of the continuum, the sales effort for complex, technical products generally requires an extensive program: calling on influencers and decision makers in various departments and different managerial levels. When the purchase involves people across the customer's organization, the sales staff often works in teams.

Qualifying the Prospect Before salespeople spend much time trying to establish a relationship with the prospective account, it is important to qualify the prospect to determine if the company is a legitimate potential customer. The process involves answering five questions:

- Does the prospect have a need for the company's products?
- Can the prospect derive added value from the product in ways that the company can deliver?
- Can the salesperson effectively contact, communicate, and work with the prospect over an extended time period (the time it takes to complete the sale and follow up after the sale)?
- Does the prospect have the financial ability and authority to make the sale?
- Will the account be profitable for the company?

Sales Presentation The **sales presentation** is the delivery of information relevant to meet the customer's needs and is the heart of the selling process. It is the process salespeople use to transition customers from interest in the product to purchase of the product.

Communicating the sales message is the number one priority of the presentation. The stereotype of a sales presentation is a salesperson talking in front of a customer or group of customers. In reality, sales presentations are carefully choreographed interactions in which the salesperson tries to discern the customer's real needs while at the same time providing critical information in a persuasive way so the customer appreciates the benefits and advantages of the product. Remember, the goal is not simply to make the sale but to create a strong value proposition that will lead to a mutually beneficial long-term relationship.[17]

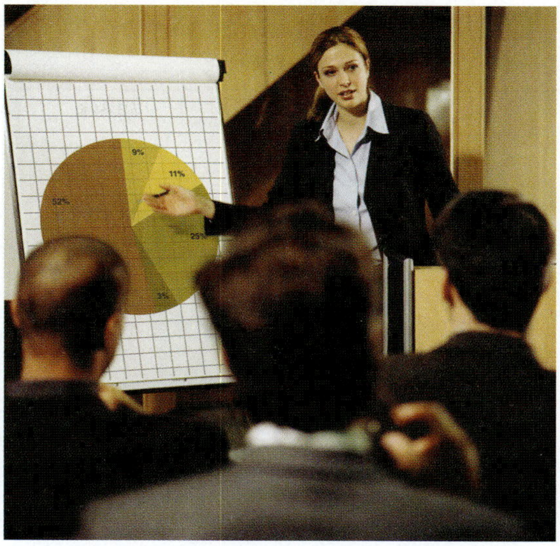

Sales presentations are an important element of personal selling.

Setting goals and objectives is the first step in communicating. Ultimately, the goal of the presentation is to secure a purchase commitment from the customer. However, the salesperson does not just walk in asking for the purchase order. Successful salespeople understand that the purchase order does not come until customers believe the company's products offer the best solution to their needs. In defining the goal, salespeople consider where the customer is in the buying process and have a clear understanding of the customer relationship.[18] New customers, for example, generally need more information about company products, policies, and procedures than existing customers. Based on an analysis of these factors, salespeople identify at least one of five principal goals for the presentation. At some point, however, the goal of the presentation will be to obtain customer action.

- Educate the customer by providing enough knowledge about the company's products.
- Get the customer's attention.
- Build interest for the company's products.
- Nurture the customer's desire and conviction to purchase.
- Obtain a customer commitment to action (purchase).

Characteristics of a Great Sales Presentation How would you respond if someone asked you, "What makes a great sales presentation?" Many people can give examples of a bad presentation, such as not listening to the customer, but not the characteristics of a great sales presentation.[19] Exhibit 14.3 identifies the four characteristics of a great presentation.

Handling Objections—Negotiating Win-Win Solutions Casual observation may suggest there are many different customer concerns; however, when

EXHIBIT 14.3 | Characteristics of a Great Sales Presentation

Characteristic	Answers the Customer Question
Explains the value proposition	What is the value-added of the product?
Asserts the advantages and benefits of the product	What are the advantages and benefits of the product?
Enhances the customer's knowledge of the company, product, and services	What are the key points I should know about this company, product, and services?
Creates a memorable experience	What should I remember about this presentation?

Source: Adapted from Mark W. Johnston and Greg W. Marshall, *Contemporary Selling*, 4th ed., 2013.

EXHIBIT 14.4 Common Customer Concerns

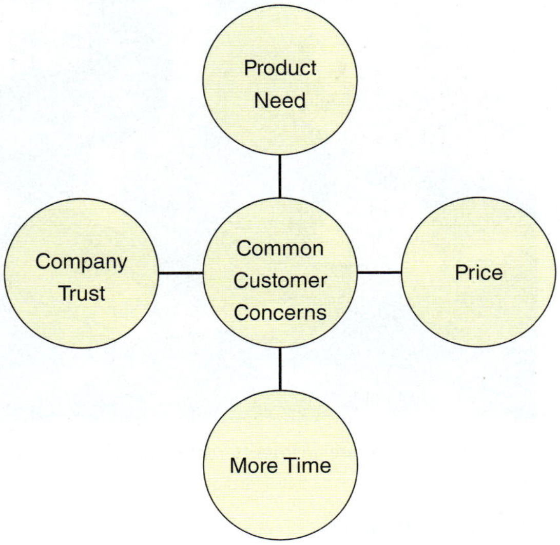

you look closely, customer anxieties fall into four areas. Customers often mask true concerns with general problems, but successful salespeople know how to identify and clarify true objections.[20] Exhibit 14.4 identifies common customer concerns.

Product Need The customer may not be convinced there is a need for the product. The customer's perspective can be summarized as, "We've always done it one way; why should we start something new now?" Key to the answer is a well-conceived value proposition that explains clearly how the product will benefit the customer and how it will be better than the existing solution.[21] It is important to remember that customers are generally not risk takers.

A much more common concern is whether the customer views the salesperson's product as a better solution than existing options. The customer is already familiar with the current products and change means learning a new product. Careful preparation is critical in dealing with questions about competitors, which is why salespeople spend a great deal of time learning about competitors' products. Cisco has developed an excellent reputation with its customers. It is leveraging that reputation with a sophisticated line of teleconferencing products. Business customers have confidence in Cisco, which translates into business opportunities.

Company Trust Personal selling is based a great deal on mutual trust between the buyer and the seller. As we discussed, most customers already have a supplier, and while they may not be totally satisfied, they are familiar with it. For example, they know the process for resolving a problem (who to call, expected wait times, costs, etc.). If the customer is unaware of the company, a common concern is the company's ability to deliver what is needed, when it's needed, and where it's needed.[22] This is a legitimate concern as the customer puts the company at risk by choosing the salesperson's company as the supplier. In other situations, customers may not object to the salesperson's company but are happy with their existing supplier.

Earning customers' trust is essential to developing long-term relationships. Major credit card company Discover was forced to pay a $14 million fine as a result of misleading telemarketing practices. The Consumer Financial Protection Bureau and the FDIC announced that Discover will refund $200 million to their credit card customers for pressuring cardholders into buying expensive payment protection and credit monitoring services. The regulatory agencies reported the company's telemarketers misled customers about the programs, enrolled customers without their consent, and led customers to believe the products were free. In some instances, the scripts suggested the cardholders would not be charged until after they had reviewed written materials, but the materials arrived after Discover had already charged the customers for the products. Roughly 3.5 million consumers were affected by these practices. Capital One was also involved in a similar situation. The company agreed to pay up to $150 million to two million consumers as a result of the bank's telemarketers deceptively pushing these same credit monitoring and payment protection services.[23]

More Time One of the most common customer objections is, "I need more time to consider the proposal." Certainly, concern about making a purchase decision too quickly is legitimate; however, the most likely scenario is that the value proposition has not been sufficiently developed.

Price Salespeople consistently report that price is the most common customer apprehension. In many cases, the customer has legitimate objections about the price of a product. Nevertheless, the price objection usually means the customer has not accepted the value proposition. In essence, if the customer does not perceive that the product benefits exceed the price, there will be no sale. The salesperson is left with two options: lower the price until it is below the product's perceived benefits or raise the perceived benefits until they exceed the price.[24]

Closing the Sale **Closing the sale** is obtaining commitment from the customer to make the purchase. The close is not a discrete event but rather a nonlinear process that begins with the approach to the customer. Research suggests salespeople make four critical mistakes in closing. First, a negative attitude about the customer or situation can affect the sales presentation and customer relationship. Second, the failure to conduct an effective pre-approach shows a lack of preparation that turns off customers. Third, too much talking and not enough listening demonstrates a lack of interest in finding out the customer's real needs. Fourth, using a "one size fits all" approach indicates the salesperson lacks creativity and is unwilling to focus on the customer's unique situation.[25]

Follow-up after the Sale One of the most critical aspects to the selling process is not what happens before the purchase decision but what happens after, the **follow-up.** Salespeople often rely on support people inside the company to help in post-sales service. Customer service personnel, product service call centers, technicians, and others are part of the follow-up process. But no matter who else has contact with the customer, the customer will hold the primary salesperson most responsible for the level and quality of service and support after the sale.

Customers expect three activities after the purchase decision: (1) delivery, installation, and initial service of the product: (2) any training needed to operate the equipment correctly: and (3) the effective and efficient disposition of appropriate customer problems that arise from the product purchase. Not meeting those expectations is a primary reason for customer complaints.[26] Any following purchase decisions are based to a large extent on the customer's experience with the product and the company.

British Telecom invested millions of dollars to upgrade its interactive customer support system. The knowledge management system includes real-time "instant messaging" support to customers with questions about service and billing problems. A critical element of the system is enhancing the information available to customer service agents as they deal with customer problems as well as improving the customer's overall experience with BT. The company still experiences significant customer disatisfaction but believes the commitment to improving customer service is critical to improving long-term customer satisfaction.[27]

Organizing the Sales Force

Since salespeople work closely with many departments inside the company, marketing managers have a real interest in working with sales managers to organize the sales force to maximize the efficiency and effectiveness of not only the sales force but also everyone in the company who interacts with the customer. The best sales structures are based on the company's objectives and strategies. In addition, as the firm's environment, objectives, or marketing strategy changes, its sales force must be flexible enough to change as well.[28]

TylrNMoblie has developed an app called WorkinBox, designed to help sales managers lead and monitor their team. It is a mobile e-mail inbox for salespeople connected to salesforce.com (now the market-leading CRM). WorkinBox lets salespeople sort their inbox by opportunity size and access the information and files they need most. This is a big productivity boost. Salespeople can turn messages into actionable tasks and update salesforce.com as they work. Trying to get actual work done from mobile e-mail is hard. For example, setting priorities is important for any successful sales effort. The 80/20 rule also plays out when evaluating sales opportunities. It's why productive salespeople bring the most focus to their most probable sales opportunities. This product helps salespeople with the selection process. Implementing a CRM system to analyze the saleforce has grown in popularity and the trend is expected to continue. WorkinBox is hoping to captialize on this opportunity.[29]

Company Sales Force or Independent Agents Maintaining a sales force is expensive, and companies are constantly assessing the most practical method to reach customers. One option is to use independent agents instead of company salespeople. It is not unusual for a company, such as IBM, to use both company salespeople and independent agents. Using independent sales agents is referred to as **outsourcing the sales force.**

The decision to use independent agents or a company sales force involves four factors:

- *Economic:* The costs and expected revenue associated with maintaining a sales force are analyzed and weighed against outsourcing to independent agents.
- *Control:* A critical factor is the amount of control senior management believes is necessary for the sales function. A company sales force offers complete control in key areas such as recruiting, training, and compensation. On the other hand, independent agents operate without direct company management supervision.
- *Transaction costs:* Finding a good replacement for a poor-performing independent sales agent can be difficult, and once one is found, it is often months before the new agent learns enough about the product and its applications to be effective in the sales job. **Transaction cost analysis (TCA)** states that when substantial transaction-specific assets are necessary to sell a manufacturer's product, the cost of using and administering independent agents is likely higher than the cost of hiring and managing a company's sales force.[30]
- *Strategic flexibility:* In general, a vertically integrated distribution system incorporating a company sales force is less flexible than outsourcing. Independent agents can be added or dismissed at short notice, especially if no specialized assets are needed to sell the product. Furthermore, it is not necessary to sign a long-term contract with independent agents. Firms facing uncertain and rapidly changing competitive or market environments and industries characterized by shifting technology or short product life cycles often use independent agents to preserve flexibility in the distribution channel.

Geographic Orientation The simplest and most common method of organizing a company sales force is geographic orientation, as illustrated in Exhibit 14.5. Individual salespeople are assigned to separate geographic territories. In this type of organization, each salesperson is responsible for performing all the sales activities in a given territory. The geographic sales organization has several advantages. First, and most importantly, it tends to have the lowest cost because (1) there is only one salesperson in each territory, (2) territories tend to be smaller than other organizational structures so travel time and expenses are minimized, and (3) fewer managerial levels are required for coordination so sales administration and overhead expenses are lower. Second, the simplicity of the geographical structure minimizes customer confusion because each customer is called on by one salesperson.

EXHIBIT 14.5 | Example of Geographic Organization

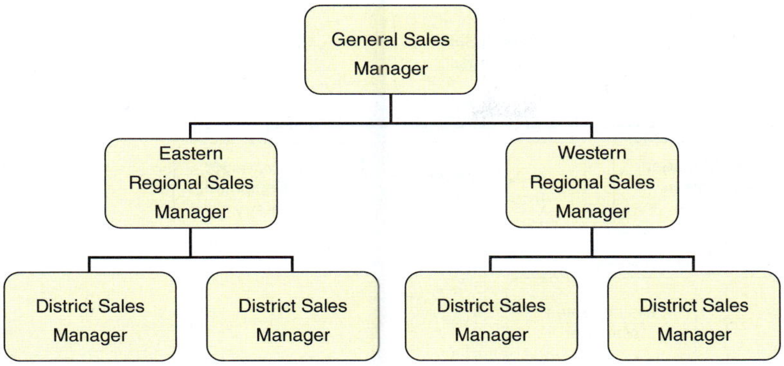

Source: Adapted from Mark W. Johnston and Greg W. Marshall, *Sales Force Management*, 11th ed., 2013. Copyright © 2013 Routledge Publishing.

The major disadvantage is that it does not encourage or support any division or specialization of labor. Each salesperson is expected to be good at many things (various customer needs, product applications and specifications).

Product Organization Some companies have a separate sales force for each product or product category (see Exhibit 14.6). The primary advantage of a product organization is that individual salespeople can develop familiarity with the technical attributes, applications, and most effective selling methods associated with a single product. Also, there tends to be a closer relationship between sales and engineering, product development, and manufacturing when salespeople focus on one product or product category. Finally, this structure enables greater control in the allocation of selling effort across various products. Management can then adjust sales assets based on the needs of individual products. The major disadvantage is the duplication of effort with salespeople across different products assigned to the same geographic territory. This generally leads to higher sales costs.

EXHIBIT 14.6 | Example of Product Orientation

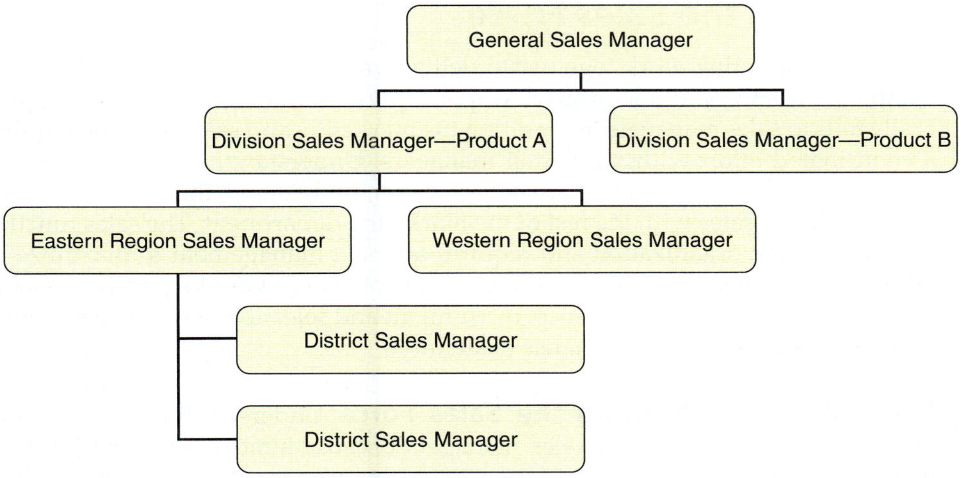

Source: Adapted from Mark W. Johnston and Greg W. Marshall, *Sales Force Management*, 11th ed., 2013. Copyright © 2013 Routledge Publishing.

EXHIBIT 14.7 | Example of Customer Orientation

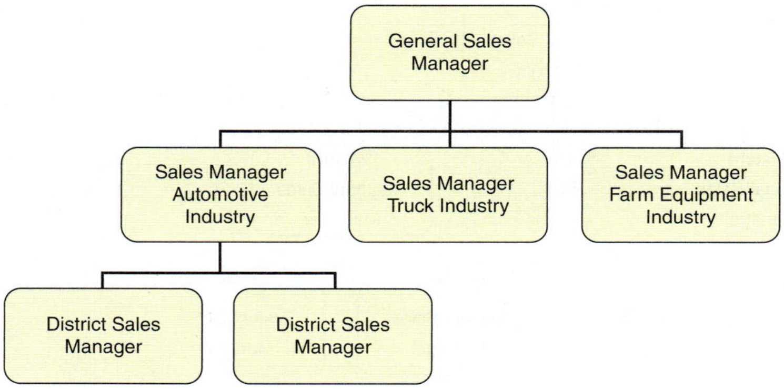

Source: Adapted from Mark W. Johnston and Greg W. Marshall, *Sales Force Management*, 11th ed., 2013. Copyright © 2013 Routledge Publishing.

Customer Type or Market Segmentation It has become increasingly popular for organizations to structure their sales force by customer type as IBM did when it created separate sales teams to call on small and large business customers. Organizing by customer type is a natural extension of creating value for the customer and reflects a market segmentation strategy (see Exhibit 14.7). When salespeople specialize in calling on a particular type of customer, they gain a better understanding of those customers' needs and requirements. They can be trained to use different selling approaches for different markets and to implement specialized marketing and promotional programs.[31]

A related advantage is that as salespeople become familiar with the customers' specific needs, they are more likely to discover ideas for new products and marketing approaches that will appeal to those customers. The disadvantage, as with product organization, is that sales costs are higher as a result of having multiple salespeople operating in the same geographic area. In addition, when customers have different departments operating in different industries, two or more salespeople from the same company may be calling on the same customer.

Managing the Sales Force

LO 14-3

Understand the major job responsibilities of sales management.

Sales and marketing work together to deliver value to the customer and achieve company objectives. While primary responsibility for managing a sales force generally falls to sales managers, integrating the marketing and sales function requires a coordinated effort with marketing managers. Understanding how salespeople are managed helps marketing managers better understand the selling function and coordinate sales with the rest of the marketing department. The sales function is unique in the organization and requires talented management to maximize its efficiency and effectiveness. Managing a sales force involves five primary responsibilities: salesperson performance, recruitment and selection, training, compensation and rewards, and performance evaluation.

Performance: Motivating the Sales Force Understanding sales agents' performance is important to sales managers because almost everything they as managers do influences sales performance one way or another. For example, how the manager selects staff members and the kind of training they receive affect their own aptitude and skills. The compensation program and the way it is administered influence motivation and overall sales performance.

It helps to understand what people want and expect from their jobs. Gen Yers entered the workforce with a different set of rules than their baby boomer parents. While still focused on high performance and high-paying jobs, they also look for positions that are fun and exciting. In essence, they are not just looking for a job but an opportunity to both enjoy their job and be well rewarded in the process. Gen Yers place a higher priority on finding the right life-work balance so the 60-hour workweek does not appeal to them, but working remotely and with flexible schedules does.[32] For marketing managers this means developing positions that offer a broader range of experiences (for example, increased travel and opportunities for faster and more frequent promotions).

As presented in Exhibit 14.8, salesperson performance is a function of five factors: (1) role perceptions, (2) aptitude, (3) skill level, (4) motivation, and (5) personal, organizational, and environmental factors.

Role Perceptions The role of a salesperson is the set of activities or behaviors he or she must perform on the job. This role is largely defined through the expectations, demands, and pressure communicated to the salesperson by role partners. These partners include people inside as well as outside the company with a vested interest in how a salesperson performs the job—top management, the salesperson's sales manager, customers, and family members. How salespeople perceive their roles has significant consequences that affect job satisfaction and motivation, which, in turn, have the potential to increase sales force turnover and hurt performance.[33]

Sales Aptitude: Are Good Salespeople Born or Made? Sales ability has historically been considered a function of (1) physical factors such as age and physical attractiveness, (2) aptitude factors such as verbal skills and sales expertise, and (3) personality characteristics such as empathy. However, there is no proof these measures, by themselves, affect sales performance. As a result, most managers believe the things a company does to train and develop its salespeople are the most important determinants of success.

Sales Skill Levels. **Sales skill levels** are the individual's learned proficiency at performing necessary sales tasks. They include such learned abilities as interpersonal skills, leadership, technical knowledge, and presentation skills. The

EXHIBIT 14.8 | Model of Salesperson Performance

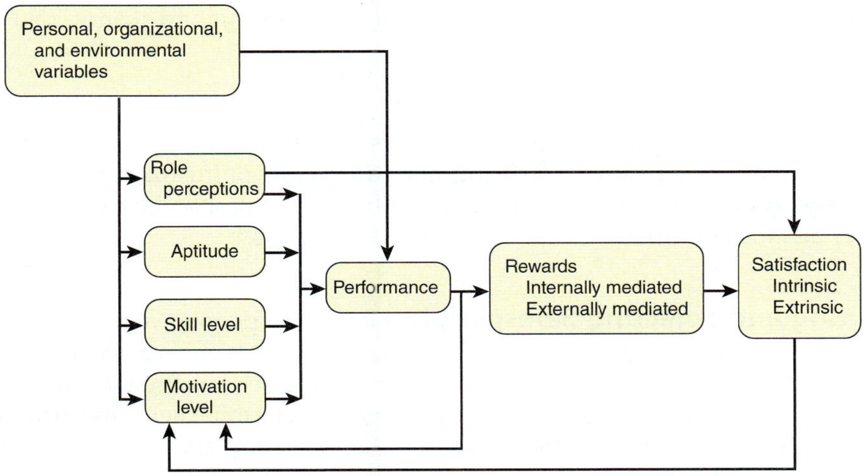

Source: Adapted from Mark W. Johnston and Greg W. Marshall, *Sales Force Management,* 11th ed., 2013.

relative importance of each of these skills and the need for other skills depend on the selling situation.[34]

Motivation. **Motivation** is how much the salesperson wants to expend effort on each activity or task associated with the sales job. Sales managers constantly try to find the optimal mix of motivation elements that direct salespeople to perform sales activities. As you would expect, motivational factors that work well with one person may not motivate another. For example, an autocratic managerial style may work with a midcareer salesperson but have a profoundly negative effect on a senior salesperson. In addition, a number of motivational factors are not directly under the sales manager's control such as personal family issues or general economic conditions.[35]

Organizational, Environmental, and Personal Factors. Organizational factors include the company marketing budget, current market share for the company's products, and the degree of sales management supervision. Personal and organizational variables such as job experience, the manager's interaction style, and performance feedback influence the amount of role conflict and ambiguity salespeople perceive.[36] In addition, the desire for job-related rewards (such as higher pay or promotion) differs with age, education, family size, career stage, and organizational climate.

Rewards. A company bestows a variety of rewards on any given level of performance. There are two types of rewards—extrinsic and intrinsic. **Extrinsic rewards** are those controlled and given by people other than the salesperson such as managers and customers. They include pay, financial incentives, security, recognition, and promotion. **Intrinsic rewards** are those salespeople primarily attain for themselves and include feelings of accomplishment, personal growth, and self-worth.[37]

Loyaltyworks is a business-to-business loyalty incentives program. It was founded on the basis that the best way to motivate customers is through incentives or rewards. CEO Steve Damerow applied this same concept to his employees. "I believe our biggest assets walk right out the door at the end of the day. We do quite a bit of dollar volume, but we do not have a lot of employees. Everything is done on the web. Our goal is to find good people and keep them. We pay 100% of health insurance, 401k match and share annual profits with all of our associates." The company also uses their RewardTrax cyber currency, which can be redeemed in over 55 countries in a shopping mall that looks and operates similar to Amazon. "We also have an integrated real time travel portal, similar to Travelocity or Expedia, where we get real time inventory of cruises, hotels, events and airlines," said Damerow.[38]

Satisfaction. Salesperson job satisfaction refers to all the characteristics of the job individuals find rewarding, fulfilling, and satisfying—or frustrating and unsatisfying. Satisfaction is a complex job attitude and salespeople can be satisfied or dissatisfied with many different aspects of the job.[39]

Recruiting and Selecting Salespeople Hiring the people who best fit the job and organization is important to long-term success, so there is a great deal of focus on recruiting and selecting qualified salespeople. The recruitment and selection process has three steps: (1) analyze the job and determine selection criteria, (2) find and attract a pool of applicants, and (3) develop and apply selection procedures to evaluate applicants.

Firms easily can be up against competitors and other industries for the best candidates. As a result, companies develop a well-coordinated recruiting strategy that, contrary to popular belief, does not seek to maximize the number of applicants. Having too many recruits overloads the selection process. The true objective of a successful recruiting strategy is to identify a few exceptionally qualified recruits.[40]

Training Sales managers work with marketing managers to identify training objectives that integrate the needs of the salesperson with corporate marketing objectives. These objectives typically include (1) improved customer relationships, (2) increased productivity, (3) improved morale, (4) lower turnover, and (5) improved selling skills. The challenge for sales managers is measuring the effectiveness of sales training.[41]

Sales training most often involves one or more of the seven topics listed in Exhibit 14.9, ranging from product knowledge to very specialized topics such as communication and customer relationship building. The key for sales managers is fitting the sales training content to the needs of the individual salespeople.

EXHIBIT 14.9 | Sales Training Topics

Source: Adapted from Mark W. Johnston and Greg W. Marshall, *Sales Force Management*, 11th ed., 2013. Copyright © 2013 Routledge Publishing.

Johnson & Johnson incorporates several online tools to help train employees. Its online "e-university" provides a variety of learning experiences for employees. In addition, personalized learning and development programs deliver specific training based on the individual's own career goals. Some of the topics included are management fundamentals, negotiation skills, and mentoring essentials. Once they have completed the learning and development program, certain employees are allowed to take additional course work in a leadership development program. Ultimately J&J wants to develop the full potential of salespeople and other employees to maximize their performance opportunities.[42]

Compensation and Rewards The total financial compensation paid to salespeople has several components designed to achieve different objectives. A **salary** is a fixed sum of money paid at regular intervals. Most firms that pay a salary also offer *incentives* **or** *incentive pay* to encourage better performance. **Incentives** are generally commissions tied to sales volume or profitability, or bonuses for meeting or exceeding specific performance targets (for example, meeting quotas for a particular product). Such incentives direct salespeople's efforts toward specific strategic objectives during the year, as well as offer additional rewards for top performers. A **commission** is payment based on short-term results, usually a salesperson's dollar or unit sales volume. Since there is a direct link between sales volume and the amount of commission received, commission payments are useful for increasing salespeople's sales efforts.[43] Exhibit 14.10 summarizes the components and objectives of financial compensation plans.

In addition to financial compensation, sales management (and management across the company) incorporates a range of **nonfinancial incentives.** Most sales managers consider promotional opportunities second only to financial incentives as effective sales force motivators. This is particularly true for young, well-educated salespeople who tend to view their sales position as a stepping-stone to a senior management position.

Evaluating Salesperson Performance Monitoring sales activity and evaluating salesperson performance are fundamental issues. Salespeople should be evaluated solely on those elements of the sales process they control. To do this

EXHIBIT 14.10 Components and Objectives of Financial Compensation Plans

Components	Objectives
Salary	• Motivate effort on nonselling activities • Adjust for differences in territory potential • Reward experience and competence
Commissions	• Motivate a high level of selling effort • Encourage sales success
Bonuses	• Direct effort toward strategic objectives • Provide additional rewards for top performers • Encourage sales success
Sales contests	• Stimulate additional effort targeted at specific short-term objectives
Benefits	• Satisfy salespeople's security needs • Match competitive offers

Source: Adapted from Mark W. Johnston and Greg W. Marshall, *Sales Force Management,* 11th ed., 2013. Copyright © 2013 Routledge Publishing.

a company develops objective and subjective measures that distinguish between controllable and noncontrollable factors.[44] For example, companies, for the most part, understand that the overall economic environment is not within the salesperson's control; however, the direct sales to a customer are quite clearly in the salesperson's control. This means that if sales are declining because the economy is not doing well, the salesperson should not be penalized; however, if sales are declining because the salesperson is not meeting the customer's needs, then he or she should be held accountable.

Microsoft, long recognized as a performance-driven, measurement-focused company, has revamped its reward and performance evaluation system. While employees are still ranked on performance and long-term potential, the company no longer uses a forced curve to evaluate performance, which means employee bonuses are not subject to a curve (if an employee performs well, he or she gets the bonus no matter the ranking). The company also offers an extensive health care plan, which even sends doctors to employee homes in an emergency.[45]

ETHICAL DIMENSION 14

Who Should We Hire?

One of the most important functions for a sales manager is the hiring of new salespeople. As we discussed in the chapter, this can be a complex and difficult task because choosing the wrong person has a number of negative outcomes (for example, lost sales and/or inefficient use of company resources). It is important to know the specific skills needed for the job (job description) as well as any personal characteristics or other information that may be useful in evaluating potential candidates.

The challenge is often determining what other information to consider in selecting new sales candidates. Most sales managers have always believed that it is important for the salesperson to have similar characteristics to their customers. For example, if a group of customers were mostly men in their forties, then sales managers would seek out similar candidates. The conventional wisdom was that customers would be more comfortable if the salesperson had similar demographic characteristics. However, in today's workplace, traditional job roles are changing and women as well as other minorities now hold many jobs historically held by other individuals.

The challenge for the sales manager is often finding qualified candidates and breaking out of existing stereotypes. Let's consider each of these issues. First, the need to identify qualified candidates can be a significant problem for companies in certain fields such as engineering. While there is certainly greater diversity in schools of engineering than there has been in the past, it is still dominated by men. Balancing the need to recruit diverse candidates for sales positions in these industries with the need to have qualified candidates in the sales territory puts significant pressure on sales managers. Second, many sales managers come out of the sales ranks and have learned sales management "on the job." As a result, it is possible to remain stuck in an "old school" view of personal selling and job roles. Together, these issues lead to some difficult ethical challenges as sales managers struggle with hiring the salespeople.[46]

Ethical Perspective

1. **Sales Manager:** Should a sales manager hire the most qualified candidate for a sales position or apply different criteria such as gender or ethnicity?
2. **Customer:** Should it make a difference if the salesperson is very different from you in terms of ethnicity, gender, or some other characteristic?
3. **HR Department:** What training should sales managers receive about the importance of diversity in the workplace, particularly as it relates to the relationship between the salesperson and the customer?

If the company fails to clearly understand the sales process and what factors are controllable/noncontrollable, it is possible, even likely, many activities critical to long-term success such as building customer satisfaction will go unmeasured. These other measures fall into two broad categories: (1) objective measures and (2) subjective measures. **Objective measures** reflect statistics the sales manager gathers from the firm's internal data. **Subjective measures** rely on personal evaluations by someone connected to the salesperson's sales process, usually the immediate sales manager or a customer. Objective measures fall into two major categories: (1) output measures and (2) input measures. **Output measures** show the results of the efforts expended by the salesperson while **input measures** focus on the efforts of salespeople during the sales process (see Exhibit 14.11).

DIRECT MARKETING

LO 14-4

Identify the role of direct marketing in integrated marketing communications (IMC).

Chapter 11 discussed direct marketing in terms of its role in the distribution network; here the focus is on direct marketing as a promotional tool. Direct marketing is among the fastest-growing marketing communication methods. As defined by the Direct Marketing Association, **direct marketing** is an interactive marketing system that uses one or more advertising media to affect a measurable response and/or transaction at any location. The term *direct marketing* includes a number of communication channels: direct mail, catalogs, telemarketing, and Internet marketing. The Internet is the most widely used direct mail tool.[47]

EXHIBIT 14.11 | Examples of Output and Input Measures

Output Measures	Input Measures
• Orders	• Calls
• Number of orders	• Total number of calls
• Average size of orders	• Number of planned/unplanned calls
• Number of canceled orders	• Time and time utilization
	• Days worked
• Accounts	• Calls per day (call rate)
• Number of active accounts	• Selling time versus nonselling time
• Number of new accounts	• Expenses
• Number of lost accounts	• Total/by category
• Number of overdue accounts	• As a percentage of sales
• Number of prospective accounts	• As a percentage of quota
	• Nonselling activities
	• Phone calls to prospects
	• Number of formal proposals developed
	• Number of service calls made

Source: Adapted from Mark W. Johnston and Greg W. Marshall, *Sales Force Managment*, 11th ed., 2013. Copyright © 2013 Routledge Publishing.

Creating a Direct Marketing Campaign

A direct marketing campaign encompasses a series of specific steps.

Set Strategy for Campaign As one element of a marketing communications strategy, the direct marketing campaign is incorporated into a broader promotional strategy. As part of that strategy, the direct marketing campaign should specify two criteria. First, what are the specific, quantifiable objectives? Direct marketing, unlike other marketing communications tools, can be measured, and it is important that marketing managers state objectives in specific, quantifiable terms. Second, marketing managers should identify the target market for the campaign and include demographic characteristics, lifestyle, and reasons direct marketing is an appropriate communications methodology for the market. At all times it is essential that the direct marketing campaign is consistent with and supports the overall marketing communications strategy.

Specify Direct Marketing Channels A number of direct marketing channels are available to marketers. As a result, a key task for marketing managers is aligning the direct marketing strategy with the most effective direct marketing media based on the unique advantages and disadvantages of each one.

Identify Qualified Target Customers Direct marketing, by nature, is more focused on specific customers than other nonpersonal communication media such as advertising or public relations. As a result, a critical step is to identify, qualify, and target a group of customers for the direct marketing campaign. There are primarily two sources of customers. The first is internally generated prospects that consist of prior customers or inquiries (through direct-mail campaigns or the company website). It is important to consider internal contacts first for two reasons. Internal names have demonstrated an interest in the company through either a purchase or an inquiry. In addition, internally generated prospects are less expensive than the second customer source—external lists from outside vendors. List companies such as InfoUSA and Dun & Bradstreet specialize in developing and selling lists to direct marketers. In addition, companies sometimes make their customer lists available for purchase for a fee. Recently, however, Yahoo and others have been criticized for this practice.

Develop and Test the Offer for the Campaign Sophisticated database management programs enable companies to create specific offers for individual customers by matching customer information with the offer. This is the basic element of a direct marketing campaign. One advantage of direct marketing is the ability to easily test alternative offer options. By targeting different individuals with unique offers, it is possible to quickly and accurately understand what messages are working well.

Analyze Results of Offer Once the campaign is underway, it is important to analyze the results. Analysis of the data can discover the revenue, cost, and overall profitability of each individual included in the campaign. No other marketing communications channel has that level of data for analysis.

Direct Marketing Channels

Direct marketing media accessible to marketing managers include e-mail, direct mail, and telemarketing, or phone marketing. Other direct media do not allow for individual targeted communication but do enable the prospect to respond immediately; an example of this is television infomercials.

Direct Mail Direct mail is one of the least expensive direct marketing channels with costs of $.75 to $2.00 per message, and despite frequent complaints about the amount of junk mail (totaling billions each year), it is still an effective channel for reaching targeted customers. Direct mail is much more effective in B2C than B2B markets because reaching the appropriate individual inside an organization is difficult.

One drawback to direct mail is the low response rate. Since it is easily discarded or, if read, not acted upon, the average direct-mail response rate as reported by the Direct Marketing Association is only 2.77 percent. Put another way, a little more than 97 percent of the direct mail is not acted on, making it relatively inefficient.

Components in a Direct-Mail Offer The contents or elements in a direct-mail offer include:

- *Outside envelope:* The offer comes in an envelope that must get the prospect's attention. Colorful illustrations, a more "personal" address, and a unique envelope feature (size, color, shape) all contribute to the prospect opening the envelope.
- *Sales collateral:* The offer is conveyed in the sales material inside the envelope. Most often this includes a letter detailing the offer and a brochure that presents a more graphic presentation of the material.
- *Contact information:* The offer gives contact information in several places. It is also important to provide multiple contact opportunities—toll-free number, response card, and website. Companies have found mentioning discounts such as coupons in the direct mail and then posting them on the website increase response rates as prospects are moved to additional action. If a response card is included, then a postage-paid return envelope is also included in the packet of material.

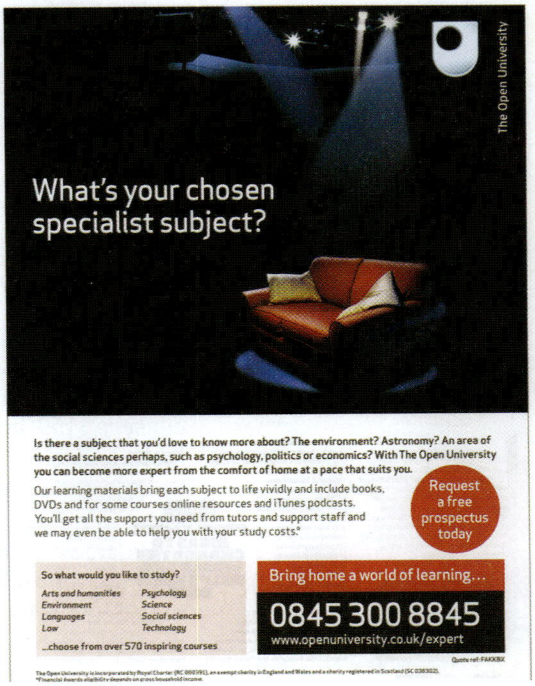

Colleges and universities prepare lots of collateral materials to attract students.

High-school students are heavily targeted by colleges, receiving direct mailings as early as their sophomore year. "We set parameters for what kinds of students we want to meet," said Nancy Spataro, director of admissions at York College of Pennsylvania, which sends out over 200,000 mailers each year and targets students in Mid-Atlantic states, including New Jersey. Colleges and universities analyze data such as SAT and ACT scores to determine potential applicants for their programs. "We have been pretty successful with our approach," she said, adding that 18 percent of the roughly 1,200-student freshman class is from New Jersey. The school expects to continue this trend of direct mailing—even as their targets become more focused on technology. If the admissions office at York College receives feedback from the potential student, it will begin sending e-mail advertisements in addition to the direct mailings. The college is willing to spend time and resources on this project because they want top-tier students.[48]

Telemarketing Telemarketing has come under a lot of criticism in recent years. As noted in Chapter 11, the National Do Not Call Registry, as well as state restrictions, severely limits "cold call" telemarketing calls. However, despite its negative reputation and high cost per contact ($1 to $3), research conducted by the Direct Marketing Association suggests telemarketing works; indeed, it had one of the highest response rates of any direct marketing channel—8.55 percent. The challenge for the telemarketer is to break through the negative initial reaction and make a personal connection with the customer. Creating a tailored sales presentation that adjusts to customer feedback is a significant advantage for telemarketers after they have established a relationship.

Successful telemarketing campaigns contain three essential elements.

1. Access to an accurate list of *qualified prospects* is critical. Research suggests a good list of prospects boosts the success rate by 60 percent.
2. The offer must persuade the prospect to *act immediately*. Enhancing the offer to encourage immediate action includes a lower price, discounts on shipping, added product features, and benefits. In addition, the offer must convey a sense of exclusivity demonstrating that the product cannot be purchased anywhere else.
3. Finally, the telemarketer must engage the prospect with the *highest ethical standards*. Given the negative perception of telemarketing and the frequent abuses of unwanted telephone solicitations, most people perceive a high degree of risk in purchasing over the phone. As a result, the telemarketer must offer, and stand behind, money-back guarantees as well as, when possible, nationally recognized brand names.

Catalogs Catalog marketers use a variety of different types of catalogs including full-line catalogs, specialty catalogs designed for small customer groups, as well as B2B catalogs to target potential buyers. The average consumer catalog purchase is $150, and more than 70 percent of Americans use catalogs. Keys to success include useful lists of customers and prospects to target, precise inventory control to monitor costs and enhance customer satisfaction, and careful brand management to maintain the company's integrity and reputation.

Seamless integration with the company's website is indispensable as consumers interact with the company through many channels. For example, the process may begin when a consumer looks at a catalog then orders online, or they may see something online and then call the company.[49] Catalog marketers have expanded globally, taking advantage of the Internet to target customers in Asia and Europe. U.S. catalog companies L.L. Bean and Lands' End have found success, particularly in Japan.

SUMMARY

An important part of integrated marketing communications (IMC) involves communicating directly with our customers (either end-user consumer or individual business customer). The most important personal communication tool is personal selling and the chapter presented the process of personal selling and the reasons why it is so important to IMC. As the chapter discussed, personal selling is a unique company function and managing the sales force presents several unique challenges. Finally, a second critical individual communication tool is direct marketing and the chapter identified the important role direct marketing plays in a comprehensive IMC strategy.

KEY TERMS

personal selling 418
trade servicer 420
missionary salespeople 420
technical selling 420
key account salespeople 421
outbound telemarketing 422
inbound telemarketing 422
sales presentation 422
closing the sale 425
follow-up 425
outsourcing the sales force 426
transaction cost analysis (TCA) 426
sales skill levels 429
motivation 430
extrinsic rewards 430
intrinsic rewards 430
salary 431
incentive pay 431
commission 431
nonfinancial incentives 431
objective measures 433
subjective measures 433
output measures 433
input measures 433
direct marketing 433

APPLICATION QUESTIONS

1. You are the vice president of sales for a $30 million manufacturer of home building materials. The company employs 50 salespeople around the country to market the company's products to hardware stores and major building contractors. The CEO believes the company needs to cut costs and wants to reduce the sales force by 50 percent. You have been asked to come in and explain why that is a bad long-term strategy for the company. Discuss why salespeople are critical to the success of the company.
2. Identify three important personal characteristics that a key account salesperson for a global manufacturer of networking hardware would need to be successful. The company sells multimillion-dollar product solutions to telecommunications companies and *Fortune* 100 global organizations.
3. You are the marketing manager for Samsung Electronics and have been asked to create a sales brochure for a new Samsung 55-inch LED TV. Pick a model and identify potential customer objections to the product. Then develop ways to address the customer objections.
4. You are vice president of sales for a medium-sized technology firm and have been asked to design a new compensation package for the company's national sales force of 50 people. Currently, they are paid solely on commission with average compensation of $75,000 to $100,000. The CEO is concerned about customer service and wants the salespeople to focus more on servicing existing customers. What compensation plan would you suggest?

MANAGEMENT DECISION CASE: Pharmaceutical Sales: Pressure Is On to Change the Selling Process

For the past few decades, pharmaceutical sales positions have represented a very nice opportunity for those interested in a sales career. Graduating college students looking to go into professional selling would be extremely lucky to secure such a job right out of college as many people get into the industry only after achieving sales success someplace else. As mentioned in the chapter, pharmaceutical salespeople are unique in that they are considered missionary salespeople who do not directly take orders from their clients—who are primarily physicians. Instead, pharmaceutical reps promote their products by educating physicians and encouraging them to write prescriptions for their drugs. Even without taking actual orders, the extent to which a salesperson succeeds at the job heavily depends on an ability to implement the personal selling process while attending to the needs of the doctor and his or her patients.

Sales territories in the pharmaceutical industry often are designed using a combination approach of product-based, customer-based, and geographic approaches. That is, in many cases a salesperson is given a geographic region in which to work and that person will call on doctors within that region who have a special need for a particular product or product line. For example, pediatricians, family practice, and internal medicine doctors see many patients for bacterial infections of the ears, sinuses, and the like that often require the use of an antibiotic for treatment. As a result, many pharmaceutical companies train salespeople in the dosage and usage characteristics of antibiotics and assign them to specific territories where they will call on all doctors who are regular heavy prescribers of antibiotics.

Regardless of how the territory is designed, the pharmaceutical salesperson still executes all of the steps of the selling process. Prospecting for customers is done and a list is usually provided by the salesperson's firm. The prescribing history of each doctor often is available from industry sources so the salesperson knows how much the doctor prescribes of his or her company's drug versus a competitor. After that it is up to the salesperson to open the relationship and begin learning more about the doctor's practice and the needs for particular medications. Asking questions of the doctor, providing information about the performance of a drug in clinical studies to educate the doctor, and responding to questions are all part of the process leading to gaining commitment to prescribe more frequently. Communicating with someone as highly educated as a doctor about a product as highly complex as a drug can be a pretty tricky process and given the demand on doctors' time, such exchanges notoriously have to occur within a 30-second to two-minute time frame!

Recently, the age-old process described above has come under fire. Much criticism of how pharmaceutical companies market to doctors has led some to believe that the process is not in the best interest of patients, the health care system, or the integrity of medicine as a whole. Pharmaceutical company practices such as paying doctors to attend "educational workshops" in exotic locations or speak as experts about a disease and course of treatment are being heavily criticized. As an example of how widespread such practices are, just three top pharmaceutical companies paid almost $466 million combined to doctors for those purposes in only one year. Consequently, one company, GlaxoSmithKline, has announced that it will no longer pay doctors to promote its products. In addition, Glaxo is eliminating paying sales representatives based on the number of prescriptions doctors write and instead is basing pay on their technical knowledge, the quality of service provided to doctors that improve patient care, and the company's overall business performance. Whether other pharmaceutical companies will follow Glaxo's lead is yet to be determined, but it's a bold move. Given evolving trends in health care, it is clear that the job of a pharmaceutical sales representative will continue to evolve over the next several years.

Questions for Consideration

1. Pharmaceutical companies historically encouraged their salespeople to take lunch into doctors' offices, the idea being that by providing lunch for doctors and their staff, the salesperson would get more than the standard two minutes of selling time. In addition, companies provide salespeople with freebies, ranging from pens and notepads to microwave popcorn, to leave at doctors' offices. What do you think of such practices? Are they ethical and do they assist with providing better patient care?

2. Now that GlaxoSmithKline has decided not to pay its salespeople based on number of prescriptions written, how do you propose they motivate their salespeople? What motivational approaches do you recommend and why do you think they are appropriate?

3. Many doctors do not work individually but instead are part of a group practice often connected to a local hospital. How would the sales process change for a pharmaceutical salesperson selling to a hospital? Be specific with your description.

Sources: Peter Loftus, "The New State of Health Care: Doctors Face New Scrutiny Over Gifts," The *Wall Street Journal*, Eastern edition, August 23, 2013, p. A.1; Jonathan D. Rockoff and Hester Plumridge, "Corporate News: Drug Firms Curb Ties to Doctors," *The Wall Street Journal*, Eastern edition, December 18, 2013, p. B.3; Katie Thomas, "Glaxo to Stop Paying Doctors to Boost Drugs," *New York Times*, December 17, 2013, p. A1.

MARKETING PLAN EXERCISE

ACTIVITY 16: Building the Interpersonal Relationship

A critical component of your company's marketing communications is the interpersonal connection to the customer. Developing an effective interpersonal communications strategy is essential and can include (1) sales force, (2) website, and (3) direct marketing. In this exercise, you will create an interpersonal communications strategy as part of the overall marketing communications plan. The following tasks are part of the strategy:

1. Review the overall marketing communications plan and determine the role of interpersonal marketing communications in communicating with target customers.
2. If personal selling is part of the marketing communications plan, create a sales strategy to include nature of sales force (company sales force or external sales team), sales structure, hiring/recruiting policies, and compensation program.
3. Determine the level of direct marketing for the company. Specifically, define the role of direct marketing in the overall marketing communications plan. Next, identify specific objectives for the direct marketing effort. Finally, create a direct marketing campaign and follow-up plan.

NOTES

1. *Market Watch,* May 2012, www.marketwatch.com/story/mindshare-launches-new-mobile-app-for-real-time-customer-feedback-2011-12-06.
2. D. Mayer and H. M Greenberg, "What Makes a Good Salesperson," *Harvard Business Review* 84, no. 7/8 (2006), pp. 164–79.
3. M. C. Johlke, "Sales Presentation Skills and Salesperson Job Performance," *Journal of Business and Industrial Marketing* 21, no. 5, pp. 311–29.
4. Chia-Chi Chang, "What Service Fails: The Role of the Salesperson and the Customer," *Psychology & Marketing* 23, no. 3 (2006), pp. 203–18; and J. T. Johnson, H. C. Barksdale Jr., and J. S. Boles, "The Strategic Role of the Salesperson in Reducing Customer Defection in Business Relationships," *Journal of Personal Selling and Sales Management* 21, no. 2, pp. 123–35.
5. B. Horovitz, "Prom Marketers Use Social Media to Push Deals," *USA Today,* April 30, 2013, www.usatoday.com/story/money/business/2013/04/30/prom-marketers-olive-garden-darden-menswearhouse-chipotle/2121791/.
6. R. G. McFarland, G. N. Challagalla, and T. A. Shervani, "Influence Tactics for Effective Adaptive Selling," *Journal of Marketing* 70, no. 4 (2006), pp. 103–17.
7. D. T. Norris, "Sales Communication in a Mobile World: Using the Latest Technology and Retaining the Personal Touch," *Business Communication Quarterly* 70, no. 4 (2007), pp. 492–510.
8. P. Declos, R. Luzardo, and Y. H. Mirza, "Refocusing the Sales Force to Cross-Sell," *The McKinsey Quarterly* 1 (2008), pp. 13–15; and R. M. Peterson and G. H. Lucas, "What Buyers Want Most from

Salespeople: A View from the Senior Level," *Business Horizons* 44, no. 5 (2001), pp. 39–45.

9. R. W. Palmatier, L. K. Scheer, and Jan-Benedict E. M. Steenkamp, "Customer Loyalty to Whom? Managing the Benefits and Risks of Salesperson-Owned Loyalty," *Journal of Marketing Research* 44, no. 2 (2007), pp. 185–201.
10. S. S. Liu and L. B. Comer, "Salespeople as Information Gatherers: Associated Success Factors," *Industrial Marketing Management* 36, no. 5 (2007), pp. 565–79; and L. Robinson Jr., G. W. Marshall, and M. B. Stamps, "An Empirical Investigation of Technology Acceptance in a Field Sales Force Setting," *Industrial Marketing Management* 34, no. 4 (2005), pp. 407–22.
11. J. Davis, "Great Sales People's Single Common Trait," *MSPmentor*, April 22, 2013, http://mspmentor.net/sales/great-sales-peoples-single-common-trait.
12. J. N. Sheth and A. Sharma, "The Impact of the Product to Service Shift in Industrial Markets and the Evolution of the Sales Organization," *Industrial Marketing Management* 37, no. 3 (2008), pp. 260–77; and P. Kriendler and G. Rajguru, "What B2B Customers Really Expect," *Harvard Business Review* 84, no. 40 (2006), pp. 22–37.
13. L. Taylor, "Back Pain, Arthritis to Dominate Chronic Pain Market: Study," *Pharma Times*, December 5, 2011, www.pharmatimes.com/Article/11-12-05/Back_pain_arthritis_to_dominate_chronic_pain_market_study.aspx.
14. P. Guenzi, C. Pardo, and L. Georges, "Relational Selling Strategy and Key Account Managers' Relational Behaviors: An Exploratory Study," *Industrial Marketing Management* 36, no. 1 (2007), pp. 121–38.
15. K. Alspach, "Prospecting for New Customers: Hubspot," *Boston Business Journal*, December 14, 2011, www.bizjournals.com/boston/blog/startups/2011/12/hubspot-amazon-personalization-marketing.html; and C. Sichtmann, "An Analysis of Antecedents and Consequences of Trust in Corporate Brand," *European Journal of Marketing* 41, no. 9/10 (2007), pp. 999–1115.
16. D. Ledingham, M. Kovac, and H. L. Smith, "The New Science of Sales Force Productivity," *Harvard Business Review* 84, no. 9 (2006), pp. 124–40.
17. L. Hershey, "The Role of Sales Presentations in Developing Customer Relationships," *Services Marketing Quarterly* 26, no. 3 (2005), pp. 41–59.
18. J. Rossman, "Value Selling at Cisco," *Marketing Management* 13, no. 2 (2004), pp. 16–23.
19. M. C. Johlke, "Sales Presentation Skills and Salesperson Job Performance," *Journal of Business and Industrial Marketing* 21, no. 5 (2006), pp. 311–28.
20. K. S. Campbell, L. Davis, and L. Skinner, "Rapport Management during the Exploration Phase of the Salesperson Customer Relationship," *Journal of Personal Selling & Sales Management* 26, no. 4 (2006), pp. 359–72.
21. J. Braselton and B. Blair, "Cementing Relationships," *Marketing Management* 16, no. 3 (2007), pp. 14–29.
22. J. E. Swan, M. R. Bowers, and L. D. Richardson, "Customer Trust in the Salesperson: An Integrative Review of Meta Analysis of the Empirical Literature," *Journal of Business Research* 44, no. 2 (1999), pp. 93–108; and J. L. M. Tam and Y. J. Wong, "Interactive Selling: A Dynamic Framework for Services," *Journal of Services Marketing* 15, no. 4/5 (2001), pp. 379–95.
23. B. Hardekopf, "Deceptive Telemarketing Practices Cost Discover over $200 Million," *Forbes*, September 25, 2012, www.forbes.com/sites/moneybuilder/2012/09/25/deceptive-telemarketing-practices-cost-discover-over-200-million/.
24. T. Nagle and J. Hogan, "Is Your Sales Force a Barrier to More Profitable Pricing . . . or Is It You?" *Business Strategy Series* 8, no. 5 (2007), pp. 365–79.
25. J. J. Belonax Jr., S. J. Newell, and R. E. Plank, "The Role of Purchase Importance on Buyer Perceptions of the Trust and Expertise Components of Supplier and Salesperson Credibility in Business to Business Relationships," *Journal of Personal Selling & Sales Management* 27, no. 3 (2007), pp. 247–60; T. V. Bonoma, "Major Sales: Who Really Does the Buying?," *Harvard Business Review* 84, no. 7/8 (2006), pp. 172–90; and E. C. Bursk, "Low Pressure Selling," *Harvard Business Review* 84, no. 7/8 (2006), pp. 150– 69.
26. G. A. Wyner, "The Customer," *Marketing Management* 14, no. 1 (2005), pp. 8–10.
27. L. Dowling, "TalkTalk Tops Ofcom Telco Complaints Table," *Total Telecom*, December 20, 2011, www.totaltele.com/view.aspx?ID=470043; and T. Furguson, "BT to Boost Online Customer Support," *BusinessWeek*, August 22, 2007, www.businessweek.com/print/globalbiz/content/aug2007/gb20070822_202845.htm.
28. A. A. Zoltners, P. Sinha, and S. E. Lorimer, "Match Your Sales Force Structure to Your Business Life Cycle," *Harvard Business Review* 84, no. 7/8 (2006), pp. 80–97.
29. S. Rosensteel, "New App Keeps Your Sales Team More Productive on the Go," *Forbes*, May 1, 2013, www.forbes.com/sites/seanrosensteel/2013/05/01/new-app-keeps-your-sales-team-more-productive-on-the-go/.

30. E. Anderson, "The Salesperson as Outside Agent or Employee: A Transaction Cost Analysis," *Marketing Science* 27, no. 1 (2001), pp. 70–86.

31. E. Waaser, M. Dahneke, M. Pekkarinen, and M. Weissel, "How You Slice It: Smarter Segmentation of Your Sales Force," *Harvard Business Review* 82, no. 3 (2004), pp. 105–22.

32. K. Weinmann, "Generation Y Isn't Impressed with Your Pension Plan and Doesn't Have Time for Your Hiring Process," *Business Insider*, December 6, 2011, http://articles.businessinsider.com/2011-12-06/strategy/30480497_1_millennials-social-media-generation; and M. Goldsmith, "Getting to Know Gen Why," *BusinessWeek*, February 28, 2008, www.businessweek.com/print/managing/content/feb2008/ca20080226_921853.htm.

33. C. F. Miao and K. R. Evans, "The Impact of Salesperson Motivation on Role Perceptions and Job Performance: A Cognitive and Affective Perspective," *Journal of Personal Selling & Sales Management* 27, no. 1 (2007), pp. 89–103.

34. W. J. Verbeke, F. D. Belschak, A. B. Bakker, and B. Dietz, "When Intelligence Is (Dys) Functional Achieving Sales Performance," *Journal of Marketing* 72, no. 4 (2008), pp. 44–57.

35. F. Jaramillo and J. P. Mulki, "Sales Effort: The Intertwined Roles of the Leader, Customers, and the Salesperson," *Journal of Personal Selling & Sales Management* 28, no. 1 (2008), pp. 37–51; and C. F. Miao, K. R. Evans, and Z. Shaoming, "The Role of Salesperson Motivation in Sales Control Systems—Intrinsic and Extrinsic Motivation Revisited," *Journal of Business Research* 60, no. 5 (2007), pp. 417–32.

36. C. Muir, "Relationship Building and Sales Success: Are Climate and Leadership Key?" *Academy of Management Perspectives* 21, no. 1 (2007), pp. 71–89; and K. LeMeunier-FitzHugh and N. F. Piercy, "Does Collaboration between Sales and Marketing Affect Business Performance?," *Journal of Personal Selling & Sales Management* 27, no. 3 (2007), pp. 207–20.

37. D. H. Lee, "The Moderating Effect of Salesperson Reward Orientation on the Relative Effectiveness of Alternative Compensation Plans," *Journal of Business Research* 43, no. 2 (1998), pp. 63–78.

38. S. Wright, "Loyaltyworks CEO Steve Damerow Improves Customer Incentives through Technology," *Investment Underground*, May 1, 2013, http://investmentunderground.com/6764/featured/loyaltyworks-ceo-steve-damerow-improves-customer-incentives-through-technology/.

39. G. R. Franke and J. E. Park, "Salesperson Adaptive Selling Behavior and Customer Orientation: A Meta-Analysis," *Journal of Marketing Research* 43, no. 4 (2006), pp. 34–50; and C. E. Pettijohn, L. S. Pettijohn, and A. J. Taylor, "Does Salesperson Perception of the Importance of Sales Skills Improve Sales Performance, Customer Orientation, Job Satisfaction, and Organizational Commitment, and Reduce Turnover?," *Journal of Personal Selling & Sales Management* 27, no. 1 (2007), p. 75.

40. R. Y. Darmon, "Controlling Sales Force Turnover Costs through Optimal Recruiting Training Policies," *European Journal of Operational Research* 154, no. 10 (2004), pp. 291–308; and P. T. Adidam, "Causes and Consequences of High Turnover by Sales Professionals," *Journal of American Academy of Business* 10, no. 1 (2006), pp. 137–42.

41. J. M. Ricks Jr., J. A. Williams, and W. A. Weeks, "Sales Trainer Roles, Competencies, Skills, and Behaviors: A Case Study," *Industrial Marketing Management* 37, no. 5 (2008), pp. 593–610; and M. P. Leach and A. H. Liu, "Investigating Interrelationships among Sales Training Methods," *Journal of Personal Selling & Sales Management* 23, no. 4 (2003), pp. 327–40.

42. Johnson & Johnson e-University website, December 26, 2011, www.jnjmedical.com.au/benefits/personal-development#euniversity; and A. McConnon, "The Name of the Game Is Work," *BusinessWeek*, August 13, 2007, www.businessweek.com/innovate/content/august2007/id20070813_467743.htm.

43. T. B. Jopez, C. D. Hopkins, and M. A. Raymond, "Reward Preferences of Salespeople: How Do Commissions Rate?," *Journal of Personal Selling & Sales Management* 26, no. 4 (2006), pp. 381–87; and S. N. Ramaswami and J. Singh, "Antecedents and Consequences of Merit Pay Fairness for Industrial Salespeople," *Journal of Marketing* 67, no. 4 (2003), pp. 46–60.

44. R. Y. Darmon and X. C. Martin, "A New Conceptual Framework of Sales Force Control Systems," *Journal of Personal Selling & Sales Management* 31, no. 3 (Summer 2011), pp. 297–310.

45. M. McQueen, "Health Costs: More Autism Coverage," *The Wall Street Journal*, March 6, 2011, p. 2, http://search.proquest.com.ezproxy.rollins.edu:2048/abicomplete/docview/855265697/fulltext/133E122CC AA6D51F471/4?accountid=13584; K. McKeough, "Best Places to Work: Benefits, Benefits, Microsoft," *Crain's Chicago Business* 31, no. 9 (2008), p. 24; and M. Conlin and J. Greene, "How to Make a Microserf Smile," *BusinessWeek*, no. 4049 (2007), pp. 56–59.

46. A. Fisher, "Why Are There Still So Few Women in Science and Tech?," *CNN Money*, March 2013,

http://management.fortune.cnn.com/2013/03/11/women-science-tech/; and J. Marder, "Why Engineering, Science Gender Gap Persists," *PBS Newshour,* April 2012, www.pbs.org/newshour/rundown/2012/04/science-engineering-and-the-gender-gap.html.

47. S. Shearman, "The Social Divide," *Marketing,* November 23, 2011, pp. 14–15; R. Ortega, "Impact of Direct to Consumers Marketing Strategies on Firm Market Value," *International Journal of Consumer Studies* 28, no. 5 (2004), pp. 466–80; and J. S. Thomas, W. Reinartz, and V. Kumar, "Getting the Most out of All Your Customers," *Harvard Business Review* 82, no. 7/8 (2004), pp. 116–29.

48. C. Joseph, "Colleges Using Direct-Mail Approach Tailored to Individual High Schoolers," NorthJersey.com, April 5, 2013, www.northjersey.com/news/201570081_Colleges_using_direct-mail_approach_tailored_to_individual_high_schoolers.html.

49. "How Can Direct Mail Keep Its Place in the Mix?" *Marketing,* October 26, 2011, p. 15; and A. Ansari, C. F. Mela, and S. A. Neslin, "Customer Channel Migration," *Journal of Marketing Research* 45, no. 1 (2008), pp. 60–75.

PART 6

Bring It all Together—Global and Performance Dimensions

chapter 15

UNDERSTAND THE GLOBAL MARKETPLACE: MARKETING WITHOUT BORDERS

chapter 16

THE MARKETING DASHBOARD: METRICS FOR MEASURING MARKETING PERFORMANCE

CHAPTER 15

Understand the Global Marketplace: Marketing without Borders

LEARNING OBJECTIVES

LO 15-1 Identify the various levels in the Global Marketing Experience Curve.

LO 15-2 Learn the essential information components for assessing a global market opportunity.

LO 15-3 Define the key regional market zones and their marketing challenges.

LO 15-4 Describe the strategies for entering new global markets.

LO 15-5 Recognize key factors in creating a global product strategy.

MARKETING IS NOT LIMITED BY BORDERS

From large multinationals to small start-up companies, business is no longer confined to a company's local market. Worldwide distribution networks, sophisticated communication tools, greater product standardization, and the Internet have opened world markets. Large companies such as Nestlé, P&G, Amazon, and General Electric leverage their considerable assets to build global companies that do business anywhere in the world (see Exhibit 15.1). At the same time, with relatively minimal investment, small companies access international markets with only a website and an international shipping company.[1]

While the opportunities have never been greater, the risks have also never been higher. Global marketing mistakes are expensive. The international competitive landscape includes sophisticated global companies as well as successful local organizations. The operating environment varies dramatically around the world creating real challenges for companies moving into new markets. Global customers demand different products, which means that successful products in a company's local market frequently have to be adapted to new markets.[2] All these factors establish global marketing as one of the most demanding but rewarding areas in marketing.

In your study of marketing management you have learned topics like marketing communications, product development, and consumer decision making; now we will consider how each is affected by global markets. Our goal in this chapter is to identify the challenges marketers face in global markets today. While it is certainly true that the global marketing manager for Huggies has different challenges than the marketing manager for a small software company, it is equally true that both need to know how marketing internationally is similar and different to marketing in their home market.

With growth in the saturated U.S. market increasingly difficult, Domino's has relied on expansion overseas. Although the company has changed aspects of its U.S. retail locations in a bid to increase sales and market share domestically (including a total overhaul of its pizza recipes, increased offerings, and new store footprints), the company's growth is increasingly a result of its international franchises. One of only eight global restaurant chains to have more than 10,000 outlets, Domino's has stores in over 100 countries—and in 70 of them, the restaurant is the country leader in pizza sales. The international market is far less saturated than the American one, and Domino's leadership says the company's products translate well internationally; bread, sauce, and cheese are almost universal. And toppings that cater to local tastes are easy to add to menus as needed. At only $200,000 to add a franchise, Domino's expects to sustain growth through international additions.[3]

EXHIBIT 15.1 | World's Largest International Companies in 2013

Company	Revenue ($ Millions)
Royal Dutch Shell	$ 484,489.0
ExxonMobil	452,926.0
Walmart	446,950.0
BP	386,463.0
Sinopec Group	375,214.0
China National Petroleum	352,338.0
State Grid	259,141.8
Chevron	245,621.0
ConocoPhillips	237,272.0
Toyota Motor	235,364.0

Source: From Fortune Global 500, July 3, 2013, Copyright 2013 Time, Inc. All rights reserved.

International brand United Colors of Benetton has a long history of promoting international togetherness. The clothing brand gets support from consumers for its causes like the Unhate Foundation.

THE GLOBAL EXPERIENCE LEARNING CURVE

An understanding of marketing beyond home markets develops over time as a company gets more international business experience. This process is referred to as *the global experience learning curve*. In some cases this happens quickly. General Motors moved into Canada in 1918, only two years after being incorporated, and eBay opened in the United Kingdom during its first year of operation. However, other companies take much longer to push into global markets. Walmart opened its first international store in Mexico City in 1991, nearly 30 years after Sam Walton opened the first store in Bentonville, Arkansas. Exhibit 15.2 lists the global expansion histories of a number of companies.

LO 15-1

Identify the various levels in the Global Marketing Experience Curve.

The global experience learning curve moves a company through four distinct stages: no foreign marketing, foreign marketing, international marketing, and global marketing. The process is not always linear; companies may, for example, move directly from no foreign marketing to international marketing without necessarily engaging in foreign marketing. In addition, the amount of time spent in any stage can vary; some companies remain in a stage for many years.

Companies with No Foreign Marketing

Many companies with *no direct foreign marketing* still do business with international customers through intermediaries or limited direct contact. In these cases, however, there is no formal international channel relationship or global marketing strategy targeted at international customers. Of course, any company with a website is now a global company as someone can visit the site from anywhere in the world, but companies with no foreign marketing consider any sales to an international customer as incidental.

EXHIBIT 15.2 | Examples of Global Companies and Their Expansion into Global Markets

Years to Expansion	U.S. Company	First Expansion
29	Walmart (est. 1962)	1991: Walmart opens two units in Mexico City.
20	Hewlett-Packard (est. 1939)	1959: HP sets up a European marketing organization in Geneva, Switzerland, and a manufacturing plant in Germany.
26	Tyson Foods (est. 1963)	1989: Tyson establishes a partnership with a Mexican poultry company, to create an international partnership.
25	Caterpillar (est. 1925)	1950: Caterpillar Tractor Co. Ltd. in Great Britain is founded.
19	Home Depot (est. 1979)	1998: Home Depot enters the Puerto Rican market, followed by entry into Argentina.
18	Gap (est. 1969)	1987: The first Gap store outside the United States opens in London on George Street.
12	Goodyear (est. 1898)	1910: Goodyear's Canadian plant opens.
10	FedEx (est. 1971)	1981: International delivery begins with service to Canada.
1	PepsiCo (est. 1965)	1966: Pepsi enters Japan and Eastern Europe.

The typical company with no foreign marketing is usually small with a limited range of products. Increasingly though, small companies move into international markets much faster than even a decade ago. This is due, in part, to domestic distributor relationships, local customers with global operations, and effective websites, which have all created international opportunities for many small companies with limited resources.

Companies with Foreign Marketing

Companies often develop a more formal international strategy by following their existing customers into foreign markets. Domestic customers with global operations may demand more service or place additional orders that require the company to work with their foreign subsidiaries. This stage of the global experience learning curve is called *foreign marketing* and involves developing local distribution and service representation in a foreign market in one of two ways. One method is to identify local intermediaries in appropriate international markets and create a formal relationship. The second approach is for the company to establish its own direct sales force in major markets, thereby expanding the company's direct market reach.

In either scenario, key activities (product planning and development, manufacturing) are still done in the company's home market, but products are modified to fit international requirements. Global markets are important enough for management to build international sales forecasts, and manufacturing allocates time specifically to international production. At this point, international markets are no longer an afterthought but, rather, an integral, albeit small, part of the company's growth model.[4]

International Marketing

When a firm makes the commitment to manufacture products outside its domestic market, it is engaged in *international marketing*. While companies can be heavily involved in international markets with extensive selling organizations and distribution networks, the decision to manufacture outside its home market marks a significant shift toward an integrated international market strategy. Global markets become an essential component of the company's growth strategy, and resources are allocated to expand the business into those markets. The company incorporates an international division or business unit that has responsibility for growing the business in targeted foreign markets.

International marketing aligns the company's assets and resources with global markets, but, in the vast majority of companies, management still takes a "domestic first" approach to the business. As a result, the corporate structure still divides international and domestic markets.

Ryanair, sometimes referred to as "Walmart on Wings," dominates the low-cost airfare market in Europe with a no-frills service that charges passengers for everything (assigned seats are extra, as is priority boarding). Also, the airline is a rolling billboard of advertisers, with passengers even seeing ads on the back of seat-back trays. In an industry where margins are already extremely narrow, Ryanair finds its profit wherever it can. An issue for the Ireland-based airline, however, is air travel taxes, which the company says are "damaging" to the airline and to travel in and out of the country in general. Although a report by the World Economic Forum ranks Ireland as the 12th most competitive country in Europe for travel—and the 19th most competitive in the world—Ryanair insists that the €3 tax per traveler leaving from Ireland has damaged the country's competitiveness. And while Ryanair's protestations may spring from self-interest—Ireland does rank 115th out of 140 for price competitiveness—the cost carrier's point may be on target.[5]

EXHIBIT 15.3 **Large U.S. Companies with over 50% of Revenue from International Markets**

Company	Percent of Sales from International Markets
Coca-Cola	71%
McDonald's	66
Hewlett-Packard	65
Dow Chemical	62
Nike	62
3M	61
Motorola	54
Caterpillar	52
Chevron	52

Global Marketing

A *global marketing* company realizes that all world markets (including the company's own domestic market) are, in reality, a single market with many different segments. This frequently happens when a company generates more than half its revenue in international markets. Exhibit 15.3 highlights companies considered traditional American companies but generate more than half their revenue outside the United States.

The most significant difference between international and global marketing organizations is management philosophy and corporate planning. Global marketers treat the world as a single, unified market with many different segments that may or may not fall along country political boundaries. International marketers, on the other hand, define markets along traditional political boundaries and, most often, assign unique status to their domestic market.

The first step in moving into global markets is to evaluate the market opportunities. Since a company's management team is usually less familiar with foreign markets, research helps fill in the blanks, providing critical information for decision makers.

With demand for luxury lower in the United States in the wake of the Great Recession, luxury brands faced slower growth (shares of Michael Kors have only grown at around 5 percent) or have lost value (Coach stocks fell over 10 percent). Tiffany's however, has performed surprisingly well. The luxury goods retailer saw a slight increase in U.S. sales, which were up 2 percent. It is the company's Asia market that has propelled its overall growth. Sales at Tiffany's are up 13 percent in Asia, with the Chinese market performing especially well. As Chinese demand for gold has grown, sales at Tiffany's jewelry have increased dramatically. To maintain its growth, the company has therefore continued to push its presence in the global market and the Asian region—a strategy that fueled its 20 percent growth in share value in 2013.[6]

Essential Information

LO 15-2

Learn the essential information components for assessing a global marketing opportunity.

Global market research focuses on five basic types of information.

Economic An accurate understanding of the current economic environment, such as gross domestic product (GDP) growth, inflation, strength of the currency, and business cycle trends, is essential. Also, depending on the company's target markets (consumer or business), additional economic data on consumer spending per capita (consumer products) or industrial purchasing trends (business products) are also needed to facilitate decision making. Exhibit 15.4 identifies the five largest economies in the world based on GDP, which is the total market value of all final goods and services produced in a country in a given year and one of the most widely used measures of economic growth.

Culture, Societal Trends Understanding a global market's culture and social trends is fundamental for consumer products and helpful for business-to-business marketers. Cultural values, symbols and rituals, and cultural differences affect people's perception of products while B2B companies must learn local cultural practices to recruit employees and establish good business relationships.[7]

Business Environment Knowledge of the business environment is essential for companies moving into foreign markets where they will invest significant resources. Ethical standards, management styles, degree of formality, and gender or other biases are all critical factors that management needs to know before entering a new market. Failure to understand the business environment can lead to misunderstanding and lost relationships as the company enters a new market. (See Exhibit 15.5 for examples.)

EXHIBIT 15.4 | Top 5 Economies Based on GDP

Top 5 Economies	GDP (purchasing power parity) (US$ trillion)
European Union	$15.70
United States	$15.66
China	$12.38
India	$ 4.74
Japan	$ 4.62

Source: *2012 CIA World Fact Book*, https://www.cia.gov/library/publications/the-world-factbook/rankorder/2112rank.html.

Political and Legal Local political changes can create significant uncertainties for a business. As witnessed in Bolivia and other countries, new governments sometimes alter the relationship of government to industry by exerting greater control and even nationalizing some industries.

Learning the legal landscape is fundamental before committing resources in a foreign market. Developing countries frequently limit the flow of money out of a country, making it harder for a foreign company to transfer money back home. Labor laws also vary widely around the world. Germany and France, for example, make it difficult to terminate someone once that person has been hired, while Great Britain's termination policies are more consistent with those of the United States.

One legal issue to consider when making foreign investments is taxes. In 2013 the Egyptian government raised taxes on luxury imports as a method to raise government revenue in a difficult political and socioeconomic situation. The decree from then President Morsi affected a wide range of products from shrimp and nuts to gambling tables, sunglasses, and fireworks. From the government's perspective, tariffs can raise revenue—a particularly important issue for the new Egyptian government, which was still trying to cement its position following the 2011 Arab Spring and a wave of uprisings. For foreign investors, however, the new tariffs are another factor to consider in determining which country to choose. While Egypt's historic reputation as a bastion of stability in the Middle East makes it a more attractive market than many of its neighbors, increased government tariff rates could detract from this.[8]

EXHIBIT 15.5 | Business Customs in Five Selected Countries

When you are doing business in...	Remember...
The Czech Republic	Relationship building is important. Start with small talk and get to know the individual you are working with.
France	You should address the French as Monsieur or Madame followed by his or her last name. Use first names only after you are encouraged to do so.
Japan	Exchanging business cards is a brief ceremony. Use both hands to accept the card and look over each side before you slip it into your jacket pocket or briefcase.
Germany	Punctuality is extremely important. Be on time or you may seem disrespectful.
Colombia	Colombians stand closer to each other than do Americans. Do not step back if you feel they are too close; you may seem rude.

Source: www.kwintessential.co.uk/etiquette/doing-business-in.html.

Specific Market Conditions Before entering a foreign market, a company has some understanding of the specific market conditions for its own products as a result of its existing business knowledge. However, it is unlikely a company has in-depth knowledge about market trends, competitors, and unique market characteristics. Unfortunately, many companies that follow customers into a particular market believe it is unnecessary to know a lot about local market conditions. This lack of understanding can limit growth opportunities. The more a company knows about the local market environment, the better it will be able to leverage its investment in that market.

Emerging Markets

World economic growth for much of the 20th century was fueled by the **developed economies** of Western Europe, the United States, and Japan. Over the past 25 years, however, while developed economies continue to grow, the most significant economic growth is found in **emerging markets**. Indeed, 75 percent of world economic growth over the next 20 years is projected to come from a new group of powerful economies, most notably China and India. These economic growth engines create market opportunities for companies, which, in turn, means marketers need to understand the unique challenges and opportunities of emerging markets.[9] Exhibit 15.6 highlights the fastest-growing economies in the world. Notice that the fastest-growing economies are small and their significant percentage growth is due in large part to the fact that the country's economy is starting from a much smaller economic base. Libya, for example, grew an amazing 121.9 percent in 2012, but that does not mean it represents a good market opportunity.

It is a cliché but still true that not all markets are created equal, and part of assessing a country's global opportunity involves understanding its stage of economic development. Economic historian Walt W. Rostow developed a classification system for evaluating markets that has been widely adopted. This classification system includes five stages of development and works best as a general guide rather than a model of specific global markets' economic development. It does not account for unique historical or current events affecting the country of interest. The final stage represents the economies of the United States, Germany, Great Britain, Japan, and other developed, industrialized countries.

Stage 1: The Traditional Society (for example, Sudan). Dependent on agriculture as the primary driver of the economy, these economies lack the capabilities to industrialize. Illiteracy is high, which hinders advances in technology.

Stage 2: Preconditions for Take-Off (for example, Romania). In these economies, new investments in infrastructure (transportation, communication, education, and health care) create the foundation for growth and encourage industrial expansion. Often these changes are driven by investments from private organizations (foreign companies looking to expand operations). Global companies target countries at this stage for production and other facilities because the cost of entry is very low. Moreover, it is possible to build a strong market position before the economy enters the next stage. In addition, countries at this stage often receive government assistance (from industrialized economies such as the United States or European Union or nongovernmental agencies such as the United Nations).

Stage 3: Take-Off (for example, The Czech Republic). The investments in infrastructure yield sustainable economic growth, which makes an economy look much more attractive to foreign investors. The economy transitions from agricultural to industrial. Banking systems, technology industries, and other "skilled" industries come into the market as business opportunities increase.

Stage 4: Maturity (for example, China). The economy, through private and public investments, seeks to maintain growth rates. As the economy grows, investments focus on expanding the infrastructure (technology and communications networks) to attract additional industrial investment. At this point, local companies begin to look outward and enter the global marketplace. Governments through legislation and public policy or investors through private development will target certain key industries to create a core global competency. Ireland, for example, identified technology and banking as key industries in the 1980s and created special incentives to attract companies in those industries. As a result Ireland is now a world leader in both technology and banking.

Stage 5: High Mass Consumption (for example, Germany). Consumption patterns shift as consumers demand higher levels of service and more durable goods. Income levels rise, creating a large population with discretionary income. Put another way, people are no longer concerned with simply surviving (food, shelter) but, rather, seek products and services that enhance the quality of their life. In other words, products are not needed but wanted.

EXHIBIT 15.6 | Fastest-Growing World Economies

Country	2012 GDP Real Growth Rate (%)
Libya	121.9
Sierra Leone	21.3
Macau	20.7
Niger	14.5
Mongolia	12.7
Afghanistan	11.0
Iraq	10.2
Timor-Leste	10.0
Bhutan	9.9
Liberia	9.0

Source: *2012 CIA World Fact Book.*

Economies that have not yet reached maturity can represent tempting investment targets as markets are less saturated and business opportunities exist. Visa and MasterCard are taking advantage of developing markets by using mobile technology. With 650 million mobile phone accounts in Africa, and 25 percent of cashless transactions taking place in developing economies, the credit card giants are taking the opportunity to invest in mobile payment technology. In 2013 Visa announced a partnership with Samsung to develop near field communication and payment technology, while MasterCard released MasterPass, a mobile wallet. The new technology is expected to be a key element in allowing Visa and MasterCard to reach users who do not use traditional credit card and banking systems: in 2012 alone, 16 percent of adults in Africa used a mobile phone to send or receive money.[10]

Marketing in Emerging Markets

The nature of emerging markets means traditional marketing methods will not be effective. For example, if the majority of a country lacks a television or radio and cannot read, traditional advertising campaigns will not work, or if a country lacks a distribution network, it will not be possible to deliver products to customers.

The challenge for marketers, particularly consumer products companies, is that demand for their products may be strong, but there is insufficient income to purchase the product and inadequate infrastructure to support sophisticated market programs. Soon after the Velvet Revolution in the Czech Republic, Estee Lauder opened a store in Prague targeted at Czech women living in the capital.[11] At first the company experienced problems because products that sold well in Western Europe and the United States simply were not being purchased. The company came to realize the products were sized and priced according to Western European standards and too expensive for the local Czech businesswoman. The solution was to sell sample sizes (which are often offered as premiums in promotional packages sold in the United States) for a fraction of the large product sizes. Czech women wanted to purchase Estee Lauder cosmetics, but at a size and price consistent with the local market.

Multinational Regional Market Zones

LO 15-3

Define the key regional market zones and their marketing challenges.

The single most significant global economic trend over the past 15 years is the emergence of regional market zones around the world. **Regional market zones** consist of a group of countries that create formal relationships for mutual economic benefit through lower tariffs and reduced trade barriers. In some cases, such as the European Union, their influence extends beyond economic concerns to political and social issues. Many countries believe membership in an economic alliance will be essential for access to markets in the future. As the world divides itself into a handful of powerful economic alliances, countries feel pressure to align with a regional market zone. Exhibit 15.7 identifies four of the largest regional market zones.

Regional market zones generally form as a result of four forces. The first and most fundamental factor is *economic.* Many small and medium-sized countries believe growth in their own country will be enhanced by forming alliances with other countries. By enlarging the trading area and creating a market zone, each country benefits economically and the market zone has more power in the global marketplace. Second, research suggests *geographic proximity* to other alliance partners is advantageous in the development of a market zone. Transportation and communication networks are more likely to connect countries close to one another, making it easier to facilitate market zone activities. Other issues such as immigration also tend to be handled more effectively when the distance between partners is minimized. The third factor is *political.* Closely related to increased economic power is increased political clout, particularly as smaller countries form broad political alliances. A prerequisite for effective political alliances among countries is general agreement on government policies. Countries with widely disparate political structures find it difficult to accommodate those differences in a political alliance. *Culture similarities,* such as having a shared language, among alliance partners also facilitate market zones as shared cultural experiences encourage greater cooperation and minimize possible conflicts from cultural disparities.

Europe The **European Union** is the most successful regional market zone and it is also one of the oldest. Founded more than 50 years ago by six countries (Belgium, France, Italy, Luxembourg, the Netherlands, and West Germany) with the Treaty of Rome, the EU now includes 28 countries spanning all of Europe (see Exhibit 15.8). In addition, five countries are seeking membership in the European Union: Iceland, Macedonia, Montenegro, Serbia, and Turkey. The process of becoming a member of the EU takes many years, and applicants must meet a wide range of economic, social, and legal criteria. One of the most difficult challenges for many member states is meeting targeted government spending and total debt limits. France and Germany (the two largest members of the EU) have both failed to meet government spending limits in recent years, and the debt limits of countries like Italy and Greece exceed the EU guidelines. With few consequences for missing EU

EXHIBIT 15.7 | Top Four Regional Market Zones

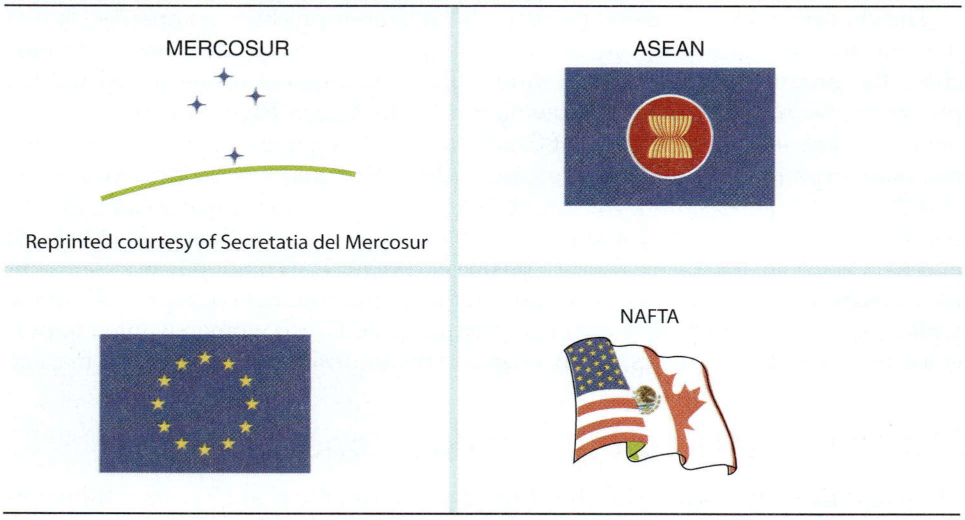

Source: Reprinted courtesy of European Commission.

EXHIBIT 15.8 | Composition of the EU since its creation

targets, many governments focus more on local country priorities than EU directives. This has been a factor in the ongoing challenges for the euro as countries like Greece experience significant budget problems. Other countries (Italy, Spain, Portugal) are also having significant problems meeting their financial obgliations.[12]

The EU has become one of the most dominant economic entities in the world, with economic output approximately equal to the United States, and its currency, the euro, is one of the leading world currencies. The European Union's influence extends far beyond economics because member countries grant the EU significant political and social power to enact laws, create taxes, and exert tremendous social influence in the lives of citizens. For example, the EU has adopted strong socially responsible policies for companies doing business in member countries. Ethical Dimension 15 examines McDonald's strategy for dealing with increased environmental and social concerns in Europe

Americas The most significant market zone in the Americas is the alliance of the United States, Canada, and Mexico, which is commonly referred to by the treaty that created the alliance, **NAFTA (North American Free Trade Agreement)**. NAFTA created the single largest economic alliance and has eliminated tariffs between the member countries for more than 19 years. Exhibit 15.9 lists NAFTA's main provisions. Many industries, such as automaking, have manufacturing plants in Mexico to supply the U.S. market. Retailers have also benefited; Gigante, a large Mexican supermarket chain, operates in the United States while Walmart, a U.S. company, has over 800 stores in Mexico.[13]

NAFTA is not the only market zone in the Americas. **MERCOSUR**, the most powerful market zone in South America, was inaugurated in 1995 and includes

ETHICAL DIMENSION 15

When Ethics Meets Good Business in Europe

Companies no longer consider ethical decisions and good business decisions to be mutually exclusive. For example, McDonald's takes a comprehensive environmental approach to its European operations with a variety of strategies targeted at increasing the environmental footprint of the company. Among the many product changes instituted by McDonald's is the sale of coffee certified by the Rainforest Alliance, a global nonprofit based in New York, at its more than 7,000 European outlets. McDonald's seeks to differentiate itself from other upscale food chains and other coffeehouses by selling a new brand of socially responsible coffee, Kenco. Steve Easterbrook, president and COO of McDonald's U.K., states, "We can offer our customers great tasting coffee that doesn't cost the earth and benefits coffee growers, their communities, and the environment."

The change to environmentally friendly coffee is the latest in a series of strategic moves designed to position McDonald's as a leader in the environmental movement. Whenever possible, the company purchases from local producers who meet established standards for animal welfare and safe environmental practices. It also bans the use of certain growth-promoting antibiotics in its poultry (a significant concern in Europe).

Increasingly, consumers consider a product's environmental impact in making their purchase decision. Is the product safe? Is the product healthy? What is the effect of the product on the environment? McDonald's research suggests consumers are willing to pay for "green" products. "Consumers more than ever want to do business with those companies that share their values, and because of our track record on environmental issues, we see lots of opportunity to close the gap between misconceptions and reality," says Bob Langert, McDonald's vice president of corporate social responsibility.

The challenge McDonald's faces is balancing environmental responsibility with consumer expectations about product quality and, in this case, tastes and value. Before making a change, McDonald's must know whether the market will accept it, which means significant product testing as well as sourcing of quality products.

McDonald's realizes that being sensitive to the health of its customers and the environment as a whole makes sense for its customers, the environment, and the company. Rita Clifton, chairman of Interbrand, U.K., notes, "Companies are increasingly trying to boost social responsibility programs because they know that not to do so is a major corporate risk."[14]

Ethical Perspective

1. **McDonald's:** Should McDonald's support the additional costs of carrying environmentally friendly coffee if it becomes unprofitable? Do you see any challenges for McDonald's in selling Kenco coffee?
2. **Consumers:** What is the price differential you would be willing to pay for McDonald's environmentally friendly gourmet coffee?
3. **Competitors:** How should Starbucks respond to this challenge by McDonald's?

EXHIBIT 15.9 | Key Provisions of NAFTA

NAFTA aims to:

- Eliminate barriers to trade in, and facilitate the cross-border movement of, goods and services between the territories of the Parties.
- Promote conditions of fair competition in the free trade area.
- Increase substantially investment opportunities in the territories of the Parties.
- Provide adequate and effective protection and enforcement of intellectual property rights in each Party's territory.
- Create effective procedures for the implementation and application of this Agreement, for its joint administration and for the resolution of disputes; and
- Establish a framework for further trilateral, regional, and multilateral cooperation to expand and enhance the benefits of this Agreement.

Source: www.mac.doc.gov/nafta/chapter1.html.

the economies of South America: Argentina, Bolivia, Brazil, Chile, Paraguay, and Uruguay. With over 200 million people and a combined GDP of more than $1 trillion, it is currently the third-largest free trade area in the world.[15] One of the drawbacks has been a limited transnational transportation network, which restricts the movement of goods between member countries. However, MERCOSUR has overcome this problem by successfully leveraging the combined economic power of the individual member countries and creating additional economic benefits for its members.

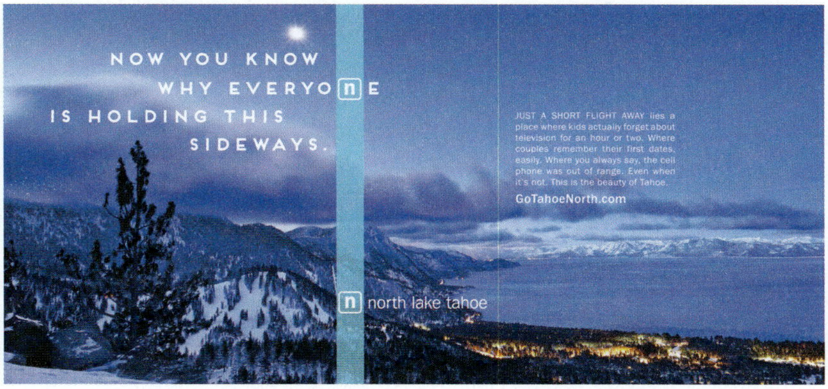

Many countries and even some cities promote their strengths for tourism and investment. North Lake Tahoe positions itself as a place to get away from technology.

Asia The most important Asian market zone is **ASEAN**, which was founded in 1967 and comprises 10 countries in the Pacific Rim (Brunei Darussalam, Indonesia, Malaysia, Philippines, Cambodia, Laos, Myanmar, Singapore, Thailand, and Vietnam). After the 1997–1998 Asian financial crisis, the group added China, Japan, and South Korea. While the relationships with these "plus 3" countries are less developed than the full member countries, the combined economic activity of all participants makes ASEAN a powerful global economic force.[16] The GDP of the 10 full members is over $600 billion, and if the "plus 3" countries are included, the combined total is over $10 trillion. ASEAN is currently leading talks to create an Asian free-trade area that would encompass "28 percent of the world's total export volume." The Regional Comprehensive Economic Partnership would be second only to the WTO in size.

Marketing in Regional Market Zones

The formation of regional market zones presents marketing managers with a number of challenges and opportunities. As market zones lower tariffs and reduce trade barriers, companies view zone members more holistically. Rather than looking at Brazil and Argentina as separate markets, companies can develop regional marketing plans that facilitate greater cost efficiencies (e.g., lowering distribution costs) and increase effectiveness of the marketing effort (e.g., creating regional advertising campaigns based on the free flow of products throughout the zone). In addition, greater market zone coordination dramatically reduces transaction costs and makes it easier for companies to determine appropriate product cost models and subsequent pricing strategies.

At the same time, however, each of these market zones suffers from internal conflicts. Lowering trade barriers, reducing tariffs, and harmonizing government spending and taxation rates among members require difficult choices that all too often governments are not willing to make. When internal conflicts (high trade barriers and tariffs or increased government spending and taxation) remain between market zone members, marketers must deal with greater marketing complexity and higher costs. In addition, while members open markets between themselves, they frequently raise barriers to other market zones and individual countries. The results are bilateral agreements with individual countries that negate the advantages of operating in a market zone.

SELECT THE GLOBAL MARKET

Conducting a thorough assessment of potential global market opportunities is an essential first step in entering the global market. Once the analysis is completed, it is time to select specific countries for future investment. Deciding which countries

Philippines-based fast-food chain Jollibee is building its brand with international expansion. The company is wildly popular in the Philippines, with 18 percent market share in metro Manila, compared to McDonald's 10 percent market share. The company began its international expansion by opening restaurants in areas where Filipinos have immigrated, such as the West Coast of the United States. Jollibee has since moved into new markets where Filipino cuisine culture is not as prevalent, such as China and Vietnam. One way the company has managed to grow so dramatically is by widening its restaurant portfolio, so that it can enter new markets with the restaurants whose product offerings are best suited to local tastes. In addition to the original Jollibee outlets, the corporation either owns outright or possesses majority stakes in Chow King (a Chinese fast-food chain), Greenwich Pizza, Mang Inasal (a Filipino barbecue chicken chain), and BK Titans—the sole franchisee of Burger King in the Philippines.[17]

to enter is difficult because the risk of failure is very high. Targeting the wrong country can lead to very high costs and unprofitable long-term investments. Walmart pulled out of the German market at an estimated cost of $400 million. On the other hand, moving too slowly into a market can hamper growth and limit profit potential in the future. eBay's decision to move slowly into China cost the company a dominant position in the market.

Identify Selection Criteria

Companies usually have a variety of different criteria for evaluating and selecting global markets. The criteria should reflect the company's commitment to ongoing corporate objectives and incorporate both market and financial targets designed to help marketing managers consider not only the marketing implications of choosing a particular country but also the financial consequences of the decision.

Market selection criteria incorporate the nature of the competitive environment, including both local and global competitors, as well as target market size and future growth rates. Marketing managers need to know which markets will be the easiest and which will be the most difficult to enter. In addition, the size and future growth potential of international markets are critical in making the long-term commitment to manufacture in an international market. On the other hand, financial criteria focus on the cost of market entry and profitability estimates over given time periods. Decision makers are particularly interested in knowing the size of the investment and the length of time it will take before the company can expect to be profitable in a new market.[18]

EXHIBIT 15.10 | Key Company Characteristics in Global Market Expansion

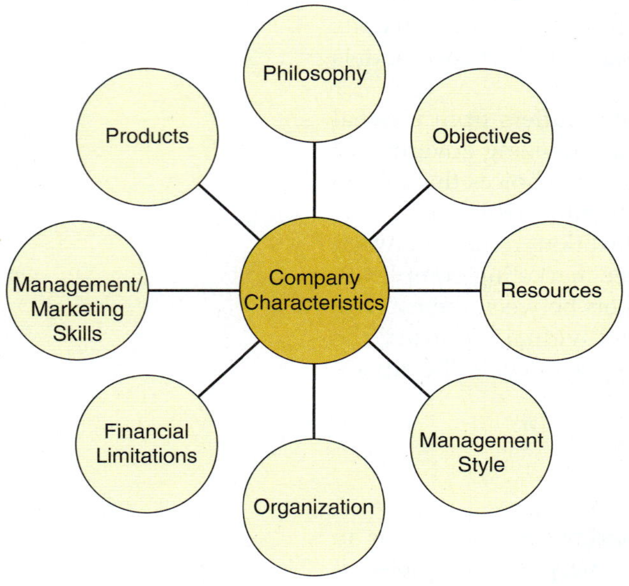

Company Review

As a marketing manager you will need to evaluate global market opportunities against key company characteristics to look for markets that maximize the company's strengths while minimizing weaknesses. Moving into new foreign markets brings greater risk to the company. As a result, decision makers must consider whether their company philosophy, personnel skill sets (principally in critical areas such as marketing and logistics), organizational structure, management expertise, and financial resources support the move into new countries (see Exhibit 15.10). Comparing the analysis of market opportunities with company characteristics drives the final selection as management looks for the best fit between each country's mix of opportunities/threats and the company's strengths/weaknesses.

DEVELOP GLOBAL MARKET STRATEGIES

After selecting a country, you must develop a comprehensive marketing strategy. International expansion requires a reassessment of existing marketing strategies. Companies often mistakenly believe they can adapt existing market strategies to new international markets. Unfortunately, successful market tactics in the company's home market often fail to translate well into foreign markets. As a result, it is necessary to construct a marketing plan specifically designed for entering global markets.

Market Entry Strategies

The first decision is how to enter the market. An entry strategy is the framework for entering a new global market, so choosing the right strategy is critical. This decision affects all other marketing decisions. In addition, deciding on a market entry strategy has long-term implications because once the strategy is selected it is difficult and expensive to change.

Entry into new global markets follows one of four basic strategies: exporting, contractual agreements, strategic alliances, and ownership. Within these basic strategies are various options. Generally, companies enter new markets by exporting because it offers minimal investment and lower risk. At the same time, potential return on investment and profitability are lower and the company has very little control over the process. As a company strengthens its international involvement there is the potential for greater financial returns and control over the process; however, risk and company investments increase.

LO 15-4

Describe the strategies for entering new global markets.

Exporting **Exporting** is the most common method for entering foreign markets and accounts for 10 percent of all global economic activity. Primary advantages include the ability to penetrate foreign markets with minimal investment and very little risk. Frequently, companies lack a coherent exporting strategy and take an opportunistic approach that simply fills orders without regard to any specific analysis or targeting.

Most people consider exporting an initial entry strategy and not a long-term approach to global marketing. However, some very large companies find exporting a viable strategy despite a global market presence. Boeing and Airbus, the two manufacturers of large jet airliners, both follow an exporting strategy, manufacturing the jets in their home markets (Boeing in the United States, Airbus in Europe) and then using a direct sales force to market their planes around the world.[19]

Internet. Without question, the Internet has expanded the global reach of every company with a website. Initially, the Internet was considered a tool for increasing domestic sales, but that has changed as Internet access has expanded worldwide. Critical to the success of the Internet market entry strategy is easy payment and credit terms offered by global credit companies such as MasterCard, Visa, and American Express. Credit cards and other financial payment systems have greatly simplified transactions, making it easier for the customer to purchase and more secure for the company to sell products anywhere in the world. Another key is the ability to deliver products anywhere in the world on time and in good working order using global delivery companies such as UPS, FedEx, and DHL. This greatly enhances customer and company confidence in a successful transaction.

Internet retailers such as Amazon.com have moved aggressively into global markets. Amazon has opened sites for Germany, the United Kingdom, Canada, Japan, France, China, Italy, Spain, and Austria. In the United Kingdom and

Germany, Amazon's sites are among the most visited commercial sites. The Internet has also expanded the international market reach of catalog retailers such as L.L. Bean and Lands' End. People in foreign markets who never have seen an L.L. Bean catalog are able to make purchases online because the company website offers instructions in several languages.[20]

Exporter and Distributor. The next of level of exporting involves having country representation, which can take several forms. **Exporters** are international market specialists that help companies by acting as the export marketing department. They generally do not have much contact with the company, but exporters provide a valuable service with their knowledge of policies and procedures for shipping to foreign markets. For small companies with little or no international experience, exporters expedite the process of getting the product to a foreign customer.

Distributors represent the company and often many others in foreign markets. These organizations become the face of the company in that country, servicing customers, selling products, and receiving payments. In many cases, they take title to the goods and then resell them. The primary advantages are that distributors know their own local markets and offer a company physical representation in a global market, saving the company from committing major resources to hire and staff its own operations. The disadvantages are lack of control since distributors do not work directly for the company and lower profitability resulting from the distributor's markup.

Direct Sales Force. Staffing a direct sales force in foreign markets is a significant step for a company moving into global markets. It is expensive to staff and maintain a local sales team in a foreign market; however, companies will often make the commitment because of the level of control and expertise offered by company-trained salespeople. For some industries, creating a direct sales force is required because customers will demand that company salespeople be in the country. This is often the case in the technology and high-end industrial product industries.

Contractual Agreements

Contractual agreements allow a company to expand participation in a market by creating enduring, nonequity relationships with another company, often a local company in that market. Most often these agreements transmit something of value such as technology, a trademark, a patent, or a unique manufacturing process in return for financial compensation in the form of a licensing fee or percentage of sales.

> In 2013, Apple announced its plans to increase its focus on the Indian market, in large part by increasing its physical presence in the country through the addition of 200 Apple franchised stores by 2015, tripling the number of Apple stores in India. In the Indian market, Apple uses licensed franchisees to run its stores. An important driver of the decision is increased mobile phone usage in India. Adding Apple Store franchises is not simply about tapping into growing demand for smartphones; there is also significant growth in the tablet market. One difficulty facing the company as it franchises in India is government regulations, one of which mandates that 30 percent of goods must be sourced locally—a condition that has so far limited the growth of Apple's physical presence in India.[23]

Licensing. Companies choose **licensing** when local partnerships are required by law, legal restrictions prohibit direct importing of the product, or the company's limited financial resources limit more active foreign participation. Companies seeking to establish greater presence in a market without committing significant resources can choose to license their key asset (patent, trademark) to another company, effectively giving the company the right to use that asset in that market. Small and medium-sized companies with a specific product competence that lack the willingness or expertise to invest heavily in foreign operations can identify a license partner in a particular foreign market to manufacture products or provide critical services such as local distribution. In addition, larger companies use this approach to help in exporting and even manufacturing products where more extensive investments are not justified. Pharmaceutical companies are global manufacturers but also license their products in a number of foreign markets. For example, Helsinn Healthcare SA and PT Kalbe Farma Tbk. signed an agreement giving Kalbe Farma the exclusive license and distribution rights in Indonesia for Aloxi, a drug that prevents nausea and vomiting after chemotherapy.[21] In these situations, there is limited direct risk to the company, though selecting the wrong licensing partner can be a major problem. On the other hand, licensing does not offer high profit potential and can limit long-term opportunities if a company awards an extended licensing contract.

Franchising. This market entry method has been growing over the last decade and enables companies to gain access to a foreign market with local ownership. The franchisor, usually a company seeking to enter a foreign market, agrees to supply a bundle of products, systems, services, and management expertise to the franchisee in return for local market knowledge, financial consideration (franchisee fee, percentage of sales, required purchasing of certain products from franchisor), and local management experience. Franchisors exert a great deal of control with extensive franchise agreements that dictate how the franchisee will operate the business.[22] In this way, the franchisor is able to maintain some level of quality control at the point of customer contact.

Franchising, as a global market entry strategy, really took off in the 1990s and has been the first point of entry for many retailers looking to expand international operations. McDonald's, Burger King, KFC, and others have created large franchising networks around the world. Nearly two-thirds of McDonald's restaurants are outside the United States. Combining low capital investments, rapid expansion opportunities, and local market expertise, franchising offers many advantages as a market entry strategy. However, there are also challenges. Worldwide, consumer tastes vary significantly and franchisors need sufficient resources to create products that will meet demands of global customers while maintaining quality control.

Strategic Alliances As a market entry strategy, **strategic alliances** have grown in importance over the past 20 years in an effort to spread risk to other partners. In some industries, strategic alliances now dominate the competitive landscape. Nowhere is this more noticeable than the airline industry. **one**world Alliance (American Airlines, British Airways, Qantas, Cathay Pacific), Sky Team (Air France, KLM, Delta, Continental, Korean Air, AeroMexico), and Star (United, Lufthansa) have created a worldwide network of airline partnerships that include code-sharing, frequent flyer mileage partnerships, and some logistical support. All these alliances are designed to make each airline stronger at its weakest point. Building a global airline is extremely expensive and it is much more cost-effective for Delta to partner with Air France to reach cities inside Europe than it is to build its own network. In reality, it would not even be possible with local legal restrictions favoring local airlines.[24] As a result, creating strategic alliances is a necessity, and airlines create broad global partnerships to extend their reach (see Exhibit 15.11).

International Joint Venture. A specific type of strategic alliance called joint venture enables many companies to enter a market that would otherwise be closed because of legal restrictions or cultural barriers.[25] Additionally, like all strategic alliances, it reduces risk by spreading risk to other partners. **Joint ventures** are a partnership of two or more participating companies and differ from other strategic alliances in that (1) management duties are shared and a management structure is defined; (2) other corporations or legal entities, not individuals, formed the venture; and (3) every partner holds an equity position. Since both partners

EXHIBIT 15.11 | Airline Strategic Alliances

STAR ALLIANCE	Air Canada, Air China, Air New Zealand, ANA, Asiana Airlines, Austrian, bmi, Egyptair, LOT Polish Airlines, Lufthansa, Scandinavian Airlines, Singapore Airlines, South African Airways, Spanair, Swiss International Air Lines, TAP Portugal, Thai Airways International, Turkish Airlines, United
SKYTEAM™	Aeroflot, Aerolineas Argentinas, AeroMexico, AirEuropa, Air France, Alitalia, China Airlines, China Eastern, China Southern, Czech Airlines, Delta, Kenya Airways, KLM, Korean Air, MEA, Saudia, Tarom, Vietnam Airlines, XiamenAir
oneworld	Airberlin, American Airlines, British Airways, Cathay Pacific, Finnair, Iberia, Japan Airlines, LAN, Malaysia Airlines, Qantas, Royal Jordanian, S7 Airlines

have equity in the joint venture and share in management duties, it is essential to choose the right partner. To avoid problems, each partner must define what it brings to the joint venture in terms of reputation, resources, and management expertise. Additional critical topics include management structure, cost sharing, and control.

Direct Foreign Investment The market entry strategy with the greatest long-term implications is **direct foreign investment**. Risks go up substantially when a company moves manufacturing into a foreign market. Although this is the riskiest market entry strategy, future market potential can position it for long-term growth. A company must consider a number of factors including:

- *Timing*—unknown political or social events, competitor activity.
- *Legal issues*—growing complexity of international contracts, asset protection.
- *Transaction costs*—production and other costs stated in various currencies.
- *Technology transfer*—key technologies are more easily copied in foreign markets.
- *Product differentiation*—differentiating a product without increasing cost.
- *Marketing communication barriers*—local market practices vary a great deal.

The size of the investment and the risk to the company mean a company should consider a wide range of costs and potential problems as well as the market opportunity. Issues like loss of product technologies can be overlooked as the company considers the opportunity to expand into new markets.[26] All too often companies have committed significant resources before they realize that a critical issue has substantially raised the investment and risk.

Organizational Structure

Once marketing managers decide on a specific market entry strategy, they must create an efficient and effective global market organizational structure. This challenge requires constant monitoring and adaptation. No one ideal structure exists. A recent study of 43 multinational U.S. companies reported they planned to make a total of 137 organizational changes to their international operations over the next five years. This suggests that the best organizational structure is, at best, a moving target that evolves over time (see Exhibit 15.12).

Before a company decides on its organizational structure, it must make two critical decisions. The first involves **decision-making authority**. As companies grow, lines of authority become longer and more complicated, so clearly defined protocols regarding which decisions are made at each level of the organization are important. A decision normally made by senior management becomes more difficult when executives are eight time zones away.[27]

The **degree of centralization** is a second critical decision since it affects resource allocation and personnel. Three primary organizational patterns employed by organizations around the world are centralized, decentralized, and regionalized. The primary advantages of a more centralized structure include greater control and, as a result, more consistency across the organization. It is also more efficient in creating centers of expertise that bring together knowledgeable people to address key organizational issues (for example, R&D, legal, and IT). Decentralized organizations, on the other hand, offer a hands-on management approach that facilitates rapid response to changing market conditions. The regional organization seeks to combine advantages of both approaches by centralizing key functions while pushing decision making closer to the global market.[28]

Once decision-making authority has been established and degree of centralization defined, companies usually adopt one of three organizational structures in building their international operations. First, **global product lines** work well for companies with a broad, diverse range of products. This model is based on the

EXHIBIT 15.12 | The Most Common International Organizational Structure

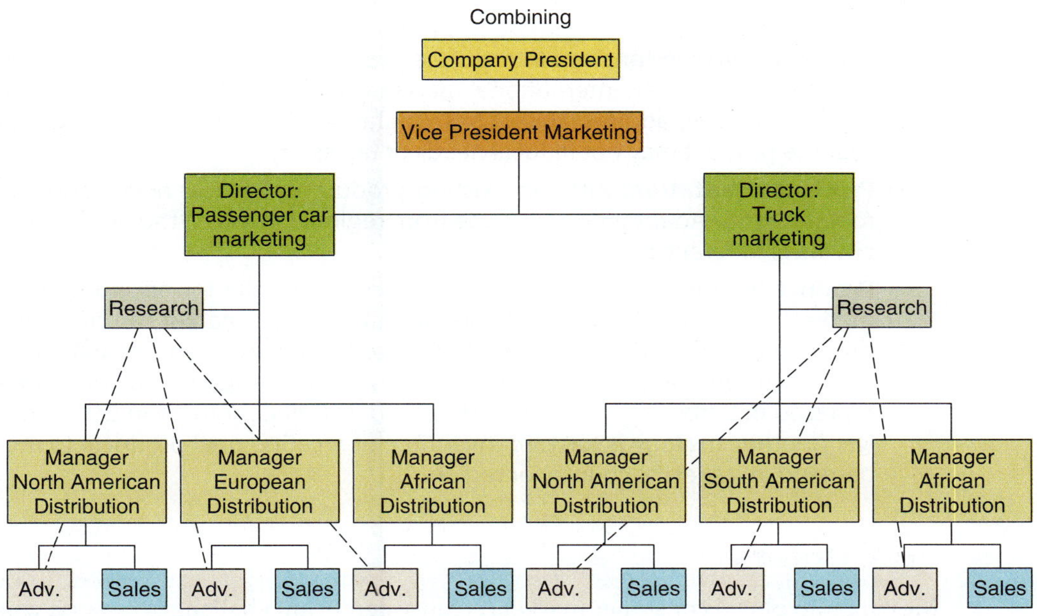

Source: Reprinted from Philip R. Cateora, John Graham, and Mary C. Gilly, *International Marketing,* 16th ed., 2013. Copyright @ 2013 The McGraw-Hill Companies.

global functionality and appeal of the products and enables companies to target similar products to customers around the world. A product line structure can also be divided by customer, providing an even closer link between product usage and customer need. The disadvantage is that some organizational functions such as the direct sales force may be duplicated in markets where the company believes there is significant market opportunity. Siemens, the large German conglomerate, maintains specialized direct sales forces by product and customer. This approach works for Siemens because its diversified product portfolio includes everything from large power generators to sophisticated medical equipment. A second structure, **geographic regions**, divides international markets by geography, building autonomous regional organizations that perform business functions in the geographic area. This model works particularly well when local government relationships are critical to the success of international operations as it affords company management a closer connection to local customers. Large construction and engineering companies such as Halliburton maintain operations geographically with specific operations in each area that are suited to the environments in which they operate. The **matrix structure** is the third form and is a hybrid of the first two. Not surprisingly, most companies today use some form of matrix structure that encourages regional autonomy while building product competence in key areas around the world.

Product

LO 15-5

Recognize key factors in creating a global product strategy.

Global market expansion is based on the belief that people or other businesses outside the company's home market will purchase its products. Acceptance of that belief depends largely on what products the company will sell in those new markets. Does it, for example, simply take its existing product with no modifications? Does it create a new product developed specifically for foreign markets, or something in between? The answers to these questions are fundamental to global market expansion.

Some products are more easily accepted than others in new markets around the world. Several consumer electronics products such as digital music players and digital cameras are essentially the same product around the world. But many products, like food, do not travel well across borders. Those products usually need to be adapted to fit local tastes. A company may select from three basic product options:[29]

- **Direct product extension:** Introduce a product produced in the company's home market into an international market with no product changes. Advantages include no additional R&D or manufacturing costs. Disadvantages are that the product may not fit local needs or tastes.
- **Product adaptation:** Alter an existing product to fit local needs and legal requirements. Adaptation can range from regional levels all the way down to city-level differences.
- **Product invention:** Create a new product specifically for an international market. Sometimes old products discontinued in one market can be reintroduced in a new market, a process known as backward invention. Cell phone manufacturers have adopted this strategy, taking phones that have been replaced in European or Asian markets and introducing them in Latin America. Another strategy is forward invention, or creating new products to meet demand in a specific country or region.

Consumers

Moving into global consumer markets creates significant challenges because companies with little international experience find it difficult to assess, develop, and market products targeted at consumers with widely different needs, preferences, and product usage demands. Even experienced global marketers sometimes fail to identify specific consumer trends in foreign markets. Four specific product issues face international consumer marketers—quality, fitting the product to the culture, brand strategy, and country of origin.

"Diet Coke" goes by "Coke Light" in many parts of the world, including Africa. However, this ad from Kenya, despite displaying a different name, displays the same fun feeling as Diet Coke in the United States.

Quality The perception of quality varies drastically around the world, which makes it hard for a company developing or adapting a product for a global market. What works in one market may fail in another, as cell phone manufacturers have learned. In Europe, Japan, and the United Sates, cell phones must have a roaming capability to be successful, but Chinese consumers do not consider it an important feature.

Global consumers are knowledgeable about product quality and have a clear understanding of what they are willing to pay for at a given quality level. Research suggests the relationship of price and quality, or the value proposition that we focus on in this book, remains a key factor in consumer decision making. The test for many organizations is providing quality when they lack control over the delivery of key quality dimensions such as service. As we discussed earlier, in many situations companies do not provide key elements of the product experience, which is one reason good international partners are so important.

Fitting the Product to the Culture Culture differences exert tremendous influence on consumer product choices and are critical in international markets. Brand names as well as product colors and features are heavily influenced by the culture in local foreign markets.

Language differences have created unique and occasionally humorous examples of marketing mistakes. When Coca-Cola introduced Diet Coke in Japan, initial sales were disappointing until the company realized that Japanese women do not like the concept of dieting and the Japanese culture relates dieting to sickness (not a desired connection with a product). The company changed the name to Coke Light, which has been much more effective around the world. Companies also have to adapt their products to fit local markets. Manufacturers of kitchen products have found the Japanese market difficult to penetrate. Mr. Coffee and Philips Electronics NV found their coffeemakers did not sell well in Japan because Asian kitchens in general are much smaller than Western kitchens. The larger coffeemakers sold in the United States did not fit on Japanese kitchen counters.

WeChat is a fast-growing social media site in China. The platform combines texting, audio and video message exchange, group messaging, and live-chat capabilities, as well as incorporating several unique features like "Shake Shake" (which allows users to connect with others who are shaking their phones at the same time) and "Drift Bottle" (through which users can send and respond to notes that are sent at random). The features allow users not only to connect with existing contacts, but to meet new people. With its growing success in China—300 million users in two years—the next question is whether the company can expand internationally. With a more globally accessible name and brand after it was rebranded from the original name (Weixin), WeChat may be more successful in other countries than other Chinese social networks. It is available in a variety of languages, and is the number one social-networking app in Thailand, Malaysia, and Saudi Arabia. WeChat is now being promoted in countries like Australia, Argentina, India, and Indonesia, and its success in those very different cultural environments may determine its further international spread.[30]

Brand Strategy As we explored in Chapter 8, companies often seek to create a unified branding strategy around the world. In some cases this is effective. Coca-Cola, Caterpillar, Apple, Kellogg, BMW, and others have created powerful global brands. As companies acquire local brands, one of the first decisions is whether to fold a local brand into a global brand. Companies have to consider local conditions, but, when possible, companies are harmonizing brands to build brand awareness and extend marketing communication dollars.

Local brands, on the other hand, offer companies distinct awareness and built-in market loyalty. Nestlé, for example, follows a local branding strategy for individual products (the company carries more than 7,000 brands) but also promotes the Nestlé corporate brand globally. It believes that local branding helps differentiate its products.

Country of Origin Increasingly, customers apply what is known as the country-of-origin effect in their purchase decisions. The **country-of-origin effect** is the influence of the country of manufacture, assembly, or design on a customer's positive or negative perception of a product.[31] "Made in Japan," "Made in Italy," "Made in the United States"—each has meaning to customers and infers that a product has certain qualities based on its country of origin. Such perceptions can change over time. Immediately after World War II, products made in Japan were considered of poor quality and inexpensive, which may seem hard to believe in light of the preeminent view of Japanese quality in the 21st century. Budweiser is a product with a very strong country-of-origin effect. Consumers around the world identify the product as American. After the purchase of Anheuser-Busch by InBev, based in Belgium, InBev announced that maintaining the strong American identity of Budweiser was a focus of the company.

Companies use ethnocentric messages to differentiate their products from foreign brands. Ford and Chrysler have both used their American heritage in advertising to foster a "buy American" feeling among consumers. Interestingly, Japanese automobiles manufactured in the United States frequently carry a higher percentage of U.S. parts than cars assembled in Mexico for American automobile manufacturers.[32] Research reports the following regarding country of origin:

- People in developed countries prefer products manufactured in their own country.
- Manufacturers from countries viewed favorably in the world tend to highlight their country of origin more than those from less developed countries.
- Countries have developed certain areas of influence in which the country of origin makes a difference, such as Japan and Germany for cars, the United States for technology, and France for wine and luxury goods.

Market Channels

One of the thorniest issues facing global marketers is getting their product to the customer.[33] American and European companies, in particular, are used to sophisticated channels of distribution that seamlessly move products from manufacturing sites to the customer at relatively low cost. Well-coordinated transportation and logistics systems lower distribution costs and increase customer choices at the point of sale.

Many companies have to rethink their distribution strategy when they enter global markets and find inadequate transportation networks, poorly organized or not easily accessible distribution systems, as well as an almost unlimited number of fundamentally different channel structures. Companies are frequently unprepared for the complexity of penetrating a foreign distribution system. The stakes are high because channel decisions are, at least in the short run, difficult and expensive to adjust. Companies able to develop successful channel strategies gain a competitive advantage in that market and effectively limit the options of other competitors.

Channel Structures Unless the product is manufactured in the country where it is sold, all products pass through a global channel of distribution (see Exhibit 15.13). The product must move from the country of manufacture through an international channel between countries to the local international market distribution channel. Obviously the manufacturer is most familiar with the distribution network in its home country. However, goods going to international markets use different intermediaries such as trading companies or international agents that require modifications to existing channels. Coordinating the movement of products between countries usually means hiring specialists familiar with legal issues as well as the most effective and efficient means of transportation. Companies have a number of transportation choices and, in addition to cost, should consider risk and length of time in transit. The producer faces the greatest challenge in the last stage, getting the product into the local channel and ultimately to the customer. International shipping specialists can help identify local distribution partners, but the company is more likely to look for channel alliances that fit overall business objectives and not simply distribution channels.

Channel Factors In selecting a channel partner, companies should consider six strategic objectives known as the Six Cs of channel strategy: Cost, capital, control, coverage, character, and continuity offer a checklist for evaluating channel options.

Cost Estimating channel costs includes (1) the initial investment in creating the channel and (2) the cost of maintaining the channel. As companies expand into new markets, many search for ways to increase the efficiency of local distribution systems by eliminating unnecessary middlemen, thereby shortening the channel to the customer.[34]

Capital An inadequate global market distribution system is expensive in terms of both adding cost to the product and creating long-term damage to the brand and the company's reputation. If a channel network is already in place, the investment is low; however, if the company needs to develop or greatly improve an existing system, the cost can be very high.

EXHIBIT 15.13 | International Channel Structure

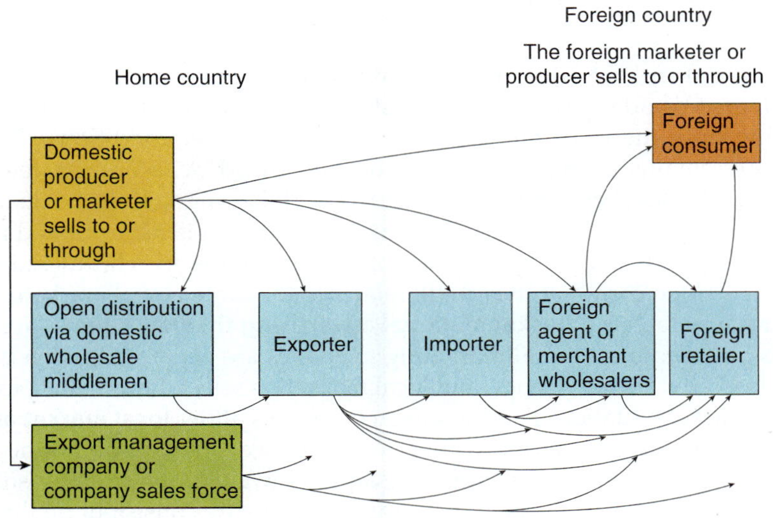

Source: Reprinted from Philip R. Cateora, John Graham, and Mary C. Gilly, *International Marketing,* 16th ed., 2013. Copyright @ 2013 The McGraw-Hill Companies.

Control The more control the company wants in the channel, the more expensive it is to maintain. As a result, companies generally look for a balance between channel control and cost. The complexity of global supply chains coupled with lack of local market knowledge make the task of creating a distribution system so expensive that all but the most accomplished global marketers rely on local distribution networks in foreign markets.

Coverage Local distribution networks around the world may lack full exposure to a given market. Even in the United States, for example, complete coverage of a consumer market necessitates multiple distribution channels. As a result, it is necessary to evaluate which distribution network best reaches the target customers, which may not necessarily be the network with the widest distribution. Targeting upper- and middle-class consumers in China requires extensive distribution in cities along the coast (Beijing, Shanghai, and Guangzhou) but minimal distribution in the rest of the country.

Character The long-term nature of channel decisions makes character an issue in selecting the best channel partner.[35] The capabilities, reputation, and skills of the local channel partner should match the company's characteristics. A service-oriented company should look for local channel partners with a reputation for excellent service and high customer satisfaction.

Continuity Changing a distribution system creates anxiety among customers and gives competitors an opportunity to take advantage of inevitable inefficiencies and disruption of service. Identifying channel partners with a long-standing presence in the market provides some security; however, the best local partners are also the most difficult to establish a relationship with as they frequently already have established involvement with competitors.

Marketing Communications

Another factor to consider is global marketing communications, which place additional demands on an organization's communication strategy. The core elements of communicating to a customer in a home market (language, images, color, cultural contextual cues) can be vastly different in foreign markets.[36] In addition, media are different and companies that rely on one form of media in their home market will have to adapt to other media.

Advertising Global market advertising follows one of four basic approaches that vary by degree of adaptation. The first strategy creates **global marketing themes** adjusting only the color and language to local market conditions. The basic ad template remains unchanged throughout the world. A second strategy, **global marketing with local content**, keeps the same global marketing theme as the home market but adapts it with local content. Local content is incorporated in a standardized template to encourage a local look and feel to the ad. This includes images as well as written copy, but the ad still relates to the same global marketing message. A third approach is a **basket of global advertising themes**. Here related but distinct ads built around several marketing messages are generated, often by the company's lead advertising agency, and local marketers select the ads that best fit their specific market situation. Finally, some companies allow **local market ad generation**. Marketers have the authorization to create local ads that do not necessarily coordinate with global marketing messages. However, this strategy still requires coordination at higher levels in the company to ensure consistent quality. It takes considerable resources to market products globally and the leading global advertisers identified in Exhibit 15.14 all spend well in excess of $2 billion advertising globally every year.

EXHIBIT 15.14 | **World's Largest Advertisers (in billions)**

Company	2012	2011	%CHG
Procter & Gamble	$10,615	$11,252	-5.7%
Unilever	7.413	7,317	1.3
L'Oréal	5,643	5,593	0.9
Toyota Motor Corp.	3,310	2,881	14.9
General Motors Corp	3,206	3,346	-4.2

Global decision making is less centralized today than it was 20 years ago, so Fossil's choice to run the same mini-magazine in issues of *Esquire* magazine that ran in countries ranging from the United States and Britain to China and Hong Kong was surprising. It's increasingly easy for companies to customize advertising to individual markets, and so the practice is increasingly common. Fossil used the eight-page mini-magazine spread to introduce a new collection of Swiss watches, and ad executives at the company felt that the appeal was universal enough to merit the investment in the international advertising. In addition, Tom Kennedy, Fossil's executive vice president, explained that in today's extremely connected world, there is no longer a way to "break in one market"—new launches will always spread through the Internet. Although the decision to pursue a global ad campaign strategy was not an easy one, ultimately Fossil felt that the possible rewards outweighed the risks.[37]

Personal Selling The salesperson–customer relationship is dramatically different around the world. In the United States, the relationship is very business-focused and less personal. In Latin America and Asia, the relationship is much more personal. Actual business negotiations often do not begin until a personal relationship has been established. Companies need sensitivity in selecting, hiring, and training their global sales force to accommodate local business cultures.

Sales Promotion A relatively small part of U.S. marketing communication budgets is allocated to sales promotion; however, this can be a significant component of marketing communication strategy in global markets. The need to stimulate consumer trial and purchase can be greater. Both PepsiCo and Coca-Cola sponsor traveling carnivals to outlying villages in Latin America with the purpose of encouraging product trial.[38]

Public Relations The expansion of global communications has greatly increased the importance of international public relations. Companies realize that dealing with crises must be done quickly and effectively as global news organizations move instantly on stories around the world. Getting the company's perspective on a story requires coordination by the company and public relations consultants before release to the public. Public relations can also enhance other elements of a marketing communications strategy.[39] When companies introduce new products, they frequently schedule them to coincide with press conferences and news cycles in other countries.

Pricing

There are three main pricing strategies. No single pricing strategy accommodates every local foreign market, so most companies follow a combination of cost-based and market-conditions-based pricing in setting a final price to market.[40]

One World Price The company assigns one price for its products in every global market. In theory, this approach enables a company to standardize other elements in the marketing mix and simplifies financial forecasting. In reality, this strategy is not followed very often. While price is constant, the cost to produce, distribute, and market the product varies dramatically, creating wide fluctuations in profit margins. Furthermore, local conditions such as competitive pressures, economic circumstances, and other local market factors can have a significant effect on the final product price.

Local Market Conditions Price The company assigns a price based on local market conditions with minimal consideration for the actual cost of putting the product into the market. Responding to the market is certainly vital in assigning the final price, but local conditions may not reflect the reality of bringing the product to market for an international company. Local competitors do not incur the transportation costs, potential tariffs, and other related expenses of bringing a product in a foreign market. As a result, companies must be particularly sensitive to local market pricing when setting their price. Strong local or even global competitors that dictate local market prices should be considered in assessing the attractiveness of a global market opportunity. One solution is to identify valued-added product features that allow a higher final price to the customer.

Cost-Based Price This strategy considers cost plus markup to arrive at a final price. While the focus on costs precludes charging an unprofitable price, it does not consider actual market conditions. If costs are high as a result of tariffs or transportation, the final price may be too high for the market.

Hyundai has successfully expanded in the global car market. However, strength in the Korean currency, the won, has put the company at a competitive disadvantage in the United States. The company is constrained by Japanese and U.S. manufacturers because their products have a price advantage relative to Hyundai models even with the additional features offered on Hyundai cars. Without the price advantage, buyers are less willing to buy a Hyundai.[41]

Price Escalation A considerable quandary for companies in global marketing is that the costs of doing business globally are often higher than in their home market. Many people are surprised that products sold in their home country frequently cost twice as much in foreign markets. Four primary forces drive higher costs and create price escalation.

- **Product export costs:** Differences in the product configuration, packaging, and documentation raise the cost of many products for international markets. A key internal cost issue is **transfer pricing**, or the cost companies charge internally to move products between subsidiaries or divisions. If companies charge too high a price internally, it can make the final product price uncompetitive because the local subsidiary must add a markup to arrive at a final price.
- **Tariffs, import fees, taxes:** Governments all around the world impose tariffs, fees, and taxes on imported products to protect industries in their home market and increase their revenue.
- **Exchange rate fluctuations:** For many years, the U.S. dollar was the standard for all international contracts, which tended to minimize currency fluctuations as everything was priced in dollars. Now, currencies float and products are priced using a market basket of currencies. Since currencies can easily float 15 to 20 percent against each other, the assigning of currency values

in international contracts is critical. Increasingly, companies want contracts written in their home currency to protect their risk of loss due to currency fluctuations.[42]

- **Middlemen and transportation costs:** Creating a channel for global markets extends the number of channel members and increases costs. Each channel partner requires compensation, which raises the final price to the customer. Moreover, transportation costs increase as the distance to a local market increases.

Global Pricing Issues In addition to price escalation, there are two other global pricing issues. The first, **dumping**, refers to the practice of charging less than actual costs or less than the product price in the company's home markets.[43] The World Trade Organization and most national governments have outlawed this practice and, if dumping is proven, a government can impose a tax on those products. Dumping is generally not a problem when global markets are strong; however, the willingness to price export goods based on marginal costs rather than full costs increases when markets weaken. The second major issue is the **gray market**, which involves the unauthorized diversion of branded products into global markets. Gray market distributors (who are often authorized distributors) divert products from low-price to high-price markets. Companies should carefully watch unusual order patterns among their distributors because that can signal a gray market problem.[44]

SUMMARY

Global marketing has become synonymous with marketing. Companies cannot rely solely on their domestic markets for long-term growth. Technology and sophisticated distribution systems make it easy for a company anywhere in the world to become an international marketer. However, companies generally go through a global experience learning curve as their international business expands.

As companies consider new international markets, their first task is to assess the market opportunity. Unlike domestic markets, companies find they often lack in-depth knowledge of international markets, which presents significant challenges.

The growth of international markets has led to the development of regional market zones that bring countries together into trade alliances and sometimes political alliances.

Developing global market strategies involves the highest levels of the company. From organizational structure, product development, distribution, and communications to pricing, companies seek to maximize the efficiencies of global market opportunities while creating effective local market strategies to satisfy local market demands.

KEY TERMS

developed economies 448
emerging markets 448
regional market zones 449
European Union 450
NAFTA (North American Free Trade Agreement) 451
MERCOSUR 451
ASEAN 453
exporting 455
exporters 456
distributors 456
contractual agreements 456
licensing 456
franchising 457
strategic alliances 457
joint ventures 457
direct foreign investment 458
decision-making authority 459
degree of centralization 459
global product lines 459
geographic regions 460
matrix structure 460
country-of-origin effect 462
global marketing themes 464
global marketing with local content 464
basket of global advertising themes 464
local market ad generation 464
transfer pricing 466
dumping 467
gray market 467

APPLICATION QUESTIONS

1. You are the marketing manager for a small company located in the United States that manufactures specialized parts for high-end ink-jet printers. The company's largest customer (Hewlett-Packard) has asked your company to supply parts to 10 of its distribution and repair sites around the world. The company has never sold products outside the United States so this represents a significant step for the company. What stage in the global experience learning curve is the company likely entering and why? Identify the activities the company should undertake at this stage.
2. You are the market research director for a consumer product company. You have been asked to evaluate China as a potential market for your company's products and begin a search of secondary data. What are types of information you would consider in assessing China? How would you find information on these issues?
3. You are the marketing manager for Oxymoron detergent and have been instructed to introduce this product into Argentina. What six factors would you need to consider in determining the proper channel of distribution for the introduction of Oxymoron detergent?

4. Compare and contrast the pricing strategy for Apple's iPhone around the world with that of the latest Samsung Galaxy. Then as marketing manager for Microsoft/Nokia, how would you price a new full-featured smartphone that will be introduced in 35 countries in the very near future? What pricing strategy would you choose and why?
5. You are the chief marketing officer for Digital Distributed Products (DDP), manufacturer of Wi-Fi hardware found on laptop computers. The company's number one distributor in Germany just called and said it is experiencing significant "gray market" products coming in from Russia. Customers are saying DDP products are available at a significant discount from the distributor's legitimate price. As the CMO how would you address this problem?

MANAGEMENT DECISION CASE: A New Global Competitor: Commercial Jetliner Production Begins in China

Manufacturing a full-size commercial jetliner with almost four million parts is a daunting task, one at which only a handful of companies in the entire world are currently succeeding (Boeing and Airbus, to name two). Nonetheless, Comac, the government-owned Commercial Aircraft Corp. of China, is vying to join the ranks of successful companies in this marketplace in roughly half the time that most industry experts think is possible. Comac is embarking on an effort to build a commercial jetliner that will compete directly with the Boeing 737 and the Airbus A320, the two most popular commercial jet products in the world. The company has consistently hawked that it will have the jet airborne in 2014, just six years after beginning the project. Many industry professionals already are predicting that the first flight will not take place at least until 2015, 2016, or 2017. Regardless of when it actually hits the market, the production and marketing of this plane are an example for how more business may be conducted in the future.

Comac's product is the C919, where the C refers to China, the number 9 in Chinese sounds similar to a different word meaning forever, and the 19 stands for the 190 passengers the plane will carry (clever, eh?). The Chinese government has been pumping money into Comac in an effort to lessen the 70 percent worldwide market share dominance enjoyed by Boeing and Airbus. This project is important to China specifically because the country is projected to surpass the United States in air passenger traffic by 2032 and they will need an additional 5,580 planes to satisfy that demand. In U.S. dollars, the value of that many planes is over $780 billion. An indicator of China's demand growth for air travel in the near term is that between 2011 and 2015 the government will construct another 80 airports and expand 100 others. Some of those new airports and expansions are occurring in such remote locations that workers are blasting the tops off of mountain ranges to create space for new runways. Suffice it to say that when demand is that acute, in both the short and long term, actions must be taken to meet the demand.

However, manufacturing a modern jetliner is not easy (as Boeing itself found with the much-delayed but finally released 787 Dreamliner). In this case, Comac has chosen a path similar to that used by both Boeing and Airbus and is partnering with suppliers from all over the world to produce different parts of the plane. Those parts will then be transported to Comac's main assembly building near Shanghai. Ten contractors working to provide components are located in the United States. Others are from Austria, England, Ireland, France, Switzerland, and Japan. Many of those suppliers have signed joint venture agreements with Comac, while others have not done so out of concern that their intellectual property and trade secrets will be compromised. Nonetheless, as Comac gets closer to actually assembling the first C919, one certainty is that its new cadre of relationships with the international partners will go a long way toward determining the project's success.

Other factors determining Comac's success include operating expenses such as fuel. Jet fuel is a major expense for the firms and governments that purchase commercial jets globally; thus, the weight of a plane is a significant concern for potential buyers. Previous attempts by other Chinese aircraft manufacturers at building a plane were abandoned because the plane was too bulky and inefficient. In addition, regulatory issues will play a big role in the success of this product and Comac will have to learn to effectively deal with the entire world network of air travel agencies. They have no experience with satisfying FAA requirements in the United States or similar requirements by government entities in other parts of the world so they have hired a consultant from the United States to help them learn to work with these systems and gain needed approvals.

Whether Comac can overcome all of these challenges to gain market acceptance of the C919 is yet to be seen. However, with 400 orders for the plane already booked (caveat—95 percent of the orders are from government-owned Chinese airlines) and with billions in cash to continue investing in the project, Comac must be taken as a serious threat to become a major player in the commercial jetliner production business.

Questions for Consideration

1. One of the suppliers working with Comac to provide parts for the C919 is a company called Parker Hannifin, which is supplying hydraulic, fuel, and flight control systems. Based on this information, what type of global market entry strategy do you believe Parker Hannifin is following with its efforts toward Comac? Support your conclusion.
2. The case mentions a potential legal issue many companies have in doing business with Chinese companies—the potential for loss of trade secrets and intellectual property rights. What other essential information do you think is necessary for companies to investigate before committing to do business with a firm based in China?
3. Comac has decided to enter an extremely competitive market with the C919. What global market strategy do you recommend for Comac as it explores the possibility of marketing its product to major airlines in the United States and Europe? That is, how will it position itself to gain orders against Boeing and Airbus?

Source: Scott Cendrowski, "China Gets Ready for Takeoff," *Fortune*, 168, no. 8 (November 18, 2013), pp. 90–99.

MARKETING PLAN EXERCISE

ACTIVITY 17: Thinking Globally; Marketing Plan Tasks

For any company doing business in a global market, it is essential to consider the unique elements of that market in developing the marketing plan. Consider the discussion in Chapter 2 as you:

- Identify possible global markets for a new product.
- Determine essential information needed to assess the market opportunity.

Keep in mind that specific marketing strategies have been presented throughout the book. However, it will be important to keep the global marketing discussion in mind as you develop your marketing plan.

NOTES

1. Peter Gabrielsson, Mika Gabrielsson, John Darling, and Reijo Luostarinen, "Globalizing Internationals: Product Strategies of ICT Manufacturers," *International Marketing Review* 23, no. 6 (2006), pp. 650–67.
2. M. Theodosiou, and L. C. Leonidou, "International Marketing Policy: An Integrative Assessment of the Empirical Research," *International Business Review* 12, no. 2 (2003), pp. 141–71.
3. Dale Buss, "Domino's Global Growth Feeds Pizza Chain's Rising Success," *Forbes,* March 9, 2013, www.forbes.com/sites/dalebuss/2013/03/09/dominos-global-growth-feeds-pizza-chains-growing-success/.
4. Katrijn Gielens and Marnik G. Dekimpe, "The Entry Strategy of Retail Firms into Transition Economies," *Journal of Marketing* 71, no. 2 (2007), pp. 196–210; and Jasmine E. M. Williams, "Export Marketing Information-Gathering and Processing in Small and Medium-Sized Companies," *Marketing Intelligence and Planning* 24, no. 5 (2006), pp. 477–92.
5. John Mulligan, "Ryanair Again Urges Scrapping of 'Damaging' Travel Tax," *Independent.ie,* March 27, 2013, www.independent.ie/business/irish/ryanair-again-urges-scrapping-of-damaging-travel-tax-29153412.html.
6. Agustino Fontevecchia, "Tiffany's Grows on China's Love for Gold as U.S. Demand for Luxury Stagnates," *Forbes,* March 22, 2013, www.forbes.com/sites/afontevecchia/2013/03/22/tiffanys-grows-on-chinas-love-for-gold-and-jewelry-as-u-s-demand-for-luxury-stagnates/.
7. Kristian Moller and Senja Svahn, "Crossing East-West Boundaries: Knowledge Sharing in Intercultural Business Networks," *Industrial Marketing Management* 33, no. 3 (2004), pp. 219–28.

8. "Egypt Raises Customs on Luxury Imports," Associated Press News, March 25, 2013, www.businessweek.com/ap/2013-03-25/egypt-raises-customs-on-luxury-imports.

9. "Growth Still Quite Strong: Inflation Remains the Key Concerns for Emergers, with Many Countries Still Tightening Policies," *Emerging Marketing Weekly,* April 14, 2008, pp. 1–13; and Luiz F. Mesquita and Sergio G. Lazzarini, "Horizontal and Vertical Relationships in Developing Economies: Implications for SME's Access to Global Markets," *Academy of Management Journal* 51, no. 2 (2008), pp. 359–71.

10. Trefis Team, "Visa and MasterCard Will Use Mobile Phones to Tap Developing Economies Growth," *Forbes,* March 6, 2013, www.forbes.com/sites/greatspeculations/2013/03/06/visa-and-mastercard-will-use-mobile-phones-to-tap-developing-economies-growth/.

11. Jennifer Hoyt, "Innovations in Beauty," *The Prague Post,* April 7, 2005, www.praguepost.cz/archivescontent/40872-innovations-in-br-br-beauty.html.

12. Cristina del Campo, Carlos M. F. Monteiro, and Joao Oliveira Soares, "The European Regional Policy and the Socioeconomic Diversity of European Regions: A Multivariate Analysis," *European Journal of Operational Research* 187, no. 2 (2008), pp. 600–12; and David Floyd, "Have 'European Politics' and EU Policymaking Replaced the Politics of Member State Countries?," *International Journal of Social Economics* 35, no. 5 (2008), pp. 338–43.

13. "Wal-Mart Banks on the 'Unbanked,'" *BusinessWeek,* December 13, 2007 and www.giganteusa.com.

14. *BBC News,* "Profile: Mercosur—Common Market of the South," May 20, 2008, http://news.bbc.co.uk/1/hi/world/americas/5195834.stm.

15. KerryCampbell, "McDonald's Offers Ethics with Those Fries," *BusinessWeek,* January 7, 2007, www.businessweek.com/globalbiz/content/jan2007/gb20070109_958716.htm?chan=search.

16. *BBC News,* "Profile Association of SouthEast Asian Nations," May 20, 2008, http://news.bbc.co.uk/2/hi/asia-pacific/country_profiles/4114415.stm.

17. Sunshine Lichauco De Leon, "Billionaire Tony Tan Caktiong Takes Jollibee Foods Global," *Forbes,* January 30, 2013, www.forbes.com/sites/forbesasia/2013/01/30/billionaire-tony-tan-caktiong-takes-jollibee-foods-global/.

18. Richard A. Owusu, Maqsood Sandhu, and Soren Kock, "Project Business: A Distinct Mode of Internationalization," *International Marketing Review* 24, no. 6 (2007), pp. 695–714; and Terence Fan and Phillip Phan, "International New Ventures: Revisiting the Influences behind the 'Born-Global' Firm," *Journal of International Business Studies* 38, no. 7 (2007), pp. 1113–32.

19. Judith Crown and Carol Matlack, "Boeing Delays Dreamliner Again," *BusinessWeek,* April 9, 2008, www.businessweek.com/print/bwdaily/dnflash/content/apr2008/db2008049_424569.htm; and Carol Matlack, "Airbus Cost-Cuts Don't Fly," *BusinessWeek,* May 7, 2008, www.businessweek.com/global-biz/content/may2008/gb2008057_379072.htm?chan=search.

20. "L.L. Bean, Inc. Reports 2007 Net Sales Results," March 7, 2008, www.llbean.com/customerService/aboutLLBean/newsroom/stories/03072008_LLBean_News.html.

21. "Helsinn Healthcare SA: Pharmaceutical Company Granted Distribution Rights for Aloxi in Indonesia," *Biotech Week,* February 9, 2005, p. 350.

22. B. Elango, "Are Franchisors with International Operations Different from Those Who Are Domestic Market Oriented?," *Journal of Small Business Management* 45, no. 2 (2007), pp. 179–85.

23. Karsten Strauss, "Apples Triples Down on India," *Forbes,* March 26, 2013, www.forbes.com/sites/karstenstrauss/2013/03/26/apple-triples-down-on-india/.

24. Sergio G. Lazzarini, "The Impact of Membership in Competing Alliance Constellations: Evidence on the Operational Performance of Global Airlines," *Strategic Management Journal* 28, no. 4 (2007), pp. 345–60; and Kerry Capell, "Skirmishing in the Open Skies," *BusinessWeek,* January 14, 2008, www.businessweek.com/print/globalbiz/content/jan2008/gb20080114_431564.htm.

25. Jane W. Lu and Xufei Ma, "The Contingent Value of Local Partners' Business Group Affiliations," *Academy of Management Journal* 51, no. 2 (2008), pp. 295–305; and Eric Rodriguez, "Cooperative Ventures in Emerging Economies," *Journal of Business Research* 61, no. 6 (2008), pp. 640–55.

26. Lance Eliot Brouthers, Yan Gao, and Jason Patrick McNicol, "Corruption and Market Attractiveness Influences on Different Types of FDI," *Strategic Management Journal* 29, no. 6 (2008), pp. 673–81; and Jan Hendrik Fisch, "Investment in New Foreign Subsidiaries under Receding Perception of Uncertainty," *Journal of International Business Studies* 39, no. 3 (2008), pp. 370–87.

27. Riki Takeuichi, Jeffrey P. Shay, and Jiatao Li, "When Does Decision Autonomy Increase Expatriate Managers' Adjustment? An Empirical Test," *Academy of Management Journal* 51, no. 1 (2008), pp. 45–60.

28. Andrea Dossi and Lorenzo Patelli, "The Decision-Influencing Use of Performance Measurement Systems in Relationships between Headquarters and

Subsidiaries," *Management Accounting Research* 19, no. 2 (2008), pp. 126–39.

29. Michael G. Harvey and David A. Griffith, "The Role of Globalization, Time Acceleration, and Virtual Global Teams in Fostering Successful Global Product Launches," *Journal of Product Innovation Management* 24, no. 5 (2007), pp. 486–501; and Thomas L. Powers and Jeffrey J. Loyka, "Market, Industry, and Company Influences on Global Product Standardization," *International Marketing Review* 24, no. 6 (2007), pp. 678–94.
30. Anita Chang Beattie, "China's Fast-Growing WeChat Shakes Up Weibo. Could It Jump to the U.S.?," *Advertising Age,* February 25, 2013, http://adage.com/article/digital/chinese-mobile-app-wechat-shake-shakes-social-crm/239938/.
31. Sadrudin A. Ahmed and Alain d'Astous, "Antecedents, Moderators, and Dimensions of Country-of-Origin Evaluations," *International Marketing Review* 25, no. 1 (2008), pp. 75–84; and Saikat Banerjee, "Strategic Brand-Culture Fit: A Conceptual Framework for Brand Management," *Journal of Brand Management* 15, no. 5 (2008), pp. 312–22.
32. "Made in the USA? The Truth behind the Labels," *Consumer Reports* 73, no. 3 (2008), p. 12.
33. Eric Gang, Robert W. Paellmatier, Lisa K. Scheer, and Ning Li, "Trust at Different Organizational Levels," *Journal of Marketing* 72, no. 2 (2008), pp. 80–98; Janice M. Payan and Richard G. McGarland, "Decomposing Influence Strategies: Argument Structure and Dependence as Determinants of the Effectiveness of Influence Strategies in Gaining Channel Member Compliance," *Journal of Marketing* 69, no. 3 (2005), pp. 66–79; Eric M. Olson, Stanley F. Slater, and G. Tomas M. Hult, "The Performance Implications of Fit among Business Strategy, Marketing Organization Structure, and Strategic Behavior," *Journal of Marketing* 69, no. 3 (2005), pp. 49–65; and Carlos Niezen and Julio Rodriguez, "Distribution Lessons from Mom and Pop," *Harvard Business Review 86,* no. 4 (2008), pp. 23–46.
34. Abel P. Jeuland and Steven M. Shugan, "Managing Channel Profits," *Marketing Science* 27, no. 1 (January/February 2008), pp. 49–54.
35. Neil Herndon, "Effective Ethical Response: A New Approach to Meeting Channel Stakeholder Needs for Ethical Behavior and Socially Responsible Conduct," *Journal of Marketing Channels* 13, no. 1 (2005), pp 63–67; and Emma Kambewa, Paul Ingenbleek, and Aad Van Tilbury, "Improving Income Positions of Primary Producers in International Marketing Channels: The Lake Victoria–DU Nile Perch Case," *Journal of Macromarketing* 28, no. 1 (2008), pp. 53–64.
36. Michelle R. Nelson and Hye-Jin Paek, "A Content Analysis of Advertising in a Global Magazine across Seven Countries: Implications for Global Advertising Strategies," *International Marketing Review* 24, no. 1 (2007), pp. 64–78.
37. Nat Ives, "As Global Print Buys Wane, an Esquire Ad Program Spans Continents," *Advertising Age,* March 28, 2013, http://adage.com/article/media/fossil-sponsors-esquire-mini-mag-spans-continents/240580/.
38. Wagner A. Kamakura and Wooseong Kang, "Chain Wide and Store Level Analysis for Cross Category Management," *Journal of Retailing* 83, no. 2 (2007), pp. 159–70.
39. Piet Verhoeven, "Who's In and Who's Out?; Studying the Effects of Communication Management on Social Cohesion," *Journal of Communication Management* 12, no. 2 (2008), pp. 124–30; and Tom Watson, "Public Relations Research Priorities: A Delphi Study," *Journal of Communication Management* 12, no. 2 (2008), pp. 104–11.
40. George S. Yip and Audrey J. M. Bink, "Managing Global Accounts," *Harvard Business Review* 85, no. 9 (2007), pp. 102–19; and Kenneth D. Ko, "Optimal Pricing Model," *Journal of Global Business Issues* 2, no. 1 (2008), pp. 143–48.
41. David Welch, David Kiley, and Moon Ihiwan, "My Way or the Highway at Hyundai," *BusinessWeek,* March 6, 2008, www.businessweek.com/print/magazine/content/08_11/b4075048450463.htm; and Moon Ihiwan, "Hyundai Pitches Luxury in the U.S.," *BusinessWeek,* April 2, 2007, www.businessweek.com/print/globalbiz/content/apr2007/ gb20070402_949571.htm.
42. Magda Kandil, "The Asymmetric Effects of Exchange Rate Fluctuations on Output and Prices: Evidence from Developing Countries," *Journal of International Trade and Economic Development* 17, no. 2 (2008), pp. 257–70.
43. Benjamin Eden, "Inefficient Trade Patterns: Excessive Trade, Cross-Hauling and Dumping," *Journal of International Economics* 73, no. 1 (2007), pp. 175–87.
44. William Vetter and C. Jeanne Hill, "The Hunt for Online Trademark Infringers: The Internet, Gray Markets, and the Law Collide," *Journal of the Academy of Marketing Science* 34, no. 1 (2006), pp. 85–88; Jen-Hung Huang, Bruce C. Y. Lee, and Shu Hsun Ho, "Consumer Attitudes toward Gray Market Goods," *International Marketing Review* 21, no. 6 (2004), pp. 598–611; and Barry Berman, "Strategies to Combat the Sale of Gray Market Goods," *Business Horizons* 47, no. 4 (2004), pp. 51–70.

CHAPTER 16

The Marketing Dashboard: Metrics for Measuring Marketing Performance

LEARNING OBJECTIVES

LO 16-1 Understand the concept of a marketing dashboard and how it improves marketing planning for a firm.

LO 16-2 Explain return on marketing investment (ROMI), including cautions about its use.

LO 16-3 Identify other relevant marketing metrics and how they are applied.

LO 16-4 Develop detailed action plans in support of the overall marketing plan.

LO 16-5 Decide on an appropriate combination of forecasting approaches.

LO 16-6 Prepare a marketing budget.

LO 16-7 Provide controls and contingency plans.

LO 16-8 Conduct a marketing audit.

THE MARKETING DASHBOARD

LO 16-1

Understand the concept of a marketing dashboard and how it improves marketing planning for a firm.

Consider how a dashboard of a car, airplane, or even a video game provides you with a lot of crucial information in real time and in a convenient format. So it should be with a **marketing dashboard**, which is a comprehensive system providing managers with up-to-the-minute information necessary to run their operation including data on actual sales versus forecast, progress on marketing plan objectives, distribution channel effectiveness, sales force productivity, brand equity evolution, and whatever metrics and information are uniquely relevant to the role of the marketing manager in a particular organization.[1] Clearly, a dashboard metaphor for this process of capturing, shaping, and improving marketing effectiveness and efficiency is a good one.[2]

> Marketing is vital to an organization and touches many aspects of a company's operations. Therefore, good metrics programs consider how marketing links to other business functions within the firm and helps executives unite these functions to support business goals. In particular, media outlets have the potential to change the way all aspects of divisions of companies interact with one another. Customers are using social media for a number of reasons including technical support, customer service, and as a way to engage with rich media content like photographs and tutorials. Shelly Stotzer, executive vice president and CMO at Highlights for Children, says although the company has been leveraging multiple channels for 67 years, it has always been hard to figure out how to optimize the various media channels. "It's difficult to anticipate needs and be there because customers have so many choices," she notes. Social media are an important channel for Highlights for Children. They are is integrated with its customer acquisition and service strategies, allowing the organization to use social channels to provide service as well as content. And importantly, these capabilities are all dependent on appropriate and accurate marketing metrics in order to assure the firm's goals for the social media usage are being met.[3]

How does a marketing dashboard manifest itself? It could appear in your inbox weekly or monthly in the form of a color printout, be beamed through cyberspace as e-mail updates, or be accessible on a password-protected website on your company intranet. Its physical form and layout should be developed within your organization *by* managers *for* managers. Search the Internet for "Marketing Dashboards" and you will be amazed at how many consulting firms come up, each working hard to convince you that its proprietary approach to a marketing dashboard is the right one for you. To successfully compete in today's market, firms must focus on marketing planning so that managers and executives have the core information about progress toward relevant goals and metrics at their fingertips *at all times.* This is what a dashboard approach delivers.

A marketing dashboard approach to enhance marketing planning delivers five key benefits summarized in Exhibit 16.1.

Goals and Elements of a Marketing Dashboard

An effective dashboard is organic, not static. The dashboard must adapt and change with the organization as objectives are clarified and redefined, as causal relationships are established between metrics and results, and as confidence in predictive measures grows. About the only thing you know for certain about your first version of a marketing dashboard is that it will likely look very different in a year or two.

[1]A number of concepts in this section are derived from the following outstanding book, which is the best single source for understanding marketing dashboards. It is highly recommended as a guidebook on the topic for marketing managers: Patrick LaPointe, *Marketing by the Dashboard Light: How to Get More Insight, Foresight, and Accountability from Your Marketing Investments,* New York: ANA, 2005.

EXHIBIT 16.1 | Benefits of a Marketing Dashboard

1. **Alignment of Marketing with the Firm**

   A marketing dashboard aligns marketing objectives with the company's financial objectives and corporate strategy through the selection of critical metrics and sharing of results.

2. **Development of Internal Relationships with Marketing**

   The marketing dashboard not only creates organizational alignment *within* marketing by linking all expenditures back to a smaller set of focused objectives, but it also clarifies the relationships *between* marketing and other organizational areas. It crystallizes roles and responsibilities to ensure everyone understands the inherent interdependencies. The result of all this alignment fosters greater job satisfaction within a culture of performance and success.

3. **Establishment of Direct Links between Marketing Spending and Profits**

   A dashboard uses graphical representations of crucial metrics in ways that begin to show, often for the first time, the causal relationships between marketing initiatives and financial results. It portrays historical data in a fashion that makes it easier for any manager to grasp and understand the implications. The result is a greater ability to make smart resource allocations and increase both the efficiency and effectiveness of marketing spending.

4. **Facilitation of Smoother Decision Making**

   A marketing dashboard fosters a learning organization whose members make decisions based on hard facts, creativity, and experiential intuition, rather than as a result of battles based on pure subjectivity. The real benefit of this evolution to a culture of "everyone has the information" is a dramatic reduction in time spent in highly politicized arguments, which greatly speeds decision making in organizations.

5. **Enhancement of Marketing's Ability to Contribute**

   A dashboard creates transparency in marketing's goals, operations, and performance, creating stronger alliances between marketing and the rest of the firm. This elevates marketing's perceived accountability, earning greater trust and confidence from the CEO, CFO, board, and other key decision makers and influencers.

Source: Patrick LaPointe, *Marketing by the Dashboard Light: How to Get More Insight, Foresight, and Accountability from Your Marketing Investments* (New York: ANA, 2005). Courtesy of Marketing NPV LLC © 2003–2008. All rights reserved.

When developing a battery of marketing metrics, don't overlook metrics related to customer service. Bank of America CEO Brian Moynihan is strongly promoting the value of high-quality customer service and its relationship to the bank's reputation. Recent marketing campaigns of the big bank have focused on humility and connecting with its clients. "Most of the people at the bank want to do positive things for people. The negative images don't always reflect the rank-and-file here. Most of our employees want to serve customers and are proud of what they do. One banker told me they feel like they can now go to a dinner party or a cocktail party and hold their head up. That's a different feel," said Moynihan. This strategy is being implemented in an effort to repair the public's often negative opinion of Bank of America (and other "big banks" as well). The marketing strategies have been created and the ball is now squarely in the court of employees to follow through. A variety of customer service metrics will be tracked to gauge the success of the initiative, and since customer service and satisfaction also directly bolster a company's brand image, metrics tracking this aspect will also be an important success indicant.[5]

Two primary goals of any dashboard are diagnostic insight and predictive foresight—with a special emphasis on the latter. Some dashboard metrics are diagnostic, looking at what has happened and trying to discern why. Probably the most important metrics you'll come to rely on, however, are predictive, using the diagnostic experience to better forecast results under various assumptions of circumstances and resource allocations.[4]

EXHIBIT 16.2 | Elements of Great Marketing Dashboards

1. **Goals and Objectives**
   These are the goals of the company, translated into a set of marketing objectives. All ideas, initiatives, and metrics should be considered in light of these.
2. **Initiative ROI and Resource Allocation**
   An important part of a marketing dashboard is measuring the incremental cash flows generated by marketing programs and action plans in the short term. In addition, the dashboard is an excellent tool to measure the efficiency of resource allocation in dollars, customers, or other appropriate units.
3. **Brand and Customer Asset Evolution**
   At least equal to the short-term results is the longer-term evolution of the corporate assets entrusted to marketing. As you have learned, key marketing assets often include the brand and customer perceptions and relationships. The dashboard can provide a read of how the assets have been growing and how they are likely to progress.
4. **Skills**
   A well-rounded dashboard tracks the skills and competencies of the marketing team against a clear set of proficiency goals.
5. **Process**
   The dashboard also provides insight into the execution of critical business processes required to deliver on the desired customer value propositions.
6. **Tools**
   Less a metric than an enabler of marketing planning success, successful dashboards employ and continuously refine tools to increase insight and reduce effort in both production and distribution.
7. **Diagnostic Insight**
   The dashboard must push beyond portrayal of *what* is happening to explain *why* it is happening, providing insight into where expectations were inaccurate and helping hone the process of setting expectations and forecasts for the future.
8. **Predictive Value**
   The difference between a helpful dashboard and a truly effective one is the degree to which it uses the diagnostic insight and predicts what is *likely* to happen on critical performance dimensions that have been identified.
9. **Efficiency and Effectiveness**
   The end goal is the enhancement of both the efficiency and the effectiveness of marketing investments, thereby improving return on marketing investment (ROMI).

Source: Patrick LaPointe, *Marketing by the Dashboard Light: How to Get More Insight, Foresight, and Accountability from Your Marketing Investments* (New York: ANA, 2005). Courtesy of Marketing NPV LLC © 2003–2008. All rights reserved.

A great marketing dashboard is comprised of the nine elements described in Exhibit 16.2.

Potential Pitfalls in Marketing Dashboards

Although taking a dashboard approach to marketing metrics goes a long way toward enabling successful marketing planning, several potential pitfalls exist in its execution, including the following:

- *Overreliance on "inside-out" measurement.* Having too many internal measures puts the focus on what you already know instead of on the unpredictably dynamic external marketplace. A focus on monitoring external factors likely to cause significant changes to the marketing plan is what makes a dashboard especially valuable.
- *Too many tactical metrics; not enough strategic insight.* Because of the focus over the past decade on holding marketing accountable for financial results, tactical, or "intermediary," metrics have proliferated. Numerous books and articles provide list after list of calculations and ratios to assess all sorts of marketing programmatic results (brand awareness, customer trial, lead conversion, etc.). Although these are valuable and having the right set of intermediary metrics on the dashboard is important, it is critical that they do not overshadow measures of strategic importance to the firm.

- *Forgetting to market the dashboard internally.* One measure of the success of a marketing dashboard is the level at which it is embraced and *used* by managers and executives throughout the firm. As we've emphasized consistently, marketing is not just a department, but rather a part of the strategic and cultural fabric of the enterprise. As such, it is important to market the dashboard internally to key stakeholders, not just to marketers. You want the percentage of senior executives who both believe in and understand what the dashboard is presenting to be very high. Obviously, the CEO should be a target for internal marketing, but just as important is your CFO. The greater the affinity a CFO has for marketing, and especially for marketing as a contributor to the firm's long-term success, the better.[6]

Toward Your Own Marketing Dashboard

The goals of the remainder of this chapter are somewhat different from the other chapters so far. Here, ideas and resources have been gathered to enhance the measurement side of the marketing planning process you have learned throughout the book, especially to aid in a marketing plan project if you are working on one for the course. Here you will learn about return on marketing investment (ROMI) and will be exposed to a sampling of other marketing metrics for your consideration. We then introduce action plans, forecasting, budgets, controls and contingency planning, and the marketing audit as important tools to enhance marketing planning. Any or all of these elements can be an integral part of, or a key informational input to, your own marketing dashboard that you can develop when you leave this course.

Creating a customizable marketing dashboard unique to each of its business customers' strategies and objectives is important to Adobe. Brad Rencher, Adobe's senior vice president and general manager of its Digital Marketing Business, believes marketers need the ability to quickly collaborate to deal with the new age of real-time marketing, when they need to reach consumers "at the last millisecond" when they're ready to make a purchase. "Candidly, marketers are struggling with their own organizations," he said. "They're not talking to each other (inside those organizations)." To address this issue, Adobe has created a product called the Marketing Cloud, which is an online collection of five major ad and marketing products such as social, analytics, and targeting. Adobe's new dashboard and related announcements, Rencher said, are intended to get various marketing organizations out of the habit of using only disparate modalities such as e-mail and spreadsheets to plan, create, execute, and measure marketing campaigns and instead get them onto a dashboard of shared tools.[7]

RETURN ON MARKETING INVESTMENT (ROMI)

LO 16-2

Explain return on marketing investment (ROMI), including cautions about its use.

CEOs today expect to know exactly what impact an investment in marketing has on a firm's success, especially financially. Hence, it has become critical to consider **return on marketing investment (ROMI)**.[8] Throughout this book we have focused on marketing as an *investment*, not as an expense, because a goal-driven investment approach to marketing maximizes the opportunity for a firm's offerings to reach their full potential in the marketplace. The alternative viewpoint—approaching

---

[8]One of the single best sources for understanding ROMI is the following book, which is highly recommended for marketing managers: Guy R. Powell, *Return on Marketing Investment: Demand More from Your Marketing and Sales Investments*, Albuquerque, NM: RBI Press, 2002. The ideas in this section are drawn from that source.

marketing as an expense tied to a percentage of historical or forecasted sales—both limits market opportunities and thwarts the ability to meaningfully plan for and measure marketing results.[9]

Similar to other investment decisions, investment decisions in marketing must consider four basic elements:

- Level of investment.
- Returns.
- Risks.
- Hurdle rates.

As with any investment, the projected results (returns minus costs) must exceed a certain investment hurdle rate for a given level of risk (both defined by the firm). Hence, ROMI represents either the revenue or the margin generated by a marketing program divided by the cost of that program at a given risk level. The ROMI hurdle rate is defined as the minimum acceptable, expected return on a program at a given level of risk. Consider an example of a relatively low-risk marketing program with costs of $1 million and new revenue generated of $5 million. This program has a ROMI of 5.0. If the company has a marketing budget of $5 million and needs to generate $20 million in revenue, then the ROMI hurdle rate for any low-risk marketing program is 4.0. This means that any marketing program must generate at a minimum $4.00 in revenue for every $1.00 in marketing expenditure. The example ROMI of 5.0 above surpasses the ROMI hurdle rate and is therefore an acceptable marketing program.[10]

Companies have to set their own hurdle rates based on differing levels of potential risk across marketing programs. Risk also tends to vary quite a bit by industry and by whether the marketing plan involves a start-up or an established product line. At its core, ROMI is a tool to help yield more out of marketing. This tool and the way of thinking promoted by the use of the tool within an organization will help marketing managers better conceptualize and execute marketing plans and programs. It puts them in a much better position to connect their planning, measurement, and results to the firm's goals and expectations and, when successful, provides gravitas for the CMO to go back to the CEO for more investment money for marketing.

Cautions about Overreliance on ROMI

Given the above, it's no wonder that ROMI is the *metric du jour* for many firms' marketing bottom line. Several offshoots of ROMI have been developed that apply the same principles to customers (ROCI), brands (ROBI), and promotion (ROPI).[11] Overall, the trend in boardrooms and executive suites of expecting more quantification of marketing's contributions has been a positive one. But remember that within the marketing dashboard concept, what organizations should be reviewing is an *array of relevant metrics,* selected for inclusion on the dashboard because together they paint a picture of firm performance. Managers should always temper the interpretation of ROMI results with review of other appropriate metrics.

In addition, it is important to remember that ROMI was originally designed for comparing capital projects, where investments are made once and the returns flow in during the periods that follow. In marketing, capital projects are analogous to discrete marketing programs or campaigns that have well-defined goals and clear points of beginning and end. However, in practice, ROMI is often applied in situations that have no clear beginning or end. Here are six other commonly expressed objections about an overreliance on ROMI:

1. While a firm may "talk the talk" of marketing as an investment, not an expense, typically marketing expenditures are not treated as an investment in a company's accounting system.

2. ROMI requires the profit to be divided by expenditure, yet all other bottom-line performance measures consider profit or cash flow *after* deducting expenditures.
3. The truth is, ROMI is maximized during the period when profits are still growing. Pursuit of ROMI during flat periods can be viewed as "causing" underperformance and suboptimal levels of activity; thus firms tend to reduce marketing reinvestment at that time in an attempt to maximize profits and cash flow. The result is a self-fulfilling prophecy of downward performance.
4. Calculating ROMI requires knowing what would have happened if the incremental expenditure hadn't occurred. Few marketers have those figures or can conjure something meaningful up to replace them.
5. ROMI has become a fashionable surrogate for "marketing productivity" in executive suites and boardrooms, yet there is mounting evidence that firms interpret the appropriate calculation of ROMI quite differently. When executives discuss ROMI with different metrics in mind, confusion results and the value of the metric degrades.
6. ROMI by nature ignores the effect of the marketing assets of the firm (for example, its brands) and tends to lead managers toward a more short-term decision perspective. That is, it typically considers only short-term incremental profits and expenditures without looking at longer-term effects or any change in brand equity.[12]

Combining a successful bottom line with a strong sense of social responsibility, Timberland promotes its earth-friendly production process to appeal to its outdoor-loving target customers.

Proceed with Caution

The expectation is that ROMI and other metrics of marketing performance will continue to proliferate, as firms home in on attempting to better quantify marketing's contribution to various dimensions of organizational success. Marketing managers should embrace the opportunity to quantify their contributions, and by taking a more holistic dashboard approach to goal-driven measurement, the potential downsides to focusing on one or a few metrics are largely mitigated.

In the end, marketing management is both a science and an art. The scientific side craves quantification and relishes the ability to provide numeric evidence of success to superiors in a firm and to stockholders. But the artistic side understands that sometimes the difference between an average new-product introduction and a world-class one rests largely on creativity, insight, and the good fortune to have a great idea that is hitting the market at just the right time.

An interesting question, given the current focus in business toward sustainability and socially responsible business practices, is how would metrics related to such aspects (say, for example, ROSI, or return on social investment) operate in tandem with other more traditional performance measures? Ethical Dimension 16 provides some insights into this important issue.

A SAMPLING OF OTHER MARKETING METRICS

This section provides a mix of metrics for your consideration. Because a variety of excellent books exist that provide hundreds of potential metrics for assessing the gamut of marketing planning activities, we provide only a sampling here. Throughout the following section, these symbols are used: $= a monetary figure; % = a percentage figure; # = a figure in units; I = an index figure, such as a comparative or average, often interpreted as a percentage.[13]

LO 16-3

Identify other relevant marketing metrics and how they are applied.

E-commerce is expected to surpass brick-and-mortar stores in the near future. Swipely, a four-year-old startup based in Providence, Rhode Island, has positioned itself to respond well in this marketplace. It acts as a traditional credit-card processor for brick-and-mortar retailers and restaurants but also adds a layer of analytics. Merchants who use the company's software can generate sales reports to see what percentage of sales comes from repeat customers. They can also create automated loyalty programs and regularly blast promotions to customers who opt in and provide an e-mail address. Angus Davis, Swipely's CEO, agrees that software is irrevocably changing the retail landscape. "The e-commerce players have lapped the offline guys," he says. But with an analytics-based system like that brought to the table by Swipely, the traditional retailers stand a decent chance of continuing to compete well with the online crowd.[14]

Market Share

Definition: The percentage of a market (defined in terms of units or revenue) accounted for by a specific product, product line, or brand.

- Unit Market Share (%) = Unit Sales (#) ÷ Estimated Total Market Unit Sales (#)
- Revenue Market Share (%) = Sales Revenue ($) ÷ Estimated Total Market Revenue ($)

Marketers need to be able to translate sales forecasts into the context of market share, which will provide evidence if forecasts are to be attained by growing with the market or by capturing share from competitors. The latter will almost always be more difficult to achieve. Market share is closely monitored for signs of change in the competitive landscape, and it frequently influences strategic or tactical marketing planning. Importantly, market share is highly dependent on how the manager defines his or her market.[15] For example, Diet Coke would report varying market share numbers depending on whether it is comparing itself to all beverages, all carbonated beverages, or diet sodas.

Penetration

Definition: A measure of brand or category popularity. It is defined as the number of people who buy a specific brand or category of goods at least once in a given time period, divided by the size of the relevant market population.

---

[13]In this section, the example formulas and descriptions are selected from the following outstanding treatise on marketing metrics, which is a must-have book for marketing managers: Paul W. Farris, Neil T. Bendle, Phillip E. Pfeifer, and David J. Reibstein, *Marketing Metrics: The Definitive Guide to Measuring Marketing Performance,* 2nd ed., Upper Saddle River, NJ: Pearson/Wharton School Publishing, 2010.

ETHICAL DIMENSION 16

When the Bottom Line Is Profit *and* Social Responsibility

A new kind of company is emerging that encompasses both profitability and social responsibility in its business model, creating not just one bottom line but two. These hybrid companies, founded by entrepreneurs who are focused as much on doing the right thing as on making a profit, are redefining traditional metrics for success. On the surface, the "do the right thing" and "maximize profit" models might seem to be incompatible, which can create challenges for entrepreneurs looking for funding.

Socially responsible companies today operate in a wide variety of industries and can include environmentally sensitive consumer products companies, organic grocers, fair trade coffee producers, and many others. These firms are often started after the founder is already committed to a social agenda. That is, the company is the tool by which the founder achieves a targeted social objective (better environment, better working conditions for the poor, etc.). Applying a socially responsible agenda frequently increases costs and suggests companies that want to follow a two-bottom-line business model need to do business at the premium end of their market or else be relegated to lower expected margins. Melinda Olson, founder of Earth Mama Angel Baby, a manufacturer of premium natural products for young mothers and babies, believes that her gross margins are 12 to 15 percent lower than those of her competitors (if she priced at parity). In addition, if a company is really going to be socially responsible it must "walk the talk." This includes using energy-friendly products and paying living wage rates to employees. While all the choices may be the right thing to do, collectively they add to the cost of running the business.

A significant challenge for entrepreneurs desiring to develop a two-bottom-line business model is finding investors who understand and are willing to support such a goal. Most investors are looking for the ROI, not the ROSI (return on social investment). As a result, many of these organizations are underfunded and fail. Another challenge is how to measure success. Investors and managers all understand traditional success metrics such as profitability, ROI, and market share. However, when the bottom line also includes a company's social responsibility, the relevant success metrics become more difficult to determine.[16]

Ethical Perspective

1. **Investors:** Should investors be concerned only with a company's profitability? What metrics might an investor use to measure the social responsibility success of a company?
2. **Entrepreneurs:** Is a two-bottom-line business model realistic in the long term? Is it sustainable?
3. **You:** Would you invest in a company with a two-bottom-line strategy (profitability and social responsibility)? Would you invest in a company without a two-bottom-line approach?

- Market Penetration (%) = Customers Who Have Purchased a Product in the Category (#) ÷ Total Population (#)
- Brand Penetration (%) = Customers Who Have Purchased the Brand (#) ÷ Total Population (#)
- Penetration Share Formula 1 (%) = Brand Penetration (%) ÷ Market Penetration (%)
- Penetration Share Formula 2 (%) = Customers Who Have Purchased the Brand (#) ÷ Customers Who Have Purchased a Product in the Category (#)

Often, marketing managers must decide whether to seek sales growth by acquiring existing category users from their competitors or by expanding the total population of category users, attracting new customers to the market. Penetration metrics help indicate which of these strategies would be most appropriate and also help monitor the success of the strategy.[17]

Margin on Sales

Definition: The difference between selling price and cost. This difference is typically expressed either as a percentage of selling price or on a per-unit basis.

- Unit Margin ($) = Selling Price per Unit ($) − Cost per Unit ($)
- Margin (%) = Unit Margin ($) ÷ Selling Price per Unit ($)

Marketing managers need to know margins for almost all decisions. Margins represent a key factor in pricing, ROMI, earnings forecasts, and analyses of customer profitability.[18]

Cannibalization Rate

Definition: Cannibalization is the reduction in sales (units or dollars) of a firm's existing products due to the introduction of a new product. The cannibalization rate is generally calculated as the percentage of a new product's sales that represents a loss of sales (attributable to the introduction of the new entrant) by a specific existing product or products.

- Cannibalization Rate (%) = Sales Lost from Existing Products (# or $) ÷ Sales of New Product (# or $)

Cannibalization rates represent an important factor in the assessment of new-product strategies, since how robbing some of the sales of Brand X by introducing Brand Y impacts overall sales must be considered in the financial projections for the introduction.[19]

Customer Lifetime Value (CLV)

Definition: The dollar value of a customer relationship based on the present value of the projected future cash flows from the customer relationship. When margins and retention rates are constant, the following formula can be used to calculate CLV:

- CLV ($) = Margin ($) × (Retention Rate [%] ÷ (1 + Discount Rate [%] − Retention Rate [%]))

Present value is the discounted sum of future cash flows. The discount rate is usually set at a corporate level, with the goal of compensating for the time value of money and the inherent risk of the particular activity. Generally, the riskier the project, the greater the discount rate to use. Techniques for setting discount rates are beyond the scope of this chapter. Suffice it to say that separate discount rates are appropriate on a by-project basis because the risk varies. A government contract might be a fairly certain project compared to a handshake agreement with a private client.[20]

Overall, CLV is an important concept in that it encourages firms to shift their focus from quarterly profits to the long-term health of their customer relationships. CLV is an important number because it represents an upper limit on spending to acquire new customers.[21]

Sales Force Effectiveness

Definition: By analyzing sales force performance, marketing managers can make changes to optimize sales going forward. Toward that end, there are a number of ways (beyond just sales volume) to gauge the performance of individual salespeople and of the sales force as a whole.[22] Among the sales force effectiveness (SFE) ratios are the following:

- SFE = Sales ($) ÷ Contacts with Clients (Number of Calls) (#)
- SFE = Sales ($) ÷ Potential Accounts (#)
- SFE = Sales ($) ÷ Active Accounts (#)
- SFE = Sales ($) ÷ Customer Buying Power ($)
- SFE = Selling Expenses ($) ÷ Sales ($)

Supply Chain Metrics

Definition: Measures of important indicators of a firm's success in its supply chain.

- Stock-Outs (%) = Outlets Where Brand or Product Is Listed but Unavailable (#) ÷ Total Outlets Where Brand or Product Is Listed (#)
- Service Level Re: On-Time Delivery (%) = Deliveries Achieved in Time Frame Promised (#) ÷ All Deliveries Initiated in the Period (#)
- Inventory Turns (I) = Product Revenues ($) ÷ Average Inventory (#)

Supply chain tracking helps ensure that companies are meeting demand efficiently and effectively.[23]

Promotions and Pass-Through

Definition: Of the promotional value provided by a manufacturer to its distributors and retailers (often referred to as "the trade"), the pass-through percentage represents the portion that ultimately reaches the end-user consumer.

- Percentage of Sales on Deal (%) = Sales with Any Temporary Discount ($ or #) ÷ Total Sales ($ or #)
- Pass-Through (%) = Value of Temporary Promotional Discounts Provided to End-User Consumers by the Trade ($) ÷ Value of Temporary Discounts Provided to the Trade by the Manufacturer ($)

Manufacturers offer many discounts to the trade with the objective of encouraging them to offer their own promotions, in turn, to their customers. If trade customers or end-user consumers do not find promotions attractive, this will be indicated by a decline in the percentage of sales on a deal. Likewise, low pass-through percentages can indicate that too many deals, or the wrong kinds of deals, are being offered.[24]

Cost per Thousand Impressions (CPM) Rates

Definition: The cost per thousand advertising impressions. This metric is calculated by dividing the cost of an advertising placement by the number of impressions (expressed in thousands) that it generates.

- CPM = Cost of Advertising ($) ÷ Impressions Generated (# in thousands)

CPM is useful in comparing the relative efficiency of different advertising opportunities or media and in evaluating the costs of overall campaigns.[25]

Share of Voice

Definition: Quantifies the advertising "presence" that a specific product or brand enjoys. It is calculated by dividing the brand's advertising by total market advertising, and it is expressed as a percentage.

- Share of Voice (%) = Brand Advertising ($ or #) ÷ Total Market Advertising ($ or #)

For purposes of share of voice, there are at least two ways to measure "advertising": (1) in terms of dollar spending or (2) in unit terms, through impressions or gross rating points (GRPs). By any of these measures, share of voice represents an estimate of a company's advertising as compared to that of its competitors.[26]

Click-Through Rates

Definition: The percentage of impressions that lead a user to click on an online ad. It describes the fraction of impressions that motivate users to click on a link, causing a redirect to another web location.

- Click-Through Rate (%) = Click-Throughs (#) ÷ Impressions (#)

Most Internet-based businesses use click-through metrics. Although these metrics are useful, they should not dominate all online marketing analysis. Unless a user clicks on a "Buy Now" button, click-throughs measure only one step along the path toward a final sale.[27]

Online advertising, such as that offered by Google, provides unparalleled opportunities for measuring marketing's success. Measurements of click-through and conversion help Google and its advertisers reduce the percentage of unwanted and irrelevant ads displayed online. Google carefully selects which ads to display to users of the search engine, sometimes even picking low-revenue ads that it thinks will be more relevant. The true measure of Google's success in this regard is the fact that searchers are now clicking more often on the ads than on the free search results. Studies have shown that even if people don't click on ads, just seeing the ad may influence a future purchase, similar to way ads work on television. Referred to as "demand generation," this approach aims to simply plant ideas in your head rather than elicit an immediate response. Google earns substantial profits from this platform and the businesses that use these services generate significant revenue.[28]

DEVELOPING EFFECTIVE ACTION PLANS

LO 16-4

Develop detailed action plans in support of the overall marketing plan.

In a marketing plan, every strategy must include an implementation element. Sometimes these are called **action plans** or programs.[29] Each must discuss timing, assign persons responsible for various aspects of implementation, and indicate the resources necessary to make the strategy happen. Budgets for the action plan must be developed based on the forecast. Then, appropriate metrics must be identified for each, along with a control process, to assess along the way to what degree the action plan is on track and contributing to the marketing strategy and achievement of the stated marketing objectives. Exhibit 16.3 provides a format for developing action plans.

Responsibility for the Action Plan

A marketing plan can't be implemented without people. And not everybody who will be involved in implementing a marketing plan is a marketer because marketing plans touch most areas of an organization. Upper management and the human resource department will need to be involved in deploying the necessary people to accomplish the plan's objectives. Reviewing the various action plans needed for implementation of a marketing plan is a great way to develop an overall human resource deployment strategy for accomplishing the marketing plan. As you know, marketing isn't just the responsibility of the marketing department and nowhere is this idea more relevant than in market plan implementation. A wide range of organizational functions—sales, production, quality control, shipping, customer service, finance, information technology, and others—will have a stake in making the plan successful. If the functions are outsourced rather than handled internally by the firm, then someone internally still must take responsibility for the outsourced aspect of the action plan.

EXHIBIT 16.3 | Format for Developing Action Plans

Title of Action Plan	Give the action plan a relevant name.
Purpose of Action Plan	What do you hope to accomplish by the action plan—that is, what specific marketing objective and strategy within the marketing plan does it support?
Description of Action Plan	Be succinct, but still thorough, in explaining the action plan. What are the steps involved? This is the core of the action plan. It describes what must be done to accomplish the intended purpose of the action plan.
Responsibility for the Action Plan	What person(s) or organizational unit(s) are responsible for carrying out the action plan? What external parties are needed to make it happen? Most importantly, who specifically has final "ownership" of the action plan—that is, who is accountable for it?
Timing for the Action Plan	Provide a specific timetable of events leading to the completion of the plan. If different people are responsible for different elements of the timeline, provide that information.
Budget for the Action Plan (Based on the Forecast)	How much will implementation of the action plan cost? This may be direct costs only, or may also include indirect costs, depending on the situation. The sum of all the individual action plan budget items will ultimately be aggregated by category to create the overall budget for the marketing plan.
Measurement and Control of the Action Plan	Indicate the appropriate metrics, how and when they will be measured, and who will measure them.

Timing of the Action Plan

Each action plan must address the timing for accomplishment of its associated tasks. This information can then be aggregated for inclusion in the overall marketing plan. Most marketing plans portray the timing of tasks in flowchart form so that it is easy to visualize when the pieces of the plan will come together. Marketers often use *Gantt charts* or *PERT charts,* popular in operations management, to portray a plan's timeline.[30] These are the same types of tools that might be used by a general contractor to map out the different elements of building a house from the ground up. Ultimately, budgets and the financial management of the marketing plan are developed around the timing of the elements of the plan so that managers know when cash outlays are required.

Budget for the Action Plan

Each action plan carries a budget item, assuming costs are involved in carrying it out. Forecasting the needed expenditures related to a marketing plan can be challenging, but one way to improve accuracy in the budgeting process overall is to ensure that estimates for expenditures for the individual action plans are as accurate as possible.[31] At the overall marketing plan level, a master budget is created and tracked throughout the marketing planning process. Variances from the budget are reported to the parties responsible for each budget item throughout the process. For example, a firm's vice president for sales might receive a weekly or monthly report showing each sales area's performance against its budget allocation. The vice president would note patterns of budget overage and contact affected sales managers to determine what actions, if any, need to be taken to get the budget back on track. The same approach would be repeated across all the functional areas of the firm on which the budget has an impact. In such a manner, the budget itself becomes a critical element of control.

Measurement and Control of the Action Plan

This portion of the action plan establishes a formal process of monitoring progress through measuring actual performance, comparing the performance to the established marketing plan objectives and metrics, and adjusting the plan on the basis of this analysis. The metrics and process a marketer uses to monitor and control individual action plans ultimately form the overall control process for the marketing plan. Unfortunately, many marketers do not consistently do a good job of measurement and control, which compromises their marketing planning. Controls are discussed in more detail later in this chapter, in the context of the overall marketing plan.

FORECASTING FOR MARKETING PLANNING

LO 16-5

Decide on an appropriate combination of forecasting approaches.

The forecast is one of the most important information tools used by marketing managers and lies at the heart of most firms' marketing planning efforts. Top management uses the forecast to allocate resources among functional areas and to control the operations of the overall firm. Finance uses it to project cash flows, to decide on capital appropriations, and to establish operating budgets. Production uses it to determine quantities and schedules and to control inventories. Human resources uses it to plan personnel requirements and also as an input in collective bargaining. Purchasing uses it to plan the company's overall materials requirements and also to schedule their arrival. And in the marketing plan itself, the forecast is used to prepare a budget and to allocate resources among the various action plans that comprise the marketing strategy.

Two broad categories of forecasting approaches are subjective and objective methods, listed in Exhibit 16.4. Each method has advantages and disadvantages in application, which are summarized in Exhibit 16.5. The decision of which method (or methods) to employ is not always as clear as a manager would like. In a typical marketing planning situation, the decision will likely depend on how much time is available, the level of technical sophistication of products, the ready availability of historical sales data, and the level of uncertainty in the external marketplace.

Subjective Methods of Forecasting

Subjective forecasting methods do not rely primarily on sophisticated quantitative (empirical) analytical approaches in developing the forecast.[32]

EXHIBIT 16.4 | Forecasting Approaches

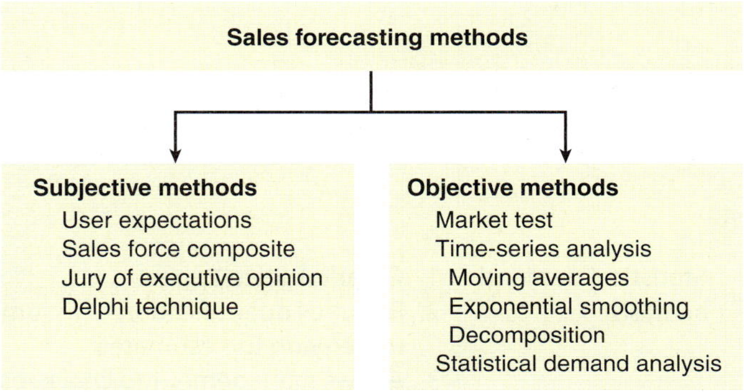

Source: Mark W. Johnston and Greg W. Marshall, *Sales Force Management*, 11th ed. (New York: Routledge), p. 144.

User Expectations The **user expectations** method of forecasting is also known as the *buyers' intentions method* because it relies on answers from customers regarding their expected consumption or purchases of the product. Data are collected through various market research methodologies discussed in Chapter 3.[33]

The user expectations method may provide estimates closer to market or sales *potential* than will other approaches. In reality, user groups would have difficulty anticipating the industry's (or a particular firm's) marketing efforts. Rather, the user estimates reflect their *anticipated needs*. From a marketing planning standpoint, the user expectations approach provides a measure of the opportunities available among a particular segment of users.

EXHIBIT 16.5 | Advantages and Disadvantages of Forecasting Approaches

Sales forecasting method	Advantages	Disadvantages
Subjective methods		
User expectations	1. Forecast estimates obtained directly from buyers 2. Projected product usage information can be greatly detailed 3. Insights gathered aid in the planning of marketing strategy 4. Useful for new-product forecasting	1. Potential customers must be few and well defined 2. Does not work well for consumer goods 3. Depends on the accuracy of user's estimates 4. Expensive, time-consuming, labor intensive
Sales force composite	1. Involves the people (sales personnel) who will be held responsible for the results 2. Is fairly accurate 3. Aids in controlling and directing the sales effort 4. Forecast is available for individual sales territories	1. Estimators (sales personnel) have a vested interest and therefore may be biased 2. Elaborate schemes sometimes necessary to counteract bias 3. If estimates are biased, process to correct the data can be expensive
Jury of executive opinion	1. Easily done, very quick 2. Does not require elaborate statistics 3. Utilizes collective wisdom of the top people 4. Useful for new or innovative products	1. Produces aggregate forecasts 2. Expensive 3. Disperses responsibility for the forecast 4. Group dynamics operate
Delphi technique	1. Minimizes effects of group dynamics 2. Can utilize statistical information	1. Can be expensive and time-consuming
Objective methods		
Market test	1. Provides ultimate test of consumers' reactions to the product 2. Allows the assessment of the effectiveness of the total marketing program 3. Useful for new and innovative products	1. Lets competitors know what the firm is doing 2. Invites competitive reaction 3. Expensive and time-consuming to set up 4. Often takes a long time to accurately assess level of initial and repeat demand
Time-series analysis	1. Utilizes historical data 2. Objective, inexpensive	1. Not useful for new or innovative products 2. Factors for trend, cyclical, seasonal, or product life-cycle phase must be accurately assessed and included 3. Technical skill and good judgment required 4. Final forecast difficult to break down into individual territory estimates 5. Ignores planned marketing effort
Statistical demand analysis	1. Great intuitive appeal 2. Requires quantification of assumptions underlying the estimates 3. Allows management to check results 4. Uncovers hidden factors affecting sales 5. Method is objective	1. Factors affecting sales must remain constant and be accurately identified to produce an accurate estimate 2. Requires technical skill and expertise 3. Some managers reluctant to use method due to its sophistication

Source: Mark W. Johnston and Greg W. Marshall, *Sales Force Management,* 11th ed. (New York: Routledge), pp. 145-46.

Sales Force Composite The **sales force composite** method of forecasting is so named because the initial input is the opinion of each member of the field sales staff. The idea is that the sales force is the closest organizational unit to the customer and will be able to come close to providing an aggregate of their customers' needs.[34] Each person states how much he or she expects to sell during the forecast period. Subsequently, these estimates are typically adjusted at various higher levels in the firm, depending on historical records of accuracy (if available). That is, when forecasting via sales force composite, organizations typically use historical information about the accuracy of the salespeople's estimates to make adjustments to the raw forecast data provided by the field sales organization. For various reasons, salespeople may be motivated to either underestimate or overestimate what they expect to sell during a period.

Much of Delta's business, as well as that of other airlines, now comes directly from Internet bookings. This has made tracking sales and customer trends and translating the information into forecasts a more straightforward process than it was when independent travel agents sold most of the tickets.

Jury of Executive Opinion The **jury of executive opinion** (or jury of expert opinion) method is a formal or informal internal poll of key executives within the firm to gain their assessment of sales potential. The separate assessments are combined into an overall forecast for inclusion in the marketing plan. Sometimes this is done by simply averaging the individual judgments, but other times differing viewpoints are resolved through group discussion toward consensus.[35] The initial views may reflect no more than the executive's hunch about what is going to happen, or the opinion may be based on considerable factual material or perhaps even an initial forecast prepared by other means.

Delphi Technique In gaining expert opinion, one method for controlling group dynamics to produce a more accurate forecast is the **Delphi technique**. Delphi uses an iterative approach with repeated measurement and controlled anonymous feedback, instead of direct confrontation and debate among the experts preparing the forecast.[36] Each individual involved prepares a forecast using whatever facts, figures, and general knowledge of the environment he or she has available. Then the forecasts are collected and the person supervising the process summarizes the forecasts (protecting the anonymity of participants). The summary is distributed to each person who participated in the initial phase. Typically, the summary lists each forecast figure, the average (median), and some summary measure of the spread of the estimates. Often, those whose initial estimates fell outside the midrange of responses are asked to express their reasons for these extreme positions. These explanations are then incorporated into the summary. The participants study the summary and submit a revised forecast. The process is then repeated. Typically, several rounds of these iterations occur until something close to consensus is achieved. The Delphi method is based on the premise that, with repeated measurements (1) the range of responses will decrease and the estimates will converge and (2) the total group response or median will move successively toward the "correct" or "true" answer.

Objective Methods of Forecasting

Objective forecasting methods rely primarily on more sophisticated quantitative (empirical) analytical approaches in developing the forecast.

Do ads for consumer products turn into sales of those products? Do the consumers exposed to TV and radio ads for specific products then purchase those advertised products more? Do these statistics change when viewers are exposed to the ads online? Media rating company Nielsen works to answer these questions with metrics designed to gauge the success of marketing strategy elements. The firm has created the Nielsen Digital Program Ratings (NDPR) system to measure TV viewership online. "The pilot for NDPR is a major milestone for the industry," SVP for Global Digital Audience Measurement at Nielsen Eric Solomon said in a statement. "As a companion product to Nielsen Online Campaign Ratings, NDPR will enable clients to better understand the online audience for their programming by harnessing the same methodology Nielsen already uses to measure the audience for related advertising." The company has also launched its Nielsen Twitter TV Ratings—a move to track TV viewership metrics solely using Twitter data.[37]

Market Test The typical **market test** (or test market) involves placing a product in several representative geographic areas to see how well it performs and then projecting that experience to the market as a whole. Often this is done for a new product or an improved version of an old product.[38]

Many firms consider the market test to be the final gauge of consumer acceptance of a new product and ultimate measure of market potential. For example, for years data from the Nielsen Company has indicated that roughly three out of four products that have been test-marketed succeed, whereas four out of five that have not been test-marketed fail. Despite this advantage, market tests have several drawbacks:

- Market tests are costly to administer and are more conducive to testing of consumer products than industrial products.
- The time involved in conducting a market test can be considerable.
- Because a product is being test-marketed, it receives more attention in the market test than it can ever receive on a national scale, giving an unrealistic picture of the product's potential.
- A market test, because it is so visible to competitors, can reveal a firm's hand on its new-product launch strategy, thus allowing competitors time to formulate a market response before full market introduction.

Time-Series Analysis Approaches to forecasting using **time-series analysis** rely on the analysis of historical data to develop a prediction for the future.[39] The sophistication of these analyses can vary widely. At the most simplistic extreme, the forecaster might predict next year's sales to be equal to this year's sales. Such a forecast might be reasonably accurate for a mature industry that is experiencing little growth or external market turbulence. However, barring these conditions, more sophisticated time-series approaches should be considered. Three of these methods are moving averages, exponential smoothing, and decomposition.

Moving Average The *moving average* method is conceptually quite simple. Consider the forecast that next year's sales will be equal to this year's sales. Such a forecast might be subject to large error if there is much fluctuation in sales from one year to the next. To allow for such randomness, we might consider using some kind of average of recent values.[40] For example, we might average the last two years' sales, the last three years' sales, the last five years' sales, or any number of other periods. The forecast would simply be the average that resulted. The number of observations included in the average is typically determined by trial and error. Differing numbers of periods are tried, and the number of periods that produces the most accurate forecasts of the trial data is used to develop the forecast model. Once determined, it remains constant. The term *moving average* is used because a new average is computed and used as a forecast as each new observation becomes available.

Exhibit 16.6 presents a moving average forecast example with 16 years of historical sales data and also the resulting forecasts for a number of years using two- and four-year moving averages. Exhibit 16.7 displays the results graphically. The entry 4,305 for 2001, under the two-year moving average method, for example, is the average of the sales of 4,200 units in 1999 and 4,410 units in 2000. Similarly, the forecast of 5,520 units in 2014 represents the average of the number of units sold in 2012 and 2013. The forecast of 5,772 units in 2014 under the four-year moving average method, on the other hand, represents the average number of units sold during the four-year period 2010–2013. Obviously, it takes more data to begin forecasting with four-year than with two-year moving averages. This is an important consideration when starting to forecast sales for a new product.

Exponential Smoothing The method of moving averages gives *equal weight* to each of the last n values in forecasting the next value, where n represents the number of years used. Thus, when $n = 4$ (the four-year moving average is being used), equal weight is given to each of the last four years' sales in predicting the sales for next year. In a four-year moving average, no weight is given to any sales five or more years previous.

Exponential smoothing is a type of moving average that, instead of weighting all observations equally in generating the forecast, weights the most recent observations heaviest. The reasoning behind this strategy is that the most recent observations contain the most information about what is likely to happen in the future, and they should therefore be given more weight.[41]

The key decision affecting the use of exponential smoothing is the choice of the *smoothing constant,* referred to as α in the algorithm for calculating exponential smoothing, which is constrained to be between 0 and 1. High values of α give great weight to recent observations and little weight to distant sales; low values of

EXHIBIT 16.6 | Moving Average Forecast Example

Year	Actual sales	Forecast sales: Two-year moving average	Forecast sales: Four-year moving average
1999	4,200		
2000	4,410		
2001	4,322	4,305	
2002	4,106	4,366	
2003	4,311	4,214	4,260
2004	4,742	4,209	4,287
2005	4,837	4,527	4,370
2006	5,030	4,790	4,499
2007	4,779	4,934	4,730
2008	4,970	4,905	4,847
2009	5,716	4,875	4,904
2010	6,116	5,343	5,128
2011	5,932	5,916	5,395
2012	5,576	6,024	5,684
2013	5,465	5,754	5,835
2014		5,520	5,772

Source: Mark W. Johnston and Greg W. Marshall, *Sales Force Management,* 11th ed. (New York: Routledge), p. 149.

EXHIBIT 16.7 Graphical Representation of Moving Average Forecast

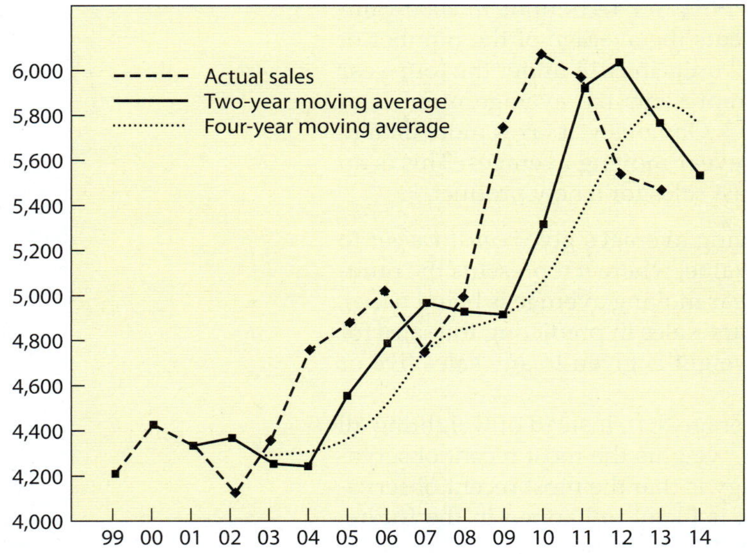

Source: Mark W. Johnston and Greg W. Marshall, *Sales Force Management*, 11th ed. (New York: Routledge), p.149.

α, on the other hand, give more weight to older observations. If sales change slowly, low values of α work fine. However, when a firm experiences rapid changes and fluctuations in sales, high values of α should be used so that the forecast series responds to these changes quickly. The value of α is normally determined empirically. First, various values of α are tried, and then the one that produces the smallest forecast error when applied to the historical series is adopted.

Decomposition The *decomposition* method of forecasting is typically applied to monthly or quarterly data where a seasonal pattern is evident and the marketing manager wishes to forecast not only for the whole year but also for each period in the year. It is important to determine what portion of any changes in sales represents an overall, fundamental change in demand and what portion is due to *seasonality* in demand. The decomposition method attempts to isolate four separate portions of a time series: the trend, cyclical, seasonal, and random factors.[42]

- The *trend* reflects the long-run changes experienced in the series when the cyclical, seasonal, and irregular components are removed. It is typically assumed to be a straight line.
- The *cyclical factor* is not always present because it reflects the waves in a series when the seasonal and irregular components are removed. These ups and downs typically occur over a long period, perhaps two to five years. Some products experience little cyclical fluctuation (canned peas), whereas others experience a great deal (housing starts).
- *Seasonality* reflects the annual fluctuation in the series due to the natural seasons. The seasonal factor normally repeats itself each year, although the exact pattern of sales may be different from year to year.
- The *random factor* is what is left after the influence of the trend, cyclical, and seasonal factors is removed.

Exhibit 16.8 shows the calculation of a simple seasonal index based on five years of sales history. The data suggest definite seasonal and trend components in the series, as the fourth quarter of every year is always the best quarter and the first quarter is the worst. At the same time, sales each year are higher than they were the previous year. One could calculate a seasonal index for each year by simply dividing quarterly sales by the yearly average per quarter. It is much more typical, though, to base the calculation of the seasonal index on several years of data to smooth out the random fluctuations that occur by quarter.

In using the decomposition method, the marketing manager typically first determines the seasonal pattern and removes its impact to identify the trend. Then the cyclical factor is estimated. After the three components are isolated, the forecast is developed by applying each factor in turn to the historical data.

Statistical Demand Analysis Time-series methods attempt to determine the relationship between sales volume and time as the basis to forecast future sales. *Statistical demand analysis* attempts to determine the relationship between sales

EXHIBIT 16.8 | Seasonal Index Calculation Example

Year	Quarter 1	2	3	4	Total	Quarter average
2010	82.8	105.8	119.6	151.8	460.0	115.0
2011	93.1	117.6	122.5	156.9	490.1	122.5
2012	92.0	122.4	132.6	163.2	510.2	127.6
2013	95.3	129.0	151.3	185.0	560.6	140.2
2014	120.1	138.1	162.2	180.2	600.6	150.2
Five-year average	96.7	122.6	137.6	167.4	524.3	131.1
Seasonal index*	73.8	93.5	105.0	127.7		

* The seasonal index equals the quarterly average divided by the overall quarterly average times 100; for the first quarter, for example, the seasonal index equals (96.7 ÷ 131.1) × 100 = 73.8.

Source: Mark W. Johnston and Greg W. Marshall, *Sales Force Management,* 11th ed. (New York: Routledge), p. 151.

and the important factors affecting sales to forecast the future. Typically, regression analysis is used to estimate the relationship. The emphasis is not to isolate all factors that affect sales but simply to identify those that have the most dramatic impact on sales and then to estimate the magnitude of the impact. The predictor variables in statistical demand analysis often are historical indexes such as leading economic indicators and other similar measures.[43] For example, Home Depot or Lowe's might use housing starts, interest rates, and a seasonal shift in demand during summer months to forecast its sales of construction materials. Today, numerous statistical software packages are available for marketing managers doing statistical demand analysis through regression. Most are user friendly and intuitive in operation. Excel, SPSS, and SAS are three popular types of software that are easily capable of statistical demand analysis.

CitizenNet analyzed how Facebook activity correlates with TV-viewing habits. For the study, the company looked at two weeks of Facebook Page Insights data leading up to the premieres of 77 TV shows from both broadcast and cable networks from 2011 and 2012. They then looked at whether the Facebook Insights metrics would correlate with Nielsen viewership for the premier episodes of each show. A regression analysis revealed that the number of Facebook actions people take leading up to a show was indeed indicative of the number of viewers that tune in to watch that show. The study's authors surmise that as consumers share more, and social platforms open up more access to user data by marketers, social identity will inevitably be more robust than cookies and other browser-based behavior. Taking an example from one of CitizenNet's own Facebook campaigns for a TV show, the study highlighted how by isolating and targeting over a hundred different audience segments, fans of Urban Outfitters were the highest-performing group. With this type of data, a show could then relay to advertisers with positive evidence that fans of Urban Outfitters are highly engaged in the content, all before the show even airs.[44]

Selecting the Appropriate Forecasting Method(s)

In preparing the forecast for a marketing plan, the marketing manager must answer two key questions: Which forecasting method(s) should be used and how accurate is the forecast likely to be? The importance of the decision is exacerbated when

Today, firms often complete their forecasting and budgeting processes through virtual meetings, thus eliminating considerable travel expense.

several methods are tried and the forecasts don't agree, which is the norm rather than the exception.

Over the years, many researchers have assessed forecast accuracy using various techniques. Some studies have been conducted within individual companies, and others have used existing data sets to which the various forecasting techniques have been systematically applied. One of the most extensive comparisons involved 1,001 time series from a variety of sources in which each series was forecast using 24 different extrapolation methods. The general conclusion was that the method used made little difference with respect to forecast accuracy. Similarly, comparisons of forecast accuracy of objective versus subjective methods tend to reach no clear conclusion as to which method is superior. Some of the comparisons seem to favor the quantitative methods, but others indicate that the subjective methods produce more accurate forecasts.

Bottom line, no single method of forecasting is likely to be superior under all conditions. Rather, a number of factors, both analytical and situational, are likely to affect the superiority of any particular technique. Analytical factors include the stability of the data series, the time horizon, the degree of structure imposed on the process, and the seasonal nature of the data. Situational factors include the volatility of the external marketplace, experience and expertise of the marketing manager in forecasting, and access to the necessary information and people required to accomplish the chosen forecasting approach. Overall, the best approach is for marketing managers to utilize multiple methods of forecasting, including a combination of subjective and objective methods, compare the results, and then make a decision on what the actual final forecast will be. Ultimately, in marketing planning the marketing manager cannot expect a final forecast to pop directly out of a statistical model, ready for use in developing strategies, action plans, and budgets. Instead, the manager must create the forecast based on multiple forms of input, ultimately relying on his or her judgment.

THE MARKETING BUDGET

LO 16-6

Prepare a marketing budget.

Chapter 12 discussed four principal methods of preparing a promotion budget. These methods are valid for overall marketing plan budgeting as well.

1. *Objective-and-task method,* which takes an investment approach in that marketing goals and objectives are set for the upcoming year and then budget dollars are secured to support the achievement of those goals and objectives. This approach is also sometimes referred to as **zero-based budgeting** because the marketing manager essentially starts the process with a blank slate and builds the budget based on the level of investment required.[45]
2. *Percent-of-sales method,* which is the most popular approach but is constraining because sales are driving budget dollars rather than marketing investment leading to sales opportunities.
3. *Comparative-parity method,* in which marketing expenditures across key competitors are assessed to arrive at a budget number.
4. *All-you-can-afford method,* which simply sets the marketing budget as whatever funds are left over after other "necessities" are funded.

Because the latter three approaches to budgeting have flaws that make them suboptimal, we encourage marketing managers to adopt a zero-based budgeting approach to marketing planning. The action planning process described earlier in this chapter facilitates the implementation of zero-based budgeting because the manager is required to justify the individual budget elements (based on the forecast) for each action plan within the overall marketing plan. These individual action plan budgets can then be aggregated into an overall budget for the marketing plan. Since these budget items are, by nature, primarily direct costs—costs attributable directly to the action plan and not inclusive of ongoing indirect or overhead costs—when the final marketing plan budget is developed, the overhead costs must be allocated to the plan on whatever basis the company uses in its accounting practices.

In practice, most marketing plan budgets are created and maintained through the use of Excel spreadsheets that provide formulaic capabilities to perform scenario analyses on a variety of contingencies and see the impact on the budget.

The marketing budget must be spread across the different kinds of media vehicles and promotional tools. Gartner, Inc. conducted a survey to determine how marketers were allocating their budgets. It included 250 marketers from U.S.-based companies with more than $500 million in annual revenue, across six industries (financial services and insurance, high-tech, manufacturing, media, retail, and health care). The results showed that digital marketing spending averaged 2.5 percent of company revenue, and these budgets were expected to increase 9 percent in the following year. "While digital marketing has been a growing area of investment in many organizations for a decade, the scope is increasing and the techniques are maturing," said Yvonne Genovese, managing vice president of Gartner for Marketing Leaders. "However, increased funding is a double-edged sword as it brings new opportunities, but it also puts more pressure on marketers to measure and attribute investments to revenue and profit growth." The majority of survey respondents were spending between 10 and 50 percent of their marketing budget on digital marketing activities, with the average at 25 percent.[46]

CONTROLS AND CONTINGENCY PLANNING

LO 16-7

Provide controls and contingency plans.

In marketing planning, the assumption is that the marketing manager moves forward to make the best possible decisions with the information that he or she has available at the time. However, a variety of uncontrollable external forces can impact the results of even the best-crafted marketing plan, sometimes very rapidly. To cope with this eventuality, **controls** must be in place from the outset of the planning process that specify the timing, procedure, and persons responsible for systematically monitoring the progress toward the goals and metrics established in the marketing plan.[47] Having goals and metrics in place without a control process to ensure that progress toward them is closely tracked is a fatal error in marketing planning. Exhibit 16.9 provides some tips for effective control.

What happens if it becomes apparent that your marketing plan is not on track to meet its goals or achieve acceptable performance metrics? And alternatively, what if evidence shows that results are *exceeding* those planned? With proper controls in place, a marketing manager should be able to detect either of these scenarios in a timely fashion, while there is still an opportunity to adjust the plan. Remember that marketing plans are not cast in stone, and the marketing manager must be willing and able to be flexible to alter any elements of the plan—from the forecast to the budget to the promotional strategy—based on unanticipated changes in the marketplace.

A convenient way to prepare for the possibility that controls will reveal significant deviations from the plan is through **contingency planning**, also called

EXHIBIT 16.9 | Tips for Effective Control

1. **Controls should involve only the minimum amount of information needed to give a reliable picture of events.**

   Too many controls create confusion. Focus on the strategic factors by following the 80/20 rule—monitor those 20 percent of the factors that determine 80 percent of the results.

2. **Controls should monitor only meaningful activities and results.**

   Regardless of measurement difficulty, if cooperation between units is important to the performance of the marketing plan, some form of qualitative or quantitative measures should be established to monitor cooperation.

3. **Controls should be timely.**

   Corrective action must be taken before it is too late. Steering controls, which are controls that monitor or measure the factors influencing performance, should be stressed so that advance notice of problems is given.

4. **Controls should be long term and short term.**

   If only short-term measures are emphasized, a short-term managerial orientation is likely.

5. **Controls should pinpoint exceptions.**

   Only those activities or results that fall outside a predetermined tolerance range should call for action.

6. **Controls should be used to reward meeting or exceeding standards rather than to punish failure to meet standards.**

   Heavy punishment of failure typically results in goal displacement. Managers will "fudge" performance reports and lobby for lower standards.

Source: J. David Hunger and Thomas L. Wheelen, *Essentials of Strategic Management*, 5th ed. Copyright © 2011. Reproduced by permission of Pearson Education, Inc., Upper Saddle River, NJ: Prentice Hall, 2011.

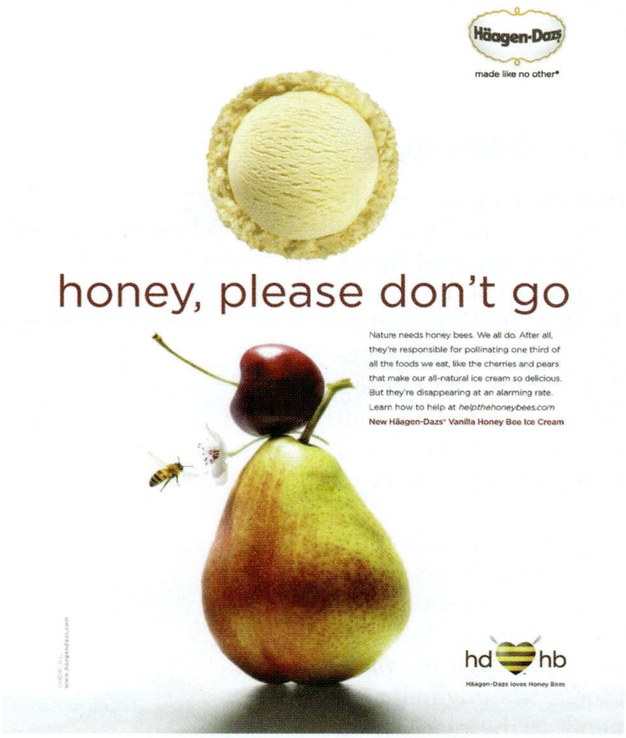

When the U.S. bee population began to diminish mysteriously a few years ago, Häagen-Dazs faced an unexpected contingency in its planning process—without honey bees, many of products cannot be produced. © HDIP, Inc.

scenario planning. Contingency planning requires the establishment of different planning options depending on the expected case, best case, or worst case.[48] The expected-case scenario is the one on which the primary plan is based. Essentially, you would prepare a response in advance as to how you would change that plan if a worst- or best-case scenario occurred. Assume that a few months into the execution of your marketing plan an unanticipated competitor enters the market with a product similar to yours at a lower price. The impact is immediate on your sales and undoubtedly you will want to adjust your marketing strategy to better compete. With a contingency plan in place, rather than starting the marketing planning process again from scratch, you can simply shift to the relevant elements of a worst-case plan, losing no time in addressing the competitive threat.

While such worst-case scenarios are certainly common, marketing managers often get caught off guard in best-case scenarios too. What if market response to your product greatly exceeds expectations and you find yourself straining production capacity and facing customers clamoring for product line extensions? A good position to be in, right? Except that without a best-case scenario plan worked out in advance, you will find yourself starting the planning process over midstream. Beginning with the forecast and through to all the planning elements, preparing contingency planning scenarios in advance is well worth the effort.

THE MARKETING AUDIT

LO 16-8

Conduct a marketing audit.

A very useful tool to aid in marketing planning is the marketing audit. A **marketing audit** systematically reviews the current state of marketing within an organization including how things are done, by whom, with what controls, and with what level of success. It uncovers what is working well and what is not working well within an organization's marketing activities, providing an invaluable snapshot of the full scope of a firm's marketing. Analysis of the results can reveal key opportunities for improvement.[49] Note that we are distinguishing a marketing audit from a *brand audit*, which includes an additional extensive external research process.

A marketing manager may wish to initiate a marketing audit when any of the following conditions are present:

- The firm is about to undergo a major rebranding initiative.
- Evidence exists of significant marketing inefficiencies and poor ROMI and other metrics.
- A new creative agency is coming onboard.
- A recent change has occurred in top management.
- Marketing has undergone a reorganization within the firm.

All units within a firm that do marketing should participate in the marketing audit. It is best administered under the direct purview of the firm's CMO. Clear objectives should be established for the audit as well as expectations about how the results will be used. This information should be communicated in advance to all participants. Exhibit 16.10 provides an example of a marketing audit instrument. Usually the instrument and instructions would be sent to the participating organizational units in advance, requesting that they gather the necessary background information and materials by a certain date. Then, the CMO or his or her designee should schedule an interview with representatives of each participating unit, either in person or by phone, to go through the audit questions. After the

EXHIBIT 16.10 | Marketing Audit Instrument

Staff and Unit

1. What is your position?
    - What are your primary responsibilities?
        - If not marketing, what is your involvement in marketing, if any?
    - What marketing experience do you have?
    - How long have you worked in this position, this unit, and this company?
2. What is the unit's purpose?

Customers

1. Are customers internal, external, or both?
2. Who are your unit's customers?
3. What are your customers' needs?
4. Do you break your customers down into segments?
    - How are segments determined?
    - Which segments are most important?
    - How much attention does each segment receive?
    - What methods do you use to communicate with different segments?
5. How often does the unit have contact with its customers?
6. Who makes contact with the customers?

(cont.)

7. Does the unit have a customer database or management system?
   Who is in charge of keeping records?
   What software is the unit currently using, and what does it do?
   How many customers does the unit have?
8. What trends in your customers have you seen in the last year?
   Have there been any recent changes in these trends?
   How has the unit adapted to these changes?
9. What future trends do you think will affect your customer base?
10. What do you know about the buying habits of your customers?
    What external factors have had an impact on these habits?
11. To the best of your knowledge, what is the customers' view of your unit?
    What do you think has shaped these perceptions?
12. What percentage of your target customers are you serving?
13. How many customers does your unit have?

Competition

1. Who do you see as your competition?
2. What are the strengths of your competition?
3. What are the weaknesses of your competition?
4. What do you find yourselves competing on (e.g., lower price, better entertainment, faster response times, etc.)?

Budget

1. Is there a marketing budget?
   How much is allocated for marketing in the budget?
   What percentage of the total unit budget is used for marketing?
   Who manages and decides how to spend this budget?
   What is the process for budget proposal and approval?
2. How much money is spent on marketing activities?
   How are these expenditures tracked?
3. Do you think the right amount of money is being allocated for marketing?
   If not, is it too much or too little, and why?
4. Do you think the money is being used effectively?
   If not, what should change?

Process

1. Does the unit have a marketing plan?
   What are the unit's marketing objectives and strategies?
2. How are marketing initiatives determined?
   Who is responsible for this?
3. How many hours a week does your unit spend on marketing?
4. Does your unit have a formal marketing position?
   If so, what is this person responsible for?
5. Could you explain the approval process for marketing activities?
   Is the process the same every time?
6. Do marketing activities require the approval of anyone outside the unit?
   If so, whose approval is needed and what unit are they in?
7. Does your unit communicate with any other departments?
8. Are there any combined efforts with other departments?
9. How aware are you of other units' marketing efforts?
10. How are logos decided on and where do they come from?
11. Who produces the content for your unit's marketing communications?
12. Does your unit use outside companies or services for marketing activities?
    What vendors are used and what are they used for?
    How does your unit decide which vendors to use?

(cont.)

Does your unit have a list of preferred vendors?

How was this list made and where did it come from?

Does your unit have any existing contracts?

With what vendors, for how much money, and for what duration?

13. Is your unit contemplating any new contracts?

Communications Audit

1. What message does your unit attempt to convey?
2. What image are you trying to project?
3. What does your unit attempt to accomplish with all of its communications?
4. Do you think the unit's communication materials are effective?
5. Do you think the unit is successful at communicating your message?
   What areas does your unit need to work on with its communications?
6. Do you think the communications are properly timed?
   How do you determine when to send out communications?
7. How effective is the unit at reaching its desired audience?
8. How consistent is the unit in the design of its materials?
9. When materials are not consistent, what is the reason for the difference?
10. Are there any special events or annual events that your unit sponsors?

Control

1. What measurements or statistics does your unit use to track marketing activities?
2. What data do you have on response rates or effectiveness of marketing efforts?
3. What forecasting methods do you use?
4. When you use publications, how do you decide how many to send out and when to send them?

Experience and Perceptions

1. How do you see your unit fitting in with the company's overall message?
2. What marketing initiatives have and have not worked for your unit in the past?
3. What is the biggest marketing challenge your unit is currently facing?
4. What current factors are impacting your unit today?
5. What do you believe are your unit's biggest strengths and weaknesses?

Credit: Thanks to Harry Antonio for creating this exhibit for *Marketing Management*.

audit results are compiled, a summarizing report should be produced and distributed to all participants.

One benefit of a marketing audit is simply getting organization members talking about marketing. It can be very useful not only for sharing best practices but also for internal marketing; for example, setting the stage for a major new branding initiative or in preparation for a change to a new creative agency.

SUMMARY

Successful marketing planning requires the application of a variety of metrics for assessing performance against the plan's goals. Marketing dashboards provide a comprehensive approach to providing managers relevant, timely, and accurate information in a convenient format for use in decision making. Action plans, forecasts, budgets, and marketing audits are all important tools and processes that marketing managers must master to maximize the potential success in marketing planning.

KEY TERMS

marketing dashboard 475
return on marketing investment (ROMI) 478
action plans 485
subjective forecasting methods 487
user expectations 487
sales force composite 489
jury of executive opinion 489
Delphi technique 489
objective forecasting methods 489
market test 490
time-series analysis 490
zero-based budgeting 494
controls 495
contingency planning 495
marketing audit 490

APPLICATION QUESTIONS

1. Pick a firm that interests you and for which you have some knowledge of its offerings.
   a. How would this firm benefit from a marketing dashboard approach?
   b. What elements would you recommend it put onto its dashboard? Why do you recommend the ones you do?
   c. How could the firm avoid some of the pitfalls potentially associated with marketing dashboards?
2. Pick any two of the marketing metrics presented in the chapter. For each, pick any brand or product and discuss how each of those brands or products would benefit from the application of each of the marketing metrics you selected. That is, what will the information reveal that will be useful in marketing planning?
3. Consider the Apple iPad. Develop one complete action plan that addresses a marketing objective to gain more iPad purchases from 50-year-old and older consumers. Be sure to complete all the elements of the action plan as shown in Exhibit 16.3 and the accompanying discussion.
4. Identify one product of interest in the B2C market and one in the B2B market. Research the products online. For each, given what you know about the products and their markets, which forecasting approaches do you believe would be most appropriate for use in developing a marketing plan? Which approaches would be least appropriate? What leads you to make these suggestions?
5. Assume that your school has decided to undertake a complete marketing audit. Review the marketing audit instrument (Exhibit 16.10) and accompanying discussion.
   a. List as many areas as you can across the entire institution that engage in marketing activities and thus should participate in the audit.
   b. As you look over the questions on the audit, do any stand out as especially important or potentially problematic when you consider what you know about your school and its marketing initiative?
   c. How would you actually administer the audit?
   d. From your perspective as a student, what aspects of marketing do you believe your school does well, and what aspects could use some improvement? What leads you to these conclusions?

MANAGEMENT DECISION CASE: Forecasting and Wannabe Blockbuster Films

Consider the intestinal fortitude it takes to invest $400 million dollars on a product before there is any verifiable prospect of making a return on that investment with certainty. Such investments are made with some regularity in the modern film industry. It seems that movie production studios are always on the lookout for the next blockbuster movie that will generate billions of dollars in sales with the hope that such movies will earn a profit. Blockbuster films often cost $200 million or more to produce and in many cases another $200 million to market worldwide. For a studio to make any money in the theaters on that investment, ticket sales must total over $800 million simply because theater margins and film distribution costs account for roughly half of the ticket price. When one considers that only 15 movies in the history of movie making have grossed over $1 billion in sales, the chances of a film studio making any money on a blockbuster are slim—particularly when one is not talking about a sequel of an established blockbuster franchise.

So what evidence do you suppose convinces film studios that they can make a profit producing and marketing a "wannabe" blockbuster film? Forecasting audience attraction and potential sales for a movie is an inexact science at best. The answer should be through a sound approach to forecasting, and, as you read in the chapter, there are numerous methods available. On the subjective forecasting side, in the movie industry a jury of executive opinion and the Delphi technique are potential subjective forecasting methods to use. Since production studio executives tend to have many years of experience in the business, they are likely to have experienced numerous film successes and failures. Consequently, it makes sense that the expertise of those executives could result in very useful input for forecasting. Also, examining user expectations may provide a reasonably accurate forecast, especially if the market research is fundamentally sound and data are collected from members of the appropriate target market.

In terms of objective forecasting approaches, a market test whereby a studio shows the movie to members of the target audience in various locations around the country before releasing it to the public has the potential to provide a useful estimate of ticket sales. However, market tests come with downsides of communicating a studio's intentions to its competitors in advance while also delaying the movie's release to the general public. Statistical demand analysis may be useful as long as the studio can determine the number of screens on which the movie will be shown, the state of the economy at the time it is released, the number of consumers in the target audience, and a host of other factors for use in the model. Having the data and expertise to implement statistical demand analysis and then convincing executives to trust a method they may not understand are potential hurdles to overcome with this method.

The recent year of 2013 is an interesting case study. With the glut of blockbuster movies released during that summer, it's no wonder so many of them were flops. Although the summer movie season rarely supports more than nine hits, 17 wannabe blockbusters were released between May and the beginning of August. As a result, it should be no surprise that *R.I.P.D.*, *Turbo, White House Down,* and *After Earth* all ended up megaflops. However, none was quite as disappointing as Disney's *The Lone Ranger,* which cost $223 million to produce and resulted in the company taking a write-off of between $160 million and $190 million. Given that the major studios have announced plans to schedule similar numbers of wannabe blockbusters for subsequent summer releases, it is certain that more big flops will occur. Be it also seems certain that regardless of the forecasting methods used, movie studios will continue to produce these big, high-budget films with the hope of having the next $1 billion box office smash.

Questions for Consideration

1. In general—not just for the movie industry—when would you most likely advocate using a jury of executive opinion or Delphi technique over the other subjective methods of user expectations and sales force composite? Alternatively, when do you think it would be more advantageous to rely on the user expectation and sales force composite methods? Be specific with your discussion.
2. Suppose you are assigned the task of developing the ticket sales forecast for the next *Hunger Games* movie. What methods of forecasting will you use and how will you justify that choice to studio executives?
3. Many studio executives believe producing a movie that builds on a franchise that has already been established in a different medium, such as comic books and *Iron Man* or toys and *Transformers,* reduces the risk of a blockbuster flop. How do you think a character in a popular comic book series or a popular line of toys may influence a ticket sales forecast for a movie based on the character or toy? That is, how would you suggest incorporating that aspect into developing a forecast for the film?

Sources: Gary Maddox, "Top of the Box-Office Movie Flops in 2013," *Sydney Morning Herald*, December 20, 2013, www.smh.com.au/entertainment/movies/top-of-the-boxoffice-movie-flops-in-2013-20131219-2zlux.html; James B. Stewart, "The Flop Looms as Studios Lean on Blockbusters," *New York Times*, May 18, 2013, p. B1; James B. Stewart, "Studios Unfazed by Colossal Wrecks," *New York Times*, December 21, 2013, p. B1.

MARKETING PLAN EXERCISE

ACTIVITY 18: Metrics

1. Select appropriate metrics for use in your marketing plan.
2. Prepare action plans in support of your marketing plan. For each action plan be sure to list budget items, and then aggregate these into an overall budget for your marketing plan. Also, be sure to specify relevant controls.
3. Select and justify the forecasting approaches you will employ in your marketing plan.
4. Develop expected-case, best-case, and worst-case scenarios for your marketing plan.

NOTES

1. A number of concepts in this section are derived from the following outstanding book, which is the best single source for understanding marketing dashboards. It is highly recommended as a guidebook on the topic for marketing managers: Patrick LaPointe, *Marketing by the Dashboard Light: How to Get More Insight, Foresight, and Accountability from Your Marketing Investments* (New York: ANA, 2005).
2. Gail J. McGovern, David Court, John A. Quelch, and Blair Crawford, "Bringing Customers into the Boardroom," *Harvard Business Review* 82, no. 11 (November 2004), pp. 70–80.
3. C. Clark, "Addressing the Challenges of Multichannel Customer Service," *1to1Media,* April 29, 2013, www.1to1media.com/view.aspx?docid=34246.
4. Thorsten Wiesel, Bernd Skiera, and Julián Villanueva, "Customer Equity: An Integral Part of Financial Reporting," *Journal of Marketing* 72, no. 2 (March 2008), pp. 1–14.
5. J. Kim, "Bank of America Customer Service Push Lifts Employees," *FierceFinance,* April 16, 2013, www.fiercefinance.com/story/bank-america-customer-service-push-lifts-employees/2013-04-16.
6. Leigh McAlister, Raji Srinivasan, and MinChung Kim, "Advertising, Research, and Development, and Systematic Risk of the Firm," *Journal of Marketing* 71, no. 1 (January 2007), pp. 35–49.
7. R. Hof, "Adobe Aims to Streamline Marketing Cloud with Pinterest-Like Social Dashboard," *Forbes,* March 6, 2013, www.forbes.com/sites/roberthof/2013/03/06/adobe-aims-to-streamline-marketing-cloud-with-pinterest-like-social-dashboard/.
8. One of the single best sources for understanding ROMI is the following book, which is highly recommended for marketing managers: Guy R. Powell, *Return on Marketing Investment: Demand More from Your Marketing and Sales Investments* (Albuquerque, NM: RBI Press, 2002). The ideas in this section are drawn from that source.
9. Claes Fornell, Sunil Mithas, Forrest V. Morgeson III, and M. S. Krishnan, "Customer Satisfaction and Stock Prices: High Returns, Low Risk," *Journal of Marketing* 70, no. 1 (January 2006), pp. 3–14; and Roland T. Rust, Katherine Lemon, and Valarie A. Zeithaml, "Return on Marketing: Using Customer Equity to Focus Marketing Strategy," *Journal of Marketing* 68, no. 1 (January 2004), pp. 109–27.
10. Behram Hansotia and Brad Rukstales, "Incremental Value Modeling," *Journal of Interactive Marketing* 16, no. 3 (Summer 2002), pp. 35–46.
11. Dominique M. Hanssens, Daniel Thorpe, and Carl Finkbeiner, "Marketing When Customer Equity Matters," *Harvard Business Review* 86, no. 5 (May 2008), p. 117; and Rick Ferguson, "Word of Mouth and Viral Marketing: Taking the Temperature of the Hottest Trends in Marketing," *Journal of Consumer Marketing* 25, no. 3 (2008), pp. 179–82.
12. Don E. Schultz, "The New Branding Lingo," *Marketing Management* 12, no. 6 (November/December 2003), pp. 8–9.
13. In this section, the example formulas and descriptions are selected from the following outstanding treatise on marketing metrics, which is a must-have book for marketing managers: Paul W. Farris, Neil T. Bendle, Phillip E. Pfeifer, and David J. Reibstein, *Marketing Metrics: The Definitive Guide to Measuring Marketing Performance,* 2nd ed. (Upper Saddle River, NJ: Pearson/Wharton School Publishing, 2010).
14. B. Stone, "To Catch Up with E-tail, Tools to Track Shoppers in the Store," *Bloomberg Businessweek,* April 25, 2013, www.businessweek.com/articles/2013-04-25/to-catch-up-with-e-tail-tools-to-track-shoppers-in-the-store#r=inn-s.
15. "Earth Mama Angel Baby Wins MACT Excellence and Green Awards," Earthmamaangelbaby.com, January 14, 2011, www.earthmamaangelbaby.com/mama-resources/reading-room/earth-mama-angel-baby-wins-mact-excellence-and-

greenawards; Anne Field, "Strategies: Mission Possible," *BusinessWeek,* December 14, 2007, www.businessweek.com/print/magazine/content/07_72/s0712038774148.htm.

16. William O. Bearden, R. Bruce Money, and Jennifer L. Nevins, "A Measure of Long-Term Orientation: Development and Validation," *Journal of the Academy of Marketing Science* 34, no. 3 (Summer 2006), pp. 456–67.
17. Kusum L. Ailawadi, Donald R. Lehmann, and Scott A. Neslin, "Marketing Response to a Major Policy Change in the Marketing Mix: Learning from Proctor & Gamble's Value Pricing Strategy," *Journal of Marketing* 65, no. 1 (January 2001), pp. 44–61.
18. Kusum L. Ailawadi, Karen Gedenk, Christian Lutzky, and Scott A. Neslin, "Decomposition of the Sales Impact of Promotion-Induced Stockpiling," *Journal of Marketing Research* 44, no. 3 (August 2007), pp. 450–67.
19. Thorsten Henning-Thurau, Victor Henning, and Henrik Sattler, "Consumer File Sharing of Motion Pictures," *Journal of Marketing* 71, no. 4 (October 2007), pp. 1–18; and Raghavan Srinivasan, Sreeram Ramakrishnan Sundara, and Scott E. Grasman, "Identifying the Effects of Cannibalization on the Product Portfolio," *Marketing Intelligence & Planning* 23, no. 4/5 (2005), pp. 359–71.
20. Paul W. Farris, Neil T. Bendle, Phillip E. Pfeifer, and David J. Reibstein, *Marketing Metrics: 50 + Metrics Every Executive Should Master* (Upper Saddle River, NJ: Pearson/Wharton School Publishing, 2006), p. 317.
21. Lynette Ryals, "Making Customer Relationship Management Work: The Measurement and Profitable Management of Customer Relationships," *Journal of Marketing* 69, no. 4 (October 2005), pp. 252–61.
22. Gary K. Hunter and William D. Perreault Jr., "Making Sales Technology Effective," *Journal of Marketing* 71, no. 1 (January 2007), pp. 16–34.
23. Cristina Gimenez and Eva Ventura, "Logistics-Production, Logistics-Marketing and Their External Integration: Their Impact on Performance," *International Journal of Operations & Production Management* 25, no. 1 (2005), pp. 20–38.
24. Robert C. Blattberg, Richard Briesch, and Edward J. Fox, "How Promotions Work," *Marketing Science* 14, no. 3 (Summer 1995), pp. 122–32.
25. Hsiao-Fan Wang and Wei-Kuo Hong, "Managing Customer Profitability in a Competitive Market by Continuous Data Mining," *Industrial Marketing Management* 35, no. 6 (August 2006), pp. 715–23.
26. Vanitha Swaminathan, Richard J. Fox, and Srinivas K. Reddy, "The Impact of Brand Extension Introduction on Choice," *Journal of Marketing* 65, no. 4 (October 2001), pp. 1–15.
27. David W. Stewart and Paul A. Pavlou, "From Consumer Response to Active Consumer: Measuring the Effectiveness of Interactive Media," *Journal of the Academy of Marketing Science* 30, no. 4 (Fall 2002), pp. 376–96.
28. M. Dickey, "Facebook's Gokul Rajaram," *Business Insider,* April 30, 2013, www.businessinsider.com/facebooks-gokul-rajaram-2013-4.
29. Jose A. Varela and Marisa del Rio, "Market Orientation Behavior: An Empirical Investigation Using MARKOR," *Marketing Intelligence & Planning* 21, no. 1 (2003), pp. 6–15.
30. Fred Anderholm III, James Gaertner, and Ken Milani, "The Utilization of PERT in the Preparation of Marketing Budgets," *Managerial Planning* 30, no. 1 (July/August 1981), pp. 18–23.
31. "Marketing on a Tight Budget: A 10-Point Action Plan," *Management Research News* 23, no. 12 (2000), p. 32.
32. J. Holton Wilson and Hugh G. Daubek, "Marketing Managers Evaluate Forecasting Models," *Journal of Business Forecasting Methods & Systems* 8, no. 1 (1989), pp. 19–23.
33. Robin T. Peterson, "How Efficient Are Salespeople in Surveys of Buyer Intentions?," *Journal of Business Forecasting Methods & Systems* 7, no. 1 (Spring 1988), pp. 11–12.
34. Kenneth B. Kahn and John T. Mentzer, "Forecasting in Consumer and Industrial Markets," *Journal of Business Forecasting Methods & Systems* 14, no. 2 (Summer 1995), pp. 21–27.
35. Ibid.
36. Zuhaimy Haji Ismael and Maizah Hura Ahamad, "Delphi Improves Sales Forecasts: Malaysia's Electronic Companies' Experience," *Journal of Business Forecasting Methods & Systems* 22, no. 2 (Summer 2003), pp. 22–25.
37. F. Bea, "Nielsen Digital Program Ratings Measures TV Viewership Online," *Digital Trends,* May 1, 2013, www.digitaltrends.com/web/nielsen-digital-program-ratings/.
38. Steve Hoeffler, "Measuring Preferences for Really New Products," *Journal of Marketing Research* 40, no. 4 (November 2003), pp. 406–20.
39. Stefan Stremersch, Gerard J. Tellis, Phillip Hans Franses, and Jeroen L. G. Binken, "Indirect Network Effects in New Product Growth," *Journal of Marketing* 71, no. 3 (July 2007), pp. 52–74.
40. Werner J. Reinartz and V. Kumar, "The Impact of Customer Relationship Characteristics on Profitable Lifetime Duration," *Journal of Marketing* 67, no. 1 (January 2003), pp. 77–99; and Wendy W. Moe and Peter S. Fader, "Modeling Hedonic Portfolio Products: A Joint Segmentation Analysis of Music

Compact Disc Sales," *Journal of Marketing Research* 38, no. 3 (August 2001), pp. 376–85.

41. Rebecca J. Slotegraaf, Christine Moorman, and J. Jeffrey Inman, "The Role of Firm Resources in Returns to Market Deployment," *Journal of Marketing Research* 40, no. 3 (August 2003), pp. 295–309.
42. Jim Burruss and Dorothea Kuettner, "Forecasting for Short-Lived Products: Hewlett-Packard's Journey," *Journal of Business Forecasting Methods & Systems* 21, no. 4 (Winter 2002/2003), pp. 9–13.
43. Guido Berens, Cees B. M. van Riel, and Gerrit H. van Bruggen, "Corporate Associations and Consumer Product Responses: The Moderating Role of Corporate Brand Dominance," *Journal of Marketing* 69, no. 3 (July 2005), pp. 35–48; and S. M. Musyoka, S. M. Mutyauvyu, J. B. K. Kiema, F. N. Karanja, and D. N. Siriba, "Market Segmentation Using Geographic Information Systems (GIS): A Case Study of the Soft Drink Industry in Kenya," *Marketing Intelligence & Planning* 25, no. 6 (2007), pp. 632–42.
44. G. Marvin, "Study: Facebook Activity Correlates to TV Viewership (Social TV's Not Just for Twitter)," *Marketing Land,* April 25, 2013, http://marketingland.com/study-facebook-activity-correlates-to-tv-viewership-social-tv-not-just-twitter-41428.
45. Myron Gable, Ann Fairhurst, Roger Dickinson, and Lynn Harris, "Improving Students' Understanding of the Retail Advertising Budgeting Process," *Journal of Marketing Education* 22, no. 2 (August 2000), pp. 120–28.
46. "Gartner Survey Shows U.S. Digital Marketing Budgets Average 2.5 Percent of Company Revenue," Gartner Inc., March 13, 2013, www.gartner.com/newsroom/id/2368315.
47. Bruce H. Clark, Andrew V. Abela, and Tim Ambler, "BEHIND the Wheel," *Marketing Management* 15, no. 3 (May/June 2006), p. 18.
48. Denis Smith, "Business (Not) as Usual: Crisis Management, Service Recovery and the Vulnerability of Organizations," *Journal of Services Marketing* 19, no. 5 (2005), pp. 309–20.
49. George Schlidge, "Marketing Audits: Why Principles of Accountability in Marketing Are Useful in Promoting Company Growth," *Journal of Promotion Management* 12, no. 2 (2006), pp. 49–52.

GLOSSARY

A

acceleration effect When small changes in consumer demand lead to considerable shifts in business product demand.

accumulating bulk A function performed by intermediaries that involves taking product from multiple sources and sorting it into different classifications for sales through the channel.

action plans The implementation element of a marketing plan that discusses issues such as timing, persons responsible, and resources necessary.

adaptive selling Being able to adjust the sales style from one sales situation to another in real time based on customer feedback.

additions to existing product lines An extension to an existing product that has already been developed and introduced to the market.

administered vertical marketing system (VMS) When the channel control of a vertical marketing system is determined by the size and power of one of its channel members.

advantages The particular product/service characteristic that helps meet the customer's needs.

advertising Paid form of relatively less personal marketing communications often through a mass medium to one or more target markets.

advertising execution The way an advertisement communicates the information and image.

advertising response function An effect in which, beyond a certain ad spending level, diminishing returns tend to set in.

advertising wearout When customers become bored with an existing advertising campaign.

agent intermediaries Intermediaries who do not take title to the product during the exchange process.

AIDA model A model designed to illustrate the hierarchy of effects in the context of customer response to marketing communications. It states that the effects build in this order: Attention (or Awareness), Interest, Desire, and Action.

allowances A remittance of monies to the consumer after the purchase of the product.

all-you-can-afford method Method of promotional budgeting that sets the promotional budget as whatever funds are left over after everything else that's considered a necessity is paid for.

ASEAN Founded in 1967, it is the most important Asian market zone and includes 10 countries running the entire length of the Pacific Rim (Brunei Darussalam, Indonesia, Malaysia, Philippines, Cambodia, Laos, Myanmar, Singapore, Thailand, and Vietnam).

aspirational purchases Products bought outside the individual's social standing.

assortment The number of different product items within a product category.

attitude Learned predisposition to respond to an object or class of objects in a consistently favorable or unfavorable way.

attitude-based choice A product choice that relies on an individual's beliefs and values to direct his or her assessment.

attribute-based choice A product choice based on the premise that product choices are made by comparing brands across a defined set of attributes.

auction pricing A pricing tactic in which individuals competitively bid against each other and the purchase goes to the highest bidder.

average-cost pricing A pricing decision made by identifying all costs associated with an offering to come up with what the average cost of a single unit might be.

awareness set A reduced set of possible alternatives a consumer considers after eliminating available options based on gathered information and personal preference.

B

backward integration When a firm merges operations back up the supply chain away from the consumer.

bait and switch When a seller advertises a low price but has no intent to actually make the lower-priced item available for sale.

banner ads Internet advertisements that are small boxes containing graphics and text, and have a hyperlink embedded in them.

basket of global advertising themes Global advertising strategy in which distinct ads built around several marketing messages are created that local marketers can select from to best fit their specific market situation.

behavioral data Information about when, what, and how often customers purchase products and services as well as other customer "touches."

behavioral segmentation Dividing consumer groups based on similarities in benefits sought or product usage patterns.

benefits The advantageous outcome from the advantage found in a product feature.

Boston Consulting Group (BCG) Growth-Share Matrix A popular approach for in-firm portfolio analysis that categorizes business units' level of contribution to the overall firm based on two factors: market growth rate and competitive position.

brand A name, term, sign, symbol, or design, or a combination of these elements, intended to identify the goods or services of one seller or groups of sellers and to differentiate them from those of competitors.

brand assets Other assets brands possess such as trademarks and patents that represent a significant competitive advantage.

brand association When customers develop a number of emotional, psychological, and performance associations with a brand. These associations become a primary purchase driver, particularly with brand loyal users.

brand awareness The most basic form of brand equity is simply being aware of the brand. Awareness is the foundation of all other brand relationships.

brand equity A set of assets and liabilities linked to a brand's name and symbol that adds to or subtracts from the value provided by a product or service to a firm or that firm's customers.

brand extensions A firm's use of knowledge of an existing brand when introducing a new product.

brand identity A summary of unique qualities attributed to a brand.

brand loyalty The strongest form of brand equity and reflects a commitment to repeat purchases.

brand personality The association between a brand and an individual's specific personality characteristics.

brand strategy The unique elements of a brand that define the products sold by a firm.

breadth of merchandise The number of different product categories offered by a retailer.

breaking bulk A shipping method used by manufacturers to better match quantities needed in terms of the space constraints and inventory turnover requirements of their buyers.

B-to-B (business-to-business) markets (B2B) Markets in which a firm's customers are other firms, characterized by few but large customers, personal relationships, complex buying processes, less price-sensitive demand.

business case analysis An overall evaluation of a product that usually assesses the product's probability of success.

buying center A number of individuals with a stake in a purchase decision who manage the purchase decision process and ultimately make the decision.

buying decision Decisions made throughout the purchase decision process that vary widely and are based on factors such as nature of the purchase, number of people involved in the decision, understanding of the product being purchased, and time frame for the decision.

buzz Word-of-mouth communication generated about a brand in the marketplace.

C

capital equipment A firm's significant, long-term investments in critical equipment or technology necessary for its manufacturing and production activities.

capital goods Major purchases in support of significant business functions.

captive pricing (complementary pricing) A pricing tactic of gaining a commitment from a customer to a basic product or system that requires continual purchase of peripherals to operate.

cash discounts A percentage discount off invoice to elicit quicker payment by the customer.

catalog retailer A retailer that offers merchandise in the form of a printed or online catalog.

category extensions When a firm uses its brand to expand into new product categories.

causal research Descriptive research designed to identify associations between variables.

census A comprehensive record of each individual in the population.

change conflict A customer's reluctance to choose change by selecting a company's product.

channel captain (channel leader) The lead player in an administered vertical marketing system (VMS).

channel conflict Disagreements among channel members that can result in their relationship becoming strained or even falling apart.

channel of distribution A system of interdependent relationships among a set of organizations that facilitates the exchange process.

channel or medium The conduit by which an encoded message travels.

channel power The degree to which any member of a marketing channel can exercise influence over the other members of the channel.

closed-ended questions Question format that encourages respondents to provide specific responses.

closing the sale Obtaining commitment from the customer to make the purchase.

clutter The level of competing messages on a particular medium.

co-branding The joining of two or more well-known brands in a common product or taking two brands and marketing them in partnership.

coercive power An explicit or implicit threat that a channel captain will invoke negative consequences on a channel member if it does not comply with the leader's request or expectations.

cognitive learning Active learning that involves mental processes that acquire information to work through problems and manage life situations.

commission Payment based on short-term results; usually a salesperson's dollar or unit sales volume.

communication The process of exchanging information and conveying meaning from one party to another.

community A group of intended visitors to the website.

comparative advertising Advertising in which two or more brands are directly compared against each other on certain attributes.

comparative-parity method Method of promotional budgeting that focuses on comparing promotion expenditures across all key competitors in the market to determine a budget number.

competitive advertising Advertising intended to build sales of a specific brand through shifting emotional appeal, persuasion, and providing information.

competitive scenario analysis Analyzing competitors using various scenarios to predict competitor behavior.

competitive strategy An organization-wide strategy designed to increase a firm's performance within the marketplace in terms of its competitors.

competitor-based pricing A pricing strategy in which a firm decides to price at some market average price in context with prices of competitors.

competitor orientation A reactive marketing strategy that uses competitor analysis as its primary driver.

complete set The very large set of possible alternatives a consumer considers during the initial search for information.

concentrated target marketing (focus or niche strategy) The target marketing approach that involves targeting a large portion of a small market.

conditioning The creation of a psychological association between two stimuli.

conformance A product's ability to deliver on features and performance characteristics promised in marketing communications.

consideration (evoked) set A refined list that encompasses the strongest options an individual considers in a purchase decision once he or she has obtained additional information and carried out an evaluation.

consumer marketing The practice of marketing toward large groups of like-minded customers.

content The materials that are included on the website.

context The overall layout, design, and aesthetic appeal of a website.

contingency planning Also called scenario planning, a planning approach that requires the establishment of different planning options depending on the expected case, best case, or worst case.

contractual agreements Enduring, nonequity relationships with another company that allow a company to expand its participation in a foreign market.

contractual VMS The binding of otherwise independent entities in the vertical marketing system legally through contractual agreements.

controls Elements put in place to ensure progress is being made in the implementation of a marketing plan. Controls must be in place from the outset of the planning process to specify the timing, procedure, and persons responsible for systematically monitoring.

convenience goods Frequently purchased, relatively low-cost products that customers have little interest in seeking new information about or considering other product options.

cooperative advertising and promotion When a manufacturer provides special incentive money to channel members for certain promotional performance.

core competencies The activities a firm can do exceedingly well.

core product The physical, tangible elements that make up a product's essential benefit.

corporate identity Consumers' perceptions of a corporation that influences their attitudes and responses toward products or services offered by it.

corporate-level strategic plan An umbrella plan for the overall direction of the corporation developed above the strategic business unit (SBU) level.

corporate vertical marketing system (VMS) The investment of a channel member in backward or forward vertical integration by buying controlling interests in other intermediaries.

cost-based price An international pricing strategy in which the firm considers cost plus markup to arrive at a final price.

cost leadership A marketing strategy in which a firm utilizes its core cost advantages to gain an advantage over competitors due to flexibility in pricing strategies as well as its ability to translate cost savings to the bottom line.

cost-plus pricing Building a price by adding standardized markup on top of the costs associated with the offering.

cost reduction A specific method for introducing lower-cost products that frequently focuses on value-oriented product price points in the product mix.

country-of-origin effect The influence of the country of manufacture, assembly, or design on a customer's positive or negative perception of a product.

creating assortments The process of accumulating products from several sources to then make those products available down the channel as a convenient assortment for consumers.

credence attributes Aspects of an offering for which customers cannot make a reasonable evaluation, even after use.

crisis management A planned, coordinated approach for disseminating information during times of emergency and for handling the effects of unfavorable publicity.

cultural values Principles shared by a society that assert positive ideals.

culture A system of values, beliefs, and morals shared by a particular group of people that permeates over time.

customer advocacy A willingness and ability on the part of a customer to participate in communicating the brand message to others within his or her sphere of influence.

customer benefit Some type of utility that a company and its products (and services) provide its customers.

customer-centric Placing the customer at the core of the enterprise and focusing on investments in customers over the long term.

customer communities Websites where customers come and share stories about their vendor experiences.

customer delight The exceeding of customer expectations.

customer expectations management The process of making sure the firm does not set customer expectations so high that they cannot be effectively met on a consistent basis.

customer loyalty A customer's commitment to a company and its products and brands for the long run.

customer marketing The practice of marketing that focuses on developing relationships with individuals.

customer mind-set An individual's belief that understanding and satisfying customers, whether internal or external to the organization, is central to the proper execution of his or her job.

customer orientation Placing the customer at the core of all aspects of the enterprise.

customer relationship management (CRM) A comprehensive business model for increasing revenues and profits by focusing on customers.

customer retention Low propensity among a firm's customer base to consider switching to other providers.

customer satisfaction The level of liking an individual harbors for an offering.

customer touchpoints Where the selling firm touches the customer in some way, thus allowing for information about him or her to be collected.

customization The degree to which the website creates a unique individual experience for each visitor.

customized (one-to-one) marketing A marketing strategy that involves directing energy and resources into establishing a learning relationship with each customer to increase the firm's customer knowledge.

D

data collection Distributing a survey to its respondents, recording the respondents' responses, and making the data available for analysis.

data mining A sophisticated analytical approach to using the massive amounts of data accumulated through a firm's CRM system to develop segments and microsegments of customers for purposes of either market research or development of market segmentation strategies.

data warehouse A compilation of customer data generated through touchpoints that can be transformed into useful information for marketing management decision making and marketing planning.

database marketing Direct marketing involving the utilization of the data generated through CRM practices to create lists of customer prospects who are then contacted individually by various means of marketing communication.

deceptive pricing Knowingly stating prices in a manner that gives a false impression to customers.

decider An individual within the buying center who ultimately makes the purchase decision.

decision-making authority An issue that arises when companies grow internationally and lines of authority become longer and more complicated, resulting in difficulty in defining decision-making protocols.

decoding process When a receiver interprets the meaning of the message's symbols as encoded by the sender.

degree of affiliation The amount of interpersonal contact an individual has with the reference group.

degree of centralization The degree to which decisions are made at the firm's home office.

delightful surprises Built-in extras in service delivery not expected by the customer.

Delphi technique A subjective method of forecasting that is done iteratively, employing repeated measurement and controlled anonymous feedback instead of direct confrontation and debate among those preparing the forecast.

demographic segmentation Dividing consumer groups based on a variety of readily measurable descriptive factors about the group.

demographics The characteristics of human populations and population segments, especially when used to identify consumer markets.

depth of merchandise The number of different product items within a product category.

derived demand Demand that originates from the demand for consumer products in business-to-business (B-to-B) marketing.

descriptive research Research designed to explain or illustrate some phenomenon.

desirability The extent and direction of the emotional connection an individual wishes to have with a particular group.

developed economies Specific economies that have fueled world economic growth for much of the 20th century, including Western Europe, the United States, and Japan.

differentiated target marketing The target marketing approach that involves developing different value offerings for different targeted segments.

differentiation Communicating and delivering value in different ways to different customer groups.

dimensions of service quality The five aspects of a service that make up its total quality, including tangibles, reliability, responsiveness, assurance, and empathy.

direct and interactive marketing Personal communication with a customer by means other than a salesperson.

direct channel A channel that has no intermediaries and operates strictly from producer to end-user consumer or business user.

direct competitors Competing firms that produce products considered very close substitutes for those of other firms' current products and services.

direct foreign investment A strategic alliance with long-term implications in which a company moves manufacturing or operations into a foreign market.

direct marketing An interactive marketing system that uses one or more advertising media to effect a measurable response and/or transaction at any location.

direct selling A form of non-store retailing that involves independent businesspeople contacting consumers directly to demonstrate and sell products or services in convenient locations.

discounts Direct, immediate reductions in price provided to purchasers.

disintermediation The shortening or collapsing of marketing channels due to the elimination of one or more intermediaries.

display ads Ads put out by companies for advertising on the Internet that include banner ads and interstitials.

distinctive competencies A firm's core competencies that are superior to those of their competitors.

distribution intensity The number of intermediaries involved in distributing the product.

distributor Represents the company and often many others in foreign markets.

diversification strategies Strategies designed to seize on opportunities to serve new markets with new products.

dumping A global pricing issue that refers to the practice of charging less than their actual costs or less than the product's price in the firm's home markets.

durability The length of product usage.

durable product Products with a comparatively long product life that are often expensive.

E

early adopter A consumer who is a product opinion leader who seeks out new products consistent with his or her personal self-image.

early majority Consumers who are product watchers who want to be convinced of the product's claims and value proposition before making a commitment to it.

e-commerce The degree to which the website allows direct purchase of products and services.

electronic commerce (e-commerce) Any action that uses electronic media to communicate with customers; facilitate the inventory, exchange, and distribution of goods and services; or facilitate payment.

electronic data interchange (EDI) Sophisticated programs that link a customer with its suppliers to manage inventories and automatically replenish supplies.

electronic retailing (e-retailing or e-tailing) The communication and sale of products or services to consumers over the Internet.

e-mail Mail communications delivered by electronic device.

emerging markets Growing economies that have developed over the last 25 years that are projected to contribute toward 75 percent of world economic growth over the next 20 years.

emotional appeal Promotional appeal that plays on human nature using a variety of human emotions and aspirations in developing promotional messages.

emotional choice A product choice based more on emotional attitudes about a product rather than rational thought.

encoding process The process in communication in which the sender translates an idea to be communicated into a symbolic message in preparation for transmittal to a receiver.

end-user purchase A category of products purchased by manufacturers that represents the equipment, supplies, and services needed to keep their business operational.

enhanced product Additional features, designs, or innovations that extend beyond the core product to exceed customer expectations.

enterprise resource planning (ERP) system A software application designed to integrate information related to logistics processes throughout the organization.

e-procurement The process of online business purchasing.

essential benefit The fundamental need met by a product.

European Union A successful regional marketing zone founded more than 50 years ago by six European countries (Belgium, France, Italy, Luxembourg, The Netherlands, and West Germany) with the Treaty of Rome that now includes 28 countries.

even pricing A pricing tactic in which the price is expressed in whole-dollar increments.

event sponsorship Having your brand and company associated with events in the sports, music, arts, and other entertainment communities.

everyday low pricing (EDLP) A pricing tactic that entails relatively low, constant prices and minimal spending on promotional efforts.

exchange The giving up of something of value for something desired.

exclusive dealing When a supplier creates a restrictive agreement that prohibits intermediaries that handle its product from selling competing firms' products.

exclusive distribution Distribution strategy built on prestige, scarcity, and premium pricing in which a producer only distributes its products to one or very few vendors.

exclusive territory The protection of an intermediary from having to compete with others selling a producer's goods.

experience attributes Aspects of an offering that can be evaluated only during or after consumption.

expert power A channel member's utilization of its unique competencies and knowledge to influence others in the channel.

exploratory research Research geared toward discovery that can either answer the research question or identify other research variables for further study. It is generally the first step in the marketing research process.

exporter International market specialist that helps companies by acting as the export marketing department.

exporting The most common method for entering foreign markets, it offers firms the ability to penetrate foreign markets with minimal investment and very little risk.

extensive information search When a consumer makes a purchase decision based on a thorough process of investigation and research.

external information sources Additional information an individual seeks from outside sources when internal information is not sufficient to make a purchase decision.

extrinsic rewards Rewards controlled and given by people other than the salesperson such as a manager and customers.

F

FAB A selling approach designed to make the company's products more relevant for customers by explaining the product's features, advantages, and benefits.

facilitating functions Activities that help fulfill completed transactions and also maintain the viability of the channel relationships.

fad Products that come and go quickly, often reaching only a limited number of individuals but creating a lot of buzz in the marketplace.

fair trade laws Laws designed to allow manufacturers to establish artificially high prices by limiting the ability of wholesalers and retailers to offer reduced or discounted prices.

family A group of two or more people living together and related by birth, marriage, or adoption.

family branding The creation of brands that have synergy between them in terms of the overall company brand.

family life cycle The changes in life stage that transform an individual's buying habits.

features Any product attribute or performance characteristic.

feedback loop Two-way communication in which a receiver can communicate reactions back to the sender.

firing a customer The shifting of investment of resources from a less attractive customer to more profitable ones.

first-mover advantage When a firm introduces a new market offering, thus defining the scope of the competitive marketplace.

fluctuating demand When the level of consumer demand is not constant, having serious implications related to the perishability of services.

FOB (free on board) Determination of title transfer and freight payment based on shipping location.

focus group A qualitative research method that consists of a meeting (either in person or increasingly online) of 6 to 10 people that is moderated by a professional who carefully moves the conversation through a defined agenda in an unstructured, open format.

follow-up A company's actions after the customer has decided to purchase the product.

food retailer Any retailer that includes food as a part of its breadth of merchandise.

form The physical elements of a product, such as size, shape, and color.

formalization The formal establishment of a firm's structure, processes and tools, and managerial knowledge and commitment to support its culture.

forward integration When a firm moves its operations more toward the end user.

franchise organization A contractual relationship between a franchisor, who is the grantor of the franchise, and the franchisee, who is the independent entity entering into an agreement to perform at the standards required by the franchisor.

franchising A contractual agreement in which a firm provides a contracted company in a foreign market with a bundle of products, systems, services, and management expertise in return for local market knowledge, financial consideration, and local management experience.

frequency The average number of times a person in the target market is exposed to the message.

functional-level plans Plans for each business function that makes up one of the firm's strategic business units (SBUs). These include core business functions within each SBU such as operations, marketing, finance, as well as other pertinent operational areas.

G

gap model A visual tool used in the measurement of service quality that identifies and measures the differences between consumer and marketer perceptions of a provided service.

gatekeeper An individual who controls access to information and relevant individuals in the buying center.

GE business screen A popular approach for in-firm portfolio analysis that categorizes business units' level of contribution to the overall firm based on two factors: business position and market attractiveness.

gender roles Behaviors regarded as proper for men and women in a particular society.

general warranty Broad promises about product performance and customer satisfaction.

generic strategy An overall directional strategy at the business level.

geographic regions An international organizational structure that divides international markets by geography, building autonomous regional organizations that perform business functions in the geographic areas.

geographic segmentation Dividing consumer groups based on physical location.

geo-location marketing The use of geographic data to drive marketing messaging and other marketing decisions.

global marketing themes Global advertising strategy in which a basic template is used for global ads that allows for slight modifications depending on local markets.

global marketing with local content Global advertising strategy in which a firm keeps the same global marketing theme as the home market but adapts it with local content.

global product lines Products that are sold across country borders.

goals General statements of what the firm wishes to accomplish in support of the mission and vision.

go-to-market mistake When a company fails to stop a bad product idea from moving into product development.

government Local, state, and federal entities that have unique and frequently challenging purchasing practices for manufacturing firms.

gray market A global pricing issue that references the unauthorized diversion of branded products into global markets.

growth phase A stage of the product life cycle marked by rapid expansion as competitors come into the market and customers learn, understand, and begin to adopt the product.

H

harvesting A product strategy that involves a measured but consistent investment reduction in a product.

high-involvement learning The learning process in which an individual is stimulated to acquire new information.

high mass consumption An economy characterized by rising income levels, creating a large population with discretionary income, which results in consumers that demand higher levels of service and more durable goods.

high/low pricing A pricing strategy in which the retailer offers frequent discounts, primarily through sales promotions, to stated regular prices.

household life cycle (HLC) A structured set of chronological activities a particular household follows over time.

I

impulse goods Goods whose sales rely on the consumer seeing the product, feeling an immediate want, and being able to purchase now.

inbound logistics The process of sourcing materials and knowledge inputs from external suppliers to the point at which production begins.

inbound telemarketing When a prospective customer contacts a company for more information.

incentives Generally commissions tied to sales volume or profitability, or bonuses for meeting or exceeding specific performance targets.

in-depth interview A qualitative research method that consists of an unstructured (or loosely structured) interview with an individual who has been chosen based on some characteristic of interest, often a demographic attribute.

indirect channel A channel that contains one or more intermediary levels.

indirect competitors Competing firms that offer products that may be substituted based on the customer's need and choice options.

inelastic demand When changes in demand are not significantly affected by changes in price.

influencer An individual, either inside or outside the organization, with relevant expertise in a particular area who provides information used by the buying center in making a final buying decision.

information search The process consumers use to gather information to make a purchase decision.

initiator The individual who starts the buying decision process.

innovation diffusion process How long it takes a product to move from first purchase to last purchase (the last set of users to adopt the product).

innovator A consumer who is a product enthusiast who is among the first to try and master a new product.

input measures The efforts of salespeople during the sales process.

inseparability The characteristic of a service in which it is produced and consumed at the same time and cannot be separated from its provider.

institutional advertising Advertising that promotes industry, company, family of brands, or some other issues broader than a specific product.

institutions Nongovernmental organizations driven by the delivery of service to the target constituency, rather than by profits.

instrumental performance The actual performance features of the product in terms of what it was promised to do.

intangibility The characteristic of a service in which it cannot be experienced through the physical senses of the consumer.

integrated marketing communications (IMC) A strategic approach to communicating the brand and company message to targeted customers in ways that are clear, concise, and consistent and yet are customizable as needed to maximize the impact on a particular audience.

intensive distribution A distribution strategy designed to saturate every possible intermediary, especially retailers.

interactive marketing An Internet-driven relationship between companies, their brands, and customers. Interactive marketing enables customers to control information flow and encourages customer-company interaction as well as a higher level of customer service.

intermediaries Organizations that play a role in the exchange process between producers and consumers.

internal information sources All information stored in memory and accessed by the individual regarding a purchase decision.

internal marketing The treating of employees as customers and developing systems and benefits that satisfy their needs to promote internal service quality.

international joint ventures A strategic alliance formed by legal entities consisting of a partnership of two or more participating companies that share management duties and a defined management structure in which every partner holds an equity position.

interstitials Graphic, visually interesting Internet advertisements that move across the web page.

intrinsic rewards Those rewards salespeople primarily attain for themselves; they include feelings of accomplishment, personal growth, and self-worth.

involvement A significant outcome of an individual's motivation that mediates the product choice decision. It is activated by three elements: background and psychological profile, aspirational focus, and the environment at the time of purchase decision.

J

joint venture A partnership of two or more participating companies that differs from other strategic alliances in that (1) management duties are shared and a management structure is defined; (2) other corporations or legal entities, not individuals, formed the venture; and (3) every partner holds and equity position.

jury of executive opinion Subjective method of forecasting that relies on a formal or informal poll of key executives within the firm to gain their assessment of sales potential.

just-in-time (JIT) inventory control system An inventory management system designed to balance levels of overstock and stock-out in an effort to reduce warehousing costs.

just noticeable difference (JND) The amount of price increase that can be taken without impacting customer demand.

K

key account salespeople Salespeople responsible for the firm's largest customers.

L

laggard A consumer who is a product avoider and evades adoption until there is no other product choice.

language An established system of ideas and phonetics shared by members of a particular culture that serves as their primary communication tool.

late majority Consumers who are product followers and are price sensitive, are risk averse, and generally prefer products with fewer features.

learning Any change in the content or organization of long-term memory or behavior.

legitimate power A channel member's ability to influence other members based on contracts or other formal agreements.

licensing When a firm offers other manufacturers the right to use its brand in exchange for a set fee or percentage of sales.

lifestyle An individual's perspective on life that manifests itself in activities, interests, and opinions.

lifetime value of a customer The measurement of important business success factors related to long-term relationships with customers.

limited information search When a consumer makes a purchase decision based on incomplete information and/or lack of personal knowledge.

line extensions Introducing a new product to an existing product line.

line of visibility The separation between activities customers see and those they do not in the process of service delivery.

local market ad generation Global marketing strategy in which a firm allows local marketers to create local ads that do not necessarily coordinate with its global marketing messages.

local market conditions price An international pricing strategy in which the firm assigns a price based on local market conditions with minimal consideration for the actual cost of putting the product into the market.

long-term memory Enduring memory storage that can remain with an individual for years or even a lifetime.

loss leader products Products sacrificed at prices below costs in an effort to attract shoppers to the retail location.

low-involvement learning The learning process in which an individual is not prompted to value new information, characterized by little or no interest in learning about a new product offering.

low-price guarantee policy A pricing strategy used by retailers that guarantees consumers the lowest price for any given product by matching the sales price of competitors.

loyalty programs Programs that reinforce the customer's benefits of purchasing at the retailer.

M

macroeconomics The study of economic activity in terms of broad measures of output and input as well as the interaction among various sectors of an entire economy.

management research deliverable The definition of what management wants to do with marketing research.

market creation Approaches that drive the market toward fulfilling a whole new set of needs that customers did not realize was possible or feasible before.

m-commerce Sales generated by a mobile device.

market deterioration The third and final phase of the maturity stage of the product life cycle in which the market starts to lose customers and competitors begin to feel the pressure of overcapacity in the market.

market development strategies Strategies designed to allow for expansion of the firm's product line into heretofore untapped markets, often internationally.

market expansion When a firm that operates in closely related markets expands into new markets to compete more directly.

market information system (MIS) A continuing process of identifying, collecting, analyzing, accumulating, and dispensing critical information to marketing decision makers.

market makers Websites that bring buyers and sellers together.

market mavens Individuals who have information about many kinds of products, places to shop, and other facets of markets, and initiate discussions with consumers and respond to requests from consumers for market information.

market orientation The implementation of the marketing concept, based on an understanding of customers and competitors.

market penetration strategies Strategies designed to involve investing against existing customers to gain additional usage of existing products.

market research The methodical identification, collection, analysis, and distribution of data related to discovering then solving marketing problems or opportunities and enhancing good decision making.

market segmentation Dividing a market into meaningful smaller markets or submarkets based on common characteristics.

market share The percentage of total category sales accounted for by a firm.

market space A powerful new communication channel that encourages customer-company interaction and a higher level of customer service.

market stability The second phase of the maturity stage of the product life cycle in which a product experiences no market growth as the market reaches saturation.

market test Objective method of forecasting that involves placing a product in several representative geographic areas to see how well it performs and then projecting that experience to the market as a whole.

market-driven strategic planning The process at the corporate or strategic business unit (SBU) level of a firm that acts to marshal the various resource and functional areas toward a central purpose around the customer.

marketing The activity, set of institutions, and processes for creating, communicating, delivering, and exchanging offerings that have value for customers, clients, partners, and society at large.

Marketing (big M) The dimension of marketing that focuses on external forces that affect the organization and serves as the driver of business strategy.

marketing (little m) The dimension of marketing that focuses on the functional or operational level of the organization.

marketing audit A systematic review of the current state of marketing within an organization.

marketing concept Business philosophy that emphasizes an organization-wide customer orientation with the objective of achieving long-run profits.

marketing control The process of measuring marketing results and adjusting the firm's marketing plan as needed.

marketing dashboard A comprehensive system of metrics and information uniquely relevant to the role of the marketing manager in a particular organization. Dashboards provide managers with up-to-the-minute information necessary to run their operation.

marketing intelligence The collecting, analyzing, and storing of data from the macro environment on a continuous basis.

marketing management The leading and managing of the facets of marketing to improve individual, unit, and organizational performance.

marketing metrics Tools and processes designed to identify, track, evaluate, and provide key benchmarks for improvement of marketing activities.

marketing mix (4Ps of marketing) Product, price, place, and promotion—the fundamental elements that comprise the marketer's tool kit that can be developed in unique combinations to set the product or brand apart from the competition.

marketing plan The resulting document that records the marketing planning process in a useful framework.

marketing planning The ongoing process of developing and implementing market-driven strategies for an organization.

marketing's stakeholders Any person or entity inside or outside a firm with whom marketing interacts, impacts, and is impacted by.

markup on cost The addition to the price of an offering after costs have been considered.

markup on sales price Using the sales price as a basis for calculating the markup percentage.

mass customization Combining flexible manufacturing with flexible marketing to greatly enhance customer choice.

mass marketing The classic style of consumer marketing in which a firm views all consumers as equal reactors to a firm's marketing strategies.

materials Natural or farm products that become part of the final product.

materials, repairs, operational (MRO) Products used in everyday business operations that are not typically considered to be a significant expense for the firm.

materials requirement planning (MRP) The overall management of the inbound materials from suppliers to facilitate minimal production delays.

matrix structure An international organizational structure that encourages regional autonomy among organizations while building product competence in key areas around the world.

maturity An economy that, through private and public investments, has reached the point where it seeks to maintain its growth rates.

maturity stage A stage of the product life cycle in which a product is in the transition from high growth to relative sales decline. There are three phases in the maturity stage: relative market expansion, market stability, and market deterioration.

mechanical observation A variation of observational data that uses a device to chronicle activity.

memory Where people store all past learning events.

merchandise category An assortment of items considered substitutes for each other.

merchant intermediaries Intermediaries who take title to the product during the exchange process.

MERCOSUR Inaugurated in 1995, it is the most powerful market zone in South America and includes the major economies of South America: Argentina, Bolivia, Brazil, Chile, Paraguay, and Uruguay.

message transmission Placing a communication into some channel or medium so that it can make its way to the intended receiver.

microeconomics The study of individual economic activity.

microsite A more focused site from a company's primary site that addresses specific topics such as new product introductions or targeted products within a large product.

minimal information search When a consumer makes a purchase decision based on very little information or investigation.

minimum markup laws Laws that require retailers to apply a certain percentage of markup to their products for sale.

mission statement The verbal articulation of an organization's purpose, or reason for existence.

missionary salespeople Salespeople who do not take orders from customers directly but persuade customers to buy their firm's product from distributors or other suppliers.

modifications to existing products Creating newer, better, faster versions of existing products that target, for the most part, existing customers.

modified rebuy A buying decision in which a customer is familiar with the product and supplier in a purchase decision but is looking for additional information because of one or more of three circumstances: the supplier has performed poorly, new products have come into the market, or the customer believes it is time for a change.

moment of truth The face-to-face time between customer and service provider.

monopolistic competition When there are many companies offering unique products in different market segments.

monopoly When a market is controlled by a single company offering one set of products.

moral appeal Promotional appeal that strikes a chord with a target customer's sense of right and wrong.

motivation The stimulating power that induces and then directs an individual's behavior.

MRO supplies (maintenance, repair, operating) The everyday items that a company needs to keep running.

multiattribute model A model that measures an individual's attitudes toward an object by evaluating it on several important attributes.

N

NAFTA (North American Free Trade Agreement) Created to eliminate tariffs between Canada, Mexico, and the United States, and which stands as the single largest economic alliance today.

national brands Products created, manufactured, and marketed by a company and sold to retailers around the country and the world.

network organization (virtual organization) Organization that eliminates many in-house business functions and activities in favor of focusing only on those aspects for which it is best equipped to add value.

new dominant logic for marketing A shift in worldview from the traditional goods versus services dichotomy to recognition of both goods and services as "offerings" that create value for consumers.

new purchase A buying decision in which the purchase of a product or service by a customer is for the first time.

new-to-the-world product A product that has not been available before or bears little resemblance to an existing product.

nimble To be in a position to be maximally flexible, adaptable, and speedy in response to the many key change drivers affecting business.

noise The distortion or interference that can occur at any stage of a communication process.

nondurable product Products that are usually consumed in a few uses and, in general, are of low cost to the consumer.

nonfinancial incentives Sales force motivators beyond financial compensation.

nonprobability sampling The selection of individuals for statistical research in which the probability of everyone in the population being included in the sample is not identified.

non-store retailer A retailer that uses alternative methods to reach the customer that do not require a physical location.

nonverbal communication The means of communicating through facial expressions, eye behavior, gestures, posture, and any other body language.

North American Industrial Classification System (NAICS) A system developed by the United States, Canada, and Mexico that classifies companies on the basis of their primary output to define and segment business markets.

O

objective forecasting methods Forecasting methods that rely primarily on sophisticated quantitative (empirical) analytical approaches.

objective measures Statistics the sales manager gathers from the firm's internal data.

objective-and-task method Method of promotional budgeting that takes an investment approach in that goals are set for the upcoming year and then promotional dollars are budgeted to support the achievement of those goals.

objectives Specific, measurable, and potentially attainable milestones necessary for a firm to achieve its goals.

observational data The documentation of behavioral patterns among the population of interest.

odd pricing A pricing tactic in which the price is not expressed in whole dollar increments.

offering A product or service that delivers value to satisfy a need or want.

oligopoly When a market is controlled by more than one company in an industry that is either standardized or differentiated.

one world price An international pricing strategy in which the firm assigns one price for its products in every global market.

one-price strategy A pricing tactic in which the price marked on a good is what it typically sells for.

one-to-one marketing Directing energy and resources into establishing a learning relationship with each customer and connecting that knowledge with the firm's production and service capabilities to fulfill that customer's needs in as customary a manner as possible.

online database Data stored on a server that is accessed remotely over the Internet or some other telecommunications network.

open-ended questions Question format that encourages respondents to be expressive and offers them the opportunity to provide more detailed, qualitative responses.

opinion leaders Individuals with expertise in certain products or technologies who classify, explain, and then bestow information to a broader audience.

organizational factors Organization-wide beliefs and attitudes that factor into a purchase decision.

organizational learning The analysis and refinement phase of the CRM process that is based on customer response to the firm's implementation strategies and programs.

original equipment manufacturer (OEM) Manufacturing firms that sell products that are used as integral manufacturing components by their customer companies.

out supplier A company that is not on a firm's list of approved suppliers.

outbound logistics The process of a product's movement from production by the manufacturer to purchase by the end-user consumer.

outbound telemarketing Calling potential customers at their home or office, either to make a sales call via telephone or to set up an appointment for a field salesperson.

output measures The results of the efforts expended by the salesperson.

outsourcing (third-party logistics, 3PL) Handing over one or more of its core internal functions, such as most or all of its supply chain activities, to other (third-party) companies that are experts in those areas allows the firm to better focus on its core business.

outsourcing the sales force Using independent sales agents to sell a company's products.

P

partner relationship management (PRM) strategies A strategic alliance that includes connectivity of inventory, billing systems, and market research among marketing channel members.

parts Equipment that is either fully assembled or in smaller pieces that will be assembled in larger components and then used in the production process.

penetration pricing A pricing strategy in which a firm's objective is to gain as much market share as possible.

perceived quality The conveyed perception of quality of a brand that is either positive or negative.

percent-of-sales method Method of promotional budgeting that allocates funding for promotional activities to certain products as a function of their forecasted sales revenues.

perception A system to select, organize, and interpret information to create a useful, informative picture of the world.

perceptual maps A visual tool used in positioning that allows for comparing attributes to gauge consumer perceptions of each competitor's delivery against those attributes.

perishability The characteristic of a product or service in which it cannot be stored or saved for future use.

personal factors The needs, desires, and objectives of those involved in a purchase decision.

personal selling A two-way communication process between salesperson and buyer with the goal of securing, building, and maintaining long-term relationships with profitable customers.

personality An individual's set of unique personal qualities that produce distinctive responses across similar situations.

physical distribution (logistics) The integrated process of moving input materials to the producer, in-process inventory through the firm, and finished goods out of the firm through the channel of distribution.

pioneering advertising Advertising intended to stimulate primary demand, typically during the introductory or early growth stages of an offering.

portfolio analysis A tool used in strategic planning for multibusiness corporations that views SBUs, and sometimes even product lines, as a series of investments from which it expects maximization of returns.

positioning The communication of sources of value to customers so they can easily make the connection between their needs and wants and what the product has to offer.

post-purchase dissonance A feeling of doubt or anxiety following a recent purchase, generally attributed with high-involvement, large purchases.

preferred state An individual's desires that reflect how he or she would like to feel or live in the present time.

prestige pricing A pricing tactic that lends prestige to a product or brand by virtue of a price relatively higher than the competition.

price bundling A pricing tactic in which customers are given the opportunity to purchase a package deal at a reduced price compared to what the individual components of the package would cost separately.

price elasticity of demand The measure of customers' price sensitivity estimated by dividing relative changes in quantity sold by relative changes in price.

price points Prices established to convey the differences in benefits offered as the customer moves up and down the product line.

price skimming A pricing strategy in which a firm enters a market at a relatively high price point, usually in an effort to create a strong price-quality relationship for the product.

price war When a company purposefully makes pricing decisions to undercut one or more competitors and gain sales and net market share.

price-fixing When companies collude to set prices at a mutually beneficial high level.

pricing objectives The desired or expected results associated with a pricing strategy that is consistent with other marketing-related objectives.

primary data Data collected specifically for a particular research question.

primary group A reference group an individual has frequent contact with.

primary target markets Market segments that clearly have the best chance of meeting ROI goals and the other attractiveness factors.

private-label brands Products managed and marketed by retailers, also known as store or house brands.

probability sampling The specific protocol used to identify and select individuals from the population in which each population element has a known nonzero chance of being selected.

product advertising Advertising designed to increase purchase of a specific offering.

product choice The end result of evaluating product alternatives in the purchase decision process.

product deletion Discontinuing the production of a product.

product demand Demand within business markets affected by three critical dimensions: derived demand, fluctuating demand, and inelastic demand.

product development strategies Strategies designed to recognize the opportunity to invest in new products that will increase usage from the current customer base.

product expansion When a firm leverages its existing expertise (technical product experience or supply chain) to create new products for existing or new markets.

product life cycle (PLC) The life of a product that includes four stages: introduction, growth, maturity, and decline.

product line A group of products linked through usage, customer profile, price points, and distribution channels or needs satisfaction.

product line pricing (price lining) A pricing tactic in which a firm affords the marketing manager an opportunity to develop a rational pricing approach across a complete line of related items.

product mix The combination of all the products offered by a firm.

production orientation The maximization of production capacity through improvements in products and production activities without much regard for what is going on in the marketplace.

professional services Services that require specialized training and certification that are typically self-regulated by industry or trade groups.

profitability analysis A thorough analysis that accounts for all costs associated with bringing a product to market to determine short- and long-term product profitability.

promotion Various forms of communication to inform, persuade, or remind.

promotion mix The elements of promotion, including advertising, sales promotion, public relations (PR), personal selling, direct marketing, and interactive marketing.

promotion mix strategies Decisions about which combination of elements in the promotion mix is likely to best communicate the offering to the marketplace and achieve an acceptable ROI for the marketer.

promotional allowances Sales promotions initiated by the manufacturer and carried out by the retailer, who is then compensated by the manufacturer.

promotional appeal The connection an offering establishes with customers; includes rational appeals, emotional appeals, and moral appeals.

promotional campaign Promotional expenditures to a particular creative execution aimed at a particular product or product line during a specified time period.

psychographic segmentation Dividing consumer groups based on variables such as personality and AIOs: activities, interests, and opinions.

psychological pricing Creating a perception about price merely from the image the numbers provide the customer.

public relations (PR) Systematic approach to influencing attitudes, opinions, and behaviors of customers and others.

publicity An unpaid and relatively less personal form of marketing communications, usually through news stories and mentions at public events.

puffery Relatively minor embellishments of product claims to bolster the persuasive message.

pull strategy Promotional and distribution strategy in which the focus is on stimulating demand for an offering directly from the end user.

pure competition When there are many companies offering essentially the same product in the market.

push strategy Promotional and distribution strategy in which the focus is on stimulating demand within the channel of distribution.

Q

qualitative research Less structured research not meant to be used for statistical analysis that can employ methods such as surveys and interviews to collect data.

quantitative research Research used to develop a measured understanding using statistical analysis to assess and quantify the results.

quantity discounts Discounts taken off an invoice price based on different levels of product purchased.

R

rational appeal Promotional appeal that centers on the benefits an offering can provide to a customer.

reach The percentage of individuals in a defined target market that are exposed to an ad during a specific time period.

real state An individual's perceived reality of present time.

receiver The individual who is the target of the communication.

reducing transactions The process of lowering the number of purchasing transactions carried out by a firm by utilizing the services of intermediaries.

reference group A group of individuals whose beliefs, attitudes, and behavior influence (positively or negatively) the beliefs, attitudes, and behavior of an individual.

reference pricing A pricing strategy in which a firm gives customers comparative prices when considering purchase of a product so they are not viewing a price in isolation from prices of other choices.

referent power A channel member's ability to influence other members based on respect, admiration, or reverence.

regional market zones A group of countries that create formal relationships for mutual economic benefit through lower tariffs and reduced trade barriers.

relationship orientation Investing in keeping and cultivating profitable current customers instead of constantly having to invest in gaining new ones.

relationship-based enterprise A firm that strives to facilitate long-term, win-win relationships between buyers and sellers.

relative market expansion The first phase in the maturity stage of the product life cycle in which product category sales continue to grow but at a rate significantly less than the growth stage.

reliability The percentage of time a product works without failure or stoppage.

repairability The ease of fixing a problem with a product.

repeat purchase A function of total demand that considers the number of products purchased by the same customer.

replacement purchase A function of total demand that considers the number of products purchased to replace existing products that have either become obsolete or malfunctioned.

reposition existing products A "new" product approach that targets new markets with existing products.

repositioning Using the marketing mix approach to change present consumer perceptions of a firm's product or service.

request for proposal (RFP) The document distributed to potential vendors that outlines an organization's product or service needs. It serves as a starting point from which vendors put together their product solution.

research design A framework for a study that directs the identification of a problem and collection and analysis of data.

research problem The definition of what information is needed to help management in a particular situation.

resellers Companies that buy products and then resell them to other businesses or consumers for a profit.

retail positioning The retailer's brand image in the consumer's mind.

retail target market The group of consumers targeted by a retailer.

retailer cooperative (co-op) The binding of retailers across a variety of product categories to gain cost and operating economies of scale in the channel.

retailer experience The overall experience a consumer has shopping at a retail location or online.

retailing Any business activity that creates value in the delivery of goods and services to consumers for their personal, nonbusiness consumption and is an essential component of the supply chain.

return on customer investment (ROCI) A calculation that estimates the projected financial returns from a customer. It is a useful strategic tool for deciding which customers deserve what levels of investment of various resources.

return on marketing investment (ROMI) What impact an investment in marketing has on a firm's success, especially financially.

reverse auctions When sellers bid prices to buyers and the purchase typically goes to the lowest bidder.

reverse logistics The process of moving goods back to the manufacturer or intermediary after purchase.

reward power A channel member's ability to coerce vendors by offering them incentives.

S

salary A fixed sum of money paid at regular intervals.

sales contests Short-term incentive programs designed to motivate salespeople to accomplish specific sales objectives.

sales experience The level of ease a consumer experiences in purchasing and returning merchandise at a retailer.

sales force composite Subjective method of forecasting that relies on the opinion of each member of the field sales staff.

sales orientation The increase of sales and consequently production capacity utilization by having salespeople "push" product into the hands of customers.

sales presentation The delivery of information relevant to meet the customer's needs.

sales promotion An inducement for an end-user consumer to buy a product or for a salesperson or someone else in the channel to sell it.

sales skill levels The individual's learned proficiency at performing necessary sales tasks.

sample A subgroup of the population selected for participation in research.

SBU-level strategic plan Planning that occurs within each of the firm's strategic business units (SBUs) designed to meet individual performance requirements and contribute satisfactorily to the overall corporate plan.

search ads Paid advertisements featured in Internet search engine results based on analysis of keywords entered in the search field.

search attributes Aspects of an offering that are physically observable before consumption.

seasonal discounts Discounts that reward the purchaser for shifting part of the inventory storage function away from the manufacturer.

SEC 10-K report A document filed with the Securities and Exchange Commission (SEC) that reports detailed information about a firm's operations and strategies.

secondary data Data collected for some other purpose than the problem currently being considered.

secondary group A reference group with which an individual has limited contact.

secondary target markets Market segments that have reasonable potential but for one reason or another are not best suited for development immediately.

selective awareness A psychological tool an individual uses to help focus on what is relevant and eliminate what is not relevant.

selective distortion The process in which an individual can misunderstand information or make it fit existing beliefs.

selective distribution A distribution strategy in which goods are distributed only to a limited number of intermediaries.

selective perception Different meanings assigned to the same message by different receivers that are based on an array of individual differences.

selective retention The process of placing in one's memory only those stimuli that support existing beliefs and attitudes about a product or brand.

sender The source of the message in communication.

service A product that represents a bundle of benefits that can satisfy customer wants and needs without having physical form.

service blueprints Complete pictorial designs and flow charts of all of a service's activities from the first customer contact to the actual delivery of the service.

service economy An economy that is predominantly comprised of service-related jobs.

service encounter The time period during which a customer interacts in any way with a service provider.

service failure When a service fails to meet the quality level promised by the provider.

service quality The formalization of the measurement of customer expectations of a service compared to perceptions of actual service performance.

service recovery The restoring of service quality to a level at or above the customer's expectations following a service failure.

service sector The portion of an economy that is comprised of service-related jobs.

service-profit chain The formalization of linkages between employee and customer aspects of service delivery.

SERVQUAL A measurement instrument designed to reflect the five dimensions of service quality.

shopping experience The consumer's holistic experience while looking for and evaluating products during the purchase decision process.

shopping goods Products that require consumers to do research and compare across product dimensions like color, size, features, and price.

short-term memory The information an individual recalls at the present time. Sometimes referred to as working memory.

showrooming Consumers going into a store and taking advantage of a product demonstration and the expertise of the salesperson and then buying the product from an online retailer at a lower price.

situation analysis An analysis of the macro- and micro-level environment within which a firm's marketing plan is being developed.

SKU (stock-keeping unit) Unique identification numbers used in tracking products through a distribution system, inventory management, and pricing.

slotting allowance (shelf fee) Extra incentives paid to wholesalers or retailers by the manufacturer for placing a particular product into inventory.

social class A ranking of individuals into harmonized groups based on demographic characteristics such as age, education, income, and occupation.

societal marketing The concept that, at the broadest level, members of society at large can be viewed as a stakeholder for marketing.

sorting The process of classifying products for sale through different channels.

specialty goods Unique products in which consumers' purchase decision is based on a defining characteristic.

specific warranty Explicit product performance promises related to components of the product.

sponsorships Spaces sold on high-traffic websites that enable companies to subsidize some section of the web page on the site.

stability pricing A pricing strategy in which a firm attempts to find a neutral set point for price that is neither low enough to raise the ire of competition nor high enough to put the value proposition at risk with customers.

stand-alone brands Brands created to be separate from a company brand that can insulate the company if there is a problem with the brand.

stock-out When an item is not in stock.

stop-to-market mistake When a product that is a good idea is prematurely eliminated during the screening process and ultimately never introduced to the market.

store brands Brands created by retailers for sale only in their store locations.

straight rebuy A buying decision that requires little evaluation because the products are purchased on a consistent, regular basis.

strategic alliances A market entry strategy designed to spread the risk of foreign investment among its partners. Examples of strategic alliances would be international joint ventures or direct foreign investment.

strategic marketing The long-term, firm-level commitment to investing in marketing—supported at the highest organization level—for the purpose of enhancing organizational performance.

strategic type Firms of a particular strategic type have a common strategic orientation and a similar combination of structure, culture, and processes consistent with that strategy. Four strategic types are prospectors, analyzers, defenders, and reactors—depending on a firm's approach to the competitive marketplace.

strategic vision Often included within a firm's mission statement, it is a discussion of what the company would like to become in the future.

strategy A comprehensive plan stating how the organization will achieve its mission and objectives.

style The look and feel of a product.

subculture A group within a culture that shares similar cultural artifacts created by differences in ethnicity, religion, race, or geography.

subjective forecasting methods Forecasting methods that do not rely primarily on sophisticated quantitative (empirical) analytical approaches.

subjective measures Personal evaluations by someone connected to the salesperson's sales process.

supplier choice Selecting between multiple suppliers offering similar product configurations by examining their qualifications.

supply chain A complex logistics network characterized by high levels of coordination and integration among its members.

supply chain management The process of managing the aspects of the supply chain.

survey A quantitative research method that employs structured questionnaires given to a sample group of individuals representing the population of interest and intended to solicit specific responses to explicit questions.

sustainability The practicing of business that meets humanity's needs without harming future generations.

sustainable competitive advantage The resulting advantage a firm has when it invests in distinctive competencies.

SWOT analysis A convenient framework used to summarize key findings from a firm's situational analysis into a matrix of strengths, weaknesses, opportunities, and threats.

symbolic performance The image-building aspects of the product in terms of how it makes the consumer feel after purchase.

T

tactical marketing Marketing activities that take place at the functional or operational level of a firm.

tangibility The physical aspects of a product.

target marketing Evaluating market segments and making a decision about which among them shows the most promise for development.

target return on investment (ROI) A pricing strategy in which a bottom-line profit is established first and then pricing is set to achieve that target.

target return pricing A pricing decision made by considering fixed and variable costs and then demand forecasting to determine the price per unit.

technical selling Selling that requires a salesperson to have technical understanding of the product or service.

television home shopping A form of non-store retailing that involves showcasing products on a television network that can be ordered by the consumer.

tertiary target markets Market segments that may develop emerging attractiveness for investment in the future but that do not appear attractive at present.

time-series analysis Objective method of forecasting that relies on the analysis of historical data to develop a prediction for the future.

total demand The cumulative demand for a product over a given time period.

trade discounts An incentive to a channel member for performing some function in the channel that benefits the seller.

trade servicer Resellers such as retailers or distributors with whom the sales force does business.

trade show An industry- or company-sponsored event in which booths are set up for the dissemination of information about offerings to members of a channel.

traditional society A society dependent on agriculture as the primary driver of the economy; these economies lack the capabilities to industrialize and have high rates of illiteracy, which hinders advances in technology.

transaction cost analysis (TCA) A tool that measures cost of using different types of selling agents.

transfer pricing The cost companies charge internally to move products between subsidiaries or divisions.

transportation and storage Commonly provided intermediary functions for producers that do not perform these functions themselves.

tying contract A formal requirement by the seller of an intermediary to purchase a supplementary product to qualify to purchase the primary product the intermediary wishes to buy.

U

undifferentiated target marketing (mass market) The broadest approach to target marketing that involves offering a product or service that can be perceived as valuable to a very generalized group of consumers.

uniform delivered pricing When the same delivery fee is charged to customers regardless of geographic location within a set area.

unsought goods Products that consumers do not seek out and often would rather not purchase at all.

user Actual customers of a product or service who have a great deal of input at various stages of the buying decision process but are typically not decision makers.

user expectations Subjective method of forecasting that relies on answers from customers regarding their expected consumption or purchase of a product.

utility The want-satisfying power of a good or service. There are four types of utility: form utility, time utility, place utility, and ownership utility.

V

VALS™ (Values and Lifestyles) A psychographic instrument developed by Strategic Business Insights that divides U.S. adults into groups based on their primary motivation and resources.

value A ratio of the bundle of benefits a customer receives from an offering compared to the costs incurred by the customer in acquiring that bundle of benefits.

value chain The synthesis of activities within a firm involved in designing, producing, marketing, delivering, and supporting its products or services.

value co-creation The combining of capabilities among members of a value network to create value.

value network An overarching system of formal and informal relationships within which the firm participates to procure, transform, and enhance, and ultimately supply its offerings in final form within a market space.

value pricing A pricing strategy in which a firm attempts to take into account the role of price as it reflects the bundle of benefits sought by the customer.

value proposition The whole bundle of benefits a company promises to deliver to the customer, not just the benefits of the product itself.

value-creating activities Activities within a firm's value chain that act to increase the value of its products and services for its customers. These can take the form of either primary activities or support activities.

variability The characteristic of a service in which its service quality can only be as good as that of its provider.

variable pricing A pricing tactic in which customers are allowed or encouraged to haggle about prices.

variety The number of different product categories offered by a retailer.

vending machine retailing The selling of merchandise or services that are stored in a machine then dispensed to the consumer when the payment has been made.

vendor reliability A vendor's ability to meet contractual obligations including delivery time and service schedules.

vertical marketing system (VMS) Vertically aligned networks behaving and performing as a unified system.

viral marketing Entertaining and informative messaging created by a firm intended to be passed among individuals and delivered through online and other media channels.

W

wholesaler cooperative When retailers contract for varying degrees of exclusive dealings with a particular wholesaler.

workload method A method for determining the correct size of a company's sales force based on the premise that all salespeople should undertake an equal amount of work.

Z

zero-based budgeting An investment approach in that marketing goals and objectives are set for the upcoming year and then budget dollars are secured to support the achievement of those goals and objectives.

zone pricing When shippers set up geographic pricing zones based on the distance from the shipping location.

PHOTO CREDITS

CHAPTER 1

Page 7: Courtesy Waste Management, Inc.
Page 11: Image courtesy of The Advertising Archives.
Page 15: Image courtesy of The Advertising Archives.
Page 16: UNICEF Sweden. Agency: Forsman & Bodenfors. Photo: UNICEF/Asad Zaidi.
Page 20: © Imeh Akpanudosen/ Getty Images.

CHAPTER 2

Page 27: Image courtesy of The Advertising Archives.
Page 30: Courtesy U. S. Army.
Page 34: FRESH STEP ® is a registered trademark of The Clorox Pet Products Company. Used with permission. FRESH STEP ® advertisement. © 2013 The Pet Products Clorox Company. Reprinted with permission. Photographer: Jill Greenberg.
Page 37: Courtesy JetBlue.
Page 40: Photo Courtesy of Southwest Airlines..
Page 46: © Jason Knott/Alamy.

CHAPTER 3

Page 63: Apple, Inc.
Page 67: Courtesy Salesforce.com.
Page 70: Image courtesy of The Advertising Archives.
Page 78: © BlueMoon Stock/Punch-Stock RF.
Page 81: Courtesy Photodex Corporation.
Page 83: Copyright © 2013. SAS Institute Inc. All rights reserved. Reproduced with permission of SAS Institute Inc., Cary, NC, USA.

CHAPTER 4

Page 95: © Image Source, all rights reserved. RF.
Page 98: Image courtesy of The Advertising Archives.
Page 102: Image courtesy of The Advertising Archives.
Page 105: © Purestock/SuperStock RF.
Page 118: © McGraw-Hill Education/ Mark Dierker, photographer.
Page 120: Courtesy Nolet Spirits, USA.
Page 122: © McGraw-Hill Educaton/Jill Braaten, photographer.

CHAPTER 5

Page 131: Image courtesy of The Advertising Archives.
Page 135: Courtesy powwownow. co.uk.
Page 139: Image courtesy of The Advertising Archives.
Page 142: Courtesy Airbus.
Page 147: © Stockbyte/Getty Images RF.
Page 149: Courtesy Deere & Company.

CHAPTER 6

Page 160: Image courtesy of The Advertising Archives.
Page 165: Image courtesy of The Advertising Archives.
Page 172: Courtesy Dallas Farmers Market and Firehouse Ad Agency. Ryan Smith, art director; Greg Hunter, writer/ creative director; Tripp Westbrook, executive creative director; Richard Thompson, illustrator.
Page 179: Courtesy Breitling SA.
Page 183: Image courtesy of The Advertising Archives.
Page 185: Courtesy Hilton Hotels.

CHAPTER 7

Page 199: © Image Club RF.
Page 201(top left): © McGraw-Hill Education RF.
Page 201(top right): © AP Photo/BMW.
Page 201(center left): © McGraw-Hill Education/ Mark Dierker, photographer.
Page 201(center right): © McGraw-Hill Education/Jill Braaten, photographer.
Page 205: © Detail Nottingham/Alamy.
Page 206 (shower): © Nalinratana Phiyanalinmat/Alamy.
Page 206 (taxi): © Lou-Foto/Alamy.
Page 206 (gas pumps): © David Muscroft/Super-Stock/Alamy RF.
Page 206 (Crest): © McGraw-Hill Education/Jill Braaten, photographer.
Page 206 (boots): © PhotoSpin/Alamy RF.
Page 206 (a/c): © McGraw-Hill Education/Jill Braaten, photographer.
Page 207 (bicycle): © Dann Tardif/LWA/Corbis.
Page 208: © Eric Carr/Alamy.
Page 214: © HDIP, Inc.
Page 220: © McGraw-Hill Education/Jill Braaten, photographer.
Page 222: © McGraw-Hill Education/ Mark Dierker, photographer.
Page 223: Image courtesy of The Advertising Archives.
Page 226: © McGraw-Hill Education/Jill Braaten, photographer.

CHAPTER 8

Page 241 (top): © Antony Nettle/Alamy.
Page 241(center): © McGraw-Hill Education/ John Flournoy, photographer.
Page 241(bottom): © McGraw-Hill Education/Jill Braaten, photographer.
Page 244: © Erica Simone Leeds RF.
Page 248(top): © McGraw-Hill Education/ Mark Dierker, photographer.
Page 248(bottom): Image courtesy of The Advertising Archives.
Page 249(all): © McGraw-Hill Education/ Suzie Ross, photographer.
Page 252: © McGraw-Hill Education/ Mark Dierker, photographer.
Page 253(all): © McGraw-Hill Education/Jill Braaten, photographer.
Page 254(all): © McGraw-Hill Education/Jill Braaten, photographer.
Page 257: © McGraw-Hill Education/Jill Braaten, photographer.

CHAPTER 9

Page 266: Image courtesy of The Advertising Archives.
Page 271: Image courtesy of The Advertising Archives.

Page 276: Image courtesy of The Advertising Archives.

Page 278: American Academy of Dermatology. Photography: Gregory Heisler. Ad Agency: Houlihan Madison Most.

CHAPTER 10

Page 301: Image courtesy of The Advertising Archives.

Page 303: Courtesy The ParkingSpot.com.

Page 305: Image courtesy of The Advertising Archives.

Page 312: Image courtesy of The Advertising Archives.

CHAPTER 11

Page 323: Image courtesy of The Advertising Archives.

Page 327: © Andre Jenny/Alamy.

Page 335: Image courtesy of The Advertising Archives.

Page 338: © Cultura Limited/SuperStock RF.

Page 340: © Kevin Foy/Alamy.

Page 343: Courtesy Ferguson Enterprises.

Page 347: Image courtesy of The Advertising Archives.

Page 350: Image courtesy of The Advertising Archives.

CHAPTER 12

Page 362: Apple, Inc.

Page 364: © McGraw-Hill Education/Mark Dierker, photographer.

Page 369: Image courtesy of The Advertising Archives.

Page 371: Courtesy Voss USA, Inc.

Page 375: Image courtesy of The Advertising Archives.

Page 377: Image courtesy of The Advertising Archives.

Page 378: Courtesy of The Salvation Army USA.

Page 381 : Courtesy WWF.

Page 387(top): © McGraw-Hill Education/Mark Dierker, photographer.

Page 387(bottom): Image courtesy of The Advertising Archives.

CHAPTER 13

Page 399: Courtesy Taco Bell.

Page 401: Courtesy ConAgra Foods.

Page 402: Courtesy Geico.

Page 405: Courtesy Michelin North America.

Page 408: Image courtesy of The Advertising Archives.

CHAPTER 14

Page 415: Image courtesy of The Advertising Archives.

Page 418: © Digital Vision/Punchstock RF.

Page 419: © Fred de Novelle/Photononstop/Getty Images.

Page 421: © Image Source/Getty Images RF.

Page 433: Image courtesy of The Advertising Archives.

CHAPTER 15

Page 444: Image courtesy of The Advertising Archives.

Page 453: Courtesy of School of Thought, Inc..

Page 461: Image courtesy of The Advertising Archives.

CHAPTER 16

Page 480: Image courtesy of The Advertising Archives.

Page 489: Courtesy Delta Airlines.

Page 494: © Blend Images/Ariel Skelley/Vetta/Getty Images RF.

Page 496: © HDIP, Inc.

COMPANY INDEX

A

A.C. Nielsen; *see* Nielsen Co.
Ace Hardware, 332
Acer, 304
Acura, 250
Adobe, 84, 478
Advanced Micro Devices (AMD), 149, 296
Adventist Health System, 143
Aeroflot, 458
AeroMexico, 457, 458
Aerospace Corp., 142
Air Canada, 458
Air China, 458
Air France, 222, 457, 458
Air New Zealand, 458
Airbus, 138, 142, 207, 223, 455
AirTran Airways, 39, 40
Alitalia, 458
Allegiant, 42
Allstate Insurance, 103
Amana, 167
Amazon.com, 6, 71, 99, 183, 260, 329, 340, 349, 383, 386, 428, 443, 455
AMD; *see* Advanced Micro Devices
American Academy of Dermatology, 278
American Airlines, 200, 457, 458
American Express, 165, 250, 251, 348, 386, 398, 455
Amway, 347
ANA, 458
Anheuser-Busch, 30–31, 418, 419, 462
Aon Hewitt, 270
Apple Computer, 18, 49, 63, 119, 125, 136, 161, 183, 184, 186, 199, 201, 202, 204, 210, 221, 222, 242, 245, 325, 349, 362, 366, 367, 371, 372, 374, 387, 389, 401, 456, 462
AppliedMicro, 149
Asiana Airlines, 458
Atmospheric and Space Technology Research Associates, 142
AT&T, 103, 221, 245, 398
Audi, 104, 183, 257, 383
Austrian Airlines, 458
Autodesk, 218
Avery Paper, 253
Avis, 269, 401
Avon, 168, 327, 347

B

Badgeville, Inc., 145
Bain & Company, 79
Bang and Olufsen, 204
Bank of America, 79, 246, 398, 476
Barnes & Noble, 100, 251, 346, 349
Bay Bread, LLC, 225
Bazooka, 17
BCG; *see* Boston Consulting Group
Bed Bath & Beyond, 309
Bell Labs, 221
Benihana, 268
Bennetton, 444
Berkshire Hathaway, 398
Best Buy, 208, 212, 329, 349, 383
Biogen Idec Inc., 298
Birchbox, 114
Blackberry, 219
Blockbuster, 290
Bloomin' Brands, Inc., 278
Bloomingdale's, 240
bmi, 458
BMW, 69, 112, 151, 174, 183, 201, 221, 247, 257, 375, 378, 462
Boeing, 142, 148, 207, 223, 295, 367, 418, 455
Bombardier, 160, 205, 207
Bose, 174
Boston Consulting Group (BCG), 33–34
Boston Market, 268
BP, 243
Brand Z, 245
Braum's Ice Cream and Dairy Store, 332
Braun, 70
Breitling, 179
Bright House Networks, 305
British Airways, 222, 457, 458
British Telecom (BT), 423
BT; *see* British Telecom
Burberry, 14, 15
Burger King, 181, 401, 457
Butlins Hotel, 301

C

Caesars Entertainment, 19–20, 271, 272–274
California Milk Advisory Board, 399
California Milk Processor Board, 116
Calxeda, 149
Campbell's Soup Co., 122, 211
Canadian Tire Corp., 270
Canon, 255, 374
Capital One, 422
Carnival Cruise Line, 244
Carrefour, 345
Carrier, 206
Caterpillar, 284, 366, 374, 444, 446, 462
Cathay Pacific, 457, 458
Chanel, 335
Chaparral, 242
Chevron, 72, 446
Chicken of the Sea, 387
Chik-fil-A, 183
China Aviation Supplies Holding Co., 138
China Mobile, 245
China Southern Airline, 458
Chrysler, 257, 373, 390, 398, 462
CI Travel, 331
Cirque du Soleil, 364
Cisco Systems, 150, 246, 419, 422
CitizenNet, 493
Clinique, 334
Clorox Pet Products Company, 34
CNet.com, 349, 383, 388–389
Coach, 445
Coca-Cola, 8–9, 102, 123, 164, 208, 218, 244, 245, 251–252, 254, 374–375, 390, 401, 446, 461, 462, 465, 481
Comcast, 305, 398
Condé Nast, 389
Constellation Brands, 256
Continental Airlines, 457, 458
Continuum, 252
Costco, 121, 251, 343, 344, 383
Cox Communications, 305
Cube, 218
CUTCO, 376
Czech Airlines, 458

D

Dallas Farmers Market, 172
Danskin, 333
Dasani, 215
Dean Foods, 209
Dell, 119, 123, 184, 211–212, 242, 244, 249, 327, 347, 387
Deloitte, 145, 409
Delta Air Lines, 200, 457, 458, 489
DeSantis Breindel, 271
DHL, 347, 455
DHL Supply Chain, 339
Diageo, 242
Dillard's, 335
DIRECTV, 401
Discover, 422
Disney; *see* Walt Disney Company
Dixons Retail Plc, 295–296
Domino, 254
Domino's Pizza, 443
Dos Equis, 362
Doubletree Hotels, 278
Dow Chemical, 446
Dreamworks, 6
Dun & Bradstreet, 433
Dunkin' Donuts, 45, 219, 297
Duracell, 103

E

Earth Mama Angel Baby, 482
EasyJet, 180
eBay, 49, 145, 296, 309, 349, 444, 454
Edmunds.com, 383, 384, 388
Efficient Frontier, 84
Egan Construction, 304
Egyptair, 458
EHarmony, 179
Electronic Arts, 228
Embassy Suites, 185
EMC Corp., 145
Emirates Air, 266
Enron, 4
Epic Healthcare, 420
ESPN, 388
Estee Lauder, 216, 449
E-Trade, 349
Eveready, 103
Evian, 201, 215
Expedia, 428
ExxonMobil, 243

F

Facebook, 8, 16, 28, 164, 165, 221, 232, 242, 247, 249, 267, 363, 372, 386, 387, 400, 416, 493
Fairmont Kea Lani, 304
FedEx, 180, 184, 239, 241, 258, 331, 347, 444, 455
Ferguson, 343
Ferrari, 259
Fiat, 398
Fidelitone, 337
Finnair, 458
Folger's, 390
Ford Motor Company, 10, 132, 133, 135, 221, 246, 257, 398, 462
Forever 21, 104
Fossil, 465
Fox, 165
Foxconn, 325
Frito-Lay, 105, 169, 251, 334
Frontier Airlines, 42

G

Gap, 13, 415, 444
Gartner, Inc., 495
GE; *see* General Electric
GEICO, 16, 181
GENCO, 331
General Dynamics, 240
General Electric (GE), 9, 11–12, 32–33, 34, 35, 131, 211, 418, 443
General Mills, 209
General Motors (GM), 103, 108, 131, 132, 199, 257, 381, 398, 444
Gerber Life Insurance, 185
GfK SE, 74
Giant Bicycles, 213
Gillette, 167, 250, 305
Girl Scouts of the USA, 16
Givenchy, 169
GM; *see* General Motors
Goodyear, 133, 135, 444
Google, 49, 72, 202, 221, 244, 245, 296, 304, 384, 388, 485
GoPro, 105, 106

H

H&M, 104
H&R Block, 171
Häagen-Dazs, 212–213, 214, 496
Halliburton, 460
Harley-Davidson Motorcycles, 73, 74–75, 76, 77, 78, 113, 114, 183, 247, 259–260
Hasbro, 250
HBO, 305
H-E-B grocery stores, 330, 341
Heineken, 254
Heinz, 248, 254
Helsinn Healthcare SA, 457
Hermes, 169
Hertz Rental Car, 269, 401
Hewlett-Packard (HP), 36, 49, 71, 119, 131, 149, 210, 211–212, 222, 242, 244, 305, 388, 444, 446
Highlights for Children, 475
Hilton, 374
Hilton Grand Vacation Club, 267
Hollister, 199
Home Depot, 142, 444, 493
Hon Hai Precision Industry, 325
Honda Motor Co., 103, 246, 247, 301–302, 374, 387
HP; *see* Hewlett-Packard
HSN, 348, 385
HTC, 14
Hubspot, 420
Hulu, 6
Hyundai, 123, 258, 466

I

Iberia, 458
IBISWorld, 83
IBM, 49, 241, 245, 347, 417, 419, 424, 426
I:CO, 104
IDEO, 252
IMS Health Inc., 74
InBev, 462
Information Resources, 80
InfoScan, 80
InfoUSA, 433
Intel, 136, 141, 149, 247, 296, 399
Inter IKEA, 251
Interbrand, 260
Interbrand, U.K., 452
Intuit, 267
Ipsos, 74

J

J. D. Power and Associates, 80, 81, 103
Jackson Hewitt, 375
Japan Airlines, 458
JCPenney, 5
J.Crew, 210
Jeffrey's, 335
JetBlue Airways, 34–36, 37, 38–39, 41–42, 43, 45–46, 280–281, 295, 399
Jimmy Dean, 27
John Deere, 149, 349
Johnson & Johnson, 109, 118, 178, 203, 330, 350, 377, 398, 429
Johnson Products, 168
Jollibee, 454
Jordache, 183
JP Morgan Chase, 398, 405

K

Kalbe Farma Tbk, 457
Kamatsu, 374
Kantar Group, 74
Kashi, 253
Kellogg, 209, 408, 462
Kelly Blue Book, 383
Kenco, 452
Kenneth Cole, 335
Kentucky Fried Chicken (KFC), 457
Ketel One, 120
KFC; *see* Kentucky Fried Chicken
Kia Motors, 308
KidCare TV, 222
Kiehl's, 307
Kimberly-Clark, 220, 253
Kitchen Aid, 208
KLM Royal Dutch Airlines, 457, 458
Klout, 386
Kmart, 40, 335
Kohl's Department Stores, 120
Korean Air, 457, 458
Kraft Foods, 209, 253
Krispy Kreme, 45
Kroger Co., 334, 341, 345

L

Lacoste, 239
LAN, 458
Lands' End, 382, 434, 456
L'eggs, 252
Lego Group, 46, 167
Lendingtree.com, 351
Lenovo, 131, 141
Lever Brothers, 242, 248
Levi Strauss, 219
Lexis/Nexis, 83
Lexus, 112, 257
LG Electronics, 202
LinkedIn, 387

L.L. Bean, 327, 382, 434, 456
L'Oréal, 108, 160, 168, 307, 398
LOT Polish Airlines, 458
Lowe's, 241, 493
Loyaltyworks, 428
Lucky Brand, 382
Lufthansa, 457, 458

M

Macy's, 335, 374, 398
MakerBot Industries, 218
Mall of America, 44
Marketing Science Institute (MSI), 19, 20
Marlboro, 245
Marriott, 192, 251, 304–305, 367, 368
Marriott Vacation Club, 267
Mars Candy, 403
Martha Jefferson Hospital, 75
Mary Kay, 347, 418
MasterCard, 449, 455
Match.com, 179
Mattel, 232
Maxim, 362
Maytag, 377
Mazola, 254
McAfee, 384
McDonald's, 73, 74, 101, 164, 181, 182, 184, 245, 297, 334, 367, 374, 401, 408, 446, 451, 452, 454, 457
McKesson, 328
MediaMark Research, Inc. (MRI), 173
Medio Systems, 100
Men's Wearhouse, 416
Mentos, 390
Mercedes-Benz, 68, 69, 112, 221, 243, 257–258, 383
Merrill Lynch, 348, 349
MetLife, 106
Metro AG, 345
Michael Kors, 445
Michelin, 115, 405
Microsoft, 18, 49, 66, 72–73, 84, 221, 228, 242, 245, 296, 299, 430
Millward Brown, 84
Mindshare, 415
MMGY Global, 80
Motorola, 27, 119, 202, 446
Mr. Coffee, 70, 219, 461
MRI; *see* MediaMark Research, Inc.
MSI; *see* Marketing Science Institute

N

NASCAR, 408
Navteq, 151
NBC Universal, 165, 369–370
Neiman Marcus, 335
Nemours Children's Hospital, 109
Nepal Airlines Corp., 138
Nestlé, 334, 443, 462
Netflix, 6, 71, 290–291
Nielsen Co., 68, 74, 80, 86, 171, 228, 247, 490, 493
Nike, 4, 9, 325, 362, 446
Nintendo, 299
Nissan, 98, 246, 308
Nokia, 119, 151, 207
Nordstrom, 81, 268, 334
Nortel Networks, 351
Northrup Grumman, 153–154
Norton, 384
Novartis AG, 298

O

Odyssey Software, 221
OfficeMax, 135
OKCupid, 179
Oklahoma City Thunder, 274
Old Spice, 390
Olive Garden, 99
One Laptop Per Child (OLPC), 296
OneWorld Alliance, 457, 458
Openfield, 339
Oracle Corp., 131, 139, 145, 147
Orangina, 369
Orlando Utility Commission, 409
Outback Steakhouse, 278–280, 282, 284, 288

P

P&G; *see* Procter & Gamble
Palm, 199
Panasonic, 342
Panera Bread Co., 8, 241, 297
Paramount, 95
ParkingSpot, 303
PayPerPost, 388
PepsiCo, 249, 251, 254, 401, 444, 465
Pfizer, 256, 398, 418
Philips Electronics NV, 331, 461
Photodex, 81
Pinterest, 247, 416
Pizza Hut, 15
Porsche, 204, 259
Post Cereal, 63
Powwownow, 135
PPR, 172
Priceline.com, 309
PricewaterhouseCoopers, 117
Procter & Gamble (P&G), 108, 133, 168, 178, 228, 242, 246, 250, 251, 253, 257, 312, 330, 332–333, 341, 381, 387, 390, 398, 399, 418, 443
Professional Research Consultants, 75
Progressive Insurance, 181
Proteus Digital Health, 131
Pulte Homes, 63, 276

Q

Qualcomm, 325
Quantas, 457, 458
QuestionPro, 84
QVC, 329, 348

R

Ralcorp, 63
Ralph Lauren, 239
Ray-Ban, 246
Raytheon Aircraft, 78
Reckitt Benckiser, 178
Red Cross, 143
Reddit.com, 389
Regal, 242
Research in Motion, 219
Rinker, 242
Rite-Aid, 31
Ritz-Carlton, 174, 183, 192, 199, 268, 269, 288, 305, 367, 368
Robert Mondavi, 97
Robitussin, 257
Rolex, 208
Royal Bank of Scotland, 271
Royal Dutch Shell, 243
Royal Jordanian Airlines, 458
Ryanair, 445

S

Saks Fifth Avenue, 335
Salesforce.com, 67, 187
Sam's Club, 121, 344
Samsung Group, 28, 69, 102, 119, 145, 184, 202, 207, 210, 242, 304, 325, 375, 401, 449
SanDisk, 253, 325
SAS, 83, 84, 493
Satmetrix, 79
SBI; *see* Strategic Business Insights
Scandinavian Airlines, 458
Scent-Air Technology, 239–240
Schwarz Unternehmens, 345
Scotts Miracle-Gro Company, 324
Sea Ray, 242
Sea World, 109
Sears, 300–301
Sharp Electronics Corp., 131, 202, 342
Shell; *see* Royal Dutch Shell
Siemens, 460
Singapore Airlines, 458
Sky Team, 457, 458
SmartDesign, 252
Sonic, 385
Sony, 95, 119, 208, 299, 325, 383
South African Airways, 458
Southwest Airlines, 38, 39, 40, 42, 148, 169, 179, 183, 200, 201, 202, 268, 272, 283, 288, 295, 296, 301, 366
Spanair, 458
Spark Networks, 179
Spirit Airlines, 42
Sprint Nextel, 100
SPSS, 84, 493

SRI International, 142
Star Alliance, 457, 458
Starbucks, 9, 100, 119, 199, 225, 247, 251, 297, 385, 452
State Farm Insurance, 16, 181, 266–267
Stella and Dot, 363
Strategic Business Insights (SBI), 172–173
Subway, 332
Survey Monkey, 78
Swipely, 481
Swiss International Air Lines, 458
Symantec, 221

T

Taco Bell, 169, 399
TAP Portugal, 458
Target Corp., 63, 89–90, 99, 112, 162, 166, 170, 250, 308, 309, 315, 330, 341, 344, 349, 398
TechniPak, 337
Tesco, 345
Tesla, 220
Texas Instruments Inc., 149
Thai Airways International, 458
Thomas Global Register, 146
3M, 210, 211, 212, 221, 446
Tiffany & Company, 335, 445
Timberland, 122, 206, 480
Time Warner, 95, 305, 398
Timex, 208
T-Mobile, 100
Tommy Hilfiger, 239
Toshiba, 323
Toyota Motor, 103, 148, 199, 246, 301–302, 308, 370, 374, 398
Trader Joe's, 226
Travelocity, 428
Treuhand KG, 345
Tupperware, 347, 363, 418
Turkish Airlines, 458
Twitter, 8, 28, 165, 267, 386, 387, 388, 416
TylrNMoblie, 423–424
Tyson Foods, 444

U

United Airlines, 200, 457, 458
Universal Orlando Resort, 95
UPS, 180, 329, 331, 347, 455
Urban Outfitters, Inc., 174, 493
USAA Insurance, 204

V

Verizon Wireless, 100, 103, 125, 305, 398
Victorinox, 257
VIPDeals, 388
Visa, 245, 449, 455
Volcom, 172
Volkswagen, 183, 383
Voss Water, 306–307, 335, 371

W

Walgreens, 174, 306, 328
Wallhogs.com, 388
Walmart, 16, 29–30, 63, 99, 131, 133, 174, 179, 183, 208, 209, 211, 247, 300–301, 308, 333, 334, 338, 340, 341, 344, 345, 348, 351, 398, 444, 454
Walt Disney Company, 6, 18, 49, 95, 232, 247, 250, 268, 350–351, 398
Waste Management, Inc., 8
Wayfair, 309
WeChat, 461
Wegmans, 341
Weight Watchers, 378
Wella Corporation, 168
Wendy's, 181, 397
Whirlpool, 70, 204
White Wave Foods, 248–249
Whole Foods Markets, 28
Williams-Sonoma, 348
Wilson's Leather Stores, 343
Wohler Associates, 218
WorldCom, 4
Wyndham Hotels, 250

Y

Yahoo, 72, 112, 383, 384, 433
YO! Sushi, 312
Yum Brands, 101

Z

Zappos, 337
Zara, 342
Zephyrhills Water, 215
Zillow, 383
Zoomerang, 78
Zumba, 113

NAME INDEX

A

Aaker, David, 243, 261
Aaker, Jennifer L., 127
Abela, Andrew V., 503
Abrahams, Marc, 234
Achrol, Ravi S., 355, 356
Adidam, P. T., 439
Agarwal, Ritu, 320
Ahamad, Maizah Hura, 503
Ahmed, Sadrudin A., 471
Ahmed, Zafar U., 128
Ahn, Jae Hyeon, 358
Ailawadi, Kusum L., 51, 319, 320, 502
Aitken, Robert, 261
Ajzen, I., 126
Akerson, Dan, 199
Albaum, Gerald, 91
Alcaniz, Enrique Bigne, 357
Aldas-Maznazo, Joaquin, 128
Algesheimer, Rene, 358
Allenby, Greg M., 195
Almquist, Eric, 195
Alspach, K., 438
Amato, Christie H., 126
Ambler, Tim, 503
Amir, On, 128
Amrouche, N., 262
Anderholm, Fred, III, 503
Anderson, Erin, 355, 438
Anderson, Eugene W., 196
Anderson, Hilding, 92
Anderson, Natanya, 28
Angulo, Natalia, 24
Ansari, Asim, 357, 439
Ansoff, H. Igor, 44
Antonio, Harry, 499
Ariely, Dan, 319
Armancioglu, Nukhel, 235
Armstrong, Barbara, 91
Armstrong, Katrina, 126
Arnold, Eric J., 51
Arnold, G., 292
Artis, L., 356
Auh, Seigyoung, 24
Aurand, Timothy W., 196
Avci, Turgay, 393
Avlonitis, George J., 319, 320

B

Babakus, Emim, 393
Bachman, Justin, 23
Bagozzi, Richard P., 194
Baker, Kenneth G., 91
Baker, L., 319
Bakker, A. B., 438
Balazs, Anne L., 194
Ball, Brad, 52
Ballantyne, David, 261
Banerjee, Saikat, 261, 471
Bang, Hae-Kyong, 394
Bansal, Harvir S., 291
Baracli, H., 155
Barboza, David, 355
Bardlow, Eric T., 195
Barksdale, Hiram C., Jr., 154, 437
Barone, Michael J., 23
Barr, A., 319
Barr, Terry Feldman, 292
Barry, James M., 155
Barry, Thomas E., 194
Bascoul, Ganael, 90
Bashkansky, E., 355
Baskin, Jonathan Salem, 413
Basligil, H., 155
Bateman, Connie R., 91
Baurer, Hans H., 128
Bawa, Kapil, 236
Baxter, Andrew, 356
Bayon, Tomas, 195
Bayus, Barry L., 194
Bea, F., 503
Bean, Shawn, 127
Bearden, William O., 502
Beasty, Colin, 92
Beattie, Anita Chang, 471
Beatty, Rich, 195
Becker, Christine, 128
Bell, Jim, 91
Bell, Simon J., 24
Bello, Daniel C., 355
Belonax, J. J., Jr., 438
Belschak, F. D., 438
Bendle, Neil T., 481, 502
Benioff, Marc, 187
Bennett, Peter D., 326
Bennett, Roger, 90
Berens, Guido, 503
Bergin, Richard, 91
Berkowitz, J., 413
Berman, Barry, 472
Berner, Robert, 356
Berry, Leonard L., 265, 279, 283, 291, 293
Bettencourt, Lance A., 234
Bettman, James R., 128
Bevil, DeWayne, 261
Bhagat, Parimal S., 126
Bharadwaj, Neeraj, 23
Bharadwaj, Sundar, 24, 355
Bhattacharya, C. B., 194, 394
Bink, Audrey J. M., 472
Binken, Jeroen L. G., 503
Birchall, Jonathan, 261
Bird, Monroe M., 154
Birk, Matthias M., 155
Bishop, Terrence R., 196
Bitner, Mary Jo, 24
Blair, B., 438
Blair, Edward, 91
Blair, Margaret Henderson, 413
Blattberg, Robert C., 502
Block, Melissa, 91
Blyth, Bill, 92
Boartwright, Peter, 356
Boddy, Clive, 91
Bohlmann, Jonathan D., 194
Bojovic, Van, 394
Boles, James S., 154, 437
Bolton, Lisa E., 126
Bolton, Ruth N., 155, 195, 292
Bond, Phillip, 355
Bonfrer, André, 413
Bonoma, Thomas V., 177, 438
Booms, Bernard H., 24
Boone, Louis E., 23
Borden, Mark, 128
Borden, Neil H., 23
Borle, Sharad, 356
Bourdeau, Brian L., 291
Bourette, S., 292
Boush, David M., 127
Bowers, M. R., 438
Boyd, Dermot, 329
Boyer, Kenneth K., 356
Brace, Ian, 127
Bradlow, Eric T., 394
Brady, Michael K., 291
Brands, Robert F., 235
Brannon, J. Isaac, 320
Brasel, S. Adam, 127
Braselton, J., 438
Braun, Curt C., 262
Bregier, Fabrice, 138
Brewster, Mike, 155
Bridges, Wesley, 356
Briesch, Richard, 502
Brodie, John, 261
Brodie, Roderick J., 193, 196
Brouthers, Lance Eliot, 471
Brown, Stanley A., 196
Brown, Stephen W., 156
Brown, Tom J., 262, 292

Broyles, Sheri J., 127
Bruell, Alexandra, 128
Buehrer, Richard E., 394
Burgess, Thomas F., 90, 196
Burkink, Tim, 356
Burnsed, Brian, 194
Burrows, Peter, 127
Burruss, Jim, 503
Bursk, E. C., 438
Burton, Mark, 319, 394
Buskirk, Bruce, 195
Buss, Dale, 470

C

Caceres, Ruben Chumpitaz, 154
Cagogan, John W., 90
Calantone, Roger, 235, 236
Callan, Cheryl, 378
Campbell, K. S., 438
Campbell, Kerry, 470
Capell, Kerry, 471
Capillure, Eva M., 128
Cardy, Robert L., 51
Carey, John, 155
Carey, Susan, 318
Carlson, Brad D., 262
Carlson, David C., 394
Carmon, Ziv, 319
Caro, Felipe, 357
Carpenter, Jason M., 355
Carter, Adrienne, 155
Carter, B., 394
Carter, Theresa, 413
Casserly, Meghan, 128
Cateora, Philip R., 459, 463
Cerquides, Jesus, 155
Chabowski, Brian R., 155
Chahal, M., 393
Chaison, Gary, 52
Challagalla, G. N., 437
Chan, Felix T. S., 155
Chan, Tat Y., 194
Chang, Chia-Chi, 437
Chang, Chiaho, 155
Chang, Chingching, 413
Chang, Wei-Lun, 236, 262
Chang, Y. H., 155
Chao, Raul O., 235
Charan, Ram, 51
Chatterjee, D., 156
Chatterjee, Subimal, 394
Chen, Chuniai, 234
Chen, Li, 357
Chen, Qimei, 194
Chen, Yuxin, 320
Chesley, Bruce, 142
Cheung, Christy M. K., 358
Chibe, Phil, 31
Chilcott, Tim, 357
Childers, Terry L., 128, 261
Chintagunta, Pradeep K., 320, 355
Chiou, Jyh-shen, 23
Chitturi, Ravinda, 234
Choi, Kyong-Ae, 320
Chou, S. Y., 155
Chu, Jeff, 128
Chu, Junhong, 355
Chuang, Pao-Tiao, 293
Chun, Rosa, 23
Chute, Matthew, 324
Clark, Bruce H., 503
Clark, C., 501
Clark, Patrick, 22
Clark, Terry, 24
Clarkson, Jonathan, 283
Clift, Robert, 52
Clifton, Rita, 452
Colao, J. J., 320
Colby, Charles L., 51
Colgate, Mark, 236
Colias, Mike, 154
Collins, Matalie, 357
Comer, Lucette B., 90, 437
Comiteau, Jennifer, 91
Commandeur, Harry R., 235
Conlin, M., 439
Connor, John M., 320
Coolidge, Carrie, 128
Cooper, Donald R., 65, 82
Cooper, Lee G., 355
Copestake, Stephen, 155
Coppett, John I., 394
Corriveau, Gilles, 356
Coulter, Keith S., 320
Court, David, 501
Cova, Bernard, 23, 355
Coviello, Nicole E., 193, 196
Cowley, Elizabeth, 127
Cox, Anthony D., 261
Cox, Dena S., 261
Coyles, Stephanie, 50
Cravens, David W., 196, 364
Crawford, Blair, 501
Crosby, Lawrence A., 292
Cross, Bob, 9
Crown, Judith, 470
Cunha, Marcus, Jr., 127, 319
Curry, Andrew, 196
Custance, Paul, 261
Cuttler, Andrea, 23

D

Dahl, Darren W., 128, 195
Dahlgaard, Jens J., 234
Dahneke, M., 438
Dai, Fan, 155
Dalrymple, Jim, 357
Damerow, Steve, 428
Dan, Avi, 262
Danaher, Peter J., 193, 196, 413
Darlin, Damon, 91
Darling, John, 470
Darmon, R. Y., 439
Dasteel, J., 293
D'Astous, Alain, 471
Daubek, Hugh G., 503
Davies, Gary, 23
Davis, Angus, 481
Davis, J., 437
Davis, John, 127
Davis, L., 438
Davis, Scott, 196
Dawar, Niraj, 262
Day, George, 24, 196
De Groot, Cristiaan, 235
De Jong, Ad, 92
De Leon, Sunshine Lichauco, 470
De Ruyter, Ko, 92
De Soriano, Yani, 127
De Waal, Gerrit Anton, 235
Declos, P., 437
DeGraba, Patrick, 320
Dekimpe, Marnik G., 470
Del Campo, Cristina, 470
Del Rio, Marisa, 503
Dempsey, John, 216
Demuth, Lee G., III, 235
DeNavas-Walt, Carmen, 194
Denegri-Knott, Janice, 91
Desai, Kalpesh Kaushik, 292
Desai, Preyas S., 234
Deshpande, Rohit, 194
Desouza, Kevin C., 52
Detior, Brian, 126
Deutschman, Alan, 127
Deutskens, Elisabeth, 92
Dewsnap, Belinda, 90
Dhar, Sanjay, 413
Dholakia, Nikhilesh, 357
Dholakia, Paul M., 358
Dholakia, Ruby Roy, 357
Diamantopoulos, A., 91
Dibb, Sally, 194
Dickey, M., 503
Dickinson, Roger, 503
Dickson, Peter R., 195
Dietz, B., 438
D'Innocenzio, Anne, 23
Dion, Paul, 155
Dishman, Lydia, 357
Dobbelstein, Thomas, 319
Donavan, D. Todd, 413
Donnelly, James H., 24, 275
Donovan, D. Todd, 292
Donthu, Naveen, 355, 356
Dossi, Andrea, 471
Dowling, L., 438
Draganska, Michaela, 319
Dreze, Xavier, 319
Droge, Cornelia, 23, 235
Dror, S., 355

Drucker, Peter F., 6–7, 18, 23, 27
Druehl, Cheryl T., 235
Drury, Colin, 320
Du, Rex Y., 127, 194
Dube, Jean-Pierre, 320
Dubinsky, Karen, 51
Dudney, Robert S., 155
Duffy, Dennis L., 357
Dugal, Lisa Feigen, 128
Dugan, Kelli, 155
Duggan, Kris, 145
Duhigg, Charles, 90, 355
Durland, Maryann, 52
Durmusoglu, Serdar S., 235

E

East, Robert, 127
Easterbrook, Steve, 452
Eden, Benjamin, 472
Edwards, Jim, 262
Edwards, Yancy, 195
Einhorn, Bruce, 318
Eisingerich, Andreas B., 234, 358
Elango, B., 471
Elgin, Ben, 91
Elliot, Stuart, 23, 261
Elliott, Chris, 318
Emerson, M. F., 50
Erat, Sanjiv, 236
Erdem, Tulim, 319
Escalas, Jennifer Edson, 128
Esch, Franz Rudolph, 261
Espejel, Joel, 261
Etzel, Michael J., 355, 356
Evans, Kenneth R., 292, 438, 439
Evans, Malcolm, 127

F

Fader, Peter S., 394, 503
Fairhurst, Ann, 503
Fan, Terence, 470
Fandos, Carmina, 261
Farris, Paul W., 195, 481, 502
Farzad, R., 52
Fassnacht, Martin, 292
Fassoula, Evangelia D., 24
Fatt, Chen Kehng, 128
Faulds, David J., 195
Feick, Lawrence F., 127
Feldman, David, 195
Fenech, Tino, 357
Fennell, Geraldine, 195
Fergie, 97
Ferguson, Rick, 502
Fernandez, Joe, 386
Fernandez, Teresa M., 90
Field, Anne, 395, 502
Findlay, Christopher, 234
Fine, Jon, 395
Finkbeiner, Carl, 502
Fisch, Jan Hendrik, 471
Fishbein, M., 126
Fisher, A., 439
Fishman, Charles, 128
Fitzsimmons, C., 319
Flavian, Carlos, 261
Floyd, David, 470
Fontevecchia, Agustino, 470
Ford, Henry, 10
Forehand, Mark R., 194
Fornell, Claes, 502
Foster, Lauren, 127
Fournier, Susan, 127
Fox, Edward J., 502
Fox, Richard J., 503
Foxall, Gordon R., 127
Frank, Anne, 379
Franke, George R., 394, 439
Franses, Phillip Hans, 503
Frazier, Gary L., 195
Frean, Alexandra, 291
Frederick, James, 195
Freestone, Oliver M., 126
Frei, Frances X., 292
French, John R. P., 333, 356
Friedman, Thomas L., 51, 356
Furguson, T., 438
Furrer, Olivier, 91

G

Gable, Myron, 503
Gabrielsson, Mika, 470
Gabrielsson, Peter, 470
Gaertner, James, 503
Gallien, Jeremie, 357
Gang, Eric, 471
Gao, Tao, 154
Gao, Yan, 471
Gara, T., 319
Garcia, Rosanna, 236
Gardiner, Stanley C., 356
Garfield, Bob, 393
Garrido-Rubio, Ana, 319
Gaskin, Steven, 413
Gaus, Patrick, 261
Gedenk, Karen, 502
Geisart, Tim, 417
Genovese, Yvonne, 495
George, William R., 24, 275
Georges, L., 438
Ghosh, Amit K., 292
Gielens, Katrijn, 470
Gilbert, Richard J., 356
Gill, Dee, 395
Gill, Donna, 155
Gilles, Laurent, 128
Gilly, Mary C., 459, 463
Gimenez, Cristina, 502
Girotra, Karan, 235
Goel, Rajeev K., 234
Goel, S. K., 356
Gohmann, Stephan F., 195
Gokey, Timothy C., 50
Goldenberg, Barton, 24
Golder, Peter N., 235
Goldsmith, M., 438
Goldsmith, Ronald E., 394
Gomez, Selena, 40
Gong, James J., 126
Goode, Caroline, 127
Goodstein, Ronald C., 194
Goodwin, Ross, 52
Goolsby, Jerry R., 51, 189, 196
Gorchels, Linda, 196
Gordon, Jonathan, 235
Gosain, Sanjay, 320
Goudreau, J., 235
Goyal, Anita, 292
Goyal, S. K., 356
Grabov, P., 355
Grabow, Amy, 27
Grace, Debra, 292, 357
Graham, John, 459, 463
Grant, John, 23
Grant, Susan, 262
Grasman, Scott E., 502
Green, David, 126
Green, Penelope, 234
Greenberg, D. M., 437
Greenberg, H. M., 437
Greene, J., 439
Grewal, Dhruv, 23, 319
Grewal, Rajdeep, 51
Griffith, David A., 471
Griffiths, G. H., 357
Grossman, Mindy, 385
Grow, Brian, 91
Gruca, Thomas S., 24
Grunbacher, Paul, 235
Guenzi, P., 438
Guilding, Chris, 320
Gupta, Pola B., 23
Gupta, Suraksah, 262
Gustafsson, Anders, 50, 194, 196
Gustin, Sam, 49
Gutierrez-Cilian, Jesus, 193

H

Haggett, Steve, 319, 394
Hall, Emma, 195
Hall, Lorna, 357
Handfield, Robert B., 235
Hanlon, P., 52
Hann, Il-Horn, 320
Hanna, Joe B., 356
Hansen, Havard, 156
Hansotia, Behram, 502
Hanssens, Dominique M., 502
Hardekopf, B., 438
Harlam, Bari, 51, 320

Harmancioglu, Nukhet, 235
Harrington, Roseanne, 409
Harris, Lynn, 503
Hartley, Steven, 214
Harvey, Michael G., 471
Harvey, Paul, 373
Hasselt, C. V., 234
Hauser, John R., 235, 413
Hausman, Angela, 236
Havila, Virpi, 355
He, Chuan, 320
Heaney, Joo-Gim, 394
Heide, Jan B., 355
Heitmeyer, J., 126
Helm, Anna, 318
Henderson, Naomi R., 91
Henkoff, Ronald, 291
Henn, Steve, 91
Henning, Victor, 502
Henning-Thurau, Thorsten, 502
Hensgen, Tobin, 52
Herman, Andreas, 50
Hernandez Ortega, Blanca, 156
Herndon, Neil, 471
Hershey, L., 438
Heskel, Julia, 291
Heskett, James L., 269, 270, 274
Hess, James D., 319
Hesseldahl, Arik, 194
Hewett, Kelly, 262
Hewlett, Bill, 49
Hill, C. Jeanne, 472
Hill, Logan, 195
Hinghley, Martin, 261
Ho, Shu Hsun, 472
Ho, Teck H., 293
Hoch, Stephen J., 394
Hoeffler, Steve, 503
Hof, R., 502
Hof, Robert D., 92
Hofstetter, Joerg, 355
Hogan, J., 438
Holahan, Catherine, 126
Hollenbeck, Candice R., 126
Holmes, Stanley, 23
Holmlund, Maria, 155
Holstein, William J., 292
Homburg, Christian, 292
Homer, Pamela Miles, 261
Hong, Paul, 155
Hong, Wei-Kuo, 502
Hopkins, Christopher D., 194, 439
Horner, Pamela Miles, 127
Horovitz, B., 437
Hosford, Christopher, 155
Hotchin, Jim, 339
Houston, Mark B., 51
Howard, A., 357
Howard, Daniel J., 319
Hoyer, Wayne D., 24, 128, 292
Hoyt, Jennifer, 470
Hozier, George C., Jr., 91
Hsu, Tiffany, 126
Hu, Haiyan, 357
Huang, Jen-Hung, 472
Huang, Jun-Ying, 394
Huang, Rong, 262
Huang, Stephen Chi-Tsun, 357
Huber, Frank, 50
Huff, Sid L., 196
Hult, G. Tomas M., 51, 155, 356, 471
Hunger, J. David, 37, 43, 50, 51, 195, 496
Hunter, Gary K., 502
Hupfer, Maureen E., 126
Hurd, Mike, 36
Huston, John, 320
Hutt, Michael D., 51

I

Ihiwan, Moon, 472
Im, Subim, 194, 195
Immegart, Ryan, 172
Immelt, Jeffrey, 32, 34
Indounas, Kostis A., 319, 320
Ingenbleek, Paul, 90, 471
Inglis, Robert, 52
Inman, J. Jeffrey, 263, 503
Intrieri, Jane, 91
Iqbal, Zafar, 235
Irani, Tracy, 413
Ismael, Zuhaimy Haji, 503
Ives, Nat, 471

J

Jackson, Stuart E., 356
Jacobs, Laurence W., 395
Jacobson, Robert, 261
Jagger, Mick, 159
Jaggi, Chandra K., 356
Jagpal, Sharan, 236
Jain, Chaman L., 51
Jain, Dipak C., 319
Jain, Shallendra Pratap, 263
Jamil, M., 236
Janiszewski, Chris, 127, 319
Jansen, Bernard J., 358
Jaramillo, F., 439
Jasper, Cynthia R., 357
Javalgi, Ravshekhar G., 292
Jayachandran, Satish, 51, 356, 393
Jayaraman, Vaidyanathan, 356
Jedidi, Kamel, 236
Jeuland, Abel P., 471
Jimenez Martinez, Julio, 156
Jin, Hyun Seung, 413
Jing, Bing, 261
Jocumsen, Graham, 92
Johanson, Jan, 355
Johlke, M. C., 437, 438
Johnson, Devon S., 355
Johnson, J. T., 437
Johnson, James P., 128
Johnson, Josh, 337
Johnson, Julie T., 154
Johnson, Lester W., 355
Johnson, Michael D., 50, 194, 196
Johnson, Ron, 5
Johnson, William, 155
Johnston, Mark W., 24, 127, 421, 425, 426, 427, 429, 430, 432, 487, 488, 491, 493
Johnston, Wesley J., 156, 193, 196
Jolie, Angelina, 97
Jones, Thomas O., 270, 274
Jopez, T. B., 439
Jordan, John, 90
Joseph, C., 439
Joshi, Yogesh V., 236
Judd, L. Lynn, 356

K

Kaehler, George, 330
Kahn, Kenneth B., 503
Kale, Sudhir N., 194, 292
Kalliny, Morris, 236
Kalra, Ajay, 194
Kalyanam, Kirthi, 356
Kamakura, Wagner A., 127, 194, 471
Kambewa, Emma, 471
Kamdar, Nipoli, 320
Kandemir, Destan, 236
Kandil, Magda, 472
Kane, Yukair Iwatani, 234
Kang, Cecilia, 92
Kang, Wooseong, 471
Kang, Yong Soon, 394
Kannan, P. K., 90
Kapferer, Jean-Noel, 128
Kaplan, Julee, 234
Karanja, F. N., 503
Karatepe, Osman M., 393
Karray, Salma, 413
Karunaratna, Amal R., 355
Kavadias, Stylianon, 235, 236
Keane, Michael P., 319
Keaveney, Susan M., 273
Keh, Hean Tat, 90
Keliner, Peter, 91
Kelleher, Herb, 268
Keller, Kevin Lane, 355
Kelton, Christina M. L., 357
Kennedy, Karen Norman, 51, 52, 189, 196
Kennedy, Tom, 465
Kenning, John, 135
Kent, Robert J., 394
Keown, Charles F., 395
Kerin, Roger, 214
Kerin, Roger A., 319
Kerr, D., 395
Kesmodel, David, 234
Ketchen, David J., Jr., 155

Ketzenberg, Michael, 355
Kiema, J. B. K., 503
Kiley, David, 472
Kilgore, Patricia, 196
Kim, J., 502
Kim, MinChung, 395, 502
Kim, Myonung Soo, 358
Kim, Namwoon, 194
Kim, Sang Yong, 413
Kim, Stephen Keysuk, 355
Kimmel, Allan J., 320
Kin, Yoo Jin, 262
King, Ceridwyn, 292
King, Martin Luther, Jr., 379
King, Stephen F., 90, 196
Kingston, William, 261
Kirchhoff, David, 378
Kitchen, Phillip J., 393
Klassen, Kenneth J., 292
Klein, Karen E., 261
Klugsberger, Peter, 194, 292
Ko, Kenneth D., 472
Koca, Cenk, 194
Kock, Soren, 470
Koening, Harold F., 292
Kopalle, Praveen K., 319
Koschat, Martin A., 357
Kotabe, Masaaki, 155
Kovac, M., 438
Kretschmer, Tobias, 234, 358
Kriendler, P., 438
Krishna, Aradhna, 357
Krishnan, Balaji, 318
Krishnan, M. S., 502
Kuehnast, Don, 291
Kuettner, Dorothea, 503
Kulviwat, Songpol, 24
Kumar, Niraj, 155
Kumar, Pratyush, 357
Kumar, Sameer, 357
Kumar, V., 24, 195, 196, 439, 503
Kumcu, Erdogan, 319
Kurtz, David L., 23
Kuruzovich, Jason, 320
Kuyumcu, Harun Ahmet, 319
Kwon, Kyong-Nan, 262

L

Laforge, Marc, 205
Lager, Marshall, 155
Laker, Freddie, 92
Langert, Bob, 452
Langner, Tobia, 261
LaPointe, Patrick, 475, 476, 477, 501
Laran, Juliano, 127
Laroche, Michael, 292
Larsen, John P., 413
Lassk, Felicia G., 189, 196
LaTour, Michael S., 356
Lau-Gesk, Loraine, 262
Lawson, Rob, 195
Layne, Ken, 196
Lazzarini, Sergio G., 470, 471
Le Bon, Joel, 90
Leach, M. P., 439
LeClaire, J., 292
Ledingham, D., 438
Lee, Bruce C. Y., 472
Lee, D. H., 439
Lee, Matthew K. O., 358
Lee, Mi-Hee, 262
Lee, Stephen, 261
Lee, Sungho, 356
Lee, Yikuan, 319
Lee Soon-am, 308
Lehmann, Donald R., 319, 502
Lei, Jing, 262
LeMeunier-FitzHugh, K., 439
Lemmink, Jos, 262
Lemon, Katherine N., 51, 155, 195, 502
Lennon, John, 379
Leonidou, Leonidas C., 155, 470
Levav, Jonathan, 128
Levine, Adam, 40
Levisohn, Ben, 194, 234
Levy, Michael, 319
Lewin, Jeffrey E., 156
Lewis, Bob, 196
Li, Jiaotao, 471
Li, Ling-yee, 413
Li, Ning, 471
Li, Shan, 127
Liang, Wen-ko, 127
Liao, Kun, 155
Lichtenstein, Donald R., 357
Lin, Yan-Shu, 320
Lin, Yu-Shan, 394
Lindgreen, Adam, 261
Lindridge, Andrew, 194
Lindsey, Charles D., 263
Lindsey-Mullikin, Joan, 23
Littman, Margaret, 292
Liu, A. H., 439
Liu, Mei-Ling, 127
Liu, Sandra S., 90, 437
Liu, Tsung-Chi, 262, 357
Liu, Yuping, 195
Loane, Sharon, 91
Locander, Willam B., 52, 261
Lodish, Leonard M., 194
Lofgren, Zoe, 389
Loft, Scott, 274
Lopex-Sanchez, Maite, 155
Lorimer, S. E., 438
Loveman, Gary W., 270, 271, 274
Lovett, Mitchell J., 23, 24
Loyka, Jeffrey J., 471
Lu, Jane W., 471
Lubatkin, Michael, 262
Lucas, G. H., 437
Ludacris, 30
Ludewig, Dirk, 262
Luechauer, David L., 261
Lueg, Jason E., 127
Lunde, Brian, 292
Luo, Xueming, 319, 355
Luo, Yadong, 356
Luostarinen, Reijo, 470
Lusch, Robert F., 24, 193, 234, 291, 324, 356
Lutzky, Christian, 502
Luzardo, R., 437

M

Ma, Xufei, 471
MacDonald, Jason B., 23, 24
Madden, Lance, 195
Madden, Thomas J., 262
Madrigal, Robert, 127
Magid, Julie Manning, 261
Magion-Muller, Katja, 127
Mahajan, Vijar, 234
Mainkar, Avinash V., 262
Malkewitz, Keven, 262
Manchanda, Rajesh V., 262
Mandhachitara, Rujirutana, 394
Manning, Kenneth C., 23
Manrakhan, Shalini, 154
Mantel, Susan Powell, 394
Maras, Eliot, 357
Marder, J., 439
Marinova, Detelina, 196
Marshall, Greg W., 24, 127, 421, 425, 426, 427, 429, 430, 432, 437, 487, 488, 491, 493
Martin, Ingrid M., 262
Martin, James, 416
Martin, X. C., 439
Martin De Hoyos, Ja Jose, 156
Martin-Herran, G., 262
Marvel, Howard P., 356
Marvin, G., 503
Marzill, T., 51
Maslow, Abraham, 99–101
Mason, Charlotte H., 194
Massey, Joseph Eric, 413
Matin, Sajjad, 91
Matlack, Carol, 470
Matta, Shashi, 262
Matthews, Candace, 347
Matthews, N., 356
Mattioli, D., 24
Maurer, Dan, 267
Maxham, James G., III, 357
Mayzlin, Dina, 358
Mazumdar, Tridib, 319
McAlexander, James H., 292
McAlister, Leigh, 395, 502
McCafferty, Stephen, 356
McCarthy, E. Jerome, 23
McChesney, Fred S., 320
McClure, James, 319

McClymont, Hoda, 92
McConnon, A., 439
McDevitt, Paul, 394
McDonnell, John, 126
McFarland, R. G., 437
McGarland, Richard G., 471
McGoldrick, Patrick J., 126
McGoldrick, Peter J., 357
McGovern, Gail J., 501
McGregor, Jena, 292, 293
McKeough, K., 439
McLean, Piper, 194
McNally, Regina C., 235
McNaughton, Rob, 91
McNeilly, Kevin M., 292
McNicol, Jason Patrick, 471
McNiven, Malcolm A., 23
McPartlin, Sue, 128
McPhee, Wayne, 51
McQueen, M., 439
McQuitty, Shaun, 291
Meese, Alan J., 356
Meichtry, Stacy, 234
Mela, Carl F., 357, 439
Melewar, T. C., 262
Melirovich, Gavriel, 234
Mendes, Eva, 70
Mentzer, John T., 503
Mercer, David, 51
Meredith, Geoffrey, 194
Merrilees, Bill, 357
Merunka, Dwight, 90
Mesquita, Luiz F., 470
Metters, Richard, 355
Miao, C. F., 438, 439
Michel, George, 268
Milani, Ken, 503
Mild, Andreas, 394
Miles, Raymond E., 38, 39
Milk, Harvey, 379
Miller, Kenneth E., 154, 261
Miller, Thomas W., 91
Minaj, Nicki, 40
Miniard, Paul W., 23
Mintzberg, Henry, 47, 52
Miquel, Salvador, 128
Mirella, M., 127
Mirza, Y. H., 437
Mishra, Debi Prasad, 394
Mitchell, Mark Andrew, 194
Mithas, Sunil, 502
Mittal, Vikas, 196
Mizik, Natalie, 261
Moe, Wendy W., 503
Mol, Michael J., 155
Moller, Kristian, 470
Money, R. Bruce, 502
Monga, Alokparna Basu, 262
Monplaisir, Leslie, 234
Monroe, Kent B., 319
Monteiro, Carlos M. F., 470
Montgomery, Alexandra, 127
Moon, Young Sook, 394
Moore, Geoffrey A., 235
Moorman, Christine, 503
Mooth, Rob, 235
Moreau, Page, 195, 236
Morgan, Michael S., 292
Morgan, Neil A., 196
Morgeson, Forrest V., III, 502
Morsi, Mohammed, 447
Mortimer, Kathleen, 394
Mosley, Richard W., 51
Mossberg, Walter, 112
Mourali, Medhi, 292
Moutot, Jean Michel, 90
Mowen, John C., 292
Moynihan, Brian, 476
Mucha, Zofia, 413
Muir, C., 439
Mulki, J. P., 439
Mulligan, John, 470
Mulvey, Michael S., 357
Muniz, Albert M., Jr., 234
Murray, Andy, 271
Murray, Jamie, 271
Murray, Janet Y., 155
Murray, Lynn, 292
Murthy, D. N. P., 263
Musyoka, S. M., 503
Mutyauvyu, S. M., 503

N

Nadeem, Mohammed M., 128
Nagle, T., 438
Naito, Masa K., 320
Nambisan, Priya, 262
Nambisan, Satish, 262
Nancarrow, Clive, 127
Nathanson, Doug, 270
Natter, Martin, 394
Neeleman, David, 35, 36, 42, 280, 281
Neff, Jack, 90, 234, 357
Negroponte, Nicholas, 296
Nelson, Michelle R., 471
Nepal, Bimai, 234
Neslin, Scott A., 319, 357, 439, 502
Netemeyer, Richard G., 318, 357
Neu, Wayne A., 156
Nevins, Jennifer L., 502
Newell, Stephen J., 394, 438
Newkirk, Margaret, 261
Newman, Kara, 261
Ng, Hwei Ping, 90
Nguyen, Thi Mai, 90
Nicholas, Chris, 331
Niederhoffer, Kate, 235
Niezen, Carlos, 471
Nix, Nancy, 356
Nonn, Jim, 304
Noor, Muhammed A., 235
Norris, D. T., 437
Nurmilaakso, Juha Mikka, 156
Nussbaum, Bruce, 235

O

Obama, Barack, 389
O'Cass, Aron, 357
O'Connor, Gina Colarelli, 319
Ohta, Hiroshi, 320
Ojala, Marydee, 155
Olson, Eric M., 51, 471
Olson, Melinda, 482
Ortega, R., 439
Orth, Ulrich R., 262
Ostrower, J., 234
Owusu, Richard A., 470

P

Packard, Dave, 49
Padgett, Dan, 357
Padmanabhan, V., 194
Paek, Hye-Jin, 471
Palmatier, R. W., 437, 471
Palmeri, Christopher, 261
Palumbo, Frederick A., 194
Pancras, Joseph, 355
Pant, S., 156
Paparoidamis, Nicholas G., 154
Parasuraman, A., 51, 279, 283, 293
Pardo, C., 438
Parekh, R., 51
Park, J. E., 439
Parker, Robert P., 155
Parry, Tim, 393
Pasquale, Margaret K., 357
Patelli, Lorenzo, 471
Pati, Niranjan, 234
Patterson, Paul G., 126, 195
Pattikawa, Lenny H., 235
Paulssen, Marcel, 155
Pavlou, Paul A., 503
Pavlovsky, Bruno, 335
Payan, Janice M., 471
Pearl, Daniel, 379
Pearson, Ann, 126
Pearson, David, 127
Pearson, J. Michael, 126
Pekkarinen, M., 438
Pennanen, Kyosti, 358
Peppers, Don, 14, 24, 195
Perlman, Jerry, 113
Perreault, William D., Jr., 502
Perriello, Brad, 395
Peters, Cara, 126
Peters, T., 395
Petersen, J. Andrew, 24, 195
Petersen, Kenneth J., 235

Peterson, R. M., 437
Peterson, Robin T., 503
Pettijohn, C. E., 439
Pettijohn, L. S., 439
Pettis, Brad, 218
Pfeifer, Philip E., 481, 502
Phan, Phillip, 470
Piercy, Nigel F., 196, 364, 439
Plank, R. E., 438
Plaskitt, Sarah, 195
Plepler, Richard, 305
Plumer, Brad, 91
Polcha, Andrew E., 51, 52
Polo-Redondo, Yolanda, 319
Ponder, Nicole, 127
Pons, Frank, 292
Popescu, Ioana, 319
Porter, Michael E., 28, 29, 37, 38, 41, 42, 51, 178, 179, 182, 183, 196, 295, 302, 323
Powell, Guy R., 478, 502
Powell, Shaun, 23
Powers, Thomas L., 154, 195, 471
Prebble, Dean Richard, 235
Price, Linda L., 127
Procter, David B., 90
Proctor, Bernadette D., 194
Proenca, Joao F., 90
Prospero, Michael A., 128
Pu, Pearl, 357
Pullig, Chris, 318
Pullins, Ellen Bolman, 394
Putrevu, Sanjay, 195

Q

Quade, Michael, 156
Quelch, John A., 501

R

Rabiser, Rick, 235
Rabojohn, Neil, 358
Ragatz, Gary L., 235
Raghunathan, Rajagopal, 234
Raj, S. P., 319
Rajguru, G., 438
Ralph, David L., 195
Ralston, Roy W., 318
Ramani, Girish, 24
Ramasamy, Bala, 261
Ramaseshan, B., 155, 261
Ramaswami, S. N., 439
Ramdas, Kamalini, 234
Randall, Taylor, 234
Ranger, Steve, 92
Ranstad, Evan, 234
Rao, Akshay R., 128
Rao, Ramesh K. S., 23
Rauyruen, Papassapa, 154
Raven, Bertram, 333, 356
Ravichandran, T., 156
Ravid, B., 355
Rawwas, Mohammed Y. A., 394
Raymond, Mary Anne, 394, 439
Rebeliein, Robert P., 357
Reda, Susan, 357
Reddy, Srinivas K., 503
Reed, Americus, II, 126
Rego, Lopo L., 24
Reibstein, David J., 481, 502
Reichheld, Frederick F., 51, 79, 185, 196
Reid, David A., 394
Reinartz, Werner, 196, 439, 503
Reingen, Peter H., 51
Reis, Dayr, 234
Reisinger, D., 319
Rencher, Brad, 478
Reuter, Joseph, 44
Reutterer, Thomas, 394
Reyes-Moro, Antonio, 155
Reynolds, N. L., 91
Ricadela, Aaron, 196, 236
Richard, James E., 196
Richards, Keith, 159
Richardson, L. D., 438
Richey, R. Glenn, Jr., 357
Ricks, J. M., Jr., 439
Rindfleisch, Aric, 319
Ringland, Gill, 196
Roberts, A., 319
Robinson, L., Jr., 437
Rodgers, Aaron, 181
Rodgers, Shelly, 194
Rodriguez, Eric, 471
Rodriguez, Julio, 471
Rodriguez-Escudero, Ana Isabel, 193
Rodriguez-Pinto, Javier, 193
Rodruguez-Aguilar, Juan A., 155
Rogers, C., 394, 395
Rogers, Martha, 14, 24, 195
Rogers, Robert A., 91
Rogosky, Mark, 235
Rohleder, Thomas R., 292
Rokkan, Aksel I., 355
Romaniuk, Jenni, 126
Roos, Inger, 50, 194, 196
Roren, T., 263
Rosa, Jose Antonio, 195
Rosenbloom, Bert, 355
Rosensteel, S., 438
Roskos-Ewoldsen, David R., 127
Rossman, J., 438
Roster, Catherine A., 194
Rostow, Walt W., 448
Roter, Catherine A., 91
Rotfeld, Herbert Jack, 91
Roth, Martin S., 262
Rowley, Jennifer, 355
Rudelius, William, 214
Rukstales, Brad, 502
Rust, Roland T., 51, 502
Rutherford, Brian N., 154
Ryals, Lynette, 502

S

Sa Vinhas, Alberto, 355
Sabin, Rob, 234
Sabol, Barry, 292
Sacks, Daniell, 128
Salkowitz, R., 413
Salle, Robert, 23, 355
Samuelsen, Bendik M., 156
Sanchez-Franco, Manuel J., 319
Sandhu, Maqsood, 470
Sanz Blas, Silvia, 357
Saqib, Najam, 262
Sarigollu, Emine, 262
Sasser, W. Earl, Jr., 270, 274
Sattler, Henrik, 502
Sauer, Nicola E., 128
Sauers, Dale G., 356
Saunders, John, 235
Saunders, Paula M., 23
Savin, Sergei, 320
Sawhney, Mohanbir, 51, 196
Scanlon, Jessie, 262
Schaafsma, Sjoerd, 355
Schaninger, Charles M., 195
Schau, Hope Jensen, 234
Scheer, L. K., 437, 471
Schewe, Charles D., 194
Schilli, Bruno, 155
Schindler, Pamela S., 65, 82
Schindler, Robert M., 320
Schlesinger, Leonard A., 270, 274
Schlidge, George, 503
Schlimgen, Jennifer, 91
Schmidt, Glen M., 235
Schmidt, JoAnn, 91
Schmidt, Stacy M. P., 195
Schmitt, Bernd H., 261
Schouten, John W., 292
Schroeder, Jonathan E., 91
Schubert, Petra, 156
Schultz, Don E., 393, 502
Schultz, E. J., 24, 51, 90, 196, 262, 394
Schulze, William S., 262
Schweidel, David A., 195, 394
Sears, Diane, 155
Seeley, Tina, 319
Seetharaman, P. B., 194
Seggie, Steven H., 24
Seiders, Kathleen, 320
Sembhy, R., 355
Sen, C. G., 155
Sen, Sankar, 155, 194, 394
Sethi, Rajesh, 235
Setijono, Djoko, 234
Shaffer, Ian, 232
Shah, Niraj, 309

Shammen, Asif, 155
Shannon, S., 318
Shaoming, Z., 439
Shapiro, Benson P., 177
Sharma, Arun, 24, 438
Sharma, Bishnu, 51
Shaver, Eric F., 262
Shay, Jeffrey P., 471
Shearman, S., 439
Shen, C. Y., 155
Sherman, Lauren, 195
Shervani, T. A., 437
Sheth, Jagdish N., 24, 438
Shiv, Baba, 319
Shocker, Allan D., 194
Shoemaker, Robert, 236
Shugan, Steven M., 413, 471
Shughart, William F., II, 320
Sichtmann, C., 438
Sierra, Jeremy J., 291
Silayoi, Pinya, 262
Silver, Jon, 126
Silverman, Ed, 262
Siminitiras, A. C., 91
Simon, Bill, 345
Sinclair, Janas, 413
Singh, Jagdip, 292, 439
Singh, Nanua, 234
Singh, Vishal, 320
Sinha, Indrajit, 319
Sinha, P., 438
Sirdeshmukh, Deepak, 292
Sirgy, M. Joseph, 154
Siriba, D. N., 503
Siseth, Pal R., 156
Sisodia, Rajendra S., 24
Sjodin, Henrik, 236
Skiera, Bernd, 501
Skinner, L., 438
Skinner, Lauren R., 357
Slater, Robert, 51
Slater, Stanley F., 51, 471
Slavin, Stephen, 136
Slotegraaf, Rebecca J., 263, 503
Smalley, Karen, 24
Smidts, Ale, 90
Smith, Alan D., 356
Smith, Amy K., 292
Smith, Denis, 52, 503
Smith, H. L., 438
Smith, J. Brock, 236
Smith, Jeremy, 23
Smith, Jessica, 194
Smith, John, 324
Smolker, Rachel, 155
Snow, Charles C., 38, 39
Soares, Joao Oliveira, 470
Solem, O., 263
Sood, Suresh, 261
Sorescu, B., 235
Sorvillo, Nick, 236
Souchon, Anne L., 90
Southwick, R., 51
Souza Fontana, Mariadel Mar, 235
Spanjol, Jelena, 235
Sparrow, Nick, 92
Spataro, Nancy, 434
Speece, Mark, 262
Speed, Richard J., 318
Sperduti, A., 234
Spink, Amanda, 358
Srinivasan, Raghavan, 502
Srinivasan, Raji, 395, 502
Staelin, Richard, 413
Stagg, Chris, 235
Stainburn, Samantha, 156
Stamps, M. B., 437
Stan, Simona, 292
Stanford, Duane, 23
Stanley, Sarah M., 127
Starvish, Maggie, 91–92
Stedman, Craig, 91
Steenkamp, Jan-Benedict E. M., 437
Steinberg, Brian, 194, 394
Stelter, Brian, 91
Sterling, Jay U., 154, 195
Stewart, David W., 23, 262, 503
Stobbe, Mike, 126
Stock, Ruth Maria, 24
Stogner, Sam, 416
Stokes, David, 91
Stone, B., 502
Story, Louise, 127
Stotzer, Shelly, 475
Strauss, Karsten, 471
Stremersch, Stefan, 503
Stride, Helen, 261
Stuyck, Jules, 320
Sudharshan, D., 91
Sudhir, K., 355
Suh, Jaebeom, 413
Sullivan, Chris T., 292
Sullivan, P., 126
Sullivan, Ursula Y., 193
Sun, Baohong, 319
Sundara, Sreeram Ramakrishnan, 502
Suter, Tracy A., 262
Svahn, Senja, 470
Swaidan, Ziad, 394
Swaminathan, Vanitha, 503
Swan, J. E., 438
Swift, Ronald S., 196
Synodinos, Nicolaos E., 395

T

Takeuichi, Riki, 471
Talley, K., 24
Tam, J. L. M., 438
Tamilla, Robert D., 356
Tanner, Christian, 156
Tansuhaj, Patriya, 51
Tapp, Alan, 91
Taudes, Alfred, 394
Tayles, Mike, 320
Taylor, A. J., 439
Taylor, Charles R., 394
Taylor, L., 438
Taylor, Ronald D., 127
Taylor, Sam, 261
Teich, Ira, 194
Tellis, Gerald J., 235, 503
Terryn, Evelyne, 320
Terwiesch, Christian, 235, 320
Theodosiou, M., 470
Thiagarajan, Palaniappan, 127
Thilenius, Peter, 355
Thirkell, Peter C., 196
Thomas, Dave, 397
Thomas, Jacquelyn S., 193, 196, 439
Thomas, M. W., 234
Thorpe, Daniel, 502
Tichy, Noel, 51
Till, Brian D., 127
Tiltman, David, 91
Timberlake, Cotton, 24
Timberlake, Justin, 30–31
Tinson, Julie, 127
Todd, Sarah, 195
Tokman, Mert, 357
Toran Torres, Francisco, 357
Trebilcock, Bob, 355
Trejos, Nancy, 193
Trivedi, Minakshi, 292
Tsai, Ming-tiem, 127
Tsao, Hsiu-Yuan, 261
Tse, David K., 319
Turner, Gregory B., 194
Twiggy, 11

U

Ulrich, Karl T., 235
Ulwick, Anthony W., 234
Urban, Glen L., 235, 413
Utke, Scott, 17

V

Van Auken, Stuart, 194
Van Bruggen, Gerrit H., 90, 503
Van De Valde, Doug, 408
Van Den Butte, Christophe, 236
Van der Stede, Wim A., 126
Van Dyck, Tom, 320
Van Hoof, Tim, 181
Van Riel, Cees B. M., 503
Van Tilbury, Aad, 471
Vance, A., 291
Vance, Ashley, 235
Vanheule, Marc, 319
Varadarajan, P. Rajan, 51, 356, 393
Varela, Jose A., 503

Vargas, Vicente, 355
Vargo, Stephen L., 24, 193, 234, 291, 324
Vaught, Bobby C., 356
Vega, Tanzina, 262
Ventura, Eva, 502
Verbeke, W. J., 195, 438
Vergara, Sofia, 40
Verheoven, Piet, 472
Verhoef, Peter C., 50, 155, 195, 196
Verwaal, Ernst, 235
Vetter, William, 472
Vilcassim, Naufel J., 355
Villanueva, Julián, 501
Villarejo-Ramos, Angel F., 319
Vinod, Ben, 320
Viswanathan, Madhubalan, 195, 261
Viswanathan, Siva, 320
Vitell, Scott J., 394
Volpp, Kevin G., 126
Voorhees, Roy Dale, 394
Voss, Glenn B., 320
Vriens, Marco, 24

W

Waaser, E., 438
Walker, Beth A., 51
Wall, Chuck, 24
Wallendorf, Melanie, 194
Walley, Keith, 261
Walton, Sam, 444
Wan, Wan Jamaliah, 394
Wang, Guangping, 318
Wang, Hsiao-Fan, 502
Wang, Jeff, 194
Wangenheim, Florian V., 195
Wansink, Brian, 394
Want, Chung-Yu, 262
Ward, David, 92
Warden, Clyde A., 357
Wathne, Kenneth H., 355
Watson, Tom, 472
Weaver, Dianne Altman, 91
Webster, Frederick E., Jr., 356, 393
Weeks, W. A., 439
Wehmeyer, Kai, 92
Weinberger, Joshua, 92
Weinmann, K., 438
Weissel, M., 438
Welch, David, 234, 472
Welch, Jack, 35, 36
Wells, William D., 194
Wernle, Bradford, 154
West, Kanye, 30
Wetzels, Martin, 92
Wheelen, Thomas H., 37, 43, 50, 51, 195, 496
Wheeler, David, 51
Whipple, Thomas W., 292
White, J. Chris, 51, 356, 393
White, Joseph B., 127
White, Katherine, 128
Whitman, Meg, 36, 49, 149
Wiedmann, Klaus-Peter, 262
Wieners, Brad, 194
Wierenga, Berend, 90
Wiersema, Fred, 15, 24
Wiesel, Thorsten, 501
Wiesenfeld, David, 235
Wilkie, Joe, 236
Williams, Dennis, 395
Williams, J. A., 439
Williams, Jasmine E. M., 470
Williams, Jerome D., 126
Williams, Patti, 195
Williamson, Nicholas C., 355
Wilson, J. Holton, 503
Wilson, R. Dale, 92
Wiman, Alan R., 320
Winchester, Maxwell, 126
Wingfield, Nick, 291
Wolffle, Ralf, 156
Wong, Veronica, 235
Wong, Y. J., 438
Wood, Charles M., 194
Wood, Stacy L., 236
Woodall, Regina D., 51
Woodman, Nicholas, 106
Woods, Tiger, 4
Woodside, Arch G., 261
Woodward, K., 395
Workman, John P., Jr., 195
Worthy, Sheri Lokken, 127
Wright, S., 439
Wu, Bob T., 394
Wu, Wann-Yih, 357
Wu, Yaozhong, 319
Wyner, Gordon A., 91, 195, 438

Y

Yang, Jerry, 112
Yang, Jun, 234
Yang, Moonhee, 127
Yang, Sha, 195
Yang, Xiz, 128
Yavas, Ugar, 393
Yeung, Matthew, 261
Yip, George S., 472
Yoo, Boonghee, 356, 394
Young, Laurie, 196
Young, Robert B., 292
Young, S. Mark, 126
Yu, Seongjae, 50

Z

Zabin, Jeff, 51, 196
Zaccour, G., 262, 413
Zacharia, Zach, 356
Zaheer, Srilata, 154
Zamiska, Nicholas, 234
Zeithaml, Valarie A., 51, 275, 279, 283, 293, 502
Zhang, Jie, 357
Zhao, Miao, 357
Zheng, Yu-Sheng, 293
Zielke, Stephan, 319
Zimmer, Greg, 253
Zinkhan, George M., 91, 395
Zoltners, A. A., 438
Zoratti, Sandra, 24
Zwick, Detiev, 91

SUBJECT INDEX

A

Accumulating bulk, 328
Acquisitions, 178
Action for Healthy Kids, 408
Action plans, 485–487, 494–495
Action stage, 372
Activities, interests, and opinions (AIOs), 97–98, 172
Additions to existing product lines, 218
Administered VMS (vertical marketing systems), 332–333
Advertising; *see also* Internet advertising
  cooperative, 406–407
  costs, 376–377
  definition, 361
  diminishing returns, 397–398
  execution approaches, 402–403
  in foreign markets, 464–465
  frequency, 401–402
  institutional, 399
  largest advertisers, 397, 398, 465
  location-based targeted, 100
  low-involvement settings, 115
  media selection, 401–403
  metrics, 484–485
  music, 105
  opinion leaders in, 112–113
  product, 399–401
  pros and cons, 365
  reach, 401–402
  spending, 397
  subliminal stimuli, 104
  television, 377, 403
  in video games, 164
Advertising agencies; *see* Creative agencies
Advertising execution, 402–403
Advertising response function, 397–398
Advertising wearout, 397
Aesthetics, package design, 255
African Americans
  marketing to, 108, 168
  population, 168
Age groups; *see* Generational groups
Age segmentation, 163–164
Agent intermediaries, 326, 327
AIDA model, 370–372
AIOs; *see* Activities, interests, and opinions
Airlines
  service recovery, 280–281, 283
  strategic alliances, 457, 458
Allowances, 311
  promotional, 312, 330, 407
  slotting, 336
All-you-can-afford method, 380, 494
AMA; *see* American Marketing Association
American Indians, 168
American Marketing Association (AMA)
  brand definition, 239
  historical definitions of marketing, 8
  marketing definition, 7, 10, 17–18, 27
  viral marketing definition, 389
Anti-Defamation League, 379
ASEAN (Association of Southeast Asian Nations), 453
Asia, cultural differences, 70
Asian Americans, 168
Aspirational purchases, 111–112
Association of Southeast Asian Nations; *see* ASEAN
Assortments, product, 328–329, 341, 343
Assurance, 284
Attention, 370–371
Attitude-based choices, 120
Attitudes, 102
Attribute-based choices, 120
Auction pricing, 309
Audits
  brand, 497
  marketing, 497–499
Auto industry
  luxury carmakers, 111–112
  warranties, 257–258
Average-cost pricing, 310–311
Awareness set, 119

B

B2B; *see* Business-to-business markets
B2C; *see* Business-to-consumer marketing
Baby boomers, 96, 97, 105, 165–166
Bait and switch practices, 315
Basket of global marketing themes, 464
Behavioral data, 78
Behavioral segmentation, 174–176
Beliefs, of consumers, 102
Benefits
  definition, 27
  essential, 200, 201
  sought by consumers, 174
Big M marketing, 17–18, 30–31
Biofuels, 134
Blogs, 372, 388, 407
Boston Consulting Group (BCG) Growth-Share Matrix, 33–34
Brand assets, 244
Brand associations, 244, 367–368
Brand audits, 497
Brand awareness, 243, 374
Brand connections, 246–247
Brand equity
  benefits, 245–247
  dimensions, 243–245
Brand experience, role of scent, 239–240
Brand identity, 243
Brand loyalty, 243–244
  benefits, 247
  brand strategies and, 244
  maintaining, 374–375
Brand personalities, 105–106
Brand sponsors, 241
Brand strategies
  for global marketing, 462
  increasing brand equity, 244
Branding decisions, 247
  co-branding, 250–251
  licensing, 250
  national or store brands, 250
  stand-alone or family branding, 248–250
Branding strategy, 239
Brands; *see also* Products
  boundaries, 242–243
  in business markets, 239
  definition, 239
  family, 248–250
  global, 245, 462
  local, 462
  logos, 239, 252, 367
  most valuable, 245
  national, 250
  roles, 239–242
  of service firms, 267
  store (private-label), 250
  testing, 226
  trademark protection, 241, 252
  warranties and, 257–258
Breadth of merchandise, 343
Breaking bulk, 328, 341–342
British Paralympic Association, 409
Budgets; *see also* Costs
  action plan, 486, 494–495
  all-you-can-afford method, 380, 494
  comparative-parity method, 380, 494
  marketing, 494–495
  objective-and-task method, 379, 494
  percent-of-sales method, 379–380, 494
  promotion
    allocation, 364, 376–377, 495
    preparation, 378–380
  zero-based, 494–495
Bureau of Labor Statistics, 265
Business case analysis, 224
Business customs, in foreign markets, 446–447
Business-to-business (B2B) markets
  brands, 239
  buying centers, 138–140
  buying decision process, 133–134
    modified rebuys, 137
    new purchases, 137–138

post-purchase evaluation, 150–151
problem recognition, 144
product choice, 147–149
product specifications, 144–145
purchase decision, 147–150
sales proposals, 147
search for suppliers, 145–146
straight rebuys, 143–144
supplier choice, 149–150
buying situations
modified rebuys, 137, 144
new purchases, 137–138, 144
straight rebuys, 136–137, 143–144
channels of distribution, 327, 328
differences from consumer markets, 132, 133
buying process, 133–134
customer number and sizes, 133
customer relationships, 132
decision process, 133–134
geographic concentration, 133
product demand, 135–136
supply chain complexity, 134
electronic commerce, 350–351
end user purchases, 142
industry classifications, 140–141
largest, 131
marketing communications, 144
new product market testing, 227
personal selling
relationships, 132, 144, 415–416
sales positions, 418–419
skills needed, 418
players, 140–143
governments, 143
institutions, 143
manufacturers, 131, 141–142, 204–205
resellers, 142–143
product classifications, 204–205
sales promotion, 405–407
segmentation, 176–177
technology use, 132, 151, 350–351
Business-to-consumer (B2C) marketing; *see also* Consumer decision process; Retailers
adoption of new products, 228–230
channels of distribution, 327
differences from business markets, 132, 133
buying process, 133–134
customer number and sizes, 133
customer relationships, 132
decision process, 133–134
geographic concentration, 133
product demand, 135–136
supply chain complexity, 134
e-retailing, 348–350
new product market testing, 226–227
personal selling, 418
sales promotion, 405, 406
segmentation
behavioral, 174–176
demographic, 163–172
gender, 98–99, 166–167
geographic, 161–162
multiple approaches, 176
psychographic, 172–174
Buying centers
definition, 138
marketing challenges, 139–140
participants, 138–139
pursuing, 139–140
Buying decisions, in B2B markets, 133–134, 136–138
Buzz, 389–390, 407–408

C

Call centers; *see* Telemarketing
Cannibalization rates, 483
Capital equipment, 142
Capital goods, 205
Captive pricing, 305
Cash discounts, 311
Catalog retailers, 346–347, 434, 455–456
Category extensions, 249
Causal research, 76
Cell phones; *see also* Mobile communications devices
advertising on, 100
text messaging, 385
Census Bureau; *see* U.S. Census Bureau
Censuses, 79
Centers for Disease Control, 101
Centralization, in global marketing, 459
Change drivers, 14–15
customer information power, 15–16
distinction of Big M and little m marketing, 17–19
focus on payback of marketing investment, 19–20
generational value shifts, 16–17
product glut and customer shortage, 15
Channel captains (leaders), 332–333
Channel conflict, 333
Channel power, 333–334
Channels
communication, 368
direct marketing, 431, 433–434
Channels of distribution; *see also* Intermediaries; Market channels; Retailers
approaches, 336
control, 336
definition, 326
direct, 327
disintermediation, 331–332
electronic, 331–332
to end-user consumers, 327
indirect, 328
international, 462–464
legal issues, 339–340
logistics, 328, 336–339
to organizational buyers, 327, 328
prioritization of functions, 336
vertical marketing systems, 332–333, 336
Chief marketing officers (CMOs), 18, 20
China
food exports, 209
manufacturing plants, 325
product quality issues, 209
social media, 461
stem cell medicine, 277
Cities
largest, 161, 162
population growth, 70, 161, 163
Classes, social, 111–112, 170
Click fraud, 72
Climate, 161, 162
Closed-ended questions, 79
Closing sales, 423
Clutter, 402–403
CLV; *see* Customer lifetime value
Co-branding, 250–251
Coercive power, 333
Cognitive learning, 105
Commissions, 429
Communication
channels, 368
customer feedback, 368–369, 415, 417
decoding process, 368
definition, 366
encoding process, 367–368
feedback loops, 368–369
message transmission, 368
noise, 369
nonverbal, 107–108
in personal selling, 416–417
process model, 366–369
receivers, 368
senders, 367
Communications, marketing; *see also* Advertising; Direct marketing; Integrated marketing communications; Personal selling; Promotion; Public relations; Sales promotion
AIDA model, 370–372
in B2B markets, 144
customer expectations management, 281–282
elements, 361
in foreign markets, 464–465
hierarchy of effects model, 370–372
influence on external information sources, 118
labeling, 256–257
packaging, 252, 255
product introductions, 224, 228
product items vs. lines, 212–213
Companies; *see also* Multinational corporations
advertising spending, 397, 398, 464–465
customer-centric, 12–13, 31, 188–189, 270
Company websites; *see* Websites, company
Comparative advertising, 401
Comparative-parity method, 380, 494
Compensation, of salespeople, 429, 430
Competitive advantage
differential, 183
sustainable, 38

Competitive advertising, 400
Competitive forces, 178
Competitive strategies, 37–38
  cost leadership, 38, 295, 302–303
  differentiation, 38
  focus (niche), 38, 180, 299
  low cost, 179, 182
Competitor analysis, 41–42
Competitor-based pricing, 300–301
Competitors
  brand roles for, 241–242
  collecting information on, 73
  price wars, 300–301, 314
  promotion budgets, 380
  promotion mix decisions and, 376
Complaints, customer, 123
Complementary pricing, 305
Complete set, 118–119
Concentrated target marketing, 180
Conditioning, 104–105
Conformance quality, 208
Consideration (evoked) set, 119
Consumer decision process, 95, 96
Consumer decision process, factors in
  cultural, 106–108
  external forces, 106
  internal forces, 95, 96
  involvement levels, 114–115
  personal characteristics, 95–96
    demographics, 95–96, 97
    family life cycle stages, 97
    lifestyles, 97–99
    occupations, 97
  psychological attributes, 96, 99
    attitudes, 102, 120
    emotions, 119
    learning, 104–105
    motivation, 99–101
    perceptions, 102–104
    personality, 105–106
  situational, 108–109, 120–121
  social, 109
    class, 111–112
    families, 110–111
    opinion leaders, 112–113
    reference groups, 113
  time, 109, 121
Consumer decision process stages, 115–116
  evaluating alternatives, 119–120
  information search, 116–119
  post-purchase assessment, 121–123
  problem recognition, 116
  product choice decisions, 120–121
Consumer demand, 135–136
Consumer Financial Protection Bureau, 422
Consumer goods, 203–204
Consumer marketing; *see* Business-to-consumer marketing; Positioning; Segmentation; Target marketing
Consumers; *see also* Customers
  complaints, 123
  early adopters, 229, 230
  early majority, 230
  in foreign markets, 460–462
  innovators, 229, 230
  laggards, 229, 230
  late majority, 230
  sales promotion to, 405, 406
Contingency plans, 46, 495–496
Contractual agreements
  in foreign markets, 456–457
  franchising, 332, 334, 456, 457
  licensing, 250, 456–457
Contractual VMS (vertical marketing systems), 332, 336
Controls, 487, 495, 496; *see also* Audits
Convenience goods, 203, 335
Cooperative advertising and promotion, 406–407
Cooperatives, 332
Core competencies, 37–38
Core products, 200
Corporate identity, 367
Corporate VMS (vertical marketing systems), 332, 336
Corporate-level strategic planning, 32
Cost leadership strategy, 38, 295, 302–303
Cost per thousand impressions (CPM) rates, 484
Cost reduction, 219
Cost-based price strategy, 466
Cost-plus pricing, 309–310
Costs; *see also* Budgets
  advertising, 376–377
  average-cost pricing, 310–311
  channel, 463
  distribution, 467
  of exporting, 466
  of international distribution, 463, 466–467
  transportation, 338, 467
Countries; *see also* Cultures, foreign
  developing, 69, 296
  economic development stages, 448–449
  emerging markets, 448–449
  fastest-growing, 448, 449
  top five economies, 446, 447
Country-of-origin effect, 462
CPM; *see* Cost per thousand impressions
Creating assortments, 328–329, 341
Creative agencies
  full-service, 404
  public relations, 407
  roles, 404
  value added, 372–373
  website development, 404
Credence attributes, 275–276
Crisis management, 409
CRM; *see* Customer relationship management
Cultures
  company, 188–189
  definition, 106–107
  influence on consumer decisions, 106–108
  subcultures, 108
  values, 107
Cultures, foreign
  differences, 70, 461
  language differences, 86–87, 461
  researching, 446
  similarities, 450
Customer acquisition, 185
Customer advocacy, 272
Customer communities, 350, 351
Customer delight, 278
Customer expectations
  actual, 279–280, 282
  gap analysis, 279–280, 282
  management's perceptions of, 279–280
  for product experience, 200
Customer expectations management, 272, 281–282
Customer lifetime value (CLV), 185–186, 483
Customer loyalty
  definition, 185
  digital programs, 81
  measuring, 79
  programs, 175–176, 272–274, 406
  satisfaction and, 185, 272, 273
  segmentation by degree, 175–176
  value proposition and, 28
Customer mind-set, 189, 271
Customer orientation, 13, 189; *see also* Customer-centric culture
Customer profitability, 67, 185
Customer relationship management (CRM)
  customer-centric culture, 188–189
  data mining, 78, 187
  definition, 184
  example, 44
  integration into marketing planning, 185, 187
  metrics, 185–186
  objectives, 185
  process cycle, 186
    analysis and refinement, 187
    customer interaction, 187
    knowledge discovery, 186–187
    marketing planning, 187
  sales proposals, 147
  uses of data, 67, 184–185
Customer retention, 28, 185, 272
Customer satisfaction
  assessing, 123
  definition, 185
  loyalty and, 185, 272, 273
  measuring, 28, 282
  product evaluation, 123
Customer service; *see* Services
Customer switching, 28
Customer touchpoints, 186, 188–189
Customer-centric culture, 188–189
Customer-centric enterprises, 12–13, 31, 270
Customers; *see also* Consumers
  brand roles for, 239–241
  building relationships, 417
  feedback, 368–369, 415, 417

firing, 186
information power, 15–16
new product ideas, 221
prospecting, 419–420
shortages, 15
switching behavior, 272, 273
as value network members, 325–326
Customized (one-to-one) marketing, 180
Cyclical factors, 492

D

Dashboard; *see* Marketing dashboard
Data; *see also* Information
behavioral, 78
confidential, 65, 188, 350, 400
observational, 78
primary, 77
secondary, 77, 80–81, 85–86
Data collection, 77–78, 81, 86–87
Data mining, 78, 187
Data warehouses, 186–187
Database marketing, 187
Databases, online, 83
Deceptive pricing, 315
Deciders, 139
Decision-making authority, in global marketing, 459
Decoding process, 368
Decomposition forecasting method, 492
Degree of affiliation, 113
Degree of centralization, in global marketing, 459
Delightful surprises, 278
Delphi technique, 489
Demand; *see also* Forecasting
in business markets, 135–136
consumer, 135–136
derived, 135
estimating for new products, 224
fluctuating, 135–136, 269
inelastic, 136
price elasticity, 300
statistical analysis, 492–493
Demographic segmentation, 163
ages, 163–164
educational, 170
family and household, 167
genders, 98–99, 166–167
generational group, 165–166
geodemographics, 171–172
incomes, 169
occupations, 169–170
PRIZM clusters, 171–172
racial and ethnic groups, 167–169
social classes, 170
variables, 163, 164
Demographics
ages, 97, 98, 110, 163–164
aging of society, 96
city populations, 70, 161, 162
data collection, 68–70
definition, 68, 95
ethnicity and race, 69–70
family life cycle stages, 97
impact on consumer decisions, 95–96
migration, 70
occupations, 97
population growth, 69, 161
Depth of merchandise, 343
Derived demand, 135
Descriptive research, 76, 77–78, 79
Desirability, 113
Desire, 371–372
Developed economies, 448
Developing countries
emerging markets, 448–449
laptop computers for children, 296
population growth, 69
Differentiation; *see also* Product discrimination; Segmentation
of markets, 160, 179–180
of products, 13
sources, 183
strategy, 38
Dimensions of service quality, 283–284
Direct channels, 327
Direct foreign investment, 458
Direct mail, 403, 433–434
Direct marketing; *see also* Telemarketing
campaigns, 432–433
catalog retailers, 346–347, 434, 455–456
channels, 431, 433–434
customer prospecting, 420
definition, 361, 431
pros and cons, 365
target customers, 432–433
Direct Marketing Association, 431, 433
Direct product extension, 460
Direct sales forces, in foreign markets, 456
Direct selling, 347
Discounts, 311–312, 484
Disintermediation, 331–332
Disruptive innovation, 218
Dissonance, post-purchase, 122
Distinctive competencies, 38
Distribution channels; *see* Channels of distribution
Distribution costs, 467
Distribution intensity, 334–335
Distributors, 143, 221, 326, 456
Diversification strategies, 44–45
Diversity, 431
DOD; *see* U.S. Department of Defense
Dodd–Frank Wall Street Reform and Consumer Protection Act, 73
Dumping, 467
Durability, 208
Durable products, 203

E

Early adopters, 229, 230
Early majority, 230
E-commerce; *see* Electronic commerce; Internet
Economic conditions, 70–71, 446
Economic development stages, 448–449
Economic forces, 450
Economy, service sector, 265
EDI; *see* Electronic data interchange
EDLP; *see* Everyday low pricing
Educational segmentation, 170
Egypt, tariffs, 447
Electronic commerce; *see also* Interactive marketing; Websites, company
advantages and disadvantages, 349–350
business-to-business, 350–351
definition, 348
e-retailing, 348–350
exporting, 455–456
flash sales, 309
growth, 349, 383
luxury brands, 169
mobile devices and, 385
product reviews, 349, 388–389
showrooming, 346
Electronic data interchange (EDI), 151, 350–351
E-mail advertising, 384, 385
Emergencies, 409
Emergency goods, 203
Emerging markets, 448–449
Emotional appeals, 377–378
Emotional choices, 119
Empathy, 284
Employees; *see also* Salespeople
customer service skills, 271
internal marketing and, 366
loyalty, 271
satisfied, productive, and loyal, 271
Employment
retailing, 340
services jobs, 265
Encoding process, 367–368
End-user purchases, 142
Enhanced product, 200–202
Enterprise resource planning (ERP) systems, 337–338
Environmental issues
biofuels, 134
green products, 9, 452
packaging, 252
pollution, 71–72
product disposal, 122–123
E-procurement, 151, 350–351
E-retailing, 348–350
ERP; *see* Enterprise resource planning systems
Essential benefits, 200, 201
Ethanol, 134
Ethical issues
biofuels, 134
click fraud, 72
corporate scandals, 36
e-commerce, 242
green products, 9, 452
hiring salespeople, 431

Ethical issues—*Cont.*
imported food products, 209
labor standards compliance of suppliers, 325
online information collection, 400
paid product reviews, 388
pricing, 306
privacy, 65, 86, 100, 188, 350, 400
product claims, 184
product usage, 242
in promotion, 400
social responsibility, 296, 480, 482
stem cell medicine, 277
video games, 164
Ethnic groups
as consumers, 108
diversity, 69–70
segmentation, 167–169
subcultures, 108
in United States, 69–70, 108, 168
European Union (EU), 70, 450–451
Even pricing, 307
Event sponsorships, 408–409
Everyday low pricing (EDLP), 308
Exchange rate fluctuations, 467
Exchanges, 8
Exclusive dealing, 339–340
Exclusive distribution, 335
Exclusive territories, 340
Expectations; *see* Customer expectations
Experience attributes, 275
Expert power, 334
Exploratory research, 76, 77, 79
Exponential smoothing, 491–492
Exporters, 455–456
Exporting strategy, 455–456, 466–467; *see also* Foreign markets
Extensive information search, 117
External forces, 69
External information sources, 117–118
Extrinsic rewards, 428

F

Facilitating agents, 326
Facilitating functions, 330–331
Fads, 215
Fair trade laws, 315
Families
decision making, 110–111
definition, 110
gender roles, 110–111
influence on consumer decisions, 110–111
structures, 110, 167
traditional, 110
Family and household segmentation, 167
Family branding, 248–250
Family life cycle, 97, 110, 167
FCC; *see* Federal Communications Commission
FDA; *see* Food and Drug Administration
FDIC; *see* Federal Deposit Insurance Corporation
Features, product, 205–207
Federal Communications Commission (FCC), 100
Federal Deposit Insurance Corporation (FDIC), 422
Federal Trade Commission (FTC), 256, 314
Feedback, customer, 368–369, 415, 417
Feedback loops, 368–369
Firing customers, 186
First-mover advantages, 39
Fluctuating demand, 135–136, 269
FOB pricing, 312–313
Focus groups, 77, 83, 181
Focus strategy, 38, 180, 299
Follow-up, 423
Food and Drug Administration (FDA), 209, 255–256
Food retailers, 341, 344, 345
Forecasting
accuracy, 493–494
importance, 487
objective methods, 487, 489
accuracy, 494
advantages and disadvantages, 488
market tests, 490
statistical demand analysis, 492–493
time-series analysis, 490–492
selecting method, 493–494
subjective methods, 487
accuracy, 494
advantages and disadvantages, 488
Delphi technique, 489
jury of executive opinion, 489
sales force composite, 489
user expectations, 487
Foreign direct investment, 458
Foreign marketing, 445
Foreign markets; *see also* Global marketing
consumers, 460–462
country-of-origin effect, 462
direct sales forces, 456
distributors, 456
economic environments, 446
emerging markets, 448–449
entering, 445
market channels, 462–464
marketing research, 84–87, 446–448
quality perceptions, 461
Form, product, 205, 208
Form utility, 27
Formalization, 188–189
4Ps of marketing, 12; *see also* Pricing; Products; Promotion
Franchise organizations, 332
Franchising, 334, 456, 457
Frequency, advertising, 401–402
FTC; *see* Federal Trade Commission
Functional discounts, 311–312
Functional-level plans, 34–35

G

Gap Model of Service Quality, 278–282
Gatekeepers, 139–140
GE Business Screen, 33, 34
Gender roles, 98–99, 110–111
Gender segmentation, 98–99, 166–167
General warranties, 257
Generation X, 165–166
Generation Y, 16, 165–166, 372, 427
Generational groups, 165–166
baby boomers, 96, 97, 105, 165–166
GI generation, 165, 166
millennials, 97, 165, 166, 372
populations, 110
promotional strategies for, 372
teenagers, 400
values, 16–17, 166
Generational segmentation, 165–166
Generic strategies, 37
Geodemographic segmentation, 171–172
Geographic concentration, 133
Geographic proximity, 450
Geographic regions, 460
Geographic segmentation, 161–162
Geo-location marketing, 385
GI generation, 165, 166
Global brands, 245, 462
Global marketing; *see also* Foreign markets
challenges, 443, 449
communications, 464–465
company characteristics and, 454–455
learning curve, 444–446
market channels, 462–464
market entry strategies, 455
contractual agreements, 456–457
direct foreign investment, 458
exporting, 455–456, 466–467
strategic alliances, 457–458
market research, 446–448
organizational structure, 459–460
pricing strategies, 466–467
product strategies, 460
in regional market zones, 453
selecting markets, 453–455
strategies, 445, 455
Global marketing themes, 464
Global marketing with local content, 464
Global product lines, 459–460
Goals, 35, 44
Go-to-market mistakes, 222
Governments
as customers, 143
information sources, 80, 83
Gray market, 467
Green marketing, 9, 40–41, 104
Green packaging, 252
Green products, 9, 452

H

Hierarchy of effects model, 370–372
Hierarchy of Needs, 99–101
High-involvement learning, 114
High/low pricing, 308

Hispanics, 69–70, 108, 168–169; *see also* Ethnic groups
HLC; *see* Household life cycle
Home sales parties, 363
House brands; *see* Private-label (store) brands
Household life cycle (HLC), 110, 111; *see also* Family life cycle
Household segmentation, 167

I

IMC; *see* Integrated marketing communications
Immigrants, 169
Import tariffs, 447, 453, 466
Importance-performance analysis matrix, 282, 283
Impulse goods, 203, 335
Inbound logistics, 337
Inbound telemarketing, 420
Incentive pay, 429
Income segmentation, 169
Incomes, occupations and, 170
In-depth interviews, 77
Indirect channels, 328
Industrial revolution, 10
Industry advertising, 399
Industry classifications, 140–141, 343
Inelastic demand, 136
Influencers, 139, 140, 386
Information; *see also* Data; Demographics; Market information systems; Marketing research
  on business environment, 68, 69
  on foreign markets, 446–447
  internal sources, 66–68
  need for, 63–64
  perception of, 102–104
  privacy, 65, 86, 100, 350
Information power, 15–16
Information searches
  alternatives set, 118–119
  by consumers, 116–119, 349
  extensive, 117
  external, 117–118
  internal, 117
  limited, 117
  minimal, 117
  sources, 117–118
Information systems; *see* Customer relationship management; Market information systems; Software
Initiators, 138–139
Innovation; *see also* New products
  creating new market segments, 161
  diffusion, 228–230
  disruptive, 218
  packaging designs, 252, 253–254
  sustaining, 218
Innovation diffusion process, 228–230
Innovators, 229, 230
Input measures, 431, 432
Inseparability of services, 267–268
Institutional advertising, 399
Institutions, 143
Instrumental performance, 123
Intangibility
  product characteristics, 203
  of services, 266–267
Integrated marketing communications (IMC), 361; *see also* Communications, marketing
  budget allocations, 364
  creative agency roles, 404
  decision making, 363, 364
  definition, 362
  internal marketing and, 366
  promotion mix decisions, 364, 375–377
  rise of, 362
Intensive distribution, 335
Interactive marketing; *see also* Direct marketing; Internet advertising; Social media; Websites, company
  challenges, 381, 404
  definition, 361
  ethical issues, 400
  importance, 381
  integration with print catalogs, 434
  privacy issues, 400
  pros and cons, 365
  viral marketing, 389–390
Interest, 371
Intermediaries; *see also* Channels of distribution
  agents, 326, 327
  distributors, 221, 326, 456
  functions
    facilitating, 330–331
    physical distribution, 328–329
    transaction and communication, 329–330
  merchant, 326, 327
  need for, 327
  number of, 334–335
  resellers, 142–143
  as source of marketing information, 330
  types, 326–327
Internal information search, 117
Internal information sources, 66–68
Internal marketing, 269–271, 366
International marketing, 445; *see also* Global marketing
Internet; *see also* Electronic commerce; Social media; Websites, company
  auction sites, 309
  blogs, 372, 388, 407
  buzz on, 389–390
  consumer research on, 117, 349
  customer prospecting, 420
  dating sites, 179
  disintermediation, 331–332
  e-mail, 384, 385
  e-procurement, 151, 350–351
  focus groups, 83
  global marketing, 455–456
  growth, 455
  market research data on, 80, 83
  marketing alcohol, 242
  mobile use of, 86, 384–385
  privacy issues, 400
  product reviews, 349, 388–389
  search engines
    advertising on, 146, 384, 485
    optimization tools, 146
    supplier searches, 146
  security issues, 350
  surveys, 78, 81, 83–84
  tracking user activity, 400
  women's use, 99
Internet advertising
  analytics, 84
  for B2B markets, 146
  banner ads, 384
  click fraud, 72
  click-through rates, 384, 485
  decisions, 384
  display ads, 384
  e-mail, 384, 385
  interstitials, 384
  paying bloggers, 388
  pros and cons, 403
  response rates, 384
  search-related, 146, 384, 485
  on social media, 247, 400
  sponsorships, 384
Interviews, in-depth, 77
Intrinsic rewards, 428
Inventory
  just-in-time, 338
  management, 338
  of retailers, 342
  stock-outs, 337, 484
  turns, 484
Investment
  direct foreign, 458
  promotion as, 377, 379
Involvement levels, 114–115
Issue sponsorships, 408

J

Japan Vending Machine Manufacturers Association, 348
JIT; *see* Just-in-time inventory management
JND; *see* Just noticeable differences
Jobbers, 326
Joint ventures, 251, 457–458
Jury of executive opinion, 489
Just noticeable differences (JND), 313
Just-in-time (JIT) inventory management, 338

K

Key account salespeople, 419
Knowledge discovery, 186–187

L

Labeling; *see also* Packaging
  information included, 255–256
  legal requirements, 255–256
  marketing role, 256–257

Laggards, 229, 230
Language
culture and, 107
differences, 86–87
Spanish, 169
Late majority, 230
Latin America, MERCOSUR, 453
Learning
definition, 104
high-involvement, 114
influence on consumer decisions, 104–105
low-involvement, 115
organizational, 187
Legal environments of foreign markets, 447
Legal issues
collecting information on, 72–73
labeling, 255–256
pricing practices, 314–315
privacy, 188, 400
supply chain management, 339–340
telemarketing restrictions, 72, 434
trademarks, 241, 252
Legitimate power, 334
Licensing
brands, 250
in foreign markets, 456–457
Life cycles
family, 97, 110, 167
household, 110, 111
product; *see* Product life cycle
Lifestyles
gender roles, 98–99, 110–111
influence on consumer decisions, 97–99
psychographic segmentation, 172–174
trends, 98, 99
Lifetime value of customer, 185–186, 483
Limited information search, 117
Line of visibility, 287
Literacy rates, 87
Little m marketing, 17, 18–19, 30–31
Local market ad generation, 464
Local market conditions price strategy, 466
Logistics, 328
inbound, 337
inventory management, 338
order processing, 337–338
outbound, 337
reverse, 337
third-party providers, 331–332
transportation, 338–339
warehousing and materials handling, 338
Logos, 239, 252, 367; *see also* Brands; Labeling
Long-term memory, 103–104
Loss leader products, 315
Loyalty; *see also* Brand loyalty; Customer loyalty
employee, 271
programs, 81, 175–176, 272–274, 406

M

Macroeconomics, 71
Magazine advertising, 403
Management; *see* Marketing management; Sales forces
Management research deliverable, 74
Manufacturers
in China, 325
as customers, 131, 141–142, 204–205
Manufacturers' agents, 326
Margin on sales, 482–483
Market channels; *see also* Channels of distribution
discounts and allowances, 311–312, 336, 484
in foreign markets, 462–464
Market creation, 18
Market development strategies, 44–45
Market entry strategies, 455
contractual agreements, 456–457
direct foreign investment, 458
exporting, 455–456, 466–467
strategic alliances, 457–458
Market information systems (MISs)
definition, 64
external information, 68
competition, 73
demographic data, 68–70
economic conditions, 70–71
natural world, 71–72
political/legal environment, 72–73
technology, 71
internal information sources, 66–68
Market makers, 351
Market mavens, 112–113
Market orientation, 13
Market penetration pricing strategy, 298
Market penetration strategies, 44–45
Market research; *see* Marketing research
Market research companies, 73–74, 80
Market segmentation; *see* Segmentation
Market share, 298, 481
Market skimming pricing strategy, 298–299, 303
Market testing, 226–227, 490
Market-driven strategic planning, 32–33
Marketing
AMA definition, 7, 8, 10, 17–18, 27
Big M, 17–18, 30–31
definition, 6–7
history, 10–13
little m, 17, 18–19, 30–31
misconceptions, 3–6
return on investment, 478–480
strategic, 17–18, 30–31
tactical, 18–19, 30–31
visibility, 4–5
Marketing audits, 497–499
Marketing communications; *see* Communications, marketing; Integrated marketing communications
Marketing concept, 11–12
Marketing control, 45–46
Marketing dashboard; *see also* Metrics
benefits, 475, 476
definition, 475
developing, 478
elements, 476
forms, 475
goals, 476
pitfalls, 477–478
Marketing intelligence, 68
Marketing management
chief marketing officers, 18, 20
as core business activity, 6
promotion roles, 372–373
budget development, 378–380
goal setting, 373–375
media selection, 378
message development, 377–378
promotion mix decisions, 375–377
results measurement, 380
target identification, 373
Marketing metrics; *see* Metrics
Marketing mix, 12
Marketing planning, 30; *see also* Budgets; Forecasting
action plans, 485–487, 494–495
contingency plans, 46, 495–496
controls, 487, 495, 496
effective, 31
framework, 32
goals and objectives, 44
implementation, 45–46
integration of CRM, 185, 187
link to firm's business plan, 32–33
market research, 43–44
new products, 223–224
as ongoing process, 46–47
participants, 46
situation analysis, 39
competitive environmental factors, 41–42
external environmental factors, 39–41
internal environmental factors, 42
SWOT analysis, 42–43
strategic, 30–31
strategy development, 44–45
tactical, 30–31
tips, 46–47
Marketing plans, 30
Marketing research, 43–44
costs by country, 85
definition, 73
in foreign markets, 84–87, 446–448
importance, 73
technology, 82–84
use in decision making, 64–65
Marketing research process, 74
data analysis, 81–82
data collection, 81
problem definition, 74–75
reports, 82
research design
activities, 75
data collection, 77–78
data types, 77
information content, 78–79

research types, 75–76
sampling plans, 79–80
secondary data, 80–81
Marketing strategies, 44–45
Markup on cost, 309–310
Markup on sales price, 310
Maslow's Hierarchy of Needs, 99–101
Mass customization, 14, 180
Mass marketing, 179
Materials, 123, 204, 338; *see also* Inventory
Materials, repairs and operational (MRO) purchases, 142, 204–205
Materials requirement planning (MRP), 338
Matrix structure, 460
Maturity stage, product life cycle, 298
M-commerce, 385
Mechanical devices, 78
Mechanical observation, 78
Media; *see also* Advertising; Social media
advertising spending, 397
as communication channels, 368
costs, 376–377
pros and cons, 402, 403
selection, 378, 401–403
Medicine, ethical issues, 277
Memory, 103–104, 105, 117
Men, Internet use, 99; *see also* Gender
Merchant intermediaries, 326, 327
MERCOSUR, 453
Message transmission, 368
Metrics; *see also* Marketing dashboard
advertising, 484–485
cannibalization rate, 483
click-through rates, 485
cost per thousand impressions, 484
customer lifetime value, 185–186, 483
customer loyalty, 79
importance, 19–20
margin on sales, 482–483
market share, 481
penetration, 481–482
planning, 487
promotion, 380
promotions and pass-through, 484
return on customer investment, 186, 479
return on marketing investment, 478–480
return on social investment, 480, 482
sales force effectiveness, 483
share of voice, 484
supply chain, 484
Microeconomics, 71
Microsites, 383
Middlemen, 326, 467; *see also* Intermediaries
Migration, 70
Millennials, 97, 165, 166, 372
Minimal information search, 117
Minimum markup laws, 315
Minorities; *see* Ethnic groups
MISs; *see* Market information systems
Mission statements, 35–36
Missionary salespeople, 418
Mobile communications devices, 86, 100, 384–385; *see also* Cell phones; Social media
Mobile payments, 385
Modified rebuy situations, 137, 144
Moments of truth, 278, 287
Moral appeals, 378
Motivation
involvement with product, 114–115
of salespeople, 428, 429
theories, 99–101
Moving average forecasting method, 490–491, 492
MRO; *see* Materials, repairs and operational
MRP; *see* Materials requirement planning
Multiattribute model, 102
Multinational corporations; *see also* Global marketing
advertising spending, 465
international revenue, 446
largest, 443
organizational structures, 459–460
Multinational regional market zones; *see* Regional market zones

N

NAFTA (North American Free Trade Agreement), 451–452
NAICS; *see* North American Industrial Classification System
National Archives and Records Administration, 83
National Association of State Purchasing Officials, 143
National brands, 250
National Do Not Call Registry, 72, 434
National Realtors Association, 86
Native Americans, 168
Natural world, 71–72; *see also* Environmental issues
Near field communication (NFC), 385
Negotiations, 421–423
Neighborhood types, 172
Network organizations, 324; *see also* Vertical marketing systems
Networks, value, 323–326
New dominant logic for marketing, 265–266
New media; *see* Interactive marketing; Social media
New products; *see also* Product development
business case analysis, 224
cannibalization rates, 483
company perspective, 218–219
consumer adoption, 228–230
customer's perspective, 219
definition, 218
failures, 219
idea sources, 220–222
launching, 228
marketing strategies, 223–224
pricing strategies, 298
reasons for success or failure, 219–220
screening ideas, 222–223
New purchase situations, 137–138, 144, 224
Newspaper advertising, 403
New-to-the-world products, 218
NFC; *see* Near field communication
NGOs; *see* Nongovernmental organizations
Niche strategy, 38, 180, 299
Nimble operations, 325
Noise, 369
Nondurable products, 203
Nonfinancial incentives, 429
Nongovernmental organizations (NGOs), 143
Nonprobability sampling, 79, 80
Non-store retailers, 346
catalog retailers, 346–347, 434, 455–456
direct selling, 347
vending machines, 348
Nonverbal communication, 107–108
North American Free Trade Agreement (NAFTA), 451–452
North American Industrial Classification System (NAICS), 140–141, 343

O

Objective measures, 431
Objective-and-task method, 379, 494
Objectives, 35, 44
Observational data, 78
Occupational segmentation, 169–170
Occupations, 97
Odd pricing, 307
OEM; *see* Original equipment manufacturer
Offerings, 12
One world price strategy, 466
One-price strategy, 307–308
One-to-one marketing, 14
Online communications; *see* Interactive marketing; Internet advertising; Social media; Websites, company
Online databases, 83
Open-ended questions, 79
Operant conditioning, 105
Opinion leaders, 112–113
Order processing, 337–338
Organizational factors, 150
Organizational learning, 187
Organizational structure
for global marketing, 459–460
sales forces, 423–426
Original equipment manufacturer (OEM) customers, 141; *see also* Manufacturers
Out suppliers, 137
Outbound logistics, 337
Outbound telemarketing, 420, 434
Outdoor advertising, 403
Output measures, 431, 432
Outsourcing
ethical issues, 325
global, 325
logistics, 331–332
promotion, 372–373, 377
sales forces, 373, 424
Ownership utility, 27

P

Packaging
    aesthetics, 255
    colors, 255
    designing, 226, 255
    effective, 255
    environmentally sensitive, 252
    importance, 251
    information communicated, 252, 255
    innovative designs, 252, 253–254
    labeling, 255–257
    objectives, 251–253
    security, 252
    testing, 226
Partner relationship management (PRM) strategies, 333
Parts, 204
Pass-through percentage, 484
Penetration, 481–482
Penetration pricing, 298
Perceived quality
    brands and, 244, 246
    in foreign markets, 461
Percent-of-sales method, 379–380, 494
Perceptions
    definition, 102
    influence on consumer decisions, 102–104
    selective, 368
    selective awareness, 103
    selective distortion, 103
    selective retention, 103–104
    subliminal stimuli, 104
Perceptual maps, 182–183
Perishability of services, 269
Personal circumstances, influence on consumer decisions, 109
Personal factors, 149–150
Personal selling
    activities, 416–417
    advantages, 415–416
    in B2B markets
        relationships, 132, 144, 415–416
        sales positions, 418–419
        skills needed, 418
    in consumer markets, 418
    costs, 377, 415
    customer needs, 422
    definition, 361
    in foreign markets, 465
    key success factors, 417
    process, 419
        closing sales, 423
        follow-up, 423
        handling objections, 421–423
        opening relationships, 420
        prospecting, 419–420
        qualifying prospects, 420
        sales presentations, 420–421
        stages, 419
    pros and cons, 365
Personality
    brand, 105–106
    definition, 105
    influence on consumer decisions, 105–106
    theories, 105
Physical distribution, 328–329; *see also* Distribution channels; Logistics
Physical surroundings
    influence on consumer decisions, 108–109, 120
    of retail stores, 109
Pioneering advertising, 399–400
Pioneers, 215
Place utility, 27
Planning; *see* Action plans; Marketing planning
PLC; *see* Product life cycle
Politics
    collecting information on, 72–73
    in foreign markets, 447
    influence on formation of regional market zones, 450
Population growth; *see also* Demographics
    in cities, 70, 161, 163
    in less developed countries, 69
Portfolio analysis, 33–34
Positioning, 180–181
    definition, 159
    differential competitive advantage, 183
    errors, 183–184
    perceptual maps, 182–183
    repositioning, 182, 218–219
    value pricing and, 301–303
Positioning strategies, 159, 181
Post-purchase dissonance, 122
Post-purchase evaluation
    by business customers, 150–151
    by consumers, 121–123
Power, channel, 333–334
PR; *see* Public relations
Predatory pricing, 315
Preferred state, 116
Presentations; *see* Sales presentations
Prestige pricing, 306–307
Price bundling, 305–306
Price discrimination, 314–315
Price elasticity of demand, 300
Price escalation, 466–467
Price lining, 303–305
Price points, 303–304
Price pressure, 313–314
Price skimming, 298–299, 303
Price wars, 300–301, 314
Price-fixing, 314
Price-quality positioning map, 302–303
Pricing
    changes, 313–314
    customer concerns, 423
    customer perceptions, 295
    decisions, 296–297
    discounts and allowances, 311–312, 336, 484
    ethical issues, 306
    geographic aspects, 312–313
    legal issues, 314–315
    setting exact prices
        average-cost pricing, 310–311
        cost-plus pricing, 309–310
        markup on sales price, 310
        target return pricing, 311
    tactics, 303
        auction pricing, 309
        bundling, 305–306
        captive pricing, 305
        everyday low pricing, 308
        high/low pricing, 308
        odd/even pricing, 307
        one-price strategy, 307–308
        prestige pricing, 306–307
        product line pricing, 303–305
        reference pricing, 306
        variable pricing, 307–308
Pricing objectives, 297
Pricing strategies
    competitor-based, 300–301
    for global marketing, 466–467
    market penetration, 298
    market skimming, 298–299
    for new products, 298
    objectives and, 297, 298
    penetration pricing, 298
    price skimming, 298–299, 303
    profit maximization, 299–300
    stability pricing, 301
    target return on investment, 299–300
    value pricing, 301–303
Primary data, 77, 86
Primary groups, 113
Primary target markets, 178
Print media, 397, 403
Privacy, 65, 86, 100, 188, 350, 400
Private-label (store) brands, 250
PRIZM clusters, 171–172
PRM; *see* Partner relationship management
Probability sampling, 79
Problem recognition, 116
Problems, research, 74–75
Product adaptation, for global marketing, 460
Product advertising, 399–401; *see also* Advertising
Product choice, 147–149
Product classifications, 202
    business goods, 204–205
    consumer goods, 203–204
    durability, 203
    tangibility, 203
Product demand, in business markets, 135–136; *see also* Demand
Product development; *see also* New products
    designs, 210
    for global markets, 460

mistakes, 222
models, 225–226
testing, 223, 226–227
Product development process
opportunity definition, 223–224
opportunity development
market testing, 226–227
product development, 225–226
product launch, 228
opportunity identification, 220–223
Product development strategies, 44–45
Product discrimination, 205, 206–207
conformance quality, 208
durability, 208
features, 205–207
form, 205, 208
performance quality, 207–208
reliability, 208–209
repairability, 209
style, 210
Product glut, 15
Product invention, for global marketing, 460
Product items
distinction from products, 200
marketing communications, 212–213
in product lines, 210–211
Product life cycle (PLC)
caveats, 215
maturity phase, 298
profitability, 215
promotion mix decisions across, 375, 376
sales revenue, 215
stages, 214, 216–217
timeline, 215
use of, 213
Product line pricing, 211–212, 303–305
Product lines, 210–211
global, 459–460
marketing communications, 212–213
pricing decisions, 211–212, 303–305
Product mix, 211
Product reviews, online, 349, 388–389
Product specifications, 144–145
Product usage
consumer experiences, 122
ethical issues, 242
segmentation by, 176
Production orientation, 10
Product-Market Matrix, 44–45
Products; *see also* Brands; New products; Packaging
attributes, 182, 205–207
characteristics, 199–202
consumer research on, 116–119, 349
core, 200
customer involvement, 114–115
defining, 199, 223
differentiation, 13
disposal, 122–123
enhanced, 200–202
essential benefits, 200, 201
for global marketing, 460
green, 9, 452
mass customization, 14, 180
multiple, 210–211
offerings, 12
performance, 123
vs. product items, 200
repositioning, 218–219
returns, 337
upgrades or modifications, 218
Professional services, 276
Profit maximization pricing strategy, 299–300
Profitability
customer, 67, 185
of new products, 224
over product life cycle, 215
Promotion; *see also* Sales promotion
budgets
allocation, 364, 376–377, 495
preparation, 378–380
ethical issues, 400
in foreign markets, 465
to generational groups, 372
goals, 373–375, 379
as investment, 377, 379
marketing manager's role, 372–373
budget development, 378–380
goal setting, 373–375
media selection, 378
message development, 377–378
promotion mix decisions, 375–377
results measurement, 380
target identification, 373
metrics, 380, 484
outsourcing, 372–373, 377
pull strategy, 336, 364–365
push strategy, 336, 364–365
Promotion mix; *see also* Integrated marketing communications
AIDA model stages and, 370, 371
decisions, 375–377
elements, 361
for product life cycle stages, 375, 376
pros and cons of elements, 364, 365
traditional decision making, 362–363
Promotion mix strategies, 362
Promotional allowances, 312, 330, 407
Promotional appeals, 377–378
Promotional campaigns, 362
Prospecting for customers, 419–420
Psychographic segmentation, 172–174
Psychographic variables, 172
Psychological attributes, 96, 99
attitudes, 102, 120
emotions, 119
learning, 104–105
motivation, 99–101
perceptions, 102–104
personality, 105–106
Psychological pricing, 307
Public relations (PR)
core functions, 407–409
crisis management, 409
definition, 361
event sponsorships, 408–409
in-house departments, 407
international, 465
issue sponsorships, 408
pros and cons, 365
Public relations firms, 407; *see also* Creative agencies
Publicity, 407–408
Puffery, 374
Pull strategy, 336, 364–365
Purchasing agents and departments, 138, 139
Purpose marketing, 8
Push strategy, 336, 364–365

Q

Qualifying prospects, 420
Qualitative research, 77; *see also* Focus groups
Quality; *see also* Service quality
conformance, 208
perceptions in foreign markets, 461
perceptions of brands, 244, 246
price-quality positioning map, 302–303
product performance, 207–208
warranties, 257–258
Quantitative research, 77; *see also* Surveys
Quantity discounts, 312
Questions
closed-ended, 79
open-ended, 79

R

R&D; *see* Research and development
Race and ethnicity segmentation, 167–169; *see also* Ethnic groups
Racial groups, 69–70, 168; *see also* African Americans
Radio advertising, 403
Rainforest Alliance, 452
Random factors, 492
Rational appeals, 377
Reach, 401–402
Real state, 116
Receivers, 368
Recycling, 104, 123
Reducing transactions, 329
Reference groups, 113, 170
Reference pricing, 306
Referent power, 334
Regional market zones, 449–450
ASEAN, 453
European Union, 70, 450–451
influences on formation, 450
marketing in, 453
MERCOSUR, 453
NAFTA, 451–452

Regulations, telemarketing, 72, 434; *see also* Legal issues
Relationship orientation, 13–14
Reliability
- product, 208–209
- service delivery, 283
- supplier, 149

Repairability, 209
Repeat purchases, 224
Replacement purchases, 224
Repositioning, 182, 218–219
Requests for proposal (RFPs), 145, 146, 147
Research; *see* Marketing research
Research and development (R&D), 221; *see also* Product development
Research problems, defining, 74–75
Resellers, 142–143; *see also* Distributors
Responsiveness, 283–284
Retailer cooperatives, 332
Retailers
- characteristics, 343–344
- co-branding, 250–251
- in distribution channel, 326
- inventories, 342
- loyalty programs, 81
- non-store, 346
  - catalog retailers, 346–347, 434, 455–456
  - direct selling, 347
  - television home shopping, 348
  - vending machines, 348
- online; *see* Electronic commerce
- personal selling, 418
- physical surroundings, 109, 120
- pricing, 308
- product assortments
  - creating, 328–329, 341
  - depth, 343
  - social class of customers and, 112
- product variety, 341, 343
- purchases, 142–143
- services
  - levels, 345–346
  - of stores, 342, 343–344
- store
  - advantages, 344–346
  - food, 341, 344, 345
  - general merchandise, 344–345
  - salespeople, 418
  - services, 342, 343–344
  - specialty, 343, 344

Retailing
- definition, 340
- economic importance, 340–341
- employment, 340
- growth, 340–341
- roles, 341–342
- top global markets, 341

Retention, customer, 28, 185, 272
Return on customer investment (ROCI), 186, 479
Return on investment (ROI), target, 299–300
Return on marketing investment (ROMI), 478–480
Return on social investment (ROSI), 480, 482
Revenue; *see* Sales revenue
Reverse auctions, 309
Reverse logistics, 337
Reward power, 334
Rewards
- extrinsic and intrinsic, 428
- for salespeople, 428, 429

RFPs; *see* Requests for proposal
Risk tolerance, 150
ROCI; *see* Return on customer investment
ROI; *see* Return on investment
ROMI; *see* Return on marketing investment
ROSI; *see* Return on social investment

S

Safety
- food, 209
- product, 208

Salaries, 429
Sales; *see also* Personal selling
- in foreign markets, 465
- unit, 224

Sales aptitude, 427
Sales force composite, 489
Sales force effectiveness (SFE), 483
Sales forces; *see also* Personal selling; Salespeople
- brokers, 329, 373
- costs, 377
- effectiveness measures, 483
- in foreign markets, 456, 465
- independent agents, 424
- as information sources, 67–68
- managing, 426
  - compensation and rewards, 429, 430
  - motivation, 428
  - performance, 426–428
  - performance evaluation, 429–431
  - recruitment and selection, 428–429, 431
  - training, 429, 431
- manufacturers' representatives, 329
- new product ideas, 220–221
- organizing, 423
  - customer orientation, 426
  - geographic orientation, 424–425
  - product orientation, 425
- outsourcing, 373, 424
- positions, 418–419
- separation from marketing organization, 373
- technical selling, 418–419

Sales forecasts; *see* Forecasting
Sales information systems, 67–68
Sales orientation, 11
Sales presentations
- characteristics of great, 421
- definition, 420
- goals, 420–421
- skills needed, 417

Sales promotion
- in B2B markets, 405–407
- to consumers, 405, 406
- definition, 361
- in foreign markets, 465
- pros and cons, 365
- purpose, 404–405
- trade shows, 144, 406

Sales proposals, 147
Sales revenue
- estimating for new products, 224
- market share, 481
- over product life cycle, 215

Sales skill levels, 427–428
Salespeople; *see also* Personal selling; Sales forces
- compensation and rewards, 429, 430
- diverse backgrounds, 431
- information management, 417
- job satisfaction, 428
- key account, 419
- motivation, 428, 429
- performance, 426–428
- performance evaluation, 429–431
- recruiting and selecting, 428–429
- retail, 418
- role perceptions, 427
- skills needed, 416–417, 427–428
- training, 429

Salvation Army, 378
Samples, 79–80, 86
Sarbanes-Oxley (SOX) Act of 2002, 36
SBA; *see* Small Business Administration
SBUs; *see* Strategic business units
Search attributes, 274–275
Search engines
- advertising on, 146, 384, 485
- optimization tools, 146
- supplier searches, 146

Seasonal discounts, 312
Seasonal index, 492, 493
Seasonality, 492
SEC; *see* Securities and Exchange Commission
Secondary data
- advantages and disadvantages, 80–81
- definition, 77
- in foreign markets, 85–86
- sources, 80

Secondary groups, 113
Secondary target markets, 178
Securities and Exchange Commission (SEC), 72–73, 86
Segmentation; *see also* Demographic segmentation; Target marketing
- business markets, 140, 176–177
- consumer markets
  - behavioral, 174–176
  - demographic, 163–172
  - gender, 98–99, 166–167

geographic, 161–162
multiple approaches, 176
psychographic, 172–174
creating new segments, 161
criteria for effective, 161
definition, 159
logic behind, 160
purpose, 160
Selective awareness, 103
Selective distortion, 103
Selective distribution, 335
Selective perception, 368
Selective retention, 103–104
Selling; *see* Personal selling; Sales
Senders, 367
Service agreements; *see* Warranties
Service attributes, 274, 275
credence, 275–276
experience, 275
importance, 276–277
search, 274–275
Service blueprints, 284, 287–288
Service economy, 265
Service encounters, 278
Service failure, 280
Service quality
definition, 278
delivery, 280–282
dimensions, 283–284
failures, 280
gap analysis, 278–282
internal services, 269–271
measuring, 283–284
SERVQUAL instrument, 283–284, 285–287
Service recovery, 280–281
Service sector, 265
Service-profit chain, 269, 270
internal service quality, 269–271
revenue and profit growth, 272–274
satisfied, productive, and loyal employees, 271
service value for external customers, 272
Services
characteristics, 266
inseparability, 267–268
intangibility, 266–267
perishability, 269
variability, 268–269
customized, 268
definition, 265
as differentiator, 265
free trials, 267
pricing strategies, 305, 308
professional, 276
of retailers
levels, 345–346
stores, 342, 343–344
SERVQUAL instrument, 283–284, 285–287
SFE; *see* Sales force effectiveness
Share of voice, 484
Shelf fees, 336
Shopping goods, 204, 335
Short-term memory, 103
Showrooming, 346
SIC; *see* Standard Industrial Classification
Silent Generation, 165, 166
Situation analysis, 39
competitive environmental factors, 41–42
external environmental factors, 39–41
internal environmental factors, 42
SWOT analysis, 42–43
Six Cs of channel strategy, 463–464
SKUs; *see* Stock-keeping units
Slotting allowances, 336
Small Business Administration (SBA), 143, 380
Smartphones; *see* Mobile communications devices
SMSAs; *see* Standard metropolitan statistical areas
Social class segmentation, 170
Social classes, 111–112
Social media
advertising on, 247, 400
buzz on, 407–408
in China, 461
marketing strategies, 249
online communities, 389
opportunities and threats, 386
privacy issues, 400
product review sites, 388–389
promotion strategies, 363
social networks, 386–387
teenagers' use, 400
trends, 247
viral marketing, 389–390
Social responsibility, 296, 480, 482
Societal marketing, 9
Software; *see also* Customer relationship management; Market information systems; Technology
enterprise resource planning systems, 337–338
Excel spreadsheets, 493, 495
marketing research, 82–84
sales systems, 67–68
statistical, 84, 493
Solution sellers, 419
Sorting, 328
Specialty goods, 204
Specific warranties, 257
Sponsorships
event, 408–409
issue, 408
Stability pricing, 301
Stakeholders, 7–8, 42
Stand-alone brands, 248
Standard Industrial Classification (SIC) codes, 140
Standard metropolitan statistical areas (SMSAs), 161, 162; *see also* Cities
Staple goods, 203
State and local governments, 143
Statistical demand analysis, 492–493
Statistical software, 84, 493
Stem cell medicine, 277
Stock-keeping units (SKUs), 200
Stock-outs, 337, 484
Stop-to-market mistakes, 222
Storage intermediaries, 329, 338
Store (private-label) brands, 250
Store retailers; *see also* Retailers
advantages, 344–346
food, 341, 344, 345
general merchandise, 344–345
salespeople, 418
services, 345–346
specialty, 343, 344
Straight rebuy situations, 136–137, 143–144
Strategic alliances, 457–458
Strategic business units (SBUs), 32–34
Strategic fit, 178
Strategic marketing, 17–18
Strategic planning
corporate-level, 32
functional-level plans, 34–35
market-driven, 32–33
portfolio analysis, 33–34
SBU-level, 32–33
Strategic types, 38–39
Strategic visions, 35
Strategies; *see also* Competitive strategies
definition, 36–37
generic, 37
marketing, 44–45
organizational, 37–39
Styles, product, 210
Subcultures, 108
Subjective measures, 431
Supermarkets, 341
Supplier choice, 149–150
Suppliers; *see also* Business-to-business markets
electronic networks, 350–351
labor standards compliance, 325
out, 137
preferred, 137, 145
reliability, 149
searching for, 145–146
Supplies, 204
Supply chain management, 323
Supply chains; *see also* Channels of distribution
complexity, 134
definition, 134, 323
metrics, 484
Surveys, 77–78
customer satisfaction, 282
delivery methods, 79
electronic, 78, 81, 83–84
in foreign markets, 86–87
positioning studies, 181
questionnaire design, 78–79
questions, 79
Sustainability, 9, 40–41; *see also* Environmental issues
Sustainable competitive advantage, 38
Sustaining innovation, 218

SWOT analysis, 42–43
Symbolic performance, 123

T

Tactical marketing, 18–19
Tangibility, of products, 203
Tangibles, in services, 283
Target marketing; *see also* Positioning; Segmentation
- approaches
  - concentrated, 180
  - customized, 180
  - differentiation, 179–180
  - undifferentiated, 179
- definition, 159, 177
- steps, 177
  - approach selection, 179–180
  - market segment analysis, 177–178
  - profiles of target markets, 178

Target markets
- abandoning, 178
- primary, 178
- profiles, 178
- promotion mix decisions, 375–376
- secondary, 178
- tertiary, 178

Target return on investment, 299–300
Target return pricing, 311
Tariffs, 447, 453, 466
TCA; *see* Transaction cost analysis
Technical selling, 418–419
Technology; *see also* Internet; Mobile communications devices; Software
- in B2B markets, 132, 151, 350–351
- changes caused by, 71
- electronic data interchange, 151, 350–351
- marketing research, 82–84
- new products, 218

Teenagers, 400
Telemarketing
- abuses, 422
- costs, 434
- customer prospecting, 420
- inbound, 420
- outbound, 420, 434
- regulations, 72, 434
- response rates, 434
- success factors, 434

Television
- advertising, 377, 403
- home shopping, 348
- in pediatricians' waiting rooms, 222
- ratings, 80

Tertiary target markets, 178
Test markets, 226–227, 490
Text messaging, 385
Third-party logistics, 331–332
Time, influence on consumer decisions, 109, 121
Time utility, 27
Time-series analysis, 490–492
Touchpoints, 186, 188–189
Trade discounts, 311–312
Trade servicers, 418
Trade shows, 144, 406
Trademarks, 241, 252
Training, sales, 429
Transaction cost analysis (TCA), 424
Transfer pricing, 466
Transportation
- costs, 338, 467
- in foreign markets, 463
- intermediaries, 329
- methods, 338–339

Trends, 492
Trust, 149, 422
Tying contracts, 340

U

Undifferentiated target marketing, 179; *see also* Mass marketing
Uniform delivered pricing, 313
Unions, 42
Unit sales, 224
U.S. Air Force, 142
U.S. Army, 30
U.S. Census Bureau, 80, 85, 95, 168, 169–170, 343
U.S. Department of Defense (DOD), 143, 153–154
U.S. Postal Service (USPS), 313
Unsought goods, 204
Upgrades or modifications to existing products, 218
Usage patterns, segmentation by, 174–176; *see also* Product usage
User expectations method, 487
Users, 138
Utility, 27

V

VALS (Values and Lifestyles), 172–174, 175
Value
- benefits-cost ratio, 27
- definition, 8

Value chain, 28–30, 323
Value co-creation, 324
Value equation, 344
Value networks, 323–326
Value offering; *see* Pricing; Products; Services
Value pricing, 301–303
Value propositions, 28, 461; *see also* Positioning
Value-creating activities, 28–29
Values
- of consumers, 102
- cultural, 107
- generational, 16–17, 166

Values and Lifestyles (VALS), 172–174, 175
Variability, of services, 268–269
Variable pricing, 307–308
Variety, product, 341, 343
Vending machines, 348
Vendors; *see* Business-to-business markets; Suppliers
Vertical integration, 332
Vertical marketing systems (VMSs), 332–333
Video gaming, 164, 299
Viral marketing, 389–390
Virtual organizations, 324
Visions, strategic, 35
VMSs; *see* Vertical marketing systems

W

Warehousing, 338; *see also* Storage intermediaries
Warranties
- brands and, 257–258
- costs and benefits, 257–258
- general, 257
- message conveyed to customer, 258
- specific, 257

Website advertising; *see* Internet advertising
Websites, company; *see also* Electronic commerce; Internet
- for B2B markets, 146, 151
- communication, 383
- connection, 383
- content, 381–382, 383
- context, 382
- customer communities, 350, 351, 383, 389
- customer interface dimensions, 382–383
- customization, 383
- development, 404
- integration with print catalogs, 434
- messages, 381–382
- microsites, 383

Wholesaler cooperatives, 332
Wholesalers, 326
Women; *see also* Gender
- Internet use, 99
- purchasing roles, 98–99

Word-of-mouth advertising, 390; *see also* Buzz; Viral marketing
World Economic Forum, 445
World Trade Organization (WTO), 467
World Wildlife Fund, 381

Y

York College of Pennsylvania, 434

Z

Zero-based budgeting, 494–495
Zone pricing, 313